About the Authors

Eric Smith is currently Senior Content Developer at inquiry.com (http://www.inquiry.com), the Internet's leading site for information technology professionals. He is directly responsible for Ask the VB Pro (http://wwwinquiry.com/thevbpro), which is the premier resource for Visual Basic developers. Prior to joining inquiry.com in 1995, Eric was a Senior Consultant with Andersen Consulting in Chicago, Illinois.

Yusuf Malluf, born April 24, 1979, is a senior student at Moriarty High School, Moriarty, NM. He has used computers for around ten years and is proficient in several programming languages, including C, FORTRAN, and Visual Basic; several scripting languages, such as Visual Basic Script, JavaScript, and HTML; and ActiveX/OLE technology. Yusuf was a contributing author in Que's *Special Edition: Using VBScript*. In New Mexico, Yusuf has participated in the New Mexico Supercomputer Challenge sponsored by New Mexico Technet (http://www.nm.org) and LANL, and in the Adventures in Supercomputing sponsored by SNL. He doesn't do too many things in his spare time because he rarely has any.

Jeffrey P. McManus is a professional developer, corporate trainer, and technical writer. A native Californian, he attended the University of California, Santa Barbara. He currently resides in San Francisco.

Art Scott is a Senior Software Developer for Advisor Technology Services, providing Portfolio Management Software. His prior experience involves software development for Hospital Database Systems; Pipeline Measurement and 3D Graphical Systems; Software Design for NASA Shuttle Cargo Bay Systems; Software Development and Hardware Design for Petro-Chemical Systems; and United States Naval Tactical Data System Hardware Maintenance. Art is also a certified Master Ordance Repair (MOR) Combat Direction System Supervisor for Shipboard overhauls, repair, and testing of Naval Shipboard Computer Systems.

Art's software experience includes Visual Basic Applications Development, Visual C++ Custom Controls, and Business Logic Development, as well as Internet/Intranet ActiveX Development. He also publishes Shareware Custom controls, which are currently available on his Web site at http://www.advdisk.com.

Trademark Acknowledgments

Dedications

From Eric Smith:

For my family: Jodi, Mom, Dad, and Drew.

From Jeffrey McManus:

To the Nelson family: Tom, Pam, and Opie; and the Chen family: John, Whittnee, and Max. Thanks for your love and support; you do nice work.

From Art Scott:

To my wife, Terri—without her continued support, this would not be possible.

Acknowledgments

From Eric Smith:

I'd like to thank all the folks at New Riders for their help, support, pestering, and nagging involved in getting this book to the shelves. Since it was my first book, I was expecting to be swamped with all sorts of writing terminology. All the people there made it really easy for me to write; I just had to write and they took care of the rest. Special thanks go to Danielle Bird, Sean Angus, Suzanne Snyder, and Gina Brown for putting up with me through these months. It was worth it.

I'd also like to thank the users of Ask the VB Pro (`http://www.inquiry.com/ thevbpro`). If it wasn't for the thousands every day who come see and appreciate my work on that site, I'd never have considered writing this book. Special thanks go to Jim LeValley, who originally asked me to write the book based on what he saw at the site.

Finally, thanks to all the people who provided moral support throughout this ordeal. Special thanks go to MaryBeth and Ray, two of my co-workers at `inquiry.com`. To Jodi, thanks for listening through all the revisions and edits and outline changes. Finally, thanks to God for giving me the strength to do this and everything else in my life.

Contents at a Glance

Table of Contents

10 Debugging Your Script   259

Part III: ActiveX Controls

11 HTML Extensions for ActiveX Controls   277

14 Creating ActiveX Controls with the Visual Basic Control Creation Edition   457

Part IV: Advanced Internet Programming

Introduction

From being a topic discussed only in universities, the Internet is now becoming a part of everyday life. Anything you want to know is probably sitting out there somewhere. Don't call directory assistance—use one of many World Wide Web phone directories. Need help with your kitchen appliance? Take a look at the manufacturer's web site and you have instant answers. Want to ask famous celebrities their deepest, darkest secrets? You can log-on to an online service and ask your questions in a virtual auditorium.

Until just recently, however, World Wide Web pages have just been static and unchanging. Someone created them with a text editor and copied them to a web site. With the advent of scripting languages, times are changing. Imagine going to a web page that customizes itself based on who you are. How about a catalog that has gathered your preferences based on previous orders and shows you the items you are more likely to purchase? These pages offer unlimited possibilities for business and recreation, and people are already making them happen. This book is designed to help you start building those pages for your own web site, using Microsoft's Visual Basic Scripting Edition, more commonly known as VBScript.

Besides learning about VBScript, you will also learn about the ActiveX technology. ActiveX is Microsoft's vision for expanding the capabilities of the user's browser. ActiveX components automatically download into your browser as they are needed. You do not have to find plug-ins or other software—Microsoft's browser does the work for you. You will learn how to use ActiveX components in your own pages to make your pages more useful. You will also learn about the underlying structure used to design and implement these components. By learning this structure, you can better use the controls in your own applications.

As you will learn in this book, VBScript is Microsoft's vision for "activating the Internet." However, Microsoft has realized that other technologies like Java, JavaScript, and the myriad of plug-ins for browsers cannot be ignored. Instead of trying to compete with all of these valuable assets, they have decided to cooperate. As a result, VBScript is able to utilize a growing number of these technologies just as it utilizes its own capabilities. In addition, Microsoft has offered to license VBScript to anyone who wants to implement it on the variety of platforms used on the Internet. This means that your VBScript pages can be used on Windows PCs, Macs, Unix workstations, and any other machine that has a VBScript-compatible browser running on it. For the millions of Microsoft Visual Basic programmers out there, this is a huge market that few have yet to explore.

One of the main reasons this book was written was the lack of information on both VBScript and ActiveX. Microsoft's documentation for VBScript is currently only available online, and much of it is still missing or incorrect. ActiveX controls are made by a large number of software companies, so all the documentation is written differently and available in different places.

Who Should Read This Book

This book is designed to be a comprehensive tutorial and reference to Microsoft VBScript and all its related technologies. You will find the complete VBScript language documented and illustrated in this book. You will also find real-world examples you can use in your own development.

Because this book is written as a tutorial, web page designers with no programming experience will be able to use it to learn Microsoft VBScript.

Many Visual Basic programmers will want to make the transition to this very different language. If you are a Visual Basic programmer, you will appreciate the time and effort taken in this book to help you learn this language. Many chapters contain sections devoted to the additions and differences in VBScript as compared to Visual Basic.

Much of the complexity of the full version of Visual Basic has been removed, making VBScript a much easier language to learn quickly. This will undoubtedly allow

VBScript to be adopted more quickly. Current Visual Basic programmers will want more details about what they can and cannot do in VBScript that they may have done under Visual Basic. All of the omissions and additions to VBScript from Visual Basic will be covered in detail in this book. Visual Basic programmers will also see how to adopt existing code for web pages and back-end server use. You will see how to leverage your investment in Visual Basic for new uses on the Internet.

In addition, this book will be a complete reference to the technical details of VBScript and ActiveX for those more interested in the implementation details of VBScript. Microsoft has made all of the documentation available on the VBScript web site, but many people don't always have an Internet connection available. This book will help you develop your pages off-line by providing you with all the available documentation on VBScript and ActiveX.

What's In This Book

The chapters in this book are divided into five sections.

Part I: VBScript, ActiveX, and the Internet

Chapter 1: Introduction to VBScript and ActiveX

This chapter introduces you to the new technologies of VBScript and ActiveX. You also learn the basic terminology that is used throughout the book.

Chapter 2: HTML Fundamentals for VBScripting

This chapter teaches you the basics of Hypertext Markup Language (HTML), which is the language used for creating documents for the Internet. Besides the basic tags that you may already be familiar with, this chapter shows you the additional tags used for VBScript and ActiveX.

Chapter 3: The ActiveX Control Pad

This chapter introduces you to Microsoft's ActiveX Control Pad, the easiest way to build ActiveX controls into your pages. This product, if you do not already have it, is included on the CD-ROM for your convenience.

Chapter 4: Introduction to Using ActiveX Controls in Web Pages

This chapter shows you the basics of adding controls to your web pages. You learn the HTML tags to use, as well as the other necessary components required to put a control to use for you.

Part II: Programming with VBScript

Chapter 5: VBScript Language Elements

This chapter introduces you to the basic elements of the VBScript language. You learn about variables, constants, data types, and comments. While this may seem familiar to Visual Basic programmers, there are some distinct differences between VBScript's data types and those used in Visual Basic. Watch for the **VB Version Notes** throughout this and all other chapters.

Chapter 6: VBScript Functions and Operators

This chapter covers all the built-in functions included in the VBScript language, such as those used for math, string, and logical expressions.

Chapter 7: Looping and Decision Structures

This chapter covers the structures you use to change the flow of code within your program. From Do loops to For loops, you will learn all the structures in this chapter.

Chapter 8: Building Procedures and Functions

No program using Visual Basic or VBScript would be complete without using procedures or functions. This chapter shows you how to use both constructs in your VBScript code.

Chapter 9: Programming with Events

As in Visual Basic, much of VBScript revolves around responding to events generated by the user. This chapter introduces you to all of the common events used in the primary ActiveX controls. You also learn how to write code to deal with these events.

Chapter 10: Debugging Your Script

No one writes perfect VBScript code every time. For the errors that always pop up when you least expect them, this chapter teaches you how to use VBScript's debugging features to kill those bugs dead.

Part III: ActiveX Controls

Chapter 11: HTML Extensions for ActiveX Controls

This chapter shows you how to take advantage of some HTML extensions recently added to support VBScript and other scripting languages. These extensions make it easier to integrate your code with your web pages.

Chapter 12: Using the Built-In ActiveX Controls

In this chapter, you learn how to use the ActiveX controls that are installed with Internet Explorer. By learning these controls, you build a foundation for learning other controls that are on the market today.

Chapter 13: ActiveX Controls Reference

In this chapter, you are given information on a large number of ActiveX controls. Each of these controls is included on the CD. With the information provided in this chapter, you will be able to start using the controls immediately.

Chapter 14: Creating ActiveX Controls with the Visual Basic Control Creation Edition

This chapter provides you with all the information you need to start creating your own ActiveX controls using the Visual Basic 5.0 Control Creation Edition, which is available from Microsoft for free! The chapter walks you through all the steps for creating and distributing your own ActiveX controls using Visual Basic.

Part IV: Advanced Internet Programming

Chapter 15: Enhancing HTML Forms with VBScript

Do you ever get tired of waiting for the server to respond from a form's input? Use this chapter to make your input forms more responsive and error-proof. This chapter shows you how to enhance basic HTML forms to provide all sorts of validation and other convenience features for the user.

Chapter 16: Web Database Access

This chapter discusses ODBC (Open Database Connectivity), and introduces an application that enables you to view and update information in a database through your web browser.

Chapter 17: Server-Side Scripting

This exciting new technology allows the server to perform VBScript code before the user ever sees the page. This expands the scope of opportunities by enabling databound forms and other solutions that previously required many lines of CGI programming.

Chapter 18: Integrating Java Applet Objects

VBScript plays well with others, Java applets included. This chapter shows you how to integrate Java applets within your VBScript code so that you can script them also.

Part V: Appendices

Appendix A: Installing Microsoft Internet Explorer 3.0

If you have not yet installed Internet Explorer 3.0, this appendix shows you how. The appendix also shows you some of the many features of this powerful web browser.

Appendix B: Glossary

This appendix contains a complete glossary to all the terms used in this book and in Internet development, in general.

New Riders Publishing

The staff of New Riders Publishing is committed to bringing you the very best in computer reference material. Each New Riders book is the result of months of work by authors and staff who research and refine the information contained within its covers.

As part of this commitment to you, New Riders invites your input. Please let us know if you enjoy this book, if you have trouble with the information and examples presented, or if you have a suggestion for the next edition.

Please note, however: New Riders staff cannot serve as a technical resource for VBScript or ActiveX, or for questions about software- or hardware-related problems. Please refer to the documentation that accompanies your software or to the applications' Help systems.

If you have a question or comment about any New Riders book, there are several ways to contact New Riders Publishing. We will respond to as many readers as we can. Your name, address, or phone number will never become part of a mailing list or be used for any purpose other than to help us continue to bring you the best books possible.

You can write us at the following address:

New Riders Publishing
Attn: Publisher
201 W. 103rd Street
Indianapolis, IN 46290

If you prefer, you can fax New Riders Publishing at:

317-817-7448

You can also send electronic mail to New Riders at the following Internet address:

`bjones@newriders.mcp.com`

New Riders Publishing is an imprint of Macmillan Computer Publishing. To obtain a catalog or information, or to purchase any Macmillan Computer Publishing book, call 800-428-5331 or visit our web site at `http://www.mcp.com`.

Thank you for selecting *Inside VBScript with ActiveX*!

PART I

VBScript, ActiveX, and the Internet

CHAPTER 1

Introduction to VBScript and ActiveX

By Art Scott

Visual Basic Scripting Edition, commonly referred to as VBScript, did not mysteriously appear out of nowhere. Rather, VBScript was derived from Visual Basic, which has a history that dates back several years. The other topic of this book, ActiveX, has a history too. Although ActiveX is a relatively new term, the principles behind it are not.

This chapter teaches you about the history of both VBScript and ActiveX. You learn about VBScript's Visual Basic background, as well as ActiveX's background. In this chapter, you will do the following:

◆ Explore the evolution of Visual Basic

◆ Delve into the history of ActiveX

◆ Begin to dig into VBScript

The purpose of this chapter is to overview the history of Visual Basic and ActiveX. In doing so, many terms may be used with which you are not familiar. In future chapters, many of these terms will be explained in detail.

Evolution of Visual Basic

In 1965 John Kemeny and Thomas Kurtz, two Dartmouth professors, developed "Beginner's All-purpose Symbolic Instruction Code," (BASIC). BASIC was created because an interactive language was needed. *Interactive* means programmers can type commands and experience immediate results. Instead of using punch cards, students of Kemeny and Kurtz sat at teletype terminals, typed their programs followed by "run," and the results were instantaneously printed out. A benefit of this immediate feedback was that it helped programmers feel free to experiment with new commands and features, and thus encouraged new ideas.

In the late 1970s, true personal computers were being sold by companies like Tandy, Apple, Commodore, and Atari, each of which had its own version of BASIC interpreters stored in the read-only memory (ROM). A small company called Microsoft also had a version of BASIC that was loaded into random-access memory (RAM). Many people turned to BASIC because it was simple to learn; they also spent hours typing in BASIC listings from magazines and books or translating them from one machine to another.

Programmers soon became frustrated with how slow BASIC was because BASIC was interpreted and not compiled. In BASIC, each program instruction had to be decoded each time it was run; therefore, the results were slow. Other problems existed as well. BASIC was not suited to structured programming because all variables were global and BASIC did not have the self-contained procedures and modules needed for structured programming.

The Development of QuickBasic

In the mid 1980s, Microsoft addressed these concerns by coming out with QuickBasic, a language that was compiled rather than interpreted. QuickBasic supported the following:

◆ Procedures—reusable routines within a program.

◆ Modules—reusable routines that are not necessarily in the main program.

◆ Long user-defined functions—reusable routines that can receive parameters and return values.

Rather than having a program that ran from top to bottom, functionality could now be split apart, thus making a program smaller and more efficient. Moreover, QuickBasic offered an integrated programming environment—meaning that programmers could edit, compile, run, debug, and revise programs from the same screen.

Although QuickBasic was powerful and easy to use and learn, there was a problem with the overall platform (MS-DOS) in which programmers were working. MS-DOS did not contain any built-in user interfaces; rather it was a character-based environment. Character-based environments do not use any real graphical presentation—only simple lines and characters are possible. This made MS-DOS hard to use because it required precise typing from the user and limited what the programmer could display to the user. To make MS-DOS programming easier, BASIC programmers began to implement menus, dialog boxes, and screen windows and to utilize the mouse as a pointing device. BASIC, however, provided some major obstacles to this development:

◆ There were no standards for this type of programming, which required users to relearn the programming interface each time they used a new program.

◆ Each program acted as if it were the only program the user would ever run. Each could occupy all the computer's resources without making any allowances for any other programs that may be running on the system or may be run by the user at another time.

The Emergence of Windows

Microsoft decided early on that the character-based PC was reaching the end of its usefulness; in 1985, Microsoft produced a clunky, unconvincing visual interface—the text-based Windows 1.0. In 1987, Microsoft upgraded Windows with Windows 2.0. This was graphical; the visual appearance of Windows along with the development tools and the debugger were improved.

In 1990, Windows 3.0 demonstrated the Graphical User Interface (GUI) that meant PC users had a consistent interface for each application. But this friendliness did not extend to programmers. At that time, Windows programming versus DOS programming was both different and difficult for the following reasons:

◆ Windows programming used *messages* and graphics, not as an afterthought, but in conjunction with menus, windows, and buttons that could be activated at any time by the user.

◆ With Windows, everything was a graphical object: menus, windows, buttons, list boxes, combo boxes, text boxes, scroll bars, pictures and even text.

◆ No longer were users controlled by the applications. Applications were controlled by the user by means of pointing and clicking with a mouse.

◆ Programming in Windows required programming in "C" plus using special development tools including a Software Development Kit (SDK).

Note Soon the programming tools for Windows began to catch up with the programmers' need. Borland's Turbo C++ for Windows, Turbo Pascal for Windows, Microsoft's QuickC for Windows, and Microsoft's Visual Basic were all early programming tools for Windows.

The Evolution of Visual Basic

Microsoft's Visual Basic, released in 1991, provided a different programming paradigm:

◆ It used Windows to design Windows programs.

◆ It used the Visual Basic language as the code behind the windows.

◆ It used custom controls to provide code reusability and ease-of-use for Windows objects.

Using Windows to design Windows programs means that the user selects and customizes graphical objects, such as menus, windows, dialog boxes, buttons, list boxes, combo boxes, text boxes, scroll bars, pictures, and even text. The user interface does most of the work, and the mouse provides a tool programmers can use to visually construct interface layouts quickly and efficiently.

With the Visual Basic Controls (VBX) technology being an intimate part of Visual Basic, this standardization created an industry based just on the VBX technology. The initial version of Visual Basic was shipped with 16 VBX controls: text boxes, list boxes, and so forth. These controls provided a plug-and-play control that enabled developers to focus on the application and not on the Windows API programming operating system.

The Development of VBX Controls

Along with Visual Basic (VB), the Control Development Kit (CDK) was released, which enabled commercial developers to develop other VBX controls for the growing Windows marketplace. The success of these controls is basically due to the standard interface that can be used right out of the box with few or no problems.

The VBX Custom Control extended the Visual Basic Toolbox, and provided events, methods, and properties fully supported by the Visual Basic environment. These controls are actually 16-bit Windows dynamic-link libraries (*.DLLs), that were designed to interact with Visual Basic.

When writing VBXs, you have to determine:

◆ How the control is displayed and printed

◆ The control's properties and what happens when the user sets a property

◆ The control's events

◆ The behavior of the control's methods

With each new operating system, a new version of Visual Basic has been introduced, each adding features and supporting more operating system capabilities. The only exception has been Visual Basic 4.0, which has a 16-bit and a 32-bit architecture. To better support the 32-bit architecture, the VBX was replaced with the OLE Custom Control, which you can compile as either a 16-bit or a 32-bit control.

The Development of OLE Custom Controls

The development of OLE custom controls was not only an important step in 32-bit system architecture, but it also gave the corporate developer the capability to create complex programs quickly, as well as reuse functionality. A corporate OLE custom control can be as simple as an AboutBox—enabling a whole company to display one Aboutbox for all software products, thus ensuring that when its company logo or address changes, everyone in the company will have these changes as they occur.

Until recently, creating OLE custom controls required the use of more complex languages such as C++ or Java. Using these more technical languages prevented programmers who only knew Visual Basic from creating their own OLE custom controls. With version 5.0, Visual Basic programmers are finally able to create their own OLE custom controls—now called ActiveX controls—using Visual Basic code.

Introduction to ActiveX

OLE Custom controls were renamed to ActiveX controls; however, ActiveX is more than just these controls. Most of the ActiveX technology that Microsoft introduced has a large foundation on the other technologies that Microsoft has developed over the past few years. In fact, ActiveX can be considered as simply the Internet-enabling of Microsoft technology. Microsoft has positioned their object technology as the core of most of these technologies. This object technology includes the capability for applications to communicate with each other or with objects that provide canned functionality.

The Evolution of Object Technology

In the past, users frequently were forced to utilize more than one application to manipulate data and were at the mercy of each application and its specific requirements. Each application acted as though it were the only application that the user would ever use. When users' data requirements were not met by the application, users had to either find workarounds to change the data requirements, learn and use another application that promised better results, or write user-specific code.

The Emergence of OLE

Microsoft introduced Object Linking and Embedding (OLE—pronounced "olé") in 1991. OLE Version 1.0 introduced the compound document concept.

OLE Version 1.0 was defined as a set of extensible protocols that enabled one application to use the services of another application in a seamless manner. The applications that used OLE could either link or embed information from documents that were created from other applications. A Word document, for example, within Microsoft Word for Windows could have a spreadsheet from Microsoft Excel embedded within it. This spreadsheet could be edited and manipulated just as if Excel were being used; however, it would still be a part of the Word document.

> **Note** The application that presents the document is the *container*. It is called a container document even though it is not the original application that created the document. Container documents are still connected to the originating application.

In 1993, Microsoft released OLE Version 2.0. This version of OLE exposed system features through Windows objects instead of API functions. Windows objects are exposed to interface methods that other applications may utilize. These methods may live anywhere: within an application, within a dynamic link library (DLL file) loaded into an application's memory space, within another application, or on another machine. OLE 2.0 also introduced the following:

◆ An interapplication drag-and-drop protocol

◆ In-place editing of embedded objects

◆ Object programmability

◆ Uniform Data Transfer (UDT)

◆ Structured storage for objects

Introducing OCX Controls

The next step in OLE's evolution replaced the *.VBX custom control with OLE Custom Controls, (*.OCX). An OLE custom control is an object with three distinct attributes:

◆ **Properties.** A control characteristic that describes a feature or part of the control such as its name, size, or color.

◆ **Events.** The outside actions to which a control can respond such as clicking or dragging.

◆ **Methods.** A function that an application can call to change the appearance, behavior, or properties of a control.

These three attributes are contained in a single file that is identified by an .OCX extension. These changes provided for the following:

◆ 16- and 32-bit support

◆ Utilization by any language that supports OLE

◆ Portability

◆ Multiple key assignments

◆ Property information retrieval

An OLE custom control is contained within a rectangle. This control acts as a server and is considered the ActiveX document. In the example, the Master1.OCX control is attached to the Visual Basic 4.0 application container, but it is confined to the area within the rectangle. The Visual Basic 4.0 application is considered the ActiveX container.

The new ActiveX document (OLE Document Object) Server takes over the entire client area of the container application. It can adjust clients' menus and appears as if it is the container application. ActiveX documents are mechanisms that are able to run within any frame and are container-independent.

An ActiveX document object provided from a server is a full-scale, conventional document that is embedded as an object within a container. Unlike embedded objects, ActiveX documents have complete control over their pages, and the user can use the full power of the application to edit them. Unlike embedded objects, ActiveX documents exploit the complete native functionality of the server (application) that creates them.

When a document is "activated" the document looks and acts as if the user were running the stand-alone application that normally manages that particular document type—complete with toolbars, menus, and all other user interface elements. Documents can be opened and saved without the user being concerned about low-level operating system concepts. The user does not have to be an experienced computer professional to use this system.

Users can create documents by using the full horsepower of their favorite applications; yet they can treat the resulting project as a single entity that can be uniquely named, saved, and transmitted to co-workers for review or editing. In the same way, a user of an Internet browser can treat the entire network, as well as local file systems, as a single document-storage entity and have the capability to browse the documents in that storage entity from a single location.

Introduction to VBScript

In the "Introduction to ActiveX" section, we discussed objects. These objects can be manipulated through scripting languages. Earlier, in the "Evolution of Visual Basic" section, we discussed graphical objects and how Visual Basic was being ported to other applications. VBScript (Visual Basic Scripting Edition) is the newest member of Microsoft's Visual Basic programming languages that bring ActiveX scripting to the web.

Note The term *scripting* refers to programming language that provides control of another host application. The language is interpreted rather than compiled—in other words, the browser has to decode each programming instruction. In the past, this meant that the program executed slowly. Today, however, this factor is circumvented because we have faster machines, interfaces, and multiple platform capability—the latter of which means, for example, that a Macintosh can run the scripts as an X86 Intel machine without any code changes.

Microsoft's Internet Explorer reads VBScript programs that are embedded within HTML web pages. HTML cannot interpret VBScript, but it can call the interpreter who can execute the VBScript language. This capability extends the web page and breaks the limitation barriers that HTML previously had.

If you have Visual Basic experience, you should notice that the following VBScript code contains the familiar BASIC syntax:

```
Sub cmdMyButton_OnClick
......' Add your Visual Basic Scripting code here
......MsgBox "Hello World, this site is now under construction."
End Sub
```

VBScript is a subset of Visual Basic. This means that many of Visual Basic's functions that manipulate clients, memory, disk drives, and so forth, have been eliminated so that Internet code does not destroy the client's machine. Don't worry—as a scripting language, VBScript is still very powerful, and you haven't lost any capabilities.

VBScript enables the user to interact with the web page, not just view the document within the browser. *Interact* means that users—those who are using your web pages—can visit your site and respond to questions from your site. Moreover, with VBScript, your interactive web page can do such things as the following:

◆ Verify the user's input prior to sending the data to the server.

◆ Provide interactive multimedia feedback to your users.

◆ Calculate data, such as sales tax.

You can integrate VBScript, HTML, ActiveX Controls (OLE controls such as calendars, edit boxes, and Active Movie), and Java applets all within the same web page.

VBScript provides many advantages. Web pages built completely with HTML gather information and process all the information on the server. This is accomplished when the user presses the SUBMIT button on the HTML form. With VBScript, the web page can validate all necessary fields without having the server return a message to the client stating that "not all required edit boxes contained proper information."

With VBScript, you can also build a web page that performs all its actions on the client's station.

Another advantage of VBScript is that it talks to host applications by means of ActiveX Scripting, a process that prevents Internet applications and browsers from the need to write special code for each component.

ActiveX Scripting does the following:

◆ It enables the host to compile scripts.

◆ It obtains and calls entry points.

◆ It manages the namespace available to the developer.

VBScript Licensing

At the time of this book's publication, you are able to obtain a no-cost VBScript license to use in your Internet products. These browser implementations of VBScript provide support for 16-bit, 32-bit, and Macintosh operating systems. VBScript can also be used as a general scripting language in other applications as well.

There are currently two types of VBScript Editions that you can use in your application:

◆ **Binary**—a ready-to-run, or compiled version.

◆ **Source**—a version that can be used to port VBScript to platforms that do not currently support the Binary Edition of VBScript.

Binary VBScript

Select this license if all you want to do is add VBScript to your application. This is the license you need to do the VBScript programming in this book. Obtaining this license provides you with the following advantages:

◆ If your application is distributed over the Internet, your users can download VBScript binary from Microsoft at `http://www.microsoft.com`.

◆ Your users can download the latest version of VBScript at any time, keeping up with new features.

◆ You can add your own objects and runtime functions to VBScript without modifying VBScript.

◆ Applications that share binary VBScript share a single copy of the DLL in memory.

VBScript Source Code

Select this license if you want to port VBScript to a platform that is not yet supported by VBScript. With this license, you are required to sign an agreement with Microsoft, which you can obtain from `http://www.microsoft.com`.

At the time this book was written, VBScript was supported on the following platforms:

◆ Windows 3.1

◆ Windows 95

◆ Windows NT for Intel-based computers

◆ Windows NT for PowerPC-based computers

◆ Windows NT for DEC Alpha-based computers

◆ Power Macintosh

Choose this license if your platform is not listed above, but remember to check with `http://www.microsoft.com/vbscript/` for platform support updates.

Summary

From its simple beginnings, BASIC has evolved and become a solution to many programming needs, and with this, Visual Basic continues to add value to today's complex applications. In 1965, Professor Kemeny and Professor Kurtz believed that a simpler way of programming would make computers more accessible to everyone. And 31 years later that concept is still holding true. BASIC has weathered the times and grown up by adapting itself to fit the needs of the user, students, commercial control builders, code reuse, Windows designing Windows, today's Internet developers, and it will continue into the 21 century.

At one time, scripting would have been considered a slow way of doing business because it is interpreted. But even this old concept has value in today's Internet market place. Why? Because interpreted means that it is *not* restricted to any particular platform. Interpreted means that the browser can and will decode the instructions providing the client user with the same presentation no matter what computer hardware is being used.

Programming and the Internet are being brought together to form one seamless part. If we were to keep with HTML only, we would not be able to drop a spreadsheet or database into a web page. We would also be limited to the static nature of HTML pages. We would not be happy with just HTML—we are demanding documents, hyperlinks, HTML, OLE objects, spreadsheets, FTP, MIME, and URLS to interact so that we can interact with each other. VBScript allows for a more dynamic interaction with users. It allows the manipulation of objects on web pages and direct feedback to users. Using the power of ActiveX controls, more powerful and impressive web pages can be created with less effort.

In the following chapters, you not only become familiar with the VB Scripting languages, but you also learn how to incorporate VBScript into your web pages. You discover how to incorporate ActiveX controls into your pages to gain their functionality. As added bonuses, you learn how to use Visual Basic 5.0 Control Creation Edition to create your own ActiveX controls using Visual Basic code, and how to apply VBScript to the server-side of an Internet system. Although the information in this chapter has been primarily technical and historical, you jump into actively learning VBScript in the next chapter.

CHAPTER 2

HTML Fundamentals for VBScripting

By Eric Smith

Now that you know how to use Internet Explorer, you are ready to start creating your own Visual Basic script pages. As you will see, creating pages is a fairly simple task. With just a text editor and the information from this chapter, you will build your first VBScript page.

This chapter covers the following topics:

◆ **The basics of creating pages with HTML and using intrinsic components, such as check boxes and text boxes, on your pages.** *HTML* stands for *Hypertext Markup Language*, which is the simple system of letter codes (called tags) you can use to create a web page. Every page that you load in your browser contains HTML tags. These tags control everything from the font size to the background colors.

◆ **How to use the HTML tags that are required for using VBScript in your pages.** Because VBScript is added directly to your web pages, you have to separate the code sections from the web page content. There are several special tags that are used specifically for marking the beginning and end of your code blocks.

- ◆ **How to embed VBScript code into your documents.**

- ◆ **How to generate output to the user.**

- ◆ **How to accept input from the user and utilize it in your VBScript code.**

All these initial pages are created with a basic text editor, such as Notepad or WordPad. Later chapters show you how to use some of the available tools for building active HTML documents. One of these tools, called the ActiveX Control Pad, is described in Chapter 3, "The ActiveX Control Pad." The Control Pad enables you to edit web pages and to add active content to pages using the ActiveX controls. You learn how to save and create your pages so that Internet Explorer can open them correctly.

Text Editing Basics

HTML pages are text files with the .HTM or .HTML file name extension. You create HTML documents by using a simple text editor, such as Notepad or WordPad. Because most HTML editing tools do not support the latest version of HTML and the associated tags, sometimes the best way to add a particular feature is to add it yourself.

In this chapter, you use both Notepad and WordPad to edit your documents. Notepad, the simple Windows text editor, is one of the most common ways to edit documents because most Windows-based computers already have it installed. Notepad is also a favorite of programmers because the program loads extremely fast (even on a slow machine), and it saves files in plain text by default, which simplifies the document creation process.

WordPad, a new accessory program introduced with Windows 95, replaces Windows Write, which was available under Windows 3.x. Although WordPad can handle much larger files and has more options for formatting, it has a much longer initial start time than Notepad and does not save files as simple text by default.

> **Note** To be sure that files from WordPad are being saved as text, remember to choose Text Document as the document type.

Simplifying Your Windows Workspace

Throughout this book, you create many HTML documents while you work through the examples in the book. (All the documents used in this chapter are available on the CD-ROM that is included with this book.) To help you work more efficiently, you will see how to make some modifications to Windows Explorer so that you can quickly open and edit HTML documents in Notepad and WordPad.

Windows 95 has several special folders used by the Windows 95 operating system in the main Windows directory, including the Send To folder. Any shortcuts placed in this folder are displayed automatically in the Send To menu, which displays when you click your alternate mouse button on a file shown in Windows Explorer.

> **Note**   Windows Explorer is not the same as Internet Explorer. Windows Explorer is used to browse the files on your hard drives, floppy drives, and your local area networks. Internet Explorer is a separate program used specifically to browse the Internet.
>
> However, the next revision of Internet Explorer (version 4.0) is going to combine these two tools into one. You will have one Explorer program that can look at files on your local machine in the same way that it looks at files on the Internet. This unified browser, when released, will simplify the Internet for casual users. See Microsoft's Internet Explorer web site at http://www.microsoft.com/ie/ie.htm for more details about Internet Explorer 4.0.

To help speed the editing and viewing cycle, you should create three shortcuts in the Send To folder: Notepad, WordPad, and Internet Explorer. The quickest way to create a shortcut is as follows:

1. In Windows Explorer, find the program for which you want to create a shortcut.

2. Click on the file that you want.

3. While holding down the Ctrl key, drag the file to the Send To folder in the main Windows 95 directory. As you drag the file, a plus sign appears beside the icon representing the file. The plus sign displays if the Ctrl key is depressed.

Create a shortcut for the three programs mentioned previously. To test your work, you can click on any file with the alternate mouse button and view the Send To menu. The three additional programs are listed in the Send To menu.

Learning the Basic HTML Tags

Now that your workspace has some helpful shortcuts, you are ready to learn about the basic HTML tags that you use with VBScript.

Almost all tags operate in pairs. The first half of the pair is enclosed between the left angle bracket (<)and the right angle bracket (>). The second half of the pair is also enclosed between the angle brackets, but it has a forward slash (/) as the second character, such as</HTML>. The tag with the slash signifies the end of a pair.

Overall Formatting Tags

The first tags discussed are for the overall formatting of your document. These tags help to separate your document into logical parts: the header, the body, and VBScript code blocks.

◆ **<HTML>...</HTML>.** The <HTML> tag encloses the HTML text on your page. The <HTML> tag should be the first line in your document, and the </HTML> tag should be the last line. Although most browsers operate correctly without these tags in the correct places, you should always put them into any HTML document you create.

◆ **<HEAD>...</HEAD>.** The <HEAD> tags enclose all the heading information on your page. The <TITLE> tag, explained next, is normally the only item that is placed between the <HEAD> tags. However, the <META> tag, a special tag used by certain types of programs, is also occasionally placed in this area. The <META> tag is reserved for special functions supported by the more advanced browsers. The <META> tag can cause the browser to reload a page at a particular time interval, for instance. The <META> tag can also contain keywords or other information used by web spiders and search engines. No matter what the <META> tag is used for, the <META> tag should be placed between the <HEAD> and </HEAD> tags.

◆ **<TITLE>...</TITLE>.** Any text placed between the <TITLE> tags is put in the title bar of your Internet browser. All documents should be given a title, especially any that are put on an Internet server. With the advent of the web spider, all documents are eventually found and indexed. If your document has no title, the spider lists it as "no title" without any other information. Anyone creating a bookmark or a shortcut to your page will have "no title" as one of his bookmarks. If you ever want someone to return to your page, you should make sure that he knows what your page is.

Note   Because the World Wide Web is a series of pages connected by links, various companies have created programs that follow these links and determine what content is contained on pages. These programs are called spiders because they *crawl* the web, just like a spider crawls on its spiderweb.

For instance, if you wanted to publicize a web site, you would submit it to a search engine such as AltaVista (http://www.altavista.digital.com). AltaVista's spider goes to your page and records what content is on the page. It then determines what pages your page links to and then records the content from the linked pages. Eventually, the spider finds a page that it has already recorded and then it stops traversing your pages.

All of the content recorded is indexed so that it can be searched. Indexing basically translates your pages into a series of keywords. AltaVista can then provide a list of pages that contain those keywords.

◆ **<BODY>...</BODY>.** Just as the <HEAD> tags contain all the heading information for the page, the <BODY> tags enclose all the primary content on the page. The <BODY> tags are used to enclose any VBScript code on the page.

◆ **<SCRIPT LANGUAGE="VBScript">...</SCRIPT>.** The <SCRIPT> tag is used to identify VBScript code within an HTML document. Because several scripting languages are available for HTML documents, the LANGUAGE parameter must always be given with VBScript as the selected language.

Warning   The *VBScript* in the <SCRIPT> tag is a recent change to the VBScript language. Previous versions of VBScript required the language parameter to be *VBS* and not *VBScript*. Unfortunately, any older pages with *VBS* as the language parameter do not function correctly under the latest version of Internet Explorer 3.0.

All the tags discussed in this section, except for the <SCRIPT> tags, are designed to be used only once in an HTML document. However, you can have multiple <SCRIPT> tags throughout your document. Later in this chapter you will learn about the various ways to embed VBScript code in your document.

Tags That Modify Text Appearance

The next group of tags are used to modify the appearance of text in your document. This list does not include every tag in this category; rather, it is a list of the most commonly used tags.

◆ **<Hn>...</Hn>.** All the heading tags are designed to enable font sizes to be easy to scale. You replace the variable *n* with any number from 1 through 6, with 1 being the largest font size and 6 being the smallest. Some guides advocate using these tags in order; that is, you would use <H2> only if you have used <H1>. However, this method does not always work correctly. Because of the wide variance of font sizes between computers and browsers, spacing can be extremely difficult to maintain if you use only the upper headings. As with much of HTML, the best way to learn what works is to try out various fonts and styles on different browsers to determine the best combination for your page.

◆ **<B>...</B>.** Text between these tags is given a boldface font. However, depending on other font options that can be selected, the font may not appear to be bold. For instance, many computers cannot display italics and bold together. If you have both of these options selected for your text, some users will only see italics.

- ◆ **<I>...</I>.** The <I> tag changes the enclosed text to an italicized font. Again, depending on the font, this tag may give an illegible result—especially at smaller font sizes such as <H5> or <H6>.

- ◆ **<U>...</U>.** Text between the <U> tags is underlined with a single line.

- ◆ **<BLOCKQUOTE>...</BLOCKQUOTE>.** The <BLOCKQUOTE> tag creates an indented paragraph. This tag is one of the more useful tags because you can nest multiple <BLOCKQUOTE> tags to produce multiple indentation levels. Paragraphs are indented from both the left and right margins.

- ◆ **<P>...</P>.** The <P> tag embeds a blank line in a block of text. However, the <P> tag is sometimes ignored based on other tags that it may precede or follow. For instance, if the <P> tag immediately precedes an <H2> tag, the <P> will be ignored. This is because the <H2> tag automatically adds a blank line just before the text that the <H2> tag encloses. The best advice to remember when using the <P> tag is to try it in your page to see how it behaves.

- ◆ **
.** The <BR> tag adds a line break to your page without adding any blank space. This tag can be useful when you do not have room or when you need room for white space between elements on a page. Unlike many of the other HTML tags discussed in this section, the <BR> tag is not used in a pair. Instead, you just add a single <BR> tag to add a line break to your page.

- ◆ **<CENTER>...</CENTER>.** Any text or other elements placed between a <CENTER> tag pair is centered relative to the edges of a page element's cell. This cell can be on the edges of the browser or the sides of a table cell.

- ◆ **<A HREF=url>.** The anchor tag is one of the most common tags used. This tag is used to specify a hyperlink to another page or address. You can use any valid URL in this type of tag, which includes the mailto:, ftp:, and http: style of links. The following code shows some examples of the anchor tag in use:

```
<A HREF="http://www.inquiry.com/thevbpro">

<A HREF="mailto:webmaster@mcp.com">

<A HREF="ftp://ftp.cica.indiana.edu/">
```

- ◆ **<HR>.** Using this tag adds a horizontal rule to an HTML document. The horizontal rule is used to break up logical blocks of text or other elements on a page. The <HR> tag does not have a corresponding </HR> tag; rather, the <HR> tag is used by itself to add the horizontal rule to a page.

On the CD

The CD-ROM contains a document with examples of all of these tags to help you see how they work together and how they appear when viewed in your browser. This document is designed to help you see the differences between various fonts and alignment options. The HTML code is included here for reference. This example, located in the \Examples\Chapter2 folder on the CD-ROM, is named HTMLSample.HTML.

```
<HTML>
<HEAD>
<TITLE>Inside VBScript - Chapter 2 - HTML Fundamentals for VBScripting</TITLE>
</HEAD>
<BODY>
<BLOCKQUOTE>
This example is designed to show you the differences between the various font
styles, appearances, and formatting options.  This document begins with the
HTML, HEAD, and TITLE tags. As you can see, putting text in a BLOCKQUOTE tag
indents it from both sides.  This paragraph is followed by a horizontal rule to
separate it from the rest of the page.
</BLOCKQUOTE>
<HR>
<H1>This line is formatted with the H1 style.  It is the largest font size
available using this type of tag.  </H1>
<HR>
<H2>You are now viewing text in the H2 style. When you change font sizes from
H1 to H2, for instance, white space is automatically added. This lets you avoid
putting in a separate paragraph tag.  </H2>
<HR>
<H3>
This is text formatted with the H3 tag. You can insert paragraph tags into text
formatted with one of the heading tags.
<P>
You can also insert simple paragraph breaks,
<BR>
just like this. You don't have to worry about spacing text in a particular way
-- your browser will automatically format the text for you. You    can    put
many spaces or
line
breaks
in
your
HTML
and your browser will reformat it correctly. This feature is useful when you
have lots of long anchors to other pages that don't fit on one line.
</H3>
<HR>
```

```
<H4>This text is formatted with the H4 tag.  Remember that you can increase all
of the fonts proportionally by clicking the Font toolbar button on Internet
Explorer, or by selecting a font size family from the Fonts submenu under the
View menu.
</H4>
<HR>
<H5>This text is formatted with the H5 tag.  Depending on the way your
browser's fonts are configured, this font may not be very clear.
</H5>
<HR>
<H6>This is H6 text, and it may be even less clear.  Both H5 and H6 text should
only be used for items such as copyright notices at the bottoms of pages or
other items that the user doesn't normally need to read carefully.
</H6>
<HR>
<BLOCKQUOTE>
Now you are viewing the default font again within the BLOCKQUOTE tag.  By using
the <B>bold</B> tag, you can emphasize certain words, or <B>entire sentences
that are important to the reader.</B>  <I>Italicized text</I> is also useful
for emphasis, as is <U>underlined text.</U>  All of these formatting options
are available at all the other font sizes, as well.
</BLOCKQUOTE>
<CENTER>
Finally, all of these text items can be centered with the CENTER tag.  If you
resize your window, you will notice that this text is centered between the
edges of the window.
</CENTER>
<BLOCKQUOTE>
Those are just a few ways you can use these basic HTML tags to create profes-
sional looking documents.  Before you are done editing your document, always be
sure to end the document with the /BODY and /HTML tags.  Most browsers will
work without them; however, it is a good practice to begin following.
</BLOCKQUOTE>
</BODY>
</HTML>
```

You will be introduced to more HTML tags throughout this book. Even though you will be learning more tags that are specifically for VBScript, you also need to be familiar with the basic tags introduced in this chapter. Without these tags, you will not be able to create HTML documents to contain your VBScript code and ActiveX controls. In addition, learning basic HTML will prepare you for future changes to the HTML language.

Learning the Intrinsic Controls

Besides text tags, HTML provides a number of elements that are used to build forms for users to complete. Because these controls do not require additional controls, they are called *intrinsic controls*. These controls are similar to those included with Visual Basic. The intrinsic controls are

Push button

Check box

List box

Drop-down list box

Radio button

Text box

Creating a Form in HTML

You have to use several tags before you can use any other intrinsic controls in your HTML document. The first of these are the <FORM> and </FORM> tags. These tags mark the beginning and end of a form, as shown in the following example.

```
<FORM ACTION="/cgi-bin/dosomething.cgi" METHOD="POST">
```

The two parameters of the <FORM> tag are critical to the operation of the HTML form. The first, the ACTION parameter, specifies a program that is used to process the data input to the form. The second parameter, the METHOD parameter, specifies how the data should be passed to the back-end program. The POST method sends the data to the program via environment variables. The GET method sends the data to the back-end program via the actual URL. All the input parameters are added to the end of the URL, and the back-end program is responsible for decoding them.

After the <FORM> tag has been added to your document, you can begin adding the intrinsic controls. All the controls must be placed between the <FORM> and </FORM> tags.

Using the Text Box Control

The text box is probably the most common form control you use. To add a text box to your form, use the following HTML tag:

```
<INPUT TYPE=text NAME="parm_topic" SIZE=50 MAXLENGTH=50>
```

Many of the intrinsic controls begin their tags with the keyword INPUT. The next parameter, TYPE, indicates that this control is a simple text box. The SIZE parameter determines how large the control is on the page. The SIZE parameter specifies the length in characters, so that the actual size on the page will vary, based on the font size that the browser uses. The MAXLENGTH parameter indicates how much text can be put into the control, regardless of how large the control appears to be on the page. This parameter is also expressed in characters. In the previous example, 50 indicates that this box can contain no more than 50 characters. As shown in the preceding sample, the entire tag is enclosed in angle brackets.

The NAME parameter is extremely important to both normal form processing and in VBScript. This parameter is the name that your VBScript code can refer to in order to access the data the user has entered into this control. All the intrinsic controls include the NAME property.

You may have noticed that the TYPE parameter value is not enclosed in quotes, but the NAME parameter is. In this example, both of them could have been enclosed in quotes. The general rule to follow is this: If the value you are using contains spaces, you must enclose the value in double quotes. If the value does not contain spaces, you can omit the double quotes. In addition, the parameters are not case-sensitive.

Note   Any parameter values that include spaces must be enclosed in double quotes.

Using the Multiple Line Text Box

For larger pieces of text, a single line is not sufficient. For these instances, you can use the multiple line text box. The HTML tag to insert this control is:

```
<TEXTAREA NAME="data_Question" COLS=50 ROWS=3>
```

Instead of a SIZE and MAXSIZE parameter, the TEXTAREA tag uses the COLS and ROWS parameters that specify how many columns and rows should display on-screen. For this control, the maximum length can be unlimited, or you can set the MAXLENGTH property to control the maximum amount of text a user can enter. The entire tag, with all its parameters, needs to be enclosed in angle brackets.

When you use this tag, you need to add a final </TEXTAREA> to complete the tag. If you leave off the final </TEXTAREA>, any text following the tag will be inserted into the multiple line text box.

Using the Push Button

As with other types of dialog boxes, the push or command button is typically used either to cancel the action or to submit the data to the program for processing. The same is true of the push button. You can have three kinds of push buttons, depending on what TYPE parameter is used in the INPUT tag: SUBMIT, RESET, or BUTTON. Of these, the BUTTON parameter is used exclusively with VBScript code.

The SUBMIT Button

The HTML tag for a button using the SUBMIT type is shown in the following example:

```
<INPUT TYPE=submit VALUE="Submit">
```

For this type of button, the VALUE parameter contains the text that should be put on the button itself. By using the TYPE parameter, you indicate that this button is used to submit data to the program specified in the initial <FORM> tag. As with the other controls, push buttons can be assigned names by using the NAME parameter.

The RESET Button

A button using the RESET type is used to clear the form. An example of the tag used to provide this type of button on your form is

```
<INPUT TYPE=reset VALUE="Clear Form">
```

By using a TYPE=reset parameter, you specify that this button, when clicked, erases the data in the form. When you create a form, you should always include a reset button. If no button exists to clear the form's data, the user has to erase all the data manually.

The BUTTON Button

The final type of button, used with VBScript, uses the TYPE parameter called BUTTON. These buttons are ones that have VBScript code attached to them and do not use the default actions for submitting or clearing the form. An example of this type of button is

```
<INPUT TYPE=BUTTON VALUE="Press This Button" NAME="btnTest">
```

If you use this type of button on a form with no VBScript code, the button does nothing. However, with VBScript, the button performs whatever code is assigned to it in the appropriate event handler. Event handlers and assigning VBScript code to buttons will be discussed later in this chapter and in Chapter 9, "Programming with Events."

Using the Check Box

The check box is used for data that requires a Yes/No or True/False answer that is exclusive of other options. To add a check box to your form, use the following HTML tag:

```
<INPUT TYPE="checkbox" NAME="SubscriberMailList" VALUE="SubscriberMailList"
CHECKED>
```

For the check box control, the VALUE parameter specifies the value given to the control when it is checked. When the control is not checked, no value is assigned to the control. If you add the optional parameter CHECKED to this tag, the check box will be checked when the form first loads or when it is cleared by the reset button.

 For choices where the user is to pick only one from a number of options, the radio button should be used instead of the check box.

Using the Radio Button

The radio button enables the user to choose only one of a group of options. It is called a radio button because it functions like the buttons on older types of car radios: only one of the station selector buttons can be pressed at once, and you can easily see which button is pressed. This control is also known as an *option button*. The HTML tag to add this type of control is shown here:

```
<INPUT TYPE="radio" VALUE="DirectMail" NAME="SubscriberHowFound">
```

As with the check box control, you can add the CHECKED parameter to this tag initially to choose one of a group of radio buttons. To make a group of radio buttons function together, they all need to have the same name. By using the NAME property correctly, you can provide multiple groups of radio buttons on your document. In Visual Basic, you would have to group the radio buttons inside a frame to provide this function. In HTML, you just need to give them all the same NAME property. When you choose one of the radio buttons in a group, the value of the control equals the VALUE property of the selected radio button.

Note   All radio buttons in a group must have the same value for their NAME properties.

Using the List Box and Drop-Down List Box

In HTML, the standard list box and the drop-down list box are essentially the same control. The only difference is the inclusion of the SIZE parameter in the HTML tag for the standard list box. An example of a drop-down list box follows:

```
<SELECT NAME=data_Version>
     <OPTION>Select Your Version</OPTION>
     <OPTION>------------------</OPTION>
     <OPTION>VBScript</OPTION>
     <OPTION>Version 3.0 Standard</OPTION>
     <OPTION>Version 3.0 Professional</OPTION>
     <OPTION>Version 4.0 Standard</OPTION>
     <OPTION>Version 4.0 Professional</OPTION>
     <OPTION>Version 4.0 Enterprise</OPTION>
</SELECT>
```

This HTML tag creates a drop-down list box with all the items specified in the <OPTION> tags. The list is terminated by the </SELECT> tag.

If you want to make this list into a standard list box, all you have to do is add the SIZE parameter to the <SELECT> tag, like this:

```
<SELECT NAME=data_Version SIZE=3>
     <OPTION>Select Your Version</OPTION>
     <OPTION>--------------------</OPTION>
     <OPTION>VBScript</OPTION>
     <OPTION>Version 3.0 Standard</OPTION>
     <OPTION>Version 3.0 Professional</OPTION>
     <OPTION>Version 4.0 Standard</OPTION>
     <OPTION>Version 4.0 Professional</OPTION>
     <OPTION>Version 4.0 Enterprise</OPTION>
</SELECT>
```

The addition of the SIZE parameter creates a standard list box on your form that is three rows in height but still contains all the entries specified in the <OPTION> tags within the <SELECT> tags. After the user chooses a particular option, the control specified by the NAME property has the value shown in the list box. This value is one of the items specified in an <OPTION> tag.

By default, the drop-down list box selects the first item. To specify a different item, change its <OPTION> tag to <OPTION SELECTED>. When the form displays, the item with the SELECTED parameter is shown in the drop-down list box as the selected item.

Using Hidden Input Fields

The last type of intrinsic control is not really a control at all. In cases where you need to pass additional information to a back-end server, for instance, you can add hidden input fields to your form. An example of this type of field follows:

```
<INPUT NAME="parm_dest_email" VALUE="webmaster@inquiry.com" TYPE="hidden">
```

This data is passed to the back-end program, just like any of the other controls' data, but the user cannot change it. This type of field is useful for sending configuration or location information to a generic program that you use for sending mail.

On the
CD

To show what the intrinsic controls look like in your browser, load the FormSample.HTML file from the \Examples\Chapter2 directory on the CD-ROM. The HTML code is included here for reference, and a picture of the browser window is shown in figure 2.1. One of each of the intrinsic controls is demonstrated in this document.

> **Note**   Although you can view this form in your browser, it will not work because no program exists to process the input data. You learn about processing the data in later chapters.

```
<HTML>
<HEAD>
<TITLE>Ask the VB Pro - Ask a Question</title>
</HEAD>
<BODY>

<BLOCKQUOTE>
Enter the information below to submit your question.
</BLOCKQUOTE>
<HR>
<FORM ACTION=/global-bin/question.pl METHOD=POST>
<INPUT NAME="parm_dest_email" VALUE="thevbpro@inquiry.com" TYPE="hidden">
<INPUT NAME="parm_back_url" VALUE="thevbpro" TYPE="hidden">
<INPUT NAME="parm_proname" VALUE="VB Pro" TYPE=hidden>
<TABLE>
<TR><TD>Full Name:</TD>
<TD><INPUT TYPE=text NAME="parm_sender_name" SIZE=40 MAXLENGTH=40></TD></TR>
<TR><TD>E-Mail Address:</TD>
<TD><INPUT TYPE=text NAME="parm_sender_email" SIZE=40 MAXLENGTH=40></TD></TR>
<TR><TD>Question Topic:</TD>
<TD><INPUT TYPE=text NAME="parm_topic" SIZE=50 MAXLENGTH=50></TD></TR>
```

```
<TR><TD>VB Version:</TD>
 <TD><SELECT NAME=data_Version>
       <OPTION>Select Your Version</OPTION>
       <OPTION>----------------------</OPTION>
       <OPTION>VBScript</OPTION>
       <OPTION>Version 3.0 Standard</OPTION>
       <OPTION>Version 3.0 Professional</OPTION>
       <OPTION>Version 4.0 Standard</OPTION>
       <OPTION>Version 4.0 Professional</OPTION>
       <OPTION>Version 4.0 Enterprise</OPTION>
</SELECT></TR>

<TR><TD>Difficulty:</TD>
<TD><INPUT TYPE=radio NAME="difficulty" VALUE="Low">Low
<INPUT TYPE=radio NAME="difficulty" VALUE="Medium" CHECKED>Medium
<INPUT TYPE=radio NAME="difficulty" VALUE="High">High
</TR>

<TR><TD>Question:</TD>
<TD><TEXTAREA NAME="data_Question" COLS=50 ROWS=3></TEXTAREA></TD></TR>
</TABLE>
<INPUT TYPE="CHECKBOX" NAME="SubscriberMailList" VALUE="SubscriberMailList"
CHECKED>
I would like to be on the Ask the VB Pro mailing list.
<CENTER>
<FONT SIZE=+1>
<INPUT TYPE=submit VALUE="Submit"> <INPUT TYPE=reset VALUE="Clear Form">
</FONT>
</CENTER>
</FORM>
<HR>
<CENTER>
<font SIZE=-1>
<i>
Comments, questions or
problems?  <a HREF="mailto:webmaster@inquiry.com">webmaster@inquiry.com</a><br>
Copyright &copy; 1996 by inquiry.com, Inc.  All rights reserved.<br>
</i>
</font>
</center>
</BODY></HTML>
```

Figure 2.1

The Intrinsic Controls example, as it appears in Internet Explorer.

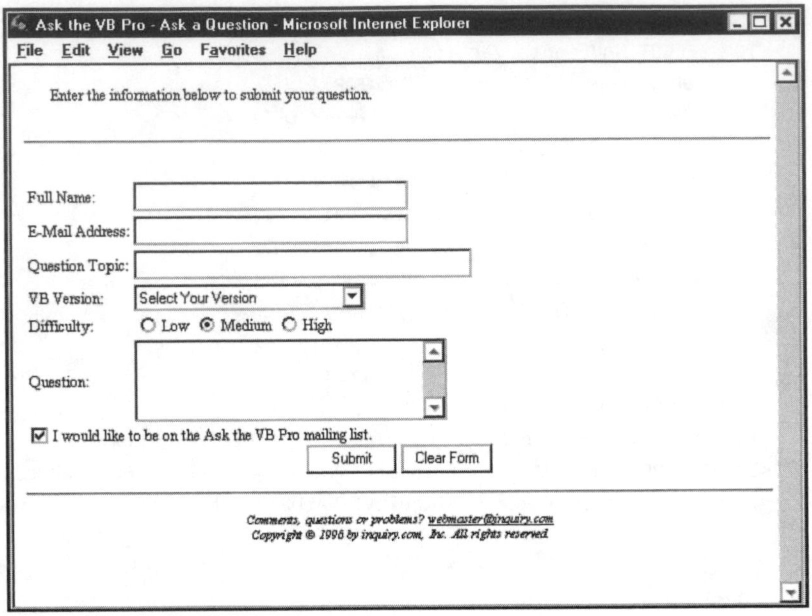

Creating a Table

For the preceding code example, an HTML table is used to easily arrange the controls and associated labels. Using tables is very easy—you only have to learn three tags to start.

◆ The first tag is the <TABLE> tag, which starts the definition of a table. The </TABLE> tag is its counterpart and goes at the end of a table's definition.

◆ The next tag is <TR>, which stands for table row. Each row of a table has a <TR> starting the row and a </TR> ending it.

◆ Within a row, you have fields. Each field is surrounded by <TD> and </TD> tags.

For best results, all rows in a table should have the same number of fields. This example uses a table with two columns: the first column contains the label identifying the control on the right, and the second column contains the actual control.

The table automatically sizes each column to the widest item, and each row is sized to the tallest item in the row. For example, the large multiple line text box and the caption Question: are in one row. The caption is centered vertically beside the text box. To see the borders of the table, you can add BORDER=1 to the initial <TABLE> tag. You will be seeing more tables used in examples throughout this book.

Learning Basic VBScript

Now that you have seen how the intrinsic controls and some basic HTML tags can be used to create an HTML document, you are ready to learn how to add VBScript code to use the data the user has entered. In this section, you learn some statements that you can use to perform basic input and output with data from the user.

Adding VBScript Code to a Document

HTML is read and evaluated by the browser exactly as the browser reads the file: it starts at the top and works its way down the page. VBScript code works the same way. As the browser reaches each block surrounded by <SCRIPT> tags, it evaluates whether it should immediately execute the code. In the example that follows, the VBScript code in the page executes as soon as the page is loaded.

```
<HTML>
<SCRIPT LANGUAGE=VBScript>
Document.Write "This is a test"
</SCRIPT>
</HTML>
```

When the page is loaded, "This is a test" is written on the top of the page. No user input is required to activate the code in this example. This method, which is known as *inline code*, can be useful in certain circumstances.

> **Tip** You can use inline code on a page that displays "Good Morning," "Good Afternoon," or "Good Evening," based on the time of day. Inline code does not require any input from the user and it executes immediately.

If you have written code that requires user input first, you may want to use another method of adding code. By adding an event handler for a control, you tell the browser to execute code when a particular event, like a button click, occurs. Refer to Chapter 9 for more information on writing event handlers. In the example that follows, the user is prompted to enter his name in the text box and to press the push button. The user's input then displays in a message box. The code for this example is in the \Examples\Chapter4 directory on the CD-ROM in the file named IOSample.HTML.

On the CD

```
<HTML>
<HEAD>
<SCRIPT LANGUAGE=VBScript>
Sub btnSubmit_Click
      MsgBox "Your name is " & Document.NameForm.txtName.value & "!"
End Sub
</SCRIPT>
</HEAD>
<FORM NAME="NameForm">
Enter your name: <INPUT TYPE=text NAME=txtName SIZE=40><P>
<INPUT TYPE=BUTTON NAME=btnSubmit VALUE="Press When Done!"
onClick="btnSubmit_Click">
</FORM>
</HTML>
```

In the preceding example, the code that processes the user's click on a button is in a
subroutine. Internet Explorer reads the code but does not execute it immediately.
However, Internet Explorer keeps a reference to the code so that when the user clicks
the button, Internet Explorer runs the piece of code that displays the user's name.

You learn more about the particulars of writing code later in this chapter and subsequent chapters, but you now see the differences in placement of code and how it
affects the user's use of a page.

Processing User Input

You can accept user input in the following two ways:

◆ Form fields

◆ InputBox function

This section goes into more detail on how and why the preceding form field example
worked. The results of this code in Internet Explorer are shown in figure 2.2.

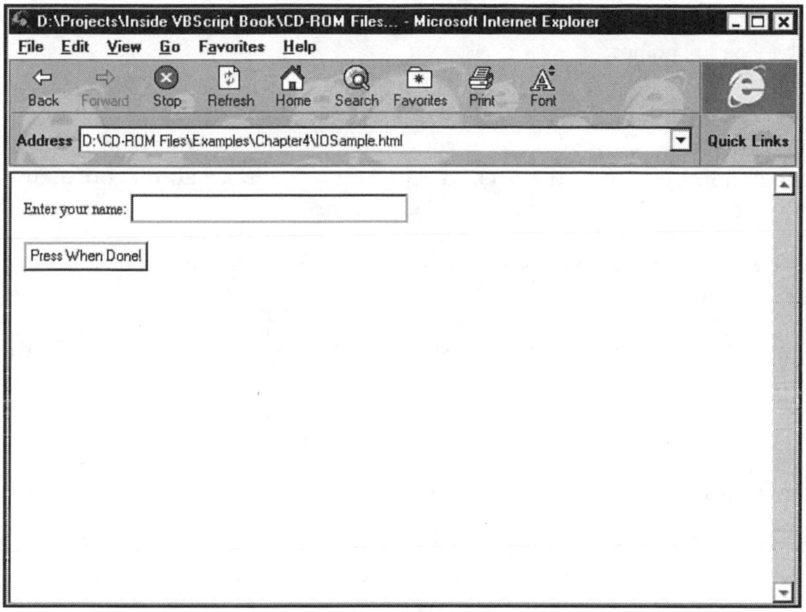

Figure 2.2

The IOSample.HTML example, as it appears in Internet Explorer.

MsgBox Function

The HTML tag for the submission button has additional parameters: ONCLICK and LANGUAGE. Because you can have multiple script languages in a single document, the language that is executed must be specified for the button. If no language is specified, Internet Explorer defaults to executingthe JavaScript code. The ONCLICK parameter specifies the subroutine name to execute when the user clicks the button with the ONCLICK parameter defined.

In the btnSubmit_Click subroutine, the user's name is displayed by the MsgBox function, which displays a message box. To access the value of the text box in the form, you cannot simply use the name of the text box; rather, you must fully specify the name of the text box. The <FORM> tag now has a NAME parameter, which names it NameForm. You use this name in combination with the overall Document object to specify the text box's name. The Document object is a way to store all the information in an HTML page so that it can be accessed through code. All page elements can be accessed through the Document object. For example, the resulting name of the text box in this page is Document.NameForm.txtName.

Moreover, you have to specify the Value property as the one to retrieve. Under Visual Basic, you frequently can specify only the control name, and then Visual Basic retrieves the default property of the control. This functionality does not work in VBScript. If you do not add the Value property to the end of Document.NameForm. txtName, you get a runtime error from Internet Explorer.

Note When referring to form elements or control properties, you must always refer to them by their full names.

After you have accessed the value of the text box, the MsgBox function can be used to display the value. The value of the text box is concatenated with the text Your name is using the concatenation operator—the & character. You learn more about concatenation later in Chapter 6, "VBScript Functions and Operators."

All of the options available to the MsgBox function are documented in the following section for your reference.

The MsgBox function's syntax is shown here, with all of the available options for both text and graphical formatting.

```
MsgBox(prompt [, options][, title])
```

The MsgBox function syntax has these arguments:

◆ **Prompt.** This parameter holds the actual message you want to display in the message box. If the message has multiple lines, you can concatenate a new line character where you want the line break, as shown in this example:

```
MsgBox "Message Line 1" & Chr(13) & "Message Line 2"
```

This will cause two lines to be displayed in the message box as follows:

```
Message Line 1
Message Line 2
```

◆ **Options.** This parameter is used to specify which options should be used to format the message box. If this parameter is set to 0, the only button to display will be the OK button. Using the numbers in the following table, you can choose which buttons and icons should be displayed in the message. For instance, if you wanted the warning query icon with the Abort, Retry, and Ignore buttons you would add 2 + 32 to get 34 as the value of the Options parameter.

Parameter	Result
0	Display OK button only
1	Display OK and Cancel buttons
2	Display Abort, Retry, and Ignore buttons
3	Display Yes, No, and Cancel buttons
4	Display Yes and No buttons
5	Display Retry and Cancel buttons

16	Display Critical Message icon
32	Display Warning Query icon
48	Display Warning Message icon
64	Display Information Message icon
0	First button is default
256	Second button is default
512	Third button is default
768	Fourth button is default

0—The *application modal* means that the user must respond to the message box before continuing to work in the current application.

4096—The *system modal* means that all applications are suspended until the user responds to the message box.

◆ **Title.** Use this parameter to title the message box that is shown to the user. If you do not provide a title, the words **Visual Basic** appear in the message box's title bar.

The MsgBox function can return one of the following values, based on the button the user presses:

Parameter	Result
1	OK button chosen
2	Cancel button chosen
3	Abort button chosen
4	Retry button chosen
5	Ignore button chosen
6	Yes button chosen
7	No button chosen

InputBox Function

The other method you have available to get user input is the InputBox function. This function displays a dialog box that contains a place for the user to enter a response to your query. An example of an InputBox function is shown in figure 2.3.

On the
CD

The InputBox function returns the input value to the calling code. You can then take that value and put it in a variable or manipulate it immediately. A simple example of this function follows. The returned value from InputBox is immediately displayed in a message box. This example is named `InputBox.HTML` and is located in the `\Examples\Chapter2` directory on the accompanying CD-ROM.

Figure 2.3

An example of a VBScript InputBox.

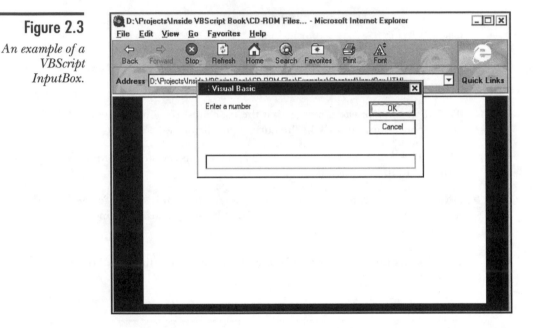

```
<HTML>
<SCRIPT LANGUAGE=VBScript>
MsgBox "You entered " & InputBox("Enter a number")
</SCRIPT>
</HTML>
```

Alternatively, you can store the result of the InputBox function in a variable and process it in another piece of code. The full function description for the InputBox function is printed here for your reference.

```
InputBox(prompt[, title][, default][, xpos][, ypos])
```

The InputBox function syntax has these arguments:

◆ **Prompt.** This parameter holds the actual message you want to display in the message box. If the message has multiple lines, you can concatenate a new line character where you want the line break, as shown in this example:

```
MsgBox "Message Line 1" & Chr(13) & "Message Line 2"
```

This will cause the two lines to be displayed in the message box as follows:

```
Message Line 1
Message Line 2
```

◆ **Title.** Use this optional parameter to title the message box that is shown to the user. If you do not provide a title, the words **Visual Basic** appear in the message box's title bar.

◆ **Default.** This optional parameter can be used to set the initial string shown in the text box portion of the InputBox displayed to the user. If this parameter is left blank, the text box is empty.

◆ **Xpos.** This optional parameter can be used to set the horizontal position of the InputBox when it displays. This parameter is set in pixels.

◆ **Ypos.** This optional parameter can be used to set the vertical position of the InputBox when it is displayed to the user. This parameter is also set in pixels.

Summary

This chapter has provided you with an introduction to HTML and how it can be used to create useful web pages. You have also learned the basics of creating forms and adding VBScript code to forms to provide additional functionality. You learned your first few VBScript functions, including the MsgBox and InputBox functions.

CHAPTER 3

The ActiveX Control Pad

By Eric Smith

In the early days of the World Wide Web (before 1995), few companies exhibited the corporate presence that currently exists. Microsoft, for example, had only a simple presence that supported limited technical information and product details. After the introduction of web browsers, such as Netscape, the World Wide Web began to grow tremendously. As a result, every Internet-savvy company scrambled for domain names that would later become household names.

Interestingly, Microsoft did not reserve www.windows95.com, which would have been the logical choice for the site for their flagship product introduced in 1995, Windows 95. A Windows 95 shareware-download site actually controls the name.

Although Internet sites became bigger and more graphical in 1995, Microsoft's site remained basically the same. Internet Explorer 2.0's capabilities fell far behind those of Netscape. Most web sites began to support Netscape's advanced features (such as frames), but almost no sites even mentioned Internet Explorer as a supported browser. Netscape's stock went public that same year and initiated the Internet stock frenzy, but Microsoft appeared to be asleep at the Internet switch.

In early 1996, however, Microsoft implemented a counter-attack on every front that Netscape controlled. A buggy, rough Internet Explorer 3.0 was released in alpha test, which is the initial public release of a software title. This early version included support for ActiveX, as well as many features such as frames that Netscape had supported exclusively until then. Shortly afterward, Microsoft released other tools, including the ActiveX Control Pad, which assists programmers and non-programmers alike in creating "activated" pages through reusable components and controls instead of writing everything from scratch.

The ActiveX Control Pad also enables you to tap into the ActiveX framework for access to everything in an ActiveX-enhanced HTML document. The Control Pad also gives the designer the ability to control other non-ActiveX components, such as Java applets, through a common interface. As Visual Basic developers will find, the ActiveX Control Pad resembles Visual Basic's interface for developing Windows applications. In this chapter, you learn that the Control Pad provides a number of useful tools, all of which can be accessed by developers of all skill levels.

Introduction to the Interface

When you first start the ActiveX Control Pad, a window that resembles a simple word processor appears (see fig. 3.1). This window provides only basic text editing capabilities. Features common in other programming tools, such as auto-indent, are missing from this tool.

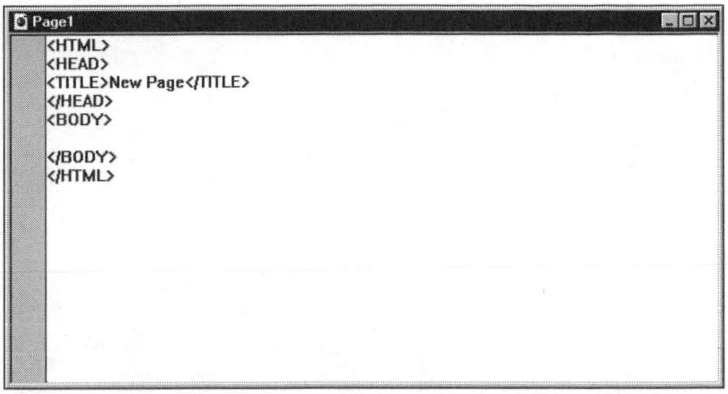

Figure 3.1

The ActiveX Control Pad as it appears when you start it.

All the functions of the Control Pad are accessible from the menus on this screen. In addition, certain common functions exist on the toolbar. (These functions are common to most Microsoft or Windows programs. If you are already familiar with the basic menu choices, skim this section and skip to the "Creating a Document with the ActiveX Control Pad" section.) There are a few differences in the menus for the ActiveX Control Pad. This section discusses the functions on both the menus and the toolbars listed here:

◆ File menu

◆ Edit menu

◆ View menu

◆ Format menu

◆ Tools menu

◆ Window menu

◆ Help menu

◆ ActiveX Control Pad toolbar

File Menu

The File menu contains the following menu items:

◆ New HTML

◆ New HTML Layout

◆ Open...

◆ Close

- ◆ Save

- ◆ Save As...

- ◆ Save All

- ◆ Print

- ◆ Recently Used File List

- ◆ Exit

This section discusses each of these menu items.

New HTML

The ActiveX Control Pad has the capability to edit both HTML documents and HTML layout files. As you have learned, HTML documents are simple text files that contain Hypertext Markup Language tags, which indicate how a page should be displayed to someone using a web browser. By selecting New HTML, you indicate that you want to create a new web page. Later sections of this chapter detail the HTML layout file.

When you select New HTML or start the ActiveX Control Pad, the ActiveX Control Pad by default creates a new HTML document that contains the following tags:

```
<HTML>
<HEAD>
<TITLE>New Page</TITLE>
</HEAD>
<BODY>

</BODY>
</HTML>
```

 Note The ActiveX Control Pad starts each page on a good note by including the recommended tags for every web page, regardless of the content.

Because the ActiveX Control Pad supports MDI (Multiple Document Interface), it enables you to open more than one document at a time. The Window menu, which is discussed later in this chapter, contains a list of currently open documents.

New HTML Layout

Although simple HTML does not provide any real layout capabilities, Microsoft's
Internet Explorer does support a special type of file, called a layout file. This file
stores information about how text should be displayed; it also contains information
about controls that should be on the page, where exactly the controls should be
placed, and what the text should look like. The layout file is currently only supported
in Internet Explorer 3.0, so if you need to maintain usability with Netscape, this
feature does not work in your case.

The ActiveX Control Pad enables you to create and edit HTML layout files so you can
take advantage of the more complex layering and layout capabilities supported by
Internet Explorer 3.0. By using the Control Pad's Visual Basic-like interface, you can
layer text, graphics, and other controls with an ease that you only dreamed about with
simple HTML. Later in the chapter, you learn how to use this part of the editor.

Open...

To continue editing a previously created document, use the Open...menu choice.
You can select both HTML documents (with .HTM or .HTML extensions) or HTML
layout files (with .ALX extensions).

Close

To close a window within the Control Pad, select the Close menu choice from the
window by highlighting the title bar and then selecting Close. If you do not first select
the window you want to close, the Control Pad closes the last window you used. This
choice is identical to clicking the Close button (the X button) in the upper-right
corner of the window.

Save

Selecting Save from the menu saves the current window's contents. If the document is
new, the system prompts you for a file name. If the document already had a file name,
selecting Save saves the document under the same name.

Save As...

You always receive a file name prompt when you select Save As.... This feature
enables you to save the current copy of a document you are editing when you want to
preserve the original, unedited copy.

Save All

When you select this menu choice, the Control Pad saves all the files currently being edited. If any of the documents are new and have no file names, the system prompts you to name each new document.

Print

The Print selection enables you to print an HTML document. However, this menu choice does not currently support printing HTML layout documents. There is no information currently available about new features planned for later versions of the ActiveX Control Pad, unfortunately.

The Recently Used File List

As with most Windows applications, the system offers you a list of your most recent files just above the Exit command on the File menu. Select one of these recent files to open the file automatically.

Exit

To shut down the ActiveX Control Pad, select Exit from the menu, or click the Close button (the X button) in the upper-right corner of the outermost ActiveX Control Pad window.

Edit Menu

The Edit menu contains the following choices, each of which are explained in this section. The detailed sections that follow note whether a menu choice is available only in the HTML document editing mode or the HTML layout editing mode.

- ◆ Undo
- ◆ Redo
- ◆ Cut
- ◆ Copy
- ◆ Paste
- ◆ Delete
- ◆ Select All
- ◆ Insert ActiveX Control

- ◆ Insert HTML Layout

- ◆ Edit Object

- ◆ Group

Undo

As you edit an HTML document or HTML layout file, the ActiveX Control Pad provides a limited Undo capability that enables you to reverse the last action performed. Unlike Microsoft Word 95, however, the function only affects the very last change. After you select Undo, the Undo menu choice becomes unavailable and the Redo menu choice appears on the Edit menu. (The Undo command returns to the menu when you make a new change.)

Redo

By selecting the Redo menu choice, you reverse the Undo operation; essentially, you restore the document to the way it was before you selected Undo. After you select Redo, the Undo menu choice appears on the menu again and the Redo command becomes unavailable. This menu choice exists in both editing modes.

Cut

As with most other Windows applications, the Control Pad enables you to select text to be removed from the document and placed on the Windows Clipboard. You can then use the Paste function to retrieve the text in other windows or applications. This menu choice exists in both editing modes.

Copy

The Control Pad enables you to select text to be copied from the document and placed on the Windows Clipboard. You can then use the Paste function in another window or application to retrieve the text. This menu choice exists in both editing modes.

Paste

Select the Paste command to retrieve the last text you placed on the Clipboard and insert it into the currently active document. When you edit an HTML layout file, you can cut, copy, and paste such objects as controls or graphics. This menu choice exists in both editing modes.

Delete

The Delete menu choice removes the currently selected text or object. When an object is deleted, it cannot be retrieved unless you immediately select the Undo command.

Select All

Use the Select All command to highlight (select) all the text or screen objects in the currently active window. This choice exists in both editing modes.

Insert ActiveX Control

Besides enabling you to create separate layout files that are not part of HTML documents, the Control Pad also enables you to insert control references directly into your HTML document. When you select this menu choice, the system presents you with a list of all the ActiveX controls registered on your machine. After you select a control from the list, the system displays the control so you can edit its properties.

After you close the editing window, an OBJECT tag that contains the correct CLASSID tag and its parameters is inserted into your HTML document. The CLASSID tag uniquely identifies the control you selected so that another user's system recognizes the control as either already installed on the system or needing to be downloaded. This function is discussed in more detail later in this chapter.

Insert HTML Layout

This menu choice enables you to select an HTML layout file to include in your HTML document. Selecting this menu choice initiates a dialog box that prompts you to select an HTML layout file to include. After you select a file, the OBJECT tag that contains the class ID for the layout control is inserted into your document, as with any ActiveX control.

Edit ActiveX Control/Edit HTML Layout

After you insert either an ActiveX Control or HTML layout file into your HTML document, an icon appears on the left side of the window near each OBJECT tag. This icon indicates that you can edit the properties of the object. To edit the properties of the control you inserted, either click the icon or select Edit ActiveX Control/ Edit HTML Layout when the cursor lies within the OBJECT tag's text. The menu choice then changes from Edit ActiveX Control to Edit HTML Layout, depending on the type of object in your document.

Group/Ungroup

The Group option exists when you edit an HTML layout file. Select multiple controls by using the Shift key in combination with your mouse button, and then select Group. This causes the system to treat all the controls as one. At this point, for example, you can move all the controls together. To break up the group, select Ungroup. Both Group and Ungroup toggle based on the currently selected screen object.

View Menu

The View menu contains the following menu choices. Only the Toolbar and Status Bar options appear while you edit an HTML document. The other choices appear when you edit an HTML layout file.

◆ Toolbar

◆ Status Bar

◆ Grid

◆ Toolbox

◆ Properties

◆ Custom Properties

Toolbar

This menu choice enables you to turn the display of the main toolbar on and off. Programmers with small screens may find it useful to hide the toolbar, especially because the menu choices duplicate all the functions of the toolbar.

Status Bar

This menu choice enables you to show or hide the status bar, which is at the bottom of the Control Pad window. When you select menu choices, the status bar displays Help text for each menu choice. The status bar also displays the status of the NumLock, CapsLock, and ScrollLock keys. Because most keyboards contain lights that indicate their status, the status bar often is redundant and can be removed to add screen space.

Grid

You might find it useful when editing an HTML layout file to have a frame of reference for aligning controls. Selecting the Grid menu choice displays a grid of points on all HTML layout files you are editing. In addition, you can specify both the size of the grid and options that force controls to "snap" to the grid and automatically align with particular points. Select these options under the Options menu by choosing HTML Layout. These and other options are discussed later in this chapter.

Toolbox

The toolbox may appear as a familiar sight for Visual Basic programmers. The toolbox contains all the controls that you can insert into your HTML layout file. In addition, you can expand or contract the toolbox by clicking on it with your right or alternate mouse button. From the pop-up menu that appears, you can add and remove controls to your system, much as an artist adds and removes colors from his palette.

Properties

In HTML Layout editing mode, you can view a selected control's properties by selecting the Properties command. Properties are values, such as color and font, that can be modified to describe various attributes of the control. Visual Basic programmers who are familiar with the F4 key that brings up properties will find that this shortcut key currently is not supported. However, you can click your right mouse button (or left, if your mouse is left-handed) on any control to open a pop-up menu containing many of the same choices that exist on the Control Pad's menus.

Custom Properties

This menu choice is available only when you highlight a non-standard control. For the basic Microsoft-supplied controls, this menu choice is not available. Furthermore, selecting this menu choice may accomplish nothing in cases when the highlighted control does not contain any custom properties. In other cases, the system displays a Property sheet for the control's special properties.

Format Menu

The Format menu is only available while you edit an HTML layout file; the Format menu includes the following choices:

- Align
- Make Same Size
- Size
- Horizontal Spacing
- Vertical Spacing
- Snap To Grid
- Send To Back
- Move Backward
- Move Forward
- Bring To Front

Align

This menu choice enables you to align controls on the selected window in a number of ways. For this menu choice to appear, you must select more than one control.

Selecting an option from this group produces a column of controls:

Lefts—Aligns controls based on their leftmost points; similar to left-justified text.

Centers—Aligns controls at their horizontal midpoints.

Rights—Aligns selected controls based on their rightmost points; similar to right-justified text.

Selecting one of the following group of options produces a horizontal line of controls:

Tops—Aligns selected controls based on their topmost points.

Middles—Aligns selected controls based on their vertical midpoints.

Bottoms—Aligns selected controls based on their bottom-most points.

This menu option exists as long as you select at least one control:

To Grid—Aligns each control with the closest grid point.

Make Same Size

Three submenu choices enable you to match vertical or horizontal sizing for a group of selected controls. For these choices to exist, you must select more than one control.

Height—Makes all selected controls the height of the tallest control selected.

Width—Makes all selected controls the width of the widest control selected.

Both—Makes all selected controls the height and width of the tallest and widest controls, respectively.

Size

The available submenu from this menu choice enables you to control the sizing on one or more controls. These choices exist when you select at least one control:

To Fit—Resizes each selected control to the minimum size required to display its contents. For instance, this option resizes a label control to correspond to the size of the text it contains.

To Grid—Sizes the control so that all four corners are aligned with a point on the grid. Even if no grid appears, the control is sized to a grid that would be displayed. For this reason, you may find it useful to display the grid while designing your document.

Horizontal Spacing

When creating a line of controls, such as those on dialog boxes, you may find it tedious to attempt to manually space each control. The Control Pad provides a submenu for spacing control lines automatically. These options exist when you select more than one control:

Make Equal—Positions the controls evenly between the leftmost and rightmost controls.

Increase—Evenly increases the distance between each selected control.

Decrease—Evenly decreases the distance between each selected control.

Remove—Removes all space between all the selected controls.

Vertical Spacing

The Vertical Spacing submenu enables you to vertically position columns of controls without counting the pixels between them. These menu choices are available when you select more than one control:

Make Equal—Positions selected controls evenly between the top and bottom controls.

Increase—Evenly increases the distance between each of the selected controls.

Decrease—Evenly decreases the distance between each of the selected controls.

Remove—Removes all space between all the selected controls.

Snap To Grid

The Snap To Grid menu choice enables you to force controls to align to the grid points on the window. This helps in aligning controls on your document.

Send To Back

Because the ActiveX Control Pad enables you to stack controls on top of one another, the Send To Back command enables you to move one of the controls to the bottom of the stack.

Move Backward

The Move Backward menu choice enables you to push a control one level closer to the bottom of the stack of controls on the document.

Move Forward

You can use the Move Forward menu choice to bring a control one level toward the top of the stack of controls on a document.

Bring To Front

The Bring To Front menu command forces a control to the top of a stack of controls.

Tools Menu

The Tools menu choices exist in both editing modes. The following choices are available on this menu:

◆ Script Wizard

◆ Options

Script Wizard

This menu choice calls up the ActiveX Control Pad's Script Wizard, which enables you to add and modify code attached to each of the controls drawn on your HTML layout document. In addition, you can use Script Wizard with the controls you inserted into your HTML document. You learn more about the Script Wizard later in this chapter.

Options

From the Options command's submenu, you can set two groups of options:

◆ HTML Layout options—You can set the horizontal and vertical size of the editing grid, as well as the default values of the Snap To Grid and Show Grid options, from this dialog box. These options are used initially when you create or open an HTML layout file.

◆ Script options—This dialog box enables you to select the default view for the Script Wizard and the default language, whether it be VBScript or JavaScript.

Window Menu

The Window menu's primary function involves maintaining a list of the open windows in the ActiveX Control Pad's editing area. You can choose to cascade or tile the windows. Cascading the windows causes each to become the same size and aligns them with their title bars visible and slightly offset from one another. Tiling the windows causes each window to resize so it fills the window, in the same way tiles cover a ceiling or floor.

Help Menu

The Help menu contains the following menu choices:

- ◆ Control Pad Topics

- ◆ HTML Reference

- ◆ VBScript Reference

- ◆ About ActiveX Control Pad

Control Pad Topics

Selecting this menu choice displays the Help file's index. From this index, you can access any of the Help topics in the Help file.

HTML Reference

Selecting HTML Reference actually starts your default web browser to enable you to view the HTML pages that contain the HTML reference documentation, which can be installed separately. If you have not yet installed this documentation (available on the CD-ROM), the system notifies you.

VBScript Reference

This menu choice starts your browser, which enables you to view the HTML documentation of the VBScript language. This documentation is not included with the basic installation of the ActiveX Control Pad; you must install it separately. Documentation is, however, included on the CD-ROM.

About ActiveX Control Pad

When you choose this command, a dialog box appears that displays basic product information, such as the copyright, title, and version number.

ActiveX Control Pad Toolbar

As with most Windows applications, the toolbar provides quick access to the most common functions of the application. Because all the buttons on the toolbar represent menu choices already documented, the following list contains only the button names:

◆ New	◆ Redo
◆ Open	◆ Bring To Front
◆ Save	◆ Move Forward
◆ Cut	◆ Move Backward
◆ Copy	◆ Send To Back
◆ Paste	◆ Script Wizard
◆ Delete	◆ Help
◆ Undo	

If you don't know what a button does, simply move your mouse over the button. The screen displays a yellow box (known as a ToolTip) that indicates the button's function.

Creating a Document with the ActiveX Control Pad

In creating HTML documents, the ActiveX Control Pad functions much like any other text editor. The Control Pad does not have any special functions for inserting HTML tags, but, as the previous section discussed, it does enable you to insert ActiveX controls or HTML layout files into the documents.

Because Chapter 2 details text editors, this chapter discusses creating HTML layout files and using ActiveX controls in your documents.

Building an HTML Layout File

If you are familiar with HTML coding, you know that text layout is not easy. You must rely on tables and other simple formatting tags to perform complex formatting.

Furthermore, unlike a desktop publishing program, HTML does not enable you to position text at certain points on the page.

Using the HTML Layout control gives you considerable control, however, over the placement of your text. This section discusses how you can take advantage of these enhanced features.

In this section, you learn how to create a simple HTML layout file that you can then insert into a standard HTML document. The following example appears in the same format as a newsletter, with multiple columns and blocks of text on the page. Although some formatting used in this HTML layout file can be accomplished using <TABLE> and other simple HTML tags, the ActiveX Control Pad provides a much easier interface for creating complex formats in your documents. In addition, some formats exist through the ActiveX Control Pad that do not exist in simple HTML. The example in the next section illustrates some of these formats.

Drawing the Controls

To begin this tutorial, do the following:

1. Start the ActiveX Control Pad. By default, the Control Pad creates a new HTML document. For now, leave that document alone; you will use it after the HTML layout file is complete.

2. From the File menu, select New HTML Layout. Your screen should look like figure 3.2

Figure 3.2

A blank HTML layout file, ready for editing.

In this example, you will create a simulated three-column newsletter for a web page. Although the text contained in the columns is irrelevant, you will gain important skills during the tutorial. The basic format of this newsletter appears in figure 3.3.

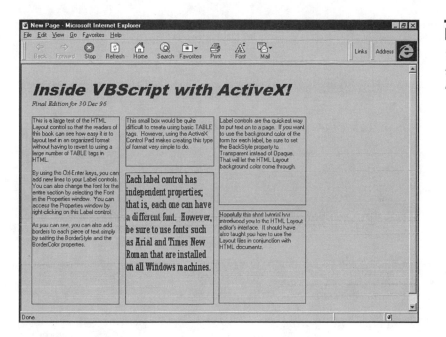

Figure 3.3

*This is what the
newsletter will
look like.*

Each box is created by the simplest of all the controls in the toolbox: the Label
control. Use this control for all static, or unchanging, text on a page. You can include
multiple lines in the Label control, and you can also embed blank lines in the control
by pressing Ctrl+Enter.

> **Note**   You must press Ctrl+Enter to add a blank line to a Label control. Simply pressing the
> Enter key does not work.

To begin creating the newsletter, follow these steps:

1. Click the Label control.

2. Hold down the primary mouse button in the HTML Layout control and drag the
   mouse to create a box at the top of the window. When the box is large enough,
   release the mouse button. The program draws a box labeled **Label1** at the top of
   the window. **Label1** is the default ID of the control, and the ID property is the
   same as the control's name. You can name the control anything you want, as long
   as the name does not currently exist on the form. In this example, you do not
   need to rename the controls.

3. Next, draw another Label control that will constitute the left column of the
   newsletter, as shown in figure 3.3. When you release the mouse button, this Label
   control is named **Label2**.

4. Continue adding Label controls in the same format as shown in figure 3.3. The four Label controls are named **Label3, Label4, Label5,** and **Label6,** respectively (see fig. 3.4).

Figure 3.4

The blank newsletter HTML layout file after the Label controls have been added to it.

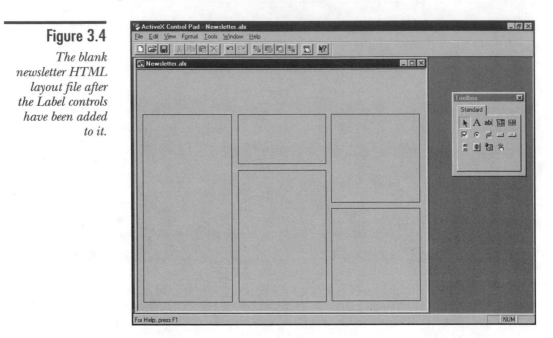

5. Click the pointer icon in the toolbox to switch back to selection mode. (If you clicked on the HTML layout document without changing to the pointer, additional controls would automatically be created. This behavior differs from Visual Basic, which switches back to pointer mode when you click on a form or control.)

Setting the Properties

As mentioned previously, each control has a number of properties you can set. Properties are values that control characteristics about each control, such as font or color.

To continue the tutorial, follow these steps:

1. Close the Toolbox window by clicking Close (the X button) in the upper-right corner of its window, or by selecting the Toolbox command from the View menu.

2. Click the topmost Label control and then select Properties from the View menu.

Each property on each Label control works independently from the others. For example, each label may contain a different font and color. The following list details the properties and their definitions. These properties are common to many other ActiveX controls as well.

◆ Accelerator—This property enables you to select a letter to move the input focus to the control. For Label controls, the focus moves to the control immediately following the Label in the tab order.

◆ AutoSize—When you set this property to True, the box around a control resizes to fit the contents of the control. To establish borders around a control, leave this property set to False.

◆ BackColor—The BackColor property specifies the background color for a control. You can select from the normal color palette or other colors, such as Window Border, that are used by the system. By selecting one of these named colors, you ensure that your controls appear similar to other controls in the user's workspace.

◆ BackStyle—This property determines whether the system uses the background color of the control or the background color of the graphic behind the control. Setting this property to Transparent enables the graphic or color behind the control to show through.

◆ BorderColor—This sets the color of the control's border, if a border is used. To use a border, set the BorderStyle property to a value other than None.

◆ BorderStyle—This property determines whether the control has a border. In most cases, leave this property at None. In this example, however, you will establish a border around the text you add to the document.

◆ Caption—For Label and other simple controls, the Caption is the text displayed in the Label. Although initially set to the ID of the control, this property is not the name of the control. In fact, changing the ID of the control does not cause the Caption to change.

◆ CodeBase—Because you may need to download all the controls you use on an HTML layout page, the CodeBase property enables you to set the URL from which the control can be downloaded.

◆ Enabled—This property determines whether a control can be used. For Label controls, setting this property to False simply changes the color of the Label to a light gray. The Enabled property typically is used when another control follows the label. With this property, the Label becomes disabled to show, for example, that the text box next to it is not available.

◆ Font—This property enables you to set font characteristics, such as font name, size, and weight (bold or italic). When selecting a font, be sure to use fonts, such as Arial or Times New Roman, which are common to all Windows machines. Because some computers may not have fonts you specify, the browser will choose a font to substitute when one is not available.

◆ ForeColor—This property specifies the foreground color of the control. For controls such as the Label, this color is the color of the text in the Label.

◆ Height—This property determines the height of the control, which is specified in pixels.

Note Unlike Visual Basic, which expresses control positions in twips, VBScript and ActiveX work in pixels.

◆ ID—This property sets the name of the control. You can use this name when you write VBScript code to use the control in a program.

◆ Left—This establishes the horizontal position of the control, which is specified in pixels.

◆ MouseIcon—If you use a custom mouse pointer specified in the MousePointer property, the MouseIcon property holds the file name for that graphic.

◆ MousePointer—This property determines what mouse pointer is shown when the mouse rests over this control. In most cases, this property should remain at the default value. By leaving it at its default value, Internet Explorer automatically provides the correct cursor at different points. For instance, when you move your mouse pointer over an URL, the cursor changes to a hand instead of an arrow.

◆ Picture—This property specifies the file name of a picture to be displayed in the control.

◆ PicturePosition—This property determines how and where the picture should be displayed within the control. Available choices include the following:

LeftTop	AboveCenter
LeftCenter	AboveRight
LeftBottom	BelowLeft
RightTop	BelowCenter
RightCenter	BelowRight
RightBottom	Center
AboveLeft	

◆ SpecialEffect—This property enables you to add display effects to the control. Available choices include the following:

> Flat—This is the default setting. Any text in the control is shown "flat;" that is, without any shadows around it.
>
> Raised—This setting causes the text to appear higher than the form itself. The text appears to be on top of a button that is raised up above the form.
>
> Sunken—This setting is the reverse of the Raised setting. The text is shown sunken into the form within a rectangle.
>
> Etched—This setting makes the text appear within a narrow box that appears to be sunken into the form.
>
> Bump—This setting is the reverse of the Etched setting. Instead of the narrow box sunken into the form, the box appears to be raised above the form.

◆ TabIndex—When the user navigates a form with the Tab key, you can specify the order in which controls receive the focus by specifying the TabIndex for each control. The flow through a form normally occurs left-to-right, top-to-bottom. The upper-left control should exhibit a TabIndex of zero.

◆ TabStop—In some cases, such as when a web site contains a text box that cannot be edited, you will not want the user tabbing to a control. To block this action, set the TabStop property to False. If the user uses the Tab key, he will skip the control. However, setting the TabStop does not prevent him from using the mouse to click in a control.

◆ Top—This property sets the vertical position of the control on the HTML layout file, which is specified in pixels.

◆ Visible—This property determines whether a control is visible to the user.

◆ Width—This establishes the width of the control, which is specified in pixels.

◆ WordWrap—This property specifies whether long pieces of text wrap around the right-hand edge of the control to a new line.

Although this list of properties is not exhaustive, many of these properties are used in other controls that are explored in this book. If these controls contain additional properties, they will be explained when the control is used.

To change the property value for a property, double-click it in the Properties window.

Note Be sure to double-click the value in the Properties window. Unlike Visual Basic, which operates under a single click, the ActiveX Control Pad requires you to double-click the property in the list to edit it.

For our example, the topmost Label control, Label1, should contain the Font property of Arial, Black, 24 point, Italic. This font provides the banner for the newsletter.

All the other Label controls can contain any font you want: Experiment with the font settings to view the different fonts.

In addition, each Label control should display a BorderColor property set to blue. To do so, double-click the BorderColor property in the Properties window. Select your favorite shade of blue from the Color Selector dialog box.

You also need to set the BorderStyle property of the Label controls to 1-Single. By using the multiple-select capabilities of the Control Pad, you can make these changes to all the Label controls in one step. Here's how:

1. Click Label2, and then press the Ctrl key.

2. Click each of the other Label controls in succession.

3. When you select Label2 through Label5, set the preceding properties. The changes will appear on all five Label controls.

Now that you have set the important properties for the text boxes, you can enter text into the boxes. To do so, follow these steps:

1. Click the mouse on one of the Label controls and wait approximately one second. The border of the Label changes to a hatched border, as shown in figure 3.5.

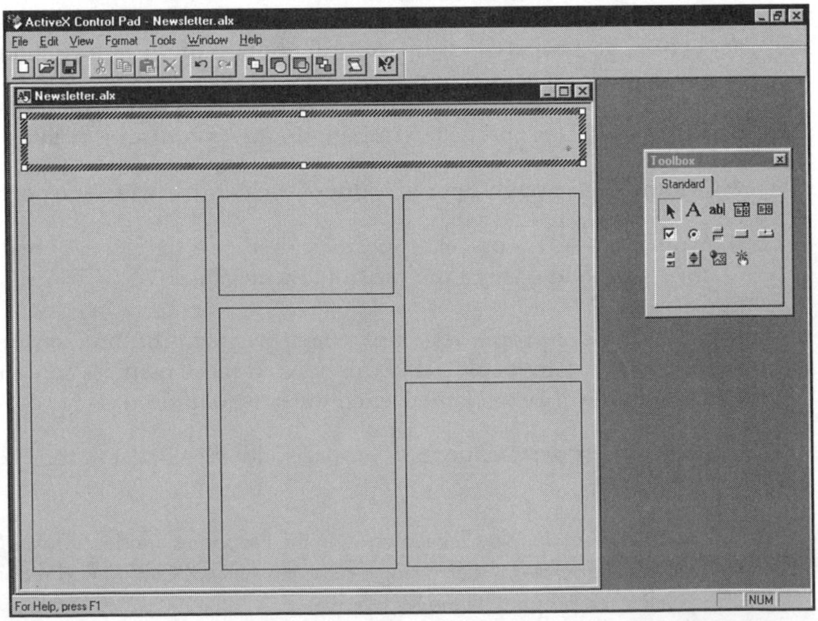

Figure 3.5

The Label control is ready to be edited, as indicated by the hatched border around it.

2. Insert text into the Label control. As you type, the text automatically wraps to another line. To insert a blank line, remember to use the Ctrl+Enter key sequence. When you finish adding text to the Label control, you can click another Label control. The hatching appears around the next control you click.

Your HTML layout file may appear similar to figure 3.6.

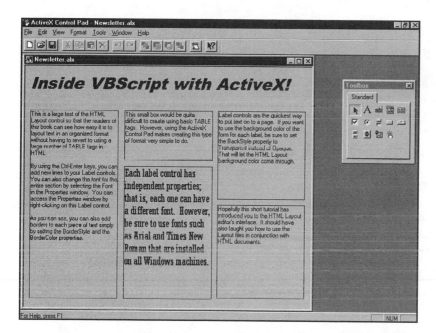

Figure 3.6

The completed HTML layout file for the newsletter document.

3. At this point, you have finished creating the newsletter layout file. Save the file as newsletter.alx on your hard drive by selecting the Save option from the File menu.

Remember the location of the file; next, you learn how to add it to the HTML document that is still waiting for you in the Control Pad.

Inserting the HTML Layout File

Now that you have completed the HTML layout file, you can insert it into your HTML document. To do so, follow these steps:

1. Position the cursor on the blank line following the <BODY> tag.

2. Select Insert HTML Layout from the Edit menu. The dialog box defaults to the same directory in which you just saved your layout file.

3. Select that file and click OK.

A tag resembling the following code will appear in the HTML document:

```
<OBJECT CLASSID="CLSID:812AE312-8B8E-11CF-93C8-00AA00C08FDF"
ID="Newsletter_alx" STYLE="LEFT:0;TOP:0">
<PARAM NAME="ALXPATH" REF VALUE="file:D:\Newsletter.alx">
 </OBJECT>
```

Although this may initially look like nonsense, the tag is easy to understand. The first part of the tag, CLASSID, is a unique identifier assigned by Microsoft to the HTML Layout control. Microsoft currently controls the class IDs used for controls. This single point of control ensures that these IDs remain unique. The next part of the tag, ID, names the object so that it can be used within VBScript or JavaScript code in the document. STYLE provides basic formatting information for the web browser. The next tag, the parameter tag, specifies the pathname to the HTML layout file inserted into this document. Most controls contain at least one parameter tag. Finally, the </OBJECT> tag closes the object reference.

As you can see, the ActiveX Control Pad already knows how to format the lengthy OBJECT tag so that you don't have to. You don't have to memorize the class IDs or otherwise know where to find them. (Incidentally, the class IDS are found in the Windows 95 Registry.) If you search the Registry for the class ID generated by the Control Pad, you will find helpful information about the control, such as its file name and location on your hard drive.

As mentioned previously, an icon beside the OBJECT tag, which was inserted into your HTML document, indicates that you can edit the object, an HTML layout file, by clicking this icon or by selecting Edit HTML Layout from the Edit menu.

To finish editing this HTML document, follow these instructions:

1. Change the title of the page to **My Newsletter**. To do so, change the text between the <TITLE> and </TITLE> tags.

2. Save the HTML document to your hard drive as `newsletter.htm`.

Viewing the Finished Product

Now that you have successfully created your first HTML Layout file, you can view the fruits of your labors. Start Internet Explorer 3.0 and open the `newsletter.htm` file. The document shown in the browser window (see fig. 3.7) is identical to the one you just finished creating with the ActiveX Control Pad.

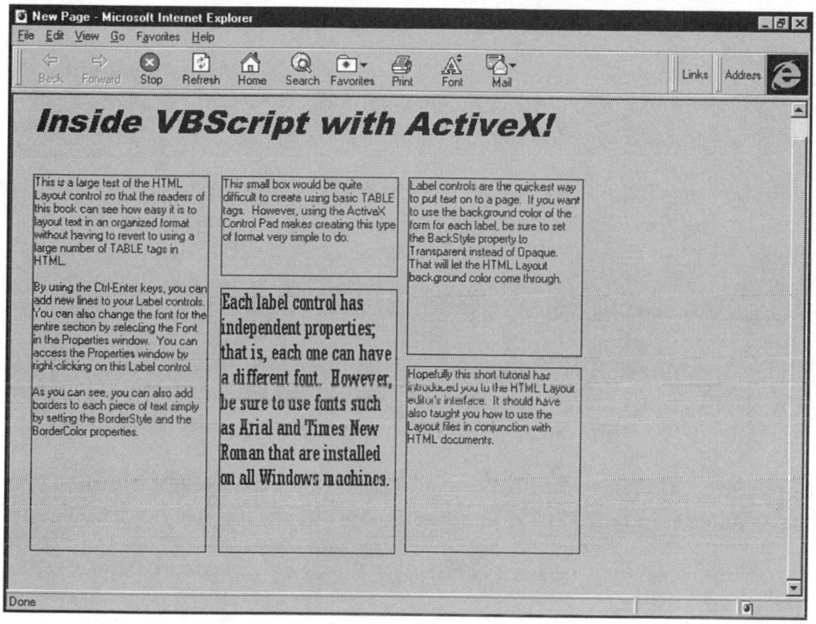

Figure 3.7

The completed document, as seen in Internet Explorer 3.0.

One of the major benefits of using the HTML Layout control is that you no longer have to line up text on the document by trial and error. Simply draw the text in the desired location, and the browser displays it accordingly. The method does have a drawback: browsers that do not support ActiveX cannot view this document. NCompass offers a plug-in for Netscape users that enables them to view ActiveX content, but users not on Windows 95 still may not be able to view the content. On a good note, Microsoft has recently announced support for alternative platforms, including Unix and Macintosh, for ActiveX controls. However, this support will not be available until 1997 or 1998.

Adding Code to the Document

Although you can use the ActiveX Control Pad for simple documents, such as the one you just created, its real power comes in adding VBScript code to make the controls function. This section describes how to use the Script Wizard to add code and create a more active newsletter.

One of the best ways to ensure a web site's success is to produce new content every day. Even if the changes are minor, visitors form the impression that the web site is active, and they will more likely return. One of the easiest ways to implement daily changes to your web site is to input dates on your documents that automatically change to the current date. You will add this example to the newsletter page.

To begin, follow these instructions:

1. Click the Edit HTML Layout menu choice to reopen the newsletter layout file. As with most newsletters, the date normally follows the title of the newsletter. Likewise, the date for this newsletter falls under the banner.

2. Add a new Label control beneath the top banner. (You may have to move the banner up to ensure that the new label fits.) Size the label so that it reaches halfway across the page from the left side.

3. Because this control actually contains code behind it, you should assign the control a meaningful name. Set the ID property of this new Label control to **lblDate**. (Lbl is an abbreviation for Label, and Date indicates that this Label contains the date.) Also, change the font to Times New Roman, 10 point, Italic, to make the date appear differently than the rest of the text on the document.

4. Finally, double-click the Caption property and then press the Delete button. When the document initially loads, the default caption should not be displayed.

5. Close the Toolbox window; that Label control is the only new control that needs to be added to this example.

Using the Script Wizard

Now you are ready to start the Script Wizard. Select Script Wizard from the Tools menu, or click the Script Wizard toolbar button. The editing window is hidden, and the Script Wizard window shown in figure 3.8 appears.

This window includes three primary parts. The first pane in the upper-left corner, which is labeled with "1. Select an Event," enables you to select the event for which the code should be executed. This tree/outline control lists each control on the document. All the label controls, including the new lblDate control, are listed there.

The control Layout1 is the HTML layout file itself. This file contains only one event: onLoad. This event is triggered when the document is first loaded and is similar to Form_Load in Visual Basic. Use the onLoad event to set the current date for the newsletter by following these steps:

1. Click the plus sign next to the Layout1 entry, and then click the displayed onLoad event entry.

2. Now that you have specified the event you want to add code for, look at the right pane, labeled "2. Insert Actions." This pane enables you to select actions to perform on the objects on the document. To view some of the available actions, click the plus sign next to lblDate. *Actions*, also known as *methods*, are next to an exclamation point icon.

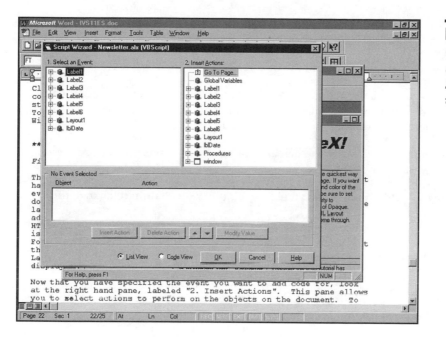

Figure 3.8

*The ActiveX
Control Pad
Script Wizard
window.*

The following actions exist for the Label control:

◆ SetFocus—For controls that accept input, the input focus moves to this control. For Label controls, the input focus is set to the control immediately following the Label in the tab order.

◆ Bring To Front—This action causes the control to appear at the top of the control stack on the document.

◆ Hide Control—This action causes the control to disappear from the user's view. The user can still access the control, but he cannot input data.

◆ Send To Back—This action moves the control to the bottom of the control stack on the document.

◆ Show Control—This action causes the control to be displayed to the user.

As with the properties of the Label control, many of these actions exist for other controls discussed in this book. Each new action will be explained as needed.

To show you how to use these simple actions, imagine that you wanted to hide the lblDate control when the form loaded. You would follow these steps:

1. Select the Hide Control action under the lblDate control listed on the right side.

2. Click the Insert Action button, and this action appears in the pane labeled "3. On Layout1 OnLoad Perform the Following Actions."

3. To remove an action listed in the box, select it and click Delete Action.

You can also rearrange the actions by selecting an action and then clicking the up and down arrows to move it around in the box. Finally, you can add actions that set control properties. To do so, follow these instructions:

1. Select one of the properties, such as Caption. A dialog box appears, requesting the new value for the control.

2. After you enter a value, you can use the Modify Value button to change this value.

3. Select one of the actions, and then press the Modify Value to change the value you entered.

Note For non-programmers, the List View of the Script Wizard provides a simple interface to the event structure of VBScript and ActiveX.

Although the List View interface works well for simple actions, you simply cannot perform many functions without writing a little bit of code. Such is the case for your newsletter.

To add the code, follow these steps:

1. Select the lblDate's OnLoad event.

2. Click the Code View option button at the bottom of the screen. The bottom half of the Script Wizard changes to reveal the code view portion of the Script Wizard, as shown in figure 3.9.

3. In the Code View window, set the caption of the lblDate control to Date, which returns the current date. Enter the following code in the Code View window:

```
lblDate.Caption - Date
```

4. Click OK, and save the HTML layout file. If you still have Internet Explorer open, reload the newsletter.htm file. The results of this piece of code appear immediately, as shown in figure 3.10.

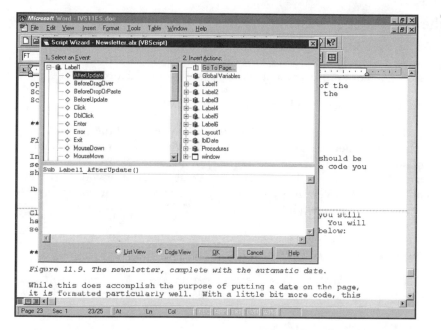

Figure 3.9

Code View mode of the Script Wizard.

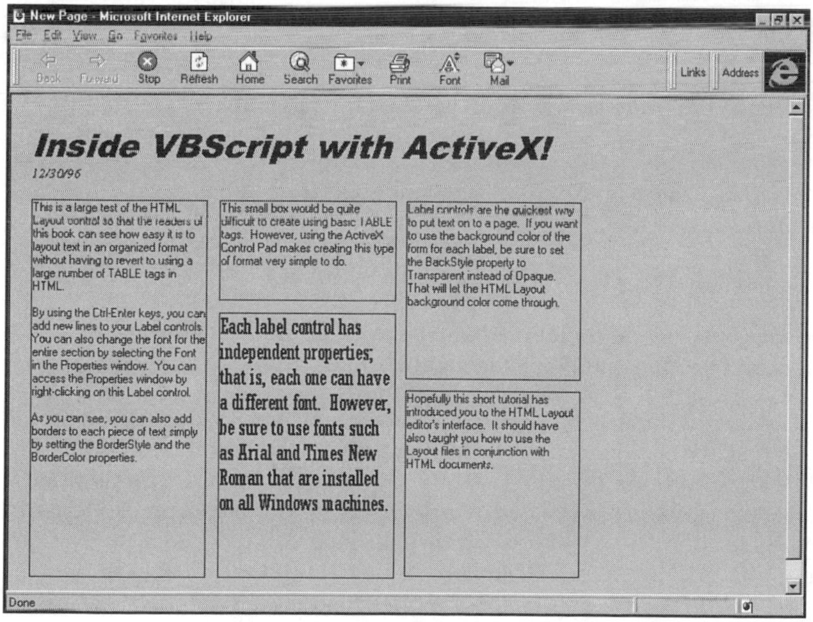

Figure 3.10

The newsletter, complete with the automatic date.

Adding the Newsletter's Finishing Touches

Although the previously listed steps accomplish the purpose of putting a date on the page, they also are an example of good formatting. With more code, however, the newsletter looks even more professional. Follow these steps to add more code:

1. Return to the ActiveX Control Pad, and edit the HTML Layout again.

2. Click the Script Wizard button, and select the OnLoad event of the Layout1 object. The code you entered in the Code View window does not appear in the List View mode because the code was simple enough for the Script Wizard to understand. However, this will not always be the case. When your code becomes more complex, the List View mode will display, indicating that the code is custom-written and thus cannot be viewed in List View mode.

3. For the enhanced date, switch to Code View mode again. The following piece of code provides a better-looking date for the newsletter:

```
lblDate.Caption = "Final Edition for " & Day(Date) & " " _
    & Mid("JanFebMarAprMayJunJulAugSepOctNovDec", (Month(Date) * 3) - 2,
    ➥3) _
    & " " & Right(Year(Date), 2)
```

Instead of simply displaying 12/30/96 as the date, the date appears as **Final Edition for 30 Dec 96**.

4. Add this code to the Code View window for the OnLoad event of the Layout1 control.

5. Click the List View radio button to view the message, indicating that you have added a custom action.

6. When you have finished, close the Script Wizard window.

7. Press the Save button, and then reload the page in Internet Explorer to view the results of your work. It should look like figure 3.11.

As you can see, adding just a little bit of code can make your page look as if it is constantly being updated, even if it isn't. Providing active content for your visitors ranks as a nice feature, but don't use these features just to use them. Learning when to use enhanced features is just as important as learning how to use them. To learn these techniques, look at other pages created through ActiveX and VBScript. To find more sites using VBScript and ActiveX controls, visit VBScript Central at http://www.inquiry.com/vbscentral. The VBScript Gallery page lists over 100 sites that employ all sorts of VBScript and ActiveX controls for page enhancement.

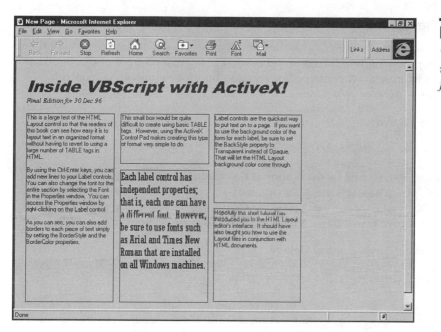

Figure 3.11

The newsletter with the new date format.

Expanding Your ActiveX Toolbox

One of the most convenient parts of the ActiveX framework is the ease with which you can add new controls to your development toolbox. Hundreds of controls are available to do everything from graphics effects to live stock tickers. In addition, these controls are relatively inexpensive when compared to the development time required to reproduce their functionality.

This chapter is designed to show you some of the other controls available. All the controls in this chapter are free. You must purchase many other controls before you use them. Because the ActiveX market is growing so quickly, a list of controls in this book would be quickly out of date. So, this section provides a sourcelist of common locations from which you can obtain information about the latest controls available.

Tips for Using ActiveX Controls

The controls in this section are not included with either the ActiveX Control Pad or Internet Explorer; you must install them. One of the most exciting technologies included with Internet Explorer is its automatic component download feature. All the complexities of installing and registering controls in Windows 95 is handled automatically. However, downloading components does pose some problems, which are explained and solved in this section.

Getting the Controls

Before you can start developing with the controls, you must first find and install them on your computer. Finding the controls is easy. There are a number of places on the Internet to obtain ActiveX controls. You can also purchase commercial controls through several different companies.

◆ **Ask the VB Pro**

```
http://www.inquiry.com/thevbpro
```

This site, maintained by the author of this chapter, contains a wealth of information about Visual Basic, VBScript, and ActiveX. The site also maintains an ActiveX controls repository that is constantly growing. You can submit controls and send your Visual Basic, VBScript, and ActiveX questions to the VB Pro.

◆ **Microsoft ActiveX Control Gallery**

```
http://www.microsoft.com/activex/gallery/
```

This site is Microsoft's listing of ActiveX controls. Although it is not particularly large as of this writing, getting a control from this site assures that the control is good quality. Microsoft does a good job of screening their site's content.

One nice feature of these pages is the large number of working examples. If, for instance, you want to use one of the freely available controls posted, just load the example—the control automatically downloads for your use.

◆ **clnet's ActiveX.Com**

```
http://www.activex.com
```

One of the largest and best computer and technology sites on the Internet is clnet. The site's organizers also produce a television show that helps provide a complete experience for the user. They recently launched `activex.com`, which is designed to be a control repository (like Microsoft's Control Gallery). Although fairly new, this site is sure to be as much of a success as another clnet site, `shareware.com`.

◆ **Xtras, Inc.**

```
http://www.xtras.com
```

Xtras, formerly known as VBXtras, has been selling components almost since the day Visual Basic created the component software industry. It is by far the largest marketer of commercial controls for Visual Basic. Recently, they have added a new market: ActiveX controls. Like the Visual Basic controls they still sell, the ActiveX controls are offered at discounted prices.

◆ **ActiveXpress**

`http://www.activexpress.com`

This site, published by CMP Publications, is more than just a control repository. It also provides news, reviews, and articles about the controls, their manufacturers, and the industry in general. CMP is building this new section on the success of their TechWeb site (`http://techweb.cmp.com`).

◆ **atOnce WebTools Store**

`http://www.webtools.atoncesoftware.com`

This site combines the best features of a public control repository with its online ordering and fulfillment services. After you purchase a control, you can download it immediately. In this age of instant gratification, this is a great service. They have a well-organized control repository that lists which controls are free, are demonstration versions, or are commercially priced.

Installing the Controls

For commercial controls you either receive on disk or download, installing them is easy because they all include instructions or setup programs that do the work for you. For the smaller controls such as those available from Microsoft's ActiveX Gallery pages, installation is slightly more difficult.

As mentioned previously, the easiest way to install a control on your machine is to find a page that uses the control and allow Internet Explorer to automatically download the control for you. (IE already knows how to get the control and place it in the correct location for use by itself and other programs, such as the ActiveX Control Pad.)

If, however, you obtain the control file, which ends in .OCX, and need to install it on your machine, there are two steps you need to take:

1. Copy the control file only into the `\Windows\OCCache` directory, which should already be on your hard drive if you have been using Microsoft Internet Explorer. If not, create the directory using Windows Explorer.

2. Now you need to register the control. According to the ActiveX specification, controls must be able to self-register; this is how Internet Explorer can install the controls when it downloads them. The controls are simply registering themselves. However, you must "encourage" the controls to do this. A Microsoft-supplied program called `REGSVR32.EXE` is the Registration Server that causes a control to register itself.

To use this program, locate it on your hard drive. (If it is not there, you can use the copy that is on the CD-ROM.) Copy it to your \Windows\System directory. Then, drag the .OCX file on top of the REGSVR32 program. You receive a message indicating that the registration of the control was successful. You are done registering the control, and you can use it with Internet Explorer and the ActiveX Control Pad.

As you can tell, it is much easier and more reliable to retrieve the control from a web page and allow Internet Explorer to install it.

Making Controls Available for Download

If you are creating pages for use on the Internet, you need to know how to make your controls available for other people to download. Every ActiveX control has at least one property in common: the CodeBase property. This property indicates where the control is located; it also holds an URL pointing to the control's location on a server somewhere on the Internet.

In the following example, which uses the Gradient control from Microsoft, you can see that the CodeBase property is used to specify the location of the control.

```
<OBJECT ID="iegrad1"
   CLASSID="clsid:017C99A0-8637-11CF-A3A9-00A0C9034920"
   CODEBASE="http://activex.microsoft.com/controls/iexplorer/iegrad.ocx"
   TYPE="application/x-oleobject"
   WIDTH=100 HEIGHT=50>
   <PARAM NAME="StartColor" VALUE="#0000ff">
   <PARAM NAME="EndColor" VALUE="#000000">
   <PARAM NAME="Direction" VALUE="0">
</OBJECT>
```

This particular example uses a full URL, including the host name. However, you can reduce this down to just a simple file name, as long as the control file itself is in the same directory as your HTML document.

You do not have to use a Microsoft Windows NT server to support controls on your pages. For many people using Unix web servers, this is a great feature. All the relevant information about the controls is actually in the HTML document you have created.

For Visual Basic Programmers:

Using the List View Window

As a Visual Basic programmer, you see similarities in the ActiveX Control Pad. These similarities include the Control toolbox and the user interface provided for arranging your controls. One of the major advances in the ActiveX Control Pad is the List View window. For simple actions, such as showing or hiding controls, the List View window is useful for new and experienced programmers alike. In addition, the hierarchical tree of controls and events makes it much easier to find the particular event or property you need to use. Many of these features will probably be in future versions of Visual Basic.

Summary

This chapter introduced you to all the features of the ActiveX Control Pad. You created a simple HTML document and an HTML layout file, embedded the file in an HTML document, and wrote code to enhance the operation of the page. Many other controls exist within the ActiveX Control Pad, however, and the next chapter discusses these controls in more detail.

CHAPTER 4

Introduction to Using ActiveX Controls in Web Pages

By Yusuf Malluf

This chapter shows you the basics of how and why to integrate ActiveX technology into your Internet site's web pages. Several ActiveX controls, along with their functionality, will be introduced. Other tools, ActiveX controls, resources, and methods to foster creativity in your web pages will be examined as well. Specifically, you will learn about the following topics:

◆ **How and why to make your web pages interactive**. The era for static, unchanging web pages is over! Welcome to the world of interactive web pages where you can truly make your pages lively and dynamic. You will become aware of the leading tools available to you for increasing the level of interactivity in your web pages in the first section, "Making Your Web Pages Interactive." The phenomenal ActiveX architecture will be examined along with real, detailed examples.

◆ **The mechanics of ActiveX technology**. This section shows you how ActiveX controls work inside a web page, what security measures exist for installing ActiveX controls on your system, and a few brief examples of ActiveX controls in web pages.

Making Your Web Pages Interactive

This section explores the different factors that have contributed to the increasing number of interactive web pages. These factors include the Microsoft Internet Strategy, the key differences between static and dynamic web pages, and the bedrock of interactive web pages: ActiveX technology. Several of Microsoft's ActiveX controls included with Internet Explorer 3.0 and with the Control Pad are also explored.

Microsoft's Internet Strategy

Originally, Microsoft's "Internet Strategy" was to provide an easy and efficient way for Windows 95 users to access the Internet through the Microsoft Network (MSN). Since this venture in early 1995, Microsoft has rapidly changed its strategy. Microsoft realized it could not tame cyberspace through a proprietary solution, so Microsoft broadened its entire spectrum—beginning with one of the first releases of ActiveX-enabled technology, code-named "Sweeper." Microsoft began focusing more on overall interactivity between the PC and the Internet. The result is a powerful and stable multiplatform technology including the easily accessible tools to harness this technology, with MSN being just a sideshow.

This high usability of ActiveX technology on the Internet and how it was brought about can, in effect, be credited to the Microsoft Corporation. Microsoft's latest products, Internet software and operating systems, take advantage of the ActiveX technology. You can also communicate across the Internet information of all types, such as Word documents, presentations, and spreadsheets, in addition to making some of the most interactive and visually appealing pages. Figure 4.1 illustrates a Microsoft Word document being accessed across the web. This example uses the Microsoft Word object to display the document, which demonstrates how simple it is to access resources through your web browser.

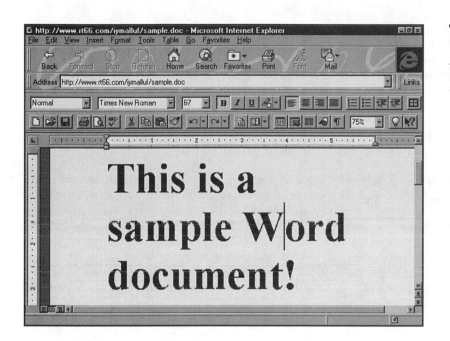

Figure 4.1

A Microsoft Word document inside the web browser.

Promotion of Interactivity

In less than three years, the World Wide Web has evolved into a powerful system of interaction, commerce, communication, and play. The main reason is that the public has realized the importance of the Internet and has taken advantage of the technology. ActiveX technology has taken the level of interactive capability a step further by following a standard architecture. This section deals with the ActiveX framework, or the architecture behind ActiveX, and explores how to use ActiveX controls with web pages and VBScripting through detailed examples.

The ActiveX Framework

The ActiveX architecture is based on the idea that numerous container programs (objects) exist within the operating environment and can be referenced by one or a multitude of applications. The Internet Explorer 3.0 Browser, for instance, is not one single program itself—it is an application interface that calls or references the Internet Explorer Browser Shell object, which incidentally was installed with Internet Explorer. In fact, anyone who has an understanding of an OLE-capable programming language, such as Visual Basic 4 and MS VC++, can embed the Browser Shell object in their application and can manipulate its methods and properties to create a browser application.

All ActiveX and OLE objects used by applications are registered with your operating system. However, if you access a web page across the Internet that contains ActiveX controls that are not registered with your system, Internet Explorer attempts to download the object if the location of this object is specified (see the CODEBASE attribute of the <OBJECT> tag in Chapter 11, "HTML Extensions for ActiveX Controls"). Then your system attempts to register the control. This is also true for any application that resides on your system; if it requires a certain OLE or ActiveX object, then it would have to be registered with your machine for the application to function properly.

The entire structure of Windows 95 and Windows NT (Workstation and Server) rests on OLE and ActiveX technology. ActiveX is a less-complicated rendition of OLE technology and is ideally designed and suited for the Internet and a wide variety of applications and other programs. The dynamic nature of ActiveX technology and its ease of creation and use enables ActiveX to effectively establish its presence on the Internet. Additionally, VBScript, JavaScript, and any other add-ons to Internet Explorer are OLE objects as well. VBScript and JavaScript are currently the primary mechanisms for manipulating ActiveX controls in web pages (this is further discussed in Chapter 11).

Note VBScript and JavaScript are called *sandbox* languages. They are called this because their functionality is severely limited to prevent malicious abuse on users' machines.

It is possible to create an inexhaustible variety of different tools and controls that can be inserted and used interactively in web pages with ActiveX controls. ActiveX controls enable greater interaction from the user, which enables him or her to access many different programs that can enable a number of things expected in highly personalized web pages. Some of these include online catalogs, discussion centers, shopping malls, customized ordering systems, and games from inside your browser. Let's examine the fundamental differences between an interactive, dynamic web page and a static one.

Static versus Dynamic Web Pages

Figures 4.2 and 4.3 demonstrate the differences between standard pages with relatively no interaction and pages that utilize ActiveX technology and VBScript. Figure 4.2 is of a plain HTML page that does not use any ActiveX technology. The second web page, on the other hand, makes good use of ActiveX technology, using scrolling marquees, Label controls, and pop-up menus—not to mention frames and sound (see fig. 4.3).

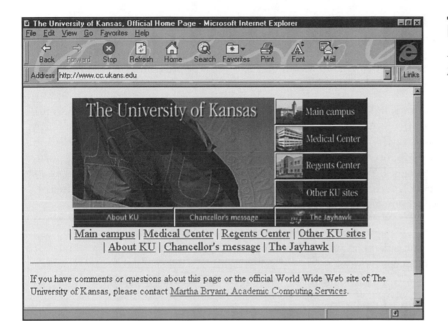

Figure 4.2

A static HTML page.

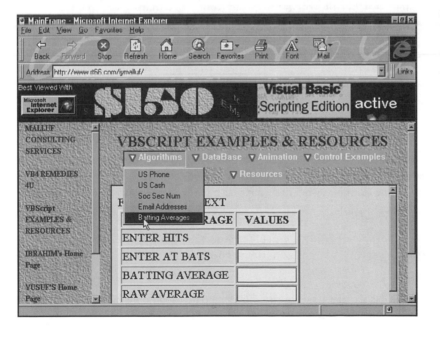

Figure 4.3

A dynamic web page, enhanced by ActiveX technology.

These examples demonstrate the classical contrast between a static page and an interactive web page. Many web pages on the Internet utilize ActiveX, but many web sites remain with the static model for fear that their page will not be rendered correctly on different browsers. The leading and most popular browsers, however, are Internet Explorer and Netscape Navigator.

Internet Explorer fully supports the ActiveX technology, VBScript, Java applets, and JavaScript. Internet Explorer boasts many features, such as highly integrated security, rating systems, a variety of different "helper" applications, and style sheets. Netscape Navigator only supports Java and JavaScript, has several plug-ins, and some support for style in web pages. You can, however, get a plug-in off the Internet that will enable you to use ActiveX technology and VBScript. The next section examines the uses of various ActiveX controls.

 Note You can pick up an ActiveX/VBScript plug-in from `http://www.ncompasslabs.com` for Netscape Navigator.

Utilizing ActiveX Controls

As mentioned previously, ActiveX controls can do many interesting things in web pages. With Visual Basic Script, you are all set to design fascinating web pages. An HTML interface that uses ActiveX has been designed for you to use so that you may examine and better understand the various uses of ActiveX controls. This interface enables you to view several controls, including the Chart control, the Marquee control, the Forms 2.0 controls, the Label control, the Image control, and a few others. The functionality of each of these controls and their contribution to more interactive web pages will be explained in the following sections. Figure 4.4 illustrates the interface.

Note The following eight code listings are the interface you will be using to examine ActiveX controls and to learn how to use them in interesting ways. The interface and the following examples work best with 800 by 600 pixel resolution with 256 colors or greater.

This code listing (07acxvb01.htm) is an HTML interface designed with ActiveX controls for the next several examples in this section.

Note Listings in this chapter are referenced by the name used on the book's accompanying CD-ROM.

```
<HTML>
<HEAD>
<STYLE>
TH {color: brown, font-family: Arial; text-align: center}
</STYLE>
<TITLE>This is a demonstration</TITLE>
</HEAD>
<BODY BGCOLOR="tan">
<CENTER>
    <OBJECT ID="IeLabel1" WIDTH=400 HEIGHT=40
     CLASSID="CLSID:99B42120-6EC7-11CF-A6C7-00AA00A47DD2">
        <PARAM NAME="_ExtentX" VALUE="8864">
        <PARAM NAME="_ExtentY" VALUE="2196">
        <PARAM NAME="Caption" VALUE="Choose an ActiveX Control">
        <PARAM NAME="Angle" VALUE="0">
        <PARAM NAME="Alignment" VALUE="4">
        <PARAM NAME="Mode" VALUE="1">
        <PARAM NAME="FillStyle" VALUE="0">
        <PARAM NAME="FillStyle" VALUE="0">
        <PARAM NAME="ForeColor" VALUE="#556B2F">
        <PARAM NAME="BackColor" VALUE="#C0C0C0">
        <PARAM NAME="FontName" VALUE="Arial">
        <PARAM NAME="FontSize" VALUE="24">
        <PARAM NAME="FontItalic" VALUE="0">
        <PARAM NAME="FontBold" VALUE="0">
        <PARAM NAME="FontUnderline" VALUE="0">
        <PARAM NAME="FontStrikeout" VALUE="0">
        <PARAM NAME="TopPoints" VALUE="0">
        <PARAM NAME="BotPoints" VALUE="0">
    </OBJECT>
</CENTER>

<!-- Begin Table and ActiveX Menu Interface -->
<TABLE BORDER="0">
<TR>
<TH>Demonstration Window</TH>
<TH>Technical Information</TH>
</TR>
<TR>
<TD>
        <IFRAME WIDTH="400" HEIGHT="300" NAME="frame1"
            SRC="mainpage.htm" SCROLLING="NO"
            ALIGN="LEFT">
        </IFRAME>
```

```
</TD>
<TD>
        <IFRAME WIDTH="300" HEIGHT="300" NAME="frame2"
                    SRC="maintpage.htm">
        </IFRAME>
</TD>
<TR>
<TD ALIGN="CENTER" COLSPAN="2">
    <OBJECT ID="pmenu3" WIDTH=71 HEIGHT=27
     CLASSID="CLSID:52DFAE60-CEBF-11CF-A3A9-00A0C9034920">
        <PARAM NAME="_ExtentX" VALUE="1879">
        <PARAM NAME="_ExtentY" VALUE="714">
        <PARAM NAME="Caption" VALUE="Chart">
    </OBJECT>
    <SCRIPT LANGUAGE="VBScript">
<!--
Sub pmenu5_Click()
        IeLabel1.Caption = "MS Forms Demo"
        window.frames(0).navigate "formpage.htm"
        window.frames(1).navigate "formtech.htm"
end sub
-->
    </SCRIPT>
    <OBJECT ID="pmenu5" WIDTH=71 HEIGHT=27
     CLASSID="CLSID:52DFAE60-CEBF-11CF-A3A9-00A0C9034920">
        <PARAM NAME="_ExtentX" VALUE="1879">
        <PARAM NAME="_ExtentY" VALUE="714">
        <PARAM NAME="Caption" VALUE="Forms 2.0">
    </OBJECT>
    <OBJECT ID="pmenu4" WIDTH=71 HEIGHT=27
     CLASSID="CLSID:52DFAE60-CEBF-11CF-A3A9-00A0C9034920">
        <PARAM NAME="_ExtentX" VALUE="1879">
        <PARAM NAME="_ExtentY" VALUE="714">
        <PARAM NAME="Caption" VALUE="Image">
    </OBJECT>
    <OBJECT ID="pmenu2" WIDTH=71 HEIGHT=27
     CLASSID="CLSID:52DFAE60-CEBF-11CF-A3A9-00A0C9034920">
        <PARAM NAME="_ExtentX" VALUE="1879">
        <PARAM NAME="_ExtentY" VALUE="714">
        <PARAM NAME="Caption" VALUE="Label">
    </OBJECT>
```

```
    <OBJECT ID="pmenu1" WIDTH=71 HEIGHT=27
     CLASSID="CLSID:52DFAE60-CEBF-11CF-A3A9-00A0C9034920">
        <PARAM NAME="_ExtentX" VALUE="1879">
        <PARAM NAME="_ExtentY" VALUE="714">
        <PARAM NAME="Caption" VALUE="Marquee">
    </OBJECT>
    <SCRIPT LANGUAGE="VBScript">
<!--
Sub pmenu6_Click()
call window.navigate("07acxvb01.htm")

end sub
-->
    </SCRIPT>
    <OBJECT ID="pmenu6" WIDTH=71 HEIGHT=27
     CLASSID="CLSID:52DFAE60-CEBF-11CF-A3A9-00A0C9034920">
        <PARAM NAME="_ExtentX" VALUE="1079">
        <PARAM NAME="_ExtentY" VALUE="714">
        <PARAM NAME="Caption" VALUE="RESET">
    </OBJECT>
    <SCRIPT LANGUAGE="VBScript">
<!--
Sub pmenu7_Select(item)
select case item

    case 1
        call pmenu3_Click()

    case 2
        call pmenu5_Click()

    case 3
        call pmenu4_Click()
    case 4
        call pmenu2_Click()
    case 5
        call pmenu1_Click()

    case 6
        call pmenuG_Click()
end select
end sub
-->
```

```
</SCRIPT>
<OBJECT ID="pmenu7" WIDTH=71 HEIGHT=27
 CLASSID="CLSID:52DFAE60-CEBF-11CF-A3A9-00A0C9034920">
    <PARAM NAME="_ExtentX" VALUE="1879">
    <PARAM NAME="_ExtentY" VALUE="714">
    <PARAM NAME="Caption" VALUE="CLICK-ME">
</OBJECT>
<SCRIPT LANGUAGE="VBScript">
<!--
Sub pmenu4_Click()
window.frames(0).navigate "pictpage.htm"
window.frames(1).navigate "picttech.htm"
IeLabel1.Caption = "IE Picture Control"
end sub
-->
    </SCRIPT>
</TD>
</TR>
</TABLE>
<!-- End Table and ActiveX Interface  -->
    <SCRIPT LANGUAGE="VBScript">
'These procedures manipulate the buttons on the button menu
call InitClickMe()
Sub InitClickMe()
call pmenu7.AddItem("Chart", 1)
call pmenu7.AddItem("Forms 2.0", 2)
call pmenu7.AddItem("Image", 3)
call pmenu7.AddItem("Label", 4)
call pmenu7.AddItem("Marquee", 5)
call pmenu7.AddItem("RESET", 6)
end sub

Sub pmenu1_Click()
    window.frames(0).navigate "marqueepage.htm"
    window.frames(1).navigate "http://www.microsoft.com/activex/gallery/ms/
    ➥ieprog/marquee.htm"
    IeLabel1.Caption = "Notice the Marquee"
end sub

Sub pmenu2_Click()
    window.frames(0).navigate "labelpage.htm"
    window.frames(1).navigate "http://www.microsoft.com/activex/gallery/ms/
```

```
       ➥ieprog/label.htm"
       IeLabel1.Caption = "The Label Example"
end sub

Sub pmenu3_Click()
       window.frames(0).navigate "chartpage.htm"
       window.frames(1).navigate "http://www.microsoft.com/activex/gallery/ms/
       ➥ieprog/chart.htm"
       IeLabel1.Caption = "Chart Example"
end sub
       </SCRIPT>
</CENTER>
</BODY>
```

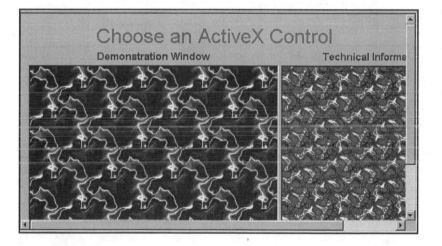

Figure 4.4

An illustration of the ActiveX interface on an HTML page.

The ActiveX interface consists of two frames and a button menu, and is driven by VBScript. The frame on the left is used to display the demonstration of the ActiveX control being viewed, while the frame on the right displays technical information about the control. The content in these frames is loaded and accessed through the Internet Explorer 3.0 Object Model when one of the buttons on the menu below the frames is clicked.

The button menu consists of seven options; they are (in order from left to right) Chart, Forms 2.0, Image, Label, Marquee, RESET, and CLICK-ME. The first five buttons, when clicked, load an ActiveX control's demonstration and technical information. The RESET button, when clicked, resets the page to its original status—two blank frames with a background pattern and no demonstrations. Finally, the CLICK-ME button, which has a small v-shaped icon on the right of it, is a menu itself, containing the previous six options. This final button serves no greater purpose than the other six except it demonstrates that the menu can be a pop-up menu in addition to a series of buttons.

The Chart Control

The Chart control has 20 chart styles and five color schemes. Different chart styles of this data are being displayed by means of an ActiveX Timer control, which is essential to many ActiveX controls. During design time of the page, an interval for the timer is set in milliseconds. At every specified interval, the timer method is launched. When this method is launched, a series of VBScript procedures are executed (in the case of the chart example, the style number corresponding to the chart style is changed.) The data being used in the chart is the number of cars and trucks produced from 1955 to 1960 (in 1,000s) in the U.S. (see fig. 4.5). The following code is the chart example displayed in the interface and can be accessed from the CD under chartpage.htm (in Chapter 4).

Figure 4.5

Clicking the Chart button displays the chart demo.

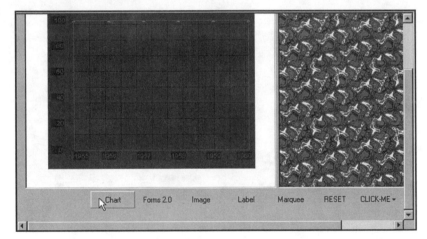

```
<HTML>
<HEAD>
    <SCRIPT LANGUAGE="VBScript">
<!--
Sub InitChart()
'the following properties set the
'row labels for the chart
iechart1.RowIndex = 0
iechart1.RowName = "1955"
iechart1.RowIndex = 1
iechart1.RowName = "1956"
iechart1.RowIndex = 2
```

```
iechart1.RowName = "1957"
iechart1.RowIndex = 3
iechart1.RowName = "1958"
iechart1.RowIndex = 4
iechart1.RowName = "1959"
iechart1.RowIndex = 5
iechart1.RowName = "1960"
end sub

-->
    </SCRIPT>
<TITLE>New Page</TITLE>
</HEAD>
<BODY BGCOLOR="#FDF5E6">
<CENTER>
<!-- the object declaration inserts the label chart into
     the page and sets most of the properties of the chart -->
    <OBJECT ID="iechart1" WIDTH=331 HEIGHT=251
    CLASSID="CLSID:FC25B780-75BE-11CF-8B01-444553540000">
        <PARAM NAME="_ExtentX" VALUE="8758">
        <PARAM NAME="_ExtentY" VALUE="6641">
        <PARAM NAME="Rows" VALUE="6">
        <PARAM NAME="Columns" VALUE="2">
        <PARAM NAME="ChartType" VALUE="5">
        <PARAM NAME="Data[0][0]" VALUE="7942">
        <PARAM NAME="Data[0][1]" VALUE="1246">
        <PARAM NAME="Data[1][0]" VALUE="5807">
        <PARAM NAME="Data[1][1]" VALUE="1112">
        <PARAM NAME="Data[2][0]" VALUE="6120">
        <PARAM NAME="Data[2][1]" VALUE="1100">
        <PARAM NAME="Data[3][0]" VALUE="4247">
        <PARAM NAME="Data[3][1]" VALUE="874">
        <PARAM NAME="Data[4][0]" VALUE="5599">
        <PARAM NAME="Data[4][1]" VALUE="1124">
        <PARAM NAME="Data[5][0]" VALUE="6703">
        <PARAM NAME="Data[5][1]" VALUE="1202">
        <PARAM NAME="HorizontalAxis" VALUE="0">
        <PARAM NAME="VerticalAxis" VALUE="0">
        <PARAM NAME="hgridStyle" VALUE="1">
        <PARAM NAME="vgridStyle" VALUE="1">
        <PARAM NAME="ColorScheme" VALUE="3">
        <PARAM NAME="BackStyle" VALUE="1">
```

```
            <PARAM NAME="Scale" VALUE="89">
            <PARAM NAME="DisplayLegend" VALUE="-1">
            <PARAM NAME="BackColor" VALUE="4210688">
            <PARAM NAME="ForeColor" VALUE="32768">
        </OBJECT>
    </CENTER>
<!-- The following is the script that manipulates
      the chart -->
    <SCRIPT LANGUAGE="VBScript">
<!--
Sub IeTimer1_Timer() 'the timer event procedure
' the following if-then conditional is used to
' scroll through the different chart styles
if iechart1.ChartType = 17 then
      iechart1.ChartType = 0
else
      iechart1.ChartType = iechart1.ChartType + 1
end if


end sub 'end of timer event procedure
'the following event procedure is for the IeChart click
'event. When the chart is clicked, the interval property
'of the timer is increased so the charts take longer to
'display
Sub IeChart1_Click()
      Timer1.Interval = Timer1.Interval + 10
end Sub
-->
    </SCRIPT>
    <OBJECT ID="IeTimer1" WIDTH=39 HEIGHT=39
      CLASSID="CLSID:59CCB4A0-727D-11CF-AC36-00AA00A47DD2">
        <PARAM NAME="_ExtentX" VALUE="1032">
        <PARAM NAME="_ExtentY" VALUE="1032">
        <PARAM NAME="Interval" VALUE="2000">
    </OBJECT>
<!-- The following minor script calls the IntiChart procedure
      defined at the beginning, which sets the properties for the
      chart -->
    <SCRIPT LANGUAGE="VBScript">
            call InitChart()
    </SCRIPT>
</BODY>
</HTML>
```

When the user clicks on the "Chart" button, a chart is displayed in the demonstration frame, and, if you are connected to the Internet, Microsoft's information on its Chart control is displayed. The ActiveX Chart is obviously a useful control. For starters, the method of entering data for the chart is extremely simple and, instead of using unconventional and sometimes disproportionate images of charts, you can display an accurate chart on-screen for the user to view. Also, if the data for the chart needs to be added or updated, it can be done manually through VBScript or with another program, because the chart's data does not have to be internal; the chart's data can also be accessed via an URL. The comments in the code listing explain how each detail of the code works.

Note Are the graphs flashing by too quickly? Just click on the graph to slow down the graph slide show. Clicking on the graph increases the timer's interval, thus making the displaying of different chart styles slower. You will understand how timers and other ActiveX controls work more thoroughly as you delve into later chapters of this book.

The Microsoft Forms 2.0 Controls

This section does not cover one, but several controls collectively called the Forms 2.0 controls. If you are familiar with the Visual Basic or C++ programming environment, then you know what these controls are. If not, they are a group of controls that are for user input and interaction. Forms controls range from very simple controls, such as the label and text box controls, to more complex controls, such as the combo box and tab strip controls.

Fourteen form controls are included with the ActiveX Control Pad, and some controls, such as the panel control, do not function properly yet. The fourteen controls are: check boxes, combo boxes, command buttons, frames, labels, list boxes, multipage controls, option buttons, panel control, scroll bars, spin buttons, tab strips, text boxes, and toggle buttons. The Forms 2.0 controls were designed to complement the ActiveX Layout control. The Forms 2.0 controls work very well with the Layout control.

The first code listing (formpage.htm) in this section is the HTML document in which an HTML Layout control is inserted. The second listing (layout2.alx) in this section is the layout file referenced by the Layout control in formpage.htm. The Forms 2.0 controls used in this particular example are the command button, label button, spin button, tab strip control, and the text box (see fig. 4.6).

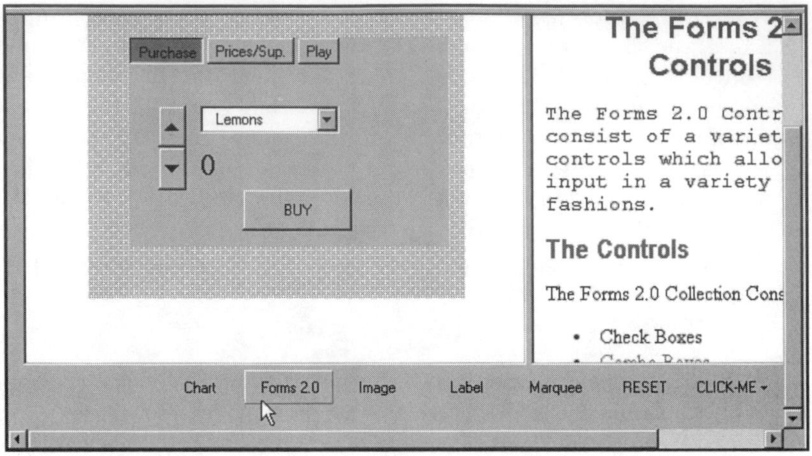

Figure 4.6

Clicking the Forms 2.0 button on the menu displays this example.

The controls and the code used to manipulate them in the Layout file (layout2.alx) are used in the example to create the interface to the somewhat popular lemonade stand game. You start out by buying lemon juice, sugar, water, and cups. The combo box is used in selecting the supplies that you want to purchase, and the spin button is used to select how many units the player wants to purchase. The label control is used to display the number of units of each product purchased. These units are arbitrary, and you can set in code how many cup-worths of lemonade each unit is capable of yielding. After the player clicks the Buy button, the code can be manipulated to subtract the total amount of money spent from the user's amount and proceed with the rest of the game.

The following code (formpage.htm) is the HTML document for the Forms 2.0 demonstration (the code in the Utilizing ActiveX controls section).

```
<HTML>
<HEAD><TITLE>New Page</TITLE></HEAD>
<BODY BGCOLOR="F0F8FF">
<CENTER>
<OBJECT CLASSID="CLSID:812AE312-8B8E-11CF-93C8-00AA00C08FDF"
ID="layout1_alx" STYLE="LEFT:0;TOP:0">
<PARAM NAME="ALXPATH" REF VALUE="layout2.alx">
 </OBJECT>
</CENTER>
</BODY>
</HTML>
```

> **Note** All files mentioned in this chapter can be accessed from the CD as well (under Chapter 4).

The following code is the Layout file (layout2.alx) containing all the controls referenced by formpage.htm, the previous code listing.

```vbscript
<SCRIPT LANGUAGE="VBScript">
<!--
Sub InitBuyBox() 'this sub initializes the combo-list box
                 'which is populated with the products the
                 'user can buy
    call ComboBox1.AddItem("Lemons", 0)
    call ComboBox1.AddItem("Sugar", 1)
    call ComboBox1.AddItem("Water", 2)
    call ComboBox1.AddItem("100 Cups", 3)
    ComboBox1.ListIndex = 0
end sub
-->
</SCRIPT>
<SCRIPT LANGUAGE="VBScript">
<!--

Sub CommandButton1_Click() 'this is the event procedure of
                           'the command button and performs
                           'different tasks based on which
                           'tab you are in
select case TabStrip1.SelectedItem.Index
'this select case determines what tab you are in, and relays the
'appropriate message to the status bar when you press the button
    case 0
        window.status="Ok, You bought it!"
    case 2
        window.status="Have fun!!!"
end select
end sub
-->
</SCRIPT>
<SCRIPT LANGUAGE="VBScript">
<!--
' variable declarations
dim Supl(4)
Money = 200
```

```
Sub ComboBox1_Change()
'the sub procedure handles what to display in the label
'controls when a different product is selected
Call WhatDisplay()
end sub
-->
</SCRIPT>
<SCRIPT LANGUAGE="VBScript">
<!--
'the following two event procedures manipulate the spin button
'control that increments or decrements amount of the current
'product being bought
Sub SpinButton1_SpinDown()
Supl(ComboBox1.ListIndex) = Supl(ComboBox1.ListIndex) - 1
Label1.Caption= Supl(ComboBox1.ListIndex)
end sub
Sub SpinButton1_SpinUp()
Supl(ComboBox1.ListIndex) = Supl(ComboBox1.ListIndex) + 1
Label1.Caption= Supl(ComboBox1.ListIndex)
end sub
-->
</SCRIPT>
<SCRIPT LANGUAGE="VBScript">
<!--
'the following subroutines are used to initialize the 3 different
'tabs and display what is on them.
Sub TabInit1() 'this procedure initializes objects on the 2nd tab
call RemoveAll(1)
call WhatDisplay()
ComboBox1.Top = 41.25
ComboBox1.Left = 33
Label3.Left = 94
Label3.Top = 74.25
Label2.Left = 33
Label2.Top = 107.25
Label1.Top = 74.25
Label1.Left = 49.5
TextBox1.Top = 107.25
TextBox1.Left = 148.5end sub
Sub TabInit2() 'this procedure initializes objects on the 3rd tab
      call RemoveAll(2)
end sub
```

```
Sub RemoveAll(x) 'removes the unneeded objects for each tab
select case x
        case 0
                'Remove all the other controls
                Label3.Left = -10000
                Label2.Left = -10000
                TextBox1.Left = -10000
        case 1
                CommandButton1.Left = -10000
                SpinButton1.Left = -10000
        case 2
                Label1.Left = -10000
                ComboBox1.Loft = -10000
                CommandButton1.Left = -10000
                SpinButton1.Left = -10000
                Label3.Left = -10000
                Label2.Left = -10000
                TextBox1.Left = -10000
end select
end sub
Sub TabInit0()
'This procedure Initializes the first Tab
        Call RemoveAll(0)
        call WhatDisplay()
        Label1.Left = 66
        Label1.Top = 83
        ComboBox1.Left = 66
        ComboBox1.Top = 58
        CommandButton1.Left = 91
        CommandButton1.Top = 107
        SpinButton1.Left = 41
        SpinButton1.Top = 58
        end sub
Sub TabStrip1_Change()
'this event procedure for the tabstrip calls the appropriate
'initialization sub procedure when one of the tabs is selected
   select case TabStrip1.SelectedItem.Index
        case 0
                call TabInit0()
        case 1
                call TabInit1()
```

```
      case 2
            call TabInit2()
   end select
end sub
-->
</SCRIPT>
<SCRIPT LANGUAGE="VBScript">
<!--
Sub WhatDisplay()
'this sub handles the display for the labels in the first 2 tabs
select case TabStrip1.SelectedItem.Index
'the TabStrip1.SelectedItem.Index property indicates which
'tab you currently have selected
      case 0
'in the first tab (case 0), just the arbitrary units
'of each product are displayed
        select case ComboBox1.ListIndex
      case 0
    Label1.Caption= Supl(ComboBox1.ListIndex)
      case 1
    Label1.Caption= Supl(ComboBox1.ListIndex)
      case 2
    Label1.Caption= Supl(ComboBox1.ListIndex)
      case 3
    Label1.Caption= Supl(ComboBox1.ListIndex)
        end select
      case 1
'the second tab displays how many cup-worths of lemonade each
'arbitrary unit is capable of producing
        select case ComboBox1.ListIndex        case 0
    Label1.Caption= Supl(ComboBox1.ListIndex)*200
      case 1
    Label1.Caption= Supl(ComboBox1.ListIndex)*150
      case 2
    Label1.Caption= Supl(ComboBox1.ListIndex)*100
      case 3
    Label1.Caption= Supl(ComboBox1.ListIndex)*100
        end select
end select
end sub
Sub layout1_OnLoad()
```

```
'this sub contains a for…next loop that just sets all
'the elements in the Supl(3) array to 0
for i = 0 to 3
    Supl(i) = 0
next
end sub
-->
</SCRIPT>
<!-- The following is the section where all of the objects
     are declared -->
<DIV BACKGROUND="#cbdaa7" ID="layout1"
STYLE="LAYOUT:FIXED;WIDTH:224pt;HEIGHT:172pt;">
    <OBJECT ID="TabStrip1"
     CLASSID="CLSID:EAE50EB0-4A62-11CE-BED6-00AA00611080"
STYLE="TOP:17pt;LEFT:25pt;WIDTH:190pt;HEIGHT:124pt;TABINDEX:0;ZINDEX:0;">
        <PARAM NAME="ListIndex" VALUE="0">
        <PARAM NAME="BackColor" VALUE="11000523">
        <PARAM NAME="Size" VALUE="6703;4374">
        <PARAM NAME="Items" VALUE="Purchase;Prices/Sup.;Play;">
        <PARAM NAME="TabStyle" VALUE="1">
        <PARAM NAME="TipStrings" VALUE=";;;">
        <PARAM NAME="Names" VALUE="Tab1;Tab2;Tab3;">
        <PARAM NAME="NewVersion" VALUE="-1">
        <PARAM NAME="TabsAllocated" VALUE="3">
        <PARAM NAME="Tags" VALUE=";;;">
        <PARAM NAME="TabData" VALUE="3">
        <PARAM NAME="Accelerator" VALUE=";;;">
        <PARAM NAME="FontCharSet" VALUE="0">
        <PARAM NAME="FontPitchAndFamily" VALUE="2">
        <PARAM NAME="FontWeight" VALUE="0">
        <PARAM NAME="TabState" VALUE="3;3;3">
    </OBJECT>
    <OBJECT ID="SpinButton1"
     CLASSID="CLSID:79176FB0-B7F2-11CE-97EF-00AA006D2776"
STYLE="TOP:58pt;LEFT:41pt;WIDTH:17pt;HEIGHT:50pt;TABINDEX:1;ZINDEX:1;">
        <PARAM NAME="Size" VALUE="600;1764">
        <PARAM NAME="Max" VALUE="200">
    </OBJECT>
    <OBJECT ID="Label1"
     CLASSID="CLSID:978C9E23-D4B0-11CE-BF2D-00AA003F40D0"
STYLE="TOP:83pt;LEFT:66pt;WIDTH:58pt;HEIGHT:25pt;ZINDEX:2;">
        <PARAM NAME="VariousPropertyBits" VALUE="8388627">
```

```
              <PARAM NAME="Caption" VALUE="0">
              <PARAM NAME="Size" VALUE="2046;882">
              <PARAM NAME="FontName" VALUE="MS Serif">
              <PARAM NAME="FontHeight" VALUE="360">
              <PARAM NAME="FontCharSet" VALUE="0">
              <PARAM NAME="FontPitchAndFamily" VALUE="2">
              <PARAM NAME="FontWeight" VALUE="0">
      </OBJECT>
      <OBJECT ID="CommandButton1"
       CLASSID="CLSID:D7053240-CE69-11CD-A777-00DD01143C57"
STYLE="TOP:107pt;LEFT:91pt;WIDTH:66pt;HEIGHT:25pt;TABINDEX:3;ZINDEX:3;">
              <PARAM NAME="Caption" VALUE="BUY">
              <PARAM NAME="Size" VALUE="2328;882">
              <PARAM NAME="FontCharSet" VALUE="0">
              <PARAM NAME="FontPitchAndFamily" VALUE="2">
              <PARAM NAME="ParagraphAlign" VALUE="3">
              <PARAM NAME="FontWeight" VALUE="0">
      </OBJECT>
  <OBJECT ID="ComboBox1"
  CLASSID="CLSID:8BD21D30-EC42-11CE-9E0D-00AA006002F3"
➥STYLE="TOP:58pt;LEFT:66pt;WIDTH:83pt;
              HEIGHT:16pt;TABINDEX:4;ZINDEX:4;">
              <PARAM NAME="VariousPropertyBits" VALUE="746604571">
              <PARAM NAME="DisplayStyle" VALUE="3">
              <PARAM NAME="Size" VALUE="2928;564">
              <PARAM NAME="MatchEntry" VALUE="1">
              <PARAM NAME="ShowDropButtonWhen" VALUE="2">
              <PARAM NAME="FontCharSet" VALUE="0">
              <PARAM NAME="FontPitchAndFamily" VALUE="2">
              <PARAM NAME="FontWeight" VALUE="0">
      </OBJECT>
      <OBJECT ID="Label2"
  CLASSID="CLSID:978C9E23-D4B0-11CE-BF2D-00AA003F40D0"
  STYLE="TOP:41pt;LEFT:239pt;
  WIDTH:66pt;HEIGHT:17pt;ZINDEX:5;">
              <PARAM NAME="VariousPropertyBits" VALUE="8388627">
              <PARAM NAME="Caption" VALUE="Set Price:">
              <PARAM NAME="Size" VALUE="2328;600">
              <PARAM NAME="FontHeight" VALUE="240">
              <PARAM NAME="FontCharSet" VALUE="0">
              <PARAM NAME="FontPitchAndFamily" VALUE="2">
              <PARAM NAME="FontWeight" VALUE="0">
```

```
    </OBJECT>
    <OBJECT ID="TextBox1"
     CLASSID="CLSID:8BD21D10-EC42-11CE-9E0D-00AA006002F3"
STYLE="TOP:99pt;LEFT:231pt;WIDTH:50pt;HEIGHT:17pt;TABINDEX:6;ZINDEX:6;">
        <PARAM NAME="VariousPropertyBits" VALUE="746604571">
        <PARAM NAME="Size" VALUE="1764;600">
        <PARAM NAME="FontCharSet" VALUE="0">
        <PARAM NAME="FontPitchAndFamily" VALUE="2">
        <PARAM NAME="FontWeight" VALUE="0">
    </OBJECT>
    <OBJECT ID="Label3"
     CLASSID="CLSID:978C9E23-D4B0-11CE-BF2D-00AA003F40D0"
STYLE="TOP:74pt;LEFT:230pt;WIDTH:63pt;HEIGHT:17pt;ZINDEX:7;">
        <PARAM NAME="VariousPropertyBits" VALUE="8388627">
        <PARAM NAME="Caption" VALUE="Cups Worth">
        <PARAM NAME="Size" VALUE="2928;600">
        <PARAM NAME="FontHeight" VALUE="240">
        <PARAM NAME="FontCharSet" VALUE="0">
        <PARAM NAME="FontPitchAndFamily" VALUE="2">
        <PARAM NAME="FontWeight" VALUE="0">
    </OBJECT>
</DIV>
<SCRIPT LANGUAGE="VBScript">
Call InitBuyBox()
</SCRIPT>
```

The tab strip is used in the previous listing example, but a different style is being used
for it. By default, a tab strip is a series of tabs in the upper-lefthand corner, but the
Style property was changed to buttons instead of tabs during design time. When the
second tab, or button, is clicked, a text box appears in which you can set the price as
indicated on the screen. When you click the combo box and select an item, the
number displayed is no longer in units, but a number representing how many cups of
lemonade each product can contribute to. Values representing each unit have been
coded already, but you can change them to anything. When the third "Play" button is
clicked, nothing is on-screen because this example is not a fully functioning game,
but merely a demonstration of an interface for the game. Putting the entire game
here would go beyond the scope of this chapter. This example, however, should give
you a feel for how Form controls are used.

Note   A full version of the program will be available in the near future at http://
www.rt66.com/iymalluf/yusuf. There will be a stand-alone version available, as
well.

Tip   The tab strip control, in the previous example, is a versatile tool to use. Controls are not placed on tabs or changed automatically when a tab is clicked. You have to change controls through code by manipulating the Left and Top properties of the Form controls. You can place the first tab's set of controls on the tab itself, but you must move them off and move the other controls on during runtime.

Assigning one of the Top or Left properties a value of –10,000 would remove it from the screen. Assigning the control to its original position on the tab strip would bring it back. This method is best done when the Change or Click event of the tab strip control occurs, as shown in the previous code.

All these controls are used in an HTML layout file and are inserted through the ActiveX Layout control, another tool that enables you to have WYSIWYG control over where you place controls on the page. The Layout control has an .alx extension (as opposed to an HTML document's .htm or .html extension) and uses HTML tags associated with style sheets, like the <DIV> tag. Like all other ActiveX controls, the HTML Layout control has properties, events, and methods you can manipulate.

The Image Control

The following code(pictpage.htm) is the HTML file for the Image control example used in 07acxvb01.htm, which is the interface discussed earlier in the chapter. Figure 4.7 illustrates the layout file and the page listing that references the layout file.

```
<HTML>
<HEAD>
    <SCRIPT LANGUAGE="VBScript">
<!--
Sub Procedure1()
'this procedure sets properties of the image tag
'such as the background color (BackColor) and the
'path of the picture (PicturePath).
Image1.PicturePath = "pictdemo.bmp"
Image1.BackColor = "8421504"
end sub
-->
    </SCRIPT>
<TITLE>New Page</TITLE>
</HEAD>
<BODY TOPMARGIN="0" LEFTMARGIN="0" BGCOLOR="#CD853F">
    <SCRIPT LANGUAGE="VBScript">
<!--
Sub WhichShape(x,y)
```

```
'this sub procedure determines which shape the mouse is
in based on coordinates and relays a message to the
'status bar
window.status = x & ":" & y 'this is the output for the
'status bar in the form of coordinate x : coordinate y
'the following conditinal determines which shape the mouse is
'in by the x and y arguments passed to the sub.
  if (x - 187.5)^2 + (Y - 56.75)^2 <= 784 then 'blue circle
     window.status="blue circle"
elseif (x > 47.5 and y > 27.2) and (x < 125.85 and y < 106.45) then
     window.status="slate-blue square"
                  'blue square
elseif ((((x   133.35)^2)/47.5^2) + (((y - 163.2)'2)/28 2)) =< 1 then
     window.status="royal-blue ellipse"
                  'ellipse
elseif ((x < 7.5 and y < 207.5) or (x > 215.85 and y > 0)) then
     window.status="dark-gray rectangle"
'rectangles (actually, just the background color of the
'image tag)
  end if
end sub
'the following event procedure handles the moving of the mouse
Sub Image1_MouseMove(Button, Shift, X, Y)
call WhichShape(x,y)
end sub
-->
    </SCRIPT>
<CENTER>
<!-- the object definition for the image control -->
    <OBJECT ID="Image1" WIDTH=270 HEIGHT=270
     CLASSID="CLSID:D4A97620-8E8F-11CF-93CD-00AA00C08FDF">
        <PARAM NAME="BorderStyle" VALUE="0">
        <PARAM NAME="SizeMode" VALUE="3">
        <PARAM NAME="SpecialEffect" VALUE="3">
        <PARAM NAME="Size" VALUE="7938;7403">
        <PARAM NAME="VariousPropertyBits" VALUE="19">
    </OBJECT>
</CENETER>
    <SCRIPT LANGUAGE="VBSCRIPT">
call procedure1()'procedure to initialize the image tag
    </SCRIPT>
</BODY>
</HTML>
```

Figure 4.7

*This is an
illustration of the
image control.*

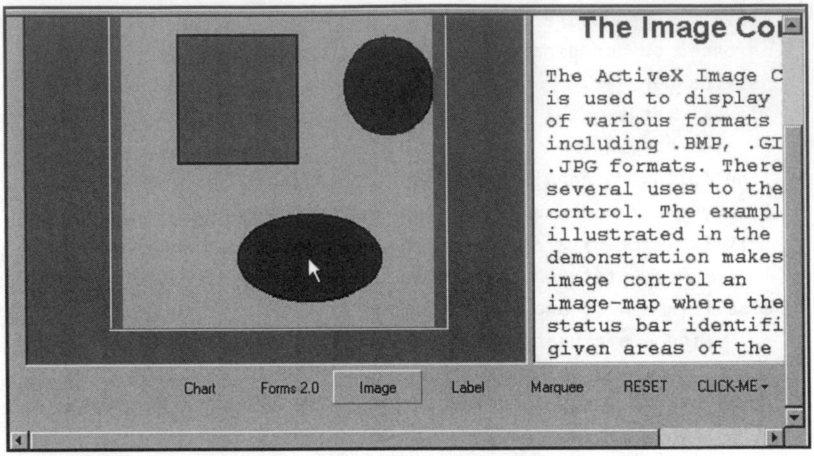

The Microsoft ActiveX Image control is a versatile tool. The Microsoft ActiveX Image control used in pictpage.htm is slightly different than the one that is part of the Forms 2.0 collection of controls. It is different in the following ways:

◆   The Microsoft ActiveX Image control supports metafiles (.wmf), bitmaps (.pmp), GIFs (.gif), and JPEGS (.jpg). The image control belonging to the Forms 2.0 collection also supports icons (*.ico).

◆   The picture specified for the Forms Image control is inline (part of the file) and the picture specified with the Microsoft ActiveX Image control is another URL. This is why the ActiveX Image control is more portable.

In pictpage.htm, the ActiveX Image Object's MouseMove event was used, which returns the coordinate location of the mouse pointer and information stating whether the mouse button is being held down or the shift key is being pressed.

The picture displayed in pictpage.htmis referenced by the control through the PicturePath property, which specifies the URL of the picture.

When the mouse pointer moves over a certain area (in this picture, the areas are obvious—the circle, square, and ellipse), the status bar reports. If you run this example and move your mouse over the ellipse, the status bar indicates that you are in a royal blue ellipse. Likewise, if you move into the square, the status bar tells you your location. This example is rather simple, but in your web projects, you may find the image control handy in a variety of ways—the tool demonstrated here is obviously an image map because certain areas are defined within the picture, and the script responds differently when your pointer is in those areas.

> **Tip**
>
> `pictpage.htm` demonstrated that you can define areas on an image and have Visual Basic Script respond to those areas differently, but how? It would be helpful if you knew several formulas used in analytic (coordinate) geometry. One of the most common of these formulas is the distance formula, where x and y are the coordinates of the mouse, and d is the distance between the two points:
>
> ```
> distance = (x-x₁)² + (y-y₁)² = d²
> ```
>
> You can use this formula to section off different areas through a conditional structure in Visual Basic Script (an if-then-else structure). The distance formula is actually the formula for a circle too, where d is the radius of the circle, x₁ and y₁ are the center coordinates of the circle, and x and y are the coordinates of the mouse. `pictpage.htm` shows you how these formulas are used with an if-then-else structure.

The Label Control

The Label control is probably one of the most interesting and useful of the ActiveX controls because you can do so much with it. The Label control has many useful properties, such as the angle property, which indicates the angle of the text, and the series of properties that enable you to abnormally shape the form of the label. To utilize all of these properties, the label control has a series of events you can use, such as the click, double-click, and MouseOver events. The only method of the Label control is the about box, which indicates who created the control, when, and so on. When you click on the buttons below the frames in `07acxvb01.htm`, notice that the heading at the very top changes from "Choose an ActiveX control" to whatever is appropriate for the button you pressed. If, for example, you clicked the button "Label," then the heading would change to "The Label Example."

In `labelpage.htm`, three of the Label control's properties are taken advantage of—its size, caption, and angle. These three properties can be manipulated through a timer control. At every interval, five degrees is added to the angle until the Label rotation nearly reaches 360 degrees. Although it is spinning positively (in a counter-clockwise direction), the Label's size is gradually increased to 72pt, and when it has almost reached 360 degrees, the rotation is reversed (five degrees are being subtracted instead of being added), the size decreases, and the caption changes from "It's Coming!" to "It's Going!" This entire process is accomplished through the timer control and VBScript. You can easily add random color changes by randomly choosing an integer from zero (black) to 16,777,215 (white) every time the `Timer` method is called for the ForeColor property. Figure 4.8 illustrates the previously mentioned technique found in labelpage.htm, the following listing.

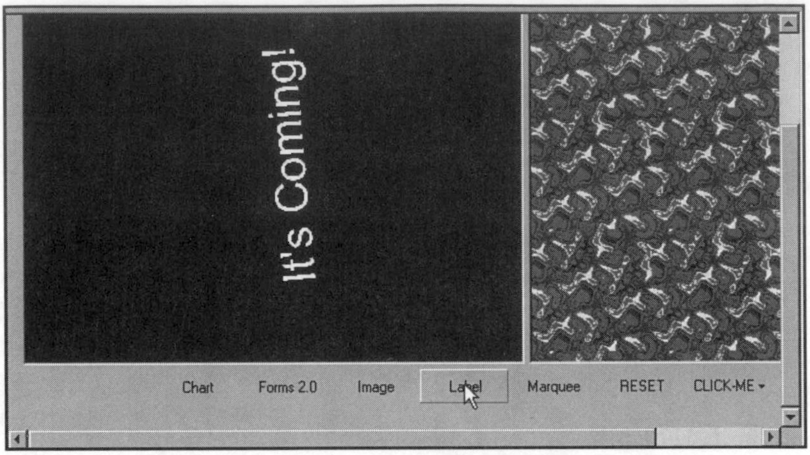

Figure 4.8

This figure illustrates the Label control used in 07acxvb01.htm.

This listing is the Label control example (`labelpage.htm`).

```html
<HTML>
<HEAD>
<TITLE>New Page</TITLE>
</HEAD>
<BODY BGCOLOR="black">
    <OBJECT ID="IeLabel1" WIDTH=400 HEIGHT=250
     CLASSID="CLSID:99B42120-6EC7-11CF-A6C7-00AA00A47DD2">
        <PARAM NAME="_ExtentX" VALUE="3625">
        <PARAM NAME="_ExtentY" VALUE="2461">
        <PARAM NAME="Caption" VALUE="It's Coming!">
        <PARAM NAME="Angle" VALUE="0">
        <PARAM NAME="Alignment" VALUE="4">
        <PARAM NAME="Mode" VALUE="1">
        <PARAM NAME="FillStyle" VALUE="0">
        <PARAM NAME="FillStyle" VALUE="0">
        <PARAM NAME="ForeColor" VALUE="#FFFFFF">
        <PARAM NAME="BackColor" VALUE="#C0C0C0">
        <PARAM NAME="FontName" VALUE="Arial">
        <PARAM NAME="FontSize" VALUE="12">
        <PARAM NAME="FontItalic" VALUE="0">
        <PARAM NAME="FontBold" VALUE="0">
        <PARAM NAME="FontUnderline" VALUE="0">
        <PARAM NAME="FontStrikeout" VALUE="0">
        <PARAM NAME="TopPoints" VALUE="0">
        <PARAM NAME="BotPoints" VALUE="0">
    </OBJECT>
    <SCRIPT LANGUAGE="VBScript">
```

```
<!--
dim AngleVal
dim SizeVal

AngleVal = 5
SizeVal = 1
Sub IeTimer1_Timer()
IeLabel1.Angle = IeLabel1.Angle + AngleVal
IeLabel1.FontSize = IeLabel1.FontSize + SizeVal
if (IeLabel1.Angle > 350) then
        AngleVal = AngleVal * -1
        SizeVal = SizeVal * -1
        IeLabel1.Caption = "It's Going!"
elseif (IeLabel1.Angle < 5) then
        AngleVal = AngleVal * -1
        SizeVal = SizeVal * -1
        IeLabel1.Caption = "It's Coming!"
end if
end sub
-->
    </SCRIPT>
    <OBJECT ID="IeTimer1" WIDTH=39 HEIGHT=39
     CLASSID="CLSID:59CCB4A0-727D-11CF-AC36-00AA00A47DD2">
        <PARAM NAME="_ExtentX" VALUE="1005">
        <PARAM NAME="_ExtentY" VALUE="1005">
        <PARAM NAME="Interval" VALUE="100">
    </OBJECT>
</BODY>
</HTML>
```

The Marquee Control

The ActiveX Marquee control enables you to scroll a specified HTML document in a horizontal, vertical, or diagonal direction. This control becomes very useful in announcements and other pieces of information that you want to get across to your user—a scrolling document catches a user's attention.

The Marquee control does not contain as many properties as other controls, but is still very handy. It is one of the few controls that can contribute to an interactive web page without the use of any Visual Basic Script (in this example, no Visual Basic Script was used). You can have any HTML elements scrolled through the Marquee control, but it does not scroll any ActiveX controls.

The marquee object includes the following important properties:

- ◆ szURL
- ◆ ScrollPixelsX and ScrollPixelsY
- ◆ ScrollDelay property

The szUrl property is used to identify the location of the file that the marquee is supposed to scroll. The ScrollPixelsX and ScrollPixelsY properties are used to specify how many pixels are to be scrolled by in a given unit of time (if the number specified for these properties is larger, then more pixels are drawn to the screen quicker, where X is in the horizontal direction and Y is in the vertical direction). The ScrollDelay property specifies the delay interval between subsequent drawings of pixels. Large intervals between drawings leads to a slower marquee. Figure 4.9 illustrates the following code listing (marqueepage.htm).

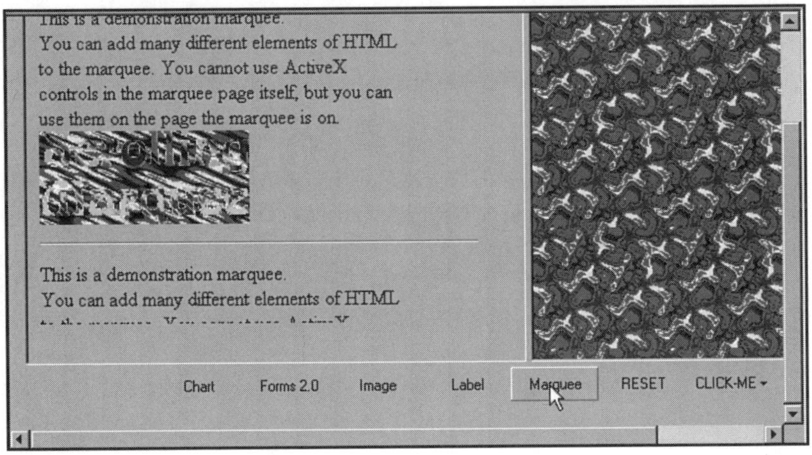

Figure 4.9

Illustrates the marquee example in the interface 07acxvb01.htm.

```
<HTML>
<BODY BGCOLOR="wheat">

<OBJECT
    ID="Marquee1"
    CLASSID="CLSID:1A4DA620-6217-11CF-BE62-0080C72EDD2D"
    TYPE="application/x-oleobject"
    WIDTH=350
    HEIGHT=250
>
    <PARAM NAME="szURL" VALUE="scrollme.htm">
    <PARAM NAME="ScrollPixelsX" VALUE="0">              <PARAM
```

```
➥NAME="ScrollPixelsY" VALUE="10">
   <PARAM NAME="ScrollDelay" VALUE="50">
      <PARAM NAME="Whitespace" VALUE="0">
</OBJECT>

</BODY></HTML>
```

The following file, `scrollme.htm`, is the file accessed by the marquee in the preceding code.

```
<HTML>
<BODY BGCOLOR="wheat" TOPMARGIN="0" LEFTMARGIN="0">
<HR>
This is a demonstration marquee.<BR>
You can add many different elements of HTML<BR> to
the marquee. You cannot use ActiveX<BR> controls in the marquee
page itself, but you can <BR>use them on the page the marquee is on.

<IMG SRC="image1.jpg" ALIGN="left">
<BR CLEAR="all">
</BODY></HTML>
```

What Tools Are Available?

Fortunately, you can use a variety of tools to simplify the process of developing and optimizing your web pages and their active content.

Tools not only refer to applications that aid you in the process of making your pages more interactive, but also to the ActiveX controls that you use in your web pages. Besides the common ActiveX controls supplied by Microsoft through their browser or through their site, many other companies distribute ActiveX controls that you can integrate into your web pages to further their interactive capability. This section examines the following tools:

◆ Microsoft's FrontPage

◆ Microsoft's ActiveX Control Pad

◆ Adobe Acrobat ActiveX Reader

◆ Black Diamond Consulting's Surround Video

◆ Microhelp's OCX Tools 5.0

Microsoft's FrontPage

FrontPage is a full Internet site manager that enables you to effortlessly create web pages with rich, streaming content. FrontPage has a management tool that graphically shows you how all the pages on your site are organized, indicating which links a document refers to or is referred by.

It also includes a personal web server that is fully functional and includes several Bot programs such as a chat client, a search program, an HTML insert Bot, a feedback Bot, and many others. Additionally, FrontPage also uses the latest HTML elements, including frames and tables. No direct support exists, however, for ActiveX and VBScript, and it is a commercial product by Microsoft. FrontPage does enable you to easily create good looking pages and would be an excellent complement to the ActiveX Control Pad, which primarily deals with ActiveX controls and scripting capabilities.

Note Check out *Designing Web Pages with FrontPage 97* (New Riders, 1996) for more information about FrontPage, or go to: `http://www.microsoft.com/frontpage/`.

The ActiveX Control Pad, if you will remember, is used specifically for inserting ActiveX controls in your web pages and for manipulating these controls through script. If you are not too HTML-savvy or lack design skills to make your site appealing beyond the use of ActiveX controls, then it would be a good idea to use FrontPage.

The design and layout of a page is just as important as the content of the page itself. A poor layout or page structure will give the semblance of a poor page in general, and it is very important not to present your pages this way. FrontPage, besides being an excellent organization tool, also contains provisions for spicing up your pages, including several wizards that enable you to graphically create tables and frames in your pages. Additionally, FrontPage uses a template system that enables you to choose a feel for your web pages from a variety of predefined styles.

The ActiveX Control Pad

The ActiveX Control Pad, discussed in Chapter 3, "The ActiveX Control Pad," is an excellent tool to use to start integrating ActiveX controls and scripting capability into your web pages—and even more so for the price: free. As you will remember, the interface of the ActiveX Control Pad is very nice to work with. Besides the standard toolbars, which provide a graphical way of accessing all the features of Control Pad, you can insert script and objects where you want in the HTML document with a click of a button. The interface for setting the properties for the different objects is similar to Visual Basic's interface. The HTML Layout control enables WYSIWYG control over controls that are used within the Layout control. The script wizard enables you to manually, or by using the interface, insert code into your document.

Adobe Acrobat ActiveX Reader

A variety of ActiveX controls are available that are useful to a web site developer or a Net surfer. Adobe Systems, Inc., for instance, (http://www.adobe.com) has made an ActiveX control of their popular Adobe Acrobat Reader, which enables you to view Adobe Portable Document Format (.PDF) files inside the browser. This ActiveX control offers the means of viewing .PDF files inside the browser instead of by using a helper application for viewing.

Black Diamond Consulting's Surround Video

Another company, Black Diamond Consulting, Inc., has developed a 3D imaging tool, Surround Video, which enables pictures to be viewed with a 3D motion perspective. The following figure displays an ActiveX control designed by Superscape (http://www.superscape.com)—another third-party developer. This control is used to display 3D worlds inside the browser. Figure 4.10 illustrates a 3D world viewed with the Superscape Control.

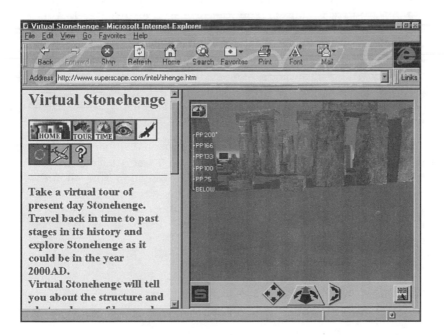

Figure 4.10

Displaying 3D worlds inside your browser.

Microhelp's OLE Tools 5.0

Microhelp, a popular control and OLE creator for programmers of Visual Basic and other visual languages, has developed a set of over 25 controls that you can use within web pages. These controls range from the simple text boxes and buttons to a card deck, clock, AVI player, and many others. The name of this control suite is OLE Tools 5.0 and it is a commercial product.

> **Note**   The Microsoft ActiveX Gallery contains a repository of over 100 ActiveX controls that you can use in your web pages. The location is `http://activex.microsoft.com/gallery`.

Some General Tips for Stylish and Appealing Web Pages

One question you must ask yourself is, "Do I really need ActiveX controls, enhanced styles, and so forth for my web pages?" In some cases, you will not need this technology. If, for example, you are a professor, and your primary audience uses Lynx-based text-only browsers or low-technology Internet browsers to access the information you publish, then there is really no need for ActiveX controls. If, of course, you want to publish your syllabus, schedule, and lesson plans in a user-friendly format, and the audience is capable of using advanced technology, then the benefit increases.

Determine where you need a certain control and why it suits that purpose. ActiveX controls may look good on a web page, but are they effective?

Obviously, some pages' sole purpose is to show off ActiveX controls and to help other people know how they are used. Their uses, however, can be more specific. As you become familiar with the ActiveX controls discussed in this section, you will understand their usefulness and how to apply them. Keep in mind that using an ActiveX control for every purpose in a web page may not be feasible. As you use ActiveX controls, you will discover more uses for them than those demonstrated in the previous section.

Inline Scripting Capabilities

Although ActiveX and inline scripting capabilities are independent of each other, most of the capability of either rests with the fact that they integrate so smoothly together. The timer control, for example, would be useless if it wasn't for the capability of the scripting engines to utilize that control. With a scripting language such as JavaScript or VBScript, which this book primarily focuses on, you can easily access and manipulate the events, methods, and properties of an ActiveX control in a page.

The following example demonstrates an *inline* script (a script that is embedded in a page, as opposed to one that is located on a server) that uses VBScript (vbscode.htm).

```
<HTML>
<HEAD>
<TITLE>New Page</TITLE>
</HEAD>
<BODY>
<H2 ALIGN="CENTER">A Simple Visual Basic Script Program</H2>
<INPUT TYPE="text" NAME="lookatme" VALUE="Nothing here">
<INPUT TYPE="button" NAME="button" VALUE="ClickMe">

<SCRIPT LANGUAGE="VBScript">
sub button_OnClick
        lookatme.value = "Something New!"
end sub
</SCRIPT>
</BODY>
</HTML>
```

This next code, `javacode.htm`, demonstrates the JavaScript inline scripting language.

```
<HTML>
<HEAD>
<TITLE>New Page</TITLE>
</HEAD>
<BODY>
<H2 ALIGN="CENTER">A Simple Java Script Program</H2>
<INPUT TYPE="text" NAME="lookatme" VALUE="Nothing here">
<INPUT TYPE="button" NAME="button" VALUE="ClickMe" onClick="dostuff()">

<SCRIPT LANGUAGE="JavaScript">

function dostuff()
```

```
{
     lookatme.value = "Something New!";
}
</SCRIPT>
</BODY>
</HTML>
```

The previous two scripts essentially do the same thing. When the user presses the button, the contents of the text box change. Notice how the syntax is very different in each of the listings. Visual Basic Script is a BASIC-like language that is loose in syntax but lacks some minor functionality of JavaScript, and JavaScript is more of a C-like language—requiring curly braces {} to encapsulate functions, stricter syntax, and so on.

Utilizing Style Sheets

A great enhancement to web pages is style sheets. Certain HTML tags that are part of the style sheet superset are used to align and to position controls on the page in an HTML layout control, which is the mechanism that enables controls to overlap.

Additionally, you can use these same style tags in a regular HTML page to position ActiveX controls. Just encapsulate the control with a <DIV> or <SPAN> tag and set the positioning and alignment properties of the tags to position the control on an HTML page.

Style sheets enable a developer to standardize a look and feel of a collection of web pages without the extraneous effort of inserting many <FONT> tags and other HTML tags to achieve the same task. In the <STYLE> block that is encapsulated in the <HEAD> block, for example, you can define various attributes for a tag. You can additionally define a class in the <STYLE>, which a tag can refer to, as shown in the following code:

```
<HTML>
<HEAD>
     <TITLE>This is a page that uses style sheets</TITLE>
     <STYLE>
          P {color: blue; font-size: 14pt}
     </STYLE>
</HEAD>
<BODY>
<!-- The following text is affected by the style defined above -->
<P>This text is 14pt and blue</P>
</BODY>
```

This, of course, is a simple example of how to use style sheets, but it shows how style sheets work. Attributes such as color and size are set in one area and they affect that tag throughout the whole document. It is also possible to create an external style sheet and to link it to all your documents so that they use the same style.

You should evaluate your need to use style sheets as you did your need to use ActiveX controls.

In many instances, web developers and designers try to make use of a new tool or control where it is not necessary, and it may distract and hinder the user from the original purpose of the page. A web developer, for example, may define styles for all the heading tags and other style tags, although his page only requires and uses one or two tags that need style. The developer also might use highly contrasting foreground and background colors, which hinders the user from viewing content and discourages him or her from that page. Fully understanding how to use and implement such tools and technologies will permit you to avoid these errors.

> **Note** A resource page with information on style sheets, HTML, and more can be found at `http://www.microsoft.com/workshop/author/default.htm`.

Appropriate Uses of Graphics and Sound

Besides ActiveX controls, sound and graphics are what make a page interesting. Many graphics and sound archives are available on the Internet. Other alternatives are to purchase a few good graphics programs and perhaps a MIDI sequencer, or a suite of programs that combine these capabilities. Microsoft may introduce such products in the near future.

The same general principles that apply to ActiveX controls and style sheets also apply to sound and graphics. Use sound and graphics where they have the most effect and where they are appropriate. A page that, for instance, presents mixed forms of images—color photographs as opposed to black-and-white ones, high-resolution images as opposed to low resolution—will not have a uniform feel and may confuse or disturb the user. Of course, it might be a little discouraging to a user if he hears a Monty Python clip on a business-related page; the user may question the seriousness of the page and the company, and were he a potential investor, might decide not to invest.

It is not impossible for a heterogeneous set of images and sounds to exist on a set of web pages, but the presence of such might make it difficult for your site to achieve its intended purpose.

Using VRML in Web Sites

Another great resource to use in making your web pages more appealing and interactive is the Virtual Reality Modeling Language (VRML). This technology—integrated into the browser through ActiveX—enables you to create 3D, polygon-based "worlds" that you can explore on-screen or just view. These worlds can be anything from a company logo to a landscape.

> **Note** Two good books about VRML written by Mark Pesce, one of VRML's creators, are *VRML: Browsing and Building Cyberspace* and *VRML: Flying through the Web.* Both are available from New Riders Publishing.

To fully understand VRML you must have a pretty good understanding of geometry, matrices, transformations, and some trigonometry. Most of VRML is expressed mathematically—you define an object, such as a sphere, in terms of the location of its center and its radius in a defined 3D "space" that is the world. Some of the current VRML worlds consist of many, many polygon-based shapes, and others are simple.

> **Note** The VRML ActiveX plug-in and further information on VRML can be found through the Internet Explorer site at: http://www.microsoft.com/ie/default.htm.

Putting Multimedia Presentations Online

Microsoft has integrated the capability of its robust presentation package, PowerPoint, into an ActiveX control, which gives you the capability to put your full multimedia presentations online for people to view. Like VRML, the PowerPoint application works inside the web browser, enabling you to view the presentation from inside the browser. If you have PowerPoint installed and have downloaded the PowerPoint Player and Publisher, the next steps will show you how to create a presentation viewed on a web page—if you haven't installed PowerPoint, see the following note. You can use the file powpt1.ppt included on the CD-ROM for this tutorial.

1. Launch PowerPoint (see fig. 4.11).

2. Load the powpt1.ppt file from the CD-ROM or wherever the file is located (see fig. 4.12).

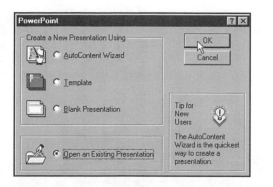

Figure 4.11

Loading PowerPoint.

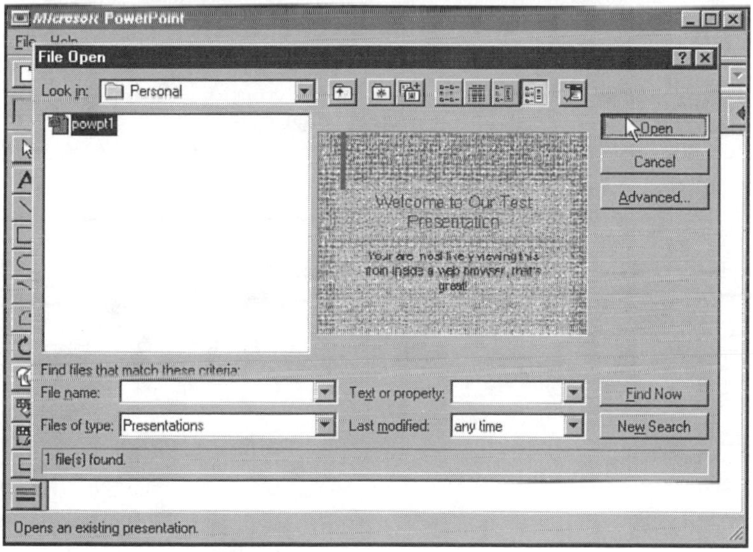

Figure 4.12

Loading the PowerPoint presentation file.

3. Go to the File Menu and click on the Export as PowerPoint Animation option (see fig. 4.13).

4. Enter the necessary information—the name of the file where it is requested and where to create it on your system (see fig. 4.14).

5. When you click OK, a skeleton HTML file containing the necessary syntax for inserting the animation is created, along with the accompanying PowerPoint Animation (.ppz) file (see fig. 4.15).

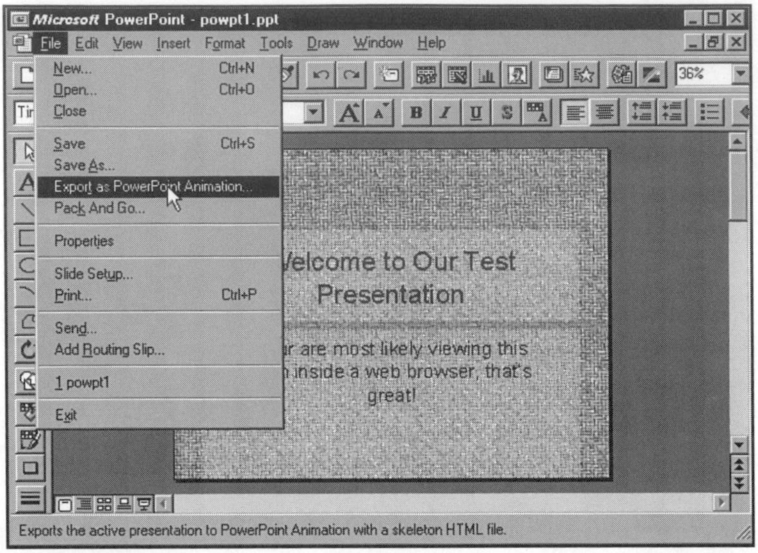

Figure 4.13

Getting ready to create the .ppz file and the HTML skeleton file.

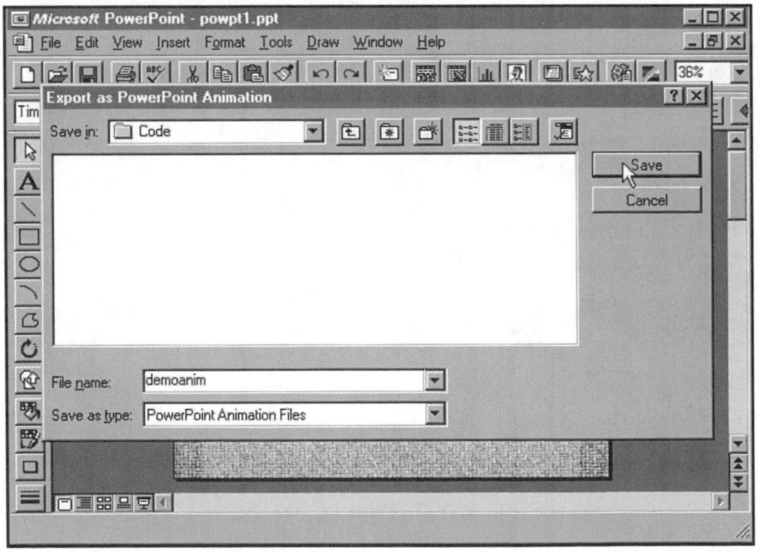

Figure 4.14

Entering the appropriate information.

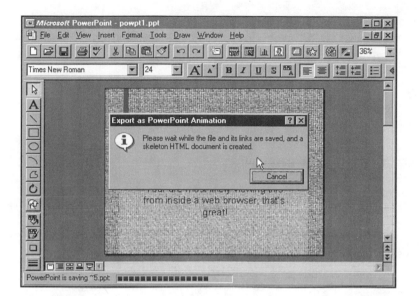

Figure 4.15

Creating the files.

This code (demoanim.htm) is the skeleton HTML file produced through the previous steps.

```
<HTML>
<HEAD>
<TITLE>Untitled</TITLE>
<META NAME="GENERATOR" CONTENT="Microsoft PowerPoint Animation Publisher 1.0">
</HEAD>
<BODY>
<CENTER>
<OBJECT CLASSID="clsid:EFBD14F0-6BFB-11CF-9177-00805F8813FF" WIDTH=360
➥HEIGHT=270>
<PARAM NAME="File" VALUE="demoanim.ppz">
<EMBED WIDTH=360 HEIGHT=270 SRC="demoanim.ppz"></EMBED>
<NOEMBED>This page contains a Microsoft PowerPoint Animation that your browser
➥was unable to view.<A HREF="demoanim.ppz">Click here to open demoanim.ppz
➥fullscreen</A></NOEMBED>
</OBJECT>
</CENTER>
<! Note: Both "PPZ" and "PPT" files are supported.>
<BR>
<A HREF="demoanim.ppz">Click here to view demoanim.ppz in a larger size</A>
<BR>
<BR>
<HR>
```

```
This page contains a Microsoft PowerPoint Animation. If you can't see it, <A
HREF="http://www.microsoft.com/mspowerpoint/">download</A> Microsoft PowerPoint
➥Animation Player today and
learn how <B>YOU</B> can create multimedia for the Web!
</BODY>
</HTML>
```

The resulting HTML file should look similar to the preceding code example. Now you have a PowerPoint presentation embedded in the browser. Figure 4.16 illustrates what the PowerPoint presentation file should look like in a web browser. To view the presentation, launch the skeleton HTML file generated by PowerPoint. demoanim.htm is an ordinary HTML file and you can modify the file like you would any other HTML file.

Figure 4.16

*The HTML file
with the
PowerPoint
presentation.*

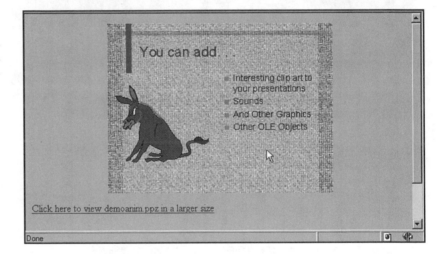

This presentation contains sound that you should hear when you reach the second slide. The presentations viewed here are treated like normal presentations, except that they are viewed from within the Internet Explorer browser.

These tools illustrate a few ideas that can aid you in making your pages interactive, regardless of whether or not you choose to use ActiveX technology. The next section examines how ActiveX controls work and what makes them safe to download on your machine.

Note   You can obtain PowerPoint's ActiveX plug-in and further information regarding PowerPoint from `http://www.microsoft.com/powerpoint/internet/player/`.

Using ActiveX Controls—How Do They Work?

You understand what ActiveX controls can do for you; now you want to know how they work. The ActiveX controls, formerly known as OCX or OLE controls, are a series of container programs that can act as applications themselves, but can behave like a normal application inside other programs. OCX, OLE, and ActiveX controls (a newer, and simpler model of the OLE 2 model) are all collectively grouped as ActiveX controls.

ActiveX Control Security on the Internet

ActiveX technology used on your machine enables you to use this same technology on the Internet in web pages: you are able to insert different controls or entire applications if they are ActiveX programs. As mentioned before, many ActiveX controls are available on the Internet, and when you decide to use a particular control off the Internet, you must download it. The control is then registered with your system and it can be used by any application that resides on your system, in addition to the browser. This process is known as *component downloading*.

Some limitations and important questions exist, however, that you should ask regarding downloading ActiveX controls to your machine.

◆ Several ActiveX controls cannot be used or distributed unless you have a license from the developer of that control. The license gives you permission to use the control in your own pages, according to the terms of the agreement. You can download a control, and it will be registered with your machine as a result of the downloading; however, you cannot use the control if you do not have a license for it.

Another reason for ActiveX controls having licensing schemes is that there has to be some way to verify that the controls are safe on web pages. Examples of such controls are those that act beyond the browser in manipulating user files and similar actions.

◆ How do you know that the code that makes this control is safe and from a viable, trustworthy source? Just as easily as a trustworthy company can distribute its ActiveX components, the malevolent one can distribute controls as well. So what measures does one take to prevent receiving destructive and harmful controls that may contain viruses? The answer lies with code signing and the Authenticode technology proposed by Microsoft. Here is a brief look at this security solution.

> **Note** You can receive additional information on ActiveX controls from Microsoft's ActiveX site at: `http://activex.microsoft.com`.

Code Signing

The concept of *code signing*, or associating a control with the person or company who developed it, is used to identify the authenticity of an ActiveX control developed by an individual or an organization. This concept is clearly needed now because of the diverse amount of data on the Internet, especially executables in the form of ActiveX controls. ActiveX controls enable powerful uses of the Internet, but also exhibit high potential damage to your computer system.

Originally, only a few types of data could be downloaded—text files, hypertext files, graphics, and sounds. The user was alerted if the file was different than this, but during the time of static browsers and web content, there wasn't really a concept of ActiveX controls and plug-ins.

The fact that the user downloading the code does not know who produced the component, whether it has been modified, or contains viruses is all the more reason to have *digital signatures*, or code that has been authenticated by its owner, in downloadable ActiveX components, or other executables. To enable digital signatures, an Internet software developer making these components must obtain a digital certificate from a Cetificate Authority (CA), which the developer can then use to sign all the Internet distributed components that he or she may publish.

The process of code signing and digital signatures is simple to accomplish. It works as follows:

◆ First, the developer obtains a digital certificate for use with all the Internet executables that are developed. These credentials may include the developer's name, company (if applicable), the developer's web site, e-mail address, and other contact information. This enables the user to determine whether the code that is being downloaded is from a trustworthy source. Additionally, it gives the user more confidence and assurance because he or she knows from where it is actually coming.

◆ Next, a one-way hash algorithm is run on the executable, creating a digest that is of fixed length. This digest is created with information provided from the original executable that was designed. A variety of items specific to each executable are considered, which presents an unlimited possibility of digests. This is very important in forming the private key for that program, which is the next process.

◆ A *private key* is created from this digest and is encrypted by using RSA data security encryption technology. Generating two similar private keys is impossible. The private key generated, based on various aspects of the executable from the digest, is used to represent the original, non-tampered, unmodified state of the program. This private key is then combined with the certificate obtained from the Certificate Authority to create the digital signature for the program.

◆ Finally, the developer merges the digital signature with the executable and it is ready to be distributed on the Internet. This program is placed on a web page with the <OBJECT> tag or by other means and is ready to be downloaded by the user. The user can now make the decision of whether or not to install the component or to discard it. When downloaded from the Internet with a browser such as Microsoft Internet Explorer 3.0, the certificate pops up, verifying that the code has been signed and shows to whom the program belongs.

The private key included with the executable is compared to a public key generated by your system on the executable as well. If the keys are identical, then the certificate will appear and verify that this executable is the original code. If these keys are not identical, then the system warns you that the original program and the one that is downloaded are different—a probable sign for a virus. If no certificate exists, then the browser gives the user a critical warning and suggests that the component should not be installed. At this point, the user may choose to install or get rid of the component.

The Authenticode Standard

Authenticode is the proposed standard for implementing code signing and digital signatures. The Authenticode standard is currently supported by over 40 major companies and Verisign Incorporated is a certified Certificate Authority (see fig. 4.17). Authenticode uses the general method for establishing a digital signature, but sets up criteria for people who obtain and use the certificate. This criteria sets up certain guidelines that the developer must agree upon.

Note By default, Microsoft Internet Explorer is set to a high security level that enables only signed code to be downloaded on your machine. This can be changed, however, though it is not recommended that you do so unless you have to, such as when you need to test your components before authentication.

Figure 4.17

An Authenticode certificate from Verisign, Inc.

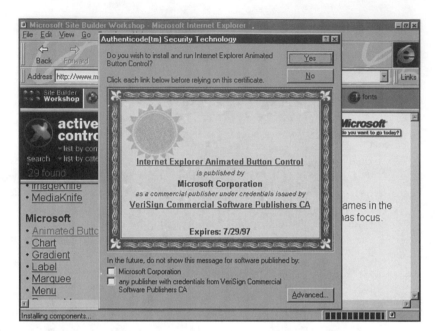

There are obviously two different types of developers—the individual developer and the company- or corporation-based developer. The circumstances for obtaining a certificate for each varies. The annual commercial license through Verisign for a company is significantly more expensive than for an individual. Yearly renewals for these licenses are less expensive. The commercial license requires the company to have a Dun and Bradstreet (a credit rating agency) credit check. Additionally, the license can be used with an infinite number of executable programs that a company chooses to distribute through the Internet as components. Users will likely trust a corporation's product more than an individual developer's because corporations are more concerned with their image.

The individual developer, through the Verisign CA, can obtain a Certificate of Authentication for a very small annual fee. The problem is whether the average user will feel comfortable downloading a component from an individual user. This requires a decision, but both the individual and corporate class of developers have to make an agreement with a CA stating their programs are trustworthy, and have no malicious code or known viruses. The developer must examine and verify the product. The developer agrees to these terms. This is the primary mechanism by which authenticated code is deemed trustworthy.

Note Verisign's web site is at: `http://www.verisign.com` and direct questions can be addressed to: `verisign@microsoft.com`.

More information on the Authenticode Standard and digital signatures can be found at: `http://www.microsoft.com/intdev/security/misf8.htm`.

Required Software for ActiveX

This section examines all the software that ActiveX requires and clearly details why you need it. The following is a list of software that you will need:

◆ Windows 95 or Windows NT 4.0 (Workstation or Server).

◆ The latest version of the ActiveX Control Pad and the HTML Layout control—these are grouped together.

◆ The latest version of Microsoft Internet Explorer 3.0 (preferred) or Netscape Navigator with the NCompass Labs plug-in.

Operating Systems

The most popular operating system, Windows 95, is probably what you are using. It was initially designed to be more functional and harmonious with the Internet than its predecessors—WFW and Win 3.1. Windows is a powerful and convenient operating system to use on a variety of different PCs and does integrate well with the Internet. Windows 95 takes full advantage of OLE and ActiveX controls, which makes an entire web development center at your machine ideal. With Windows 95, you can use all the tools that are covered in this section without any difficulties.

Note You can get information about Windows 95 from: `http://www.microsoft.com/windows/`.

Windows NT 4.0, on the other hand, is a power user's operating system. Windows NT Workstation and Server is catered to the Internet and networking more than Windows 95, and is Microsoft's flagship operating system. Workstation comes with a peer web server (Internet Information Server) that enables you to put up a web server with a ten user access limit. NT Workstation's initial purpose is not to be a web server, but to be a workstation or client similar to but more powerful than Windows 95.

If you have Windows NT Server, then obviously one of your intentions is to have a decent web server for your local intranet and possibly for the Internet too. Windows NT Server provides you with the maximum power of a server operating system, while not limiting you to a boring and inefficient interface at the same time. Many of the popular development and productivity packages, such as the entire MS Back Office Suite, enable you to have an extensive Internet service, whatever it may be. Most, if not all of the tools mentioned here work without a problem in both NT Workstation and NT Server.

Note You can get information about Windows NT Server from: `http://www.microsoft.com/ntserver/` and NT Workstation from: `http://www.microsoft.com/ntworkstation/`.

Web Browsers

Microsoft Internet Explorer 3.0 should be the browser that you use. It is the first and only browser that completely supports ActiveX technology to date; the browser itself is an ActiveX control embedded in the Internet Explorer application. Additionally, both VBScript and JavaScript are native to the browser and component downloading and code signing is supported completely. You have full control to manipulate the scripting object model of the browser and any ActiveX controls embedded in an HTML document. In addition to this, Explorer offers a very aesthetic and useful interface that is pleasing to the user. What's better than that is if you have an organization that works mostly with an intranet and the Internet you can obtain the Microsoft Internet Explorer Registration kit that enables you to customize Internet Explorer for distribution in your organization with no license or royalty costs.

Note You can obtain the latest version of Microsoft Internet Explorer 3.0 from: `http://www.microsoft.com/ie/`.

If you do not choose to use Internet Explorer (not recommended), however, you can always use Netscape Navigator v3.0 or later with the NCompass Labs ActiveX and Visual Basic Script plug-in. ActiveX and VBScript are not officially supported by Netscape currently.

Note You can get the latest version of Netscape Navigator from: `http://home.netscape.com` and the ActiveX control and VBScript plug-in from: `http://www.ncompasslabs.com/`.

The ActiveX Control Pad and the Layout Control

The ActiveX Control Pad and the Layout control are definitely the most important tools you need to work with ActiveX and VBScript. The ActiveX Control Pad, as previously mentioned, enables you to insert any ActiveX control that is registered on your system into an HTML document. The ActiveX Control Pad also includes many features that make it powerful, including a scripting wizard and an extensive help system, which has documentation on many of the common ActiveX controls and other topics that can aid you greatly.

The ActiveX Layout control gives you full control over the placement of ActiveX components in the region defined by the Layout control in an HTML page. The layout file is separate from the HTML document and it contains all the controls and their positions in a file with an .alx extension. The Layout control is inserted in the HTML page, and that control is used to load the file into the HTML document and to initiate its boundaries on the browser's screen.

> **Note** You can get the ActiveX Control Pad from: `http://www.microsoft.com/workshop/author/cpad/default.htm`.

> **Tip** When you develop your applications, take the strain out of them by using the ActiveX Control Pad's script wizard. Through it, you will be able to know all of an object's public properties, methods, and events. The interface also enables you to manage your code more efficiently.

PART II

Programming with VBScript

CHAPTER 5

VBScript Language Elements

By Eric Smith

This chapter introduces you to the basic language elements of VBScript:

◆ Constants

◆ Data types

◆ Variables

◆ Comments

These elements are the building blocks of the more complex programming that you learn about in later chapters. If you are already familiar with these terms, you may skip this section. However, if you have never programmed before, read this introduction to these basic building blocks of programming.

The first basic element you learn in this chapter is called the *constant*. As its name suggests, a constant has the same value while the program is running. This constant might be an interest rate or the number of months in the year. Whatever it is, the value does not change.

In contrast to the constant, a variable's value may change while the program is running. A *variable* can store any type of information—text and numbers. A variable can also store a logical value; that is, the values of True and False. Variables are extremely useful for programming because they can be used as a placeholder in calculations. A variable used in a calculator application, for example, could be used to store the last number the user entered. That variable could then be used in a calculation to get a result the user requested. Anytime you see a variable, imagine that it can always be replaced by an actual numeric value or text value.

Many types of data exist that you may use in your programs. Each distinct form of data, whether it is text or numeric, is known as a *data type*. Visual Basic supports many data types, and you learn about them later in this chapter.

Finally, you learn about *comments* and how to document your code. Comments are simply remarks that can be entered with your code. These remarks are ignored by the computer as it runs your program. Because the computer ignores your comments, you may add whatever comments you need. If you are building web pages for your own use, commenting your code might not seem important. However, if you found a technique for coding something and want to remember why you did it, comments would be extremely useful. You may be working with other people on your web pages and need to document what changes you made to the page. You may just want to make a list of your own changes to your web page. Comments are a good thing to learn about for many reasons.

With these basic definitions in mind, keep reading to learn more specifics about using these building blocks in your code.

Using Built-In Constants

As its name suggests, a *constant* maintains the same value while a program is running. Constants are used in Visual Basic and in VBScript to hold values such as the names of the days of the week or the name of your web site. Whatever it is, the value does not change.

Besides the constants you might define, VBScript has a number of built-in constants that have been predefined. If you are familiar with Visual Basic, it is interesting to note that VBScript does not have the enormous number of built-in constants that Visual Basic does. However, it does have several constants that are important and frequently used.

The following constants are always available to your VBScript code without any additional definitions. The documentation for each is available here for reference.

◆ **Empty.** The Empty keyword is used to indicate an uninitialized variable value. Empty is not the same thing as Null.

◆ **Nothing.** The Nothing keyword in VBScript is used to disassociate an object variable from any actual object. Use the Set statement to assign Nothing to an object variable, as shown in the following example:

```
Set MyObject = Nothing
```

By setting a variable to Nothing, you indicate to VBScript that you are done using the object to which the variable refers. VBScript frees up the memory and other system resources that were assigned to that object. However, if you have several variables that refer to the same object, VBScript does not free up the system resources until all the variables referring to an object are set to Nothing.

◆ **Null.** The Null keyword is used to indicate that a variable contains no valid data. Null is not the same thing as Empty.

◆ **True.** The True keyword has a value equal to –1.

◆ **False.** The False keyword has a value equal to 0.

The difference between Null and Empty may be confusing, so here is a real-world example of how to use these two constants. Think of a variable as a box or container into which data may be placed. If the variable is set to Empty, that is equivalent to the container being empty. The container is ready to hold data, but it just isn't holding any at that point. If your variable is set to Null, the box is holding invalid data. Null values are common when you are accepting user input. If the user did not enter data for a particular field, the value for the field is Null.

Defining Constants

If you need to define your own constants, you can declare a variable and set it equal to a particular value. VBScript has several restrictions on the numbers at which you can set your variables. You cannot use exponent-based real numbers (6.02E+23), nor can you use trailing data type characters (256&).

| Warning | A note for Visual Basic programmers: You cannot use the Visual Basic *Const* keyword to define constants because it does not exist in VBScript. |

It is possible to define all the constants that Visual Basic provides and add them to your HTML document; however, you have to remember that the user has to download that page over the Internet. On a 28,800 baud modem, a page downloads at approximately 2.5 KB per second. All the unused constants you have put into your page are just wasting the user's time without providing any benefit.

Using the Variant Data Type

As mentioned previously, VBScript supports one data type—the Variant type. The Variant type is designed to store any of the different data types. Unlike Visual Basic or other programming languages, you do not have to declare variables with a particular type in VBScript. This feature can be both convenient and problematic. The Variant data type is convenient because you can put any type of data in a Variant variable. It is problematic because you do not know what type of data is in the variable without checking it first. Visual Basic variables are defined with a particular type, so you always know what type of data it is holding.

Because all variables are of the same data type, many of Visual Basic's data type conversion functions (such as the Int and Fix functions) are not available nor are they necessary with VBScript. You cannot create custom data types by using the Type keyword, as you can with Visual Basic. To declare a variable (which will automatically be of the Variant type), use the Dim keyword, as in the following example:

```
Dim X, Y, Z
```

Because you cannot determine a data type by the type of variable, VBScript provides the following functions that are designed to deal with Variant data variables:

- Dim

- IsArray

- IsDate

- IsEmpty

- IsNull

- IsNumeric

- IsObject

- VarType

These functions enable you to determine what type of data is stored in a Variant. They are also very useful in validating user input, as illustrated by the example in the next section.

Variant Testing Functions

The functions in this group that begin with *Is* are simplified versions of the VarType function. The VarType function returns a value indicating the type of data stored in a

Variant. Each one of the return values can be tested by one of the Is functions. For instance, the IsNumeric function determines if a Variant is one of the numeric types of data, which include integers, floating-points, and currency values. IsDate tests for data that is in a date format.

In the following example, the data the user entered is tested to verify that it is numeric. The program displays a message with the results of this test. This example is on the accompanying CD-ROM and is titled NumericValidation.HTML.

On the CD

```
<HTML>
<FORM NAME="NumberInput">
Enter a number: <INPUT TYPE=text NAME=txtNumber SIZE=40><P>
<INPUT TYPE=BUTTON NAME=btnSubmit VALUE="Press When Done!"
➥ onClick="btnSubmit_Click" language="VBScript">
</FORM>
<SCRIPT LANGUAGE=VBScript>
Sub btnSubmit_Click
     If IsNumeric(Document.NumberInput.txtNumber.Value) then
          MsgBox "Your number was " & Document.NumberInput.txtNumber.Value & "."
     Else
               MsgBox "You did not enter a number."
     End If
End Sub
</SCRIPT>
</HTML>
```

The IsNumeric function tests the data in the txtNumber text box. If IsNumeric is True, the program displays the number to the user. Otherwise, the message "You did not enter a number" is displayed to the user.

Note   Always be sure to test the Value and not the control itself. In the previous example, the *control* was the text box created by the <INPUT> tag. If you test the control itself, it will never be numeric or any other type. The VarType function correctly indicates that it is an object, which is not an expected response. The expected action would be for the VarType function to look at the data stored in the object and return the type of that data. However, the VarType function will not search that far into the control. It will only look at the control itself.

This technique is used for the other data types, too. Use the appropriate Is function to test for the required data type. Alternatively, you use the VarType function instead of the Is function. In the previous example, using the VarType function instead of the IsNumeric function would have been identical functionally, but the code would have

On the CD

been much longer. If the IsNumeric function is not used, you have to test for each type of numeric value, as shown in the following example, `VarTypeExample.HTML` on the accompanying CD-ROM:

```
<HTML>
<FORM NAME="NumberInput">
Enter a number: <INPUT TYPE=text NAME=txtNumber SIZE=40><P>
<INPUT TYPE=BUTTON NAME=btnSubmit VALUE="Press When Done!"
➡ onClick="btnSubmit_Click" language="VBScript">
</FORM>
<SCRIPT LANGUAGE=VBScript>
Sub btnSubmit_Click
    Dim iReturn
    iReturn = VarType(Document.NumberInput.txtNumber.Value)
    If iReturn >= 2 And iReturn <= 6 Then
        MsgBox "Your number was " & Document.NumberInput.txtNumber.Value & "."
    Else
            MsgBox "You did not enter a number."
    End If
End Sub
</SCRIPT>
</HTML>
```

All the VarType related functions, as well as the Dim keyword, are documented here.

Dim

Dim is a keyword that declares variables and allocates storage space. The syntax for the Dim statement is as follows:

```
Dim varname[([subscripts])][, varname[([subscripts])]] . . .
```

The Dim keyword accepts the following parameters:

Parameter	Description
varname	This is the name of the variable you want to create. The name cannot contain spaces or other punctuation characters. It can contain numbers and upper or lowercase letters; however, the first letter of the variable name must be a letter.

Parameter	Description
subscripts	The subscripts for the variable are used when you are declaring arrays. Each dimension of the array should be separated by a comma from the previous dimension, as in these examples:

```
Dim A(5)
Dim B(5, 6)
Dim C(5, 2, 1)
```

 Note The lower bound of an array is always zero. This is different from Visual Basic, where you can specify the lower and upper bounds of your arrays.

Variables declared with Dim outside of a subroutine or function are available globally to all subroutines and functions. Any variables declared within a subroutine or function are only available to that subroutine or function.

You can also use the Dim statement with empty parentheses to create a dynamic array. After declaring a dynamic array, use the ReDim statement within a procedure to define the number of dimensions and elements in the array. If you redeclare a dimension for an array variable whose size is explicitly specified in a Dim statement, an error occurs.

When variables are initialized, a numeric variable is initialized to 0, and a string is initialized to a zero-length string. To store a zero-length (empty) string in a variable, do it as shown in this example:

```
Dim A
A = ""
```

 Tip When using the Dim statement in a procedure or function, it is good programming practice to put the Dim statement at the beginning of the procedure or function.

IsArray

IsArray is a function that returns a Boolean value, which indicates whether a variable is an array. The syntax for IsArray is as follows:

```
IsArray(varname)
```

The varname argument can be any variable. IsArray returns True if the variable is an array; otherwise, it returns False. IsArray is especially useful with variants containing arrays.

IsDate

IsDate is a function that returns a Boolean value, which indicates whether an expression can be converted to a date. The syntax for IsDate is as follows:

```
IsDate(expression)
```

The expression argument can be any date or string expression recognizable as a date or time. IsDate returns True if the expression is a date or can be converted to a valid date. If the expression is not a date or a valid date, a False value returns. In Microsoft Windows, the range of valid dates is January 1, 100 A.D. through December 31, 9999 A.D.; the ranges vary among operating systems.

IsEmpty

IsEmpty is a function that returns a Boolean value, which indicates whether a variable has been initialized. IsEmpty's syntax is the following:

```
IsEmpty(expression)
```

The expression argument can be any expression. However, because IsEmpty determines whether individual variables are initialized, the expression argument is most often a single variable name. IsEmpty returns True if the variable is uninitialized or set to Empty. Otherwise, the IsEmpty function returns False. In addition, False is always returned if the expression contains more than one variable.

IsNull

IsNull is a function that returns a Boolean value, which indicates whether an expression contains no valid data (Null). The syntax for IsNull is as follows:

```
IsNull(expression)
```

The expression argument can be any expression. IsNull returns True if the expression contains no valid data. If the expression is not Null, IsNull returns False. If you are using an expression with more than one operand, IsNull will return False if any one of the operands is Null.

The Null value indicates that the variable contains no valid data. Null is not the same as Empty. Empty indicates that a variable has not yet been initialized. Null is also not the same as a zero-length string, which is sometimes referred to as a null string.

Note   Use the IsNull function to determine whether an expression contains a Null value. Expressions that you expect to evaluate to True under some circumstances, such as If Var = Null and If Var <> Null, are always False because any expression containing a Null is itself Null and, therefore, False.

IsNumeric

IsNumeric is a function that returns a Boolean value, which indicates whether an expression can be evaluated as a number. IsNumeric's syntax is as follows:

```
IsNumeric(expression)
```

The expression argument can be any expression. IsNumeric returns True if the entire expression is recognized as a number. If it is not a number, IsNumeric returns False. IsNumeric returns False if the expression is a date expression.

IsObject

IsObject is a function that returns a Boolean value, which indicates whether an expression references a valid OLE Automation object. The syntax for IsObject is the following:

```
IsObject(expression)
```

The expression argument can be any expression. IsObject returns True if the expression is a variable of an Object subtype or a user-defined object; otherwise, it returns False.

VarType

VarType is a fucntion that returns a value indicating the subtype of a variable. VarType's syntax is as follows:

```
VarType(varname)
```

The varname argument can be any variable. Values returned by VarType represent the variable subtypes in the following table:

Value	Variable type description
0	Empty (uninitialized)
1	Null (no valid data)
2	Integer
3	Long integer
4	Single-precision floating-point number
5	Double-precision floating-point number
6	Currency
7	Date

continues

Value	Variable type description
8	String
9	Automation object
10	Error
11	Boolean
12	Variant (used only with arrays of Variants)
13	Non-Automation object
17	Byte
8192	Array

The VarType function never returns the value for Array by itself. The function is always added to some other value to indicate an array of a particular type. For example, the value returned for an array of integers is calculated as 2 + 8192, or 8194. If an object has a default property, VarType (object) returns the type of its default property.

Using Arrays in VBScript

In addition to using single variables, you can also create and use arrays of Variant variables. To do so, use the Dim keyword and add a number of dimensions to the variable declaration, as follows:

```
Dim arrInputData(4, 3)
```

These dimensions create an array that has 12 cells. You can think of a two-dimensional array as a grid, where the first number is the width and the second number is the height, or vice versa. To access a particular cell, add the index values to the variable name in the following manner:

```
Document.Write arrInputData(0, 2)
```

For this example, the first dimension can have values from 0 to 3, and the second dimension can range from 0 to 2. Unlike Visual Basic, all VBScript array indexes begin at 0. Visual Basic enables you to specify the lower bound on any array.

Note As documented in the Dim keyword description, you can create an array with up to 60 dimensions. However, because most people think in only three dimensions, using more than three dimensions makes your data storage routine hard to visualize.

Array Functions

VBScript has the following useful functions that help your code handle arrays:

> Redim
>
> LBound
>
> UBound
>
> Erase

The first useful function is the ReDim statement. In many cases, you may be adding an indeterminate amount of data and need a place to store the data. Because you cannot use user-defined types, a multidimensional array often works well. However, you need to be able to enlarge and reduce the size of your array as data is entered or deleted. The ReDim statement is used to adjust the size of the array. In the following example, the array arrInputData is enlarged from 10 elements to 20:

```
Dim arrInputData(10)
'
' More code
'
ReDim Preserve arrInputData(20)
```

 Tip   If you are defining your variable and do not know how many elements the array is, define the array with a single item. You can use ReDim later to enlarge the array to the correct size.

One restriction on the ReDim statement is that it can change only the final dimension of a multidimensional array. For example, if arrInputData in the preceding example was defined as (10, 20), the array would always have to remain 10 cells wide, but you could enlarge or reduce the height of the array from 20 cells high by using the ReDim statement.

Another important note about the preceding example: the ReDim statement, by default, automatically erases all the data in your array when you use it. To prevent this behavior, add the Preserve keyword. Any existing data is left alone, and new blank cells are added. Obviously, if you reduce the size of your array, any data in the cells that were downsized is lost.

Warning   Always use the Preserve keyword with the ReDim statement to prevent the loss of data in your array.

Because the array is aware of its upper and lower bounds, you can use these values within your code and avoid having to use a separate counter. The LBound and UBound functions return the lower and upper bounds of an array. You can then use this information, for example, to add a new row to an existing array. Both of these functions can take an optional argument to specify which dimension you are interested in retrieving. If no dimension is given, the first dimension is assumed.

Finally, a simple way to erase an array that you have been using is the Erase statement. Just give the Erase statement the name of your array, and Erase empties the array of all data.

All the array handling functions are documented in this section for reference.

ReDim Statement

The ReDim statement is used to enlarge and reduce dynamic array variables that were previously created with the Dim statement. The syntax for this statement follows:

```
ReDim [Preserve] varname(subscripts) [, varname(subscripts)] . . .
```

The following table contains an explanation for the parts of the ReDim statement.

Part	Description
Preserve	This keyword saves the data in the array when the array is resized. The default behavior (when this keyword is missing) is to erase the array when it is resized.
varname	This is the name of the variable you want to create. The name cannot contain spaces or other punctuation characters. It can contain numbers and upper or lowercase letters; however, the first letter of the variable name must be a letter.
subscripts	The subscripts for the variable are used when you are declaring arrays. Each dimension of the array should be separated by a comma from the previous dimension, as in these examples:

```
ReDim A(5)
ReDim Preserve B(5, 6)
ReDim C(5, 2, 1)
```

The lower bound of an array is always zero.

You can use the ReDim statement repeatedly to change the number of elements and dimensions in an array.

The ReDim statement can only resize one dimension of an array. If you have an array of one dimension, that dimension can be resized. However, for arrays with multiple dimensions, only the last dimension can be resized. Look at the following example:

```
ReDim X(1, 2, 3)
```

In this case, only the last dimension can be changed from its current size of 3. If you reduce the size of your array, any data stored in the eliminated rows will be lost. The data will be lost even if you use the Preserve keyword.

When you resize your array and omit the Preserve keyword, all the cells of the array are cleared. If you look at the value as a number, it will be zero. If you look at the string value of the cell, it will equal the empty string, represented by double quotes ("").

Erase Statement

The Erase statment re-initializes the elements of fixed-size arrays and frees dynamic array storage space. The syntax for the Erase statement follows:

```
Erase array
```

The array argument is the name of the array variable to be erased. All the cells in the array will be cleared. If you view the contents of a cell after it has been cleared, it will be 0 (if printed as a numeric) or " " (if printed as a string).

Erase frees the memory used by dynamic arrays originally created by the Dim statement and modified by the ReDim statement. If you want to reuse a dynamic array variable, you must use the ReDim statement to set the array's size.

LBound Function

The LBound function returns the smallest available subscript for the indicated dimension of an array. The syntax for the LBound function is as follows:

```
LBound(arrayname[, dimension])
```

The following table contains an explanation for the parameters of the LBound function.

Part	Description
arrayname	Name of the array variable
dimension	This parameter is a whole number indicating which dimension you want.
	Use 1 for the first dimension, 2 for the second, and so on. If you omit this parameter, dimension 1 is returned.

The LBound function is used with the UBound function to determine the size of an array. Use the UBound function to find the upper limit of an array dimension. The default lower bound for any dimension is always 0.

UBound Function

The UBound function returns the largest available subscript for the indicated dimension of an array. The syntax for the UBound function appears as follows:

```
UBound(arrayname[, dimension])
```

The following table contains an explanation for the parameters of the UBound function.

Part	Description
arrayname	Name of the array variable
dimension	This parameter is a whole number indicating which dimension you want.
	Use 1 for the first dimension, 2 for the second, and so on. If you omit this parameter, dimension 1 is returned.

The UBound function is used with the LBound function to determine the size of an array. Use the LBound function to find the lower limit of an array dimension.

The default lower bound for any dimension is always 0. The table after the following example shows some sample results from the UBound function.

```
Dim B(5,3,4)
```

Statement	Return Value
UBound(B, 1)	4
UBound(B, 2)	2
UBound(B, 3)	3

Using Variables

A variable can store any type of information, both text and numbers. A variable can also store a logical value; that is, True or False. Variables are extremely useful for programming because they can be used as a placeholders in calculations. For example, a variable used in a calculator application could be used to store the last number the user entered. That variable could then be used in a calculation to get a result the user requested. Anytime you see a variable, just imagine that it can always be replaced by an actual numeric or text value.

You have seen some variables in the examples in the previous sections. You have also seen how to create variables for use in your code. Another important item to learn about is variable scope. *Variable scope* refers to the parts of a program where a variable is valid. With VBScript, you can declare variables in two places—within a procedure or function definition or outside of these declarations.

A variable declared within a procedure or function definition is valid only within that definition. You cannot directly access that variable from another procedure or function without passing the variable to the second routine as a procedure or function parameter. You learn more about parameters in Chapter 8, "Building Procedures and Functions."

 Tip Variables that need to be accessible throughout the program should be declared outside of all the procedure and function declarations but within the <SCRIPT> tags marking the VBScript code in a document. These variables are considered global to the program and can be accessed throughout without redeclaring them.

Visual Basic has a feature that enables variables to be used without having previously declared them. This feature is a holdover from some of the original versions of BASIC. However, this feature is responsible for more coding errors than almost anything else in Visual Basic. For programmers who are more comfortable declaring their variables before using them, VBScript's Option Explicit statement forces you to declare every variable you use. When Option Explicit is added to your code (outside of the procedure and function declarations), any variable that is not declared generates an error. One habit you should learn immediately is to add Option Explicit to your VBScript code. Option Explicit prevents numerous errors that occur when you start using one variable, misspell it elsewhere, and wonder why your results are wrong. In the following code fragment, you can see that the Option Explicit statement should be placed immediately after the <SCRIPT> tag and should be placed outside of any subroutine or function declarations.

```
<HTML>
<SCRIPT LANGUAGE=VBScript>
Option Explicit
... rest of your code ...
```

Tip Always use Option Explicit to force yourself to declare all your variables before you use them.

Adding Comments to Your Code

No matter how experienced a programmer is, deciphering someone else's code is never an easy job. However, if the code is well documented with inline comments, the task becomes more palatable. You can use either of the following Visual Basic methods to add comments to code within your <SCRIPT> tags:

♦ Precede text with a single quote.

♦ Precede any line with the Rem keyword.

This example shows the most common way to add comments—a single quote preceding your comment within your code.

```
<SCRIPT LANGUAGE=VBScript>
Sub btnSubmit_Click
'
' This event determines if the data entered is numeric
'
     If IsNumeric(Document.NumberInput.txtNumber.Value) then
          MsgBox "Your number was " & Document.NumberInput.txtNumber.Value & "."
     Else
             MsgBox "You did not enter a number."
     End If
End Sub
</SCRIPT>
```

HTML also provides a comment tag, as shown in the following example. The comment tag is useful for text outside of VBScript code blocks.

```
<HTML>
<!-- This document has an example of a comment in it. -->
</HTML>
```

By preceding your text with the <!-- tag and ending it with the --> tag, that part of your document is considered a comment by the browser.

For Visual Basic Programmers:
The major change introduced in this chapter for Visual Basic programmers is the fact that no data types exist in VBScript other than Variant data types. For programmers who are comfortable with declaring variables of certain types, this omission of data

types can be unnerving. However, with judicious use of the VarType and the other Variant testing functions, you can keep track of your data reasonably well. Another tip to keep in mind—give your variables names with prefixes (such as i for integer, s for string, and so on) to keep them organized. Few instances will cause a different type of data to be stored in a variable originally designed to store integer data. However, it never hurts to check your variables before you perform type-specific functions or conversions on them. This final check will prevent runtime errors while a user is viewing your pages.

Summary

In this chapter, you were introduced to the basic building blocks of VBScript programming: constants, variables, data types, and comments. *Constants* are values that don't change while your program is running. *Variables* are used to store data. *Data types* are the different forms for the data that you use, and *comments* help document what your code does. Learning these basic elements now is critical to your understanding of the concepts presented in this book.

CHAPTER **6**

VBScript Functions and Operators

By Eric Smith

In this chapter, you are introduced to many functions that are used to manipulate numeric, date, logical, and character values. The VBScript language contains numerous functions to process these four types of data. As you learned in the previous chapter, all variables classify as Variants; each function in this chapter is designed to accept Variants as function parameters. However, if you use a mathematical function on a variable that actually contains character string data, the screen displays an error message. Therefore, it is important to know how to use Variant handling functions, such as IsNumeric and VarType, before you attempt to use data of an unknown type. After you have determined that a variable corresponds to a particular type of data, you can use the appropriate group of functions to manipulate it.

Implicit Type Conversion

When VBScript adds an integer to a floating-point number, the *implicit type conversion* process changes the precision of one or more of the values in the calculation so that all operands are of the same precision. For example, if you add an integer to a single-precision number, the result would be a single-precision number, as illustrated in this example:

In the expression 1 + 1.52 = 2.52, the implicit conversion would make the equation look like this: 1.00 + 1.52 = 2.52.

Although this concept usually does not rank as a crucial one to remember, ignoring it can introduce errors into your calculations. For instance, if you calculate numbers and round them before you add them, you most likely gain a different result than if you add the original values before you round them. The following is an example of this error-producing behavior:

```
<SCRIPT LANGUAGE=VBScript>
Dim IntegerValueA, FloatValueA
Dim IntegerValueB, FloatValueB

IntegerValueA = 6
FloatValueA = 0.3

IntegerValueB = 8
FloatValueB = .6

Document.Write CInt(IntegerValueA * FloatValueA) + CInt(IntegerValueB *
➥ FloatValueB)

Document.Write (IntegerValueA * FloatValueA) + (IntegerValueB * FloatValueB)
➥ </SCRIPT>
```

In this example, the values 7 and 6.6 are generated for the two calculations. Although these results are not the expected ones, this behavior is easy to regulate with the appropriate type-conversion functions. In most cases, you will know the type of data before you store it in a variable. Naming your variables to reflect the type of data that is stored makes it easier to track down this kind of error when you are debugging your VBScript code.

Mathematical Operators

You are already familiar with most of VBScript's mathematical operators. However, VBScript contains some slightly different symbols for several operations. The language uses symbols for certain operations, such as the modulus function, that do not normally carry symbols.

Addition and Subtraction Symbols

As with mathematics, VBScript uses the plus (+) sign for the addition operation; the minus (−) sign represents subtraction. Both symbols can represent positive and negative numbers and can be used with all types of numeric data.

```
Document.Write 1 + 2
```

This example will print a result of 3, and the following example will print 1.

```
Document.Write 2 - 1
```

Multiplication Symbol

VBScript uses the asterisk (*) to represent the multiplication operation. This operator can be used with all types of numeric data.

This example will print a result of 18.

```
Document.Write 6 * 3
```

Division Symbols

Note | *Integer division*—This type of division rounds the two numbers to integer values and produces an integer result. Any remaining decimal values are discarded.

VBScript provides two different division operators. For normal division, use the forward slash (/) character between the operands. VBScript also provides *integer division* (\). Integer division rounds the two numbers (which need not be integers) to integer values and produces the result as an integer. Decimal values are truncated. Standard decimal division does not round or truncate the operands or the result. An example of the difference follows:

```
Document.Write 5.6 / 2
```

This example uses standard decimal division and its expected result is 2.8.

```
Document.Write 5.6 \ 2
```

In this example, integer division produces a result of 3. The process rounds 5.6 to 6, and division produces the result of 3.

With integer division, you can calculate the number of pages filled by a certain number of lines. Use integer division to divide the number of lines by the number of lines per page. The result is the number of full pages produced.

In general, integer division should only be used when you are dividing other integers. Using integer division with non-integers can produce unexpected results, as in the previous examples.

Modulus/Remainder Function

Using the previous example for a basis, imagine that you need to know how many lines the last page of the document holds. The *modulus function* calculates this value by producing the remainder left when dividing the two integers. Because the modulus function deals with remainders not logically associated with point numbers, you should avoid using the function with non-integer values. When used with non-integers, the function rounds both operands before processing the result.

The following is an example of the modulus function:

```
Document.Write 8 Mod 3
```

This statement produces the value 2, which is the remainder of dividing 8 by 3.

```
Document.Write 8 Mod 2
```

This statement produces the value 0, which is the remainder of dividing 8 by 2.

Exponentiation Operator

VBScript provides a function equivalent to assigning an exponent to a number. The caret (^), placed between two operands, raises the first number to the power specified by the second. This operator can be used with all valid numeric operands.

The following are some examples:

```
Document.Write 8 ^ 2
```

This statement produces the value 64, which is 8 squared.

```
Document.Write 4 ^ 0.5
```

This statement produces the value 2, which is the square root of 4. The square root is symbolized by taking a number to the ½ power.

```
Document.Write 4 ^ -0.5
```

This statement displays the value 0.5, which is 4 to the –0.5 power.

Grouping Expressions

As in mathematics, the left and right parenthesis characters [(,)] can be used to group expressions that should be evaluated out of their normal order. For reference, the following list displays the correct order for operators. When operators from more than one of the groups listed below come together in the same expression, arithmetic operators are always evaluated first. Comparison operators follow, and logical operators are evaluated last. When in doubt about the order that an expression will actually be evaluated, use parentheses to group the expression in the correct manner. For example, the following expression will be evaluated by the system as 4 + (3 * 5):

4 + 3 * 5

However, you might require this expression to be evaluated as (4 + 3) * 5. The first, and correct, evaluation yields 19, but the alternate interpretation produces 60 as the answer. Grouping symbols are especially important when you are creating complex expressions, as in this example that calculates the hypotenuse of a right triangle:

c = (a * a + b * b) ^ 0.5

In this case, it is not immediately obvious which parts of the expression should be calculated first. VBScript, according to the rules of operator precedence, multiplies a * a first, b * b next, and then adds the results. However, if this order is not carried out, the result would be incorrect.

◆ **Arithmetic Operator Precedence**

Exponentiation (^)

Negation (–)

Multiplication and Division (*,/)

Integer Division

Modulo Arithmetic (Mod)

Addition and Subtraction

String Concatenation

◆ **Comparison Operator Precedence**

Equality (=)

Inequality (<>)

Less Than (<)

Greater Than (>)

Less than or Equal to (<=)

Greater than or Equal to (>=)

Is Operator

◆ **Logical Operator Precedence**

Not

And

Or

Xor

Eqv

Imp

&

Comparison Operators

Six operators are used when comparing numeric expressions:

Operator	Definition
=	Equal to
<>	Not equal to
<	Less than
<=	Less than or equal to
>	Greater than
>=	Greater than or equal to

These operators are valid for numeric, string, and date expressions. Unlike Visual Basic, which generates the words **True** and **False**, VBScript displays a 0 for false or a −1 for true when printing a logical expression.

Mathematical Functions

These functions only deal with numeric data. Later in this chapter, you learn about the many functions used to convert data from one type to another. They are:

◆ Absolute Value function

◆ Sine function

◆ Cosine function

◆ Tangent function

◆ Arctangent function

◆ Exponent function

◆ Logarithm function

◆ Square Root function

◆ Sign function

◆ Random Number function

◆ Base Conversion functions

◆ Integer Conversion functions

Absolute Value Function

This function produces the absolute value of a number, which is the number without a positive or negative sign attached to it. The following examples illustrate the absolute value function:

```
Document.Write Abs(-50)    ' Prints 50
Document.Write Abs(100)    ' Prints 100
Document.Write Abs(0)      ' Prints 0
```

Sine Function

The sine function evaluates an angle and displays the ratio of the side opposite the angle to the hypotenuse of the triangle. Both the input argument and the return value must be expressed in radians. The returned radian value will fall between –1 and 1, inclusive.

To convert radians to degrees, multiply the value by 180/pi. Similarly, multiply by pi/180 to convert degrees to radians. For reference, pi is approximately equal to 3.141592654.

```
Document.Write Sin(3.1415926 / 2)
```

This statement produces the value 1, which is the sine of pi/2 radians, or 90 degrees.

Cosine Function

The cosine function evaluates an angle and displays the ratio of the side adjoining the angle to the hypotenuse of the triangle. Both the input argument and the return value must be in radians. The returned radian value will fall between –1 and 1, inclusive.

```
Document.Write Cos(3.1415926535/3)
```

This statement produces the value 0.5, which is the cosine of pi/3 radians, or 60 degrees.

Tangent Function

The tangent function evaluates an angle and displays the ratio of the side opposite the angle to the side adjoining the angle. Both the input argument and the return value must be in radians.

```
Document.Write Tan(3.1415926535/4)
```

This statement produces the value 1.0, which is the tangent of pi/4 radians, or 45 degrees.

Arctangent Function

The arctangent function evaluates an angle and displays the inverse tangent of the angle. Both the input argument and the return value must be in radians.

```
Document.Write Atn(3.1415926535/4)
```

This statement produces the value 0.66577375001447, which is the arctangent of pi/4 radians.

Exponent Function

This function accepts any number as an argument and displays the value produced by raising *e* to that exponent. *e* represents the base of natural logarithms and equals approximately 2.71828182845905.

```
Document.Write Exp(1)
```

This statement produces the value 2.71828182845905, which is *e* raised to the power of one.

Logarithm Function

This function produces the natural logarithm of a number. The logarithm function is the inverse of the exponent function described previously in this section. By calculating the logarithm of the exponent function of a number, you produce the original number, as the following example illustrates:

```
Document.Write Exp(Log(15))
```

This statement generates the value 15. To determine a logarithm for a base other than *e*, use the following conversion:

$$\text{Logn}(x) = \text{Log}(x) / \text{Log}(n)$$

For example, to determine the base 10 logarithm of 100 use the following code:

```
Document.Write Log(100) / Log(10)
```

This produces the value 2, which is the exponent to which you raise 10 to obtain 100.

Square Root Function

This function produces the square root of a number, which is identical to raising a number to the 0.5 power. The square root function is included primarily for convenience and readability.

```
Document.Write Sqr(100)
```

This statement generates the value 10, which is the square root of 100.

Sign Function

This function returns the sign of a number and the sign indicates whether the number is positive, negative, or 0. Positive numbers return 1, negative numbers return –1, and 0 returns 0, as in these examples:

```
Document.Write Sgn(-50)      ' Prints -1
Document.Write Sgn(100)      ' Prints 1
Document.Write Sgn(0)        ' Prints 0
```

Random Number Function, Randomize Statement

To obtain a random number for your program, use the Rnd function. This function returns a value greater than or equal to zero but less than one. However, if you enter the following code in a page, you see that the Rnd function is not necessarily random.

```
<HTML>
<SCRIPT LANGUAGE=VBScript>
Document.Write Rnd()
</SCRIPT>
</HTML>
```

Each time you reload the page, you expect to see a different number on the screen. Without any arguments, the Rnd function always displays the same initial number. Further calls to the Rnd function in the same code returns each successive number in the random number sequence.

Sometimes you want a truly random number. To ensure this, follow the Randomize statement that uses the system timer to generate a sequence of random numbers. Under this process, reloading the page results in a different number each time.

```
<HTML>
<SCRIPT LANGUAGE=VBScript>
Randomize
Document.Write Rnd()
</SCRIPT>
</HTML>
```

In addition to random number generation feature of the Rnd function, specifying a number for the function's argument can help you predict that function's behavior. Table 6.1 displays the function's behavior with each type of input.

Table 6.1
Rnd Function Parameter Options

If number is...	Rnd generates...
Less than zero	The same number every time, using the number as the seed
Greater than zero	The next random number in the sequence
Equal to zero	The last random number retrieved from the sequence
Not supplied	The next random number in the sequence

To generate a number from one to ten, use the following formula:

Int((upperbound – lowerbound + 1) * Rnd + lowerbound)

In this example, the code would look like this:

```
Document.Write Int((10 - 1 + 1) * Rnd + 1)
```

Base Conversion Functions

For converting numbers to octal or hexadecimal representations, VBScript provides several convenient functions. These functions produce strings that display the results of the conversion. Hexadecimal and octal numbers are used frequently when dealing with the operating system. One common example of hexadecimal numbers is in specifying colors. Because every color can be represented by three numbers that specify the red, green, and blue components of the color, the resulting value is often written in hexadecimal. For instance, FFFFFF is the same as 255, 255, 255, which is white. Hex numbers like this are used frequently in HTML tags to specify colors for text and HTML elements. The following examples illustrate the functions:

```
Document.Write Hex(65536)    ' Prints 10000
Document.Write Oct(400)      ' Prints 620
```

If you need to specify an octal or hexadecimal number in your code, prefix the number with &O or &H, respectively, as in these examples:

```
Document.Write &H10000    ' Prints 65536
Document.Write &O620      ' Prints 400
```

Integer Conversion Functions

Besides the CInt function that you learn about later in this chapter, VBScript also provides the Int and Fix functions. Each of these functions truncates the number given and produces an integer result. However, the functions differ when dealing with negative numbers. Int removes the decimal portion and displays the first negative integer that is less than the input number. Fix removes the decimal portion and displays the first negative integer that is greater than the input number. The following examples illustrate this difference:

```
Document.Write Int(65.3)    ' Prints 65
Document.Write Fix(65.3)    ' Prints 65


Document.Write Int(65.6)    ' Prints 65 - does not round number
Document.Write Fix(65.6)    ' Prints 65 - does not round number


Document.Write Int(-10.5)   ' Prints -11
Document.Write Fix(-10.5)   ' Prints -10
```

Logical Operators

Logical operators are used to compare expressions and numbers. They can be used to create *Boolean expressions*. A Boolean expression is a mathematical expression that consists exclusively of true/false conditions. By evaluating each part of a Boolean expression, you get a result of True or False.

> **Note** A Boolean expression is a mathematical expression that consists exclusively of True or False conditions. By evaluating each part of a Boolean expression, you get a result of True or False.

Not Operator

The Not operator is useful for simple negation. If the argument for this function is originally True, it will become False, and vice versa. The Not operator typically precedes an expression, as in this example:

```
If Not (A < 4) Then ...
```

Because the expression generated by the Not operator can be confusing to read, many logical expressions can be reversed. For example, the code could be rewritten as follows:

```
If  A  >=  4  Then  ...
```

In this case, the opposite of "less than" is "greater than or equal to." The reversal creates an expression that is easier to read and debug, if necessary.

Table 6.2
Result Table for Not Operator

Expression1	Result
True	False
False	True

And Operator

The And operator is used to evaluate two Boolean expressions together. When you link the two expressions with "And" the resulting expression is only True if both operands are True. Otherwise, the expression displays a result of False. The following examples illustrate the operator's behavior.

Table 6.3
Result Table for And Operator

Expression1	Expression2	Result
True	True	True
True	False	False
False	True	False
False	False	False

```
If (3 < 5) And (5 > 6) Then ...    ' Because 5 is less than 6, this expression
                                   ' is False.
If True And (3 < 5) Then ...       ' Both operands are True, so the expression
                                   ' is True.
```

Or Operator

As with the And operator, the Or operator joins two Boolean expressions. The operator returns True if either expression is True.

Table 6.4
Result Table for Or Operator

Expression1	Expression2	Result
True	True	True
True	False	True
False	True	True
False	False	False

The following examples illustrate the Or operator:

```
If (3 < 5) Or (5 > 6) Then ...    ' The first expression is True, as is the
                                  ' entire expression.
If true Or (3 < 5) Then ...       ' Both operands are True, so the expression is
                                  ' True.
```

Xor Operator

The Xor, or Exclusive Or, operator is also used to join two expressions. This operator displays True if one of the two expressions is true. However, if both expressions are true or both false, this operator displays False. Although the Xor operator is not as common as the And and Or operators, VBScript supports it to enable other more complex binary logic calculations.

Table 6.5
Result Table for Xor Operator

Expression1	Expression2	Result
True	True	False
True	False	True

Expression1	Expression2	Result
False	True	True
False	False	False

Eqv Operator

The Eqv operator performs a logical equivalence on two Boolean expressions. If the two expressions are either both true or both false, the Eqv operator displays True. Otherwise, it displays False.

Table 6.6
Result Table for Eqv Operator

Expression1	Expression2	Result
True	True	True
True	False	False
False	True	False
False	False	True

Imp Operator

The Imp operator performs a logical implication on two Boolean expressions. A logical implication can be defined as such: if A is True AND B is False, then (A Imp B) is False, otherwise A Imp B is True. The results of the operator, based on the operands, are shown in Table 6.7.

Table 6.7
Result Table for Imp Operator

Expression1	Expression2	Result
True	True	True
True	False	False

continues

Table 6.7, Continued
Result Table for Imp Operator

Expression1	Expression2	Result
True	Null	Null
False	True	True
False	False	True
False	Null	True
Null	True	True
Null	False	Null
Null	Null	Null

String Operators

String operators will probably be the most common operators that you use, because so much of VBScript deals with string processing. These operators can be used to combine and compare string expressions.

◆ Concatenation operator

◆ Comparison operators

Concatenation Operator

The ampersand (&) character is used to concatenate two strings together, as in this example:

```
Document.Write "This is a test" & " of string concatenation."
```

These two strings appear as one on the output screen. However, depending on how the text is formatted, the strings may appear to be split.

If you build a string piece by piece, you can concatenate on one piece at a time, as in this example:

```
Dim StringVariable
StringVariable = "This is the beginning of the string. "
StringVariable = StringVariable & "This is the next part of the string. "
etc.
```

Comparison Operators

As discussed, all comparison operators can be used with strings. However, because these operators check for strict equality, each character in each string must be identical. If two strings appear the same except for capitalization, both strings must be converted to the same capitalization style before you can compare them and produce a valid result. The following example illustrates the process:

```
If UCase(StringVar1) = UCase(StringVar2) Then ...
```

Alternatively, you can use the StrComp function to compare two strings. You learn about the UCase and StrComp functions in the next section.

String Functions

Because VBScript and Internet Explorer support multiple languages (including some such as Unicode that contains double-byte characters), many of the string functions come in several versions. Functions with a B suffix operate on byte data in a string. Functions with a W suffix are designed to operate on Unicode strings. You will discover that each variation behaves differently as you learn about each available string function.

In general, if you are going to support Unicode characters in your Web pages, you should use the W-suffixed functions. Otherwise, just use the version without a suffix.

Asc, AscB, AscW Functions

> **Note**   *ASCII value*—The ASCII value of a character is a number between 0 and 255, based on a standard set up by the American National Standards Institute (ANSI). This value is consistent across all operating systems and computer languages.

All characters are assigned a numerical value. By accessing this number, you can use it in comparisons to determine whether a particular range of characters was entered. This value, known as the *ASCII value* for the American Standard Code for Information Interchange, is a code developed by the American National Standards Institute (ANSI). Each character corresponds to a number from 0 to 255. By using the Asc function, you can retrieve this number and manipulate it in various ways. For instance, to determine whether a particular letter falls between A and Z, use the following example:

```
If Asc(strChar) >= Asc("A") And Asc(strChar) <= Asc("Z") Then ...
```

The Asc function displays the ASCII value of the first character in the string you pass to it. To determine a particular ASCII value for a character, use the Asc function as follows:

```
Document.Write Asc("A")
```

This statement produces the value 65, which is the ASCII value of "A." Because ASCII values are case-sensitive, the following statement produces the value 97:

```
Document.Write Asc("a")
```

The inverse of this function is the Chr function, which is discussed in the next section.

VBScript provides two Variants of this function: AscB and AscW. As mentioned in the introduction to this section, AscB works with byte data and produces the ASCII value of the first byte of the string. AscW is somewhat of a misnomer, however, because the function does not actually produce the ASCII value of the first character as AscB does. Instead, AscW returns the Unicode value, a 32-bit value used in large character set languages such as Japanese and Chinese. Unicode is supported by several operating systems, including Windows NT.

Chr, ChrB, ChrW Functions

The Chr function is used to retrieve the character assigned to a particular ASCII value. This function is the inverse of the Asc function, which returns the ASCII value of a character. The following statement displays the capital letter A on the screen:

```
Document.Write Chr(65)
```

As with the Asc function, the Chr function contains two Variants: ChrB and ChrW. ChrB displays a single byte generated by the input character's number. ChrW displays the assigned character for a 32-bit Unicode character code.

InStr, InStrB Functions

The InStr function is used to locate one string within another. The function contains four parameters (*startpos, datastring, searchstring, comparemode*), two of which are optional.

◆ **startpos.** Position to start search. The first character of the string is position 1. If a position is omitted, the search begins at position 1. This is an optional parameter.

◆ **datastring.** String to search within.

◆ **searchstring.** String to locate within *datastring.*

◆ **comparemode.** 0—Exact, or binary, comparison. 1—Case insensitive search. If a figure is omitted, the function performs a binary comparison. This is an optional parameter.

The InStr function displays the position at which the *searchstring* is found, or it is one of the following values:

Table 6.8
InStr Return Values

If	InStr returns
datastring is zero-length	0
datastring is Null	Null
searchstring is zero-length	Start
searchstring is Null	Null
searchstring is not found	0
searchstring is found within datastring	Position at which match is found
startpos > searchstring's length	0

The following examples illustrate the InStr function:

```
Document.Write InStr("alphabet", "l")' Prints 2
Document.Write InStr("alphabet", "a")' Prints 1 - finds first instance of a
Document.Write InStr("alphabet", "q")' Prints 0
Document.Write InStr("alphabet", "bet")    ' Prints 6
```

This function also contains a version to process byte data: InStrB. Instead of displaying the character position, InStrB displays the byte position of the substring when found.

Len, LenB Function

The Len function determines the length of a string. The function counts all characters, including leading and trailing spaces. The following example illustrates the Len function:

```
Document.Write Len("This is a test.")' Prints 15
```

As with the InStr function, the Len function contains the LenB version, which counts the number of bytes in a string.

Left, LeftB Functions

The Left function is used to produce a certain number of characters, beginning at the first position, or left side, of the string. The Left function operates under two parameters (*string*, and *characters*), both of which are required:

◆ **string.** String from which to retrieve characters

◆ **characters.** Number of characters to retrieve

When you combine the Left function with the InStr function, you can perform some fairly complex string manipulations. For instance, perhaps you need to determine the Internet access protocol for a URL. In a URL, the protocol is the first piece of the URL, thus for http://www.microsoft.com, the protocol is http. By using the InStr function, you can retrieve the protocol code from the string using the Left function.

```
Document.Write "Protocol: " & Left("http://www.microsoft.com",
➥ InStr("http://www.microsoft.com", ":") - 1)
```
This example displays "Protocol: http." By subtracting 1 from the return value of InStr, you can remove the colon from the result.

The Left function also contains a version that processes byte data, instead of retrieving characters, the LeftB function retrieves a specified number of bytes.

Mid, MidB Functions

The Mid function, similar to the Left function, is used to extract a certain number of characters, beginning at an arbitrary position within a string. The Mid function operates within three parameters (*string, startpos,* and *characters*), all of which are required.

◆ **string.** String from which to retrieve characters

◆ **startpos.** Position to begin retrieving characters

◆ **characters.** Number of characters to retrieve

In this example, both the Left and Right functions can be replaced with the Mid function when they are combined with the Len function. The following is the conversion code:

```
Left("test string", 3)
```

is the same as

```
Mid("test string", 1, 3)
```

And:

```
Right("test string", 4)
```

is the same as

```
Mid("test string", Len("test string") - 4 + 1, 4)
```

The Mid function contains a version that processes byte data. Instead of retrieving characters, the MidB function retrieves a specified number of bytes at a specified byte position.

Right, RightB Functions

The Right function retrieves a specified number of characters starting from the last, or right-most, position in the string. As with the Left function, the Right function operates within two parameters (*string,* and *characters*), both are required.

◆ **string.** String to retrieve characters

◆ **characters.** Number of characters to retrieve

The Right function contains a version that processes byte data. Instead of retrieving characters, the RightB function retrieves a specified number of bytes.

Space Function

As you might have guessed, the Space function offers a quick way to generate multiple space characters. Because manually counting spaces in a literal string can be difficult, the Space function provides a more error-free method to create a number of spaces.

The following example illustrates the Space function:

```
Document.Write Len(Space(50))          ' Will print 50 —same number of spaces
                                       ' generated
```

Essentially, the Space function is shorthand for the String function, which generates a given number of any one character. The String function is discussed later in this section.

StrComp Function

The StrComp function performs a string comparison on the two strings accepted as parameters. The StrComp function operates within three parameters (*string1*, *string2*, and *comparemode*), one of which is optional.

◆ **string1, string2.** Strings to compare.

◆ **comparemode.** 0—Exact, or binary, comparison. 1—Case-insensitive comparison. If a value is omitted, the function performs a binary comparison.

StrComp performs a comparison between two strings and produces one of the following results:

Table 6.9
StrComp Results

If	StrComp returns
string1 is less than string2	−1
string1 is equal to string2	0
string1 is greater than string2	1
string1 or string2 is Null	Null

The following examples illustrate the StrComp function:

```
Document.Write StrComp("apple", "banana")     ' Prints -1, because apple
                                              ' comes before banana

Document.Write StrComp("banana", "apricot")   ' Prints 1, because banana
                                              ' comes after apricot
```

```
Document.Write StrComp("Apricot", "banana")    ' Prints 1, because capital
                                               ' letters come before
                                               ' lowercase letters
Document.Write StrComp("banana", "Banana", 1)  ' Prints 0 because a case-
                                               ' insensitive search
                                               ' determines that they are equal
Document.Write StrComp("banana", "Banana", 0)  ' Prints 1 becausecapital letters
                                               ' come before lowercase
                                               ' letters
```

As mentioned previously, you can use the comparison operators with strings to determine many of these relationships. However, to perform case-insensitive comparisons, you must convert both strings to either uppercase or lowercase with the UCase and LCase functions.

String Function

The String function is used to generate a certain number of repeated characters. The Space function, discussed previously, is similar to this function, except that the Space function generates only space characters. The String function operates within two parameters (*string*, and *repeat*), both of which are required.

◆ **string.** String to duplicate

◆ **repeat.** Number of times to repeat string

The String function duplicates the first character of *string*. The function cannot be used to duplicate a pattern of two or more characters. The following example illustrates the String function:

```
Document.Write String("*", 5)        ' Prints ***** on the screen
```

LTrim, RTrim, Trim Functions

LTrim, RTrim, and Trim remove unwanted spaces from your strings.

◆ **LTrim.** Removes leading spaces from the string. The Ltrim function stops removing spaces when it locates a non-space character.

◆ **RTrim.** Removes trailing spaces from the string and stops when it locates the last non-space character in the string.

♦ **Trim function.** Combines the Ltrim and RTrim functions and removes spaces from both ends of the string.

Note that these functions only remove the spaces on either end of the string, not the spaces within the string.

UCase, LCase Functions

As in a previous example, the UCase function is designed to change all the letters in a string to uppercase letters. The LCase function accomplishes the opposite result and converts all the letters in a string to lowercase letters. The following examples illustrate the Ucase and Lcase functions:

```
Document.Write UCase("banana")            ' Prints "BANANA"
Document.Write LCase("ThIs iS All MiXed Up") ' Prints "this is all mixed up"
```

Date and Time Functions

The Date and Time functions display the current date and time on your local machine. These functions do not return the current date and time on the remote server, if you are viewing a page across a network. Both functions display the output in whatever format the Windows Control Panel application currently specifies.

♦ **DateSerial Function.** The DateSerial function is used to convert a particular month, day, and year into a Date Variant variable. This function requires three parameters (*year, month,* and *day*):

   ♦ **year.** Any numeric expression between 100 and 9999

   ♦ **month.** Any numeric expression

   ♦ **day.** Any numeric expression

Considerable concern surrounds whether the turn of the century will affect dates stored in computers. It is therefore important to point out that Windows supports the year 100 through the year 9999. If the initial two digits are omitted from a year expression, the system automatically prefixes the value with "19." The following examples illustrate the Date function:

```
Document.Write DateSerial(1996 - 5, 5, 1)    ' Prints May 1, 1991
Document.Write DateSerial(1996, 15, 2)       ' Prints March 2, 1997
```

Although the numbers can fall outside the normal range for days and months, neither the day nor the month can be larger than 32,767 or smaller than −32,767. In both cases, the function displays an error message.

◆ **DateValue Function.** The DateValue function is used to convert a string that contains a date into a Date subtype variable. The DateValue function can operate within a variety of formats and uses the settings in the Control Panel to determine whether the month or the day is specified first before converting the string. In addition, the DateValue function can handle abbreviated dates and appends the current year if the year is omitted from the string. The function ignores time information that accompanies the date. The following examples illustrate the DateValue function:

```
Document.Write DateValue("Dec 7, 1941")     ' Prints 12/7/41
Document.Write DateValue("6/19/70")         ' Prints 6/19/70
Document.Write DateValue("06/19/1970")      ' Prints 6/19/70
```

◆ **TimeSerial Function.** The TimeSerial function operates similarly to the DateSerial function, by converting hours, minutes, and seconds to a Date subtyped variable.

  ◆ **Hours.** Any numeric expression

  ◆ **Minutes.** Any numeric expression

  ◆ **Seconds.** Any numeric expression

The function indicates midnight as 0 hours, and 23 hours represents 11:00 p.m. As with the DateSerial function, the TimeSerial function automatically converts too-large numbers into valid ones. For instance, the value 46 hours becomes 22 hours.

◆ **TimeValue Function.** As with the DateValue function, the TimeValue function converts a string that contains a common time format into a Date subtyped variable. The TimeValue function can accept times in both 12-hour clock and 24-hour clock formats.

◆ **Now Function.** The Now function displays the current date and time on your computer. Essentially, the Now function performs the operations of both the Date and Time functions.

◆ **Year Function.** The Year function displays a whole number between 100 and 9990, inclusive, to indicate the current year.

◆ **Month Function.** The Month function displays a whole number between 1 and 12, inclusive, to indicate the current month.

◆ **Day Function.** The Day function displays a whole number to indicate the current day of the month.

◆ **Weekday Function.** The Weekday function displays a whole number to indicate the day of the week. The function considers Sunday as day one, but an optional second argument following the date parameter enables you to determine another day of the week for day one.

◆ **Hour Function.** The Hour function displays a whole number between 0 and 23, inclusive, to indicate the current hour.

◆ **Minute Function.** The Minute function displays a whole number between 0 and 59, inclusive, to indicate the current minute.

◆ **Second Function.** The Second function displays a whole number between 0 and 59, inclusive, to indicate the current second.

The preceding seven functions can be used to create custom date and time formats, as the following example illustrates:

```
Document.Write "This document was created on day " & Day(Now) _
& " of month " & Month _
& " of year " & Year _
& ", during minute " & Minute _
& " of hour " & Hour & "."
```

Conversion Functions

Because all variables in VBScript classify as type Variant, conversion functions become less important for data storage and more important for formatting output data either for display or for input to other functions. VBScript provides a conversion function for each subtype of data, these functions appear in the following table. Each function accepts a Variant as an argument and displays a value in the subtype named by the function.

Function Name	Action
CBool	Converts to subtype Boolean
CByte	Converts to subtype Byte
CDate	Converts to subtype Date
CDbl	Converts to subtype Double
CInt	Converts to subtype Integer

Function Name	Action
CLng	Converts to subtype Long Integer
CSng	Converts to subtype Single
CStr	Converts to subtype String

Although the variable's type will always be Variant, these functions enable you to change the subtype of data stored in that variable. After you have converted the subtype, you can use the appropriate group of functions for that data. If a function is not assigned the correct subtype of data, you will get an error like `Type Mismatch Error`.

For Visual Basic Programmers:
Functions and Types

In general, the functions presented in this chapter are identical to their Visual Basic counterparts. The first primary difference is the lack of types other than the Variant type. Having one type makes it somewhat difficult to use these functions, because you must be sure of the data that is stored in a variable. If you do not check your variables, you might end up passing string data to a numerical function, which would result in an error.

The second major difference between Visual Basic and VBScript is VBScript's support of both Unicode and Byte operators, as in AscW and AscB. Although most users of VBScript won't need to worry about Unicode characters, having the support for byte characters can help to simplify or eliminate the problems you might have had before these functions were available.

CHAPTER 7

Looping and Decision Structures

By Eric Smith

N ow that you have learned the functions and expressions that you can use within VBScript, it is time to use them in some complex structures. VBScript supports five looping and decision structures that you learn about in this chapter. The structures include the following:

♦ If/Then/Else

♦ For/Next

♦ Select/Case

♦ Do/Loop

♦ While/Wend

You also learn which structures you can use that are not supported. In some cases, this lack of support requires some code rewriting, and this chapter covers how to convert from some of the unsupported structures.

If/Then/Else Structure

If you have ever done any programming, you are probably very familiar with the If/Then/Else decision structure because it is one of the most common programming constructs used. Even if you are not a programmer, you are already familiar with the concept as it is used in language. For example, these sentences use the If/Then/Else structure:

If your car's gas tank is empty, you need to get gas. Otherwise, you do not have to stop at the gas station.

Three separate pieces make up these sentences:

> "If your car's gas tank is empty,"
>
> "You need to get gas."
>
> "Otherwise, you do not have to stop at the gas station."

The first clause is known as the *conditional expression*. If this condition is true, the second clause occurs. If the condition in the first clause is false, the third clause occurs. These three pieces of this statement correspond directly to the three keywords of the If/Then/Else construct. The conditional expression in the first clause follows the If keyword. The second clause follows the Then keyword. Finally, the third clause follows the Else keyword. If this sentence was formatted in a computer program, it would look like this:

```
If (Your car's gas tank is empty) Then
        You need to get gas
Else
        You do not have to stop at the gas station.
End If
```

The sentence structure converts easily to code, as shown in this example. For this reason, the If/Then/Else structure is the most understandable of all the structures that are discussed in this chapter because it is used so often in the real world.

The basic syntax of the If/Then/Else construct is as follows:

```
If logical-expression Then statement1 Else statement2
```

 You can use any valid logical expression in the If/Then/Else statement. Refer to Chapter 6, "VBScript Functions and Operators," for more information on creating logical expressions.

If the `logical-expression` is True, `statement1` is executed. If the `logical-expression` is False `statement2` is executed. A simple example of this expression follows:

```
If A > B Then Document.Write "Variable A is greater" Else Document.Write
"Variable B is greater"
```

In some cases, you may not have an Else condition that requires code. In the cases where you do not need to use the Else condition, you can simplify the statement and omit the Else condition. You may, for instance, want to check a condition and do something only if the condition is True. An example of omitting the Else clause looks like the following:

```
If A > B Then Document.Write "Variable A is greater and we don't care about
variable B."
```

Using the End If Statement

What if `statement1` actually needs to be multiple statements? VBScript provides a way to format the If/Then/Else condition to enable multiple statements in a more readable format. An example of the multiple-line format is as follows:

```
If A > B Then
   Document.Write "Variable A is greater." & "<P>"
   Document.Write "Variable B is less than or equal to variable A."
Else
   Document.Write "Variable B is greater." & "<P>"
   Document.Write "Variable A is less than or equal to variable B."
End If
```

In the preceding example, you see the addition of the End If statement. End If is used at the end of the final section of the If/Then/Else structure. If you are using the Else clause, End If follows the end of the Else code block. If the Else clause has been omitted, as in the following example, the End If statement follows the `Then` code block.

```
If A > B Then
   Document.Write "Variable A is greater." & "<P>"
   Document.Write "Variable B is less than or equal to variable A."
End If
```

Enhancing Readability in If/Then/Else Code

Notice that the code within the If/Then/Else block is indented in the preceding example. Typically, the code should be indented three or four spaces. The indents help readability by showing which code is associated with which conditions. When you learn about nested If/Then/Else structures, you see the need for this sort of formatting.

As you learned in the preceding chapter, logical expressions can be quite complex. Any valid logical expression can be used in the If/Then/Else statement, as in the following example that verifies a character is an uppercase letter:

```
Dim strCharacter
strCharacter = "E"
If Asc(strCharacter) >= Asc("A") And Asc(strCharacter) <= Asc("Z") Then
   Document.Write "The letter is an uppercase letter."
Else
   Document.Write "The letter is not an uppercase letter."
End If
```

Note   *Continuation character*—The continuation character, the underscore character, is used to split long lines into multiple small lines. The character can be in the same place as a space within a statement. For instance, the following line of code:

```
If Asc(strCharacter) >= Asc("A") And Asc(strCharacter) <= Asc("Z")
Then
```

can be rewritten with a continuation character like this:

```
If Asc(strCharacter) >= Asc("A") _
And Asc(strCharacter) <= Asc("Z") Then
```

In cases where you have long conditions or statements, the continuation character can make your code easier to read.

In some cases, the condition may be so long that it scrolls past the right edge of your window. Lengthy conditions are common, but not being able to see the entire condition makes it prone to errors. When you have a lengthy condition, you can use the *continuation character* to split the line into multiple lines. The continuation character is the underscore character (_). The following example shows how this character can be used:

```
Dim strCharacter
strCharacter = "E"
If (Asc(strCharacter) >= Asc("A") And Asc(strCharacter) <= Asc("Z")) _
```

```
   Or (Asc(strCharacter) >= Asc("a") And Asc(strCharacter) <= Asc("z")) Then
      Document.Write "The character is a letter."
Else
      Document.Write "The character is not a letter."
End If
```

 You can use the underscore continuation character to split any line between any space as long as you are not splitting a string enclosed in quotes.

Nested If/Then/Else Structures

Within an If/Then/Else structure, you can have other If/Then/Else structures. These structures are called *nested* when this format is used. In the preceding example, you may need to determine whether the character is actually a number. The following example shows how to nest an additional If/Then/Else condition to determine whether the character is a number:

```
Dim strCharacter
strCharacter = "E"
If (Asc(strCharacter) >= Asc("A") And Asc(strCharacter) <= Asc("Z")) _
   Or (Asc(strCharacter) >= Asc("a") And Asc(strCharacter) <= Asc("z")) Then
   Document.Write "The character is a letter."
Else
   If Asc(strCharacter) >= Asc("0") And Asc(strCharacter) <= Asc("9") Then
      Document.Write "The character is a number."
   Else
      Document.Write "The character is not a letter or a number."
   End If
End If
```

Note the placement of the two End If statements. One follows the outside If/Then/Else construct at the very end of the sample. This End If closes the structure that began at the top of the sample. The second End If closes the structure within the Else clause of the first If/Then/Else structure. Formatting your code consistently makes reading the code much easier. Imagine trying to decode the following piece of code that lacks any formatting:

```
Dim strCharacter
strCharacter = "E"
If (Asc(strCharacter) >= Asc("A") And Asc(strCharacter) <= Asc("Z")) _
Or (Asc(strCharacter) >= Asc("a") And Asc(strCharacter) <= Asc("z")) Then
Document.Write "The character is a letter."
Else
```

```
If Asc(strCharacter) >= Asc("0") And Asc(strCharacter) <= Asc("9") Then
Document.Write "The character is a number."
Else
Document.Write "The character is not a letter or a number."
End If
End If
```

Even in this simple example, quickly finding the decision blocks is difficult. As your code becomes more complex, reading code formatted in this manner becomes impossible.

Using the ElseIf Keyword

The preceding example brings up a good question: What happens when the nesting goes too deep? The following example illustrates this question:

```
If condition Then
    If condition2 Then
        If condition3 Then
```

In some cases, the structure can be flattened by using the ElseIf keyword. If you are using mutually exclusive possibilities, as in the example that checked a character against several ranges, you can use ElseIf to create a much simpler structure. The structure in the preceding example changes as follows when you add the ElseIf keyword:

```
Dim strCharacter
strCharacter = "E"
If (Asc(strCharacter) >= Asc("A") And Asc(strCharacter) <= Asc("Z")) _
    Or (Asc(strCharacter) >= Asc("a") And Asc(strCharacter) <= Asc("z")) Then
    Document.Write "The character is a letter."
ElseIf Asc(strCharacter) >= Asc("0") And Asc(strCharacter) <= Asc("9") Then
    Document.Write "The character is a number."
Else
    Document.Write "The character is not a letter or a number."
End If
```

This type of structure is similar to a series of filters that are designed to trap smaller and smaller particles. The first If clause traps certain cases, the ElseIf clause traps others that didn't match the first, and so on. Finally, cases that didn't match any of the first conditions are handled by the final Else clause. In this example, the code traps letters and numbers. All other cases are handled by the final condition.

For/Next Structure

The computer excels at performing repetitive tasks. For coding these structures, VBScript provides the For/Next structure to perform loops where the beginning and ending values are known. For loops where a logical condition should be evaluated to determine the end of the loop, you can use the While/Wend or Do/Loop structures, which are discussed later in this chapter.

The basic format of this structure is as follows:

```
For loopvariable = startvalue To endvalue
   <statements that should be repeated>
Next
```

The statements within the For and Next statements execute once for each value between startvalue and endvalue. While the loop is executing, the variable loopvariable increments by 1 after each iteration. In the following example, all the values between 1 and 5 print on-screen.

```
Dim loopVar
For loopVar = 1 To 5
   Document.Write loopVar & "<P>"
Next
```

The starting and ending values must be numbers; however, they are not restricted to being simple numbers. You can use expressions that evaluate to numbers, as in the following example, which prints all the letters from A to Z by looping through the ASCII values of the letters:

```
Dim loopVar
For loopVar = Asc("A") To Asc("Z")
   Document.Write Chr(loopVar) & "<P>"
Next
```

The loopvar function is assigned the ASCII (numeric) values of the letters from A to Z. The Chr function returns the actual character assigned to an ASCII value.

The For/Next structure enables negative numbers to be used as starting or ending values, as in the following example:

```
Dim loopVar
For loopVar = -5 To 5
   Document.Write loopVar & "<P>"
Next
```

Using the Step Keyword

In cases where you need to increment by a value other than 1, you can use the Step keyword to indicate how much each iteration should increment the counter. The following example counts by two to 20:

```
Dim loopVar
For loopVar = 0 To 20 Step 2
    Document.Write loopVar & "<P>"
Next
```

The Step value can also be negative to make a loop iterate backwards. To step backwards by one, for example, you would use a Step value of –1.

The For loop keeps iterating as long as the counter variable is less or equal to the ending value given in the loop. In the preceding example, the value 20 is the last value printed because the next value in the sequence, 22, is greater than 20.

You don't have to end exactly on the ending value. For instance, in this example, the counter is never given the value 21, but will be given 22. Because 22 is greater than 21, the loop will terminate when it passes the ending value.

```
Dim loopVar
For loopVar = 0 To 21 Step 2
    Document.Write loopVar & "<P>"
Next
```

Note   The If/Then/Else and If/ElseIf/Else structures are identical to those used in Visual Basic. No changes were made for the VBScript version of this structure.

Exiting For/Next Loops Prematurely

In certain cases, it may be necessary to exit the For/Next loop before reaching the ending value. In these cases, you can use the Exit For statement to exit the loop and continue at the first line following the Next keyword. Although exiting a loop in this manner is considered by some to be poor programming style, it often simplifies the logic for the reader of your code. In the following example, the For loop exits when it matches the first letter of the string held in the stringVar variable:

```
Dim loopVar
Dim stringVar
stringVar = "Components"
```

```
For loopVar = Asc("A") to Asc("Z")
 <statements>
  If Left$(stringVar, 1) = Chr(loopVar) Then Exit For
   <statements>
Next
```

Nested Loops

For/Next structures, like all other programming structures, can be nested. For instance, to generate a grid, you can create code, as in the following example:

```
Dim xVar, yVar

For xVar = Asc("A") to Asc("Z")
   For yVar = 1 to 10
      Document.Write Chr(xVar) & yVar & Space(1)
   Next  ' yVar
   Document.Write "<P>"
Next  ' xVar
```

A few interesting things about this example are worth mentioning. For each time that the outer loop is executed, the inner loop is completely executed; that is, it iterates through all the values from 1 through 10 before the next iteration of the outer loop. The resulting output appears as follows:

```
A1 A2 A3 A4 A5 A6 A7 A8 A9 A10

B1 B2 B3 B4 B5 B6 B7 B8 B9 B10

C1 C2 C3 C4 C5 C6 C7 C8 C9 C10

D1 D2 D3 D4 D5 D6 D7 D8 D9 D10

E1 E2 E3 E4 E5 E6 E7 E8 E9 E10

F1 F2 F3 F4 F5 F6 F7 F8 F9 F10

G1 G2 G3 G4 G5 G6 G7 G8 G9 G10

H1 H2 H3 H4 H5 H6 H7 H8 H9 H10

I1 I2 I3 I4 I5 I6 I7 I8 I9 I10

J1 J2 J3 J4 J5 J6 J7 J8 J9 J10
```

To move to a new line after the inner loop finishes executing, a paragraph tag is printed right after the inner loop finishes. Because the Document.Write function prints characters without any formatting, insert the <BR> tag and force a line break at the end of each logical row.

> **Note**
>
> In nested loops, you can become confused about which Next keyword matches with the appropriate For keyword. In Visual Basic, the variable name is normally placed with the Next keyword; however, VBScript does not support this placement. Therefore, you must place a comment next to the Next keyword to indicate the loop it matches. This comment is a handy trick that you can use to help you debug your code. By placing the comments consistently, your nested loops become much easier to read.

Select/Case Structure

In cases where you have a number of items that you want to match a variable against, you can code it as an If/Then/Else or an If/ElseIf/Else structure. However, if some of the items have the same action to be performed, you end up with a lot of duplicated code. To eliminate the duplication, the Select/Case structure enables you to create a list of values to test against and perform various actions based on the results. An example of Select/Case structure follows:

```
Dim stringVar
stringVar = "B"

Select Case stringVar
   Case "A":
      Document.Write "Letter is A"
   Case "B", "C":
      Document.Write "Letter is B or C"
   Case Else:
      Document.Write "I don't know what letter it is"
End Select
```

The equivalent code, using If/ElseIf/Else statements, appears as follows:

```
Dim stringVar
stringVar = "B"

If stringVar = "A" Then
   Document.Write "Letter is A"
```

```
ElseIf stringVar = "B" Or stringVar = "C" Then
   Document.Write "Letter is B or C"
Else
   Document.Write "I don't know what letter it is"
End If
```

For short lists, either structure can be used. However, in the cases where you are testing for multiple items to perform the same action (as in the preceding example for B or C), the Select/Case structure is much easier to use and change later. You can separate each of the items in the acceptable list with commas (as in the first example), and any matching value causes the statements below it to be executed. You can add items to any of the Case statements more easily than you can add additional ElseIf clauses to an already large If/ElseIf block.

Using the Case Else Keyword

In cases where you are evaluating a user's input, you should assume that the user may type invalid characters. The `Case Else` keyword enables you to have a generic case that catches all values not handled in a previous case. Note that only one Case can be matched for any given value. In the following example, the first Case is matched and `"Letter is A or B"` is printed on-screen. This event occurs even though the letter *B* can be matched by either of the first two Case statements.

```
Dim stringVar
stringVar = "B"

Select Case stringVar
   Case "A", "B":
      Document.Write "Letter is A or B"
   Case "B", "C":
      Document.Write "Letter is B or C"
   Case Else:
      Document.Write "I don't know what letter it is"
End Select
```

Besides string values, you can use the Select/Case structure to match any valid values.

Performing Blank Actions

In cases where you do not want to perform any statements when a value is matched, you can leave the statement section blank, as in the following example. If the letter is *A*, no action is taken. This method is used when a large number of values is checked. In these cases, you can add a blank action for the sake of completeness to show that you did consider the value but that no action was required.

```
Dim stringVar
stringVar = "B"

Select Case stringVar
   Case "A":
     ' No action is required
   Case "B", "C":
     Document.Write "Letter is B or C"
   Case Else:
     Document.Write "I don't know what letter it is"
End Select
```

In cases where you use a placeholder, a comment is usually used to explain your actions to later users of the code. Otherwise, users may think that you introduced an error into your code.

Using the Underscore Character

If you are writing a Case condition for a large number of choices, you can use the underscore character to format your lines easily, as in the following example:

```
Dim stringVar
stringVar = "B"

Select Case stringVar
   Case "A":
     ' No action is required
   Case "B", "C", _
        "D", "E", _
        "F", "G":
     Document.Write "Letter betwen B and G"
   Case Else:
     Document.Write "I don't know what letter it is"
End Select
```

The underscore character enables you to combine the conditions into more logical groups and save yourself from having to write multiple conditions that have the same actions. As always, the fewer times that you use the same code translates into fewer possibilities for errors.

Note The Select/Case structure is identical to the Visual Basic version and syntax. No changes were made for the VBScript version of this structure.

Do/Loop Structure

As mentioned in the preceding section, every For/Next loop can be written as a Do/Loop structure. However, the Do/Loop structure offers more possibilities than the For/Next loop. For instance, you can exit the loop based on a logical condition instead of just when the counter reaches an ending value that you previously specified. In the following example, which emulates the behavior of the For/Next structure, the loop iterates as long as the loop variable is less than a given value:

```
Dim loopVar
loopVar = 1
Do
    <statements>
    loopVar = loopVar + 1
Loop While loopVar <= 5
```

Just as the For/Next loop initializes the counter variable to the starting value, the value of loopVar is set to the starting value before entering the loop. At some point within the loop, loopVar increments. Finally, at the end of the loop, the counter is checked to determine whether the loop should continue.

The Do/Loop structure can be written by using the Until keyword. The Until keyword essentially reverses the logic in the condition. For example, the preceding example can be rewritten using the Until keyword as follows:

```
Dim loopVar
loopVar = 1
Do
    <statements>
    loopVar = loopVar + 1
Loop Until loopVar > 5
```

Using this keyword is similar to reversing the logic when you have a complex If/Then/Else condition. As mentioned before, your syntax is clearer when you use fewer symbols and keywords. In this case, the condition Until loopVar > 5 is clearer than While loopVar <= 5 because you only have to determine whether the number is larger than 5 and not larger or equal to 5. You have fewer possibilities for confusion about how large the counter can become before exiting the loop.

Reversing Operators

In several examples, you needed to reverse the logic of a condition. All logical operators can be reversed and used in an alternative manner. Table 7.1 contains several examples of reversing operators.

Table 7.1
Converting Logical Expressions

Original Condition	Converted Condition	
If X < 5	reversed would become	If Not(X >= 5)
If X = 5	reversed would become	If Not(X <> 5)
If X > 5	reversed would become	If Not(X <= 5)
If X >= 5	reversed would become	If Not(X < 5)
If X <= 5	reversed would become	If Not(X > 5)
If X <> 5	reversed would become	If Not(X = 5)

In these conversions, the original logic stays the same, but the condition can be used with a different keyword. If, for example, you want to change a While condition to an Until condition, you first follow the rules given previously. Then because the Until keyword uses the opposite condition of the While keyword, you would use the reversed condition without the Not keyword. Look at the following steps to see how a condition can be reversed:

1. The original code statement is as follows:

```
Do
 <statements>
   loopVar = loopVar + 1
Loop While loopVar <= 5
```

2. You can reverse the condition by using the information in table 7.1 The condition now becomes the following:

```
Loop While Not(loopVar > 5)
```

3. Finally, you replace the While Not keywords with Until, as follows:

```
Loop Until loopVar > 5
```

Following these rules, you can reverse any condition to make it easier to read. In cases where you have a compound condition that uses the And or Or keywords, the conversion is slightly more difficult. However, you still follow the same steps. Look at these examples to see how the conversion is done for the keywords:

```
Do While (Asc(stringVar) >= Asc("A")) And (Asc(stringVar) <= Asc("Z"))
```

To reverse this condition, follow these steps:

1. Change the And keyword to Or, or vice versa, as follows:

```
(Asc(stringVar) >= Asc("A")) Or (Asc(stringVar) <= Asc("Z"))
```

2. Reverse the conditions on either side of the And/Or operator, as follows:

```
Not(Asc(stringVar) >= Asc("A")) Or Not(Asc(stringVar) <= Asc("Z"))
```

3. Using the rules about reversing operators, simplify the condition. Each Not operator reverses the conditions on either side of the Or keyword. After the simplification has happened, the condition becomes the following:

```
(Asc(stringVar) < Asc("A")) Or (Asc(stringVar) > Asc("Z"))
```

At this point, you can use this condition in the Do Until clause, as follows:

```
Do Until (Asc(stringVar) < Asc("A")) Or (Asc(stringVar) > Asc("Z"))
```

If you look at this condition logically, it still uses the same logic. The loop should continue until the ASCII value of stringVar is outside the range bounded by the letters *A* and *Z*. In the unreversed condition, the character has to be between the letters. In the reversed condition, the letter has to be outside the range. Either way, the same effect is achieved.

The previous examples are designed to give you some good methods to convert and simplify your logic. Boolean math has many other complex rules for converting expressions, but this is the main rule you probably need to use.

Exiting the Loop

When the condition is checked at the end, use the Do/Loop structure so that the program enters the loop immediately without checking any condition first. Checking the condition at the end of the loop guarantees that the statements within the Do/Loop structure are executed at least once. However, sometimes you will have statements that should not execute at all. In these cases, the logical expression following the Loop keyword can be repositioned to follow the Do keyword. By checking the exit condition first, the entire block of statements can be skipped when dictated by conditions in the program. In the following example, the preceding structure has been rewritten with the alternative method just described:

```
Dim loopVar
loopVar = 1
Do Until loopVar > 5
```

```
   <statements>
   loopVar = loopVar + 1
Loop
```

If `loopVar` is initially set to 6, the statements within the Do/Loop structure do not execute. The exit condition is met when the program flow reaches the Do Until statement. This example can be written by using the `While` keyword in place of the `Until` keyword. Again, when you make the replacement, you have to reverse the logic of the exit condition, as in the following example:

```
Dim loopVar
loopVar = 1
Do While loopVar <= 5
   <statements>
   loopVar = loopVar + 1
Loop
```

Both of the previous two examples are programmatically identical. They both stop iterating when the counter reaches 6.

Nesting the Do/Loop Structure

As with all the other looping structures, you can also nest the Do/Loop structure. In the following example, the For/Next example has been rewritten to use two Do Until loops instead of the For/Next loops that were used before:

```
Dim xVar, yVar

xVar = Asc("A")
Do Until xVar > Asc("Z")
   yVar = 1
   Do Until yVar > 10
      Document.Write Chr(xVar) & yVar & Space(1)
      yVar = yVar + 1
   Loop ' yVar loop
   Document.Write "<P>"
   xVar = xVar + 1
Loop ' xVar loop
```

The `Loop` keywords are commented to indicate which loop they match. The statements within each loop are also indented so that you can tell which loop they belong to. If you do not indent and comment this code, it will look something like this:

```
Dim xVar, yVar
xVar = Asc("A")
Do Until xVar > Asc("Z")
yVar = 1
Do Until yVar > 10
Document.Write Chr(xVar) & yVar & Space(1)
yVar = yVar + 1
Loop
Document.Write "<P>"
xVar = xVar + 1
Loop
```

As you can see, several more lines are needed to perform the same functions that the For/Next structure performs automatically. You have to manually initialize your counters to their starting values, manually increment them, and manually reset them (for the inner loop) each time you want to use them again.

Exiting the Do/Loop Prematurely

Finally, as with the For/Next statement, you will have some cases where it is easier to exit the loop when a condition is met. For instance, you may be using a For loop and have multiple exit conditions. If one of the optional exit conditions is met, you can use Exit For to exit immediately instead of waiting until the end of the loop. In these cases, the Exit Do statement can be used to exit the current Do/Loop structure. The Exit Do statement exits the current loop. If you have nested loops, you must use one Exit Do statement for each Do/Loop structure you have to exit.

Note The Do/Loop structure, with all its variations, is identical to the Visual Basic version and syntax. No changes were made for the VBScript version of this structure. All variations of this structure (using the While or Until keywords) are also valid for Visual Basic.

While/Wend Structure

The final looping structure supported by Visual Basic is the While/Wend structure. This structure is identical to the Do While <condition>/Loop structure variation. The Wend stands for End While and takes the place of the Loop keyword in the previous examples. The following example uses the Do While keywords:

```
Dim loopVar
loopVar = 1
Do While loopVar <= 5
   <statements>
   loopVar = loopVar + 1
Loop
```

The preceding example can be rewritten by using the While/Wend structure as follows:

```
Dim loopVar
loopVar = 1
While loopVar <= 5
   <statements>
   loopVar = loopVar + 1
Wend
```

Unlike the Do/Loop structure, the While/Wend structure does not have an `Exit` keyword that enables you immediately to exit the currently iterating loop. For this and several other reasons, you should use the Do/Loop structure instead of the While/Wend structure. The While/Wend structure is included primarily for compatibility and consistency with Visual Basic.

Note The While/Wend structure is identical to the Visual Basic version and syntax. No changes were made for the VBScript version of this structure.

For Visual Basic Programmers:

Unsupported Looping Structures

Visual Basic programmers are probably familiar with many structures that are not supported in VBScript. These unsupported structures include the following:

- ◆ **DoEvents.** This keyword forces the Visual Basic event queue to be processed. Using this keyword helps to better control the visual interface to your Visual Basic program.

- ◆ **For Each/Next.** This structure is used to iterate through a collection of objects in much the same way that the For/Next structure is used to iterate through a list of values. Because the Collection object is not supported by VBScript, the For Each/Next structure cannot be used either.

◆ **GoSub/Return.** This structure is similar to the subroutines and functions that are used in Visual Basic. GoSub is similar to a subroutine, but it works based on line numbers that were formerly used in BASIC coding. Because line numbers and line labels are unsupported, GoSub cannot be used.

Warning | Line numbers and line labels are not supported in VBScript.

◆ **GoTo.** For the same reason that the GoSub keyword does not work, GoTo requires a line number or a label to function.

◆ **On Error GoTo.** This common error handling construct is unsupported in VBScript because it requires a line label to work correctly. VBScript, as you learn in Chapter 9, "Programming with Events," does support the On Error Resume Next statement, which enables the program to continue even after a runtime error occurs. Any error handling has to be handled inline.

◆ **With/End With.** The With/End With structure is used in combination with user-defined types and objects. It is used to execute a series of statements on an object or variable declared with a user-defined type. Because user-defined types are not supported in VBScript, this operator is not needed.

The five structures introduced in this chapter are identical to those used in Visual Basic. However several key constructs are missing: GoTo, On Error GoTo, GoSub/Return, For Each/Next, With/End With, and DoEvents. However, these omissions can be supplemented by other similar structures that are supported in VBScript. Some of these omissions, such as the For Each/Next and With/End With, are omitted because they are not needed. Both of these structures deal with the Collection object, which is not supported in VBScript.

Summary

This chapter introduced you to the basic flow control structures used in VBScript. Using the If/Then/Else, Do/Loop, While/Wend, For/Next, and Select/Case structures and the examples from this chapter, you will be able to use these structures in your own VBScript pages to control how code is executed. Understanding these structures is important because this book's examples will be using them extensively.

CHAPTER 8

Building Procedures and Functions

By Eric Smith

Now that you have learned about many of the structures you can use in your coding, you can start building useful codes to use in your HTML documents. As you write your VBScript code, you will undoubtedly create pieces of code that can be used multiple times throughout your documents. However, you don't want to copy codes from page to page, because you might introduce errors into the code in the process.

To alleviate this problem, this chapter introduces you to functions and subroutines. Functions and subroutines enable you to modularize your code so that pieces of the code can be changed without affecting other parts of the code. You can put useful pieces of code into a common location so that it can be used from multiple places in a HTML document.

You can also use subroutines and functions to perform pieces of more complex operations. This makes the code more readable and logical so that others can follow the flow of the code more easily. In this chapter, you learn how to use these and many other functions and subroutines.

The Subroutine Structure

VBScript provides two different ways to create reusable blocks of code. The first is the subroutine structure. Several examples of subroutines are built into the VBScript language. The first one you should be familiar with is the *Document.Write subroutine*. It prints output to the current HTML document.

> **Note** Document.Write subroutine—This subroutine will produce output within the current HTML document.

> **Note** MsgBox command—This built-in function can display message boxes to the user. This function is also useful for debugging code.

Another example is the *MsgBox command*. It displays a message box, and when the user clicks a button, it exits. The MsgBox command can be used as a function. This process is discussed in the next section.

The main distinguishing factor of the subroutine versus the function is that the subroutine does not return a value to the calling code. All the functions described in previous chapters, such as the Asc and Mid functions, return a value that can be processed by your code. Functions are the same way—they return a value based on processing performed within the function code.

To create a subroutine, use the following format:

```
Sub subroutine-name (parameters)
    <statements go here>
End Sub
```

Calling a Subroutine

To call a subroutine, you can use several different formats. Look at the example that follows to see the different ways to call a subroutine.

```
<SCRIPT LANGUAGE=VBScript>
Sub DisplayMessageBox ()
    MsgBox "This message box was displayed from the DisplayMessageBox
➥subroutine."
End Sub
Sub Main ()
    DisplayMessageBox
```

```
    Call DisplayMessageBox()
End Sub
</SCRIPT>
```

> **Note** The main distinguishing factor of the subroutine versus the function is that a subroutine does not return a value to the calling code. Even if a function is called with no parameters, it always returns a value to the calling code.

The first method for calling a subroutine is to use the name of the subroutine. The alternative method is to use the `Call` keyword. Both ways are equally valid; however, when adding parameters to the subroutine call, you might notice some differences.

Both subroutines and functions can accept parameters. *Parameters* are a special type of variable used only with subroutines and functions. To use a parameter in a subroutine or function, perform the following steps:

1. In the subroutine or function declaration, list the parameters you want to use. Each parameter should be separated by commas within a pair of parentheses.

2. When you call the subroutine or function, any values you want to pass as parameters should be listed following the subroutine or function name.

> **Note** When you are declaring parameters within your function or subroutine declarations, you do not have to specify a type for each parameter. The *As type clause*, used in Visual Basic, is not necessary in VBScript because all variables are of type Variant.

The following example illustrates this two-step procedure:

1. The `DisplayMessageBox` subroutine has one parameter: `strMessage`. It is listed following the subroutine name within a pair of parentheses.

2. In the `Main` subroutine when `DisplayMessageBox` is called, the actual message is listed following the subroutine name. In this case, the message `"This is the first message to be printed"` is stored in the `strMessage` parameter within the `DisplayMessageBox` subroutine.

```
<SCRIPT LANGUAGE=VBScript>
Sub DisplayMessageBox (strMessage)
   MsgBox strMessage, 64, "DisplayMessageBox Subroutine"
End Sub
Sub Main ()
   DisplayMessageBox "This is the first message to be printed."
```

```
   Call DisplayMessageBox("This is the second message to be printed.")
End Sub
</SCRIPT>
```

In the subroutine definition, the `strMessage` parameter is equivalent to a variable that was declared within the subroutine. You do not have to declare the parameter again, as you would a regular variable. The `strMessage` parameter serves double duty as the first parameter to the MsgBox statement. The second parameter, 64, indicates that the information icon should display in the message box. The final parameter is the value for the title of the message box.

 Because all variables are of type Variant, parameters do not have the *As type* following them in the subroutine declaration. This is different from Visual Basic where all parameters must either have a type declared or an Integer type assumed.

 All the valid values for the MsgBox command are described in Chapter 2, "HTML Fundamentals for VBScripting."

Now that a parameter has been added to the `DisplayMessageBox` routine, the method that calls it has also changed. In the first method, the `Call` keyword is not used, and the message to be printed follows the name of the subroutine.

```
DisplayMessageBox "This is the first message to be printed."
```

When using this method, no parentheses are used. However, when using the `Call` keyword, parentheses are required.

```
Call DisplayMessageBox ("This is the second message to be printed.")
```

The subroutine is not restricted to a single parameter; you can use any number of parameters in each subroutine. When using multiple parameters, separate them with commas. If the previous example is modified so that the title of the message box can be specified, the two parameters are separated by commas in the subroutine declaration.

```
<SCRIPT LANGUAGE=VBScript>
Sub DisplayMessageBox (strMessage, strTitle)
   MsgBox strMessage, 64, strTitle
End Sub

Sub Main ()
   DisplayMessageBox "This is the first message to be printed.", "First
   ➥Message"
   Call DisplayMessageBox("This is the second message to be printed.",
"Second Message")
```

```
End Sub
</SCRIPT>
```

Although commas are used to separate arguments in subroutine declarations, commas are also required when listing the arguments passed to the subroutine. When using the first method to call the subroutine, each argument follows the name of the subroutine and is separated by commas, as in this example:

```
DisplayMessageBox "This is the first message to be printed.", "First Message"
```

When using the Call keyword, the arguments are separated by commas within a single set of parentheses:

```
Call DisplayMessageBox("This is the second message to be printed.",
    ➡"Second Message")
```

Passing Variables to Subroutines

Like variables, subroutines have a scope where they are available within a program. In VBScript, all subroutines and functions that are declared in a document can be called from within any block of code in the same document. The calls can come from different <SCRIPT> blocks, where the subroutine or function is defined. In some languages, functions are declared within other functions' declarations. Neither Visual Basic nor VBScript support this and make all subroutines and functions globally available within the same HTML document.

In the previous examples, simple strings were used as parameters to the Display-MessageBox subroutine. Variables can be used as parameters. However, passing variables to subroutines might cause some unexpected behavior. In this example that appears correct, a runtime error is generated.

```
<SCRIPT LANGUAGE=VBScript>
Sub ModifyValue(intValue)
    intValue = 10

End Sub

Dim intValue

intValue = 5

ModifyValue intValue

Document.Write intValue

</SCRIPT>
```

A runtime error generates because VBScript is preventing you from changing a variable that passes to the subroutine by reference. *Passing by reference* means that any changes to the variable's value within a subroutine changes the original variable. By default, all variables pass to subroutines by reference. However, VBScript prevents you from assigning a new value to a parameter that is passed by reference. In certain cases, this is not the desired behavior. In the following example, this behavior is changed using the ByVal keyword, which instructs VBScript that the parameter's value is to be used and no changes should be made to the original variable.

```
<SCRIPT LANGUAGE=VBScript>
Sub ModifyValue(ByVal intValue)

    intValue = intValue * 10
    MsgBox "Value calculated by ModifyValue: " & intValue

End Sub

'
' Main processing begins here
'
    Dim intValue
    intValue = 5

    ModifyValue intValue

    MsgBox "Value following ModifyValue: " & intValue

</SCRIPT>
```

In this example, the first message box that displays shows the value 50 (the value of intValue—5 multiplied by 10). Although the calculation is stored in the intValue variable within the subroutine, the change is not permanent. The ByVal keyword in the subroutine declaration prevents the subroutine from making permanent changes to the variable's real value. To verify that this works, the second message box displays the value 5, the same value as intValue contained before it passed to the ModifyValue subroutine.

Note | Unlike Visual Basic, parameters cannot be set to new values within subroutines. This is a major change from Visual Basic. However, this might change in future versions of the language. Currently, any assignments to a parameter passed by reference generate this runtime error: `Cannot assign to non-ByVal argument`.

To be able to assign values to variables within subroutines, the variables must be declared globally and cannot be passed as parameters to the subroutine.

Exiting a Subroutine Prematurely

As is the case with some of the looping structures, you may need to exit a subroutine immediately. To do this, use the `Exit Sub` keyword. This causes execution of the current subroutine to stop. The next line executed is the one immediately following the call to the exited subroutine. Here is an example of using the `Exit Sub` keyword:

```
<SCRIPT LANGUAGE=VBScript>
Sub AddOne(ByVal intValue)
   If IsNull(intValue) Then Exit Sub

   intValue = intValue + 1
   MsgBox "New value is " & intValue

End Sub


'
' Main processing begins here
'
   Dim intValue
   intValue = 5

   AddOne Null

   AddOne intValue

</SCRIPT>
```

Before any actions are taken using the `intValue` parameter, the `AddOne` subroutine is checked to see if it is Null. Null values cause unexpected results in most functions and may cause runtime errors in your code. In this case, adding a value to Null results in Null, an incorrect result.

The first time that AddOne is called, it is called with a Null value. The first line of the AddOne subroutine checks the parameter against Null. Because the parameter is Null, the subroutine is exited and control passes through the second call to AddOne in the main processing code. The second call to AddOne passes a legal value of 5, and the message box displays 5 + 1, which is 6.

For Visual Basic Programmers:

Simulating Optional Parameters in Subroutines

In Visual Basic, subroutines can have *Optional* parameters. You may omit these parameters in cases where they are not needed. VBScript does not support optional parameters. Using the technique previously explained, you can simulate optional parameters. The DisplayMessageBox subroutine discussed at the beginning of this chapter can be modified to have an optional title parameter. If the title parameter is set to Null, a default value may be used. Here is the subroutine and calling code rewritten using the concept of an optional parameter:

```
<SCRIPT LANGUAGE=VBScript>
Sub DisplayMessageBox (strMessage, strTitle)
   If IsNull(strTitle) Then
      MsgBox strMessage, 64, "Application Message Box"
   Else
      MsgBox strMessage, 64, strTitle
   End If
End Sub


'
' Main processing begins here
'

   DisplayMessageBox "This message uses a custom title.", "First Message"

   DisplayMessageBox "This message uses the default title.", Null

</SCRIPT>
```

In the first call to DisplayMessageBox, the title parameter is supplied with a non-Null value, so the title "First Message" is added to the first message box. In the second call to DisplayMessageBox, the title parameter is filled with Null, so the default title of "Application Message Box" is used for the message box.

In some cases, Null is a valid value for a parameter. In these cases, a Boolean parameter may be used to indicate whether a particular argument is supplied. Using this method, the previous example is rewritten as follows:

```vbscript
<SCRIPT LANGUAGE=VBScript>
Sub DisplayMessageBox (strMessage, boolTitleSupplied, strTitle)
   If boolTitleSupplied Then
      MsgBox strMessage, 64, strTitle
   Else
      MsgBox strMessage, 64, "Application Message Box"
   End If
End Sub


'
' Main processing begins here
'

   DisplayMessageBox "This message uses a custom title.", True, "First Message"

   DisplayMessageBox "This message uses the default title.", False, Null

</SCRIPT>
```

The `DisplayMessageBox` routine checks the Boolean value of the `boolTitleSupplied` routine to determine whether the `strTitle` parameter has a usable value.

In the first call to `DisplayMessageBox`, `boolTitleSupplied` is set to True because a custom title is supplied. `DisplayMessageBox` checks `boolTitleSupplied`, determines the value is True, and uses the custom title in the `strTitle` parameter.

In the second call to `DisplayMessageBox`, `boolTitleSupplied` is set to False and the title parameter is set to Null. `DisplayMessageBox` checks `boolTitleSupplied`, determines that the value is False, and uses the default message box title instead. This prevents you from having to check parameters for Null. In cases where you are dealing with objects, checking the parameter for Null might not be the correct method.

Finally, you must have a parameter value for each parameter defined for a subroutine. In other words, if the subroutine is declared with two arguments, you must always supply it with two arguments, even if one or both are Null.

The Function Structure

Unlike the subroutine structure, which does not have the capability of returning values, the function is able to return values that can be processed by the calling code. VBScript has many built-in functions, which are described in the previous chapters. All of them take at least one parameter, like the subroutine, and they all return a value. For instance, the `Asc` function takes a character as input and returns the ASCII value of the character to the calling code. As always, all parameters are of type Variant, but the function operates on the type of data within the variant.

The basic format of the function is the following:

```
Function function-name (parameter-list)

   <statements>
   function-name = return-value

End Function
```

Within the statements of a function, the return value must be assigned to the name of the function to return it to the calling code. Do this step before exiting the function, or no value returns to the calling code.

> **Note**
>
> Because all variables are of type Variant, the *As Type* that normally follows the declaration of a function is omitted in VBScript. All functions return a Variant to the calling code. You can put whatever type of data in the Variant that is necessary.
>
> Like the subroutine structure, the *As Type* that normally follows each parameter defined for a function is omitted in VBScript. All parameters are of type Variant for functions and subroutines.

Calling Functions

Functions have a scope where they are available. In VBScript, all subroutines and functions that are declared in a document are called from any block of code within the same document. The calls can come from different `<SCRIPT>` blocks, not just the one where the subroutine or function is defined. In some languages, functions can be declared within other functions' declarations. Neither Visual Basic nor VBScript support this, and both make all subroutines and functions globally available within the same HTML document.

Because every function returns a value, functions can be called in only one way. This method is the following:

```
Dim ReturnValue
ReturnValue = RunThisFunction()
```

Any parameters that are required by the function are placed within the parentheses following the function name and separated by commas. If no parameters are needed, empty parentheses must be added to the function name, as shown in the previous example. An example of a function that requires a parameter is:

```
<SCRIPT LANGUAGE=VBScript>
Function CubeTheNumber(intNumber)

    CubeTheNumber = intNumber ^ 3

End Function


'
' Main processing begins here
'

    Dim intReturnValue
    intReturnValue = CubeTheNumber(5)
    MsgBox "The result is " & intReturnValue

</SCRIPT>
```

In the CubeTheNumber function, the result of the function is assigned to the name of the function. As you learned in the previous section, no assignments can be made to input parameters that do not have the ByVal keyword. You cannot change input parameters within a function or a subroutine. However, using the CubeTheNumber function, you can return a value by setting the name of the function equal to the value you want to return, as shown in the previous example.

The calling code stores the return value from CubeTheNumber in the intReturnValue variable, which is shown in a message box. However, you can embed the call to the CubeTheNumber function in the MsgBox call. (The code for the CubeTheNumber function remains the same.) The following example illustrates this point.

```
'
' Main processing begins here
'

    MsgBox "The result is " & CubeTheNumber(5)
```

Because the result of CubeTheNumber is a variant, it can be appended to the short description of the results, and then it displays in a message box.

Note In Visual Basic, the return value from a function normally needs to be converted to a string with the CStr or Str$ functions before being appended to another string. Because all variables are variants, they can be immediately combined.

Passing Parameters to Functions

Like the subroutine's parameters, each parameter passed to a function can be sent by reference or by value. By default, each parameter is passed by reference. To change this behavior, add the ByVal keyword in the declaration of the function, as follows:

```
<SCRIPT LANGUAGE=VBScript>
Function CubeAndMultiply (ByVal intNumber)

    intNumber = intNumber ^ 3
    CubeAndMultiply = intNumber * 2

End Function


'
' Main processing begins here
'

    Dim intReturnValue
    Dim intValue
    intValue = 5
    intReturnValue = CubeAndMultiply(intValue)
    MsgBox "The result is " & intReturnValue


</SCRIPT>
```

As you learned in the previous section, the code in the CubeAndMultiply function generates an error if the ByVal keyword is omitted. No assignments can be made to a function's parameters unless they are passed by value. This means that no changes are made to any parameter passed to any function or subroutine. In the previous example, the intNumber parameter is used to hold the partial results of the calculations, but the changes made to this parameter are not permanent. The values are used within the CubeAndMultiply function and are then discarded.

Note Another important thing to note about the assignment of the return value to the name of the function is that it can be done multiple times during the flow of a program. However, the final value assigned to the name of the function is only thing that returns to the caller. In Visual Basic, attempting to assign a value to a function's name more than once generates an error.

The Exit Function Statement

The function structure also has a method to exit immediately: the *Exit Function statement.* This statement exits the currently executing function. Before you execute this statement, assign a value to the name of the function. If a value is not assigned, no value returns when the Exit Function statement is carried out. The previous example has been rewritten here to determine if the parameter's value is greater than zero. If the parameter is less than or equal to zero, the function is immediately terminated.

```
<SCRIPT LANGUAGE=VBScript>
Function CubeAndMultiply (ByVal intNumber)

    If intNumber <= 0 Then
        CubeAndMultiply = -1
        Exit Function
    End If


    intNumber = intNumber ^ 3
    CubeAndMultiply = intNumber * 2
End Function

'
' Main processing begins here
'
    Dim intReturnValue
    Dim intValue
    intValue = 5
    intReturnValue = CubeAndMultiply(intValue)
    If intReturnValue <> -1 Then
        MsgBox "The result is " & intReturnValue
    Else
        MsgBox "The input value was zero - no operation was performed."
    End If

</SCRIPT>
```

 Flag value—A flag value is a predetermined number that is used to indicate a condition. For instance, the value −1 is often used to indicate that a task is complete.

In this example, a flag value of −1 is created to indicate to the caller that there was an error in processing. In this case, the calling code checks the return value of the function and only prints the result if it is not equal to −1.

The use of return values in this manner is one of the most popular and common uses of functions. By combining this with globally available variables, you set up a series of flags that a function returns and these flags can be interpreted consistently throughout your application. Here is the previous example using some global variables to indicate the state of processing from the function:

```
<SCRIPT LANGUAGE=VBScript>
Dim BADINPUT

Function CubeAndMultiply (ByVal intNumber)

    If intNumber <= 0 Then
        CubeAndMultiply = BADINPUT
        Exit Function
    End If

    intNumber = intNumber ^ 3
    CubeAndMultiply = intNumber * 2
End Function

'
' Main processing begins here
'
    Dim intReturnValue
    Dim intValue
    BADINPUT = -1
    intValue = 5
    intReturnValue = CubeAndMultiply(intValue)
    If intReturnValue <> BADINPUT Then
        MsgBox "The result is " & intReturnValue
    Else
        MsgBox "The input value was zero - no operation was performed."
    End If

</SCRIPT>
```

By using BADINPUT instead of a literal value of –1, you consistently check for errors in input. Every piece of code throughout this page could use the same set of return codes. The other benefit to this method is that if you need to change the values stored in your error codes, you can change them all with one line of code instead of having to find all the occurrences of –1 in your code and determining whether you need to change it.

For Visual Basic Programmers:

Simulating Optional Parameters in Functions

In Visual Basic, functions have *optional parameters*, just like subroutines. These parameters can be omitted in cases where they are not needed. VBScript does not support optional parameters in either functions or subroutines. However, you can simulate optional parameters. The DisplayMessageBox subroutine, discussed at the beginning of this chapter can be modified into a function with the ability to return the button that the user pressed in response to the message box. The subroutine and calling code are rewritten here using the concept of an optional parameter in the form of a function:

```
<SCRIPT LANGUAGE=VBScript>
Function DisplayMessageBox (strMessage, strTitle)
   If IsNull(strTitle) Then
      DisplayMessageBox = MsgBox (strMessage, 64, "Application Message Box")
   Else
      DisplayMessageBox = MsgBox (strMessage, 64, strTitle)
   End If
End Sub


' Main processing begins here
'

   Dim intReturnValue
   intReturnValue = DisplayMessageBox ("This message uses a custom title.",
   ➥"First Message")
   If intReturnValue = value Then
      ' Perform some action based on returned value
   End If

   intReturnValue = DisplayMessageBox ("This message uses the default title.",
   ➥Null)

</SCRIPT>
```

In the first call to `DisplayMessageBox`, the title parameter is supplied with a non-Null value, so the title `"First Message"` is added to the first message box. In the second call to `DisplayMessageBox`, the title parameter is filled with Null, so the default title

continues

For Visual Basic Programmers: Simulating Optional Parameters in Functions,   *continued*

of "Application Message Box" is used for the message box.

In some cases, Null is a valid value for a parameter. In these cases, a Boolean parameter can be used to indicate whether or not a particular argument was supplied. Using this method, the previous example can be rewritten as follows:

```
<SCRIPT LANGUAGE=VBScript>
Function DisplayMessageBox (strMessage, boolTitleSupplied, strTitle)
   If boolTitleSupplied Then
      DisplayMessageBox = MsgBox (strMessage, 64, strTitle)
   Else
      DisplayMessageBox = MsgBox (strMessage, 64, "Application Message Box")
   End If
End Sub


'
' Main processing begins here
'
   intReturnValue = DisplayMessageBox ("This message uses a custom title.", _
      True, "First Message")

   intReturnValue = DisplayMessageBox ("This message uses the default title.",
      ➥False, Null)
</SCRIPT>
```

The DisplayMessageBox routine checks the Boolean value of the boolTitleSupplied routine to determine whether or not the strTitle parameter has a usable value.

In the first call to DisplayMessageBox, boolTitleSupplied is set to True because a custom title has been supplied. DisplayMessageBox checks boolTitleSupplied, determines the value is True, and uses the custom title in the strTitle parameter.

In the second call to DisplayMessageBox, boolTitleSupplied is set to False and the title parameter is set to Null. DisplayMessageBox checks boolTitleSupplied, determines that the value is False, and uses the default message box title instead. This prevents you from having to check parameters for Null values. In cases where you are dealing with objects, checking the parameter for Null might not be a correct method.

Finally, when creating your own optional parameters, you must have a parameter value for each parameter defined for a function. In other words, if the function is declared with two arguments, you must always supply it with two arguments, even if one or both are Null.

CHAPTER 9

Programming with Events

By Eric Smith

When the first programmable computers were built in the 1950s and 1960s, programs required little or no input from the user. The programmer simply initiated a series of tasks, and the program terminated after completing those tasks. As programs became more interactive, users chose tasks by selecting from menus. However, each selection only led to another series of tasks to perform before the user could return to the menu for the next selection.

In today's event-driven programming, programs are more reactive. Event-driven programming means that programs respond to user actions as they occur. Instead of telling the user what to do or choose next, the event-driven program allows the user to determine the tasks to be performed. The program also responds to requests from the operating system, such as resizing a window.

This chapter discusses event-driven programming, including how to make your program respond to system- and user-generated requests, known as *events*. By using simple events and some VBScript code, you can program complex behavior into your VBScript-enhanced web pages to make a visitor's experience much richer than browsing a simple web page.

This chapter also covers the events available through the ActiveX Control Pad. Although no book can document all the third-party controls available, this chapter illustrates many of the events that are common to most controls. A fundamental understanding of those controls will prove useful when pursuing additional controls.

How Event-Driven Programming Works

Everything you see happen on the screen in an operating system such as Windows results from messages passed from the operating system to a program. For instance, when you press the Tab key to move from one field to another, you initiate a series of events. The following list illustrates the high-level flow of events for this action:

1. Pressing the Tab key triggers an event indicating that the cursor has left a field.

2. If the user changed the data in the field before he hit the Tab key, the program is notified by the operating system with a separate event.

3. When the cursor reaches the next field, the operating system sends another event to the program.

Moving your mouse or pressing the mouse button to reposition the cursor generates additional events. These events are all automatically generated by the operating system. Your program needs only to respond to these events when they occur.

Benefits of Event-Driven Programming

One of the major benefits of coding in Visual Basic instead of Windows is that the operating system sends the appropriate messages to every control to ensure that each one functions correctly. As a result, you don't have to do anything to initiate these events. Visual Basic shields you from having to send all the messages to the appropriate controls to perform something as simple as a mouse click. The Windows operating system handles the messages generated from the controls used on a document. Internet Explorer then receives and translates those system-generated messages into events that you can use in your programming. (VBScript and ActiveX use these features as well.)

As you will learn, many controls contain a wealth of events that you might not ever need to use. However, ActiveX exposes the events so that you can use them if necessary. The number of events used depends on your application's needs: A simple program, such as an animated graphic, might use only a couple events from one control, but a complicated program could use all the events from every control used in a document. You must learn how to choose the correct event to trigger a particular task to be performed at the right time. This task might seem daunting, but the skills you learn in this chapter simplify the process.

The Basics: Creating and Formatting Event Handlers

To tell VBScript that you have code for a particular event, you must create an *event handler,* which is a type of subroutine. As with other subroutines, the event handler contains a declaration, the actual code, and an End Sub keyword at the end. The following is an example of an event handler:

```
Sub Button1_Click()
      ...
      (VBScript code to be executed when this event is triggered)
      ...
   End Sub
```

All event handlers follow this format:

```
   Sub ControlID_EventName(parameter1, parameter2, ...)
      ...
      (VBScript code to be executed when this event is triggered)
      ...
   End Sub
```

The ControlID is the name of the control and is assigned by the programmer. The ActiveX Control Pad allows you to specify the identity of the control so you can reference it later with other VBScript code in the page.

Note   When you use the ActiveX Control Pad and/or VBScript, the ID parameter replaces the Name parameter normally used to name the control. Both are identical in function.

To process an event, an event handler must begin with a name of a control in the document. If you use an outdated name, the code remains unused, and you have some debugging to do. This problem occurs frequently when you name your controls, write code for them, and then rename them.

The EventName is an arbitrary name assigned to a particular event the control handles. A large number of common events can be handled by most controls, including MouseMove and Click. In addition, controls often have additional events that are only used by that control. For instance, a control designed as a timer might contain various events that indicate when a certain period of time has elapsed.

Finally, many events, such as mouse events, contain additional data. Mouse events, for example, typically include the coordinates of the mouse's location when the event occurred. The parameters for these events are specified by the manufacturer of the control. You must declare all parameters when you write the event handler to avoid runtime errors. Events can contain any number of parameters or no parameters.

Basic Control Events

Now that you have learned the basic structure for all event handlers, you will examine the events of the basic controls included on the ActiveX Control Pad. After you become familiar with the events and their codes, you will be able to use the Control Pad's interface to write more efficient event handlers.

CheckBox Control Events

TheCheckBox control allows a user to turn a selection on or off. Unlike the OptionButton control, each CheckBox control works independently and does not depend on the values of other CheckBox controls in the same document. Think of a CheckBox control like an item you might put on a salad: You can have green peppers, but it doesn't matter whether or not you put tomatoes on the salad. Each choice is independent.

Note   For Visual Basic programmers already familiar with the CheckBox control, some of the following events are new or enhanced from version 4 of Visual Basic. These differences are noted for your reference with asterisks.

The CheckBox control generates the following events that are available for scripting within the ActiveX Control Pad. The following section, "Event Documentation," describes each event in detail.

- ◆ AfterUpdate *

- ◆ BeforeDragOver *

- ◆ BeforeDropOrPaste *

- ◆ BeforeUpdate *

- ◆ Change

- ◆ Click

◆ DblClick

◆ Enter *

◆ Error *

◆ Exit *

◆ KeyDown, KeyUp

◆ KeyPress

◆ MouseDown, MouseUp

◆ MouseMove

Note The "Event Documentation" section later in this chapter describes each of the events in the following sections in detail.

ComboBox Control Events

The ComboBox, or drop-down list box, allows you to present a series of choices from which the user can select an entry. In another variation of this control, the user can type information into the text portion of the control. This control supports the following events:

◆ AfterUpdate *

◆ BeforeDragOver *

◆ BeforeDropOrPaste *

◆ BeforeUpdate *

◆ Change

◆ Click

◆ DblClick

◆ Enter *

◆ Error *

◆ Exit *

- ◆ KeyDown, KeyUp

- ◆ KeyPress

- ◆ MouseDown, MouseUp

- ◆ MouseMove

CommandButton Control Events

The CommandButton control creates buttons on the document. These buttons do not remain depressed on the screen; rather, clicking a button prompts it to go down and come back up immediately. The following list details this control's events:

- ◆ AfterUpdate *

- ◆ BeforeDragOver *

- ◆ BeforeDropOrPaste *

- ◆ BeforeUpdate *

- ◆ Change

- ◆ Click

- ◆ DblClick

- ◆ Enter *

- ◆ Error *

- ◆ Exit *

- ◆ KeyDown, KeyUp

- ◆ KeyPress

- ◆ MouseDown, MouseUp

- ◆ MouseMove

HotSpot Control Events

The HotSpot control is a unique control that allows you to detect when a mouse pointer is within a particular area. With this control, you can easily create clickable images in various areas that perform actions when the user clicks on them. This control is invisible at runtime to allow the control, graphic, or text below it to appear. This control supports the following events:

◆ Click

◆ DblClick

◆ Enter *

◆ Exit *

◆ MouseDown, MouseUp

◆ MouseEnter, MouseExit *

◆ MouseMove

Note   The Hotspot control was not available in Visual Basic, version 4. It is a new control introduced with the ActiveX Control Pad. However, the Click, DblClick, MouseDown, MouseUp, and MouseMove events function the same way with this control as they do with other controls.

HTML Layout Control Events

The HTML Layout control is essentially identical to the Visual Basic Form control: The control contains all the controls in a document. The HTML Layout control only contains the onLoad event, which can be used for code to be run when a document first loads. This control is demonstrated at the end of this chapter.

Image Control Events

The Image control displays graphics to the user. This control supports a number of formats, including the GIF (both '87 and '89), JPEG, Windows Metafile (WMF), and the Windows Bitmap (BMP) formats. Support for the JPEG and GIF formats will be welcome to Visual Basic developers who have until now been forced to obtain third-party controls to view these files in their applications. The following list details the Image control's events:

◆ BeforeDragOver *

◆ BeforeDropOrPaste *

◆ Enter *

◆ Exit *

◆ MouseDown, MouseUp

◆ MouseMove

Note The Image control was not available in Visual Basic, version 4. It is a new control introduced with the ActiveX Control Pad. This control is different from both the PictureBox and Image controls included with Visual Basic because this control supports both the GIF and JPEG formats. However, the Click, DblClick, Mouse-Down, MouseUp, and MouseMove events function the same way with this control as they do with other controls.

Label Control Events

The Label control displays text to the user. With this control, you can display multiple fonts, but it is advisable to stick to basic fonts, such as Times New Roman and Arial, that are installed with Windows. If you choose a font that is not normally installed with Windows, users who do not have this font will not see your page correctly. As of this writing, Microsoft is attempting to implement TrueType fonts that can be down-loaded to allow the user to obtain the proper font for your text. This control includes the following events:

◆ AfterUpdate *

◆ BeforeDragOver *

◆ BeforeDropOrPaste *

◆ BeforeUpdate *

◆ Click

◆ DblClick

◆ Enter, Exit *

◆ Error *

◆ KeyPress

◆ MouseDown, MouseUp

◆ MouseMove

ListBox Control Events

The ListBox control displays a list of items to a user. Typically, the ListBox works with large lists of items that would be unwieldy as CheckBox controls. Unlike the Combo-Box control, which hides its list after the user finishes, the ListBox control displays the entire list. This control includes the following events:

◆ AfterUpdate *

◆ BeforeDragOver *

◆ BeforeDropOrPaste *

◆ BeforeUpdate *

◆ Change

◆ Click

◆ DblClick

◆ Enter *

◆ Error *

◆ Exit *

◆ KeyDown, KeyUp

◆ KeyPress

◆ MouseDown, MouseUp

◆ MouseMove

OptionButton Control Events

The OptionButton control, or radio button, allows the user to choose an option from a group of selections, as the name *radio button* suggests, the control works in a manner similar to older radios. With these radios, only one station's selection button could be pressed at a time. If you picked another button, the previous one would pop back up. The OptionButton controls work the same way: If you select one option button in a group and then click on another, the first button will be deselected. This control includes the following events:

◆ AfterUpdate *

◆ BeforeDragOver *

- ◆ BeforeDropOrPaste *

- ◆ BeforeUpdate *

- ◆ Change

- ◆ Click

- ◆ DblClick

- ◆ Enter *

- ◆ Error *

- ◆ Exit *

- ◆ KeyDown, KeyUp

- ◆ KeyPress

- ◆ MouseDown, MouseUp

- ◆ MouseMove

ScrollBar Control Events

The ScrollBar control specifies values within a range. For instance, this control could be used as a volume or speed control, because both volume and speed typically exist within a range of valid values. The ScrollBar control includes the following events:

- ◆ AfterUpdate *

- ◆ BeforeDragOver *

- ◆ BeforeDropOrPaste *

- ◆ BeforeUpdate *

- ◆ Change

- ◆ Enter *

- ◆ Error *

- ◆ Exit *

- ◆ KeyDown, KeyUp

- ◆ KeyPress

- ◆ Scroll

SpinButton Control Events

The SpinButton control allows you to increase or decrease a numerical value by clicking an Up or Down button. This controls works with dialog boxes, such as the Print dialog box, which allows you to specify the number of copies by clicking the appropriate buttons. This control should only be used with small numbers; large numbers require the user to scroll too much. This control includes the following events:

- ◆ AfterUpdate *
- ◆ BeforeDragOver *
- ◆ BeforeDropOrPaste *
- ◆ BeforeUpdate *
- ◆ Change
- ◆ Enter, Exit *
- ◆ Error *
- ◆ KeyDown, KeyUp
- ◆ KeyPress
- ◆ SpinDown, SpinUp

TabStrip Control Events

The TabStrip control allows you to group controls into a tabbed dialog box so that the user can navigate between groups of options more easily. This control operates in a similar manner as the tabbed dialog boxes that are common in Windows 95 applications. This control includes the following events:

- ◆ BeforeDragOver *
- ◆ BeforeDropOrPaste *
- ◆ Change
- ◆ Click
- ◆ DblClick
- ◆ Enter, Exit *
- ◆ Error *

◆ KeyDown, KeyUp

◆ KeyPress

◆ MouseDown, MouseUp

◆ MouseMove

TextBox Control Events

One of the most common controls, the TextBox control, allows the user to enter single or multiple lines of text. TextBox supports the following events:

◆ AfterUpdate *

◆ BeforeDragOver *

◆ BeforeDropOrPaste *

◆ BeforeUpdate *

◆ Change

◆ Click

◆ DblClick

◆ Enter *

◆ Error *

◆ Exit *

◆ KeyDown, KeyUp

◆ KeyPress

◆ MouseDown, MouseUp

◆ MouseMove

ToggleButton Control Events

In many Windows 95 applications, such as Microsoft Word, certain buttons must have the capability to display their current status. For instance, the Bold button on the Microsoft Word toolbar indicates that it is active by remaining in the down position. The ToggleButton control allows you to implement these functions in ActiveX and VBScript. As with the CheckBox control, buttons can be independent of each other.

In addition, the buttons can function like OptionButton controls. For example, you can select one item in a group, such as the left/right/center buttons in Microsoft Word. This control supports the following events:

◆ AfterUpdate *

◆ BeforeDragOver *

◆ BeforeDropOrPaste *

◆ BeforeUpdate *

◆ Change

◆ Click

◆ DblClick

◆ Enter, Exit *

◆ Error *

◆ KeyDown, KeyUp

◆ KeyPress

◆ MouseDown, MouseUp

◆ MouseMove

Event Documentation

This section fully documents all the events available to the controls previously discussed. Although the events for many of the controls have the same names, the events mean slightly different things to each of the controls. These differences are noted for reference in this section.

AfterUpdate Event

When the user moves from one control to another in a document, the operating system sends a series of messages to Internet Explorer. These messages appear in the form of events within VBScript. First, the BeforeUpdate event is processed. In this event, you can undo the change to the control by setting the Cancel parameter to True. After this event is complete, the AfterUpdate event occurs. The AfterUpdate event can be used for storage or additional validation of the data that the user enters.

Unlike the BeforeUpdate event, the AfterUpdate event cannot be canceled. Finally, both the BeforeUpdate and AfterUpdate events will not be activated if you change the Value property of the control through code.

Note For Visual Basic programmers who are familiar with the unexpected events generated when a program—not the user—changes the control's data, the BeforeUpdate and AfterUpdate events are welcome additions to Visual Basic and VBScript. These two events allow you to move validation code that checks user input into a location where it won't be accidentally triggered.

The declaration for this event, which is generated by the ActiveX Control Pad, is illustrated here for reference.

```
Sub CheckBox_AfterUpdate()
```

This event, as well as the other mouse and data modification events, appears in an example at the end of this chapter. The example illustrates the interaction and timing of each event in typical user actions.

BeforeDragOver Event

Because VBScript and ActiveX function within the Windows environment, enabling your application with drag-and-drop functionality adds a whole new dimension. Using this event in combination with the BeforeDropOrPaste event allows you to monitor the user's location in the drag-and-drop operation.

The BeforeDragOver event is triggered during a drag-and-drop operation. However, this event will be triggered each time there is a small change of the mouse position or when a mouse button is pressed. Fortunately, the event parameters make it easy to determine when the state of the operation has changed, such as when the user has moved an object over a target area.

A *target area* is a control, such as the Windows 95 Desktop, that is coded to accept dropped objects. When you create a shortcut in Explorer and drag it to the desktop, the desktop becomes the target area for that shortcut.

Table 9.1 illustrates the parameters for the BeforeDragOver event. The actual declaration of this event follows the table. All these parameters are, as usual, of type Variant, but their subtypes are shown in table 9.1.

Table 9.1
BeforeDragOver Event Parameters

Name	Variant Subtype	Description
Cancel	Boolean	The Cancel parameter allows you to cancel the drag-and-drop operation. Setting this parameter to True achieves the same function as if the user were dropping the object on an area that is not a valid target.
Data	Object	This parameter is the formatted text dragged by the user and the parameter is stored in an object type known as the DataObject. DataObjects store text that is dragged from one control to another, such as text dragged within or between multiple TextBox controls. After the dragging operation, the data can be retrieved from this object and placed into the target object, when applicable.
X	Single	This is the horizontal position, of the mouse, when the event is activated. The position is measured from the left edge of the screen, and its value is expressed in points, which are $\frac{1}{72}$ of an inch.
Y	Single	This is the Y coordinate, or the vertical position of the mouse when the event is activated. The position is measured from the top edge of the screen, and its value is expressed in points, which are $\frac{1}{72}$ of an inch.
DragState	Integer	The DragState parameter allows you to determine the state of the drag-and-drop operation. This parameter can incorporate one of three values:
		◆ 0—The cursor is currently above the object receiving the event. If the user terminates the drag-and-drop operation by releasing the mouse button, the BeforeDropOrPaste event would handle the dropped data.
		◆ 1—The mouse is no longer above the current object.

continues

Table 9.1, Continued
BeforeDragOver Event Parameters

Name	Variant Subtype	Description
		◆ 2—This mouse has moved, but it still remains above the current object.
		During a drag-and-drop operation, the BeforeDragOver event uses the DragState parameter set to 0 when the mouse first passes over the object. A series of 2s follows as the user moves across the object. This series precedes a 1, which is initiated when the user moves the mouse away from the object.
Effect	Integer	The effect parameter indicates whether the source of the drag-and-drop operation can support copy or move operations. By checking this value, you can determine the operation to perform. The following list details this parameter's values:
		◆ 0—The source of the operation does not support a copy or a move operation. The only valid operation is to cancel the drag-and-drop action.
		◆ 1—The source supports a copy operation.
		◆ 2—The source supports a move operation.
		◆ 3—The source supports both a copy and a move operation.
Shift	Integer	This parameter indicates whether the user presses the Shift, Ctrl, or Alt keys during the operation. In other applications, such as Windows Explorer, dragging a file with one of these keys performs a different operation than would otherwise be performed.

Name	Variant Subtype	Description
		◆ 0—No keys are pressed.
		◆ 1—The user presses one or both Shift keys.
		◆ 2—The user presses one or both Ctrl keys.
		◆ 4—The user presses one or both Alt keys.
		These values can be added together in cases where two or more keys are pressed. The following list illustrates the combinations and the keys pressed:
		◆ 1—Shift
		◆ 2—Ctrl
		◆ 3—Shift and Ctrl
		◆ 4—Alt
		◆ 5—Alt and Shift
		◆ 6 Alt and Ctrl
		◆ 7—Alt, Shift, and Ctrl

Note

Unlike most Visual Basic mouse coordinates, which are measured in twips, VBScript and ActiveX coordinate values are expressed in points. Twips are approximately $1/1440$ of an inch, but a point is $1/72$ of an inch. Most other coordinates, such as the Top and Left properties, are specified in points.

The declaration, which is generated by the ActiveX Control Pad for this event, is shown here for reference.

```
Sub Control_BeforeDragOver(ByVal Cancel, ByVal Data, _
    ByVal X, ByVal Y, _
    ByVal DragState, ByVal Effect, _
    ByVal Shift
```

For more information on this and the other features of drag-and-drop, refer to the example documented at the end of this chapter.

BeforeDropOrPaste Event

Because VBScript and ActiveX function in the Windows environment, enabling your application with the drag-and-drop function equips the system with an added dimension. Using this event in combination with the BeforeDragOver allows you to determine when the user has dropped an object and what actions to initiate in response.

The BeforeDropOrPaste event is activated by a completed drag-and-drop operation. The parameters of this event are similar to the BeforeDragOver event, so you can determine exactly what parameters were in effect during the drag-and-drop operation.

Table 9.2 illustrates the parameters for the BeforeDropOrPaste event. The actual declaration of this event is shown following this table. All parameters are, as usual, of type Variant, but their subtypes are shown in the table that follows.

Table 9.2
BeforeDropOrPaste Event Parameters

Name	Variant Subtype	Description
Cancel	Boolean	The Cancel parameter allows you to cancel the drag-and-drop operation. Setting this parameter to True achieves the same function as the user dropping the object on an area that is not a valid target.
Action	Integer	The Action parameter indicates the action to be taken on the dropped object. ♦ 2—The user pasted the object onto the target object. This action bears similarity to the function in Windows Explorer that allows you to cut and paste files between directories. ♦ 3—The user dragged an object from a source control to this control and dropped it.
Data	Object	This parameter is the formatted text dragged by the user and is stored in an object type known as the DataObject. DataObjects store text dragged from one control to another, such as text dragged within or between multiple TextBox controls. After the dragging operation, the data can be retrieved from this object and placed into the target object, when applicable.

Name	Variant Subtype	Description
X	Single	This is the X coordinate, or the horizontal position of the mouse, when the event is activated. The position is measured from the left edge of the screen, and its value is expressed in points, which are $\frac{1}{72}$ of an inch.
Y	Single	This is the Y coordinate, or the vertical position of the mouse, when the event is activated. The position is measured from the top edge of the screen, and its value is expressed in points, which are $\frac{1}{72}$ of an inch.
Effect	Integer	The effect parameter indicates whether the source of the drag-and-drop operation can support and/or move operations. By checking this value, you can determine the operation to perform. The following list details this parameter's values. ◆ 0—The source of the operation does not support a copy or move operation. The only valid operation is to cancel the drag-and-drop action. ◆ 1—The source supports a copy operation. ◆ 2—The source supports a move operation. ◆ 3—The source control supports both a copy and a move operation.
Shift	Integer	This parameter indicates whether the user presses the Shift, Ctrl, or Alt keys during the operation. In other applications, such as Windows Explorer, dragging a file with one of these keys will perform a different operation than would otherwise be performed. ◆ 0—No keys are pressed. ◆ 1—The user presses one or both Shift keys. ◆ 2—The user presses one or both Ctrl keys. ◆ 4—The user presses one or both Alt keys.

continues

Table 9.2, Continued
BeforeDropOrPaste Event Parameters

Name	Variant Subtype	Description
		These values can be added together in cases where two or more keys are pressed. The following list illustrates the combinations and the keys pressed:

- 1—Shift
- 2—Ctrl
- 3—Shift and Ctrl
- 4—Alt
- 5—Alt and Shift
- 6—Alt and Ctrl
- 7—Alt, Shift, and Ctrl

The declaration for this event, which is generated by the ActiveX Control Pad, is shown here for reference.

```
Sub Control_BeforeDropOrPaste(ByVal Cancel, ByVal Action, _
    ByVal Data, _
    ByVal X, ByVal Y, _
    ByVal Effect, ByVal Shift
```

For more information on this and the other features of drag-and-drop, refer to the example documented at the end of this chapter.

BeforeUpdate Event

When the user moves from one control to another within a document, a series of events take place. First, the BeforeUpdate event is processed. In this event, you can undo the change to the control by setting the Cancel parameter to True. After that event is complete, the AfterUpdate event occurs. The BeforeUpdate event can be used for storage or additional validation of the data the user enters.

The BeforeUpdate's Cancel parameter, its only parameter, can be set to True to cancel the change in the control. To perform this action, use the UndoUpdate method, as shown in this example:

```
Sub Control_BeforeUpdate(ByVal Cancel)

   If (somecondition) Then
      Control.UndoUpdate
      Cancel = True
      Exit Sub
   Else
      ...
      remainder of code
   End If
```

Neither the BeforeUpdate or AfterUpdate events are activated if the Value property of the control is changed through code. For Visual Basic programmers who are familiar with the inadvertent events generated when a program—not the user—changes the control's data, the BeforeUpdate and AfterUpdate events are welcome additions to the repertoire of Visual Basic and VBScript. These two events enable you to move validation code that checks user input into a location that won't be inadvertently triggered.

The declaration for this event, which is generated by the ActiveX Control Pad, is shown here for reference.

```
Sub Control_BeforeUpdate(ByVal Cancel)
```

This event, and other mouse and data modification events, are demonstrated in an example at the end of this chapter that illustrates the interaction and timing of each event in typical user actions.

Change Event

The Change event, which is common to almost all the controls discussed in this chapter, occurs when the Value property of the control changes. Because the control's Value property changes when a user clicks the control, a Change event immediately follows a Click event. The BeforeUpdate and AfterUpdate events also are activated at the same time.

Unlike the BeforeUpdate and AfterUpdate events, the Change event is triggered by programmatic changes to the Value property of the Change event. Therefore, any validation code reserved for user actions should be incorporated into the BeforeUpdate or AfterUpdate events.

The declaration for this event, which is generated by the ActiveX Control Pad, is shown here for reference.

```
Sub Control_Change()
```

This event, and other mouse and data modification events, are demonstrated in an example at the end of this chapter that illustrate the interaction and timing of each event in typical user actions.

Click Event

This event is as simple as its name: Click events occur when the user presses the mouse down and releases it. Although a Click event occurs at the same time as a MouseDown followed by a MouseUp event, not every MouseDown event and MouseUp event will constitute a click. For instance, if the user presses the mouse button and then drags the mouse off the window, no Click event is generated.

The declaration for this event, which is generated by the ActiveX Control Pad, is shown here for reference.

```
Sub Control_Click()
```

DblClick Event

This event indicates that the user has clicked twice in rapid succession on a control. In many cases, a double-click is not a valid action. For example, the user normally does not double-click a button. Most users are familiar with double-clicking an icon to start a program in Windows Explorer.

The declaration for this event, which is generated by the ActiveX Control Pad, is shown here for reference.

```
Sub Control_DblClick()
```

Enter Event

When a user traverses a window, he generates events when he enters and leaves controls. The user generates the Enter event by setting the input focus to a control. A blinking cursor in the control indicates input focus for TextBox controls, and a dotted outline around a control indicates the input focus for the CheckBox and OptionButton controls. The Enter event immediately follows the Exit event for the control that previously contained the focus.

The declaration for this event, which is generated by the ActiveX Control Pad, is shown here for reference.

```
Sub Control_Enter()
```

This event, and other mouse and data modification events, are demonstrated in an example at the end of this chapter that illustrates the interaction and timing of each event in typical user actions.

Error Event

The Error event is activated when the control itself detects an error that cannot be handled by the calling program. In these cases, the error handling code you write for this event will handle the error correctly.

For more information on error handling and this event, please refer to Chapter 10, "Debugging Your Script."

Exit Event

When a user traverses a window, he generates events when he enters and leaves controls. The user generates the Exit event when he moves the input focus from the current control to a new control elsewhere in the document. A blinking cursor in the control indicates input focus for TextBox controls, and a dotted outline around a control indicates the input focus for the CheckBox and OptionButton controls. The Exit event immediately precedes an Enter event on the next control to gain the input focus.

The declaration for this event, which is generated by the ActiveX Control Pad, is shown here for reference.

```
Sub Control_Enter()
```

This event, and other mouse and data modification events, are demonstrated in an example at the end of this chapter that illustrates the interaction and timing of each event in typical user actions.

KeyDown, KeyUp Events

Even in the world of mouse clicks, some input still must be done with the keyboard. Every time you press a key on the keyboard, two events are triggered: KeyDown, followed by KeyUp. In addition, the KeyPress event follows the KeyDown event. However, the KeyPress event only recognizes the character that was entered. The KeyDown and KeyUp events can determine other information, such as whether the Shift, Ctrl, or Alt key was pressed at the time of the key press. These events can detect any key press, including function key, navigation key (Home, End, PageUp, and so on), and even Tab key presses. (The KeyPress event normally ignores Tab key or other function key presses.)

The identical parameters for both events are shown in table 9.3.

Table 9.3
Parameters for the KeyDown, KeyUp Events

Name	Variant Subtype	Description
KeyCode	Integer	This code refers to the key that was pressed. Refer to the following list to decode the number into a keyboard key.
Shift	Integer	This parameter indicates whether the user presses the Shift, Ctrl, or Alt keys during the operation.

◆ 0—No keys are pressed.

◆ 1—The user presses one or both Shift keys.

◆ 2—The user presses one or both Ctrl keys.

◆ 4—The user presses one or both Alt keys.

These values can be added together in cases where two or more keys are pressed. The following list illustrates the combinations and the keys pressed:

◆ 1—Shift

◆ 2—Ctrl

◆ 3—Shift and Ctrl

◆ 4—Alt

◆ 5—Alt and Shift

◆ 6—Alt and Ctrl

◆ 7—Alt, Shift, and Ctrl

The following list contains the keycodes for each character on the standard U.S. keyboard. ASCII codes range from 0 to 255; however, the characters in the 128-255 range cannot be entered directly from the keyboard.

Value	Description	Value	Description	Value	Description	Value	Description
0	Null	32	space	64	@	96	'
1	Ctrl-A	33	!	65	A	97	a
2	Ctrl-B	34	"	66	B	98	b

3	Ctrl-C	35	#	67	C	99	c
4	Ctrl-D	36	$	68	D	100	d
5	Ctrl-E	37	%	69	E	101	e
6	Ctrl-F	38	&	70	F	102	f
7	Ctrl-G	39	'	71	G	103	g
8	Ctrl-H (Backspace)	40	(	72	H	104	h
9	Ctrl-I (Tab)	41	)	73	I	105	i
10	Ctrl-J (Line Feed)	42	*	74	J	106	j
11	Ctrl-K	43	+	75	K	107	k
12	Ctrl-L (Page Feed)	44	,	76	L	108	l
13	Ctrl-M (Enter)	45	-	77	M	109	m
14	Ctrl-N	46	.	78	N	110	n
15	Ctrl-O	47	/	79	O	111	o
16	Ctrl-P	48	0	80	P	112	p
17	Ctrl-Q	49	1	81	Q	113	q
18	Ctrl-R	50	2	82	R	114	r
19	Ctrl-S	51	3	83	S	115	s
20	Ctrl-T	52	4	84	T	116	t
21	Ctrl-U	53	5	85	U	117	u
22	Ctrl-V	54	6	86	V	118	v
23	Ctrl-W	55	7	87	W	119	w
24	Ctrl-X	56	8	88	X	120	x
25	Ctrl-Y	57	9	89	Y	121	y
26	Ctrl-Z	58	:	90	Z	122	z
27	Unused	59	;	91	[	123	{
28	Unused	60	<	92	\	124	|
29	Unused	61	=	93	]	125	}
30	Unused	62	>	94	^	126	~
31	Unused	63	?	95	_	127	

The declaration for both events, which is generated by the ActiveX Control Pad, are shown here for reference.

```
Sub Control_KeyDown(ByVal KeyCode, ByVal Shift)
Sub Control_KeyUp(ByVal KeyCode, ByVal Shift)
```

These events, and other mouse and data modification events, are demonstrated in an example at the end of this chapter that illustrates the interaction and timing of each event in typical user actions.

KeyPress Event

The KeyPress event acts as a simplified version of the KeyUp, KeyDown events just described. KeyPress only recognizes printable characters, such as numbers and letters. In most applications, using this event simplifies your work. The event's only parameter, KeyAscii, is the ASCII value of the letter that was pressed. Pressing a non-character key, such as an arrow key, does not generate the KeyPress event. This simplifies your code, because you don't have to check for those types of key presses. Any keys not listed in the previous ASCII character list will not generate a KeyPress event. This includes the function keys, the arrows, and the NumLock, ScrollLock, CapsLock, Pause/Break, and PrintScrn keys.

The declaration for this event, which is generated by the ActiveX Control Pad, is shown here for reference.

```
Sub Control_KeyPress(ByVal KeyAscii)
```

This event, and other mouse and data modification events, are demonstrated in an example at the end of this chapter that illustrates the interaction and timing of each event in typical user actions.

MouseDown, MouseUp Events

The user generates a MouseDown event by pressing any of the mouse buttons. Likewise, the user generates the MouseUp event by releasing the button. Because both the Click and DblClick events respond to clicking buttons, the process follows a normal order of events:

1. MouseDown

2. MouseUp

3. Click

4. DblClick

5. MouseUp

If the user clicks the button in the normal manner, he will trigger a MouseDown event, followed by a MouseUp event, followed by the Click event. For a double-click of the mouse button, however, the DblClick event will be preceded by MouseDown, MouseUp, Click, and a MouseUp event.

These events contain identical parameters, which are explained below in table 9.4.

Table 9.4
Parameters for MouseDown and MouseUp Events

Name	Variant Subtype	Description
Button	Integer	This value indicates the buttons currently depressed. This control returns values for three distinct buttons, as follows: ◆ 1—Left button ◆ 2—Right button ◆ 4—Middle button These values can also be combined to indicate that more than one button was pressed: ◆ 1—Left button ◆ 2—Right button ◆ 3—Left and right buttons ◆ 4—Middle button ◆ 5—Left and middle buttons ◆ 6—Right and middle buttons ◆ 7—Left, right, and middle buttons In most cases, programs only support one pressed button at a time.
Shift	Integer	This parameter indicates whether the user presses the Shift, Ctrl, or Alt keys during the operation.

continues

Table 9.4, Continued
Parameters for MouseDown and MouseUp Events

Name	Variant Subtype	Description
		◆ 0—no keys are pressed.
		◆ 1—The user presses one or both Shift keys.
		◆ 2—The user presses one or both Ctrl keys.
		◆ 4—The user presses one or both Alt keys.
		These values can be added together in cases where two or more keys are pressed. The following list illustrates the combinations and the keys pressed:
		◆ 1—Shift
		◆ 2—Ctrl
		◆ 3—Shift and Ctrl
		◆ 4—Alt
		◆ 5—Alt and Shift
		◆ 6—Alt and Ctrl
		◆ 7—Alt, Shift, and Ctrl
X	Single	This is the X coordinate, or the horizontal position of the mouse, when the event is activated. The position is measured from the left edge of the screen, and the value is expressed in points, which are $\frac{1}{72}$ of an inch.
Y	Single	This is the Y coordinate, or the vertical position of the mouse, when the event is triggered. The position is measured from the top edge of the screen, and its value is expressed in points, which are $\frac{1}{72}$ of an inch.

The declaration for this event, which is generated by the ActiveX Control Pad, follows for reference.

```
Sub Control_MouseDown(ByVal Button, ByVal Shift, _
    ByVal X, ByVal Y
Sub Control_MouseUp(ByVal Button, ByVal Shift, _
    ByVal X, ByVal Y
```

These events, and other mouse and data modification events, are demonstrated in an example at the end of this chapter that illustrates the interaction and timing of each event in typical user actions.

MouseMove Event

Every time the mouse moves, it generates the MouseMove event. This event can be used for tracking, particularly when performing graphic operations. The MouseMove event also can generate ToolTips (the yellow boxes that appear when you leave your mouse over a control). The parameters for this event are identical to the MouseDown and MouseUp events and are shown below in table 9.5 for reference:

Table 9.5
Parameters for MouseMove Event

Name	Variant Subtype	Description
Button	Integer	This value indicates the buttons currently depressed. This control returns values for three distinct buttons, as follows:
		◆ 1—Left button
		◆ 2—Right button
		◆ 4—Middle button
		These values also can be combined to indicate that more than one button was pressed:
		◆ 1—Left button
		◆ 2—Right button
		◆ 3—Left and right buttons
		◆ 4—Middle buttons
		◆ 5—Left and middle buttons
		◆ 6—Right and middle buttons
		◆ 7—Left, right, and middle buttons

continues

Table 9.5, Continued
Parameters for MouseMove Event

Name	Variant Subtype	Description
		In most cases, programs only support one pressed button at a time.
Shift	Integer	This parameter indicates whether the user presses the Shift, Ctrl, or Alt keys during the operation.
		◆ 0—No keys are pressed.
		◆ 1—The user presses one or both Shift keys.
		◆ 2—The user presses one or both Ctrl.
		◆ 4—The user presses one or both Alt keys.
		These values can be added together in cases where two or more keys are pressed. The following list illustrates combinations and the keys pressed:
		◆ 1—Shift
		◆ 2—Ctrl
		◆ 3—Shift and Ctrl
		◆ 4—Alt
		◆ 5—Alt and Shift
		◆ 6—Alt and Ctrl
		◆ 7—Alt, Shift, and Ctrl
X	Single	This is the X coordinate, or the horizontal position of the mouse, when the event is activated. The position is measured from the left edge of the screen, and its value is expressed in points, which are $\frac{1}{72}$ of an inch.
Y	Single	This is the Y coordinate, or the vertical position of the mouse, when the event is activated. The position is measured from the top edge of the screen, and its value is expressed in points, which are $\frac{1}{72}$ of an inch.

The declaration for this event, which is generated by the ActiveX Control Pad, is shown here for reference.

```
Sub Control_MouseMove(ByVal Button, ByVal Shift, _
    ByVal X, ByVal Y
```

This event, and other mouse and data modification events, are demonstrated in an example at the end of this chapter that illustrates the interaction and timing of each event in typical user actions.

Scroll Event

The user activates the Scroll event on the ScrollBar control by moving the slider control. This event contains no parameters. When it occurs, check the Value property of the ScrollBar control to determine its new value.

The declaration of this event, which is generated by the ActiveX Control Pad, is shown here for reference.

```
Sub ScrollBar_Scroll()
```

This event is demonstrated in an example located at the end of Chapter 12, "Using the Built-In ActiveX Controls."

SpinUp, SpinDown Events

The user activates these two events by pressing either the up or down button on the SpinButton control. The SpinUp event indicates that the Value property has increased by the specified amount set in the SmallChange property of the control. The SpinDown event indicates that the Value property has decreased by the same amount.

The declaration of these events, which are generated by the ActiveX Control Pad, is shown here for reference.

```
Sub SpinButton_SpinUp()
Sub SpinButton_SpinDown()
```

These events, as well as the other specialized control events, are demonstrated in an example at the end of this chapter.

This event is demonstrated in an example located at the end of Chapter 12, "Using the Built-In ActiveX Controls."

Examples

Data Events Example

Many of the events just discussed deal with data entry and the events that occur as a user moves around a form. This example shows you exactly what events happen when you perform various actions in this form. The following events will be demonstrated in this example:

◆ AfterUpdate

◆ BeforeUpdate

◆ Change

◆ Enter

◆ Exit

◆ KeyDown

◆ KeyUp

◆ KeyPress

On the CD

This example is provided on the CD-ROM and is located in the `\Examples\Chapter9` folder. The file name is `DataEvents.html`.

Open the example in Internet Explorer. This simple data entry form is designed to help you learn about the data modification events. Each event will add a line to the Event Log box. To start, click in the topmost text box, which is labeled TextBox1. The following line will be added to the Event Log:

```
TextBox1 - Enter Event
```

The Enter event is triggered whenever the cursor is moved to a new location. In this case, you placed the cursor in the text box. Now click in the second text box, labeled TextBox2. The following lines will be added to the Event Log:

```
TextBox1 - Exit Event
TextBox2 - Enter Event
```

The Exit event is triggered on TextBox1 immediately before the Enter event for TextBox2 is triggered. The Exit event indicates that the cursor has been moved out of this control to somewhere else on the form. If you now click in TextBox3, you will see a similar result:

```
TextBox2 - Exit Event
TextBox3 - Enter Event
```

Finally, click on the Event Log. You will see the following entry added to the log when the cursor moves:

```
TextBox3 - Exit Event
```

The Exit event registers when you move the cursor out of TextBox3. The Event Log control also receives an Enter event; however, this program does not log events other than those that occur to the three text boxes.

Now that you see how these two events work together, you are ready to learn about the other events that occur to these text boxes. Press the Clear Log button and then put the cursor in TextBox1. Once the cursor is in TextBox1, press any letter key, such as a lowercase *a*. The following events will be generated:

```
TextBox1 - KeyDown Event, KeyCode: 65, Shift: 0
TextBox1 - KeyPress Event, KeyAscii: 97
TextBox1 - Change Event
TextBox1 - KeyUp Event, KeyCode: 65, Shift: 0
```

When you press the a key down, the KeyDown event fires first. If you look at the KeyCode, you will notice that the 65 actually is the ASCII code for the uppercase A. If you pressed the lowercase a, why does the uppercase A code display? The uppercase letter's code displays because the KeyDown and KeyUp events display the hardware code for the key. The hardware code does not always match with the ASCII values. Letters have the same hardware code as their uppercase ASCII value; that is, both lowercase and uppercase A have a code of 65. Numbers have the same hardware code as their ASCII value, and punctuation marks above the numbers will have the same hardware code as the number key they are on.

The following list lists the hardware keycodes for each key on a standard U.S. keyboard. Some of these keys may not be on your keyboard since the keycodes are standard across all keyboards, regardless of manufacturer or model.

Value	Description	Value	Description
1	Left mouse button	97	1 key
2	Right mouse button	98	2 key
3	CANCEL key	99	3 key
4	Middle mouse button	100	4 key
5	BACKSPACE key	101	5 key
6	TAB key	102	6 key

Value	Description	Value	Description
12	CLEAR key	103	7 key
13	ENTER key	104	8 key
16	SHIFT key	105	9 key
17	CTRL key	106	Multiplication sign (*) key
18	MENU key	107	Plus sign (+) key
19	PAUSE key	108	ENTER key
20	CAPS LOCK key	109	Minus sign (–) key
27	ESC key	110	Decimal point (.) key
32	SPACEBAR key	111	Division sign (/) key
33	PAGE UP key	112	F1 key
34	PAGE DOWN key	113	F2 key
35	END key	114	F3 key
36	HOME key	115	F4 key
37	LEFT ARROW key	116	F5 key
38	UP ARROW key	117	F6 key
39	RIGHT ARROW key	118	F7 key
40	DOWN ARROW key	119	F8 key
41	SELECT key	120	F9 key
42	PRINT SCREEN key	121	F10 key
43	EXECUTE key	122	F11 key
44	SNAPSHOT key	123	F12 key
45	INS key	124	F13 key
46	DEL key	125	F14 key
47	HELP key	126	F15 key
96	0 key	127	F16 key
		144	NUM LOCK key

Note Keys 96-111 are the keys on the numeric keypad.

For letters, the uppercase letter's code will be displayed. However, the computer also has to know if that key was pressed in combination with another key. The Shift parameter is used for that purpose. The Shift parameter will be a sum of the following values:

0—No modifier key was pressed

1—Shift key was pressed

2—Ctrl key was pressed

4—Alt key was pressed

In this case, you did not press the Shift or any other modifier key, so the Shift parameter is 0. The computer recognizes that if no modifier keys are pressed in combination with a letter key, then the letter should be lowercase. The KeyPress event is then triggered with the correct ASCII value for a lowercase a, which is 97.

Next, the Change event is triggered, which indicates that the contents of the TextBox were changed. Finally, the KeyUp event is triggered when you release the a key. The KeyUp event has the same parameters as the KeyDown event; that is, the Keycode and the Shift parameters. Four events for a simple keystroke? It may seem like a lot, but you gain a lot of flexibility in coding by using the appropriate event, as you will see later in this example. Try pressing other letters and watch the events as they display in the Event Log. You will see the same pattern of four events per letter that you type.

Next, try entering a capital letter. For instance, if you were to press Shift+A, the following events will be triggered and listed in the Event Log:

```
TextBox1 - KeyDown Event, KeyCode: 16, Shift: 1
TextBox1 - KeyDown Event, KeyCode: 16, Shift: 1
TextBox1 - KeyDown Event, KeyCode: 16, Shift: 1
TextBox1 - KeyDown Event, KeyCode: 65, Shift: 1
TextBox1 - KeyPress Event, KeyAscii: 65
TextBox1 - Change Event
TextBox1 - KeyUp Event, KeyCode: 65, Shift: 1
TextBox1 - KeyUp Event, KeyCode: 16, Shift: 0
```

You might notice that there are three KeyDown events with the KeyCode of 16. From the list above, keycode 16 is the Shift key. This is one of the problems with the KeyDown event: if you hold a key down, the event can be triggered multiple times. In this case, the shift key was depressed slightly before the A was pressed. Notice that when the A key was pressed, the Shift parameter was set to 1, indicating that the Shift key was pressed. As a result of the Shift key, the KeyPress event's KeyAscii parameter was set to 65, which is the ASCII value for an uppercase A. Finally, both KeyUp events were registered: The A key was released, followed by the Shift key being released.

Because the KeyDown event may repeat, programmers often put code in the KeyUp event. Because you will always only get a single KeyUp event for any key that is depressed, you do not have to account for a user holding a key down. In addition, the KeyUp event can be used to check for key presses that do not register KeyPress events. These keys include the function and arrow keys. Try pressing Ctrl+F1 while you are in TextBox1. The following events are generated:

```
TextBox1 - KeyDown Event, KeyCode: 17, Shift: 2
TextBox1 - KeyDown Event, KeyCode: 112, Shift: 2
TextBox1 - KeyUp Event, KeyCode: 112, Shift: 2
TextBox1 - KeyUp Event, KeyCode: 17, Shift: 0
```

From the table above, a keycode of 17 is the Ctrl key, and 112 is the F1 key. However, notice that there is no KeyPress or Change event triggered. This is because KeyPress only registers for printable characters; that is, letters, numbers, and punctuation. In addition, the contents of the text box were not changed by the Ctrl+F1 key press; therefore, no Change event is registered.

Knowing how the KeyUp and KeyPress events differ is important since code to watch for a function key press, for instance, will not work if it is placed in the KeyPress event. You must check for non-printable characters within the KeyUp event.

Mouse Event Example

This example is designed to show you how the three mouse events work together. These events are MouseDown, MouseUp, and MouseMove.

On the CD

This example is provided on the CD-ROM and is located in the \Examples\Chapter9 folder. The file name is MouseEvents.html.

In this example, any mouse event on the picture will be added to the event log below the picture. To begin, move your mouse pointer over the picture and then stop moving the pointer. You will see a number of events immediately listed in the event log, as shown below:

```
MouseMove Event - Button: 1, Shift: 0, X: 131.75, Y: 33.5
MouseMove Event - Button: 1, Shift: 0, X: 133.75, Y: 33.5
MouseMove Event - Button: 1, Shift: 0, X: 135.75, Y: 34.5
```

Like the KeyDown event from the previous example, the MouseMove event will trigger for every move of the mouse. While the mouse is stationary, you will not receive MouseMove events. However, if you move the mouse pointer now, the events will again be triggered. The Button parameter will be a combination of the following values:

    1—Left button

    2—Right button

    4—Middle button

In this case, Button is equal to 0, which indicates that no buttons were pressed while you were moving the mouse. To test this, press either or both buttons while your mouse is over the picture. If you press and hold the left button and then move the mouse, you will receive the following events:

```
MouseDown Event - Button: 1, Shift: 0, X: 129.75, Y: 31.5
MouseMove Event - Button: 1, Shift: 0, X: 131.75, Y: 33.5
MouseMove Event - Button: 1, Shift: 0, X: 133.75, Y: 33.5
MouseMove Event - Button: 1, Shift: 0, X: 135.75, Y: 34.5
```

When you release the left mouse button, you will receive the following event:

```
MouseUp Event - Button: 1, Shift: 0, X: 129.75, Y: 31.5
```

The MouseUp and MouseDown events both provide you information about the position of the pointer when the mouse button was pressed. In addition, the Shift parameter indicates whether a modifier key was being pressed when the mouse button was pressed or released. The Shift parameter will be a combination of the following values:

    0—No modifier key was pressed

    1—Shift key was pressed

    2—Ctrl key was pressed

    4—Alt key was pressed

Finally, click either of your mouse buttons on the picture. You will see the following events if you click the left mouse button:

```
MouseDown Event - Button: 1, Shift: 0, X: 129.75, Y: 31.5
MouseUp Event - Button: 1, Shift: 0, X: 129.75, Y: 31.5
```

These two events together are identical to a Click event. Two of these pairs together are the same as a DblClick event. By using the appropriate event for your situation, you will always get your desired results.

Drag-and-Drop Example

The final example for this chapter deals with drag-and-drop operations within Internet Explorer. Currently, only the TextBox and ComboBox controls can serve as sources for drag-and-drop information. This means that you can only start your drag-and-drop operation from either a text box or a combo box. Presumably, Microsoft will expand support of drag-and-drop to the other controls that are already available.

In this example, you will see the events that are triggered during drag-and-drop operations: BeforeDragOver and BeforeDropOrPaste. While these events may sound confusing, they are really simple to use.

On the CD

This example is provided on the CD-ROM and is located in the \Examples\Chapter9 folder. The file name is DragDropEvents.html.

First of all, open the example within Internet Explorer. Like the other examples in this chapter, this page contains two controls and an event log to help you see the events that are occurring. For your convenience, three items have been added to the combo box already. Pick one of these items by dropping the list down and clicking an item. Next, press your left mouse button down and hold it on the text in the combo box. Finally, drag it to the text box, and you will see it appear automatically. There is no code required to perform this action; however, both controls must have their DragBehavior property set to True. If the DragBehavior property is left at the default value of False, the drag-and-drop operation will not take place.

> **Note**   To enable drag-and-drop on text box or combo box controls, set the DragBehavior property to True.

When you dragged the text from the combo box to the text box, you saw a list of events that looks something like this:

```
ComboBox1 - BeforeDragOver - Cancel: False, X:30.75, Y:7.5, DragState:0,
➡Effect:3, Shift:0
ComboBox1 - BeforeDragOver - Cancel: False, X:31, Y:8.5, DragState:2, Effect:3,
➡Shift:0
ComboBox1 - BeforeDragOver - Cancel: False, X:31.75, Y:8, DragState:1,
➡Effect:0, Shift:0
TextBox1 - BeforeDragOver - Cancel: False, X:32.75, Y:8, DragState:0, Effect:3,
Shift:0
TextBox1 - BeforeDragOver - Cancel: False, X:34.75, Y:8.5, DragState:2,
➡Effect:3, Shift:0
TextBox1 - BeforeDropOrPaste - Cancel: False, X:34.75, Y:7.5, DragState:0,
➡Effect:3, Shift:0
```

As you might surmise, you receive a BeforeDragOver event while you are dragging the text, whether or not you are moving the mouse. When you release the mouse button to "drop" the text, the BeforeDropOrPaste event triggers. However, there are two intermediate states while the text is being dragged. Notice the DragState parameter's value during the operation. It starts at 0, indicating that the mouse is in range of a target and has not been moved yet. DragState's value then changes to 2, which means that the mouse pointer has changed position over that same target.

Next, DragState's value changes to 1, which means that the mouse pointer is not in range of a valid target. When your mouse pointer reaches the text box, the DragState parameter changes to 0 again, indicating that you are over a new valid target. Finally, the DragState parameter's value changes to 2, which means that the mouse pointer has changed position over that same target.

To clarify these actions, here is a short list of what happened and what the value of DragState was:

Drag and drop operation starts	DragState – 0
Start moving pointer over combo box	DragState = 2
Move pointer over window	DragState – 1
Move pointer over text box	DragState = 0
Keep moving pointer over text box	DragState = 2

For validation purposes, as long as the DragState property is 0 or 2, it means that the mouse pointer is over a valid target. Once the pointer reaches a valid target, the user releases the button and the BeforeDropOrPaste event triggers. This event indicates that data has been dropped in the control receiving the event. The control can use the parameters of the event to view the data that was dropped. However, in this example, the text box and combo box automatically accept text.

To test your understanding of these events, write down the sequence of events that should occur when you drag text from the text box to the combo box. Test your answer by dragging the text from the text box back to the combo box. If you guessed that the events would be identical, give yourself a gold star for the day. You should have seen a list of events something like the following:

```
TextBox1 - BeforeDragOver - Cancel: False, X:30.75, Y:7.5, DragState:0,
➥Effect:3, Shift:0
TextBox1 - BeforeDragOver - Cancel: False, X:31, Y:8.5, DragState:2, Effect:3,
➥Shift:0
TextBox1 - BeforeDragOver - Cancel: False, X:31.75, Y:8, DragState:1, Effect:0,
➥Shift:0
ComboBox1 - BeforeDragOver - Cancel: False, X:32.75, Y:8, DragState:0,
➥Effect:3, Shift:0
ComboBox1 - BeforeDragOver - Cancel: False, X:34.75, Y:8.5, DragState:2,
➥Effect:3, Shift:0
ComboBox1 - BeforeDropOrPaste - Cancel: False, X:34.75, Y:7.5, DragState:0,
➥Effect:3, Shift:0
```

Now that you have learned the basics of drag-and-drop operations for web pages, try modifying the example so that you know if the user has pressed the Shift or Ctrl key. (Hint: Look at the description of the Shift parameter in the first section of this chapter.)

For Visual Basic Programmers

As you may have noticed, some of Visual Basic's events have been renamed in VBScript. The GotFocus event from Visual Basic has become Enter, and the Lost-Focus event has been renamed to Exit. Frankly, the new names are clearer than the old names; however, they are different so be sure to use the new names and not the Visual Basic names.

In addition, VBScript has provided several new events, namely the BeforeUpdate and AfterUpdate events. These extremely useful events supplement the Change event and actually replace it as the best place to put your validation code. Besides the clarity of knowing when the events will fire, these events do not respond if the data in the control is changed by your program. This action, in Visual Basic, would cause the Change event to trigger and often causes unexpected results. Hopefully, these new events will find their way into Visual Basic 5.0, as well. Data validation has always been a problem in Visual Basic because of the poor control you have over the events that are triggered. The events, like Change, are too high-level to be useful. AfterUpdate and BeforeUpdate, on the other hand, give you better control over when validation should be done.

Other than those few changes, programming with events in VBScript will be fairly similar to writing programs in Visual Basic. Some of the controls may have slightly different events, but for the most part, the events all do the same things as they do in Visual Basic.

Summary

This chapter was designed to help you start using the other controls included with the ActiveX Control Pad. These controls include the text box, check box, list boxes, Scroll bar, Spin button, and Command button. With these controls in your VBScript repertoire, you can improve and enhance your web pages to make them more useful for your users.

If you are looking for more controls to expand your VBScript toolbox, check these web sites:

Microsoft ActiveX Component Gallery:
`http://www.microsoft.com/activex/gallery/`

Ask the VB Pro's VBScript Central:
`http://www.inquiry.com/vbscentral`

ActiveX.com:
`http://www.activex.com`

ActiveXpress.com:
`http://www.activexpress.com`

atOnce Software's WebTools Store:
`http://www.webtools.atoncesoftware.com`

These sites all have component repositories and allow you to download controls, many of which are free of charge.

CHAPTER 10

Debugging Your Script

By Eric Smith

One of the most neglected features of software is a robust, complete error handler. Even the best, most reviewed code is subject to the whims of operating systems, and any operating system can cause fatal, unheard of errors. For this reason, Visual Basic provides extensive error handling capabilities. Unfortunately, most of these capabilities are not included with VBScript. As you learn in this chapter, much of the error trapping must be handled manually. You are still able to catch those wily errors in your code, but it requires more work on your part.

This chapter presents information on the following topics that are related to error handling in VBScript:

◆ Basics of error handling

◆ Error propagation

◆ Err object and its properties

◆ User-generated errors

◆ How to build error handlers

◆ Trappable errors in VBScript

Preventing Web Page Explosions

If you have ever programmed in Visual Basic, you are aware of what happens when an unhandled error occurs in your program. If you are within the development environment, the program stops and a message displays. However, if you are running an executable (.EXE) file, the error displays right before the executable file crashes, without any more messages. Even end-users are becoming aware that these types of behaviors indicate a lack of testing or a poor error handling code in the program. This failure to include robust error handling casts a dark shadow on your product and your reputation as a software developer.

> **Tip**   Cardinal Rule #1 of Programming: Never let the user see the error message box on your web site.

When Visual Basic encounters an untrapped error, it displays the error to the user in a message box. The program terminates, and the user is left wondering what happened. VBScript responds similar to Visual Basic, in that any untrapped error causes Microsoft Internet Explorer to generate a message box containing the error. Seeing this error might cause a user to leave your site, never to return. Internet surfers have a very low tolerance for badly designed sites and pages. Because you want users to come back to your page and bring their friends, you need to have pages that work correctly.

Basics of Error Handling

As previously mentioned, if VBScript encounters an error in your code, it stops and displays the error message to the user. Unfortunately, the user might not have the slightest idea what the error means and might not report it to you. To prevent these errors from bringing your page to a crashing halt, you need to understand how these errors occur, and you need to know how to avoid the errors.

> **Note**   *Error handler*—An error handler is a special block of code in a function or procedure that is designed to process errors that may occur.

When an error occurs, VBScript looks in the current procedure or function for what is known as an *error handler*. The error handler is an instruction to the system explaining how the error should be handled. In VBScript, there is only one instruction you can give the system to skip the offending line and proceed to the next line. This command is *On Error Resume Next*.

On Error Resume Next—This VBScript keyword causes VBScript to continue to the next line after an error occurs. The `On Error Resume Next` keyword prevents your program from stopping immediately when an error occurs.

 In VBScript the only valid On Error command you can use is Resume Next. Any other command, such as GoTo label or Exit Function/Sub, is illegal and unsupported in VBScript. All error handling must be done inline, which means that you must manually check for errors after each statement. VBScript will not automatically transfer control to an error handler like Visual Basic does.

Note *Registered error handler*—An error handler is registered after you use the On Error statement. For VBScript, the *On Error Resume Next* keyword registers an error handler that simply transfers control to the line after an error.

When VBScript enters a subroutine or function, it encounters the On Error Resume Next command. Then the error handler is *registered*, meaning that VBScript recognizes the command given to it. All the errors are handled in the manner that you specified and execution continues at the line following the error producing line. This is an important behavior to understand.

Tip Cardinal Rule #2: When the error handling feature is turned on, the page continues to function and may be able to recover from whatever errors occur.

To illustrate this, an example is included on the accompanying CD-ROM in \Examples\Chapter 10\SimpleError.html. This example is a good representation of how error handling works.

On the CD

This example is shown here for reference:

```
<HTML>
<SCRIPT LANGUAGE=VBScript>
    On Error Resume Next
    Dim tmp
    tmp = 5 / 0
    If Err.Number <> 0 Then
        Document.Write "Error #" & Err.Number & " occurred." & "<P>"
    End If
</SCRIPT>
</HTML>
```

This example, unlike normal code, is designed to produce an error. *division by zero* is an illegal operation; therefore, the `5 / 0` line causes an error. However, because of the `On Error Resume Next` line, this error does not cause Internet Explorer to stop with an error message. If you load this example, you will see the following line on your screen:

```
Error #11 occurred.
```

`Error #11` is a division by zero error in VBScript and Visual Basic. To see the On Error Resume Next error handling in action, try commenting out the On Error Resume Next line with a single quote as the first character on the line. Internet Explorer displays an error message with the same error, but the page no longer functions correctly.

Error Propagation

You will have code that is as simple as the preceding example. In most cases, multiple subroutines are calling other subroutines. In cases where an error occurs in a subroutine, *error propagation* occurs. Error propagation describes the condition in which errors are handled when no error handler is registered in a subroutine.

For example, imagine a program that contains three subroutines labeled A, B, and C. In subroutine A, subroutine B is called, and within subroutine B, subroutine C is called. If an error occurs in subroutine C and no error handler is registered for subroutine C, the error travels to subroutine B. If no error handler processes the error in subroutine B, the error travels to subroutine A and looks for an error handler in subroutine A. If no error handler is found in subroutine A, the error displays to the user.

On the CD

This behavior is illustrated in the following example, which is on the CD-ROM. (The example is in \Examples\Chapter 10\ErrorPropagation.html.)

```
<HTML>
<SCRIPT LANGUAGE=VBScript>
    On Error Resume Next
    Call A()
    If Err.Number <> 0 Then
        Document.Write "Error #" & Err.Number & " occurred in subroutine A.<P>"
    End If

    Sub A()
        Dim tmp
        tmp = 5 / 0
```

```
        Document.Write "Passed division by zero error.<P>"
    End Sub
</SCRIPT>
</HTML>
```

When you run this example in Internet Explorer, the following line displays on-screen:

```
Error #11 occurred in subroutine A.
```

Here is what happens in this example:

1. On Error Resume Next is read and an error handler is registered by Visual Basic. Any error that occurs in this part of the code causes execution to continue at the next line.

2. Subroutine A is called.

3. No error handler registers for subroutine A; however, the error handler in the previous section of code still registers.

4. A division by zero error occurs.

5. VBScript does not find an error handler in subroutine A, so control immediately passes back to the calling code.

6. The error handler in the calling code is found. VBScript handles the error by passing control to the If statement.

7. The If statement checks the error number and displays the error message.

This example illustrates two key points:

◆ When an error occurs, execution of that subroutine stops immediately. In this example, the Document.Write statement in subroutine A is never executed because it follows the line that generated the error.

◆ After an error handler is registered, it is active for the life of that subroutine or function. Error handlers are only deregistered when VBScript encounters either the Exit Sub or Exit Function statements.

Note In the preceding example, the code at the beginning of the <SCRIPT> section is a subroutine, even though code is not preceded by the Sub keyword. This type of code is commonly known as Sub Main(), which is the name given to it in Visual Basic. Sub Main() contains a code that is executed when a program starts, or in this case, when a page loads.

For purposes of error handling, this code is treated like any other subroutine.

By modifying the previous example, you can see how error handlers in subroutines handle errors that occur. If On Error Resume Next is added to subroutine A, subroutine A handles its own error. The following code shows this and the example file is available on the CD-ROM in \Examples\Chapter 10\ NoMorePropagation.html.

On the CD

```
<HTML>
<SCRIPT LANGUAGE=VBScript>
   On Error Resume Next
   Call A()
   If Err.Number <> 0 Then
      Document.Write "Error #" & Err.Number & " occurred in subroutine A.<P>"
   End If

   Sub A()
      On Error Resume Next
      Dim tmp
      tmp = 5 / 0
      If Err.Number <> 0 Then
         Document.Write "Error #" & Err.Number _
            & " occurred in and was handled by subroutine A.<P>"
      End If
   End Sub
</SCRIPT>
</HTML>
```

The Err.Clear Method

Now that an error handler is in subroutine A, you should see the following message:

```
Error #11 occurred in and was handled by subroutine A.
```

But if you run this example as is, you see two messages:

```
Error #11 occurred in and was handled by subroutine A.
Error #11 occurred in subroutine A.
```

Does this mean that the error handler in subroutine A didn't really handle the error? No, it means that the error has not been cleared. To clear the error so that no other routines attempt to handle it, use the Err.Clear statement. Clear is a method in the Err object. A *method* is a subroutine or function that is part of an object. Other methods of the Err object are discussed later in this chapter.

Note *Err.Clear*—This method clears the contents of the Err object. Err.Clear erases the information stored in the Err object.

Note *Method*—A method is a special subroutine that performs an action on an object. In the case of error handlers, the Err object has several methods, including the Clear method.

By adding Err.Clear to the error handling code of subroutine A, the expected results are achieved in this example.

```
<HTML>
<SCRIPT LANGUAGE=VBScript>
   On Error Resume Next
   Call A()
   If Err.Number <> 0 Then
      Document.Write "Error #" & Err.Number & " occurred in subroutine A.<P>"
   End If

   Sub A()
      On Error Resume Next
      Dim tmp
      tmp = 5 / 0
      If Err.Number <> 0 Then
         Document.Write "Error #" & Err.Number _
            & " occurred in and was handled by subroutine A.<P>"
         Err.Clear
      End If
   End Sub
</SCRIPT>
</HTML>
```

Note According to Microsoft's documentation on the Err object, the Exit Sub and Exit Function statements perform the same function as the Err.Clear statement. However, in this example, if you replace Err.Clear with Exit Sub, the calling subroutine sees a number in the Err object and displays a message.

For best results, use the Err.Clear statement to explicitly clear the Err object, after you have handled the error that occurred in your subroutine.

Finally, in this example, with both On Error Resume Next statements removed, Internet Explorer displays an error message indicating a division by zero error. You should always have a top-level error handler to catch any errors that might not have been caught in another subroutine. In this example, the error handler in the main subroutine serves as a top-level error handler. It catches any error that occurs and any errors that were not caught in another subroutine.

The Err Object

As with many other things in Internet Explorer and VBScript, *objects* are used to represent real-world components. For instance, the Document object represents the entire page that is being loaded. Throughout this book, you have seen examples that print to the page by using the Document.Write statement. In this case, `Write` is a method acting on the Document object. These are just fancy names for special subroutines that are part of objects like Document.

Note *Object*—A programming structure used to represent real-world components. For instance, an inventory system might have objects representing orders and inventory items. In this section, the Err object is a convenient way to store information about errors that occur in a program.

Note *Properties*—Properties are the values stored in an object. For instance, if you had a Car object, you might also have a color and a manufacturer property associated with the object.

You use the Err.Number statement to retrieve the last error's number. Number is a property of the Err object. Just like most everything in Windows 95, the Err object has certain attributes that can be viewed and modified. These attributes are known as properties.

Note To retrieve a property, you use dot notation, as shown in Err.Number. The object is always followed by the property you want to retrieve, and the two words are separated by a period, or dot.

To help you debug your code, the Err object has a number of other properties and methods that you can use in your pages. The properties of the Err object are covered in the following sections.

Description Property

This property holds the description of the error that occurred. If the Err object represents a standard VBScript error, the Description property holds the text describing that error. In the previous examples that generated division by zero errors, the Description property holds the text division by zero. You can use this text in your code to report errors without disrupting your program.

Number Property

This property holds the current error number. For standard VBScript errors, this is the error's assigned number. In a later section dealing with user-generated errors, you see how to set this error number to a number that you have determined for a particular error condition in your code.

Source Property

This property holds the location where errors occur. This is particularly useful for debugging complex ocdes, inwhich multiple subroutines might be the cause of the error. For standard VBScript errors, this property's value will be "Microsoft VBScript runtime error", which is not particularly useful for debugging. It can be used to set the Source property for debugging.

The Err object has two methods to help debug your code: Clear and Raise. The following sections explain these methods in more detail.

Clear Method

This method resets the properties of the Err object in one step. It sets the Description and Source properties to zero-length strings, and sets the Number property to zero. The Clear method should be used within an error handling code when an error has been processed by the code and the program is ready to continue. By clearing the error, you prevent other error handling code from trying to process it.

Raise Method

The Raise method generates an error to be handled by error processing code in the same way that VBScript runtime errors are handled. As you learn in the section dealing with user-generated errors, the Err object has a great deal of flexibility. It can be used to communicate system-generated errors and to create errors. The errors that you generate can be trapped by error handlers elsewhere in your programs.

The Raise method can take the following parameters:

◆ **Number**—This *Long Integer* specifies the number of the error held in the Err object. All VBScript errors are in the range of 0–65535. When creating your own errors and error numbers, the error number must be greater than zero and less than or equal to 65535.

◆ **Source**—This parameter enables you to specify where this error occurs. In most cases, you want to set this property to a meaningful name or keyword (such as the subroutine's name) so that you can debug it later. If the Source is not specified, the default "Microsoft VBScript runtime error" puts in the Source property. This parameter is optional. However, if the Description, HelpFile, or HelpContext parameters are used, you must specify the Source property.

◆ **Description**—This parameter is the text that describes the error. For standard VBScript errors, this text generates automatically and contains the text associated with the VBScript error number in the Number property. If no description is given for an error, the default value of "Unknown Runtime Error" sets in the Description property. This parameter is optional.

User-Generated Errors

In many cases, you need to create functions and subroutines to perform various tasks. In some cases, you need to determine whether a function is performing its task correctly. One method of programming relies on trapping errors to determine whether problems might have occurred. Using this method enables the main flow of the code to be simpler. Basically, if the function did not generate an error, then it is working fine.

Although this method might work under Visual Basic, which has more robust error handling capabilities, VBScript requires you to check the Err object after each step to determine where an error occurred. In the example from the previous section, the value of the Err object is checked immediately after the call to subroutine A. If this check is not performed or is performed later, the error handling steps are different and are no longer appropriate for the error that occured as a result of subroutine A.

Even with the limitations of VBScript's error handling capabilities, the Err object provides more useful information than a return code would. These techniques are applied to the previous example to show you how to create your own errors. When an error occurs in subroutine A, this example clears the current error and then uses the `Raise` method to generate a new error that is trapped by the calling subroutine. This new error can be handled by a more robust error handler, which would not have to be part of subroutine A. This more extensive error handler could be placed in a section of code used by all the subroutines in your code. Placing it in a common area accessible to all your subroutines prevents you from having to duplicate your code. Changes to this error handler are easier to make because you only have one copy of the code to change.

```
<HTML>
<SCRIPT LANGUAGE=VBScript>
   On Error Resume Next
   Call A()
   If Err.Number <> 0 Then
      Document.Write "Error #" & Err.Number & " trapped in main subroutine.<P>"
      Document.Write "Error description: " & Err.Description & "<P>"
      Document.Write "Error source: " & Err.Source & "<P>"

   End If


   Sub A()
      On Error Resume Next
      Dim tmp
      tmp = 5 / 0
      If Err.Number <> 0 Then
         Document.Write "Error #" & Err.Number _
            & " occurred in and was handled by subroutine A.<P>"
         Err.Clear
         Err.Raise 65535, "Subroutine A() Error Handler", "Division by zero
         ➥error"
      End If
   End Sub
</SCRIPT>
</HTML>
```

In this example, the following output generates to the screen:

```
Error #11 occurred in and was handled by subroutine A.
```

```
Error #65535 trapped in main subroutine.
```

```
Error description: Division by zero error
```

Error source: Subroutine A( ) Error Handler

By using the Err object, you can easily transfer error information to the calling subroutine without using subroutine parameters or return values for functions.

Building an Error Handler

In the previous examples, error handling code was done in place. Unfortunately,
this solution does not work well for large projects. If you have 30 subroutines, for instance, do you really want to put all the error handling code after each line for all 30 subroutines? A better solution is to create an error handling subroutine for your page. The routine can then be used by all the subroutines in your document.

When you build a handler keep in mind that although you want it to be robust, you need the handler to be compact. All this code is going into a web page that the user must download. If the user has to download hundreds of lines of error handling code that will probably not be used, it is a waste of his time. However, by grouping responses to errors, you consolidate your error handling into a package that can be used in your code. An example of this type of generic error handler follows:

```
<HTML>
<SCRIPT LANGUAGE=VBScript>

On Error Resume Next
Call A()
Select Case fnCheckError()
   Case 1
      Exit Sub
   Case 2
      ' additional responses to return codes
   . . .
End Select

Function fnCheckError()
'
' For demonstration purposes, a zero return code
' indicates no error, and a one indicates a major
' error occurred and the routine should exit.
'
```

```
Select Case Err.Number
    Case 0
  fnCheckError = 0
 Case 11
        fnCheckError = 1
    Case 35
        fnCheckError = 1
    Case 92
        fnCheckError = 1
    ' more case statements for other possible errors.
 End Select


End Function
```

If an error were to occur somewhere in subroutine A and subroutine A did not have an error handler registered, the error would be passed to the fnCheckError function. The fnCheckError function is designed to provide a response for any error that may occur. The function analyzes the error that occurred and, based on the error number, returns an action code to the procedure that called the fnCheckError function. For instance, subroutine A encounters error number 11, division by zero. The error is sent to the fnCheckError function after it propagates out of subroutine A. fnCheckError determines that the division by zero error is a serious error that cannot be resolved automatically, so it returns action code 1 to the calling code. Action code 1, in this example, indicates that a serious error has occurred that will require the program to exit. As you can see in the fnCheckError code, there are a number of other errors that could require the same behavior of exiting the program.

> **Note**
> One other thing to note is that the fnCheckError function has a case for error number 0, which indicates that no error occurred. Because the error handler always has to be called manually to process an error, error number 0 is a real possibility. In this case, error number 0 causes the fnCheckError function to return action code 0, which means that there is no error and processing can continue.

Although this example is not robust, it does demonstrate how error handling can be centralized. Even though the routine that is checking for an error needs to check the return code from fnCheckError to determine what to do, the routine does not have to worry about all the possible errors. It just needs to know what to do next.

For instance, most normal VBScript runtime errors are fatal to the currently executing subroutine. For example, if you suddenly get a syntax error the page should not continue to run. The routine that is checking for the error does not have to know exactly what happened, it only needs to know that it must exit because of the error.

Trappable Errors in VBScript

Throughout this chapter, you have seen ways of dealing with the errors that may occur within your VBScript-enhanced web pages. This section wraps up this chapter with a list of the most common errors in VBScript. Each error is listed with its number, a description, and a short list of common causes of the error. Each of the numbers assigned to the errors are unique within VBScript and can be trapped within your own error handling code.

Warning If you create your own errors, be sure not to use any of these numbers to represent your custom error messages. If you do, it will be difficult to determine which error message is meaningful (the standard error message or a custom message you created).

0—No Error Detected

Many error handlers forget to account for the case in which the error handling code was invoked without a real error, error number 0. (See the *"Building an Error Handler"* section of this chapter for an example of error number 0.) For this reason, 0 represents an error-free state.

5—Invalid Procedure Call

There are a number of reasons that you may get an invalid procedure call error. The first and most common reason is that you tried to call a procedure or function with an illegal parameter. For instance, you may have tried to use a string function like Mid or Left on a numerical value. This usage error can cause an invalid procedure call error.

6—Overflow

Overflow errors are caused by setting a variable to a number that is too large for the type you selected. For instance, integers can have values between $-32,768$ and $32,767$, inclusive. If you were to set an integer variable to a value outside of that range, you would get an overflow error. Table 10.1 shows a list of the acceptable ranges for each data type.

Table 10.1
Acceptable Ranges for Data Types

Data type	Range
Byte	0–255
Boolean	True or False
Integer	–32,768 to 32,767
Long Integer	–2,147,483,648 to 2,147,483,647
Single	–3.402823E38 to –1.401298E–45 for negative values; 1.401298E–45 to 3.402823E38 for positive values.
Double	–1.79769313486232E308 to –4.94065645841247E–324 for negative values; 4.94065645841247E–324 to 1.79769313486232E308 for positive values.
Currency	–922,337,203,685,477.5808 to 922,337,203,685,477.5807.
Date	January 1, 100 to December 31, 9999, inclusive.
String	Strings may range in length from 0 to approximately 2 billion characters

9—Subscript Out of Range

This error occurs when you use arrays and use an index outside of the array boundaries. For instance, if you declare an array like this:

```
Dim arrData(10)
```

the valid indices are between zero and nine, inclusive. If you try to access an element with an index outside of that range, you get a `Subscript Out of Range` error.

11—Division by Zero

If you remember your grade school math classes, you might recall that if you divide a number by zero, the result is infinity. This is obviously not a valid result, so division by zero is an illegal operation in VBScript. Typically, division by zero errors are caused by incorrect data in your program.

35—Sub, Function, or Property Not Defined

This error is really a syntax error and should never appear to the end user. The error occurs when you call a subroutine or a function that is not defined. It can occur when you try to access an object's property that does not exist.

91—Object Variable Not Set

This error occurs when you attempt to use a property or method of an object that has not been created. If the object has not been created, you cannot use methods or properties associated with it.

92—For Loop Not Initialized

This error is also a syntax error that should be caught before the page is made available to users. This error occurs when the Next keyword is used without a matching For loop. This typically happens when you forget to remove all the components of a For loop from your code. You must always remove both the For and Next keywords.

> ***For Visual Basic Programmers:***
> The error numbers and messages used within VBScript are identical to those used in Visual Basic. However, a large number of the errors within Visual Basic do not apply to VBScript. For instance, any error dealing with files or databases will not be valid in VBScript. However, you can use the Visual Basic Help file to help you debug your code. Just do a search for trappable errors and you will be shown a list of all the errors Visual Basic recognizes. If you choose the Miscellaneous Messages section, you will see the list that this section was based on. You will also see that most of those errors do not apply to VBScript.

Summary

This chapter showed you how to deal with errors in your VBScript pages and how to prevent the user from seeing untrapped errors. With the tools and techniques covered in this chapter, you can now bulletproof your VBScript pages and prevent potential user frustration.

PART III

ActiveX Controls

CHAPTER 11

HTML Extensions for ActiveX Controls

By Yusuf Malluf

This chapter shows you how to put ActiveX components in action; in other words, it adds to what you have already learned about HTML and ActiveX controls by making your knowledge practical. Basically, this chapter provides a fresh look at inserting ActiveX controls into HTML pages; it also offers more insight into ways you can set and change attributes of ActiveX controls using inline scripting. This chapter covers the following:

♦ **A review of the HTML elements that are essential to ActiveX and VBScript.**

♦ **How to insert ActiveX controls on a web page.** With a rudimentary understanding of HTML, knowing how to insert ActiveX controls in an HTML document becomes a simple task. You merely use HTML tags for inserting objects and setting their various properties and attributes.

♦ **Setting properties of ActiveX controls.** Initializing properties for ActiveX controls is even easier than inserting them. The ActiveX Control Pad completely automates setting properties and inserting controls, thereby eliminating the risk of mistyping errors and other tedious errors.

◆ **Inserting inline script in web pages.** In addition to inserting ActiveX controls and setting their various properties in web pages, you can insert inline scripting capabilities in web pages. Using either VBScript or JavaScript, you can manipulate the ActiveX controls on the page. "Manipulation" involves more than just setting properties of ActiveX controls; you can also call methods and events that make the controls do various things.

A Brief Review of HTML

As you have learned, the Hypertext Markup Language is the medium by which information on the World Wide Web is exchanged. HTML documents are transferred through the hypertext transfer protocol (http)—as opposed to binary and other files that are transferred through the file transfer protocol (FTP), or Gopher files that are transferred through the Gopher protocol. These hypertext documents enable web developers to insert graphics, text, sound, ActiveX controls, and a variety of different entities into a document that is accessed over the Internet. This is what has made the World Wide Web so revolutionary.

Note For more comprehensive information on HTML fundamentals, see Chapter 2, "HTML Fundamentals for VBScripting."

This section provides a brief review of HTML, which should benefit you whether you come from a programming background or are relatively new to HTML. This section reviews some of the general syntax and the structure of an HTML document, as well as some information on individual entities such as frames and the HTML intrinsic controls.

Note If you feel comfortable with your knowledge of HTML, you may want to skip this section entirely and proceed to the next section: "Inserting ActiveX Controls."

Why are frames and HTML form controls (intrinsic controls) covered in this section? Frames have contributed immensely to the interactive ability of web pages. They enable a single page to consist of several "mini" browsers where each frame hosts a different document and has the capability to load new documents. Frames can also be manipulated by VBScript, as you will see in forthcoming examples.

The HTML form or intrinsic controls are also essential to VBScript and ActiveX. With the intrinsic form controls, you can insert several basic controls (such as a button or text box), and you can manipulate them with VBScript—which enables the validation of the contents of the controls and the capability to submit them. Incidentally, there is a collection of ActiveX controls that are included with the ActiveX Control Pad, which are more capable than the standard HTML form controls. These controls are collectively called the Microsoft Forms 2.0 controls and include not only input, select boxes, and push buttons, but also toggle buttons, spin buttons, the tab-strip control, and more.

> **Note** See Chapter 12, "Using the Built-In ActiveX Controls," for more information on ActiveX built-in controls and examples of ways to utilize these controls—such as creating data entry forms and clickable image maps.

General Syntax Review

This section quickly reviews the syntax of HTML in its entirety. HTML syntax is relatively simple and not at all hard to understand, especially if you are from a programming background. First, however, let's review some of the general terms used to refer to different entities in HTML:

◆ **Element**—Many people use the word "element" out of context when dealing with HTML. It can refer to a tag, an attribute, or an infinite amount of entities. According to the HTML standard, however, the word "element" is used to indicate a style or format used in HTML without the angle brackets (< and >). For instance, you can use the element *P* to make new paragraph blocks in HTML, but you use the tag *<P>* in the document for paragraphing text.

◆ **Tag**—A tag refers to an HTML element that is encapsulated within angle brackets. Tags are used in HTML documents; you use elements in style sheets and as a generic reference to a tag. Most tags come in pairs: an opening tag *<TAG>* and a closing tag *</TAG>* (where *TAG* is the element used).

◆ **Attributes**—Attributes are the properties of a tag and are placed after the tag's element in the angle brackets. In this example:

<FONT COLOR="#00FF00" SIZE="+2" FACE="Arial Black">

The name of the tag is <FONT>, and it is followed by the attributes COLOR, SIZE, and FACE. In the case of these three attributes and with most attributes, a value is assigned to the attribute like this:

AttributeName="Value"

where *AttributeName* is the name of the attribute and *"Value"* is the value of that attribute surrounded by quotations (all attribute values should be surrounded by quotations in HTML). In some cases, attributes do not have a value, and the presence of that attribute in a tag indicates an alteration of some attribute, or is a Boolean attribute that makes an attribute true or false.

The following code demonstrates the preceding components in a simple HTML document.

```
<HTML>
<HEAD>
<TITLE>This is a simple document</TITLE>
<STYLE>
P {color: teal; background: wheat; font-size: 22pt}
</STYLE>
</HEAD>
<BODY>
<H2>This is a simple HTML Document</H2>
<HR SIZE="10" WIDTH="50%" ALIGN="CENTER" COLOR="BLUE" NOSHADE>
<P> Some text will go here, and it looks different than</P><BR>
Normal text<BR>
<FONT SIZE="+3" COLOR="GOLD" FACE="Matura MT Script">This is some
more text</FONT>
<P><A HREF="http://www.microsoft.com">Microsoft</A></P>
</BODY>
</HTML>
```

Notice the variety of tags used in the previous code: <HTML>, <HEAD>, <TITLE>, <STYLE>, <BODY>, <H2>, <HR>, and <P>. There is only one element used in this document, and that is in the style sheet section (the different sections of the HTML document will be covered in the following section of this chapter).

Notice also that a few of the tags have attributes. The <HR> tag (notice that, along with the <BR> tag, it does not have a closing tag) has five attributes used. The first is the SIZE attribute, which is set to "10" (meaning 10 pixels, in this case); the next attribute is WIDTH, which specifies the width of this horizontal rule ("50%" means 50 percent of the screen); and so on. The <HR> line ends with the NOSHADE attribute, which has no value. The NOSHADE attribute specifies that there are no shading effects for the horizontal rule; in other words, shading effects are "false." The <FONT>, <P>, <H2>, and other tags are examples of tags that have closing counterparts. The previous code is illustrated in figure 11.1.

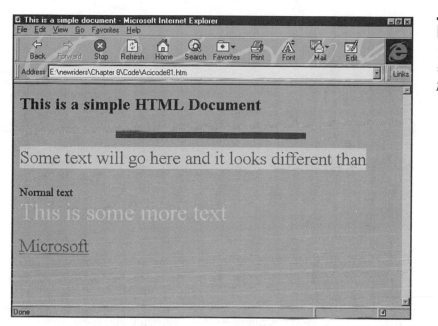

Figure 11.1

This is an illustration of the previous code.

Most HTML tags can be encapsulated in another, which means that a <P> tag can be nested in a <FONT> tag. Tags work by *inheritance*, which simply means that if a tag is nested in another tag, it inherits all the attributes of its *parent* tag (the tag that encapsulates it). The nested tag is called the *child* tag. Multiple tags can be nested within each other. Notice in the previous code that all the tags are encapsulated by the <HTML> tag, and that several of the tags are nested in the <BODY> tag. In the <BODY> tag, an <A> tag is nested by a <P> tag. The <A> tag inherits all the attributes of the <P> tag, yet it retains its own attributes that the <P> tag does not account for. Figure 11.2 should help you understand the concept of inheritance.

Figure 11.2

How inheritance works in HTML pages.

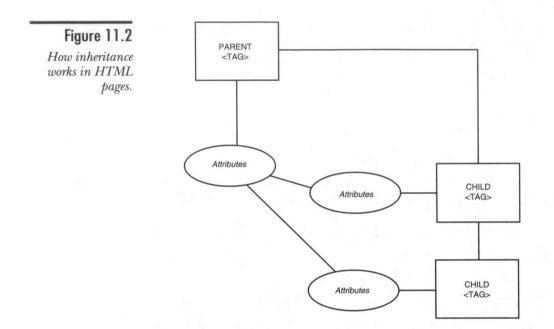

A concept that is important to understand in HTML and important to ActiveX and VBScript is *linking*. The World Wide Web couldn't exist without links, which, being the voracious web surfer you probably are, you already knew. In static HTML, you can link to other Uniform Resource Locators (URLs) simply by using the <A> tag and its HREF attribute to specify the location of the resource on the Internet. In VBScript and in many ActiveX controls, special properties exist for linking and navigating to other resources.

Document Structure

This section reviews the basic overall structure of an HTML page. It is essential to understand this simple structure because, for example, certain scripts are located in the header part of a document and behave differently than other scripts and objects that are located in the body section. There are two basic sections that comprise everything in an HTML document: the header section and the body section. In HTML, both these sections are inside or nested between the opening and closing <HTML> tags, which contain the entire document. Figure 11.3 is a graphical representation of the HTML document structure.

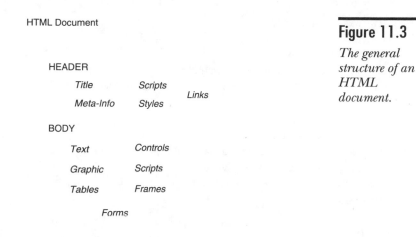

Figure 11.3

The general structure of an HTML document.

The header section is where everything regarding information about the document in general is placed; everything mentioned related to the header in this section must be nested in the <HEAD> tags. The title, which names the document, is placed here; the title is specified by the <TITLE> tag. Any links that have some sort of relationship to the document—as in a style sheet or an URL-based location of the author—are put in the header section, as well as any meta-information regarding the document, such as when the document will refresh or retrieve another URL. In addition to this, style sheets and certain scripts that are used on a global basis are included in the header section.

The body section is obviously where all the content of an HTML document is placed. Content includes text, pictures, tables, objects, scripts, and anything else that is displayed on the page. Most tags in HTML are used in the body section. Examine the following code and notice the different sections of the HTML document. This code is shown in figure 11.4.

```
<HTML>
<HEAD>
<TITLE>An HTML Document</TITLE>
<STYLE>
H1 {font-size: 16pt; font-family: Matura Mt Script Capitals;
color: darkgreen; text-align: center}
</STYLE>
</HEAD>

<BODY BGCOLOR="wheat">
```

```
<H1>This is a test</H1>
<CENTER>
<OBJECT id=iegrad1
    type="application/x-oleobject"
    classid="clsid:017C99A0-8637-11CF-A3A9-00A0C9034920"
    width=600
    height=10>
  <PARAM NAME="StartColor" value="#00ff00">
  <PARAM NAME="EndColor" value="#000000">
  <PARAM NAME="Direction" value="1">
</OBJECT>
</CENTER>

<CENTER>
<P>
<TABLE BORDER="10" BACKGROUND="test.jpg">
    <TR>
        <TD ALIGN="CENTER">
            <INPUT TYPE="Button"
                        NAME="btn1"
                        VALUE="Change Color">
        </TD>
    </TR>
    <TR>
        <TD>
            <INPUT TYPE="text" NAME="bb2" VALUE="0">
        </TD>
    </TR>
</TABLE>
</CENTER>

<SCRIPT LANGUAGE="VBSCRIPT">
randomize
    sub btn1_OnClick
        iegrad1.StartColor = randnum(255) * randnum(255) * randnum(255)
        iegrad1.EndColor = randnum(255) * randnum(255) * randnum(255)
        iegrad1.repaint
        bb2.value = iegrad1.StartColor & " --> " & iegrad1.EndColor
    end sub
```

```
   function randnum(x)
        randnum= int(rnd * x) + 1
   end function
</SCRIPT>
</BODY>
</HTML>
```

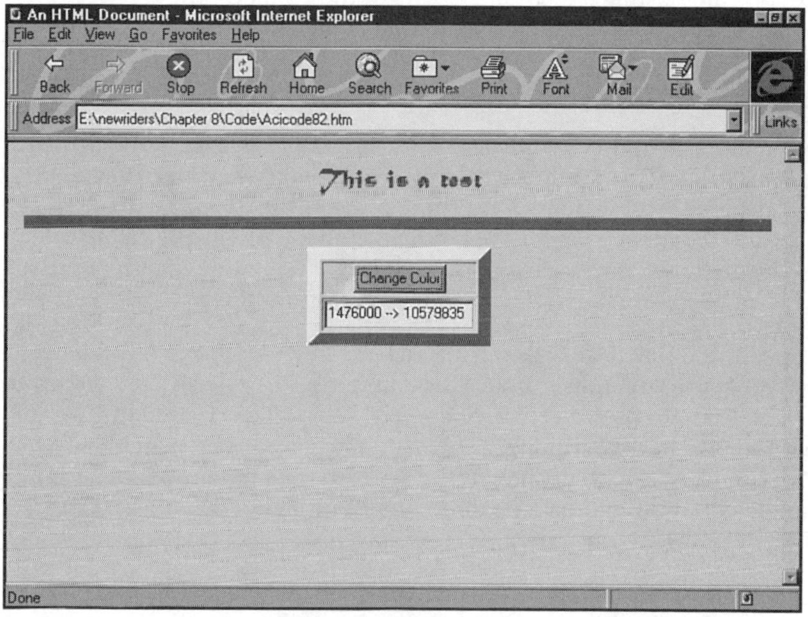

Figure 11.4

A simple HTML page with a VBScript and an ActiveX control.

This sample HTML document uses several different entities. In the header section, a style section exists that defines some styles for the H1 element such as size, color, and which font is defined for that element. The title for the document, "An HTML Document," will appear in the title bar of Internet Explorer. In the body section of this document, there are several different entities that exhibit what can exist in an HTML document.

The first thing you see in the code example and in figure 11.4 is the centered heading: This is a test. The <H1> tag's element, if you recall, was modified in the style section. It is now a smaller font than the normal <H1> tag, it is dark green instead of black, and it uses the Matura MT Script Capitals font. This is a simple tag compared to the next tag: an ActiveX Gradient control.

The ActiveX Gradient control is used in the previous code listing, and you will learn of its attributes such as CLASSID, ID, and TYPE later when the <PARAM> tag is introduced. Like all ActiveX controls, the gradient control has some properties; in this example, however, the gradient's properties that are initiated are: its starting and finishing color, its width and height, and the direction of the gradient.

After the gradient control is a table that encapsulates an HTML intrinsic button control and a text box. This is a simple table with a tiled background image. The button's function is to cause the color of the gradient to change when it is clicked. The text box reports the starting and ending colors of the gradient; they are separated by - ->. When the button is clicked, a script that changes the color of the gradient control starts running. The text box then reports the new starting and ending colors of the gradient.

When the click event for the button control occurs, the script launches a sub procedure called btn1_OnClick. This sub procedure then randomly sets the starting and ending colors of the gradient by calling a function in the <SCRIPT> tag called randnum(x) that sets the new colors for the gradient control. After this, the new colors of the gradient are set to the value of the text box. Then, the repaint method of the gradient is called to actually change the color of the gradient.

The gradient control and the <SCRIPT> tag may seem a little confusing if you have had no exposure to ActiveX or Visual Basic. However, most of the terms and concepts hinted at in this explanation of this HTML document have been reviewed in Chapter 2, "HTML Fundamentals for VBScripting." The main purpose of this example was to show you a more complete HTML document than the first example you looked at in this chapter, and to demonstrate that a plethora of different entities can easily interact and exist in an HTML document.

The next section examines the HTML intrinsic form controls, which are controls that are slightly less functional than their ActiveX counterparts. They are the most common types of controls currently used on web pages because of their original ties with the Common Gateway Interface (CGI); however, this situation is drastically changing. They are also inserted into HTML pages using "standard" HTML. Be aware that VBScript will also be used (in addition to HTML) in the next few sections, and you may want to review the previous VBScript chapters for a better understanding of how the VBScript components work.

HTML Intrinsic Controls

This section covers the form controls that are standard to the HTML language. The HTML intrinsic controls are made up of nine controls that are placed in your pages by means of three tags. These controls include the text and password boxes, check boxes, radio buttons, buttons, hidden fields, combo and drop-down boxes, text fields, and variations of these controls. The three tags used for inserting these controls are the <INPUT>, <SELECT>, and <TEXTAREA> tags. These tags should be nested in the <FORM> tag if you intend on directly submitting data to a sever-side CGI program. However, they can operate normally with VBScript without being nested in a <FORM> tag. The following list describes the HTML intrinsic controls:

◆ The *text box* is a standard input box in which you enter character or numerical data. This can be standard data or data that is hidden from the screen (for example, password data). The data contained in this text box can then be accessed by VBScript for further use, and you can submit this data to a CGI or another server program.

◆ The *button* has several uses as an intrinsic control in HTML. The button enables a form consisting of HTML controls to be submitted to a specified program and the content of the form to be reset. The button control can also serve as a plain button that calls some procedure in VBScript or JavaScript when clicked.

◆ *Check boxes* are used for simple yes-no options and for options that have more than one item to select from. The boxes are checked, indicating that the item (or items) is selected, or unchecked when the item was not selected by the user.

◆ The *radio button* is used to choose one option from a set of alternatives. Only one of the items can be selected or checked at a time, and one of the items of the set always remains checked.

◆ *Drop-down boxes* and *list boxes* enable a user to select items from a list. This list can be a drop-down box, in which the user clicks the down-arrow on the right side of the control and a list of options drops down, or it can be a list box, in which a specified number of the options appear in a scrollable box and the user can select more than one item in the collection of items. These controls are handy when you have a situation in which the user has to choose from several options and it would be too awkward to place all the other options using other controls such as check boxes in the HTML document.

◆ The *text-area* control is specified by the <TEXTAREA> tag and enables a user to enter multiple lines of data in a text field. This is handy when the user needs to relay comments or feedback to a program.

◆ The *hidden field* is a control that hides data it contains from the user. It is useful for storing data that is not necessary for the user to see certain parameters that need to be sent to a program.

Another minor control is the *image-submit* control. The image-submit control is just a variation of the submit button which is an image instead. When the image is clicked, the contents of the form are submitted and the (x, y) coordinates of the image are submitted.

The following sections remind you how to place these controls in your web pages and the syntax for these tags. The first section discusses the <FORM> tag, which is essential to submitting data to a server-side program unless you develop a work-around in VBScript that can circumvent this method. The <INPUT> tag is the tag for inserting all the controls except the drop-down and list boxes, which are inserted through the <SELECT> tag.

The <FORM> Tag

As a review, the general syntax for the form tag is as follows:

```
<FORM METHOD="MethodType" ACTION="ActionType" TARGET="FrameName"
NAME="FormName">

. . .

</FORM>
```

The <FORM> tag has three elements: METHOD, ACTION, and TARGET. The following list presents information on each of these elements:

♦ The value for the METHOD attribute, *MethodType*, can be one of two values: "GET" and "POST". These values refer to what method the information contained in the form's controls should be sent. The "GET" method submits all the data appended to the URL in a series of NAME=VALUE pairs separated by semicolons. The "POST" method submits the data to the program as a series of variables and arrays that are then processed. The METHOD attribute is required if you intend to submit data to another program on the web; if it is not used, then the method would be "GET" by default.

♦ The ACTION attribute is used to specify the location (URL) of the program. The value *ActionType* indicates this location. This URL has to be the location of some program, namely the one that was designed for your form! This attribute is required if you intend to submit the form.

♦ The TARGET attribute is used to specify which frame on the current page the results of the form submittal should be sent to. This will be explained fully in the section in this chapter called "Frames."

The <INPUT> Tag

If you recall, the general syntax for the <INPUT> tag is as follows:

```
<INPUT TYPE="ControlType" NAME="ControlName" VALUE="ValueData"
ALIGN="AlignPosition">
```

There are attributes for the <INPUT> tag specific to individual controls, and those specific attributes will be mentioned along with those controls. These three general attributes are TYPE, NAME, and VALUE. The value *ControlType* is used to specify which control to use for the attribute TYPE; these values are listed in table 11.1. The TYPE attribute is obviously required for this tag.

The attribute NAME simply gives the control a name that is used by VBScript for manipulating that control. The value *ControlName* is a name that the user gives to the control following standard VBScript conventions (i.e., no numbers or non-alphabetical characters should be the first character of the name, and the name should not be that of another object or VBScript keyword). The NAME attribute is required.

The VALUE attribute is used to indicate a control's value. For text boxes and password text boxes, *value* is what will be in the text boxes' field. This value can be initiated in HTML and set or changed by the user and VBScript. It is submitted in the form of *ControlName=value*. For buttons, *value* is what is displayed on the face of the button; it can be set in HTML and changed in VBScript. For check boxes and radio buttons, *value* is submitted to the form if that check box or radio button is selected. These values can be set in HTML and changed by VBScript. The VALUE attribute is required.

The ALIGN attribute specifies where to align the control on the page. Values for *AlignPosition* are: "RIGHT" (to the right margin of the page), "LEFT" (to the left margin of the page), and "CENTER" (centered in the page). This attribute is not required—the control is aligned to the left margin by default.

Table 11.1
Values for the TYPE Attribute of the <INPUT> Tag

Value	Control
"CHECKBOX"	This value makes the input tag a check box. The checkbox control also has the additional attribute CHECKED (no value), which indicates that the box is to be checked by default. Multiple check boxes can exist with the same name (NAME attribute). When such a set of data is submitted, a different *ControlName=value* pair is submitted for each check box.
"HIDDEN"	This value is used to make a hidden field. The hidden field is not visible to the user and is useful in sending, submitting, and containing information that the user doesn't necessarily have to see.

continues

Table 11.1, Continued
Values for the TYPE Attribute of the <INPUT> Tag

Value	Control
"IMAGE"	This is another variation of the submit button. When the image is clicked, the form in which the image rests is submitted. There are two values submitted for this control: the x and y coordinates of the image. The SRC attribute is also used with this control to specify the location of the image.
"PASSWORD"	This is another variation of the text box. The user sees asterisks instead of text when he or she types. The SIZE attribute is used to specify the size of the text box in characters (i.e., SIZE="10" would make the control 10 characters long). The MAXLENGTH attribute is used to specify the maximum length allowed, in characters, of text to be typed in the text box (i.e., MAXLENGTH="5" would only allow five characters to be typed into the text box).
"RADIO"	This value for TYPE is used to create a radio button that enables the user to select an option from a series of alternatives. If multiple radio buttons with the same name (NAME attribute) are on a page, only the selected button's name=value pair will be submitted. The radio button also has the attribute CHECKED, which is the same as the one used in the checkbox control.
"RESET"	This value for the TYPE attribute creates a button that resets the contents of the form when clicked.
"SUBMIT"	This value for the TYPE attribute creates a button that submits the contents of the form when clicked.
"TEXT"	This value is used to make a standard text box. It uses all the attributes mentioned in the password text box control.

The <SELECT> Tag

As you recall, the <SELECT> tag enables you to define two types of similar controls: list boxes or drop-down lists. The general syntax for this tag is:

```
<SELECT NAME="ControlName" SIZE="n">
<OPTION VALUE="value">

. . .

</SELECT>
```

There are two tags in this syntax. The <SELECT> tag defines the control. The attribute NAME identifies the control and ControlName is what you choose to identify it as, with proper conventions. The NAME attribute is required. The SIZE attribute specified how many entries of the list box or drop-down box should be displayed. By default, this is "1," which makes the control a drop-down box. If it is more than one, the control becomes a list box. An additional attribute MULTIPLE (no value) indicates that multiple entries can be selected if present in the select tag.

The <OPTION> tag is used to specify the entries or options of the list box or drop-down box. The attribute VALUE is used to specify the value of a selected entry. If multiple entries exist, then multiple ControlName=value pairs are submitted by the form. The <OPTION> tags are required if you want entries in your drop-down box or list box.

The <TEXTAREA> Tag

To review, the <TEXTAREA> tag is used to create a field of text that enables the user to type multiple lines of text. The general format for a text area field is:

```
<TEXTAREA NAME="ControlName" COLS="n" ROWS="w">

. . .

</TEXTAREA>
```

The <TEXTAREA> tag has the NAME attribute as well as the ROWS and COLS attributes. The NAME attribute is used to specify the name of the control, and ControlName is a name for the control of your choosing (following the proper conventions). The COLS and ROWS attributes deal with the size of the text field. The COLS attribute specifies how long the field should be in characters (i.e., COLS="20" would make the text field 20 characters wide). The ROWS attribute is to specify the height of the text field in characters (i.e., ROWS="25" would give a text area a 25-character height). All three attributes are required for the <TEXTAREA> tag. Any text that is nested inside the <TEXTAREA> tags is the default text for that text area.

Frames

As mentioned previously, frames enable you to place a series of documents inside frames in the browser window. Each of these frames can hold a different document and interact smoothly through HTML. You can control the contents of one page through another with HTML and even better with VBScript!

In this section, the general logic of HTML frames and the syntax used for implementing frames is discussed—so is the TARGET attribute and how it works with VBScript. Additionally, floating frames are covered. Floating frames can be inserted into an HTML document and behave similarly to "stationary" frames.

Standard Frames

When you use standard frames, there is one document that contains the HTML for implementing your frames; those frames are used to reference other documents that are initially displayed in the collection of frames. This base document is loaded into your browser, and then the other documents' references are loaded in their respective frame(s) as well. You can create relatively simple to very complex frame layouts on your page. These frame layouts or any collection of frames on an HTML page is called a *frameset* (named after the <FRAMESET> tag).

Syntax

The general syntax for specifying a *frameset* is:

```
<FRAMESET COLS="length" ROWS="height" FRAMEBORDER="n" FRAMESPACING="w">
    <FRAME FRAMEBORDER="n" MARGINWIDTH="width" NAME="FrameName"
            MARGINHEIGHT="height" SCROLLING="yn" SRC="DocumentURL"
              NORESIZE>
    . . .
    <FRAMESET . . .>
        <FRAME . . .>
        . . .
    </FRAMESET>
    <NOFRAMES>
        . . .
    </NOFRAMES>
</FRAMESET>
```

There is quite a bit of syntax to consider here, but it is all meaningful. Let's describe the hierarchy of this syntax first. The outermost parent tag is the <FRAMESET> tag, which acts as the container for all the frames used in the document. This tag is required to initiate the frames collection. The <FRAMESET> tag contains attributes that generally define how the frames should be rendered and how many frames should exist. The attributes defined here are inherited by children tags—unless the children tags have attributes that are different.

The next tag, the <FRAME> tag, is actually used to specify an individual frame and the contents of that frame. Some of the <FRAME> tag's attributes are the same as the

<FRAMESET> tag's attributes. If the <FRAME> tag's attributes differ from the <FRAMESET> tag's, the attributes of <FRAME> are used. Frame tags are required if you plan to put frames in your *frameset*.

Notice there is another <FRAMESET> tag nested inside the original <FRAMESET> tag. You can nest an infinite (if you really want to) amount of <FRAME> or <FRAMESET> tags, which would enable you to have complex layouts (considering that the children have priority here). Nested <FRAMESET> tags' attributes also have precedence over their parent tags' attributes, so the nested tag's attributes are used.

The <NOFRAMES> tag is used for browsers that do not support frames. All static content is encapsulated inside the <NOFRAMES> tag for interactively challenged browsers to access.

The <FRAMESET> Tag

The <FRAMESET> tag's required and most important attributes are the ROWS and COLS attributes. These attributes are used for specifying the length in columns or the width in rows of the frame, as well as how many frames are to exist under the *frameset*. Either the ROWS attribute or the COLS attribute can be used for a <FRAMESET> tag, but not both. The COLS attribute specifies the length of frames by columns (meaning each frame uses all the row space, but is metered out by its length in columns across the screen). The ROWS attribute specifies the length of the frames by rows (meaning each frame uses all the available column space and is metered out by its height in rows).

The width for each frame is specified by the ROWS or COLS attribute. These lengths are separated by commas (which imply how many frames are in the set). There are three different ways to specify the length for the frames, as follows:

◆ *Pixels*—When you define a frame's length by pixels, you are giving it a set length that may not be preferable in some cases because the browser's window can change in size and the user isn't always using the same pixel resolution as you are. For example, ROWS="200,50,100" would define three frames. The first frame is 200 pixels in height, the second is 50 pixels in height, and the final is 100 pixels in height.

◆ *Percentage of the Screen*—It is safer, sometimes, to define the length of your screens by specifying a percentage of the screen. Defining frames in this manner enables the frames to scale as the size of the browser changes. For example, if you use COLS="25%,100%", the first frame takes 25% of the available browser space (lengthwise), and the second frame consumes the rest of the space (100%).

◆ *Relative Size*—Similar to the prior method, defining the lengths of frames by relative sizes is efficient. Using this method, you define your lengths with a number followed by "*" to state the proportion of each frame's space relative to the other frames. For instance, COLS="2*,*,*" shows that there are three frames. The first frame takes up twice the length as the next two frames. Each of the second frames takes up half the space as the first frame. In short, the first frame takes 50% of the space ($\frac{1}{2}$), and the remaining two take 25% of the space ($\frac{1}{4}$).

◆ *Mix and Match*—You can use a combination of the previously mentioned methods for defining a frame's length. For example, in ROWS="200,25%,*", the first frame is 200 pixels high; the second frame takes up 25% of the available leftover space, and the third frame takes up whatever is left. Defining row and column space by proportions and by a percentage are the best ways to define frames because they are guaranteed to fit on all screens. But you may need to specify a frame in pixels if you want a graphic, control, or some other entity to fit exactly in the frame.

The FRAMEBORDER and FRAMESPACING attributes of the <FRAMESET> tag deal more with the aesthetics of the frame. Use the FRAMEBORDER attribute to specify whether you want a 3D border surrounding the frame. The value for *n* can be "1" (a frame border is present) or "0" (a frame border is not present).

The FRAMESPACING attribute is used to specify how much uniform spacing exists between each frame. The value *w* is in pixels and specifies the spacing of the frames. FRAMESPACING="10" causes each frame to be spaced 10 pixels from its neighboring frames.

The <FRAME> Tag

There are many attributes to consider here. You are already familiar with the function of the FRAMEBORDER attribute. The MARGINWIDTH property specifies the distance between the frame and the horizontal (left and right) sides of the document in pixels. For example, MARGINWIDTH="10" would make the left and right sides of the document both 10 pixels away from the margin on the left and right sides of the frame. The MARGINHEIGHT property is used to specify the distance between the frame and the top and bottom portions of the HTML document in the frame.

The NAME attribute is used to identify the frame's name. The value for FrameName can be any name following previously defined conventions. This name is used by HTML to appropriately direct links and can also be utilized by VBScript for the same purposes.

The SCROLLING attribute is used to indicate whether horizontal and vertical scroll bars should exist around the frame. The p yn can be either "yes" or "no" (specifying whether the scroll bars should exist).

The SRC attribute is used to specify the location of the initial document for that frame. The DocumentURL is the location of the HTML document or other resource to be accessed. For example, SRC="http://www.nm.org" would load the New Mexico Technet Web site into the corresponding frame.

The NORESIZE attribute (it doesn't take a value) is used to indicate whether the user is allowed to resize the given frame. The presence of this attribute prevents the user from resizing the frame.

The following code lists make an HTML document that contains frames. The various parts and functions of the document are explained after the code. Figure 11.5 illustrates these lists.

```
<HTML>
<HEAD>
<TITLE>This is the HTML document that contains the frame definitions</TITLE>
</HEAD>
<BODY>
<FRAMESET ROWS="*,25%" FRAMESPACING="6">
    <FRAME SRC="page1.htm" FRAMEBORDER="1" NAME="frame1">
    <FRAMESET COLS="*,100">
        <FRAME SRC="page2.htm"  FRAMEBORDER="1" NAME="frame2">
        <FRAME SRC="page3.htm"  FRAMEBORDER="1" NAME="frame3" SCROLLING="NO">

    </FRAMESET>
    <NOFRAMES>
        Your browser doesn't support frames? Too bad...
    </NOFRAMES>
</FRAMESET>
</BODY>
</HTML>
```

Notice that the preceding code defined two frame areas with the ROWS="*,25%" attribute in the first <FRAMESET> tag. One frame is defined under this tag, and the frame's initial document is Page1.htm. In the preceding code, notice that the next tag is not another <FRAME> tag, but another <FRAMESET> tag.

What significance does this have? Any frames defined and nested in this <FRAMESET> tag will be in the remaining 25 percent of the screen, as defined by the first <FRAMESET> tag. Notice that there are two frames, and they are defined by columns. The second frame is 100 pixels long; the first frame uses the remaining space. You can easily observe this in figure 11.5.

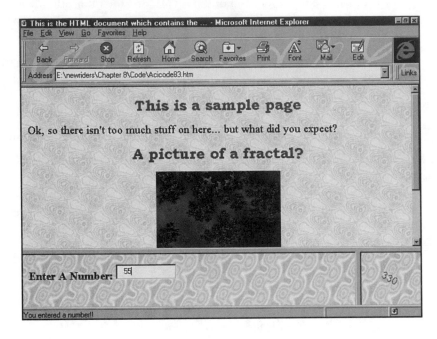

Figure 11.5

The document produced by the first code list, which contains three lists.

```
<HTML>
<HEAD>
<TITLE>This is the page used by the first frame</TITLE>
<STYLE>
H2 {color: brown; font: 18pt Bookman Old Style;  text-align: center}
</STYLE>
</HEAD>
<BODY BACKGROUND="tile1.jpg">
<BGSOUND SRC="bach1.mid">
<H2>This is a sample page</H2>
<P>
Ok, so there isn't too much stuff on here... but what did you expect?
</P>
<H2>A picture of a fractal?</H2>
<CENTER>
<IMG SRC="fractal.jpg">
```

```
</CENTER>
<HR>
</BODY>
</HTML>
```

The preceding code is a normal HTML page with some graphics and some style-sheet usage. It also plays a MIDI file when loaded.

```
<HTML>
<HEAD>
<TITLE>New Page</TITLE>
</HEAD>
<BODY BACKGROUND="tile4.jpg">
<B>Enter A Number:</B>

<OBJECT ID="TextBox1" WIDTH=96 HEIGHT=24
 CLASSID="CLSID:8BD21D10-EC42-11CE-9E0D-00AA006002F3">
    <PARAM NAME="VariousPropertyBits" VALUE="746604571">
    <PARAM NAME="MaxLength" VALUE="13">
    <PARAM NAME="Size" VALUE="2540;635">
    <PARAM NAME="FontCharSet" VALUE="0">
    <PARAM NAME="FontPitchAndFamily" VALUE="2">
    <PARAM NAME="FontWeight" VALUE="0">
</OBJECT>
<SCRIPT LANGUAGE="VBScript">
sub TextBox1_change
    if IsNumeric(TextBox1.value) = true then
        window.status = "You entered a number!!"
    else
        window.status = "not a number!!!"
    end if
end sub
</SCRIPT>
</BODY>
</HTML>
```

The longer of the two frames in the preceding code contains a Microsoft Forms 2.0 text box control. When you enter characters in the text box, a VBScript checks to see if the data you entered is a number or not. It indicates whether this data is a number through the status bar. If the data is a number, the status bar echoes: "You entered a number!!" If not, then the status bar reports: "not a number!!!"

```
<HTML>
<HEAD>
<TITLE>New Page</TITLE>
</HEAD>
<BODY BACKGROUND="tile4.jpg">
<OBJECT ID="IeLabel1" WIDTH=71 HEIGHT=49
 CLASSID="CLSID:99B42120-6EC7-11CF-A6C7-00AA00A47DD2">
    <PARAM NAME="_ExtentX" VALUE="1879">
    <PARAM NAME="_ExtentY" VALUE="1296">
    <PARAM NAME="Caption" VALUE="0">
    <PARAM NAME="Angle" VALUE="0">
    <PARAM NAME="Alignment" VALUE="4">
    <PARAM NAME="Mode" VALUE="1">
    <PARAM NAME="FillStyle" VALUE="0">
    <PARAM NAME="FillStyle" VALUE="0">
    <PARAM NAME="ForeColor" VALUE="#FF0000">
    <PARAM NAME="BackColor" VALUE="#C0C0C0">
    <PARAM NAME="FontName" VALUE="Arial">
    <PARAM NAME="FontSize" VALUE="12">
    <PARAM NAME="FontItalic" VALUE="0">
    <PARAM NAME="FontBold" VALUE="0">
    <PARAM NAME="FontUnderline" VALUE="0">
    <PARAM NAME="FontStrikeout" VALUE="0">
    <PARAM NAME="TopPoints" VALUE="0">
    <PARAM NAME="BotPoints" VALUE="0">
</OBJECT>

<OBJECT ID="IeTimer1" WIDTH=39 HEIGHT=39
 CLASSID="CLSID:59CCB4A0-727D-11CF-AC36-00AA00A47DD2">
    <PARAM NAME="_ExtentX" VALUE="1005">
    <PARAM NAME="_ExtentY" VALUE="1005">
    <PARAM NAME="Interval" VALUE="100">
</OBJECT>
<SCRIPT LANGUAGE="VBScript">
dim angrot
angrot = 5
sub Ietimer1_timer
    IeLabel1.Angle = IeLabel1.Angle + angrot
    if  IeLabel1.Angle = 0 then
        angrot = angrot * (-1)
    end if
    IeLabel1.Caption = IeLabel1.Angle
```

```
end sub
</SCRIPT>
</BODY>
</HTML>
```

The frame in the preceding code has an ActiveX control label that rotates on the lower right-hand corner of the browser screen. The timer that rotates the label calls (at a given interval) a script that increments the angle position of the text. When the text has rotated in one direction for 360 degrees, it alternates and rotates the other direction. The text's angle is reported by the control's caption.

Floating Frames

So far, only one collection of frames has been introduced: the *frameset*. Another type of frame is the floating frame. A floating frame is different from a frameset because you can use the floating frame in an HTML document, whereas the frameset is the HTML document that references other resources. You may also find that they suit your needs better than a frameset.

The general syntax for floating frames is as follows:

```
<IFRAME ALIGN="Alignment" FRAMEBORDER="n" HEIGHT="y" MARGINHEIGHT="height"
        MARGINWIDTH="width" NAME="FrameName" SCROLLING="yn"
        SRC="DocumentURL" WIDTH="x">
</IFRAME>
```

Most of these attributes, such as FRAMEBORDER, NAME, MARGINWIDTH, MARGINHEIGHT, SCROLLING, and SRC function the same as with framesets (see the previous section). The ALIGN attribute specifies the alignment of text and other entities in HTML around the frame—there are five values that can take the place of the *Alignment* placeholder in the preceding code. The value "TOP" specifies that surrounding text is aligned with the top of the frame, "BOTTOM" specifies that the text is aligned with the bottom of the frame, and "CENTER" specifies that the text is aligned with the center of the frame. The value "LEFT" aligns the frame to the flush left and causes all the text to flow around it. The value "RIGHT" is the same as "LEFT" except it aligns the frame to the right side of the screen.

The attributes WIDTH and HEIGHT are used to specify the width and height of the floating frame. WIDTH is used to specify the horizontal length of the frame in x number of pixels (or percentage). The HEIGHT attribute is used to specify the vertical length of the frame in y number of pixels (or percentage).

The following code is an example of a floating frame, illustrated in figure 11.6. The code uses VBScript to load a random URL into the frame every time the user clicks the button.

```
<HTML>
<HEAD>
<TITLE>Floating Frames Demo</TITLE>
</HEAD>
<BODY BACKGROUND="tile2.jpg">
<H2 ALIGN="CENTER">This is a floating frame</H2>
<HR WIDTH="50%" COLOR="blue">
<CENTER>
<IFRAME NAME ="framefloat" WIDTH="400" Height="200" SRC="blankhtml.htm">
</IFRAME>
</CENTER>
<HR WIDTH="50%" COLOR="blue">
<CENTER>
<INPUT TYPE="button" VALUE="Click to load a random link" NAME="b1">
</CENTER>
<HR WIDTH="50%" COLOR="blue">
<SCRIPT LANGUAGE="VBSCRIPT">
sub b1_OnClick
     window.frames(0).navigate "http://random.yahoo.com/bin/ryl"
end sub
</SCRIPT>
</BODY>
</HTML>
```

Figure 11.6

An illustration of the previous code.

This simple example waits for the user to press the button labeled: "Click to load a random link." When the user presses that button, the script then calls a program on this Internet, which chooses a random URL. The URL is displayed in the floating frame.

```
HTML>
<HEAD> '<
<TITLE>Blank Page</TITLE>
</HEAD>
<BODY BACKGROUND="tile5.jpg">
</BODY>
</HTML>
```

This code is just a blank page that is placed in the frame so it will load and display on screen. For this file to work with the previous code listing, you need to call it blankhtml.htm or another name that matches the SRC attribute of the floating frame code listing.

Obviously, this example is much simpler than the example presented in the previous section. In this example, the frame is defined with these attributes: the width is 400 pixels and the height is 200 pixels. There is also an initial page specified for the frame to load (it's an HTML document with a tiled background image). When the user clicks the button, a random URL generator is called, and the frame goes to a different URL every time the button is clicked. The URL to this random URL picker is http://random.yahoo.com/bin/ryl. The Internet Explorer's frames object model is used to indicate into which frame to place the content of the requested URL.

The TARGET Attribute

You can use the TARGET attribute in certain tags to redirect the results of the tag's action to a specified frame on the page. The TARGET attribute works with both floating and non-floating frames.

The TARGET attribute can be used in the following tags: <A> , <AREA>, <BASE>, and <FORM> tags. The <A> tag or anchor tag creates links in HTML documents. Normally, when a user clicks a link, the link loads and the original document is replaced by the document that was called through the link. Using the TARGET attribute with the <A> tag enables you to direct the content to a frame in the document instead.

The <AREA> tag is used inside the <MAP> tag to specify clickable hot-spots on a client-side image map that also request URLs across the Internet. Using the TARGET attribute in this tag enables you to direct the content to a frame on the current page.

The <BASE> attribute specifies the base location (URL) of the document and all relative links (links to other resources without a complete URL, just the name of the file they access). Use the location specified by the base attribute to access the resources. Using the TARGET attribute in this tag directs all links on the page to the frame specified by the TARGET attribute (unless the tag has a TARGET attribute that specifies otherwise).

When a form is submitted, usually a confirmation or other data is returned. When the TARGET attribute is used in the <FORM> tag, all data that is returned as a result of submitting the form is placed in the frame specified by the TARGET attribute. Table 11.2 specifies the valid attributes allowed for the TARGET attribute.

Table 11.2
A Listing of the Values Used for the TARGET Attribute

Value	Purpose
FrameName	*FrameName* is a placeholder for the name you specified for the targeted frame. When the TARGET attribute is given the name of the frame, all the content requested from the tag containing the TARGET attribute is loaded in that frame with the specified name.
[sym]blank	This value causes the content requested by the tag that contains the TARGET attribute to be loaded in a new browser window.
[sym]parent	This value causes the content requested by the tag that contains the TARGET attribute to be loaded in the parent document that the tag is in.
[sym]self	This value causes the content requested by the tag to be loaded into the frame from which it was requested.
[sym]top	This value causes the content requested to be loaded into the full body of the window.

Place this HTML tag in the body section of the previous code somewhere:

```
<A HREF="http://www.microsoft.com/" TARGET="flamefloat">Click Me!</A>
```

When you click this link, the requested resource, http://www.microsoft.com/, loads into the floating frame that has the name framefloat. Changing the TARGET attribute to [sym]blank causes a new browser window to be loaded with the specified URL (http://www.microsoft.com/).

Inserting ActiveX Controls

If you have followed the examples in this chapter and understand how HTML works, then you have a pretty good grasp of ActiveX controls already. What you have seen so far are some relatively simple uses of the ActiveX control. The timer control, which calls a procedure at a given interval, was used; the gradient control was used, and its colors were randomly changed when the user clicked the button; and the label control was rotated using the timer control and VBScript.

In this section, you will learn about more complex ActiveX controls such as the TabStrip control, the chart control, and more of the Microsoft Forms 2.0 controls. We focus on various controls in this section by using examples and more VBScript.

> **Note** Keep in mind that manually inserting any ActiveX control is a tediously painful task that can be efficiently handled by the ActiveX Control Pad.

This section covers the general syntax of the <OBJECT> tag and its child tag: the <PARAM> tag. The <PARAM> tag sets the properties of the object specified by its parent <OBJECT> tag. You can consider the <OBJECT> tag just another HTML tag, and in some respects it is; however, it behaves differently from the other tags because it actually inserts another program into your HTML page, not a picture or a sound clip.

Syntax of the <OBJECT> Tag

The <OBJECT> tag has a pretty extensive syntax that would naturally be demanded by a tag that has the capability for inserting programs in an HTML page. The syntax for the <OBJECT> tag is in the following code, and all the attributes for the tag are explained in the paragraphs that follow the code.

```
<OBJECT ALIGN="Alignment" BORDER="borderlen" CLASSID="clid"
    ➥CODEBASE="codeurl" CODETYPE="mime" DATA="datatype" HEIGHT="y"
    ➥HSPACE="xspace" ID="ObjectName" STANDBY="message"
    ➥USEMAP="mapurl" TYPE="mimetype" VSPACE="yspace" WIDTH="x">
        <PARAM NAME="ObjectPropertyName" VALUE="ObjValue">
. . .
</OBJECT>
```

The ALIGN attribute is used to specify the alignment of the object on the HTML page it is on. You can substitute the *Alignment* placeholder with one of several values mentioned in table 11.3. This attribute is not required.

Table 11.3
The Valid Values for the Alignment Attribute of the <OBJECT> Tag

Value	Position
"BASELINE"	This value for ALIGN causes the bottom of the object to be aligned with the baseline of the text.
"CENTER"	This value for ALIGN causes the object to be centered on the screen. All text begins on the line after the object.
"LEFT"	This value for ALIGN aligns the object flush left. All text is wrapped along the right side the object.
"MIDDLE"	The middle of the object is aligned with the baseline of the text when this value is used for the ALIGN attribute.
"RIGHT"	This value for the ALIGN attribute causes the object to be aligned flush right. Text wraps around the left side of the object.
"TEXTBOTTOM"	This value causes the bottom of the object to be aligned with the bottom of the surrounding text.
"TEXTMIDDLE"	This value causes the middle of the object to be aligned with the middle of the surrounding text.
"TEXTTOP"	This value aligns the top of the object with the top of the surrounding text.

The BORDER attribute draws a border around the specified object. The placeholder value *borderlen* is to be specified in pixels, indicating the uniform width of the border around the object. Some objects, such as the timer control, have no need for this attribute. The BORDER attribute is not required.

The CLASSID attribute specifies what control to use. Each control has its own, unique CLASSID setting that is used to indicate the address of the control in your registry. The CLASSID's scheme for giving unique identification to every control is based on several factors. A CLASSID is made for a control when that control is created and uses different variables, such as the time and date the control was made, who made it, and so on. No two controls can have the same CLASSID value.

The clid placeholder represents the value for the CLASSID of a control. For instance, the value "CLSID:99B42120-6EC7-11CF-A6C7-00AA00A47DD2" for the CLASSID attribute specifies the standard Label control. This attribute is required because ActiveX objects are registered with your system, and this is the method for specifying which registered ActiveX control will be used in the page.

If the users do not have the specified ActiveX control, the `CODEBASE` attribute is used to specify where they can get the ActiveX control. The value `codeurl` is used to indicate the URL of that control on the Internet. For example, `CODEBASE="http://www.microsoft.com/ie/control/ielabel.ocx"` would specify the path to the label.ocx control. This attribute is not required.

The `CODETYPE` control complements the `CODEBASE` control by specifying the media type of the control in MIME-type format (program-type/program-name). For example, `CODETYPE="application/perl5"` would specify that the control was written in perl5 (although no ActiveX controls I know of are written in perl5) and would specify if the system will handle it accordingly—if it is capable (if the system has a perl interpreter that runs the controls). `CODETYPE` is not a required attribute either.

The `DATA` attribute specifies inline data or the location of data (in the form of an URL) that the control may require. *Datatype* is the placeholder for what the data for the `DATA` attribute would be. If it is inline data, then it will be typed here. If the data is at an URL, then the location to it is entered here. The `DATA` attribute is not required unless the control specified needs it.

Warning If you use inline data, keep it to a minimum. For example, it would be ludicrous to use the image control and have the data (the image) inline, unless it were rather small.

The `HEIGHT` attribute specifies the vertical length of the control's space. This space is the maximum space the program is allowed to use in the HTML document. The placeholder value *y* is in pixels for the height of the control space. The `HEIGHT` attribute is not required; if it is not specified, the control will use as much height-space as it requires.

The `HSPACE` attribute is used to specify the separation space between the specified object and all surrounding entities, such as text, graphics, and other objects. The placeholder value *xspace* is in pixels specifying the horizontal (left and right) separations. The `HSPACE` attribute is not required.

The `ID` attribute identifies the object so it is capable of being utilized by VBScript and other objects. The placeholder value *ObjectName* is a name you choose to identify the object (following proper conventions). The `ID` attribute is not required, but is necessary if you intend to use the control with VBScript.

The attribute `STANDBY` is used to show a message while a specified control is loading and initializing on your page. The placeholder value for *message* is the message you want to relay to the user while the control is loading and setting up. For example, `STANDBY="This control is initializing, please wait"` would relay that message to the user. This attribute is not required.

The USEMAP attribute specifies an image map to be used with the control. This can be an URL to an image map location, or it can be a client-side image map on the same page. Client-side image maps are defined using the <MAP> tag. This tag is not required, either.

The TYPE attribute is used in conjunction with the DATA attribute and is used to specify the MIME type of the data. For example, TYPE="application/gif" would indicate that the data was a GIF (Graphics Information Format) image. This attribute is not required unless the control also uses the DATA attribute.

The attribute VSPACE specifies the separation space between the specified object and all surrounding entities, such as text, graphics, and other objects. The placeholder value *yspace* is in pixels and specifies the vertical (top and bottom) separations. For example, VSPACE="10" would make a 10-pixel separation between surrounding entities and the specified object. The VSPACE attribute is not required.

The WIDTH attribute specifies the horizontal length of the control's space. This space allots the maximum space across the page that the program is allowed to use. The placeholder value *x* is in pixels. The WIDTH attribute is not required; if it is not specified, the control will use as much width-space as it requires.

The <PARAM> Tag

Now let's examine the <PARAM> tag and its uses. As you know, the <PARAM> tag is used for initializing or setting the internal properties of the specified control. A property to an ActiveX control is the same as an attribute to an HTML tag. It is more suitable to call the ActiveX control's attributes "properties" because they are objects and consist of events, methods, and properties. The <PARAM> tag accomplishes the task of setting properties with two simple attributes: the NAME attribute and the VALUE attribute.

◆ The NAME attribute is used to specify what property of the object to set. These properties can be any exposed properties of the given object. Exposed or public properties are properties that can be changed by other programs and entities, whereas private properties of the object are used for internal purposes only and are not exposed or accessible to other programs or entities.

◆ The VALUE attribute is used to set the value of the property of the control specified by name. For various properties of different controls, the value for this attribute is different. For instance, the value for the "Background" color of a Label control might be the Hexadecimal color for green: "#00FF00", whereas a value of "true" might be given to another control indicating whether it is visible or not.

The next section deals with several examples utilizing Intrinsic controls, VBScript, frames, and ActiveX controls. These examples will be fully examined and the different portions of them will be explained in detail.

Examples

The following code listings demonstrate some of the uses of ActiveX controls that you haven't been exposed to—as well as the ones you have seen.

When people design pages with ActiveX controls, they often find it difficult to place the controls exactly where they want. The HTML layout control is very essential to anyone who wants to use ActiveX controls and have full leverage over them. The HTML layout control enables you to specify a variety of objects in a defined area. In this defined area, you can place the objects wherever you want; they can be placed right next to each other, they can overlap, and so on. In short, the HTML layout control enables you to disregard the HTML formatting "rules" that do not permit extra spacing or overlapping in ordinary cases.

```
<HTML>
<HEAD>
<TITLE>New Page</TITLE>
</HEAD>
<BODY>

<OBJECT CLASSID="CLSID:812AE312-8B8E-11CF-93C8-00AA00C08FDF"
ID="Layout1_alx" STYLE="LEFT:0;TOP:0">
        <PARAM
            NAME="ALXPATH"
            REF
            VALUE="file:E:\newriders\Chapter 8\Code\Layout1.alx"
            >
</OBJECT>
</BODY>
</HTML>
```

This example uses one <OBJECT> tag that is the HTML Layout control. As you can see, this control has one <PARAM> tag, and therefore, one property that is the path of the layout (.alx) file. The layout file actually contains all the specifications for the objects and their spacing, and also the scripts that control those objects, if any. So, you are inserting this layout file into another HTML document, and now all the objects and scripts specified in the layout file are part of the document as well.

The next listing is the actual layout file itself. This listing is long, so you may want to get it off the CD that accompanies this book. It is under Chapter 11 and is called Acicode89.htm. The layout file is called Layout1.alx.

```
<SCRIPT LANGUAGE="VBScript">
<!--
Sub PageOne()
      Label1.caption = "Enter a Sine Value"
      myBox.left = 116
      myBox.top = 50
      CommandButton1.left = 116
      CommandButton1.top = 91
      ToggleButton1.top = -10000
      ToggleButton1.left = 75
      Image1.top = -10000
      Image1.left = 166
end sub
show = 25
hide = 25


Sub TabStrip1_Change()

select case TabStrip1.SelectedItem.Index
    case 0
        call PageOne()
    case 1
        call PageTwo()
end select
end sub
-->
</SCRIPT>
<SCRIPT LANGUAGE="VBScript">
<!--
Function GetSine(Angle)
pi = 4 * atn(1)
GetSine = sin(Angle * pi/180)
end function
dim pi
dim SineValue
Sub PageTwo()
```

```
            Label1.caption = "Press the Button"
            myBox.left = -10000
            myBox.top = 50
            CommandButton1.left = -10000
            CommandButton1.top = 91
            ToggleButton1.top = 66
            ToggleButton1.left = 75
            Image1.top = 66
            Image1.left = 166
end sub
Sub CommandButton1_Click()
SineValue = GetSine(myBox.text)
alert SineValue
end sub
-->
</SCRIPT>
<SCRIPT LANGUAGE="VBScript">
<!--
Sub ToggleButton1_Click()
if Image1.PicturePath = "icon1.bmp" then
        Image1.PicturePath = "icon2.bmp"
else
        Image1.PicturePath = "icon1.bmp"
end if
end sub
-->
</SCRIPT>
```

The previous code snippet contains all of the scripting that manipulates the ActiveX controls in this layout file. All the script, whether it is JavaScript or VBScript, must be encapsulated within the <SCRIPT> tags, as you will see in the following section, "Manipulating Controls."

```
<DIV BACKGROUND="#8080" ID="Layout1"
STYLE="LAYOUT:FIXED;WIDTH:243pt;HEIGHT:142pt;">
     <OBJECT ID="TabStrip1"
     CLASSID="CLSID:EAE50EB0-4A62-11CE-BED6-00AA00611080"
STYLE="TOP:8pt;LEFT:17pt;WIDTH:215pt;HEIGHT:124pt;TABINDEX:0;ZINDEX:0;">
         <PARAM NAME="ListIndex" VALUE="0">
         <PARAM NAME="BackColor" VALUE="8421376">
         <PARAM NAME="Size" VALUE="7585;4374">
```

```
<PARAM NAME="Items" VALUE="Example 1;Example 2;">
<PARAM NAME="TabOrientation" VALUE="2">
<PARAM NAME="TipStrings" VALUE="This calculates the sine of a given
➥angle;This is just another example;">
<PARAM NAME="Names" VALUE="Tab1;Tab2;">
<PARAM NAME="NewVersion" VALUE="-1">
<PARAM NAME="TabsAllocated" VALUE="2">
<PARAM NAME="Tags" VALUE=";;">
<PARAM NAME="TabData" VALUE="2">
<PARAM NAME="Accelerator" VALUE=";;">
<PARAM NAME="FontCharSet" VALUE="0">
<PARAM NAME="FontPitchAndFamily" VALUE="2">
<PARAM NAME="FontWeight" VALUE="0">
<PARAM NAME="TabState" VALUE="3;3">
</OBJECT>
<OBJECT ID="MyBox"
 CLASSID="CLSID:8BD21D10-EC42-11CE-9E0D-00AA006002F3"
STYLE="TOP:50pt;LEFT:116pt;WIDTH:58pt;HEIGHT:17pt;TABINDEX:1;ZINDEX:1;">
<PARAM NAME="VariousPropertyBits" VALUE="746604571">
<PARAM NAME="Size" VALUE="2046;600">
<PARAM NAME="Value" VALUE="0">
<PARAM NAME="FontCharSet" VALUE="0">
<PARAM NAME="FontPitchAndFamily" VALUE="2">
<PARAM NAME="FontWeight" VALUE="0">
</OBJECT>
<OBJECT ID="Label1"
 CLASSID="CLSID:978C9E23-D4B0-11CE-BF2D-00AA003F40D0"
STYLE="TOP:17pt;LEFT:99pt;WIDTH:116pt;HEIGHT:17pt;ZINDEX:2;">
<PARAM NAME="BackColor" VALUE="8421376">
<PARAM NAME="VariousPropertyBits" VALUE="8388627">
<PARAM NAME="Caption" VALUE="Enter an angle">
<PARAM NAME="Size" VALUE="4092;600">
<PARAM NAME="FontHeight" VALUE="280">
<PARAM NAME="FontCharSet" VALUE="0">
<PARAM NAME="FontPitchAndFamily" VALUE="2">
<PARAM NAME="FontWeight" VALUE="0">
</OBJECT>
<OBJECT ID="ToggleButton1"
 CLASSID="CLSID:8BD21D60-EC42-11CE-9E0D-00AA006002F3"
STYLE="TOP:33pt;LEFT:297pt;WIDTH:41pt;HEIGHT:33pt;TABINDEX:3;ZINDEX:3;">
```

```
            <PARAM NAME="BackColor" VALUE="2147483663">
            <PARAM NAME="ForeColor" VALUE="2147483666">
            <PARAM NAME="DisplayStyle" VALUE="6">
            <PARAM NAME="Size" VALUE="1446;1164">
            <PARAM NAME="Caption" VALUE="ClickMe">
            <PARAM NAME="FontCharSet" VALUE="0">
            <PARAM NAME="FontPitchAndFamily" VALUE="2">
            <PARAM NAME="ParagraphAlign" VALUE="3">
            <PARAM NAME="FontWeight" VALUE="0">
      </OBJECT>
      <OBJECT ID="Image1"
        CLASSID="CLSID:D4A97620-8E8F-11CF-93CD-00AA00C08FDF"
STYLE="TOP:83pt;LEFT:297pt;WIDTH:33pt;HEIGHT:33pt;ZINDEX:4;">
            <PARAM NAME="PicturePath" VALUE="icon1.bmp">
            <PARAM NAME="BorderStyle" VALUE="0">
            <PARAM NAME="SizeMode" VALUE="3">
            <PARAM NAME="SpecialEffect" VALUE="2">
            <PARAM NAME="Size" VALUE="1164;1164">
            <PARAM NAME="PictureAlignment" VALUE="0">
            <PARAM NAME="VariousPropertyBits" VALUE="19">
      </OBJECT>
      <OBJECT ID="CommandButton1"
        CLASSID="CLSID:D7053240-CE69-11CD-A777-00DD01143C57"
STYLE="TOP:91pt;LEFT:116pt;WIDTH:58pt;HEIGHT:25pt;TABINDEX:4;ZINDEX:5;">
            <PARAM NAME="Caption" VALUE="Calculate!">
            <PARAM NAME="Size" VALUE="2046;882">
            <PARAM NAME="FontCharSet" VALUE="0">
            <PARAM NAME="FontPitchAndFamily" VALUE="2">
            <PARAM NAME="ParagraphAlign" VALUE="3">
            <PARAM NAME="FontWeight" VALUE="0">
      </OBJECT>
</DIV>
```

In this example, all the objects in this layout file are surrounded by <DIV> tags. The <DIV> tag is a style-sheet tag and is used for many different reasons. Its main purpose is to divide off sections of an HTML document so it can be dealt with differently. In this case, the <DIV> tag specifies the area with the STYLE attribute that all the controls in the layout file will consume. In each <OBJECT> tag, the attribute STYLE is again seen. This attribute specifies the exact placement of the control within the area bounded by the <DIV> tag.

There are many controls used in this example, with the most important one being the tabstrip control. From the ID attribute of the <OBJECT> tags, you should have been able to identify which <OBJECT> tag was used to insert the tabstrip control. It was the first object tag in the file and its ID is "TabStrip1." The tabstrip control is one of the nicest controls to use. These controls are a series of tabs that are attached to a box, and when different tabs are clicked, the contents in the box change. The tabstrip in this listing hosts the two examples.

The way the tabstrip works is simple: when the user clicks on the collection of tabs, the change event occurs for the control. The event handler then does what is necessary to display the new content. The sub procedure called TabStrip1_Change() is what handles the event. When a tab is clicked, all the controls that are not needed by that tab are moved off the screen and the tab's controls are moved on. The sub procedures PageOne() and PageTwo() handle the movement of the controls.

Remember that all controls have many properties, and they can be used to specify many different attributes of the object. The tabstrip control, for example, has many properties, including the number of tabs, their caption, the style of the tabs, their orientation, the width of the tab-box area, and tab tip-text. When a user positions the mouse over one of the tabs, a yellow box will appear, indicating the purpose of the tab. These are all set by properties of the tabstrip control.

The first example is rather simple. A user enters an angle in degrees and clicks the button. A message box is returned, indicating the sine of that angle (*sine* is geometrically defined as the ratio of a triangle's opposite side to the hypotenuse). The logic behind the program is also not complicated. The sub procedure CommandButton1 _Click() is called when the click event occurs for the button. This event then calls the function GetSine(Angle) that does all the mathematical work behind determining the sine of the angle, which involves converting the given angle into radians, using the intrinsic $\sin(x)$ function, and then returning the value.

The first example is on the first tab, as indicated by the tab's titles. When the second tab is clicked, the text box and the button are moved off the screen and a toggle button and an image control are moved on. The label on the first example, however, does not get moved off. The label's caption property is merely changed when the second example tab is clicked. It is very useful to conserve controls this way. If they can be used on multiple tabs, do it! The other way wastes memory and uses more code.

The second example is just as simple as the first. You start with an image. Every time the toggle button is pressed down, the image changes. Every time it is unpressed, the original image returns. The sub procedure that handles the changing of images through the toggle button is the ToggleButton1_Click() sub procedure, which then uses an if-then conditional statement to determine which image to display.

All the objects in the example file are named so you can easily figure out which object is which. You can add more to the script if you want, you can alter the properties of the tabstrip control to include another tab or several more, or you can make the tabs buttons—or any number of things.

Manipulating Controls

In this section, you learn the specifics about the <SCRIPT> tag that seems to be appearing in every example. A few more examples will emphasize the details of the <SCRIPT> tag and its related attributes. All your VBScript statements are encapsulated within the <SCRIPT> tag, and this is where they are executed.

The <SCRIPT> tag is used for not only the VBScript programming language but also the JavaScript programming language. In Chapter 4, a JavaScript program and a VBScript program were both presented, and they more or less perform the same task. Examine those listings to see how JavaScript and VBScript are used in web pages.

Remember, scripting and the <SCRIPT> tag is the mechanism you use to change and manipulate ActiveX controls. With scripting, you respond to events, call and invoke methods, and set and change procedures.

> **Note** | JavaScript and Visual Basic Script can coexist in an HTML document; you just have to define them using separate script tags.

Syntax of the <SCRIPT> Tag

The <SCRIPT> tag does not have a syntax as cumbersome as the <OBJECT> tag. In fact, the only attribute required and primarily used in the <SCRIPT> tag is the LANGUAGE attribute. The syntax of the <SCRIPT> tag is as follows:

```
<SCRIPT LANGUAGE="ScriptLanguage" EVENT="EventName" FOR="ObjectName">
. . .
</SCRIPT>
```

The LANGUAGE attribute specifies which language to use in the current <SCRIPT> tag. The value "VBScript" for the <SCRIPT> tag uses the Visual Basic Script interpreter; the value "Javascript" uses the JavaScript interpreter for the given <SCRIPT> tag.

The FOR and EVENT attributes are used together. The FOR attribute specifies what control the following <SCRIPT> tag should be used *for* (*ObjectName* represents the name of the control the script is for), and the EVENT attribute is used to specify what event to use for the control of *ObjectName*. The placeholder *EventName* is used to specify which event for the control to invoke the following script. Events are "actions" that objects receive, such as a click or a mouse-pointer moving over the object. For example:

```
<SCRIPT LANGUAGE="VBScript" FOR="IeLabel1" EVENT="OnClick">
 . . .
</SCRIPT>
```

The script is invoked when the click event occurs for the object named IeLabel1. Then, all the statements contained in the script block are executed.

Additionally, events for certain objects can be used as attributes in their respective tag to call a Visual Basic Script procedure. The LANGUAGE attribute must also be included when you desire to call Visual Basic Script statements with this method.

Examples

This section will cover some examples directly relating to the <SCRIPT> tag, which includes some of the methods previously mentioned for invoking scripts. The methods examined will be using the script tag and having a Visual Basic Script procedure enacted when its corresponding event occur, using the FOR and EVENT attributes for invoking scripts, and calling scripts by using an event for an object as that object's attribute. The following code will demonstrate all three methods using simple controls. Figure 11.7 illustrates this listing.

```
<HTML>
<HEAD>
<TITLE>New Page</TITLE>
</HEAD>
<BODY>
<INPUT TYPE="BUTTON" VALUE="ClickMe" NAME="btn1">
<!-- The input tag below uses the second technique,
    notice how the attributes are part of the tag -->
<INPUT LANGUAGE="VBScript"
      TYPE="TEXT"
      OnBlur="numcheck"
      LANGUAGE="VBScript"
      NAME="txt1" >
<SCRIPT LANGUAGE="VBScript" FOR="btn1" EVENT="OnClick">
      window.status = "Click the label to change color"
</SCRIPT>
```

```
<!-- The above script tag is an example of the third technique -->
<HR>
<!-- Below is an example of the first technique -->
<SCRIPT LANGUAGE="VBScript">
<!--
Sub NumCheck()
      if IsNumeric(txt1.value) = false then
            msgbox"this is not a number!!"
      else
            msgbox"this is a number!!"
      end if
End Sub
Sub IeLabel1_Click()
    randomize
    IeLabel1.BackColor = int((rnd * 255)*(rnd * 255)*(rnd * 255))
    IeLabel1.ForeColor =  int((rnd * 255)*(rnd * 255)^(rnd * 255))
end sub
-->
</SCRIPT>
    <OBJECT ID="IeLabel1" WIDTH=137 HEIGHT=93
    CLASSID="CLSID:99B42120-6EC7-11CF-A6C7-00AA00A47DD2">
        <PARAM NAME="_ExtentX" VALUE="3625">
        <PARAM NAME="_ExtentY" VALUE="2461">
        <PARAM NAME="Caption" VALUE="The Label Button">
        <PARAM NAME="Angle" VALUE="0">
        <PARAM NAME="Alignment" VALUE="4">
        <PARAM NAME="Mode" VALUE="1">
        <PARAM NAME="FillStyle" VALUE="0">
        <PARAM NAME="FillStyle" VALUE="1">
        <PARAM NAME="ForeColor" VALUE="#000000">
        <PARAM NAME="BackColor" VALUE="#8098B0">
        <PARAM NAME="FontName" VALUE="Arial">
        <PARAM NAME="FontSize" VALUE="12">
        <PARAM NAME="FontItalic" VALUE="0">
        <PARAM NAME="FontBold" VALUE="0">
        <PARAM NAME="FontUnderline" VALUE="0">
        <PARAM NAME="FontStrikeout" VALUE="0">
        <PARAM NAME="TopPoints" VALUE="0">
        <PARAM NAME="BotPoints" VALUE="0">
        <PARAM NAME="BackStyle" VALUE="1">
    </OBJECT>
</BODY>
</HTML>
```

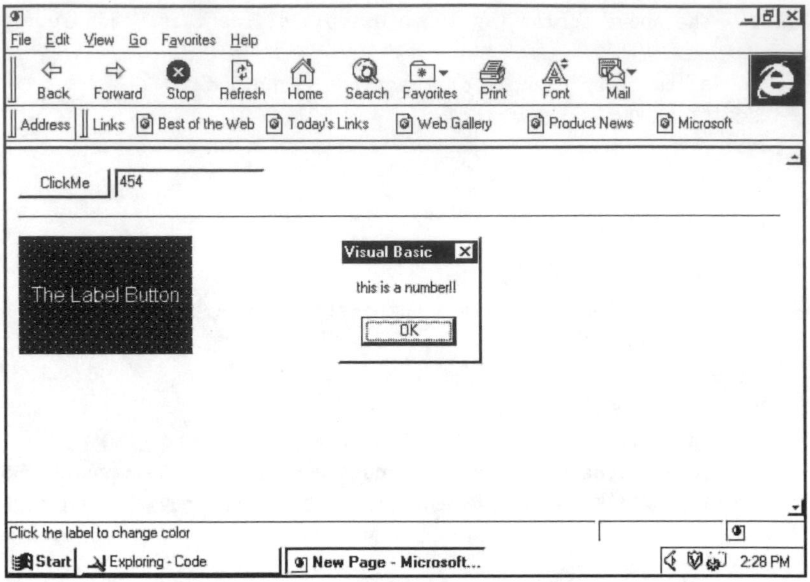

Figure 11.7

*An illustration of
the previous
listing.*

The code uses three techniques of the script tag; these are in the following list.

1. **Scripts launched through sub procedures that are event handlers.**
   This is the most common way to manipulate the events of controls through
   scripting. A sub procedure inside VBScript or JavaScript is named after the
   control and the event it handles (in the form of *ObjectName_ObjectEvent*) and the
   necessary statements in that sub procedure are executed.

2. **Events as attributes of the object's tag calling a sub procedure.** This
   is another method used to handle an event for a specific object. Specifying the
   event as an attribute of the object's tag and referencing the appropriate sub
   procedure is how this task is accomplished (in the form of *EventName="sub-
   procedure"*, where *sub procedure* is the name of the sub procedure that is in the
   <SCRIPT> tag). You must also use the LANGUAGE="VBScript" or
   LANGUAGE="JavaScript" in the object's tag as an attribute as well.

3. **Events and the object's name identified as values for
   the EVENT and FOR attributes of the <SCRIPT> tag.**
   This is the final method for handling events of objects. This
   method uses the FOR and EVENT attributes of the script tag.
   All the statements in the script tag are executed for the object
   specified by FOR and for the event specified by EVENT (in the
   form of FOR="*ObjectName*" EVENT="*EventName*").

The comments found in the code indicate when each of the previously mentioned techniques for the <SCRIPT> tag were used. Using the first technique was simple. A sub procedure called IeLabel1_OnClick() was created that would handle the Click event for the label on the page. When the label is clicked, the foreground and the background properties of the label also change.

The second technique was used with the text box intrinsic HTML control. When some characters were typed and the user left the test box (its focus was blurred), a message box would appear, indicating whether the input was a number or not a number. Notice the OnBlur="NumCheck" attribute in the text boxes' tag. The *EventName* for the object is the attribute, and it calls a sub procedure named NumCheck. This procedure then checks to determine if the input was a number or not and relays the appropriate message.

The third technique was used with the button intrinsic control on this page. Notice that there are two <SCRIPT> tags in the listing, and the first of the two contains the FOR and EVENT attributes that were mentioned. The FOR attribute specifies the name of the button and the EVENT attribute indicates what must occur for the button to execute the following code. When the OnClick event occurs for the button, the status bar tells users that they should click on the label to change its color.

CHAPTER 12

Using the Built-In ActiveX Controls

By Eric Smith

N ow that you have learned how to use the ActiveX Control Pad to build layout files to add to your HTML documents, you are ready to learn about other controls, known as *built-in controls*. These controls are available to any user with Internet Explorer 3.0. Although these controls are simple, they are key building blocks for creating more complex pages.

You have already learned how to use one built-in control: the Label control. In this chapter, you will be introduced to 12 more, including the Text Box, Image, Check Box, and others. By using these controls together, you can create data entry windows on your forms without having to worry about complex HTML formatting that never quite comes out right, no matter how many times you try. By using the ActiveX Control Pad, all the controls will appear exactly as you designed them.

To help you understand how these controls can be used, each is demonstrated in a real-world, practical example. Ever wonder how to create a graphical map of your site that a user can click on? This is just one of several examples demonstrated in this chapter.

Creating a Data-Entry Form

One of the most common types of documents on the Internet is the data-entry form. Used for everything from ordering products to sending feedback about a site, knowing how to create a data-entry form is an important skill for web developers to have.

This example demonstrates the use of several built-in ActiveX controls:

◆ the Text Box

◆ the Label

◆ the Check Box

◆ the Combo Box

◆ the Command Button

◆ the List Box

◆ the Option Button

Although this may sound like a lot of controls to show in one example, you will see how easy they are to put together to build custom forms for your own needs.

Getting Started

To begin with, figure 12.1 shows what the data-entry form will look like when it is done. This form demonstrates seven of the built-in ActiveX controls, all of which are common to Windows applications. This typical data entry form is also one you might have seen at a web site somewhere on the Internet.

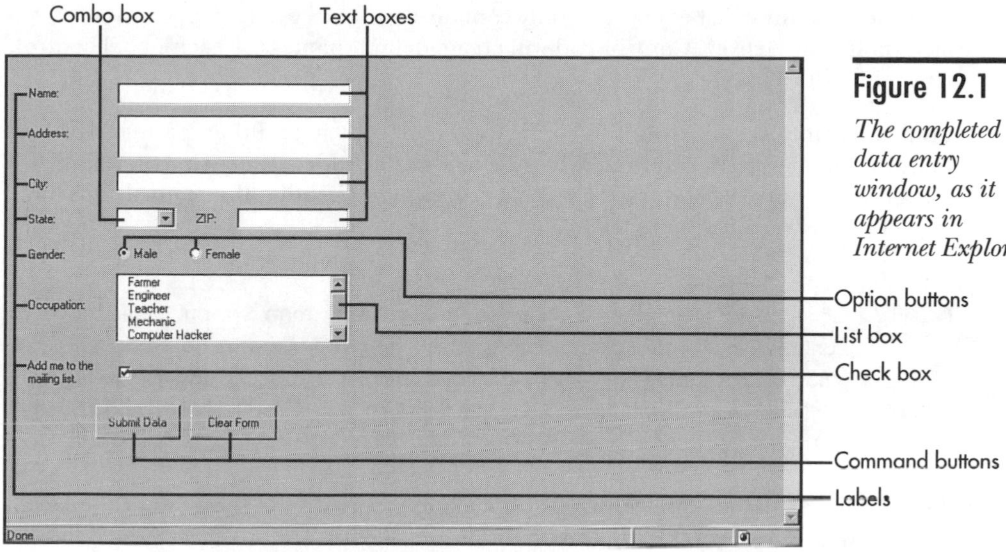

Figure 12.1

The completed data entry window, as it appears in Internet Explorer.

Now that you have seen what the finished product will eventually look like, it is time to create it with the ActiveX Control Pad.

1. If you have not done so already, start the ActiveX Control Pad and select New HTML Layout from the File menu.

2. When the blank HTML Layout file is displayed, access the Property Sheet by clicking your right mouse button on the form and selecting Properties from the pop-up menu.

3. Set the ID property of the HTML Layout to a useful name, such as DataEntryForm or frmDataEntry, if you are more familiar with the prefix naming format common in Visual Basic. The code included with the CD uses the name frmDataEntry, and that is the name used in the code shown in the book.

All the code for this example is included on the CD-ROM that accompanies this book. The files for this example are in the `\Examples\Chapter 12\` directory.

On the CD

Placing the Labels

Almost every piece of text on this form is a Label control. As figure 12.1 displays, all the text except for the labels next to the Option buttons is contained in Label controls.

By now, you are familiar with the ActiveX Control Pad's method of control placement. Click the Label control in the toolbox, and then drag a box on the Layout page. Because these Label controls only contain static text, the ID property is not important. The ActiveX Control Pad will create default names for each Label control, beginning with Label1.

A quick way to place controls is to create one label, copy it, and then paste it as many times as you need it. If you do this, be sure to set any properties (such as color, border, and so on) *before* you start making copies of it. Creating the controls this way saves you a great deal of time later.

> **Note** One popular method of "uncluttering" a Visual Basic form is to put all the Label controls into a control array. Unfortunately, this technique does not work in VBScript; each label has to have a unique name. It is normally easier to just leave the Label controls with the name created by the Control Pad (Label1, Label2, and so on).

Here is a list of all the Label controls you need to create on the form. You can place them on the form as you see fit; the figures in this section are only a suggested layout.

◆ Name:

◆ Address:

◆ City:

◆ State:

◆ ZIP:

◆ Gender:

◆ Occupation:

◆ Add me to the mailing list.

> **Note** One important thing to remember about creating pages and forms for the Internet: your page is internationally available. For this reason, do not rely on U.S. conventions for items such as zip codes or phone number formats. A zip code, for instance, is specific to the United States. A more generic label could be *ZIP/Postal Code.*
>
> In addition, phone numbers outside the U.S. are not always preceded by an area code and are not always 10 digits long. Unless you are certain that your pages will only be used by people within the United States, do not attempt to impose formats on these country-specific fields—this includes trying to validate a phone number based on where the user entered hyphens or parentheses around the numbers.

Although this example uses the Label controls without setting any properties, there are a number of properties you may want to use in your own pages. These properties are covered in more detail in Chapter 13; however, they are summarized here for reference. There are many other properties of the Label control; these are the ones that enable you to customize your labels.

◆ **AutoSize**—This property, when set to True, causes the border of the Label control to shrink or expand to fit the content of the Label.

◆ **BackStyle**—By setting this property to *Transparent*, the background color of the form shows through and appears to be the background of the Label. Using this property is much easier than setting all the color properties of each of the Labels on your form.

◆ **BackColor, ForeColor**—These properties control the background and foreground colors of the Label control. In some cases, you want to have different colors than the default values. Besides being able to specify a color, you can also instruct the control to use a color the user has already specified. These pre-selected colors include the default window background, the title bar color, and so on. This feature enables your form to conform to the user's color selections automatically.

◆ **Caption**—This is the property that contains the actual text displayed in the Label control.

◆ **SpecialEffect**—This property enables you to specify other attributes about the text to be displayed. It enables you to show the text in the label as flat (the default selection), raised, sunken, etched, or as a bump on the form.

◆ **TextAlign**—This property enables you to left-align, center, or right-align the text in the Label control.

◆ **WordWrap**—This property, which is on by default, causes text to wrap to multiple lines, as in the last Label on the form: **Add me to the mailing list**.

Adding the Text Box Controls

As with most data entry forms, there are a large number of text boxes for the user to enter data. In this form, there are four text boxes: the name, address, city, and zip code. The name, city, and zip code are single-line text boxes, and the address text box is actually a multiple-line text box. The multiple-line text box is a very useful control. Instead of having two or three separate text boxes to accommodate all the lines of the user's address, only a single box is required for the user to enter multiple lines of address information. This type of control gives the user the flexibility to enter multiple addresses, if necessary, and also is excellent for freeform text the user may need to enter.

On the CD

Because you will need to retrieve data from these controls, text boxes should be given meaningful names. A suggested format for the name is to prefix each name with *txt*, standing for Text Box. Here is the list of names used in the example included on the CD-ROM:

- ◆ txtName
- ◆ txtAddress
- ◆ txtCity
- ◆ txtZIP

Place each of these controls next to their associated labels. Be sure to size the address box large enough to accept multiple lines of text.

As with the Label control, the Text Box control has a large number of properties that can be set. Here is a summary of the more interesting properties of the text box. For a complete reference, refer to the Help file included with the ActiveX Control Pad.

Note For the data-entry form example, the only properties that need to be changed from their default values are on txtAddress. These changes are:

MultiLine: Change to **-1 - True**

ScrollBars: Change to **2 - Vertical**

- ◆ **AutoTab**—When used in combination with the MaxLength property, the cursor automatically moves from this control to the next control (in order) when the maximum number of characters has been entered. This feature can be useful for data that is a fixed length, such as customer numbers. It saves the user from needing to press the Tab key or move the mouse, thus increasing the speed in which the data can be entered into the form.

- ◆ **AutoWordSelect**—If the user has placed the cursor in the middle of a word and then begins to highlight a section of text, setting this property to True causes the current word to always be included in the selection the user is making. As with many of these options, experiment on your own to find the best behavior. This option may cause some unexpected user reactions, so be careful using it.

◆ **EnterFieldBehavior**—This property controls the behavior that occurs when the cursor enters this text box. By default, all the text in the text box is highlighted. Most Windows applications work like this, so it is best to leave this property at its default value. The alternative to this behavior is to allow the text box to recall the last selected piece of text from that text box. This essentially leaves the appearance of the control unchanged.

◆ **EnterKeyBehavior**—This property is especially important for multi-line text boxes. If the user presses the Enter key, a new line is added to a multi-line text box by default. However, if you change this property to its alternate value, you can cause the Enter key to act like the Tab key; that is, move the cursor to the next field in order. In this case, the user would have to press Ctrl+Enter to add a new line to a multi-line text box.

◆ **Locked**—By setting this property to True, it is possible to create a read-only Text Box control. This can be useful for forms in which the data is editable sometimes, and read-only other times. This is common in cases in which you want to reuse the form for both viewing and editing. By making all the fields read-only, the form becomes a viewing form—without having to create a new form.

◆ **MultiLine**—This property enables the Text Box control to accept multiple lines of text. For this property to work correctly, the WordWrap property must be set to True, which is its default value. In addition, you should set the ScrollBars property to a value that will provide at a minimum a vertical scroll bar. Because the WordWrap property is turned on, it should not be necessary to have a horizontal scroll bar also.

◆ **PasswordChar**—For cases in which you need to have a field whose data should not be visible, such as a password, set the PasswordChar property to a character such as an asterisk (*). If this property has a character in it, that character will be displayed in the text box for each character that is typed. To remove this characteristic, delete all characters from the PasswordChar property.

◆ **Text**—If you want to give the Text Box control an initial value, set the Text property to that text. It is similar to the Caption property of the Label control.

After you have created all four text boxes, place them on the layout form next to the labels you created before.

Adding the Combo Box

One of the hardest tasks in programming an application is trying to anticipate what the user *might* do. This is an especially hard task when it comes to evaluating and validating user input. For this reason, any time the user needs to choose from a list of items, the items should be displayed. Displaying the items accomplishes the following two purposes:

◆ The user does not have to memorize obscure codes or other information; the information is displayed for him when he needs it.

◆ It eliminates the chance of the user selecting an item that isn't on a predefined list. This also eliminates the need for error-checking code or validation code to check that piece of input. And of course, any time code can be eliminated, it is one less place a syntax error can occur.

For this data-entry form, you will add a combo box for the two-letter state abbreviations used by the U.S. Postal Service. The combo box is a better choice to add to data-entry forms, as in this example. It is a better choice because the box is the same height as a text box, so it looks good placed in line with the City and zip boxes. Again, with many of these aesthetic judgments, experiment with the available options and make your own choice.

> **Tip**   Typically, combo box lists should not exceed 100 items. If the list *does* exceed that recommended amount, a standard list box should be used instead.

Because the user will not be allowed to enter the state code manually, this combo box will actually be a drop-down list box. A true combo box enables the user to type in his selection, in addition to enabling him to select from a list. The Style property controls this behavior. For this example, do the following:

1. Set the Style property to 2 - DropDownList after you have drawn the Combo Box control on the form.

2. Set the ID property to cboState (cbo stands for combo box).

Here are some of the properties you can use to customize the behavior of your combo box on your own forms. (Many of the properties of the Combo Box control are identical to those of the text box, so they are not repeated here.)

◆ **BoundColumn**—The combo box can also have multiple columns. In cases where you are displaying data (area codes, for instance) where a piece of text is related to a numerical value or a text code, you can use the BoundColumn property to tell the Combo Box control which column has the code value. You can also read the BoundColumn property to determine the code value for an item selected by the user.

◆ **ColumnCount**—This property sets the number of columns to be displayed to the user in this combo box.

◆ **ColumnHeads**—In cases where you want to give a title to the columns displayed in the combo box, set this property to True. The first row of data will be used as the titles for the columns when this property is set to True.

◆ **ColumnWidths**—For this property value, a list of pixel widths separated by semicolons determines exactly how wide each column in the combo box is displayed. In addition, the values can be given in inches or centimeters by following the number with in or cm, respectively.

◆ **DropButtonStyle**—The combo box enables you to select the icon that is displayed on the button beside the text portion of the combo box. The available choices are shown in figure 12.2 for reference. Both styles 0–Plain, and 3–Reduce, are not commonly used in Windows or web applications. The most common usage is Style 1–Arrow. You may have also seen Style 2–Ellipsis. The Ellipsis style is normally used when an alternate window needs to be displayed instead of dropping down a list.

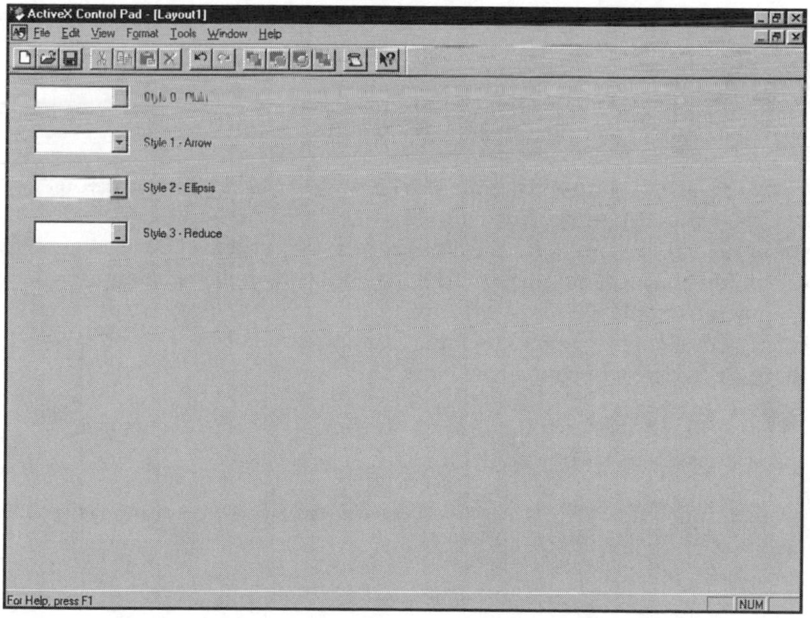

Figure 12.2

Examples of each available choice for the DropButtonStyle property.

◆ **ListRows**—This property enables you to control how many rows of data are shown when the drop button is pressed. If you had a small number of entries that you wanted to display immediately, you could set this value to the appropriate number of items.

- **ListWidth**—This property lets you set the width of the list that drops down below the combo box. If your data is unusually long, for instance, you could increase the size of this property so that the entire length of the data could be shown to the user.

- **MatchEntry**—For those of you who have used one of Intuit's products, such as Quicken or QuickBooks, you are already familiar with this feature of the combo box. For drop-down lists you can type into, the combo box automatically positions itself to an entry in the list that matches the partial string you have entered. For long lists of data, this feature is essential. This property can also be set to only match the first character that you type into the text portion of the combo box. This feature has also been used in the past in various Windows applications; however, the default behavior is more useful because there are usually many entries with the same first letter.

- **MatchRequired**—This property helps to enforce the accuracy of the user's text entry in the combo box. If this property is set to True, the user will not be able to leave the control if text is entered that does not match an entry in the list. By using this property in conjunction with the MatchEntry property, the problems that normally occur in allowing the user to type in a selection instead of just picking it from the list disappear.

- **ShowDropButtonWhen**—This property enables you to control when the drop button (the button to the right of the text portion of the combo box) is displayed on the combo box. These choices are valid for this property:

    - 0—The drop-down button is never shown to the user. However, if you never show the drop-down button to the user, the combo box does not serve its primary purpose. Because the combo box can also be used as a text box, this property setting could be used if your form is being used for view-only purposes. Like the Text Box control's Locked property, this property enables you to quickly change the purpose of the combo box without needing extra controls.

    - 1—This setting only shows the drop-down button when the cursor is focused on the combo box control.

    - 2—This setting causes the drop-down button to always be visible to the user. This is the default value for this property, as it is the most common usage of this control.

- **TextColumn**—This property works in conjunction with the BoundColumn property. Although the BoundColumn property holds the column number that is considered the code or number for the entry in the combo box, the TextColumn property holds the column number of the text associated with that code.

Adding Code to the Combo Box Control

Even with all the properties set correctly, no data will be displayed in the combo box. This is because the data has to be added at run-time. The combo box has a method named AddItem, which is used to add entries to the combo box control's list box portion. To add the code for this control, open the Script Wizard of the ActiveX Control Pad.

Because this code needs to be run before the form is actually visible to the user, it needs to be placed in the onLoad event of the frmDataEntry layout control. To add the code, do the following:

1. Select onLoad from the tree beneath the frmDataEntry item.

2. Because this is a custom action, click the Code View option button at the bottom of the Script Wizard window.

This is the code that should be added. Obviously, for a real application, you would want to add all the states' abbreviations with similar code.

```
Sub frmDataEntry_OnLoad()
cboState.AddItem "AK"
cboState.AddItem "AL"
cboState.AddItem "CA"
cboState.AddItem "CO"
cboState.AddItem "DE"
cboState.AddItem "GA"
cboState.AddItem "HI"
cboState.AddItem "IL"
cboState.AddItem "IN"
cboState.AddItem "NY"
cboState.AddItem "PA"
cboState.AddItem "VA"
```

When you are done adding this code, click the OK button to close the Script Wizard window; you return to the HTML Layout editor.

Checking What You Have Done So Far

I like to stop in the middle of lengthy tasks for a "checkpoint" to see what I have done so far. This is the way most programmers work anyway—write a bit, test, write, test, and so on.

To test your layout page, do the following:

1. First save your HTML Layout file.

2. Next, if an empty HTML document is not already visible, select New HTML from the File menu. You are going to insert your HTML Layout file into this new HTML document.

3. Do you remember where you saved the HTML Layout file? When you remember, select Insert HTML Layout from the Edit menu.

4. Find your HTML Layout file and select it in the dialog box.

5. After you have done that, save the HTML document and open it in Internet Explorer.

6. Try out the combo box and see how the state abbreviations you added in the onLoad event are now visible in the combo box. If the combo box is not working, go back to the HTML Layout editor and make sure you only set the properties discussed in this section.

Adding the Option Buttons

Option buttons, also known as radio buttons, are useful for enabling the user to select one of a group of choices, only one of which can be selected at a time (see fig. 12.3). Much the same way old car radios worked, only one button can be depressed at a time.

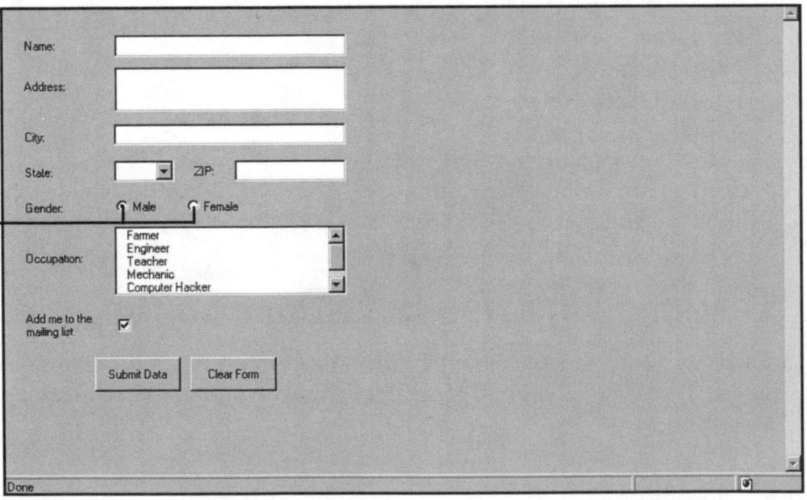

Figure 12.3

Option buttons in use in the data entry form.

Option buttons ——

Select the option button from the toolbox and draw two separate buttons on your form. Besides the graphical button, each option button also has a label that can be positioned to the left or to the right of the graphic. In the example in figure 12.3, the Gender label is placed next to the two option buttons to describe the group. This label helps describe the input the user is required to give.

The option button is a much simpler control, as compared to the combo box or text box. Many of its properties have already been covered; therefore, refer to the previous descriptions or use the online Help file included with the ActiveX Control Pad. The option button has a few unique properties worth mentioning here, though.

◆ **Alignment**—As mentioned before, the text associated with an option button can be placed to the left or right of the graphical circle. This property controls this setting.

◆ **GroupName**—In cases where you have multiple sets of option buttons, they have to be grouped so that they function independently. For instance, if we had another set of option buttons on this form for the Age group, those option buttons would have to function regardless of the setting for the Gender group. In Visual Basic, groups of option buttons are placed into another container, such as a frame or panel control. However, VBScript and ActiveX have no concept of a container that can hold other controls. For this reason, the GroupName property is used. All the option buttons in a group must have the same GroupName. In the example in figure 12.3, the GroupName has been set to optGender.

◆ **TripleState**—This property works in combination with the Value property. If this property is set to True, the option button actually has three states: selected, unselected, and partially selected. These states translate to settings in the Value property of True, False, and Empty. If the TripleState property is set to False, the user can only select from the first two choices—selected and unselected. There are very few times where the user should be able to select the third state. One case is similar to Microsoft Word or Excel, in which text or cells are highlighted and all have a different value for the same property. In this case, the option button for that property is shown as partially selected. The user can then toggle through selected, unselected, and partially selected and choose the correct option for those cells or text.

◆ **Value**—The Value property determines if the option button's graphic is filled in, empty, or partially filled in. If the Value is set to True (or -1), the graphic is shown as filled in. For a Value of False (0), the graphic is depicted as empty. If the Value property is left blank, the graphic shows as partially filled. In most cases, you should set the Value property to either True or False when you are designing the form.

For the two option buttons on this form, the example in figure 12.3 uses the names `optMale` and `optFemale`. These names can be used later in your VBScript code within this document. The `GroupName` property is not critical because there is only one group of option buttons. However, for completeness, the `GroupName` is set to `optGender`.

Adding a List Box

Besides the basic information this form is collecting about the user, it also provides a list box for the user to select his/her occupation. This control is very similar to the drop-down combo box, because both are actually list boxes.

The list box only has one property not already discussed: `MultiSelect`. This property allows a list box a variety of selection behaviors, as represented by the following:

◆ The first behavior, represented by a value of `0` in the property, enables the user to select a single item from the list. This is the simplest use of this control, and this is the default value for the `MultiSelect` property.

◆ The next possible behavior, represented by a value of `1`, enables the user to select and deselect multiple items in the list by clicking once on each item.

◆ The final behavior, represented by a value of `2`, enables the user to use the Shift and Ctrl keys to select single items or groups of items. When the Shift key is depressed, all the items between the previously selected item and the item the mouse highlights are selected. If the Ctrl key is used, the user can select single items that are not next to each other.

The other property you need to set is the `ID` property. In the code used for the figure 12.3 example, the name `lstOccupation` has been used to identify the Occupation list box. After you have done that, it is time to add code to the Layout file. Enter the Script Wizard again, and select the `onLoad` event for the `frmDataEntry` object. This code, which is nearly identical to the code used for the combo box, will add a series of occupations to the list box. This code should follow the code previously added to the `onLoad` event.

```
lstOccupation.AddItem "Farmer"
lstOccupation.AddItem "Engineer"
lstOccupation.AddItem "Teacher"
lstOccupation.AddItem "Mechanic"
lstOccupation.AddItem "Computer Hacker"
lstOccupation.AddItem "Astronaut"
```

Once again, it is time to save your work and try out your new creation. Save the HTML Layout file, and either open or reload the HTML document in Internet Explorer. You will now see the list box populated with the occupations the user can choose from. Of course, a real application would have a few more occupation choices.

Creating the Check Box

For this hypothetical data-entry form, the user has the choice to subscribe to a mailing list. Because this is a simple yes or no choice, the check box is used. You can have a large number of check boxes on your form, and each one works by itself. For this reason, the GroupName property used on the option button is not available for the check box. Other than that omission, the check box's properties are identical to those of the option button.

| **Note** | Check boxes function independently of each other; for instance, a pizza can have mushrooms, pepperoni, or both. If it has mushrooms, it doesn't mean it can't have pepperoni. This is a good illustration of how the check box works. |

For the example in this book, the check box is not given a caption. If a caption for the check box had been given, it would not have lined up with the rest of the controls on the form. For this reason, therefore, the caption property is set to nothing for our example, and a separate Label control is used to identify this control. Once you have drawn the check box, set its ID property to a meaningful name, such as chkMailingList. This control's Value property, like the option button's, will let you know if the box is checked or not.

If for some reason the graphical look of the check box does not fit in your application, you can replace it with the ToggleButton control. This control is another one of the built-in controls. It has identical properties to those of the check box, but looks like a standard command button. Experiment with this control and the check box to see which one you like better.

Adding the Command Buttons

The final controls to add to the form are the two command buttons at the bottom of the form. In general, HTML forms should always have at least two buttons:

◆ One to submit the data.

◆ One to clear the form.

Of course, you can use command buttons for any other purpose, as well. However, if you are doing data entry, experienced Internet users will be expecting to see the two buttons previously mentioned. If you do not follow this convention, be sure to label your buttons clearly.

The command button has only one property not already covered—TakeFocusOnClick. This property determines if the cursor will shift focus to the button when the user clicks the button. By default, this property is set to True so it is enabled. There may be cases, such as toolbars, in which you do not want the rectangle left on the button after the user clicks the button. In those cases, set this property to False.

The last thing you need to do is to label your two command buttons. Label one **Submit Data** and name it cmdSubmit. The other button should be labeled **Clear Form** and named cmdClear. The exact names are not critical; however, these are the names that are used in the example provided to you.

At this point, the basic data entry form is complete. All the controls should be placed, labeled, and identified by now.

1. Save your work and reload the HTML document in Internet Explorer.

2. Try out the various controls to make sure they are doing what you expected. If not, be sure the property values are set correctly. These controls are fairly simple, so you should not have any problems if the values are left at their defaults.

Building a Clickable Image Map

In many large web sites, it is easy to become lost in the wealth of information. For this reason, many sites have graphical toolbars that, when you click on them, take your browser to a starting point within the site. These toolbars are known as *image maps* because there is a coordinate system that maps each section of the graphic to a different action. These are common throughout the Internet and were one of the first advances produced when the World Wide Web was becoming more graphical from its all-text beginnings.

To create an image map, you need three things:

1. A list of locations the user can go to.

2. A series of pictures representing each location.

3. A program to relate the first two items.

This example, which uses the Image and HotSpot controls, will implement a toolbar for an HTML document. By clicking various parts of the document, you can navigate to other documents on a web site.

Designing Web Page Graphics

As you will soon see, the programming portion of the image map is a relatively simple task. The more difficult portion of the job is actually designing the graphics so that they are clear and usable. Most major web sites have multiple graphic artists on staff whose job is to design these graphics to provide consistency and clarity throughout the entire web site.

However, you don't have to hire a graphic artist to have good graphics. In fact, with some basic tools that are all freely available on the Internet, you can create all the graphics you need for your web pages. The best of these tools is called Paint Shop Pro, and it can be downloaded from http://www.shareware.com. It is by far the best shareware graphics package on the market. If you download it, start using it, and like it, be sure to support the shareware concept by registering your software with its producer, JASC, Inc. All the registration information is included in the distribution archive you download.

Graphics Tips

Here are some general tips for creating graphics for your web pages, based on personal experience with many of the best and the worst web sites on the Internet.

1. Keep them small. Remember that you have to support the slowest modems (minimum of 14.4 Kbps or 28.8 Kbps) as well as the speedy network connections. As a general rule, graphics that will take longer than 15–30 seconds to download are too large for general use. Also watch the total amount of graphics you are putting on a page. These graphics have to be downloaded one at a time; three 20 KB graphics are the equivalent of one 60 KB graphic. The best method for testing response time is to dial into your machine over a modem and time each page to verify its loading requirements.

2. Limit the number of colors you are using in each graphic. In most graphic file formats, a certain amount of space is required to store the definitions of how to show each color. By reducing the number of colors you have in your graphics, you will reduce the size of the graphic.

3. Be consistent! If you have a toolbar on the bottom of a page, use the same toolbar everywhere. Do not change items that are on similar-looking toolbars—most people refer to the graphics before they read the text. For instance, if you use a car graphic to represent one thing on a page, do not use a car graphic to represent anything else.

If you keep these simple tips in mind, you will create graphics that are functional and enjoyable, instead of graphics that are a hassle to the user of your pages.

Description of the Image Map Example

For this example, you will create an image map that has four icons on it. You can build the graphic in any paint program, but it must be saved in either GIF (Graphics Interchange Format) or JPEG (Joint Photographic Experts Group) format. The GIF format was originally pioneered on CompuServe, but is controversial because Unisys Corporation actually owns the patent on the method in which the data is stored. For this reason, the JPEG format was designed. It is an open standard that no one actually owns. This format is becoming more widely used on the Internet, and most image programs can save files in this format.

On the CD

The image map you will be using, shown in figure 12.4, is provided for you on the CD-ROM. It is actually a portion of the image map used at Macmillan Computer Publishing's home page. To view the graphic, open the file within Internet Explorer.

Figure 12.4

The image map graphic you will be using for your toolbar.

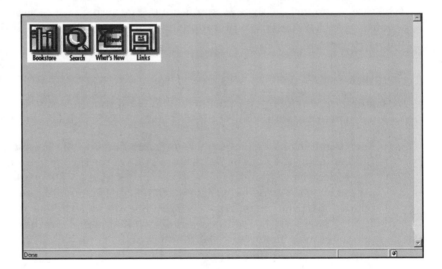

As you can see, the graphics for each section are clear and consistent, there are a limited number of colors, and the graphic is only 8 KB in size. There are four distinct graphics within this one picture: a Bookstore icon, a Search icon, a What's New icon, and a Links icon. One of the best ways to create ideas for your own web site is to get ideas from other well-done web sites. Taking other people's graphics is considered theft, but there is nothing wrong with adapting ideas used on other sites. For instance, you may see a color combination you like or a series of shapes that look good together. These are ideas you can use to build your own distinctive graphics for your own web site.

Adding the Image Control

Start the ActiveX Control Pad and create a new HTML Layout file. This form will be much smaller than the previous example, using only a single image control and four hotspot controls.

The first control you need to draw is an Image control. The Image control is able to show the standard Microsoft picture types, such as bitmap (BMP) and the Windows Metafile Format (WMF). However, neither of these formats are standards for the Internet. For this reason, the Image control can also display GIF and JPEG files. The sample image provided on the CD-ROM is a GIF image.

On the
CD

1. When you are ready to begin, draw an Image control (also known as ISImage when you see the ToolTips next to the control in the ActiveX Control Pad Toolbox window) on the form. You do not have to worry about the size of the image because you will be using the AutoSize capability of the Image control.

2. For this example, give the image control a nontrivial name, such as imgToolbar.

There are a number of properties that are important for the Image control. These are listed here with a summary of how the property applies to the Image control.

◆ **AutoSize**—This property, when set to True, causes the border of the Image control to shrink or expand to fit the content of the control. For graphics, this is especially useful so you do not have to determine the actual size of the graphic.

◆ **PicturePath**—Unlike the Visual Basic picture controls, which store the graphic as part of the executable program, the ActiveX Image control stores an URL pointing to the graphic file to be loaded. For Internet sites, this is a simple task. The URL is of the standard format, which resembles the following:

```
http://www.domain.com/filename.gif
```

For local development, you have to specify a file name. For this example, the file name of the image map graphic has been specified as follows:

```
file:///imagemap.gif
```

You must specify the following format to use files that are on your hard drive. You can specify an entire path name, as in this example:

```
file:///C:\Windows\System\Graphic.gif
```

◆ **PictureSizeMode**—This property determines how the graphic will be shown if the Image control is not the same size as the graphic itself. You have three choices for this property:

> **0 - Clip**—The image will be displayed in the control, and any part of the graphic that does not fit in the extents of the Image control will be clipped off. This behavior is similar to cropping a picture—you select a piece of the picture and not the whole thing.

> **1 - Stretch**—This method causes the graphic to stretch or shrink in both a horizontal and vertical direction to completely fill the Image control's box. This will distort the picture if the Image control is not the same size as the graphic.

> **3 - Zoom**—This causes the graphic to enlarge in the horizontal and vertical directions. However, the proportions of the graphic will be maintained so that there is no distortion caused by making the graphic wider than it was originally drawn.

◆ **PictureTiling**—If you have a small graphic on your page, you can set the PictureTiling property to True, and the graphic will be repeated multiple times in the horizontal and vertical directions so that the Image control is filled with multiple copies of the graphic. This is similar to the capability of the Control Panel of Windows 95 to tile graphics on the background of your desktop.

For this Image control, do the following:

1. Set the AutoSize property to True.

2. Set the PicturePath property to file:///imagemap.gif.

On the CD

3. Be sure to copy the image map graphic from the CD-ROM to the directory in which you are working on this file. Otherwise, the ActiveX Control Pad will not be able to find the graphic.

The next step of the process is to add hotspots to the graphic, so you must have the graphic displayed.

Adding Hotspots to the Graphic

For an image map to be functional, it has to have areas defined on it for the user to click. When the user clicks one of the icons on the image map, a new page is loaded in his browser. Although the Image control does have a Click event that it can respond to, you would have to figure out where in the image the user clicked and then provide the correct response.

Note You may be wondering how you see the graphic while you are adding the hotspots. The answer is that the graphic is always visible below the hotspot.

To simplify designers' lives, Microsoft has created the HotSpot control. This control is drawn on top of other controls, such as Image controls, and provides mouse response events (such as `Click`). By having four separate hotspots on the graphic, two purposes are accomplished:

1. No code is required to determine where the user clicked. If the event for hotspot one fires, the user must have clicked in hotspot one.

2. As the user moves his mouse over the graphic and finds a hotspot, the cursor changes accordingly. Instead of the normal arrow pointer, the cursor changes to a pointing finger, indicating the presence of the hotspot you created. This helps the user find these otherwise invisible regions on the picture.

Warning One important thing to remember when you are drawing hotspots on your graphics: *they cannot overlap.* If hotspots overlap, the user will experience unpredictable results, based on which hotspot is arranged on top. For this reason, size the hotspots as close to the graphics as possible. In this example, each graphical icon has a shadow and text beneath it. To minimize the chance of overlap, the hotspots should be placed around the rectangular icons only and not the text below the graphic. Because the cursor will change as the user enters and leaves each hotspot, there will be no problem in locating the correct region to click.

To set up the hotspots, do the following:

1. Draw one that encloses the Bookstore icon in the graphic. Only draw the box around the orange part of the graphic—not the text or the gray shadow. One important property you will want to set is the `MousePointer` property of the HotSpot control you just drew. By setting this property to something other than the default pointer, the user will be visually cued as to where the hotspot region is on the picture. In the example provided on the CD-ROM, the `UpArrow` pointer (value of `10`) is used.

On the CD

2. After you have created the first hotspot and set its `MousePointer` property, copy and paste it three additional times.

3. Move the three other hotspots so they cover each of the other graphical icons. All the icons are the same size, so all you have to do is position the hotspot.

4. Finally, give each hotspot a name. The following names are used in the example provided on the CD-ROM:

hotBookstore

hotSearch

hotWhatsNew

hotLinks

Activating the Hotspots

The last task required to make this image map work is to add some simple code for each hotspot. When the user clicks in a hotspot, your code will direct the user's browser to the correct location on Macmillan Computer Publishing's web site. Here are the URLs you will be using to access each of the four areas shown in the image map:

Bookstore   `http://www.mcp.com/bookstore/`

Search   `http://www.mcp.com/bookstore/do-searches.html`

What's New   `http://www.mcp.com/general/whats_new/`

Links   `http://www.mcp.com/refdesk/`

Surprisingly enough, the code to make your browser access a page is extremely simple.

1. Using the Script Wizard, select the Click event of the first hotspot, hotBookstore.

2. On the right hand side of the window, select **window** from the bottom of the list.

3. Open the tree below it, and then select **location**.

4. Open the tree below it and double-click on **href**.

5. When the pop-up window appears, enter in the URL for the Bookstore link, which is `http://www.mcp.com/bookstore/`.

That's all there is to it! Do the same for the other three hotspots and then save your HTML Layout file. You will need to create a new HTML document into which you can insert this layout file. (Refer to the previous section or Chapter 3 for instructions on doing this task.)

When you load your HTML document into Internet Explorer, you will see the graphic with no visible signs of the hotspots you created. However, when you move your mouse across the graphic, you will notice it changing from the up arrow pointer to the standard pointer as you cross in and out of the hotspot regions. If your Internet connection is active, you can click each of the graphics to visit various sections of Macmillan's web site.

Using the TabStrip Control

One of the major problems inherent with old terminal-based programs was the inevitable lack of screen space. For large systems, a large amount of data must be input per transaction, but there was no good way to display it all at the same time. The same problem was inherent with many applications, such as Microsoft Word 2.0. The number of customizable options was so large that many separate windows were required to let the user select from all of them.

With the advent of Microsoft Word 6.0, a new control called the tabbed dialog box was introduced. This control, using the metaphor of index cards, enabled software designers to organize related controls into groups within the tabs. Suddenly, Microsoft Word's Options dialog boxes were compressed into a single window, as shown in figure 12.5.

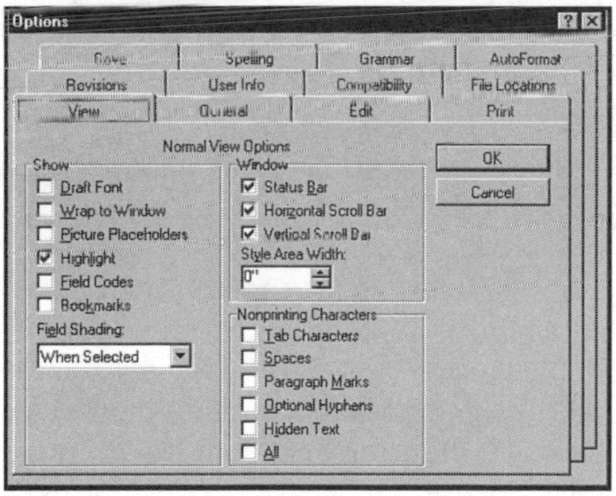

Figure 12.5

The Options dialog box from Microsoft Word 95.

If you were to take all the controls that are on this window within the tabs and try to lay them out in a single window, the result would be an absolute nightmare. In addition, you would need a screen the size of a big-screen TV to see them all!

This section shows you how to use the TabStrip control. Although the TabStrip is not appropriate for every case, the content of this section helps you learn when and how to use it in your own pages.

How the TabStrip Works

From the outward appearance of the control, it would seem that you could put controls into each page to divide them into groups. However, this is not the case. The TabStrip is simply a navigational aid and is only a graphical control. It cannot hold other controls. The TabStrip control included with Visual Basic is similar in this capability.

However, in Visual Basic, you can put controls into other containers, such as PictureBox controls, to group them. When you do this, you can shuffle groups of controls simply by bringing a group to the top of the stack. Unfortunately, there is no concept of a control container in VBScript/ActiveX. For this reason, it becomes quite difficult to use the TabStrip control effectively.

As you will see in the small example that follows, each and every control has to be manipulated manually. Each has to be raised to the top of the stack, hidden or shown at the correct times, and then lowered when the user is done with it. This fact makes it very difficult to use the TabStrip control without causing a lot of tedious work and somewhat redundant code.

Adding the TabStrip Control

Before you start drawing controls, name the HTML Layout file **frmTabExample**. Draw a TabStrip control on the form. Be sure to make it fairly large, because you will be adding controls that will appear to be within the tabs of the TabStrip. By default, the TabStrip control appears with two tabs. Later in this section, you will see how to add additional tabs to the starting two.

The TabStrip control has a number of unique properties that have yet to be discussed in this chapter. These properties are listed and explained here for reference.

◆ **MultiRow**—As you saw in the picture of the Options dialog box from Microsoft Word, it is possible that you would have a large number of tabs in a TabStrip. For this reason, the MultiRow property allows the tabs to be in more than one row. The system will automatically determine how many tabs go in each row and will automatically adjust the height and width, unless the TabFixedHeight and/or TabFixedWidth properties are set. By default, the MultiRow property is set to False.

◆ **Style**—If you do not like the look of tabs for the TabStrip, you have the option of changing the Style property to 1 - Buttons, which will cause the tabs at the top of the form to appear like ToggleButton controls. In addition, you can remove the tabs from your TabStrip by setting this property's value to 2 - None. In this case, the user will have no way to switch between tabs unless you provide another method or cause the tabs to switch programmatically.

◆ **TabFixedHeight, TabFixedWidth**—By default, the TabStrip control will automatically determine how high to make each tab. It primarily bases the size on the font size and weight. However, if you want to force the size of the tabs to be the same, you can set a value for the TabFixedHeight and/or the TabFixedWidth properties. These values will override the default sizes the control would have chosen.

◆ **TabIndex**—This property, which is read-only at design time, displays the index of the tab that is currently selected. This property can be read at runtime to determine which tab has been selected by the user.

◆ **TabOrientation**—The tabs on the TabStrip control can be placed in any orientation around the rectangle. The TabOrientation property enables you to move the tabs to the top (default choice), bottom, left, or right on the control. Placing the tabs on the right gives the effect of an address book with index tabs, for instance.

For this example, the only property you should set is the ID property. Give the control a meaningful name, such as tabControlPanel. The example you are going to build is designed to both show you how to manipulate controls with the TabStrip, as well as demonstrate how to use the SpinButton and ScrollBar controls. Every other property of the TabStrip has to be set through code.

Adding the SpinButton Control

When using most Windows applications, it is always more convenient to make controls mouse-oriented instead of keyboard-oriented. One example of this is the standard Print dialog box that is displayed in various Microsoft Office applications, as shown in figure 12.6.

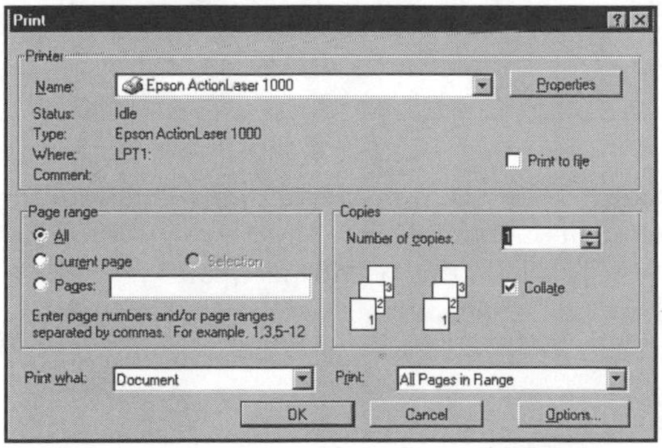

Figure 12.6

The Print dialog box from Microsoft Word 95.

As you can see, all the controls can be manipulated with the mouse only, including the number of copies. The up and down arrows beside the number of copies is called a `SpinButton` control. As the control name says, it is designed to let you quickly increase or decrease a numerical value. This control is best for small numbers, such as the number of copies that should be printed. Typically this number will not be more than two digits. Obviously you would not want to use a spin button for a user to enter his zip code, unless you wanted to help bring on carpal tunnel syndrome. However, when used correctly, the spin button is a very valuable addition to your toolbox.

For this example, the spin button is going to be used to adjust the simulated volume in this application when the user has selected Tab1. When the user selects Tab2, the spin button disappears and the scroll bar is used. For now, do the following:

1. Add a label and a text box (name it `txtVolume`).

2. Draw a SpinButton next to it, as shown in figure 12.7. Do not draw the scroll bar yet—that will be covered next.

Figure 12.7

The completed TabStrip example.

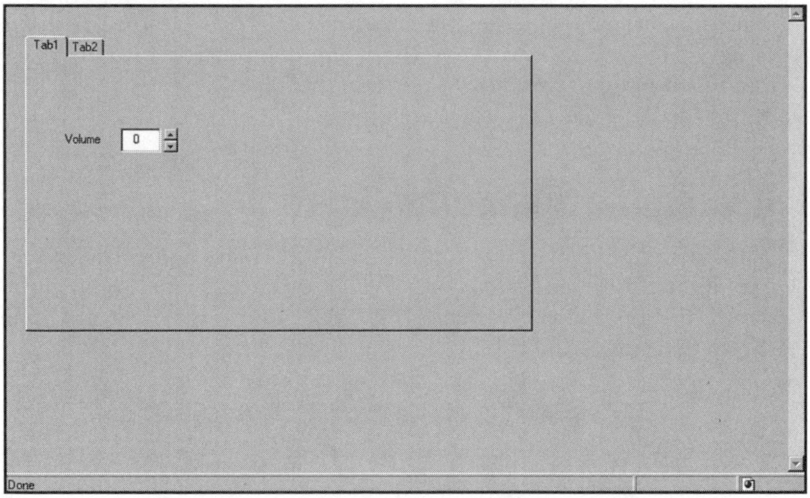

Because it is such a simple control, the main properties worth mentioning are the `Min` and `Max` properties, which control the boundaries that the spin button has. You will not be able to reduce the value less than the `Min` property, and you will not be able to enlarge the value greater than the `Max` property, as you probably guessed. For this example, do the following:

1. Set the `Min` property to `0` and the `Max` property to `100`.

2. You should also set the ID property of the SpinButton to `spinScale`.

Besides the Min and Max properties, you can also control how fast the spin button spins. The Delay property specifies this time value in milliseconds (thousandths of a second). The default value is 50. You can experiment to find a setting you like.

Adding the ScrollBar Control

The only other control you will add to this HTML Layout is a scroll bar. This scroll bar can be used just like the spin button to select a value from a range. In fact, its Min and Max properties are identical to those of the SpinButton. The other property that is unique about the scroll bar is the Orientation property. The scroll bar can be drawn either horizontally or vertically. For this example, the scroll bar will be drawn horizontally, as shown in figure 12.8.

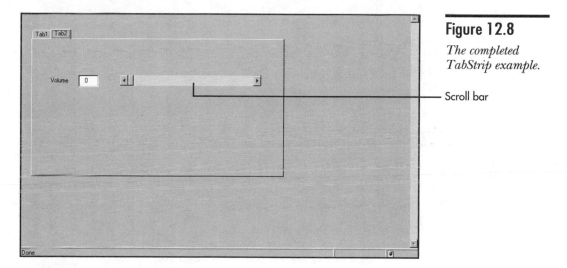

Figure 12.8

The completed TabStrip example.

Scroll bar

Be sure to set the Min property of the scroll bar to 0 and the Max property to 100, just as you did on the SpinButton. In addition, set the name of the scroll bar to sbScale.

Activating the TabStrip

As was mentioned before, the first tab, currently labeled Tab1, will show the spin button next to the text box and will omit the scroll bar. Tab2 will show the scroll bar, but hide the spin button. In order for this to work, open the Script Wizard.

Three pieces of code are required to make the TabStrip and the other controls work correctly.

1. In the onLoad event of the frmTabExample control, select the action on the right-hand side to hide the sbScale control. This code will initially hide the scroll bar when the form is loaded. You can also set the Visible property of the sbScale control to False when you return to the HTML Layout editor window.

2. In the Click event of the tabControlPanel control, add the following code in the Code View window:

```
If tabControlPanel.SelectedItem.Index = 0 Then
    spinScale.Visible = True
    spinScale.ZOrder 0
    spinScale.Value = CInt(txtVolume)
    sbScale.Visible = False
Else
    spinScale.Visible = False
    sbScale.Visible = True
    sbScale.Value = CInt(txtVolume)
    sbScale.ZOrder 0
End If
```

This code will allow the control to determine which tab has been clicked. Based on that, it will display the appropriate control. It will also synchronize the values of each control so that both the scroll bar and the spin button increase the text box in the same manner.

3. In the Change event of the sbScale control, add the following code in Code View mode:

```
txtVolume = CStr(sbScale.Value)
```

4. In the Change event of the spinScale control, add the following code in Code View mode:

```
txtVolume = CStr(spinScale.Value)
```

Steps 3 and 4 synchronize the value displayed in the text box with the value currently being held by either the scroll bar or the spin button.

That's all the code you have to write for this example. Save your work, insert the new HTML Layout file into a new HTML document, and load it into Internet Explorer.

Figure 12.9 shows what the example looks like with Tab1 selected. The spin button is visible, but the scroll bar is not. Figure 12.10 shows what the example looks like with Tab2 selected.

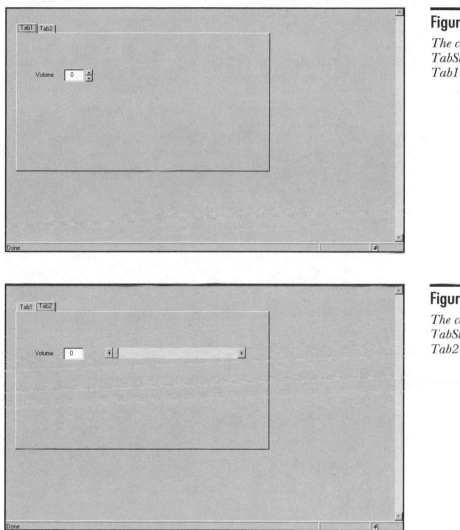

Figure 12.9

The completed TabStrip with Tab1 visible.

Figure 12.10

The completed TabStrip with Tab2 visible.

For Visual Basic Programmers:

If you are familiar with the basic controls included in Visual Basic, you will find their ActiveX counterparts almost identical. The primary differences are in property names, such as **ID** in the ActiveX control versus **Name** in the Visual Basic version. When you remember these differences, the controls function identically.

continues

For Visual Basic Programmers, *continued*

Avoid using the ActiveX control within your Visual Basic applications, however. Because of some of the minor differences in property naming, the built-in ActiveX controls will cause you problems when you attempt to use them in your application. For instance, the ActiveX picture box is able to display GIF format graphics. It may seem that you could use the ActiveX control in your Visual Basic application. However, doing so will cause your application to crash. A general rule is that you can use full-featured OCX controls in both Visual Basic applications and on web pages, but ActiveX controls should be used only for web pages.

CHAPTER 13

ActiveX Controls Reference

By Jeffrey McManus

T his chapter provides a reference to ActiveX resources. Although 32-bit software components have been around since Visual Basic 4.0 (in the form of the OCX specification), not every control makes sense in the web context, for a number of reasons—either the software developers haven't certified them as web-safe, or they simply have no relevance in a web browser. All the controls in this chapter will work in the context of a web browser.

While many of these controls are commercial, many are shareware, and a few are free. The controls listed in this chapter are generally downloadable in one way or another. In cases where a control is shareware, you'll want to check with the author to determine the registration fee before using the control in your projects.

ActiveMovie

The Microsoft ActiveMovie control is a playback engine for the most popular media types including MPEG audio and video, AVI video, WAV audio, and Apple QuickTime video.

This control is installed automatically when you perform a full install of Microsoft Internet Explorer 3.0.

A page giving detailed instructions on how to get started with the ActiveMovie control can be found on the Microsoft Web site at `http://www.microsoft.com/mediadev/ video/usingam.htm`. This page also contains a link to a help file that contains all the properties, events, and methods of the ActiveMovie control. This help file also includes information on how to embed the control in HTML Web pages.

Setting the ShowDisplay and ShowControls properties to zero suppresses the display of the ActiveMovie controls (the user can still stop and restart the video clip by right-clicking the clip, however). Setting the AutoStart property to –1 means that the clip will load and run as soon as the HTML page is loaded. Setting the PlayCount property to zero tells the ActiveMovie control to keep looping the video clip over and over. (Setting the PlayCount property to a number other than zero denotes the number of times you want the clip to loop.)

Sample Code

This code embeds and plays an ActiveMovie in an HTML document. You can play a different video file by replacing the filename `"the-head.avi"` in the FileName parameter with the URL to a video clip of your choosing.

```
<HTML>
<HEAD>
<TITLE>ActiveMovie Example</TITLE>
</HEAD>
<BODY>
<b>My Rotating Head</b>
<center>
<OBJECT ID="ActiveMovie1" WIDTH=104 HEIGHT=125
 CLASSID="CLSID:05589FA1-C356-11CE-BF01-00AA0055595A">
    <PARAM NAME="_ExtentX" VALUE="2752">
    <PARAM NAME="_ExtentY" VALUE="3307">
    <PARAM NAME="MovieWindowWidth" VALUE="100">
    <PARAM NAME="MovieWindowHeight" VALUE="121">
    <PARAM NAME="FileName" VALUE="the-head.avi">
</OBJECT>
```

If you want to suppress display of the VCR-style controls and start the video clip automatically, add the following properties (inside the <OBJECT> tags):

```
<PARAM NAME="ShowDisplay" VALUE="0">
<PARAM NAME="ShowControls" VALUE="0">
<PARAM NAME="AutoStart" VALUE="-1">
<PARAM NAME="PlayCount" VALUE="0">
```

Properties

AllowChangeDisplayMode: Indicates whether the end-user can change the display mode at runtime between time and frames.

AllowHideControls: Indicates whether the end-user can hide the control panel at runtime.

AllowHideDisplay: Indicates whether the end-user can hide the display at runtime.

Author: Contains the author of the multimedia stream.

AutoRewind: Indicates whether to automatically rewind the multimedia stream when it stops.

AutoStart: Indicates whether to automatically start playing the multimedia stream.

Balance: Specifies the stereo balance.

Copyright: Contains copyright information for this multimedia stream.

MediaPosition: Specifies the current position within the multimedia stream, in seconds.

MediaState: Specifies the current state of the player: stopped, paused, running.

Description: Contains a description for this multimedia stream.

DisplayBackColor: Specifies the color used for the control background.

DisplayForeColor: Specifies the color used for the control foreground.

DisplayMode: Indicates whether the control displays the current position in time or frames.

Duration: Specifies the duration of the multimedia stream in seconds.

EnableContextMenu: Indicates whether to enable the context menu on right click.

EnablePositionControls: Indicates whether to enable the position buttons in the control panel.

EnableSelectionControls: Indicates whether to enable the selection buttons in the control panel.

EnableTracker: Indicates whether to enable the tracker bar in the control panel.

FileName: Specifies the name of the file that contains the multimedia stream to be played.

FilterGraph: Returns an interface pointer to the current filter graph object.

FilterGraphDispatch: Returns an interface pointer to the current filter graph object.

FullScreen: Expands the area of the control so that it fills the entire screen.

ImageSourceHeight: Specifies the authored height of the source image.

ImageSourceWidth: Specifies the authored width of the source image.

MovieWindowSize: Selects the image window size and characteristics.

PlayCount: Specifies the number of times to play this multimedia stream.

Rate: Specifies the playback rate for the stream.

SelectionEnd: Specifies the ending position in this multimedia stream, in seconds, relative to the beginning of the stream.

SelectionStart: Specifies the starting position in this multimedia stream, in seconds, relative to the beginning of the stream.

ShowControls: Indicates whether the control panel is visible.

ShowDisplay: Indicates whether the status display panel is visible.

ShowPositionControls: Indicates whether the position buttons are visible in the control panel.

ShowSelectionControls: Indicates whether the selection buttons are visible in the control panel.

ShowTracker: Indicates whether the tracker bar is visible in the control panel.

Title: Specifies the title of the multimedia stream.

Volume: Specifies the audio volume.

The ActiveMovie control also supports the following properties that are common to other controls: Appearance, BorderStyle, Enabled, and hWnd. For information about these properties, please see your Visual Basic documentation.

Methods

AboutBox: Displays version and copyright information about the ActiveMovie control.

Pause: Pauses playing and maintains the current position in the multimedia stream.

Run: Plays the multimedia stream.

Stop: Stops playback and resets the position as indicated by the AutoRewind and SelectionStart properties.

Events

DisplayModeChange: Indicates the DisplayMode property has been changed.

Error: Indicates an error.

PositionChange: Indicates changes to the position, such as by the user seeking to the position using the default user interface.

StateChange: Indicates player state changes, such as a change from stopped to running, or from running to paused.

Timer: Handles timer events.

Additional Information

Microsoft

One Microsoft Way
Redmond, WA 98052 USA

Phone: 206-882-8080

Fax: 206-936-7329

http://www.microsoft.com/activex/gallery/

Information on this control: http://www.microsoft.com/mediadev/video/usingam.htm

ClassID: CLSID:05589FA1-C356-11CE-BF01-00AA0055595A

Download page: http://www.microsoft.com/msdownload/ieadd/07.htm

Animated Button

The Animated Button control displays various frame sequences of an AVI (Video for Windows clip) depending on the button state. It uses the Windows Animation Common Control. The AVI file must be RLE-compressed or 8-bit-compressed.

Sample Code

This code displays a page with an animated button based on the video clip `the-head.avi`. It cycles through different frames in the video clip when the page is loaded, when the mouse passes over the button, and when the button is clicked.

```
<HTML>
<HEAD>
<TITLE>Animated Button Example</TITLE>
</HEAD>
<BODY>
    <SCRIPT LANGUAGE="VBScript">
<!--
Sub anbtn1_Click()
 MsgBox "Thank you for clicking on my head."
end sub
-->
    </SCRIPT>
    <OBJECT ID="anbtn1" WIDTH=133 HEIGHT=133
     CLASSID="CLSID:0482B100-739C-11CF-A3A9-00A0C9034920">
        <PARAM NAME="_ExtentX" VALUE="3519">
        <PARAM NAME="_ExtentY" VALUE="3519">
        <PARAM NAME="URL" VALUE="the-head.avi">
        <PARAM NAME="defaultfrstart" VALUE="0">
        <PARAM NAME="defaultfrend" VALUE="11">
        <PARAM NAME="mouseoverfrstart" VALUE="0">
        <PARAM NAME="mouseoverfrend" VALUE="-1">
        <PARAM NAME="focusfrstart" VALUE="22">
        <PARAM NAME="focusfrend" VALUE="33">
        <PARAM NAME="downfrstart" VALUE="11">
        <PARAM NAME="downfrend" VALUE="22">
    </OBJECT>
</BODY>
</HTML>
```

States

The Animated Button control can be in any of four states:

Down: When the control receives a left-button click.

Focus: When the control gets focus.

Mouseover: When the mouse moves over the control.

Default: When neither the mouse cursor nor the focus is on the control.

> **Note** All Animated Button control states are mutually exclusive (which is somewhat confusing, because the control can have focus even when the mouse moves over it). However, the Down state has precedence over all other states, while the Default state has the least precedence. The Mouseover state has precedence over Focus. Thus, if a control has focus (that is, if it's in the Focus state) and the mouse moves over it, it goes to the Mouseover state.

Properties

URL: The URL location of the AVI file to be used.

DefaultFrStart: The start frame for the Default state.

DefaultFrEnd: The end frame for the Default state.

MouseoverFrStart: The start frame for the Mouseover state.

MouseoverFrEnd: The end frame for the Mouseover state.

FocusFrStart: The start frame for the Focus state.

FocusFrEnd: The end frame for the Focus state.

DownFrStart: The start frame for the Down state.

DownFrEnd: The end frame for the Down state.

Methods

AboutBox: Displays the About dialog box.

Events

ButtonEvent_Click: Fires when the button is clicked.

ButtonEvent_DblClick: Fires when the button is double-clicked.

ButtonEvent_Focus: Fires when the button gets the focus.

ButtonEvent_Enter: Fires when the mouse enters the button area.

ButtonEvent_Leave: Fires when the mouse leaves the button area.

Additional Information

Microsoft

One Microsoft Way
Redmond, WA 98052 USA

Phone: 206-882-8080

Fax: 206-936-7329

`http://www.microsoft.com/activex/gallery/`

Information on this control: `http://microsoft.saltmine.com/isapi/activexisv/ prmgallery/gallery-activex-info.idc?ID=141`

ClassID: clsid:0482B100-739C-11CF-A3A9-00A0C9034920

Download page: `http://microsoft.saltmine.com/activexisv/msctls/ie/ anbutton.htm`

Codebase: `http://activex.microsoft.com/controls/iexplorer/ ieanbtn.ocx#version=4,70,0,1161`

Button Control

The Protoview Button Control enables users to edit buttons for their applications. Choose from over 30 bitmaps or create your own.

Sample Code

This page displays a user input prompt, along with OK and Cancel buttons. When the user clicks a button, a message box is displayed.

```
<HTML>
<HEAD>
<TITLE>Protoview Button Example</TITLE>
</HEAD>
<BODY>
This will detonate all the nuclear weapons. Are you sure you want to do
this?<p>
    <SCRIPT LANGUAGE="VBScript">
```

```
<!--
Sub cmdOK_Click()
 MsgBox "BOOOOOOOOOM!"
end sub
-->
    </SCRIPT>
    <OBJECT ID="cmdOK" WIDTH=93 HEIGHT=28
     CLASSID="CLSID:C0000000-FFFF-1100-8005-000000000004"
     CODEBASE="http://www.protoview.com/msactivex/pics/pbtn32.ocx">
        <PARAM NAME="_Version" VALUE="65541">
        <PARAM NAME="_ExtentX" VALUE="2455">
        <PARAM NAME="_ExtentY" VALUE="741">
        <PARAM NAME="_StockProps" VALUE="79">
        <PARAM NAME="Caption" VALUE="OK">
        <PARAM NAME="Picture" VALUE="4">
    </OBJECT>
    <SCRIPT LANGUAGE="VBScript">
<!--
Sub cmdCancel_Click()
 MsgBox "The free world thanks you, Mr. President."
end sub
-->
    </SCRIPT>
    <OBJECT ID="cmdCancel" WIDTH=104 HEIGHT=28
     CLASSID="CLSID:C0000000-FFFF-1100-8005-000000000004">
        <PARAM NAME="_Version" VALUE="65541">
        <PARAM NAME="_ExtentX" VALUE="2746">
        <PARAM NAME="_ExtentY" VALUE="741">
        <PARAM NAME="_StockProps" VALUE="79">
        <PARAM NAME="Caption" VALUE="Cancel">
        <PARAM NAME="Picture" VALUE="10">
    </OBJECT>
</BODY>
</HTML>
```

Properties

BackColor: Returns or sets the background color of an object.

Caption: Returns or sets the text displayed on the face of the Button control.

ColorCodeColor: Returns or sets the color code color of the control. This property is only meaningful when you set the SpecialEffect property of the control to 2—Show Color Code.

CustomPicture: Sets or returns the picture displayed on the Button control.

DarkHighlight: Returns or sets the dark highlight color of the Button.

DarkShadow: Returns or sets the dark shadow color of the Button.

DefaultButton: Returns or sets the display style of the Button control.

Enabled: Returns or sets a value that determines whether a form or control can respond to user-generated events.

Font: Returns a Font object.

ForeColor: Returns or sets the foreground color used to display text and graphics in an object.

hWnd: Returns a handle to a Button control. Read-only at runtime, not available at design time.

LightHighlight: Returns or sets the light highlight color of the Button.

LightShadow: Returns or sets the light shadow color of the Button.

Picture: Returns or sets the picture displayed on the Button control.

RepeatButton: Returns or sets the repeat state of the Button. The repeat state specifies whether the object continues to send Button Down events while the button is pressed.

SpecialEffect: Returns or sets the display style of the Button control. Possible values are:

   0—No special effect.

   1—(Default) A picture is displayed on the button.

   2—A color code is displayed on the button.

Methods

AboutBox: Use the About command to find the version number and other pertinent information about PICS.

ResetColorScheme: Resets the color scheme of a Button object back to the original settings.

SetRedraw: Sets the redraw state of a Button object. To prevent redrawing of the Button object, set the bRedraw parameter to False. This will prevent the Button object from redrawing itself until the redraw state is set back to True. This method is useful to prevent unwanted redraws while a number of properties are being set.

Events

Click: Occurs when the user presses and then releases a mouse button over an object. It can also occur when the value of a control is changed.

KeyDown: Fires each time a key is pressed when the Button object has input focus.

KeyPress: Fires each time a key is pressed when the Button object has input focus.

KeyUp: Fires each time a key is released when the Button object has input focus.

MouseDown: Occurs when the user presses the mouse button.

MouseUp: Occurs when the user releases the mouse button.

Additional Information

ProtoView Development

2540 Route 130
Cranbury, NJ 08512 USA

Phone: 609-655-5000

Fax: 609-655-5353

http://www.protoview.com

Information on this control: http://microsoft.saltmine.com/isapi/activexisv/prmgallery/gallery-activex-info.idc?ID=190

ClassID: CLSID:C0000000-FFFF-1100-8005-000000000004

Download page: http://www.protoview.com/msactivex/pics/pbutton.htm

Codebase: http://www.protoview.com/msactivex/pics/pbtn32.ocx

 Web pages are notoriously transitory; hence, the URLs presented in this chapter may have changed by the time this book is on the shelves.

Button Menu

The menu control enables the Web author to place a menu button on the page that brings up a menu using the standard menu look and feel. The menu control fires events that the author can respond to via VBScript code.

Sample Code

This code displays a menu-driven hot list. When the user clicks the button, a menu drops down. The choices in the menu lead to other popular Web sites.

```
<HTML>
<HEAD>
<TITLE>Button Menu Example</TITLE>
</HEAD>
<BODY>
    <SCRIPT LANGUAGE="VBScript">
<!--
Sub mnuNavigate_Select(item)
' note that the 'item' value does
' not map to the 'MenuItem[x]' value
' used to populate the control.
 Select Case Item
  Case 1
  Window.location.href = "http://www.microsoft.com/"
  Case 2
  Window.location.href = "http://www.mcp.com/"
  Case 3
  Window.location.href = "http://www.well.com/user/jeffreyp/newsbabe1.html"
 End Select
end sub
-->
    </SCRIPT>
    <OBJECT ID="mnuNavigate" WIDTH=57 HEIGHT=20
     CLASSID="CLSID:52DFAE60-CEBF-11CF-A3A9-00A0C9034920"
     CODEBASE="http://activex.microsoft.com/controls/iexplorer/
```

```
➥btnmenu.ocx#Version=4,70,0,1161">
        <PARAM NAME="_ExtentX" VALUE="1508">
        <PARAM NAME="_ExtentY" VALUE="529">
        <PARAM NAME="Caption" VALUE="Navigate">
        <PARAM NAME="Menuitem[0]" VALUE="Microsoft">
        <PARAM NAME="Menuitem[1]" VALUE="Macmillan Publishing">
        <PARAM NAME="Menuitem[2]" VALUE="The News Babe Page">
    </OBJECT>
</BODY>
</HTML>
```

Properties

ItemCount: The number of menu items in the current menu (read-only).

Caption: The caption to be displayed.

Parameter Tags

Menuitem[]: The menu item to be displayed.

Caption: The caption to be displayed.

Methods

AboutBox: Displays the About dialog box.

PopUp(vx, vy): Pops up the menu. If no value is passed for the x or y positions, the current mouse position is used to display the pop-up menu. The x and y values are relative to the window, not to the screen.

Clear: Clears off all menu items.

RemoveItem(index): Removes the specified item. If the menu item does not exist, nothing is done.

AddItem(item, index): Adds the passed menu item at the specified index. If no index is passed, the item is appended to the menu.

Events

Select(item): Item indicates the menu item selected.

Click: No menu items were present, and the button was clicked.

Additional Information

Microsoft

One Microsoft Way
Redmond, WA 98052 USA

Phone: 206-882-8080

Fax: 206-936-7329

http://www.microsoft.com/activex/gallery/

Information on this control: http://microsoft.saltmine.com/isapi/activexisv/ prmgallery/gallery-activex-info.idc?ID=158

ClassID: CLSID:52DFAE60-CEBF-11CF-A3A9-00A0C9034920

Download page: http://microsoft.saltmine.com/activexisv/msctls/ie/menu.htm

Codebase: http://activex.microsoft.com/controls/iexplorer/ btnmenu.ocx#Version=4,70,0,1161

Calendar Control

The Calendar control enables users to edit the date on-the-fly. It can display one month, three months, or half a year, and has either a normal or 3D display.

Sample Code

This code simulates an online appointment-making application, displaying a calendar and a confirmation button to the user. The user picks a date from the calendar and clicks the button. The application responds by displaying the date chosen by the user in a message box.

```
<HTML>
<HEAD>
<TITLE>Protoview Calendar Example</TITLE>
</HEAD>
<BODY>
    <OBJECT ID="Calendar1" WIDTH=215 HEIGHT=139
    CLASSID="CLSID:B7733C43-8697-11CF-AACD-444553540000"
    CODEBASE="http://www.protoview.com/msactivex/pics/calctl32.ocx">
        <PARAM NAME="_Version" VALUE="65536">
        <PARAM NAME="_ExtentX" VALUE="5662">
        <PARAM NAME="_ExtentY" VALUE="3678">
        <PARAM NAME="_StockProps" VALUE="228">
        <PARAM NAME="Appearance" VALUE="1">
        <PARAM NAME="BkDayColor" VALUE="-2147483633">
        <PARAM NAME="DayColor" VALUE="-2147483630">
        <PARAM NAME="BkHighlightColor" VALUE="-2147483624">
    </OBJECT>
    <INPUT LANGUAGE="VBScript" TYPE=button VALUE="Submit" ONCLICK=" MsgBox
&quot;Thanks for signing up for your appointment.&quot; _
    &amp; &quot;Your appointment has been set for &quot; &amp;
Calendar1.Value &amp; &quot;.&quot;"
    NAME="cmdSubmit">
</BODY>
</HTML>
```

Properties

Appearance: Returns or sets the paint style of a Calendar control; read-only at run-time.

AutoSizeFont: Returns or sets a value that determines whether the font used in a Calendar control will be proportional to the size of the control.

BackColor: Returns or sets the background color of an object.

BorderStyle: Returns or sets the border style for a Calendar object; read-only at run-time.

Enabled: Returns or sets a value that determines whether a form or control can respond to user-generated events.

EnablePeriodEdit: Returns or sets a value that determines whether the period can be changed on a calendar control.

EnableYearEdit: Returns or sets a value that determines whether the year can be changed on a calendar control.

Font: Returns a Font object.

ForeColor: Returns or sets the foreground color used to display text and graphics in an object.

Format: Returns the format style for a Calendar object; read-only at runtime.

hWnd: Returns a handle to a Calendar control. Read-only at runtime; not available at design time.

ReadOnly: Returns or sets a value that determines whether the Calendar control can respond to user-generated events.

SundayColor: SundayColor returns or sets the foreground color used to display days that fall on Sunday in a Calendar control.

SundayBkColor: SundayBkColor returns or sets the background color used to display days that fall on Sunday in a Calendar control.

Value: Returns or sets the date in a Calendar object.

Methods

AboutBox: Displays the version number and other information about the control.

Events

Change: Occurs when the value of a control is changed.

Click: Occurs when the user presses and then releases a mouse button over an object. It can also occur when the value of a control is changed.

DblClick: Occurs when the user presses and releases a mouse button, and then presses and releases it again over an object.

KeyDown: Fired each time a key is pressed when the Calendar object has input focus.

KeyPress: Fired each time a key is pressed when the Calendar object has input focus.

KeyUp: Fired each time a key is released when the Calendar object has input focus.

MouseDown: Occurs when the user presses a mouse button.

MouseMove: Occurs when the user moves the mouse.

MouseUp: Occurs when the user releases a mouse button.

Additional Information

ProtoView Development

2540 Route 130
Cranbury, NJ 08512 USA

Phone: 609-655-5000

Fax: 609-655-5353

http://www.protoview.com

Information on this control: http://microsoft.saltmine.com/isapi/activexisv/ prmgallery/gallery-activex-info.idc?ID=188

ClassID: CLSID:B7733C43-8697-11CF-AACD-444553540000

Download page: http://www.protoview.com/msactivex/pics/calendar.htm

Codebase: http://www.protoview.com/msactivex/pics/calctl32.ocx

Chart

The Chart control enables you to draw various types of charts with different styles. The control can utilize data stored in a text file (via the URL property) or generated programmatically.

Sample Code

This HTML page displays consumption of three different kinds of food for police officers at three different precincts. The data for this chart is stored in a text file, food.txt.

```
<HTML>
<HEAD>
<TITLE>Chart Example</TITLE>
</HEAD>
<BODY>
<OBJECT ID="iechart1" WIDTH=500 HEIGHT=300 align=center
 CLASSID="CLSID:FC25B780-75BE-11CF-8B01-444553540000">
    <PARAM NAME="hgridStyle" VALUE="3">
    <PARAM NAME="vgridStyle" VALUE="0">
    <PARAM NAME="ColorScheme" VALUE="0">
    <PARAM NAME="BackStyle" VALUE="1">
    <PARAM NAME="Scale" VALUE="100">
    <PARAM NAME="DisplayLegend" VALUE="1">
    <PARAM NAME="BackColor" VALUE="16777215">
    <PARAM NAME="ForeColor" VALUE="16711680">
    <PARAM NAME="URL" VALUE="food.txt">
</OBJECT>
</BODY>
</HTML>
```

The contents of food.txt are:

```
11

3

3    First Precinct  Second Precinct Third Precinct

Hamburgers    6        5          8

Hot Dogs     13       12          4

Donuts        8        6         15
```

Chart Types

Pie chart
Point chart
Line chart
Area chart
Bar chart
Column chart
Stocks chart

Properties

Rows: Specifies the number of rows in the data series.

Columns: Specifies the number of columns in the data series.

HorizontalGrid: Specifies horizontal grids.

VerticalGrid: Specifies vertical grids.

ChartType: Specifies the type of chart you want. This property can take the following values:

Simple Pie—0

Pie with wedge out—1

Simple Point Chart—2

Stacked Point Chart—3

Full Point Chart—4

Simple Line Chart—5

Stacked Line Chart—6

Full Line Chart—7

Simple Area Chart—8

Stacked Area Chart—9

Full Area Chart—10

Simple Column Chart—11

Stacked Column Chart—12

Full Column Chart—13

Simple Bar Chart—14

Stacked Bar Chart—15

Full Bar Chart—16

HLC Stock Chart—17

HLC Stock Chart WSJ—18

OHLC Stock Chart—19

OHLC Stock Chart WSJ—20

RowIndex: Specifies the row index; used along with the DataItem property.

ColumnIndex: Specifies the column index; used along with the DataItem property.

DataItem: Specifies a data value; entry is identified by RowIndex and ColumnIndex properties. To specify a value of 3 for row 2, column 4, set the RowIndex property to 2, ColumnIndex property to 4, and then set the DataItem property value to 3.

ColorScheme: Specifies the predefined set of colors you would like to use. These colors will be used to fill regions. The possible values for this property are 0, 1, and 2.

BackStyle: Determines whether the background is transparent or opaque. The possible values for this property are as follows:

Transparent—0

Opaque—1

Scale: Determines the percentage scaling factor. By default, the control will perform 100 percent scaling. The value of the property should be between 1 to 100. If the specified value is invalid, the default scaling factor will be used.

RowName: Use this property along with the RowIndex property to specify a name for the row. This name will be used in legends and labels. On the HTML page, row names are specified using the RowNames <param> tag:

```
<param name="RowNames" value="Nov Dec">
```

ColumnName: Use this property along with ColumnIndex to specify a name for the column. This name will be used in legends and labels. On the HTML page, column names are specified using the ColumnNames <param> tag:

```
<param name="ColumnNames" value="Apple Orange Grapes">
```

DisplayLegend: Use this property to view or hide the legend. This property can assume one of the following values:

Show Legend—1

Hide Legend—0

GridPlacement: This property controls how grids are drawn. The grid lines can be drawn either over the chart (foreground) or below the chart (background). This property can assume one of the following values:

Grid lines in the background—0

Grid lines in the foreground—1

Data param tags: The data param tags are used to specify the data values for the chart. To specify data values for row x, use the following syntax:

```
<param name="data[x]" value="num1 num2 num3">
```

Example:

```
<param name="data[0]" value="37 75 100">
```

```
<param name="data[1]" value="91 64 200">
```

```
<param name="data[2]" value="91 64 200">
```

```
<param name="data[3]" value="37 75 100">
```

```
<param name="data[4]" value="91 64 200">
```

```
<param name="data[5]" value="91 64 200">
```

URL: This property enables you to specify a data file using an URL. The Chart control will use the data specified in the data file to draw the chart. The format of the data file is as follows:

```
chart_type\n
number_of_rows\n
number_of_columns<\tcolumn_name_0\tcolumn_name_1\tcolumn_name_2 ... >\n
<row_name_1\t>data_val_0\tdata_val_1\tdata_val_2 ...data_val_n\n
<row_name_2\t>data_val_0\tdata_val_1\tdata_val_2 ...data_val_n\n
...
<row_name_m\t>data_val_0\tdata_val_1\tdata_val_2 ...data_val_m\n
```

The first line in the data file specifies the chart type, followed by a new line. See "Chart Types" in the previous section for the types of charts you can draw and their corresponding values.

The second line in the data file specifies the number of rows in the chart, followed by a new line.

The third line specifies the number of columns followed by column names. Column names are optional. The column names show up as legends in the chart. The column name can include any alphanumeric character and space. Note that the column names should be separated only by tab characters.

Successive lines specify data values for each row. Each line starts with an optional row name followed by n numbers, where n is the number of columns. The row name can include any alphanumeric characters and space. The row name, if specified, should be followed by a tab character.

Example 1: Column names unspecified

5

5

12

Off	37	75	54	88	5	15	74	17	44	70	97	55
Win	91	64	12	45	48	80	98	80	54	37	70	23
Cons	84	95	53	24	79	32	55	90	98	98	95	7
Back	15	1	79	45	72	33	37	88	4	90	29	83
Dev	61	66	81	82	41	16	68	49	5	90	84	20

Example 2: Row names unspecified

5

5

12

Jan	Feb	Mar	Apr	May	Jun	Jul	Aug	Sep	Oct	Nov	Dec
37	75	54	88	5	15	74	17	44	70	97	55
91	64	12	45	48	80	98	80	54	37	70	23
84	95	53	24	79	32	55	90	98	98	95	7
15	1	79	45	72	33	37	88	4	90	29	83
61	66	81	82	41	16	68	49	5	90	84	20

Example 3: Both row names and column names unspecified

5

5

12

37	75	54	88	5	15	74	17	44	70	97	55
91	64	12	45	48	80	98	80	54	37	70	23
84	95	53	24	79	32	55	90	98	98	95	7
15	1	79	45	72	33	37	88	4	90	29	83
61	66	81	82	41	16	68	49	5	90	84	20

Methods

AboutBox: Displays the About dialog box.

Reload: Forces the data specified in the URL to be downloaded and read again.

Events

None.

Additional Information

Microsoft

One Microsoft Way
Redmond, WA 98052 USA

Phone: 206-882-8080

Fax: 206-936-7329

http://www.microsoft.com/activex/gallery/

Information on this control: http://microsoft.saltmine.com/isapi/activexisv/ prmgallery/gallery-activex-info.idc?ID=162

ClassID: clsid:FC25B780-75BE-11CF-8B01-444553540000

Download page: http://microsoft.saltmine.com/activexisv/msctls/ie/ chart.htm

Codebase: http://activex.microsoft.com/controls/iexplorer/ iechart.ocx#Version=4,70,0,1161

DataTable

DataTable is a high-performance grid component. Features include: editable cells, cells may have bitmaps, check boxes or combo boxes, set colors and fonts for cells, horizontal and vertical splitter windows, resize columns and rows, column sorting, region selection, built-in column searches and column totaling, 3D effects, and more.

Sample Code

This code sets up a simple data-entry interface that stores statistics pertaining to baseball pitchers. The results are stored on the page in a DataTable grid.

```
<HTML>
<HEAD>
    <SCRIPT LANGUAGE="VBScript">
<!--
Sub window_onLoad()
 Datatbl1.RowSet.Reset
 Datatbl1.ColumnSet.Add 0
 Datatbl1.ColumnSet.Add 0
 Datatbl1.ColumnSet.Add 0
 Datatbl1.ColumnSet(0).DataType = 135   ' dttString
 Datatbl1.ColumnSet(0).DataLen = 50
 Datatbl1.ColumnSet(0).Heading = "Player"
 Datatbl1.ColumnSet(1).DataType = 132   ' dttSingleFloat
 Datatbl1.ColumnSet(1).Format = "0.00"
 Datatbl1.ColumnSet(1).Heading = "ERA"
 Datatbl1.ColumnSet(2).DataType = 153   ' dttStdCheckbox
 Datatbl1.ColumnSet(2).Heading = "Injured?"
 Datatbl1.Font.Bold = True
 Datatbl1.RowSet.SelectType = 1
 Datatbl1.RowSet.AllowAutoRowInsert = True
end sub
Sub cmdAdd_OnClick()
 Dim MyData(2)
 dtAfterLast = -2
 strName = txtName.Value
 MyData(0) = strName
 MyData(1) = CStr(txtERA.Value)
 MyData(2) = chkInjured.Value
 Datatbl1.Rowset.Add dtAfterLast, MyData
End Sub
-->
```

```
    </SCRIPT>
<TITLE>Protoview DataTable Example</TITLE>
</HEAD>
<BODY>
<b>Baseball Pitcher Scouting System</b><p>
<p>
Name:
    <INPUT TYPE=TEXT NAME="txtName">
ERA:
    <INPUT TYPE=TEXT NAME="txtERA">
Injured:
    <INPUT TYPE=CHECKBOX NAME="chkInjured">
<p>
    <INPUT TYPE=BUTTON VALUE="Add Player" NAME="cmdAdd">
<p>
    <OBJECT ID="Datatbl1" WIDTH=280 HEIGHT=152 </OBJECT
     CLASSID="CLSID:4C1DF000-D3FF-11CE-84BA-484F4DF914E6"
     CODEBASE="http://www.protoview.com/msactivex/datatbl/dtbl32.ocx">
</BODY>
</HTML>
    </OBJECT>
</BODY>
```

Object Hierarchy

The DataTable object contains four objects:

- ◆ the DTRowSet object for row information

- ◆ the DTColumnSet object for Column information

- ◆ the DTCellSet object for cell information

- ◆ the DTCurCell object for current cell information

The DTRowSet, DTColumnSet, and DTCellSet objects each contain other objects used to encapsulate information about a particular item in the set. For example, the DTRowSet object contains the DTRow object, which encapsulates information about a particular row.

DataTable Properties

AboutBox: Displays an About dialog.

AllowPaintCellEvent: Returns or sets whether the PaintCell event is fired.

Appearance: Returns or sets the three-dimensional effect drawn.

BackColor: Returns or sets the DataTable background color.

BorderStyle: Returns or sets the type of DataTable border drawn.

CellSet: Retrieves the DTCellSet object.

ColumnSet: Retrieves the DTColumnSet object.

CurCell: Retrieves the DTCurCell object.

DataSource: The name of a Data control that provides database access.

DropDownType: Returns or sets the drop-down type.

DroppedState: Returns or sets whether the DataTable is fully visible.

Enabled: Returns or sets whether the DataTable can respond to user-generated events.

Font: Returns or sets the DataTable font.

ForeColor: Returns or sets the DataTable text color.

GridLineColor: Returns or sets the color of the grid lines.

HorzGridLines: Returns or sets whether horizontal grid lines are displayed.

HorzScrollBar: Returns or sets when scroll bars are displayed.

HorzSplitPane: Returns or sets whether the DataTable window is split horizontally.

hWnd: Returns a handle to the DataTable.

LeftPaneWidth: Returns or sets the width of the left pane.

Redraw: Enables or disables DataTable painting.

RowSet: Retrieves the DTRowSet object.

SelBackColor: Returns or sets the selected background color.

SelForeColor: Returns or sets the selected text color.

TopPaneHeight: Returns or sets the height of the top pane.

VertGridLines: Returns or sets whether vertical grid lines are displayed.

VertScrollBar: Returns or sets when vertical scroll bars are displayed.

VertSplitPane: Returns or sets whether the DataTable window is split vertically.

VirtualMemType: Returns or sets the virtual memory type.

VMDataKey: Returns or sets the data key of the row being fetched while processing virtual memory events.

DTColumnSet Properties

AllowResize: Returns or sets whether columns can be resized.

Count: Returns or sets the number of columns.

FirstVisible: Returns or sets the first (left-most) visible column.

HideListArrow: Returns or sets whether the arrow on a list box column is visible.

Item: Returns the specified DTColumn object.

LabelType: Returns or sets the type of row labels displayed.

NumListItems: Returns or sets the number of items visible in a column that has a drop-down list box.

SelectType: Returns or sets the column selection type.

SortAsc: Returns or sets the sorting direction.

SortCaseI: Returns or sets whether the sorting is case-insensitive.

SortEnabled: Returns or sets whether sorting is enabled.

SortKey: Returns or sets the column used for sorting.

DTColumn Properties

BackColor: Returns or sets the background color of the column.

Bound: Returns or sets whether the column is bound.

DataAlign: Returns or sets the alignment of the data in the column.

DataEdit: Returns or sets whether the column is editable.

DataLen: Returns or sets the length of the column data.

DataType: Returns or sets the type of the column data.

DefVal: Returns or sets the default value for the column.

EditAutoHScroll: Returns or sets whether the column data will scroll horizontally while editing the column.

EditAutoVScroll: Returns or sets whether the column data will scroll vertically while editing the column.

EditLowercase: Returns or sets whether characters will be converted to lowercase while editing the column.

EditMultiLine: Returns or sets whether editing is multiline for the column.

EditUppercase: Returns or sets whether characters will be converted to uppercase while editing the column.

EditWantReturn: Returns or sets whether the ENTER key can be used to move to the next line while editing the column.

Extra1: Returns or sets the first extra long for the column.

Extra2: Returns or sets the second extra long for the column.

Font: Returns or sets the font used for the column.

ForeColor: Returns or sets the text color used for the column.

Format: Returns or sets the format string used for the column.

HeadAlign: Returns or sets the heading alignment for the column.

Heading: Returns or sets the heading string for the column.

Hidden: Returns or sets whether the column is hidden.

List: Returns or sets the list of items used for a drop-down list.

Locked: Returns or sets whether the column is locked.

Name: Returns or sets the symbolic name for the column.

Overwrite: Returns or sets whether cells in the column can overwrite adjoining cells.

Resize: Returns or sets whether the column can be resized.

SelBackColor: Returns or sets the selected background color for the column.

Selected: Returns or sets whether the column is selected.

SelForeColor: Returns or sets the selected text color for the column.

Value: Returns or sets the value of the cells in the column.

Width: Returns or sets the column width.

DTRowSet Properties

AllowAutoRowInsert: Returns or sets whether rows will automatically be added to the end of the table.

AllowResize: Returns or sets whether rows can be resized.

Count: Returns or sets the number of rows in the DataTable.

FirstVisible: Returns or sets the index of the first (topmost) visible row.

HeadingType: Returns or sets the type of column headings displayed.

Height: Returns or sets the height of the DataTable rows.

Item: Returns the specified DTRow object.

SelectType: Returns or sets the type of row selection enabled.

TrapDeleteKey: Returns or sets whether the delete key will delete the current row.

TrapInsertKey: Returns or sets whether the insert key will insert a new row.

VertAlign: Returns or sets the vertical alignment of text in rows.

DTRow Properties

BackColor: Returns or sets the background color for the row.

Font: Returns or sets the font used for the row.

ForeColor: Returns or sets the text color for the row.

Height: Returns or sets the height of the row.

Label: Returns or sets the row label text for the row.

Resize: Returns or sets whether the row can be resized.

SelBackColor: Returns or sets the selected background color for the row.

Selected: Returns or sets whether the row is selected.

SelForeColor: Returns or sets the selected text color for the row.

Value: Return/sets the cell data for the row.

DTCellSet Properties

Item: Returns the specified DTCell object.

NullString: Returns or sets the string used to represent null cells.

SelectType: Returns or sets the type of cell selection enabled.

DTCurCell Properties

AllowCellEdit: Returns or sets whether the current cell can be edited.

BackColor: Returns or sets the background color of the current cell.

Column: Returns or sets the column index of the current cell.

EditValue: Returns or sets the value while editing the current cell.

EndEditClick: Returns or sets whether edit mode is ended with a mouse click.

EndEditCtrlTab: Returns or sets whether edit mode is ended with the CTRL+TAB key.

EndEditLfRtArrows: Returns or sets whether edit mode is ended with the left and right arrow keys.

EndEditTab: Returns or sets whether edit mode is ended with the TAB key.

EndEditUpDnArrows: Returns or sets whether edit mode is ended with the up and down arrow keys.

FocusPenColor: Returns or sets the color of the pen used to draw the focus rectangle.

FocusPenStyle: Returns or sets the style used when drawing the focus rectangle.

FocusPenWidth: Returns or sets the width of the pen used when drawing the focus rectangle.

Font: Returns or sets the font used for the current cell.

ForeColor: Returns or sets the text color for the current cell.

hWndEditBox: Returns the handle to the edit box while editing.

hWndListBox: Returns the handle to the list box while editing.

KeyForAbortEdit: Returns or sets the key used to abort editing.

KeyForBeginEdit: Returns or sets the key used to begin editing.

KeyForEndEdit: Returns or sets the key used to end editing.

MoveColMajor: Returns or sets whether the next cell is determined by moving to the next row in the same column.

Pane: Returns or sets the pane number of the current cell.

Row: Returns or sets the row index of the current cell.

SelBackColor: Returns or sets the selected background color for the current cell.

SelForeColor: Returns or sets the selected text color for the current cell.

SelLength: Returns or sets the number of characters selected while editing.

SelStart: Returns or sets starting point of the text selected while editing.

TabToNextCell: Returns or sets whether the TAB key can be used to move to the next cell.

Value: Returns or sets the current cell value when not in edit mode.

DTCell Properties

BackColor: Returns or sets the background color for the cell.

Font: Returns or sets the font used for the cell.

ForeColor: Returns or sets the text color for the cell.

NullFlag: Returns or sets whether the cell has a null value.

SelBackColor: Returns or sets the selected background color for the cell.

Selected: Returns whether the cell is in the selected block.

SelForeColor: Returns or sets the selected text color for the cell.

Value: Returns or sets the cell data.

DataTable Methods

Reset: Resets all DataTable information.

VMReady: Informs the DataTable that the parent is ready to receive virtual memory events.

DBAutoConfig: Deletes any existing columns and creates a new column for each field in the Recordset.

Events

AbortEdit: Occurs when editing of the current cell has been aborted.

BeforeAbortEdit: Occurs before editing is aborted.

BeforeBeginEdit: Occurs before editing is begun.

BeforeBlockSel: Occurs before a block of cells is selected.

BeforeColSel: Occurs before a column is selected.

BeforeCopy: Occurs before the contents of the selected items are copied to the clipboard.

BeforeCut: Occurs before the contents of the selected items are copied to the clipboard and the cells cleared.

BeforeDeleteRow: Occurs before a row is deleted.

BeforeEndEdit: Occurs before editing is ended.

BeforeInsertRow: Occurs before a row is inserted.

BeforePaste: Occurs before the contents of the clipboard is pasted to the DataTable.

BeforeRowSel: Occurs before a row is selected.

BeginEdit: Occurs when editing has begun on the current cell.

BlockSel: Occurs when a block of cells has been selected.

BlockUnSel: Occurs when a block of cells has been deselected.

CellFull: Occurs when the user has entered as much data as will fit in the current cell.

Change: Occurs when editing mode has ended and the cell contents have been updated with the new value.

ColAdded: Occurs when a column has been added.

ColChange: Occurs when the column index of the current cell has changed.

ColDeleted: Occurs when a column has been deleted.

ColMoved: Occurs when a column has been moved.

ColNameChanged: Occurs when the symbolic name of a column has been changed.

ColSel: Occurs when a column has been selected.

ColSize: Occurs when the size of a column has been changed.

ColUnSel: Occurs when a column has been deselected.

ComboCloseUp: Occurs when the combo box displays while editing has closed up.

ComboDropDn: Occurs when the combo box displays while editing has dropped down.

Create: Occurs when the DataTable has been created.

DeletedRow: Occurs when a row has been deleted.

Destroy: Occurs when the DataTable is about to be destroyed.

DropDn: Occurs when the DataTable has been dropped down or closed up.

EditKeyDown: Occurs when the user presses a key and the DataTable is currently being edited.

EditKeyPress: Occurs when the user presses and releases an ANSI key and the DataTable is being edited.

EditKeyUp: Occurs when the user releases a key and the DataTable is currently being edited.

Error: Fires when an error occurs within the DataTable outside of the scope of a method call or property access.

HScroll: Occurs when the DataTable has been scrolled horizontally.

InsertedRow: Occurs when a row has been inserted.

KeyDown: Occurs when the user presses a key and the DataTable is not currently being edited.

KeyPress: Occurs when the user presses and releases an ANSI key and the DataTable is not being edited.

KeyUp: Occurs when the user releases a key and the DataTable is not being edited.

LfClick: Occurs when user presses the left mouse button.

LfDblClick: Occurs when the left mouse button is double-clicked within the client area of a DataTable control.

MouseDown: Occurs when the user has pressed a mouse button.

MouseMove: Occurs when the user moves the mouse.

MouseUp: Occurs when the user has released a mouse button.

PaintCell: Occurs when a cell is about to be painted.

PosChange: Occurs when the current cell's row or column index has changed.

RowChange: Occurs when the current cell's row index has changed.

RowSel: Occurs when a row has been selected.

RowSize: Occurs when a row has been resized.

RowUnSel: Occurs when a row has been deselected.

RtClick: Occurs when the user has clicked the right mouse button.

RtDblClick: Occurs when the user has double-clicked the right mouse button.

UpdateCell: Occurs when edit mode is ending and the value of the current cell is about to be updated with the new value.

VMGetFirst: Occurs when the virtual memory table needs to retrieve the first row of data.

VMGetLast: Occurs when the virtual memory table needs to retrieve the last row of data.

VMGetNext: Occurs when the virtual memory table needs to retrieve the next row of data.

VMGetPercent: Occurs when the virtual memory table needs to retrieve a row located a specified percentage down the table.

VMGetPrev: Occurs when the virtual memory table needs to retrieve the previous row of data.

VMGetRowData: Occurs when the virtual memory table needs to retrieve a specific row of data.

VScroll: Occurs when the DataTable has been scrolled vertically.

DTColumnSet Methods

Add: Adds a column to the DataTable.

Copy: Copies a column in the DataTable.

GetColWithName: Retrieves the index of the column with the specified symbolic name.

GetSelectCount: Retrieves the number of selected columns.

GetSelect: Retrieves the index of the first column selected after the specified column.

GetVisCount: Retrieves the number of visible columns.

Move: Moves the specified column.

Remove: Removes the specified column.

SelectRange: Selects a range of columns.

DTColumn Methods

Invalidate: Invalidates the area of the column.

Search: Searches the column for the specified value.

Total: Totals the values in a column.

DTRowSet Methods

Add: Adds a row to the DataTable.

Copy: Copies a row in the DataTable.

GetSelectCount: Retrieves the number of selected rows.

GetSelect: Retrieves the index of the first selected row after the specified row.

GetVisCount: Retrieves the number of visible rows.

Move: Moves a row in the DataTable.

Remove: Removes a row from the DataTable.

Reset: Removes all DataTable rows.

SelectRange: Selects a range of DataTable rows.

DTRow Methods

Invalidate: Invalidates the area of the row.

DTCellSet Methods

GetCellAtPoint: Retrieves the pane, row, and column index of the cell located at the specified point.

GetSelect: Retrieves the selected block of cells.

SelectBlock: Selects a block of cells.

DTCurCell Methods

AbortEdit: Aborts editing of the current cell.

BeginEdit: Begins editing of the current cell.

EndEdit: Ends editing of the current cell.

MoveToNext: Moves the current cell to the next cell.

MoveToPrev: Moves the current cell to the previous cell.

DTCell Methods

GetRect: Retrieves the coordinates for the bounding rectangle of the cell.

Invalidate: Invalidates the area of the cell.

MakeVisible: Scrolls the table horizontally and vertically so that the cell becomes visible.

Additional Information

ProtoView Development

2540 Route 130
Cranbury, NJ 08512 USA

Phone: 609-655-5000

Fax: 609-655-5353

http://www.protoview.com

Information on this control: http://microsoft.saltmine.com/isapi/activexisv/
prmgallery/gallery-activex-info.idc?ID=62

ClassID: CLSID:4C1DF000-D3FF-11CE-84BA-484F4DF914F6

Download page: http://www.protoview.com/msactivex/datatbl/datatbl.htm

Codebase: http://www.protoview.com/msactivex/datatbl/dtbl32.ocx

DateEdit Control

The DateEdit control enables users to input a date in a graphical calendar format. You can display the date with a drop-down calendar, an LED display, or as an odometer.

Sample Code

This code displays a DateEdit control in an HTML page and provides confirmation to the user with a message box when a date has been selected.

```
<HTML>
<HEAD>
<TITLE>DateEdit Example</TITLE>
</HEAD>
<BODY leftmargin=8 bgcolor="#FFFFFF" VLINK="#666666" LINK="#FF0000">
<SCRIPT LANGUAGE="VBScript">
<!--
  Sub ConfirmOrder
    MsgBox "Your order will be delivered on " & DateEdit1.Value & "."
  End Sub
-->
</SCRIPT>
    <OBJECT ID="DateEdit1" WIDTH=160 HEIGHT=24
 CLASSID="CLSID:C0000000-FFFF-1100-8001-000000000102"
 CODEBASE="http://www.protoview.com/msactivex/pics/pdate32.ocx">
    <PARAM NAME="_Version" VALUE="65541">
    <PARAM NAME="_ExtentX" VALUE="4233">
    <PARAM NAME="_ExtentY" VALUE="635">
    <PARAM NAME="_StockProps" VALUE="228">
    <PARAM NAME="Appearance" VALUE="1">
</OBJECT>
    <INPUT LANGUAGE="VBScript" TYPE=BUTTON VALUE="Order" ONCLICK="Call
ConfirmOrder"
     NAME="cmdOrder">
</BODY>
</HTML>
```

Properties

Appearance: Returns or sets the paint style of a DateEdit control. Read-only at run-time.

BorderStyle: Returns or sets the border style for a DateEdit object. Read-only at run-time.

BackColor: Returns or sets the background color of an object.

DateFormat: Controls the display format of the date presented in the DateEdit control.

DayLeadingZero: Controls the way numbers below 10 are displayed in the date.

DisplayFormat: Controls the display format of the date presented in the DateEdit control.

EnableCalendar: Controls whether or not the calendar drop-down button is displayed on the DateEdit control.

Enabled: Returns or sets a value that determines whether a form or control can respond to user-generated events.

Font: Returns a Font object.

ForeColor: Returns or sets the foreground color used to display text and graphics in an object.

hWnd: Returns a handle to a DateEdit control. Read-only at runtime; not available at design time.

IgnoreKeyboard: Controls whether or not the DateEdit control will accept keyboard input.

MonthLeadingZero: Controls the way numbers below 10 are displayed in the DateEdit control.

Seperator: The character used to separate the different parts of a date when the date is shown in the mm/dd/yy, dd/mm/yy, or yy/mm/dd formats.

ShowCentury: Controls the way the year is displayed in a DateEdit control.

UseDefaultFormat: Controls the display format of the date presented in the DateEdit control.

Value: Represents the date in the DateEdit control.

Methods

AboutBox: Displays the control's About box.

GetDateString: Returns a string representation of the date.

IsNull: Returns True if the DateEdit control contains a null date.

SetDayLiteral: Sets the text used to represent the day of the week in the date string.

SetDOWLiteral: Sets the text used to represent first character of the day of the week in the abbreviated version of the date string.

SetMonthLiteral: Sets the text used to represent the month in the date string.

SetNull: Empties the DateEdit control.

Events

Change: Fires whenever the contents of the DateEdit control changes.

Click: Occurs when the user presses and then releases a mouse button over an object. It can also occur when the value of a control is changed.

HideDropDown: Fires whenever the calendar drop-down is about to be hidden.

KeyDown: Fires each time a key is pressed when the object has input focus.

KeyPress: Fires each time a key is pressed when the object has input focus.

KeyUp: Fires each time a key is released when the object has input focus.

MouseDown: Occurs when the user presses (MouseDown) or releases (MouseUp) a mouse button.

MouseMove: Occurs when the user moves the mouse.

MouseUp: Occurs when the user presses (MouseDown) or releases (MouseUp) a mouse button.

ShowDropDown: Fires whenever the calendar drop-down is about to be shown.

Additional Information

ProtoView Development

2540 Route 130
Cranbury, NJ 08512 USA

Phone: 609-655-5000

Fax: 609-655-5353

http://www.protoview.com

Information on this control: http://www.protoview.com/msactivex/pics/pdate.htm

ClassID: CLSID:C0000000-FFFF-1100-8001-000000000102

Codebase: http://www.protoview.com/msactivex/pics/pdate32.ocx

Dial Control

A variation on the scroll bar control found in Windows, the Dial control is a mouse-controlled stereo knob. Like the standard scroll bar, you can define specific ranges, or it can be "turned" up or down freely.

Sample Code

This code displays a Protosoft Dial control and a label control on a page. When the user adjusts the Dial control, the label control changes to indicate the new value of the Dial control.

```
<HTML>
<HEAD>
<TITLE>ProtoView Dial Control Example</TITLE>
</HEAD>
<BODY bgcolor="#FFFFFF" VLINK="#666666" LINK="#FF0000">
    <SCRIPT LANGUAGE="VBScript">
<!--
Sub Dial1_ThumbTrack(Position, TurnDial)
 ' Position is a parameter generated by
 '  the ThumbTrack event.
 lblVolume.Caption = "Volume: " & Position
end sub
-->
    </SCRIPT>
    <OBJECT ID="Dial1" WIDTH=115 HEIGHT=83
     CLASSID="CLSID:51FFB583-81DA-11CF-AACD-444553540000"
     CODEBASE="http://www.protoview.com/msactivex/pics/dial32.ocx">
        <PARAM NAME="_Version" VALUE="65536">
        <PARAM NAME="_ExtentX" VALUE="3034">
        <PARAM NAME="_ExtentY" VALUE="2187">
        <PARAM NAME="_StockProps" VALUE="64">
    </OBJECT>
    <OBJECT ID="lblVolume" WIDTH=137 HEIGHT=33
     CLASSID="CLSID:99B42120-6EC7-11CF-A6C7-00AA00A47DD2">
        <PARAM NAME="_ExtentX" VALUE="3625">
        <PARAM NAME="_ExtentY" VALUE="873">
        <PARAM NAME="Caption" VALUE="Volume: 0">
        <PARAM NAME="Alignment" VALUE="4">
        <PARAM NAME="ForeColor" VALUE="#FF0000">
        <PARAM NAME="BackColor" VALUE="#C0C0C0">
        <PARAM NAME="FontName" VALUE="Arial">
```

```
            <PARAM NAME="FontSize" VALUE="14">
        </OBJECT>
    </BODY>
</HTML>
```

Properties

Direction: Returns or sets the direction (clockwise or counter-clockwise) that a Dial control is turned to increase the value.

Enabled: Returns or sets a value that determines whether a form or control can respond to user-generated events.

hWnd: Returns a handle to a Dial control. Read-only at runtime; not available at design time.

MaximumRange: Returns or sets the value of the maximum range of the Dial control. The Value property can never exceed this value.

MaximumTurnRange: Returns or sets the maximum value, in degrees, of the cursor of the Dial control. The cursor is displayed as a red dot on the Dial control.

MinimumRange: Returns or sets the value of the minimum range of the Dial control. The Value property can never fall below this value.

MinimumTurnRange: Returns or sets the minimum value, in degrees, of the cursor of the Dial control. The cursor is displayed as a red dot on the Dial control.

Value: Returns or sets the value of the current position of the Dial control.

Methods

AboutBox: Use the About command to find the version number and other pertinent information about this control.

Events

Click: Occurs when the user presses and then releases a mouse button over an object. It can also occur when the value of the control is changed.

DblClick: Occurs when the user presses and releases a mouse button and then presses and releases it again over an object.

EndScroll: Occurs after the user turns the Dial control.

KeyDown: Fires each time a key is pressed when the Dial object has input focus.

KeyPress: Fires each time a key is pressed when the Calendar object has input focus.

KeyUp: Fires each time a key is released when the Calendar object has input focus.

LineDown: Occurs when the user presses the Down Arrow key while the Dial control has input focus, or clicks the button on the dial with the minus symbol on it.

LineUp: Occurs when the user presses the Up Arrow Page Down key while the Dial control has input focus or clicks the button on the dial with the plus symbol on it.

MouseDown: Occurs when the user presses (MouseDown) or releases (MouseUp) a mouse button.

MouseMove: Occurs when the user moves the mouse.

MouseUp: Occurs when the user presses (MouseDown) or releases (MouseUp) a mouse button.

PageDown: Occurs when the user presses the Page Down key while the Dial control has input focus or clicks between the red dot representing the current Value and the Minimun Turn Range.

PageUp: Occurs when the user presses the Page Up key while the Dial control has input focus or clicks between the red dot representing the current Value and the Maximum Turn Range.

ThumbPosition: Occurs when the user releases the mouse after turning the Dial control.

ThumbTrack: Occurs when the user turns the Dial control with the mouse.

Additional Information

ProtoView Development

2540 Route 130
Cranbury, NJ 08512 USA

Phone: 609-655-5000

Fax: 609-655-5353

http://www.protoview.com

Information on this control: http://www.protoview.com/msactivex/pics/dial.htm

ClassID: CLSID:51FFB583-81DA-11CF-AACD-444553540000

Codebase: http://www.protoview.com/msactivex/pics/dial32.ocx

Envoy Control For ActiveX

Envoy enables the electronic distribution of formatted documents. You can create Envoy documents from any application by printing to the Envoy print driver. When an Envoy document is loaded into a Web page, the user can choose from viewing and zooming tools by right-clicking on the embedded document.

You can see Envoy documents in action at the *New York Times* Fax site at http://www.nytimesfax.com.

This control can't be inserted using version 1.00.04 of the ActiveX Control Pad. You'll have to hand-code the VBScript in order to insert the control.

Sample Code

```
<HTML>
<HEAD>
<TITLE>Tumbleweed Envoy Control Example</TITLE>
</HEAD>
<BODY BGCOLOR=ffffff LANGUAGE="VBScript" onLoad="Init" >
<OBJECT CLASSID="CLSID:5220cb21-c88d-11cf-b347-00aa00a28331">
<PARAM NAME="LPKPath" VALUE="http://www.tumbleweed.com/lic/evyactx.lpk"> </
OBJECT>
<OBJECT
  CLASSID="clsid:92B54588-AE4A-11CF-A1DD-004095E18035"
  CODEBASE="http://www.tumbleweed.com/ftp/evyactx.cab#version=1,0,0,141"
  id=Evyocx1
  HEIGHT= 255 WIDTH=200
>
  <PARAM NAME = "DocumentName" VALUE = "http://www.tumbleweed.com/evy/
➥fallnews.evy">
  <PARAM NAME="Toolbar" VALUE=FALSE>
  <PARAM NAME="Scroll" VALUE=FALSE>
</OBJECT>
<SCRIPT LANGUAGE="VBScript" >
Dim InitState
InitState = FALSE
Sub Init
 InitState = TRUE
End Sub
Sub Evyocx1_HyperCommandClick (Processor, Command)
 If processor = "External Link" Then
  If (Right(Command, 4) = ".evy" ) Then
```

```
    Evyocx1.OpenFile Command
  Else
   Location.Href = Command
  End If
    End If
End Sub
Sub Evyocx1_ProgressChange (Percent, Status_string)
 Status = Status_string
End Sub
</SCRIPT>
</BODY>
</HTML>
```

Properties

CurrentPage: Retrieves and sets the current page of the document. The current page is always visible.

CurrentTool: Retrieves and sets the current mouse tool.

DocumentName: The file name of the Envoy document that is currently displayed in the control. This property can be changed when the container opens a new document using OpenFile(), or when the control does a hypertext jump to another Envoy document.

GreekPointSize: Retrieves and sets the threshold of character size in typographic points below which the text is rendered as a gray rectangle.

RightClickMenuState: Modifies the behavior of the mouse right-click. When it is set to 1, the mouse right-click on the document brings up a pop-up menu that enables the user to select some viewing commands or tools.

Scroll: When this property is set to 1, the control opens documents with the scrollbar; otherwise, the control opens documents without the scrollbar.

SelectionStyle: Retrieves and sets the mouse selection style of the control.

Toolbar: When this property is set to 1, the control opens a document with a default toolbar attached to each document. When it is set to 0, no toolbar is attached with the document.

ViewStyle: Retrieves and sets the viewing style of the control.

ViewZoom: Retrieves and sets the current zoom level of the control.

Methods

AboutBox: Displays the control's About box.

CommandExecute: Executes a predefined command such as open document, print document, or other viewing commands.

FindText: Starts a text search in the current document.

GetDocumentInfo: Retrieves document information specified by a key value for the current document in the control.

GetDocumentFirstVisiblePage: Returns the page number of the first visible page.

GetDocumentLastVisiblePage: Returns the page number of the last visible page.

GetDocumentPageCount: Returns the total number of pages.

GetSelectedText: Copies selected text into a string variable.

GetTotalHitCount: Returns the number of hits returned by a search.

IsCommandChecked: Checks whether a predefined command is checked in the control.

IsCommandEnabled: Checks whether the predefined command is enabled in the control.

OpenFile: Opens an Envoy document in the control.

PrintPage: Prints the current document.

Refresh: Causes the control to redraw itself.

Events

CommandStateChange: Fires when there is a predefined command state changes. This event enables the control to update its user interface.

CurrentPageChange: Fires when the current page is changed.

CurrentToolChange: Fires when the mouse tool is changed.

DblClick: Fires when the user double-clicks the control.

DocumentChange: Fires when the current document changes. This event can happen when a new document is opened but also when a cross-document hypertext jump is clicked.

HyperCommandClick: Fires when the user clicks a Hyper Command within the document.

VisibleChange: Fires to inform the container control that a change took place in the control.

ZoomChange: Fires when the zoom level within the control is changed.

Additional Information

Tumbleweed Software

2010 Broadway, Suite 200
Redwood City, CA 94063 USA

Phone: 415-369-6790

Fax: 415-369-7197

http://www.tumbleweed.com

Information on this control: http://www.tumbleweed.com/products.htm

ClassID: clsid:92B54588-AE4A-11CF-A1DD-004095E18035

Download page: http://www.tumbleweed.com/demo/eaxintro.htm

Codebase: http://www.tumbleweed.com/ftp/evyactx.cab#version=1,0,0,141

Gradient

This control shades the area with a range of colors, making the transition from a specified color to another specified color.

Sample Code

This code inserts a gradient control in an HTML page.

```
<HTML>
<HEAD>
<TITLE>Gradient Example</TITLE>
</HEAD>
<BODY>
<OBJECT ID="iegrad1" WIDTH=400 HEIGHT=20
 CLASSID="CLSID:017C99A0-8637-11CF-A3A9-00A0C9034920">
    <PARAM NAME="StartColor" VALUE="#0000FF">
    <PARAM NAME="EndColor" VALUE="#000000">
    <PARAM NAME="Direction" VALUE="0">
</OBJECT>
</BODY>
</HTML>
```

Properties

StartColor: The color with which the transition starts.

EndColor: The color with which the transition ends.

Direction:

> 0—The color transition is in the horizontal direction.

> 1—The color transition is in the vertical direction.

> 2—The color transition is toward the center.

> 3—The color transition is toward the corner.

> 4—The color transition is across diagonal down.

> 5—The color transition is across diagonal up.

> 6—The color transition is around the point specified in the StartPoint property.

> 7—The color transition is across the line joining StartPoint and EndPoint.

StartPoint: Coordinates of the start point in the format (x,y).

EndPoint: Coordinates of the end point in the format (x,y).

Methods

AboutBox: Displays the About dialog box.

Events

None.

Additional Information

Microsoft

One Microsoft Way
Redmond, WA 98052 USA

Phone: 206-882-8080

Fax: 206-936-7329

`http://www.microsoft.com/activex/gallery/`

Information on this control: `http://microsoft.saltmine.com/isapi/activexisv/prmgallery/gallery-activex-info.idc?ID=155`

ClassID: clsid:017C99A0-8637-11CF-A3A9-00A0C9034920

Download page: `http://microsoft.saltmine.com/activexisv/msctls/ie/gradient.htm`

Codebase: `http://activex.microsoft.com/controls/iexplorer/iegrad.ocx#Version=4,70,0,1161`

InterAct

InterAct is a software component used to create diagrams. Choose from an assortment of shapes, bitmaps, and lines to create your diagram. Setting colors, fonts, text, and 3D effects is easy, using the built-in diagramming editor. Advanced features like zoom in and zoom out and printing are standard features.

Sample Code

This code embeds an InterAct control in a page.

```
<HTML>
<SCRIPT language="VBScript">
Sub VBInterActIn
 interact.Zoom 1, 20
End Sub
</SCRIPT>
<SCRIPT language="VBScript">
Sub VBInterActOut
 interact.Zoom 2, 20
End Sub
</SCRIPT>
<HEAD>
<TITLE>ProtoView InterAct Example</TITLE>
</HEAD>
<BODY leftmargin=8 bgcolor="#FFFFFF" VLINK="#666666" LINK="#FF0000">
<TABLE BORDER=0 CELLPADDING=2>
<TR>
<TD ALIGN=RIGHT>
<TR><TD>
<tr>
<td align=left colspan=2><input name="idoIn"          type="button" value="Zoom
➥In"          onclick="VBInterActIn()"></td>
<td align=left colspan=2><input name="idoOut"         type="button" value="Zoom
➥Out"          onclick="VBInterActOut()"></td>
</tr>
</TABLE>
</TD></TR>
```

```
<font face="Arial,Helvetica,Geneva,Swiss" size=1>
    </font>
    <OBJECT ID="interact" WIDTH=500 HEIGHT=300
     CLASSID="CLSID:9DCCD563-29B5-11CF-BDCB-0020A90B183A"
     CODEBASE="http://www.protoview.com/msactivex/interact/pvido32.ocx">
        <PARAM NAME="_Version" VALUE="65536">
        <PARAM NAME="_ExtentX" VALUE="5292">
        <PARAM NAME="_ExtentY" VALUE="5292">
        <PARAM NAME="_StockProps" VALUE="1">
        <PARAM NAME="ScrollBars" VALUE="2">
        <PARAM NAME="EditMode" VALUE="1">
        <PARAM NAME="ToolsPalette" VALUE="1">
    </OBJECT>
<P>
</FONT>
</BODY>
</HTML>
```

Properties

BackColor: Determines the color used to paint the InterAct background.

Border: Determines whether InterAct will display a black rectangle around its edges to mark its border.

CurrentEntity: Retrieves or sets the current entity in a diagram. The current entity is the one that contains the tracking rectangle.

CurrentRelation: Retrieves or sets the current relation in the diagram.

EditMode: Returns or sets the edit mode for InterAct. When editing is disabled, entities and lines cannot be modified (moved or resized), right-clicking on InterAct will not display pop-up menus, and the tools palette will not be displayed.

FileName: Returns or sets the name of the diagram currently opened in InterAct. InterAct will update this value whenever the method ReadDiagram is invoked. If you invoke SaveDiagram and do not specify a file to save to, InterAct will use the value stored here to save the diagram, if a value is present. If you invoke ResetDiagram, this value is not reset. InterAct does not actually read or save a file if you set this property programmatically—use the methods ReadDiagram and SaveDiagram. This value does not affect palette files in any way.

GridHeight: Determines the vertical spacing of gridlines in InterAct.

GridLineColor: Determines the color used to paint gridlins in InterAct.

GridLines: Determines the vertical spacing of gridlines in InterAct.

GridWidth: Determines the horizontal spacing of gridlines n InterAct.

HorizontalScrollOffset: Determines the horizontal offset of the InterAct window. This property affects the display of the scrollbars if scrollbars are visible. Setting this property will not repaint the InterAct control. This is intentional to allow you to set both the horizontal and vertical offset without unnecessary flicker. See the InterAct Redraw property to force a repaint of the InterAct control.

hWnd: Returns a handle to InterAct. Read-only at runtime, not available at design time. The Microsoft Windows operating environent identifies each form and control in an application by assigning it a handle, or hWnd. The hWnd property is used with Windows API calls. Many Windows operating environment functions require the hWnd of the active window as an argument.

InetPath: Sets an optional path InterAct will use to locate an Internet host when executing an URL.

Modified: Determines whetherthe InterAct has been modified.

PopupMenu: Determines whether InterAct will display its built-in menus when an entity, relation, or the InterAct background is rght-clicked. By setting these properties to True, you are telling InterAct to display its own defined menus. By setting this value to False you are telling InterAct not to display its built-in menus. If you want to display your own menus, you can respond to the mouse click or double-click events.

PrinterLandscape: Determines the orientation of the printer page lines displayed by the InterAct. In landscape mode the horizontal and vertical dimensions of the page lines are reversed.

PrinterLines: Determines whether printer lines will be displayed in InterAct. Printer Lines are the solid lines displayed with a diagram. These provide a preview of a diagram when printed—showing where page breaks will occur if a multi-page diagram is printed. InterAct must be able to get access to the default printer of a workstation to properly calculate this value.

Redraw: Determines if InterAct will repaint itself when a change within a diagram occurs. This is useful for turning off redraw when a lot of changes are anticipated, such as adding several entities and relations at one time, and it is quicker to have InterAct redraw itself only after all the objects have been added rather than after each item is added. When you set redraw to True InterAct will repaint itself immediately.

RulesEnforced: Determines whether rules will be enforced in a diagram. Rules determine whether certain relations can be made between two entities. It may be desirable to have only certain entities be joined by specific relations.

ScrollBars: Determines whether horizontal and/or vertical scrollbars will be displayed on InterAct.

SnapToGrid: Determines whether entities will "snap" to the nearest grid lines for easy positioning. The upper-left corner of an entity will be moved to the nearest gridline. Even if gridlines are not being displayed, you can still have snap-to-grid enforced. Entities will be "snapped" when they are first created or whenever they are moved. If snap-to-grid is enabled in a diagram that previously did not have snap-to-grid enabled, all entities will be immediately "snapped."

ToolsPalette: Determines whether a tools palette is displayed. The tools palette is an interface that enables users to add entities and relations to a diagram, cut/copy/paste objects to the clipboard, zoom the diagram for different displays, and load or save diagrams. If the program does not display the tools palette, but intends to enable the user to access these capabilities, then the program must provide its own UI that takes advantage of the InterAct's exposed methods. The tools palette will not be displayed unless InterAct also has EditMode enabled.

VerticalScrollOffset: Determines the vertical offset of the InterAct window. This property affects the display of the scrollbars if scrollbars are visible. Setting this property will not repaint the InterAct control. This is intentional to enable you to set both the horizontal and vertical offset without unnecessary flicker.

ZoomValue: Determines the amount of zooming the InterAct control will perform on a diagram. The zoom value can be in the range 10–200. The value 100 means no zooming. The greater the zoom value, the less of the diagram you can see (you are zooming into the diagram to see more detail). The lesser the zoom value, the more of the diagram you can see (you are zooming out of the diagram to see less detail but more area). InterAct by default multiplies the zoom value by 0.8 when zooming in and 1.2 when zooming out for smooth motion.

Methods

AddEntityClass: Adds a new entity class to the diagram.

AddEntityFromClass: Adds a new entity to the diagram.

AddRelationClass: Adds a new relation class to the diagram.

AddRelationFromClass: Adds a new relation to the diagram.

AddRule: Adds a new rule to a diagram.

Copy: Copies the selected entity/entities and line(s) to the Windows clipboard.

Cut: Cuts the selected entity/entities and line(s) to the Windows clipboard.

DeleteEntity: Deletes an entity from the diagram.

DeleteEntityClass: Deletes an entity class definition from the diagram. This does not delete entities of this class that are currently being displayed in a diagram, nor does it remove any rules that refer to this class.

DeleteRelation: Deletes a relation from the diagram.

DeleteRelationClass: Deletes a relation class definition from the diagram. This does not delete relations of this class that are currently being displayed in a diagram, nor does it remove any rules that refer to this class.

DeleteRule: Deletes a rule from the diagram.

DoesEntityExist: Confirms whether a specified entity exists in the diagram.

DoesEntityClassExist: Confirms whether a specified entity class definition exists in the diagram. This does not return whether an entity of the specified class exists within the diagram.

DoesRelationExist: Confirms whether a specified relation exists in the diagram.

DoesRelationClassExist: Confirms whether a specified relation class definition exists in the diagram. This does not return whether a relation of the specified class exists within the diagram.

DoesRuleExist: Confirms whether a specified rule exists in the diagram.

DragAddEntity: Places InterAct into a mode where the user can use the mouse to drag a rectangle in InterAct for a new entity to be placed. This mimics the exact operation InterAct performs if the user clicks an entity class button on the tools palette. This method is extremely useful for users who do not want to display InterAct's tools palette, but do want to design their own palette for interaction with InterAct.

DragAddRelation: Places InterAct into a mode where the user can use the mouse to drag a new relation from a source to a destination entity. This method is extremely useful for users who do not want to display InterAct's tools palette, but do want to design their own palette for interaction with InterAct.

GetEntity: Selects an entity and prepares it to be manipulated.

GetEntityClass: Selects an entity class and prepares it to be manipulated.

GetNotifyEntity: Selects an entity and prepares it to be manipulated.

GetNotifyRelation: Selects a relation and prepares it to be manipulated.

GetNumberOfSelectedEntities: Returns the number of selected entities in a diagram.

GetNumberOfEntities: Returns the number of entities in a diagram.

GetNumberOfRelations: Returns the number of lines in a diagram.

GetRelation: Selects a relation and prepares it to be manipulated.

GetRelationClass: Selects a relation class and prepares it to be manipulated.

GetVersion: Returns the version number of the control.

IterateEntityClassFirst: Prepares InterAct to allow a program to iterate a list of entity classes available in the diagram.

IterateEntityClassNext: Returns the next entity class available in the diagram.

IterateEntityFirst: Prepares InterAct to allow a program to iterate a list of entities available in the diagram.

IterateEntityNext: Returns the next entity available in the diagram.

IterateRelationClassFirst: Prepares InterAct to allow a program to iterate a list of relation classes available in the diagram.

IterateRelationClassNext: Returns the next relation class available in the diagram.

IterateRelationFirst: Prepares InterAct to allow a program to iterate a list of relations available in the diagram.

IterateRelationNext: Returns the next relation available in the diagram.

IterateRuleFirst: Prepares InterAct to allow a program to iterate a list of rules enforced in the diagram.

IterateRuleNext: Returns the next rule enforced in the diagram.

IterateSelectedEntityFirst: Prepares InterAct to allow a program to iterate a list of selected entities available in the diagram.

IterateSelectedEntityNext: Returns the next selected entity in the diagram.

ManageClasses: Displays InterAct's built-in dialog for managing diagram classes.

ManageRules: Displays InterAct's built-in dialog for managing diagram rules.

MapDeviceToLogical: Takes a logical point in InterAct and converts it to the corresponding screen coordinate.

MapLogicalToDevice: Takes a device point in InterAct and converts it to the corresponding logical coordinate.

Paste: Pastes entities and lines from the Windows clipboard to a diagram.

PrintDiagram: Displays InterAct's built-in dialog for printing the diagram. This dialog allows a destination printer to be selected as well as pagination.

PropertyPage: Displays InterAct's built-in property page dialog for manipulating InterAct itself.

ReadDiagram: Reads a diagram from a file on disk and restores it in an InterAct object.

ReadPalette: Reads a set of entity and relation classes, as well as a set of rules associated with these classes, from a file on disk.

RedefineFromEntityClass: Causes all entities of the class ClassName to adopt the characteristics of ClassName.

RedefineFromRelationClass: Causes all relations of the class ClassName to adopt the characteristics of ClassName.

ResetDiagram: Resets InterAct, deleting all entities and relations.

ResetPalette: Resets InterAct's palette, deleting all entity and relation classes and rules associated with InterAct.

SaveDiagram: Saves a diagram to permanent storage as a file on disk. This diagram can be restored at any time.

SavePalette: Saves a diagram's palette (the collection of rules and classes used to create the diagram) to permanent storage as a file on disk.

SetToolsPaletteButtonText: Sets the text on the Options button of the default Tools Palette.

Zoom: Changes the zoom mode of InterAct. Zooming can allow more of a diagram to be visible but with less detail, or more detail in a smaller area displayed.

Events

BeforeDiagramLoaded: Fires before a diagram file is loaded.

BeforeDiagramReset: Fires before InterAct is about to reset a diagram. All relations and entities within a diagram will be deleted on reset.

BeforeDiagramSaved: Fires before a diagram is saved.

BeforeDisplayHelp: Fires when the user clicks the help button on InterAct's built-in tools palette. InterAct will by default display its help file. This event can be used to cancel the display of the InterAct help file.

BeforeDisplayManageClasses: Fires when InterAct is about to display its Manage Classes dialog.

BeforeDisplayOptionsMenu: Fires when the user clicks the Options button on the tools palette. By default InterAct displays a menu of options to choose from. This event can be used to cancel the display of the menu by InterAct.

BeforeDisplayManageRules: Fires when InterAct is about to display its Manage Rules dialog.

BeforeDisplayManageRulesButton: Fires when InterAct is about to display its Manage Classes dialog. The Manage Classes dialog has a button, Manage Rules, that will display the Manage Rules dialog. Some container applications will not want this button displayed if they do not want the user to access the Manage Rules dialog.

BeforeDisplayToolsPalette: Fires when InterAct is about to display its built-in tools palette.

BeforeHideToolsPalette: Fires when InterAct is about to hide its built-in tools palette.

BeforePaletteLoaded: Fires before a palette is loaded.

BeforePaletteReset: Fires before a palette is reset. Resetting a palette will remove all the entity and relation classes in the diagram.

BeforePaletteSaved: Fires before a palette is saved.

ClickEntity: Fires when the mouse is clicked or double-clicked on an entity.

ClickInterAct: Fires when the mouse is clicked or double-clicked on the InterAct background.

ClickRelation: Fires when the mouse is clicked or double-clicked on a relation.

DiagramLoaded: Fires after a diagram is loaded.

DiagramReset: Fires after InterAct has reset the diagram.

DiagramSaved: Fires after a diagram is saved.

EntityAddRequest: Fires when an entity object is about to be added to a diagram. If necessary, you can abort the entity addition.

EntityAdded: Fires after an entity object has been added to a diagram.

EntityDeleteRequest: Fires before an entity object is about to be deleted from a diagram.

EntityDeleted: Fires after an entity object has been deleted from a diagram.

EntityBeforeMove: Fires when the mouse is used to move an entity in a diagram. This event passes the old and new coordinates of the entity and gives the container an opportunity to change where the entity will be placed after being moved.

EntityMoved: Fires after the mouse is used to move an entity in a diagram. This event passes a reference to the moved entity, which the user can then query for its new coordinates.

PaletteLoaded: Fires after a palette is loaded.

PaletteReset: Fires after a palette is reset.

PaletteSaved: Fires after a palette is saved.

RelationAddRequest: Fires when a relation object is about to be added to a diagram. If necessary, you can abort the relation addition.

RelationAdded: Fires after a relation object has been added to a diagram.

RelationDeleteRequest: Fires before a relation object is about to be deleted from a diagram. This action can be canceled.

RelationDeleted: Fires after a relation object has been deleted from a diagram.

SelectionChange: The user has added or removed the selection from an entity or relation.

SetFocus: The input focus has been set to the InterAct control.

KillFocus: The Interact control has lost the focus.

Additional Information

ProtoView Development

2540 Route 130
Cranbury, NJ 08512 USA

Phone: 609-655-5000

Fax: 609-655-5353

http://www.protoview.com

Information on this control: http://www.protoview.com/msactivex/interact/interact.htm

ClassID: CLSID:9DCCD563-29B5-11CF-BDCB-0020A90B183A

Download page: http://www.protoview.com/msactivex/interact/interact.htm

Codebase: http://www.protoview.com/msactivex/interact/pvido32.ocx

Label

The Label control displays given text at any specified angle. It can also render the text along user-defined curves.

Sample Code

This code embeds a label control at a 45-degree angle on the HTML page:

```
<HTML>
<HEAD>
<TITLE>Label Example</TITLE>
</HEAD>
<BODY>
<OBJECT ID="IeLabel1" WIDTH=137 HEIGHT=127
 CLASSID="CLSID:99B42120-6EC7-11CF-A6C7-00AA00A47DD2"
 CODEBASE="http://activex.microsoft.com/controls/iexplorer/
 ➥ielabel.ocx#Version=4,70,0,1161">
    <PARAM NAME="Caption" VALUE="New! Improved!">
    <PARAM NAME="Angle" VALUE="45">
    <PARAM NAME="FontName" VALUE="Arial">
    <PARAM NAME="FontSize" VALUE="16">
    <PARAM NAME="FontBold" VALUE="1">
</OBJECT>
</BODY>
</HTML>
```

Properties

Caption: Specifies text to be displayed.

Angle: Specifies angle (counter-clockwise rotation) in degrees.

Alignment: Specifies how to align text in the control:

> 0—Aligned to left (horizontal) and to top (vertical)
>
> 1—Centered (horizontal) and to top (vertical)
>
> 2—Aligned to right (horizontal) and to top (vertical)
>
> 3—Aligned to left (horizontal) and Centered (vertical)
>
> 4—Centered (horizontal) and Centered (vertical)

5—Aligned to right (horizontal) and Centered (vertical)

6—Aligned to left (horizontal) and to bottom (vertical)

7—Centered (horizontal) and to bottom (vertical)

8—Aligned to right (horizontal) and to bottom (vertical)

BackStyle: Control background:

0—Transparent

1—Opaque

FontName: Name of a TrueType font.

FontSize: Size of the font.

FontItalic: Flag for italics.

FontBold: Flag for bold.

FontUnderline: Flag for underline.

FontStrikeout: Flag for strikeout.

Mode: Which mode the text will be rendered in:

0—Normal (same as the VB Label control)

1—Normal text with rotation

2—Apply the user-specified lines while rendering without rotation

3—Apply the user-specified lines while rendering, allow rotation

Param tags such as TopPoints, TopXY, BotPoints, and BotXY are provided to specify the two lines along which the text will be shown. Visual Basic properties such as TopPoints, TopIndex, TopXY, BotPoints, BotIndex, and BotXY are also supported.

Methods

AboutBox: Displays the About dialog box.

Events

Click: Triggered when the user clicks the label.

Change: Triggered when the label caption changes.

DblClick: Triggered when the user double-clicks the label.

MouseDown: Triggered when the user presses the mouse button down while the cursor is on the label.

MouseMove: Triggered when the user moves the mouse when the cursor is on the label.

MouseUp: Triggered when the user releases the mouse.

Additional Information

Microsoft

One Microsoft Way
Redmond, WA 98052 USA

Phone: 206-882-8080

Fax: 206-936-7329

http://www.microsoft.com/activex/gallery/

Information on this control: http://microsoft.saltmine.com/isapi/activexisv/prmgallery/gallery-activex-info.idc?ID=156

ClassID: clsid:99B42120-6EC7-11CF-A6C7-00AA00A47DD2

Download page: http://microsoft.saltmine.com/activexisv/msctls/ie/label.htm

Codebase: http://activex.microsoft.com/controls/iexplorer/ielabel.ocx#Version=4,70,0,1161

Marquee

The Marquee control can scroll any HTML file in either the horizontal or vertical direction. The control can be configured to change the amount and delay of scrolling. This control is built in to Internet Explorer.

Sample Code

This code consists of an HTML page with an embedded Marquee control that displays the contents of another HTML page, display.htm.

```
<HTML>
<HEAD>
<TITLE>Marquee Example</TITLE>
</HEAD>
<BODY>
<OBJECT ID="Marquee1" WIDTH=400 HEIGHT=40
 CLASSID="CLSID:1A4DA620-6217-11CF-BE62-0080C72EDD2D">
    <PARAM NAME="_ExtentX" VALUE="10583">
    <PARAM NAME="_ExtentY" VALUE="3519">
    <PARAM NAME="ScrollDelay" VALUE=300>
    <PARAM NAME="ScrollPixelsX" VALUE=5>
    <PARAM NAME="szURL" VALUE="http://99.99.99.1/activex/marquee/display.htm">
</OBJECT>
</BODY>
</HTML>
```

The file display.htm contains the following code:

```
<HTML>
<HEAD>
<TITLE>Marquee Madness </TITLE>
</HEAD>
<BODY leftmargin=8 bgcolor="#FFFFFF" VLINK="#666666" LINK="#FF0000">
<FONT FACE="ARIAL,HELVETICA" SIZE="4">
This is an example of scrolling text in a Marquee control.
</FONT>
</BODY>
</HTML>
```

Properties

ScrollStyleX: Sets the horizontal scroll style. Valid values are Bounce and Circular (default).

ScrollStyleY: Sets the vertical scroll style. Valid values are Bounce and Circular (default).

ScrollDelay: Sets the time in milliseconds between each movement of the URL in the marquee window. Valid values are positive integers. Default is 100.

LoopsX: Sets the number of times the image scrolls horizontally if ScrollStyleX is Circular, or sets the number of times the image bounces if ScrollStyleX is Bounce. Valid values are integers above or equal to –1. Zero indicates that a horizontal slide is to occur, –1 indicates that the image will never stop (infinite). The default is –1 (infinite).

LoopsY: Sets the number of times the image scrolls vertically if ScrollStyleY is Circular, or sets the number of times the image bounces if ScrollStyleY is Bounce. Valid values are integers above or equal to –1. Zero indicates that a vertical slide is to occur, –1 indicates that the image will never stop (infinite). The default is –1 (infinite).

ScrollPixelsX: Sets the number of pixels to move the URL horizontally in the marquee window; the number of milliseconds between each move is defined by the ScrollDelay property. Valid values are integers. The default is 75 pixels.

ScrollPixelsY: Vertical counterpart of ScrollPixelsX, except that the default is zero.

szURL: Sets the URL to scroll.

DrawImmediately: Determines whether you want to progressively render the URLs. Valid values are 1 (true) or 0 (false). The default is 1.

Whitespace: Sets the whitespace between URLs and/or tiled images. Valid values are non-negative integers. The default is zero.

PageFlippingOn: Determines whether the marquee will flip between multiple URLs (instead of creating one scrolling image) when the user presses the right mouse button or via the put_CurrentURL automation function. Valid values are 1 (true) or 0 (false). The default is 0.

Zoom: Sets the percentage of the original size you want the scrolling URLs to be. Valid values are positive integers. The default is 100.

WidthOfPage: Sets the width, in pixels, used to format the text of the URL. Valid values are positive integers. The default is 640.

Methods

AboutBox: Displays the About dialog box.

Pause: Stops the scrolling of the marquee.

Resume: Restarts the scrolling of the marquee.

InsertURL: Inserts a new URL after the existing URL.

DeleteURL: Deletes the URL at the specified index.

QueryURL: Gets an URL.

QueryURLCount: Gets the number of URLs in the list.

Events

OnStartOfImage: Issued just before the URL to be scrolled appears in the marquee window.

OnEndOfImage(HorizontalOrVertical): Is issued when the image has been completely scrolled. For example, it can be used to let VBScript change the contents of another control after the image has stopped moving. Because the horizontal and vertical scrolling could end at different times (different loops), which one has ended is indicated by the HorizontalOrVertical value (returns "H" for horizontal, "V" for vertical).

OnBounce(SideBouncedOff): Fires only in bounce mode, when the image being scrolled bounces off a side. SideBouncedOff returns the side it bounces off ("L" for left, "R" for right, "T" for top, and "B" for bottom).

OnScroll(HorizontalOrVertical): Fires each time the control is about to scroll the URL. HorizontalOrVertical indicates whether the horizontal or vertical scrolling is about to begin again (returns "H" for horizontal, "V" for vertical). This event is not fired for bounces or slides, nor is it fired the first time the image is scrolled.

OnLMouseClick: Fires when the user presses the left mouse button in the marquee window.

Additional Information

Microsoft

One Microsoft Way
Redmond, WA 98052 USA

Phone: 206-882-8080

Fax: 206-936-7329

`http://www.microsoft.com/activex/gallery/`

Information on this control: `http://microsoft.saltmine.com/isapi/activexisv/ prmgallery/gallery-activex-info.idc?ID=157`

ClassID: CLSID:1A4DA620-6217-11CF-BE62-0080C72EDD2D

Download page: `http://microsoft.saltmine.com/activexisv/msctls/ie/ marquee.htm`

mBED Control

The mBED Player provides access to media-rich, Web-smart interactivity. Using a text editor and standard Web formats such as gif, jpeg, and wav files, you can begin adding multimedia to your Web site today.

Sample Code

This is a generic example of how to include an mbedlet on an HTML page:

```
<OBJECT
 CLASSID="clsid:873237C3-C440-11CF-B4B6-00A02429C7EF\"
 WIDTH=XXX
 HEIGHT=YYY>
<PARAM NAME="SRC" VALUE="(URL to .mbd file)">
<EMBED SRC="(URL to .mbd file)" WIDTH=XXX HEIGHT=YYY>
</OBJECT>
```

The functionality of an mBED object (known as an "mbedlet") comes not from the properties, events, and methods of the ActiveX control, but rather from the mBED file displayed by the control. In this respect, the mBED ActiveX control is really a type of file viewer.

A guide to the syntax of the mBED file format is on the mBED Web site at `http://www.mbed.com/filefmt.html`.

Additional Information

mBED Software

185 Berry Street, #3807
San Francisco, CA 94107 USA

Voice: 415-778-0930

`http://www.mbed.com`

Information on this control: `http://microsoft.saltmine.com/isapi/activexisv/prmgallery/gallery-activex-info.idc?ID=51`

ClassID: clsid:873237C3-C440-11CF-B4B6-00A02429C7EF

Download page: `http://www.mbed.com/examples/microsoft/index.html`

Codebase: `http://www.mbed.com/control/MbedCtrl.cab#ver=1,0,0,10`

Multi-Directional Button Control

The Multi-Directional Button control allows for movement in four different directions. By incorporating four hot spots into an application, the Multi-Directional Button control makes navigating easy.

Sample Code

This example embeds a Multi-Directional Button control and a label into an HTML page. The label changes to indicate which button was pressed.

```
<HTML>
<HEAD>
<TITLE>ProtoView Multi Directional Button Control Example</TITLE>
</HEAD>
<BODY leftmargin=8 bgcolor="#FFFFFF" VLINK="#666666" LINK="#FF0000">
    <SCRIPT LANGUAGE="VBScript">
<!--
Sub Multibtn1_Left()
 lblDirection.Caption = "West"
end sub
Sub Multibtn1_Down()
 lblDirection.Caption = "South"
end sub
Sub Multibtn1_Up()
 lblDirection.Caption = "North"
end sub
Sub Multibtn1_Right()
 lblDirection.Caption = "East"
end sub
-->
    </SCRIPT>
    <OBJECT ID="Multibtn1" WIDTH=27 HEIGHT=27
     CLASSID="CLSID:1E4E86A3-83D1-11CF-AACD-444553540000"
     CODEBASE="http://www.protoview.com/msactivex/pics/mltbtn32.ocx">
        <PARAM NAME="_Version" VALUE="65541">
        <PARAM NAME="_ExtentX" VALUE="709">
        <PARAM NAME="_ExtentY" VALUE="709">
        <PARAM NAME="_StockProps" VALUE="224">
    </OBJECT>
    <OBJECT ID="lblDirection" WIDTH=115 HEIGHT=27
```

```
        CLASSID="CLSID:99B42120-6EC7-11CF-A6C7-00AA00A47DD2">
            <PARAM NAME="_ExtentX" VALUE="3043">
            <PARAM NAME="_ExtentY" VALUE="714">
            <PARAM NAME="Caption" VALUE="Direction">
            <PARAM NAME="Angle" VALUE="0">
            <PARAM NAME="Alignment" VALUE="4">
            <PARAM NAME="ForeColor" VALUE="#000000">
            <PARAM NAME="FontName" VALUE="Arial">
            <PARAM NAME="FontSize" VALUE="12">
            <PARAM NAME="FontBold" VALUE="1">
        </OBJECT>
    </BODY>
    </HTML>
```

Properties

Appearance: Returns or sets the paint style of a Multi-Directional Button control. Read-only at runtime.

BorderStyle: Returns or sets the border style for a Multi-Directional Button object. Read-only at runtime.

Enabled: Returns or sets a value that determines whether a form or control can respond to user-generated events.

hWnd: Returns a handle to a Multi-Directional Button control. Read-only at runtime, not available at design time.

Methods

AboutBox: Use the About command to find the version number and other pertinent information about the control.

Events

Click: Occurs when the user presses and then releases a mouse button over an object. It can also occur when the value of a control is changed.

DblClick: Occurs when the user presses and releases a mouse button and then presses and releases it again over an object.

Down: Occurs when the user presses and then releases a mouse button over the Down Button of the Multi-Directional Button.

KeyDown: Fires each time a key is pressed when the Multi-Directional Button object has input focus.

KeyPress: Fires each time a key is pressed when the Multi-Directional Button object has input focus.

KeyUp: Fires each time a key is released when the Multi-Directional Button object has input focus.

Left: Occurs when the user presses and then releases a mouse button over the left button of an object.

MouseDown: Occur when the user presses (MouseDown) or releases (MouseUp) a mouse button.

MouseMove: Occurs when the user moves the mouse.

MouseUp: Occur when the user presses (MouseDown) or releases (MouseUp) a mouse button.

Right: Occurs when the user presses and then releases a mouse button over the right button of an object.

Up: Occurs when the user presses and then releases a mouse button over the Up button of an object.

Additional Information

ProtoView Development

2540 Route 130
Cranbury, NJ 08512 USA

Phone: 609-655-5000

Fax: 609-655-5353

http://www.protoview.com

Information on this control: http://www.protoview.com/msactivex/pics/multibtn.htm

ClassID: CLSID:1E4E86A3-83D1-11CF-AACD-444553540000

Codebase: http://www.protoview.com/msactivex/pics/mltbtn32.ocx

Numeric Edit Control

The Numeric Edit control is a graphical number editor. Choose the look of the numbers; from a normal, LED, or odometer format. It also allows for centering and spin controls as needed.

Sample Code

This code displays a Numeric Edit control. It monitors the value of the control and displays a message when the value of the control goes beyond a predefined boundary.

```
<HTML>
<HEAD>
<TITLE>ProtoView Numeric Edit Control Example</TITLE>
</HEAD>
<BODY leftmargin=8 bgcolor="#FFFFFF" VLINK="#666666" LINK="#FF0000">
<b>Please</b> do not increase the value in this text box to a value greater
than 9.
    <SCRIPT LANGUAGE="VBScript">
<!--
Sub NumEdit1_EndSpin()
 If NumEdit1.Text >= 10 Then
  MsgBox "AIIIIIEEEEEE!!!"
 End If
end sub
-->
    </SCRIPT>
    <OBJECT ID="NumEdit1" WIDTH=93 HEIGHT=24
     CLASSID="CLSID:C0000000-FFFF-1100-8000-000000000004"
     CODEBASE="http://www.protoview.com/msactivex/pics/numed32.ocx">
        <PARAM NAME="_Version" VALUE="65541">
        <PARAM NAME="_ExtentX" VALUE="2455">
        <PARAM NAME="_ExtentY" VALUE="635">
        <PARAM NAME="_StockProps" VALUE="244">
        <PARAM NAME="Text" VALUE="1234.56">
        <PARAM NAME="Appearance" VALUE="1">
    </OBJECT>
</BODY>
</HTML>
```

Properties

Alignment: Returns or sets the alignment setting of a Numeric Edit control.

Appearance: Returns or sets the paint style of a Numeric Edit control. Read-only at runtime.

BackColor: Returns or sets the background color of an object.

BorderStyle: Returns or sets the border style for a Numeric Edit object. Read-only at runtime.

DecimalPlaces: Returns or sets the number of decimal places displayed in a Numeric Edit control.

DecimalSeperator: Returns or sets the character used to separate decimals in a Numeric Edit control.

DeltaValue: Returns or sets the increment/decrement amount that will be applied to the number in a Numeric Edit control when a spin button is pressed.

DisplayFormat: The UseDefaultFormat property controls the display format of the date presented in the Numeric Edit control.

EnableCustomFormat: Returns or sets a value that determines whether the Numeric Edit uses the Control Panel settings or user-specified settings to format the number.

Enabled: Returns or sets a value that determines whether a form or control can respond to user-generated events.

EnableSpinButtons: Returns or sets a value that determines whether the Numeric Edit control displays spin buttons.

Font: Returns a Font object.

ForeColor: Returns or sets the foreground color used to display text and graphics in an object.

hWnd: Returns a handle to a Numeric Edit control. Read-only at runtime, not available at design time.

LeadingZero: Returns or sets a value that determines whether the Numeric Edit prepends a zero to numbers less than 1.

LimitValue: Returns or sets a value that determines whether the Numeric Edit control limits the user input to a number between minimum and maximum values.

MaxValue: Returns or sets the maximum value allowed in a Numeric Edit control.

MinValue: Returns or sets the minimum value allowed in a Numeric Edit control.

NumericFormat: Returns or sets a value that determines the format of the number displayed in a Numeric Edit control.

Text: Returns or sets the textual representation of the number displayed in a Numeric Edit control.

ThousandsSeparator: Returns or sets the character used to separate thousands in a Numeric Edit control.

Methods

AboutBox: Use the About command to find the version number and other pertinent information about the control.

GetDouble, GetFloat, GetInteger, GetLong: Returns the value of a Numeric Edit control.

SetDouble, SetFloat, SetInteger, SetLong: Sets the value in a Numeric Edit control.

Events

BeginSpin: Occurs when the user presses the left mouse button over either spin button.

Click: Occurs when the user presses and then releases a mouse button over an object. It can also occur when the value of a control is changed.

DblClick: Occurs when the user presses and releases a mouse button, and then presses and releases it again over an object.

Incrementing: Occurs when the user presses and holds a mouse button over the top spin button. This event occurs continuously while the top spin button is pressed.

Decrementing: Occurs when the user presses and holds a mouse button over the bottom spin button. This event occurs continuously while the bottom spin button is pressed.

EndSpin: Occurs when the user releases the left mouse button over either spin button.

KeyDown: Fires each time a key is pressed when the Numeric Edit object has input focus.

KeyPress: Fires each time a key is pressed when the Numeric Edit object has input focus.

KeyUp: Fires each time a key is released when the Numeric Edit object has input focus.

MouseDown: Occurs when the user presses (MouseDown) or releases (MouseUp) a mouse button.

MouseMove: Occurs when the user moves the mouse.

MouseUp: Occurs when the user presses (MouseDown) or releases (MouseUp) a mouse button.

Additional Information

ProtoView Development

2540 Route 130
Cranbury, NJ 08512 USA

Phone: 609-655-5000

Fax: 609-655-5353

http://www.protoview.com

Information on this control: http://www.protoview.com/msactivex/pics/numedit.htm

ClassID: CLSID:C0000000-FFFF-1100-8000-000000000004

Codebase: http://www.protoview.com/msactivex/pics/numed32.ocx

Percent Bar Control

The Percent Bar control enables users to see the status of an ongoing process.

In their documentation, ProtoView refers to this control alternately as the "Percent Bar" control and the "Progress Bar" control. The two terms refer to the same thing.

Sample Code

This code displays a ProtoView Percent Bar and a command button. When the user clicks the command button, the value of the percent bar is blasted up to 100 percent.

```
<HTML>
<HEAD>
<TITLE>Protoview Percent Bar Example</TITLE>
</HEAD>
<BODY>
<SCRIPT LANGUAGE="VBScript">
<!--
 Sub cmdGo_OnClick()
  For x = 1 to 100
   pctProgress.Value = x
  Next
End Sub
-->
</SCRIPT>
    <OBJECT ID="pctProgress" WIDTH=160 HEIGHT=39
     CLASSID="CLSID:B1F2C8A3-7F60-11CF-AACD-444553540000"
     CODEBASE="http://www.protoview.com/msactivex/pics/pctbar32.ocx">
        <PARAM NAME="Value" VALUE="0">
        <PARAM NAME="FillColor" VALUE="8421440">
    </OBJECT>
    <INPUT TYPE=button VALUE="Go!" NAME="cmdGo">
</BODY>
</HTML>
```

Properties

Appearance: Returns or sets the paint style of a Progress Bar control. Read-only at runtime.

BorderStyle: Returns or sets the border style for a Progress Bar object. Read-only at runtime.

BackColor: Returns or sets the background color of an object.

Enabled: Returns or sets a value that determines whether a form or control can respond to user-generated events.

FillColor: Returns or sets the color of the filler bar on a Progress Bar control.

Font: Returns a Font object.

ForeColor: Returns or sets the foreground color used to display text and graphics in an object.

hWnd: Returns a handle to a Progress Bar control. Read-only at runtime, not available at design time.

Limit: Returns or sets a value that represents 100 percent in a Progress Bar control.

ShowNumbers: Returns or sets a value that determines whether the Progress Bar control displays the percent complete numbers below the progress bar.

ShowPercentComplete: Returns or sets a value that determines whether the Progress Bar control displays the percent complete number on its face.

ShowTickMarks: Returns or sets a value that determines whether the Progress Bar control displays tick marks on its face.

Value: Returns or sets a value that represents the value in a Progress Bar control.

Methods

About: Displays the version number and other information about PICS.

Events

None.

Additional Information

ProtoView Development

2540 Route 130
Cranbury, NJ 08512 USA

Phone: 609-655-5000

Fax: 609-655-5353

http://www.protoview.com

Information on this control: http://www.protoview.com/msactivex/pics/pctbar.htm

ClassID: CLSID:B1F2C8A3-7F60-11CF-AACD-444553540000

Codebase: http://www.protoview.com/msactivex/pics/pctbar32.ocx

Popup Menu

The Popup Menu control displays a pop-up menu whenever the method PopUp is called. This control fires an event when a menu item is clicked.

Sample Code

This page displays a button, which leads to a menu. Selecting a choice from the menu sends you to that Web page.

```
<HTML>
<HEAD>
<TITLE>Popup Menu Example</TITLE>
</HEAD>
<BODY>
    <SCRIPT LANGUAGE="VBScript">
<!--
Sub cmdGoTo_onClick
    Call mnuPopUp.PopUp
End Sub
Sub mnuPopUp_Click(item)
 Select Case Item
  Case 1
  Window.location.href = "http://www.theonion.com/"
  Case 2
  Window.location.href = "http://www.stim.com/"
  Case 3
  Window.location.href = "http://www.salon1999.com/"
 End Select
end sub
-->
    </SCRIPT>
    <OBJECT ID="mnuPopUp" WIDTH=0 HEIGHT=0
CLASSID="CLSID:7823A620-9DD9-11CF-A662-00AA00C066D2"
CODEBASE="http://activex.microsoft.com/controls/iexplorer/
➥iemenu.ocx#Version=4,70,0,1161">
    <PARAM NAME="_ExtentX" VALUE="2117">
    <PARAM NAME="_ExtentY" VALUE="1058">
    <PARAM NAME="Menuitem[0]" value="The Onion">
    <PARAM NAME="Menuitem[1]" value="Stim">
    <PARAM NAME="Menuitem[2]" value="Salon">
</OBJECT>
<INPUT TYPE="button" NAME="cmdGoTo" VALUE="Go To...">
</BODY>
</HTML>
```

Properties

ItemCount: The number of menu items in the current menu (read-only).

Parameter Tags

Menuitem[]: The menu item to be displayed.

Methods

AboutBox: Displays the About dialog box.

PopUp(vx, vy): Pops up the menu. If no value is passed for the X or Y positions, the current mouse position is used to display the pop-up menu. The x and y values are relative to the window, not to the screen.

Clear: Clears off all menu items.

RemoveItem(index): Removes the specified item. If the menu item does not exist, nothing is done.

AddItem(item, index): Adds the passed menu item at the specified index. If no index is passed, the item is appended to the menu.

Events

Click(item): Item clicked is one of the parameters passed.

Additional Information

Microsoft

One Microsoft Way
Redmond, WA 98052 USA

Phone: 206-882-8080

Fax: 206-936-7329

http://www.microsoft.com/activex/gallery/

Information on this control: http://microsoft.saltmine.com/isapi/activexisv/ prmgallery/gallery-activex-info.idc?ID=159

ClassID: clsid:7823A620-9DD9-11CF-A662-00AA00C066D2

Download page: http://microsoft.saltmine.com/activexisv/msctls/ie/ popup.htm

Codebase: http://activex.microsoft.com/controls/iexplorer/ iemenu.ocx#Version=4,70,0,1161

Popup Window

The Popup window control displays specified HTML documents in a pop-up window. This control can be used to provide tooltips or preview links.

Sample Code

This code pops up a "ToolTips"-style window when you move the mouse over the label control.

```
<HTML>
<HEAD>
<TITLE>Popup Window Example</TITLE>
</HEAD>
<BODY>
    <SCRIPT LANGUAGE="VBScript">
<!--
Sub lblMystery_MouseMove(Button, Shift, x, y)
 Call PopWin1.PopUp("http://99.99.99.1/activex/popwindo/remind.htm", True)
end sub
-->
    </SCRIPT>
    <OBJECT ID="lblMystery" WIDTH=215 HEIGHT=27
     CLASSID="CLSID:99B42120-6EC7-11CF-A6C7-00AA00A47DD2">
        <PARAM NAME="_ExtentX" VALUE="5662">
        <PARAM NAME="_ExtentY" VALUE="714">
        <PARAM NAME="Caption" VALUE="What could be under here?">
        <PARAM NAME="FontName" VALUE="Arial">
        <PARAM NAME="FontSize" VALUE="14">
    </OBJECT>
    <OBJECT ID="PopWin1" WIDTH=267 HEIGHT=40
     CLASSID="CLSID:A23D7C20-CABA-11CF-A5D4-00AA00A47DD2"
     CODEBASE="http://activex.microsoft.com/controls/iexplorer/
    ➥iepopwnd.ocx#Version=4,70,0,1161">
        <PARAM NAME="_ExtentX" VALUE="7064">
        <PARAM NAME="_ExtentY" VALUE="1058">
    </OBJECT>
</BODY>
</HTML>
```

Properties

None.

Methods

AboutBox: Displays the About dialog box.

Popup: Brings up the pop-up window. This method accepts the following parameters:

URL: The URL location of the page to be displayed.

Scale: [optional] Boolean value:

True: Scale the display to fit in the pop-up window.

False: Don't scale; clip display to fit in the pop-up window.

Dismiss. Removes the pop-up window, if one is currently being displayed.

Events

None.

Additional Information

Microsoft

One Microsoft Way
Redmond, WA 98052 USA

Phone: 206-882-8080

Fax: 206-936-7329

http://www.microsoft.com/activex/gallery/

Information on this control: http://microsoft.saltmine.com/isapi/activexisv/ prmgallery/gallery-activex-info.idc?ID=160

ClassID: clsid:A23D7C20-CABA-11CF-A5D4-00AA00A47DD2

Download page: http://microsoft.saltmine.com/activexisv/msctls/ie/ popupwin.htm

Codebase: http://activex.microsoft.com/controls/iexplorer/ iepopwnd.ocx#Version=4,70,0,1161

Preloader

This control downloads the file at the specified URL and puts it in the cache. The control is invisible at runtime and starts downloading when enabled. When the download is finished, the control fires a Complete event.

Sample Code

This page presents the user with a button; when the button is clicked, it preloads the file head1.gif, informing the user when the file is loaded (or if an error occurred).

```
<HTML>
<HEAD>
<TITLE>Preloader Madness</TITLE>
</HEAD>
<BODY>
    <SCRIPT LANGUAGE="VBScript">
<!--
Sub PreLoader1_Complete()
 MsgBox "Preload complete!"
 Window.location.href = "head1.gif"
end sub
Sub PreLoader1_Error()
 MsgBox "Preload error."
end sub
-->
    </SCRIPT>
    <OBJECT ID="PreLoader1" WIDTH=0 HEIGHT=0
     CLASSID="CLSID:16E349E0-702C-11CF-A3A9-00A0C9034920"
     CODEBASE="http://activex.microsoft.com/controls/iexplorer/
     ➥iepreld.ocx#Version=4,70,0,1161">
        <PARAM NAME="_ExtentX" VALUE="0">
        <PARAM NAME="_ExtentY" VALUE="0">
        <PARAM NAME="URL" VALUE="head1.gif">
        <PARAM NAME="enable" VALUE="0">
    </OBJECT>
    <INPUT LANGUAGE="VBScript" TYPE=button VALUE="Load it!"
ONCLICK="Preloader1.Enable=&quot;1&quot;"
    NAME="cmdLoad">
</BODY>
</HTML>
```

Properties

URL: The URL to be downloaded.

Enable: Enables (1) or disables (0) the control.

CacheFile: File name of the local cached file (read-only).

Bytes: The amount of data read so far in bytes (read-only).

Percentage: The amount of data read so far in percentage (read-only).

Methods

AboutBox: Displays the About dialog box.

Events

Complete: Fires when the download has been completed.

Error: Fires when the download could not be completed.

Additional Information

Microsoft

One Microsoft Way
Redmond, WA 98052 USA

Phone: 206-882-8080

Fax: 206-936-7329

http://www.microsoft.com/activex/gallery/

Information on this control: http://microsoft.saltmine.com/isapi/activexisv/
prmgallery/gallery-activex-info.idc?ID=142

ClassID: CLSID:16E349E0-702C-11CF-A3A9-00A0C9034920

Download page: http://microsoft.saltmine.com/activexisv/msctls/ie/
preload.htm

Codebase: http://activex.microsoft.com/controls/iexplorer/
iepreld.ocx#Version=4,70,0,1161

Sax Canvas Control

The Sax Canvas control allows VBScript or JScript code to draw onto the canvas using a variety of drawing instructions. From within Internet Explorer, you can now draw circles, lines, and text labels in any color or size.

Sample Code

This is the source code to a tic-tac-toe game using the Sax Canvas control.

```
<HTML>
<HEAD>
<TITLE> Sax Canvas Sample </TITLE>
</HEAD>
<BODY>
<CENTER>
    <OBJECT ID="Canvas" WIDTH=300 HEIGHT=300
     CLASSID="CLSID:1DF67C43-AEAA-11CF-BA92-444553540000"
     CODEBASE="http://www.saxsoft.com/product/canvas/
    ➡SaxCanv.ocx#Version=1,0,0,1">
        <PARAM NAME="_Version" VALUE="65536">
        <PARAM NAME="_ExtentX" VALUE="8573">
        <PARAM NAME="_ExtentY" VALUE="3916">
        <PARAM NAME="_StockProps" VALUE="13">
        <PARAM NAME="ForeColor" VALUE="0">
        <PARAM NAME="BackColor" VALUE="11206655">
    </OBJECT>
</CENTER>
    <SCRIPT LANGUAGE="VBScript">
<!--
Sub window_onLoad()
 InitBoard
End Sub
' Module level variables
Dim Field
' Draw initial board and empty field
Sub InitBoard()
 Field = "         "
 ' Draw board
 Canvas.Clear
 Canvas.BorderColor = 128
 Canvas.BorderWidth = 10
 Canvas.MoveTo 100, 10
 Canvas.LineTo 100, 290
```

```
    Canvas.MoveTo 200, 10
    Canvas.LineTo 200, 290
    Canvas.MoveTo 10, 100
    Canvas.LineTo 290, 100
    Canvas.MoveTo 10, 200
    Canvas.LineTo 290, 200
End Sub
' Make player's move and respond with your own
Sub Canvas_MouseDown(Button, Shift, x, y)
  If Field = "" Then InitBoard
  If MakeMove("X", x \ 100, y \ 100) Then
    Do
      myX = Rnd * 300
      myY = Rnd * 300
    Loop Until MakeMove("O", myX \ 100, myY \ 100)
  End If
End Sub
' Draw move and update Field variable
' Check if won, and if so, display message
' If board full or won, clear board
Function MakeMove(Player, X, Y)
  ' If the board is full, start over
  If Instr(Field, " ") = 0 Then InitBoard
  ' Check to see if it's a valid move.
  If FieldItem(X,Y) <> " " Then
    MakeMove = False
    Exit Function
  End If
  Field = Left(Field, X + 3 * Y) + Player + Mid(Field, X + 3 * Y + 2)
  If Player = "X" Then
    Canvas.BorderWidth = 16
    Canvas.BorderColor =  16711680
    Canvas.MoveTo X * 100 + 30, Y * 100 + 30
    Canvas.LineTo (X + 1) * 100 - 30, (Y + 1) * 100 - 30
    Canvas.MoveTo (X + 1) * 100 - 30, Y * 100 + 30
    Canvas.LineTo X * 100 + 30, (Y + 1) * 100 - 30
  Else
    Canvas.BorderWidth = 20
    Canvas.BorderColor = 255
    Canvas.FillColor = 11206655
    Canvas.FillStyle = 0
    Canvas.MoveTo (X * 100) + 50, (Y * 100) + 50
    Canvas.Circle 25
```

```
 End If
 If CheckMove(X, Y) Then
  If Player = "X" Then MsgBox "Congratulations!", 0, "Tic-Tac-Toe" else MsgBox
  ➥"I'm smarter than you...", 0, "Tic-Tac-Toe"
  Field = "XXXXXXXXX"           ' Force new game next time
 End If
 MakeMove = True
End Function
' Returns item at a certain position ("X", "O", or " ")
Function FieldItem(X, Y)
 FieldItem = Mid(Field, 1 + X + Y * 3, 1)
End Function
' Check if if all the items in a row are the same value
Function CheckLine(X, Y, dX, dY, Value)
 If (FieldItem(X, Y) = Value) and (FieldItem(X + dX, Y + dY) = Value) and
(FieldItem(X + 2 * dX, Y + 2 * dY) = Value) Then
  CheckLine = True
 else
  CheckLine = False
 End If
End Function
' Check if rows at a certain position contain three in a row
Function CheckMove(X, Y)
 CheckMove = CheckLine(0, Y, 1, 0, FieldItem(X, Y))  or CheckLine(X, 0, 0, 1,
FieldItem(X, Y)) or CheckLine(0, 0, 1, 1, FieldItem(X, Y)) or CheckLine(0, 2,
1, -1, FieldItem(X, Y))
End Function
-->
    </SCRIPT>
</p>
</FONT>
</BODY>
</HTML>
```

Properties

BackColor: The control's background color.

ForeColor: The color used to draw lines.

FillColor: Used to fill shapes such as rectangles or circles.

CurrentX: Indicates the horizontal position of the current pen location.

CurrentY: Indicates the vertical position of the current pen location.

BorderColor: Sets or returns the color that is used to draw lines.

BorderWidth: Sets or returns the width of the lines.

Font: Sets or returns the font style of the control.

Methods

LineTo: Draws a line from the current pen position to the specified coordinates.

MoveTo: Sets the current pen position to the specified coordinates.

Circle: Draws a circle with the current pen position as the center and the specified radius.

Clear: Clears the canvas.

Label: Draws text at the current pen position.

Events

MouseDown: Fires when a mouse button is pushed down on the control.

MouseMove: Fires when the mouse is moved over the control.

MouseUp: Fires when a mouse button is released over the control.

DblClick: Fires when the user double-clicks the control.

Additional Information

Sax Software

950 Patterson Street
Eugene, OR 97401 USA

Phone: 541-344-2235

Fax: 541-344-2459

http://www.saxsoft.com

Information on this control: http://microsoft.saltmine.com/isapi/activexisv/prmgallery/gallery-activex-info.idc?ID=35

ClassID: CLSID:1DF67C43-AEAA-11CF-BA92-444553540000

Download page: http://www.saxsoft.com/product/canvas/sample.htm

Codebase: http://www.saxsoft.com/product/canvas/
SaxCanv.ocx#Version=1,0,0,1

Sizzler

Sizzler is a control that permits users to view animated multimedia. The animated display is streaming, which means you don't have to wait for the complete file to be downloaded before it starts playing. You can create animation and add sound with the Sizzler editor; export a Sizzler file for popular browsers; preview your animation in the Animation Statistics Previewer Window; easily add your animation to any HTML page; and, play your animation with the Sizzler multimedia player.

Streaming is the process of slicing data into sequenced readable pieces so that the animation starts to play immediately, in real-time. As a result, Sizzler enables you to see the animation as it downloads, as opposed to other "store, forward, and play" technologies that force you to wait for the entire file to download before it starts playing.

The control has the following features:

◆ Animation Statistics Previewer Window enables you to preview your animation at 14.4, 28.8 Kbps, or ISDN rates before applying the animation to a Web page.

◆ Supports major browsers with Sizzler file formats: Sizzler for Netscape, Sizzler ActiveX control for Internet Explorer, Sizzler Live Object for OpenDoc technologies such as Cyberdog, and a Sizzler Java Applet.

◆ Enables you to set the speed of your animation.

◆ Enables you to create links to any URL on the Web when you click on the animation.

◆ Enables you to add sound with the ability to filter in at various points of the download, middle, end, in a certain cel.

◆ Plays audio files without interrupting the animation.

◆ Easy maintenance of Web sites because the sound file is embedded right into the sprite file.

Sizzler multimedia players and editor are available free from Totally Hip's Web site at http://www.totallyhip.com.

Sizzler animation file formats currently support the conversion of API and Windows bitmaps.

Sample Code

This code displays a sprite file of a talented monkey (downloaded from the Totally Hip Web site) and provides controls so you can programmatically start, stop, and hide the animation as it runs.

```
<HTML>
<HEAD>
<TITLE>Sizzler Demonstration</TITLE>
</HEAD>
<BODY leftmargin=8 bgcolor="#FFFFFF" VLINK="#666666" LINK="#FF0000">
<FONT FACE="ARIAL,HELVETICA" SIZE="2">
<OBJECT ID="Sizzler1" WIDTH=100 HEIGHT=51
 CODEBASE="http://www.totallyhip.com/ActiveSizzler/Control/
 ➡Sizzler.cab#Version=1,0,0,8"
 CLASSID="CLSID:088d8100-c496-11cf-b54a-00c0a8361ed8"
 HEIGHT=175 WIDTH=195>
 <PARAM NAME="Image" VALUE="http://www.totallyhip.com/activex/monkey.sprite">
</OBJECT>
<BR>
<INPUT TYPE=BUTTON VALUE="Start" NAME="BtnStart" onClick="BtnStart_OnClick"
language="VBScript">
<INPUT TYPE=BUTTON VALUE="Stop" NAME="BtnStop" onClick="BtnStop_OnClick"
language="VBScript">
<INPUT TYPE=BUTTON VALUE="Show" NAME="BtnShow">
<INPUT TYPE=BUTTON VALUE="Hide" NAME="BtnHide">

<SCRIPT LANGUAGE="VBSCRIPT">
Sub BtnAboutBox_OnClick
 Sizzler1.AboutBox()
End Sub
Sub BtnSetFile_OnClick
 Sizzler1.Image = Filename.Value
End Sub
Sub BtnStart_OnClick
 Sizzler1.Start()
End Sub
Sub BtnStop_OnClick
 Sizzler1.Stop()
End Sub
Sub BtnShow_OnClick
 Sizzler1.Show()
End Sub
Sub BtnHide_OnClick
 Sizzler1.Hide()
End Sub
</SCRIPT>
</BODY>
</HTML>
```

Properties

Image: The name of the sprite file to be displayed.

Methods

AboutBox: Displays the AboutBox.

Show: Makes the control visible.

Hide: Hides the control.

Start: Starts the animation playing.

Stop: Stops the current animation.

Events

Shown: Triggered when the control is made visible.

Hidden: Triggered when the control is hidden.

Started: Triggered when the control starts playing.

Stopped: Triggered when the control stops playing.

NewFile: Triggered when a new animation file is specified.

Additional Information

Totally Hip Software

1224 Hamilton Street, Ste. 301
Vancouver, BC V6B 2S8 Canada

Phone: 604-685-6525

Fax: 604-685-4057

`http://www.totallyhip.com`

Information on this control: `http://microsoft.saltmine.com/isapi/activexisv/ prmgallery/gallery-activex-info.idc?ID=166`

ClassID: CLSID:088d8100-c496-11cf-b54a-00c0a8361ed8

Download page: `http://www.totallyhip.com/ActiveSizzler/Gallery/Default.htm`

Codebase: `http://www.totallyhip.com/ActiveSizzler/Control/ Sizzler.cab#Version=1,0,0,8`

Stock Ticker

The Stock Ticker control is used to display changing data continuously. The control downloads the URL specified at regular intervals and displays that data. The data can be in a text or XRT format.

Sample Code

This code displays the data in the file mydata.txt in a stock ticker control.

```
<HTML>
<HEAD>
<TITLE>Stock Ticker Example</TITLE>
</HEAD>
<BODY>
<OBJECT ID="Stock1" WIDTH=267 HEIGHT=33
 CLASSID="CLSID:0CA4A620-8E3D-11CF-A3A9-00A0C9031920"
 CODEBASE="http://activex.microsoft.com/controls/iexplorer/
➡iestock.ocx#Version=4,70,0,1161">
    <PARAM NAME="_ExtentX" VALUE="7064">
    <PARAM NAME="_ExtentY" VALUE="873">
    <PARAM NAME="DataObjectName" VALUE="http://99.99.99.1/activex/sticker/
➡mydata.txt">
    <PARAM NAME="DataObjectActive" VALUE="1">
</OBJECT>
</BODY>
</HTML>


The file mydata.txt contains the following text:

XRT

MYSE  YDA       14 3/4  PDQ       7 1/8   LMNO      43

BAZDAQ         BDF    74 1/2  TNJN   69 1/2  JRK      4 1/8

Data Formats

The Stock Ticker control downloads the specified URL at regular intervals and
displays that data. The data can be in text format or XRT format.

Text format:

   XRT

   name1TABvalue1TABvalue2...CR/LF
```

```
name2TABvalue1TABvalue2...CR/LF
```

   . . .

```
XRT format: See the WOSA/XRT spec on the MSDN Library CD for details on the
XRT format. You can also specify an OLE object that generates data in the XRT
format.
```

Properties

DataObjectName: Name of the data source. This can be an URL or an OLE object.

DataObjectActive: Indicates whether the data source is active:

>   0—inactive

>   1—active

The ticker control displays data only when DataObjectActive is 1.

ScrollSpeed: The intervals at which the display is scrolled.

ScrollWidth: The amount in which the display is scrolled for each redraw.

ReloadInterval: The interval at which the URL is reloaded periodically.

ForeColor: Foreground color.

BackColor: Background color.

OffsetValues: The value (in pixels) by which the value will be offset from the name in the vertical direction.

Methods

AboutBox: Displays the About dialog box.

Events

None.

Microsoft

>   One Microsoft Way
>   Redmond, WA 98052 USA

>   Phone: 206-882-8080

>   Fax: 206-936-7329

>   `http://www.microsoft.com/activex/gallery/`

>   Information on this control: `http://microsoft.saltmine.com/isapi/activexisv/`
>   `prmgallery/gallery-activex-info.idc?ID=161`

ClassID: clsid:0CA4A620-8E3D-11CF-A3A9-00A0C9034920

Download page: `http://microsoft.saltmine.com/activexisv/msctls/ie/ticker.htm`

Codebase: `http://activex.microsoft.com/controls/iexplorer/iestock.ocx#Version=4,70,0,1161`

TimeEdit Control

The TimeEdit control features data entry control in a normal, digital, or odometer display.

Sample Code

This code displays a TimeEdit control with a button that echos the control's Time property as set by the user.

```
<HTML>
<HEAD>
<TITLE>ProtoView TimeEdit Control Example</TITLE>
</HEAD>
<BODY bgcolor="#FFFFFF" VLINK="#666666" LINK="#FF0000">
<SCRIPT LANGUAGE="VBScript">
<!--
  Sub ShowTime
    MsgBox "At the tone the time will be " & TimeEdit1.Time
  End Sub
-->
</SCRIPT>
    <OBJECT ID="TimeEdit1" WIDTH=127 HEIGHT=39
 CLASSID="CLSID:8F25C403-8346-11CF-AACD-444553540000"
 CODEBASE="http://www.protoview.com/msactivex/pics/time32.ocx">
    <PARAM NAME="_Version" VALUE="65536">
    <PARAM NAME="_ExtentX" VALUE="3351">
    <PARAM NAME="_ExtentY" VALUE="1023">
    <PARAM NAME="_StockProps" VALUE="228">
    <PARAM NAME="Appearance" VALUE="1">
    <PARAM NAME="DisplayStyle" VALUE="1">
</OBJECT>
<p>
<INPUT LANGUAGE="VBScript" TYPE=BUTTON VALUE="Time" ONCLICK="Call ShowTime"
NAME="cmdTime"><p>
</BODY>
</HTML>
```

Properties

AMString: The text string used to indicate morning (am) in a 12-hour clock format.

Appearance: Returns or sets the paint style of a TimeEdit control. Read-only at run-time.

BorderStyle: Returns or sets the border style for a TimeEdit object. Read-only at run-time.

BackColor: Returns or sets the background color of an object.

DisplayStyle: Controls the display format of the time presented in the TimeEdit control.

Enabled: Returns or sets a value that determines whether a form or control can respond to user-generated events.

Font: Returns a Font object.

ForeColor: Returns or sets the foreground color used to display text and graphics in an object.

Hour: Represents the hour of the time displayed in a TimeEdit control.

hWnd: Returns a handle to a TimeEdit control. Read-only at runtime, not available at design time.

LeadZero: Controls whether or not a zero is prepended to hours less than 10.

Minute: Represents the minute of the time displayed in a TimeEdit control.

NoHideSel: Returns or sets the selection display state of a TimeEdit control.

PMString: The text string used to indicate evening (pm) in a 12-hour clock format.

ReadOnly: Controls whether or not the TimeEdit control will accept keyboard input.

TwentyFourHourClock: Controls whether the time will be displayed as a 12-hour or 24-hour clock.

Second: Represents the second of the time displayed in a TimeEdit control.

ShowSeconds: Controls the display format of the time presented in the TimeEdit control. If set to True, the time is displayed in the hh:mm:ss format; otherwise, the time is shown in the hh:mm format.

SeperatorCharacter: The character used to separate the different parts of the time string.

Time: The string representation of the time in a TimeEdit control.

UseDefaultFormat: Controls the display format of the time presented in the TimeEdit control.

Methods

AboutBox: Use the About command to find the version number and other pertinent information about the control.

StartClock: Causes the TimeEdit control to behave like a clock (that is, the control will display the current system time and continue to update the time every second).

StopClock: Causes the TimeEdit control to stop counting time.

Events

BeforeChange: Indicates that the time in the TimeEdit control is about to be changed.

Change: Indicates that the time in the TimeEdit control has changed.

Click: Occurs when the user presses and then releases a mouse button over an object. It can also occur when the value of a control is changed.

KeyDown: Fires each time a key is pressed when the TimeEdit object has input focus.

KeyPress: Fires each time a key is pressed when the TimeEdit object has input focus.

KeyUp: Fires each time a key is released when the TimeEdit object has input focus.

MouseDown: Occurs when the user presses (MouseDown) or releases (MouseUp) a mouse button.

MouseMove: Occurs when the user moves the mouse.

MouseUp: Occurs when the user presses (MouseDown) or releases (MouseUp) a mouse button.

Additional Information

ProtoView Development

2540 Route 130
Cranbury, NJ 08512 USA

Phone: 609-655-5000

Fax: 609-655-5353

http://www.protoview.com

Information on this control: `http://www.protoview.com/msactivex/pics/ptime.htm`

ClassID: CLSID:8F25C403-8346-11CF-AACD-444553540000

Codebase: `http://www.protoview.com/msactivex/pics/time32.ocx`

Timer

The Timer control invokes an event periodically. It is invisible at runtime.

Sample Code

This code changes the color of a label control once per second.

```
<HTML>
<HEAD>
<TITLE>Timer Example</TITLE>
</HEAD>
<BODY>
    <OBJECT ID="lblChange" WIDTH=350 HEIGHT=33
     CLASSID="CLSID:99B42120-6EC7-11CF-A6C7-00AA00A47DD2"
     CODEBASE="http://activex.microsoft.com/controls/iexplorer/
➥ielabel.ocx#Version=4,70,0,1161">
        <PARAM NAME="_ExtentX" VALUE="7117">
        <PARAM NAME="_ExtentY" VALUE="873">
        <PARAM NAME="Caption" VALUE="This changes color once a second.">
        <PARAM NAME="ForeColor" VALUE="255">
        <PARAM NAME="FontName" VALUE="Arial">
        <PARAM NAME="FontSize" VALUE="14">
        <PARAM NAME="FontBold" VALUE="1">
    </OBJECT>
    <SCRIPT LANGUAGE="VBScript">
<!--
Sub Timer1_Timer()
 If lblChange.ForeColor <> 255 Then
  lblChange.ForeColor = 255
 else
  lblChange.ForeColor = 0
 end if
end sub
-->
    </SCRIPT>
    <OBJECT ID="Timer1" WIDTH=39 HEIGHT=39
     CLASSID="CLSID:59CCB4A0-727D-11CF-AC36-00AA00A47DD2">
```

```
            <PARAM NAME="_ExtentX" VALUE="1005">
            <PARAM NAME="_ExtentY" VALUE="1005">
            <PARAM NAME="Interval" VALUE="1000">
        </OBJECT>
    </BODY>
    </HTML>
```

Properties

Enabled: Enables or disables the timer.

> True—Enabled state

> False—Disabled state

Interval: Interval (in milliseconds) at which the Timer event will be triggered. When this property is set to a negative value or zero, the timer will behave as in the disabled state.

Methods

AboutBox: Displays the About dialog box.

Events

Timer: When the timer is enabled and has a positive interval, this event is invoked at every interval.

Additional Information

Microsoft

One Microsoft Way
Redmond, WA 98052 USA

Phone: 206-882-8080

Fax: 206-936-7329

http://www.microsoft.com/activex/gallery/

Information on this control: http://microsoft.saltmine.com/isapi/activexisv/ prmgallery/gallery-activex-info.idc?ID=163

ClassID: clsid:59CCB4A0-727D-11CF-AC36-00AA00A47DD2

Download page: http://microsoft.saltmine.com/activexisv/msctls/ie/ timer.htm

Codebase: http://activex.microsoft.com/controls/iexplorer/ ietimer.ocx#Version=4,70,0,1161

TreeView Control

The TreeView has many styles, as well as extended functionality over the standard TreeView control. It is also available as a 16-bit control for Windows 3.x.

The PICS TreeView OLE control is a hierarchical list box control suitable for displaying lists of items in a hierarchical manner. The TreeView control is similar to the Microsoft TreeView control; however, the PICS version adds a number of important features.

To add items to the TreeView control, use the Branches: to obtain the main Branch Object, then use the Add Method of the Branch object to add items to the list. Likewise, you can use the Remove Method of the Branch object to remove items from the list. Most operations that affect the list of items in a TreeView control are done through the methods and properties of the Branch object.

The PICS TreeView control enables you to display the list of items in a multi-column fashion, using either fixed column width or fixed number of columns styles. In addition to multicolumns, you can display tabbed text in the TreeView control. Use the UseTabStops Property to enable tab stops for the control, and use the TabPoint Property to set tab stop positions.

Bitmaps are a special and flexible feature of the TreeView control. The TreeView control comes with a set of useful prebuilt bitmaps (Standard Pictures), or you can specify your own (Custom Pictures). You can specify a default picture (either a Standard or Custom Picture) that will be used for all items in the TreeView control. In addition, you can specify a default picture (again, either Standard or Custom) for a particular level of the list. And of course, you can specify a particular picture (either Standard or Custom) that is assigned to an individual item in the list. See the StandardDefaultPicture Property or CustomDefaultPicture Property for details.

Sample Code

This code populates a TreeView control with a number of items. It responds with a message box when the user double-clicks one of the items.

```
<HTML>
<HEAD>
    <SCRIPT LANGUAGE="VBScript">
<!--
Sub window_onLoad()
Dim Root
Dim ParentNode
Dim Child
Set Root = TreeView1.Branches
```

```
Set ParentNode = Root.Add(pvtPositionInOrder, 0, "Food")
Set Child = ParentNode.Add(pvtPositionInOrder, 0, "Salad")
Set Child = ParentNode.Add(pvtPositionInOrder, 0, "Appetizer")
Set Child = ParentNode.Add(pvtPositionInOrder, 0, "Main Course")
Set Child = ParentNode.Add(pvtPositionInOrder, 0, "Dessert")
Set Child = ParentNode.Add(pvtPositionInOrder, 0, "Breath Mint")
Set ParentNode = Root.Add(pvtPositionInOrder, 0, "Instruments")
Set Child = ParentNode.Add(pvtPositionAfter, 0, "Trumpet")
Set Child = ParentNode.Add(pvtPositionAfter, 0, "Violin")
Set Child = ParentNode.Add(pvtPositionAfter, 0, "Flute")
Set Child = ParentNode.Add(pvtPositionAfter, 0, "Trombone")
Set Child = ParentNode.Add(pvtPositionAfter, 0, "Piano")
End Sub
-->
    </SCRIPT>
<TITLE>ProtoView TreeView Control Example</TITLE>
</HEAD>
<BODY bgcolor="#FFFFFF" VLINK="#666666" LINK="#FF0000">
<SCRIPT LANGUAGE="VBScript">
<!--
Sub TreeView1_LButtonDblClick(node, x, y)
 If Asc(Left(node.Text,1)) <> 1 Then
  MsgBox "You double-clicked " & node.Text & "."
 End If
end sub
-->
    </SCRIPT>
    <OBJECT ID="TreeView1" WIDTH=225 HEIGHT=236
     CLASSID="CLSID:C0000000-FFFF-1100-8007-000000000004"
     CODEBASE="http://www.protoview.com/msactivex/pics/ptree32.ocx">
        <PARAM NAME="_Version" VALUE="65541">
        <PARAM NAME="_ExtentX" VALUE="5962">
        <PARAM NAME="_ExtentY" VALUE="6244">
        <PARAM NAME="_StockProps" VALUE="228">
        <PARAM NAME="Appearance" VALUE="1">
        <PARAM NAME="Sort" VALUE="0">
        <PARAM NAME="EnableMicroBitmaps" VALUE="0">
        <PARAM NAME="EnableLines" VALUE="0">
        <PARAM NAME="AutoOpen" VALUE="-1">
        <PARAM NAME="AlwaysShowSelection" VALUE="-1">
        <PARAM NAME="StandardLevelPicture0" VALUE="0">
        <PARAM NAME="StandardLevelPicture1" VALUE="1">
```

```
        <PARAM NAME="StandardLevelPicture2" VALUE="2">
    </OBJECT>
</BODY>
</HTML>
```

The TreeView control is comprised of a number of subordinate Branch objects, accessed through the Branches collection. Most operations that affect the list of items in a TreeView control are done through the methods and properties of the Branch object.

Properties (TreeView Object)

AlwaysShowSelection: Returns or sets the selection display state of a TreeView control.

Appearance: Returns or sets the paint style of a TreeView control. Read-only at runtime.

AutoOpen: Returns or sets the auto open state of the TreeView control.

BackColor: Returns or sets the background color of an object.

BorderStyle: Returns or sets the border style for a TreeView object. Read-only at runtime.

Branches: Returns the list of items in a TreeView control. Read-only at runtime, not available at design time.

ColumnWidth: Returns or sets the width of an individual column in the TreeView control.

Count: Returns the total number of items in a TreeView control. Read-only at runtime, not available at deign time.

CustomDefaultPicture: Returns or sets the default picture displayed next to each item on the TreeView control.

CustomLevelPicture: Returns or sets the default picture dislayed next to each item on the TreeView control on a particular level.

Enabled: Returns or sets a value that determines whether a form or control can respond to user-generated events.

EnableBitmaps: Returns or sets a value that determines whether a TreeView control will display images next to each item in the control.

EnableLines: Returns or sets a value that determines whether a TreeView control will display lines connecting parent items to their children.

EnableMicroBitmaps: Returns or sets a value that determines whether a TreeView control will display a box containing either a "+" or "-" next to each item. A box with a "+" indicates that a closed item has children. Clicking the "+" with the mouse will cause the item to open (display its children in the TreeView control). A box with a "-" indicates that the item has children and is open. Clicking the "-" will cause the item to close.

Font: Returns a Font object.

ForeColor: Returns or sets the foreground color used to display text and graphics in an object.

HorizontalExtent: Returns or sets a value that determines the logical width of a TreeView control.

hWnd: Returns a handle to a TreeView control. Read-only at runtime, not available at design time.

Indent: Returns or sets the amount of space, in pixels, that each subsequent child level is indented from its parent in the TreeView control.

IntegralHeight: Returns or sets a value indicating if the control displays partial items. Read-only at runtime.

MultiColumn: Returns or sets a value indicating if the TreeView control displays the list of items in a multicolumn fashion. Read-only at runtime.

MultiColumnStyle: Returns or sets a value indicating the style of the multicolumn display.

NumberOfColumns: Returns or sets the number of columns displayed in the TreeView control.

ProportionalScrollBars: Returns or sets a value that specifies whether or not the TreeView controls scroll bars are sized proportionally to the contents of the control.

SelectMode: Returns or sets a value indicating whether a user can make multiple selections in TreeView control and how the multiple selections can be made. Read-only at runtime.

Sort: Returns a value indicating whether the elements of a control are automatically sorted alphabetically. Read-only at runtime.

StandardDefaultPicture: Returns or sets a value indicating the default picture that will be displayed next to an item in the TreeView control.

StandardLevelPicture: Returns or sets a value indicating the default picture that will be displayed next to an item in the TreeView control on a particular level.

TabPoint: Returns or sets the location of tab stops in the TreeView control.

TabPointCount: Returns the number of tab stops defined in the TreeView control. Read-only at runtime, not available at design time.

UseStateBitmaps: Returns or sets a Boolean value indicating whether or not the TreeView control uses state format bitmaps.

UseTabStops: Returns a value indicating whether the TreeView control recognizes and expands tab characters when drawing its strings. The default tab positions are 2 dialog units. (A dialog unit is a horizontal or vertical distance. One horizontal dialog unit is equal to one-fourth of the current dialog base width unit. The dialog base units are computed based on the height and width of the current system font. The GetDialogBaseUnits Windows function returns the current dialog base units in pixels.) Read-only at runtime.

VisibleCount: Returns the total number of visible items in a TreeView control. Read-only at runtime, not available at design time.

Properties (Branch Object)

CustomItemPicture: Returns or sets the default picture displayed next to an item on the TreeView control.

Data: A user defined value that can be kept with each item in a TreeView control.

IsOpen: Returns a Boolean value indicating whether or not the Branch object is open.

Level: Indicates the level the Branch object is on in a TreeView control.

StandardItemPicture: Returns or sets a value indicating the default picture that will be displayed next to a specific item in the TreeView control.

Text: Represents the text string associated with the Branch object.

Methods

AboutBox: Finds the version number and other pertinent information about this control.

BeginInPlaceEdit: Enables the user to visually edit the text of the selected item in the TreeView control.

ClearTabStops: Clears all tab stops in a TreeView control.

EndInPlaceEdit: Stops the user from visually editing the text of the selected item in the TreeView control.

Find: Searches for a specific item in a TreeView control.

GetEditHWND: Enables the user to obtain a handle to the edit control used for visual editing in the TreeView control.

Methods (Branch Object)

Add: Adds a new item to the Branch.

Clear: Removes all the child items from a Branch.

Close: Closes the Branch object according to command argument.

Get: Returns a Branch object from a related Branch object.

GetHandle: Returns the item handle (HITEM) of the TreeView control item associated with the Branch. The HITEM handle can be used with the hWnd Property to send messages directly to the TreeView control.

IsLocked: Returns a Boolean value indicating whether or not the Branch object is locked.

IsMainBranch: Returns a Boolean value indicating whether or not the Branch object is the main Branch object.

IsValid: Returns Boolean value indicating whether or not the Branch object is a valid Branch object.

Lock: Locks a Branch in a TreeView control.

Open: Opens the Branch object according to command argument.

Remove: Removes and deletes a Branch from a TreeView control.

Select: Selects or deselects the Branch object according to command argument.

Unlock: Unlocks a Branch in a TreeView control.

Events

AfterCollapse: Fires after an item has been collapsed (closed).

AfterExpand: Fires after an item has been expanded (opened).

AfterSelChange: Fires before an item is selected.

BeforeCollapse: Fires before an item is collapsed (closed).

BeforeExpand: Fires before an item is expanded (opened).

BeforeSelChange: Fires before an item is selected.

Delete: Fires when an item is about to be deleted.

InPlaceEditBegin: Fires before an item is selected.

InPlaceEditEnd: Fires before an item's text is changed from InPlaceEditing.

KeyDown: Fires each time a key is pressed when the TreeView object has input focus.

KeyPress: Fires each time a key is pressed when the TreeView object has input focus.

KeyUp: Fires each time a key is released when the TreeView object has input focus.

LButtonDblClick: Fires when the left button of the mouse is double-clicked over the TreeView control.

LButtonDown: Fires when the left button of the mouse is pressed over the TreeView control.

LButtonUp: Fires when the left button of the mouse is released over the TreeView control.

RButtonDblClick: Fires when the right button of the mouse is double-clicked over the TreeView control.

RButtonDown: Fires when the right button of the mouse is pressed over the TreeView control.

RButtonUp: Fires when the right button of the mouse is released over the TreeView control.

Additional Information

ProtoView Development

2540 Route 130
Cranbury, NJ 08512 USA

Phone: 609-655-5000

Fax: 609-655-5353

http://www.protoview.com

Information on this control: http://www.protoview.com/msactivex/pics/treeview.htm

ClassID: CLSID:C0000000-FFFF-1100-8007-000000000004

Codebase: http://www.protoview.com/msactivex/pics/ptree32.ocx

View Tracker

The View Tracker control generates a set of events whenever the control enters or leaves the viewing area. The author can use this control to automatically modify properties or functionality on the page based on sectional input.

Sample Code

This code displays message boxes when the View Tracker control scrolls into and out of the viewable area.

```
<HTML>
<HEAD>
<TITLE>View Tracker Example</TITLE>
</HEAD>
<BODY>
<OBJECT
 ID="Track1"
 CLASSID="clsid:1A771020-A28E-11CF-8510-00AA003B6C7E"
 CODEBASE="http://activex.microsoft.com/controls/iexplorer/
➥ietrack.ocx#Version=4,70,0,1161"
 WIDTH=1
 HEIGHT=1
 ALIGN="left"
>
</OBJECT>
<OBJECT
 ID="label0"
 CLASSID="clsid:99B42120-6EC7-11CF-A6C7-00AA00A47DD2"
 CODEBASE="http://activex.microsoft.com/controls/iexplorer/
➥ielabel.ocx#Version=4,70,0,1161"
 WIDTH=100
 HEIGHT=450
 VSPACE=0
 ALIGN=left
>
<PARAM NAME="Angle" VALUE="270">
<PARAM NAME="Alignment" VALUE="4" >
<PARAM NAME="BackStyle" VALUE="1" >
<PARAM NAME="BackColor" VALUE="#ff0000" >
<PARAM NAME="Caption" VALUE="Scroll to the bottom of this screen.">
<PARAM NAME="FontName" VALUE="Arial">
<PARAM NAME="FontSize" VALUE="24">
<PARAM NAME="ForeColor" VALUE="#0000ff" >
```

```
</OBJECT>
<SCRIPT Language="VBScript">
Sub Track1_OnShow
  MsgBox "The View Tracker is back on the screen"
End Sub
Sub Track1_OnHide
 MsgBox "The View Tracker control has left the screen"
End Sub
</SCRIPT>
</FONT>
</BODY>
</HTML>
```

Properties

Image: URL specifying an image for the control.

Methods

AboutBox: Displays the About dialog box.

Events

OnShow: Control falls within the view area.

OnHide: Control scrolls off the view area.

Additional Information

Microsoft

One Microsoft Way
Redmond, WA 98052 USA

Phone: 206-882-8080

Fax: 206-936-7329

http://www.microsoft.com/activex/gallery/

Information on this control: http://microsoft.saltmine.com/isapi/activexisv/
prmgallery/gallery-activex-info.idc?ID=164

ClassID: clsid:1A771020-A28E-11CF-8510-00AA003B6C7E

Download page: http://microsoft.saltmine.com/activexisv/msctls/ie/
track.htm

Codebase: http://activex.microsoft.com/controls/iexplorer/
ietrack.ocx#Version=4,70,0,1161

VivoActive Player

This is a tool that plays streaming video without a specialized server. This technology uses compressed video using an authoring tool called VivoActive Producer, which transforms AVI or QuickTime files into Vivo's own video format.

Sample Code

This is a generic example of code that will embed a Vivo video object into a Web page. Note that this code will work with both Microsoft Internet Explorer and Netscape Navigator; Vivo provides a plug-in utility for the Netscape browser, which recognizes the <EMBED> tag.

```
<OBJECT CLASSID="clsid:02466323-75ed-11cf-a267-0020af2546ea"
WIDTH=176 HEIGHT=144
CODEBASE="http://www.vivo.com/ie/vvweb.cab#Version=1,0,0,0">
<PARAM NAME="URL" VALUE="yourfile.viv">
<PARAM NAME="AUTOSTART" VALUE="true">
<PARAM NAME="VIDEOCONTROLS" VALUE="on">
<EMBED SRC="yourfile.viv" WIDTH=176 HEIGHT=144 AUTOSTART=true VIDEOCONTROLS=on>
</OBJECT>
```

Additional Information

Vivo Software

411 Waverly Oaks Road, Suite 313
Waltham, MA 02154 USA

Voice: 617-899-8900

Fax: 617-899-1400

http://www.vivo.com

Information on this control: http://microsoft.saltmine.com/isapi/activexisv/ prmgallery/gallery-activex-info.idc?ID=58

ClassID: clsid:02466323-75ed-11cf-a267-0020af2546ea#Version=1,0,0,0

Download page: http://www.vivo.com/ie/sample.htm

Codebase: http://www.vivo.com/ie/vvweb.cab

CHAPTER 14

Creating ActiveX Controls with the Visual Basic Control Creation Edition

By Michael C. Amundsen

This chapter shows you how to use the new Visual Basic 5.0 Custom Control Edition (VB CCE). Unlike previous versions of Visual Basic, VB CCE gives VB programmers the power to create their own ActiveX controls, including defining their own properties and events.

Even more important, VB CCE utilizes the new ActiveX Control specifications when creating OCX files. This means that any OCX file created with VB CCE can be used not only in Microsoft Visual Basic and Microsoft Access, but also in Microsoft Internet Explorer and any other application that can host ActiveX Controls. The first part of this chapter, "The Basics of ActiveX Control Development," outlines the creation of methods, properties, and events. You'll also learn how to use the Property Bag object to ensure that design-time properties are retained during runtime. In the next section, "Building the TextEdit ActiveX Control," you will build a simple input control that enables you to edit input as the user types in data. After you build the control, the "Distributing ActiveX Controls" section shows you how to construct standard install packages and how to create Internet installation packages.

Finally, after creating the control and building the install packages, you'll learn how to use the TextEdit control in a VB project ("Using TextEdit in a Visual Basic Project") and how to use the control in an HTML document ("Using TextEdit in an Internet Explorer Page").

The Basics of ActiveX Control Development

This section discusses the basic components of ActiveX control development. Every ActiveX control contains three basic parts:

◆ Properties

◆ Methods

◆ Events

Properties and methods will look familiar to anyone who has used Visual Basic 4.0 to build a Class Module, an OLE Server, or a Visual Basic 4.0 Add-In. However, while Visual Basic 4.0 limits programmers to the creation of DLL-type interfaces (OLE Servers), VB CCE enables you to actually register and fire off your own events.

This means you can build fully functional controls that can be placed in the Visual Basic toolbox and used in lots of places. Even better, because the controls you make with VB CCE are ActiveX (not OCX or VBX) controls, you will have a wealth of hosting platforms (Microsoft Access97 and Microsoft Internet Explorer, for example) on which you can use your newly invented controls.

Designing an ActiveX Control

Designing an ActiveX control involves planning the properties, methods, and events of the control. When designing the control, you can use any of the existing controls in your Visual Basic toolbox. In other words, you can create a control that uses the Visual Basic text box, but adds additional properties, methods, or events that make the text box behave as a unique control.

The next few sections show you how to define new properties, methods, and events
for your custom control. You will first learn how to create a simple demonstration
control. Although this control is quite simple, it shows the basics of control building.
After you learn how to build this control, you'll learn how to design and implement a
useful text box control to add to your Visual Basic and Microsoft Internet Explorer/
Visual Basic Script applications.

Starting Visual Basic Custom Control Edition

To begin creating your demonstration control, do the following:

1. Start up VB CCE. When you do, you'll be asked to select the type of project you
   want to build.

2. Select "ActiveX Control" and you'll see VB CCE open an empty UserControl
   form, ready for your design. All ActiveX controls are built using this VB CCE
   template (see fig. 14.1).

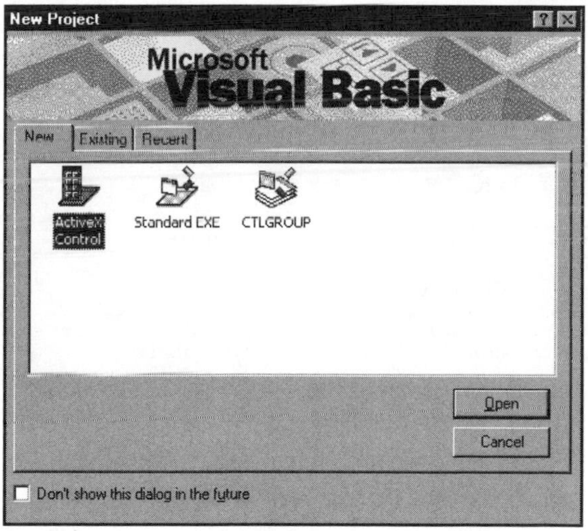

Figure 14.1

*Starting Visual
Basic 5.0 Custom
Controls Edition.*

Note ActiveX Controls are called *UserControl objects* within the VB CCE programming
environment. The term *custom control* is also frequently used to describe these
objects. All three of these names are common and used interchangeably throughout
this chapter.

For this demonstration control, you will build a simple toggle control that switches
between True and False each time you press its command button. To do this, you
need two existing controls—a command button and a label control.

It is perfectly legal to create a User Control that contains more than one existing control. In fact, this is one of the really compelling reasons to build your own custom controls. By doing so you'll be able to define ActiveX control objects that contain the functionality of several well-known controls.

Use figure 14.2 and table 14.1 as a guide for laying out your first custom control.

Table 14.1
Setting the User Control Properties

Control	Property	Setting
UserControl	Name	BooleanToggle
	ClientHeight	1425
	ClientWidth	1395
CommandButton	Name	Command1
	Caption	Push
	Height	375
	Left	240
	Top	840
	Width	975
Label	Name	Label1
	Alignment	2 - Centered
	BorderStyle	1 - Fixed Single
	Caption	True
	Height	375
	Left	240
	Top	240
	Width	975

Figure 14.2

*Laying out the
User Control.*

3. After you lay out the control, set the Project Name to "prjControl" by selecting
the Project Folder in the Project Window and then updating the Project Name
shown in the Properties Windows (see fig. 14.3).

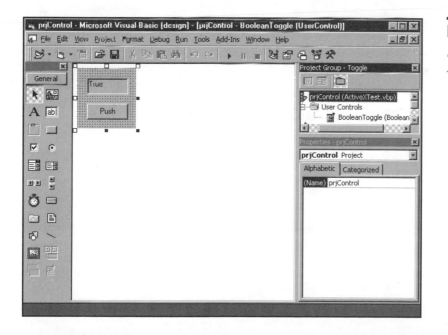

Figure 14.3

*Setting the Project
Name.*

4. Next, save the User Control as BOOLEANTOGGLE.CTL and the project file as ACTIVEXTEST.VBP.

Now you are ready to begin coding the properties, methods, and events of the BooleanToggle Control. But first, you need to add just a bit of code to the project to make sure the toggle control works properly.

Adding Base Code to the BooleanToggle Control

Here is how the BooleanToggle control operates: each time the user presses the command button, the label caption toggles between True and False. To make this happen, you need to add a short bit of code in the Command1_Click event. Open the form code window (select View, Code) and enter the following code:

```
Private Sub Command1_Click()
    '
    ' toggle the caption
    If Label1.Caption = "False" Then
        Label1.Caption = "True"
    Else
        Label1.Caption = "False"
    End If
    '
End Sub
```

This code is executed each time the user presses the command button on the User Control. This code simply checks the current caption value and switches it between True and False. Now you're ready to begin defining the properties, methods, and events of the control.

Adding Properties to the BooleanToggle Control

The next step in the process is to define one or more custom properties for the control. For the BooleanToggle example, you will add one property—the LabelBorder property. You can use this property to control the way the label's border appears.

You can use this defined property the same way you use any other Visual Basic properties. Visual Basic code enables you to read or write the property value at run-time, or use the Properties Window to modify the value at design time.

To add a custom property to the control, you need to insert some property procedures behind the control form, by following these steps:

1. Select Tools, Add Procedure to bring up the Add Procedure dialog box (see fig. 14.4).

2. After opening the dialog box, enter LabelBorder as the Name and select the Property radio button, then press OK. Visual Basic creates two property routines—one for reading the property and one for writing the property.

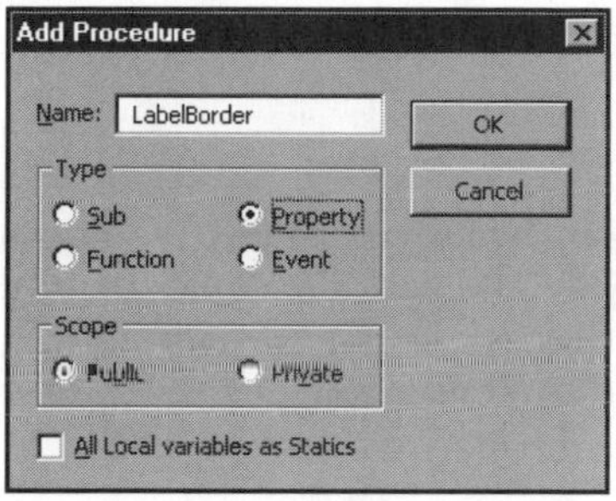

Figure 14.4

Adding a property procedure to the User Control.

Note
Be sure to open the code window of the User Control before you attempt to use the Tools, Add Procedure menu option. To open the code window, you can double-click at any location on the User Control form, select View, Code from the menu, or press the little code icon at the top border of the project window.

You must add code to these two routines to actually read and write the property. You must first, however, add a private variable to the general declarations section of the User Control. This private variable enables you to store the property value within the form itself.

Tip
In many cases, you don't need to define a private variable to store property values. However, it is a good idea to do this anyway so that you can easily keep track of property settings without having to access any underlying controls that use these values.

Add the following code to the general declaration section. Its purpose is to add a private variable to the User Control Project:

```
Option Explicit

' define private property
Private intBorder As Integer
'
```

Now that you have defined local storage for the property, you are ready to add code to the LabelBorder property methods.

1. First, open the code for the Let LabelBorder property routine and add the code shown here:

```
Public Property Let LabelBorder(ByVal vNewValue As Variant)
    '
    ' set borderstyle property
    intBorder = vNewValue
    Label1.BorderStyle = intBorder
    '
End Property
```

The first line of code accepts the value passed into it and places that value in the private storage variable. The next line of code copies the stored value into the BorderStyle property of the label control on the custom control. In this way, users can set the LabelBorder property (at design time or run time) and see the results in the label control on the custom control.

2. The next step is to add code to the Get LabelBorder property routine. This routine returns the current setting. Add the following code to the project:

```
Public Property Get LabelBorder() As Variant
    '
    ' return borderstyle property
    LabelBorder = intBorder
    '
End Property
```

This single line of code copies the stored value in the private variable into the property. This is the only custom property you'll add to the control.

After the code has been entered, save the control and project before proceeding to the next section.

Adding Methods to the BooleanToggle Custom Control

You can also define custom methods for your ActiveX controls. Methods are nothing more than Visual Basic subroutines or functions. By creating public subroutines or functions, you are actually creating methods for the control. For this example, you will add one method to the control. This method pops up a dialog box that shows the status of the control. In production applications, you can add methods that perform calculations, use properties to open files, or produce other results.

To add a new method to your control, complete the following steps:

1. Select Tools, Add Procedure.

2. Enter **ShowStatus** as the Name. Be sure the Sub radio button is selected before you press the OK button.

Now enter the following code into the ShowStatus method.

```
Public Sub ShowStatus()
    '
    ' execute a method
    MsgBox Label1.Caption, vbInformation, "BooleanToggle Control"
    '
End Sub
```

As mentioned earlier, this method simply displays a message box showing the status of the control. This is the only method you will define to complete this project. Save this control and project before going on to the next section.

Adding Events to the Boolean Toggle Custom Control

The next step in the process of creating this control is to define an event for it. Events are also known as *system messages*. By defining an event, you are actually defining a system message that is sent out at a time determined by your code. This message is then received by your Visual Basic program that hosts the control. You can add code behind the event message; this code executes each time the message is received.

Note You use event messages in every Visual Basic program. The Command1_Click event is a good example.

The first step in defining an event is to place a single line of code in the general declaration area. This code line uses the new Event keyword. Modify the general declaration area of your User Control to match the following code, which defines a User Control Event.

```
Option Explicit

' define private property
Private intBorder As Integer

' define an event
Public Event Toggle()
```

By defining the Toggle event, you can see a new code event in the Visual Basic form that hosts this ActiveX control. It looks like this:

```
Sub BooleanToggle1_Toggle()

End Sub
```

This is just like the code for the command1_Click event or any of the other well-known Visual Basic events.

Now that the event is defined, you need to add code to your project to fire off your message so that your Visual Basic program receives it. Because you want to fire off the event each time the control switches from True to False, you must add code to the Label1_Change event. Enter the following code to fire the Toggle event message.

```
Private Sub Label1_Change()
    '
    ' fire off new event
    RaiseEvent Toggle
    '
End Sub
```

Notice the use of the RaiseEvent keyword. RaiseEvent sends out the Toggle message. After adding this code, save the project. You're almost ready to test the control. You need to add a bit more code, however, to make sure the User Control behaves correctly in both runtime and design-time modes.

Using the Property Bag Object

One of the challenges of building ActiveX controls is that they exist in both runtime (while the program is running) and design-time (while the Visual Basic editor is running) modes. Most control properties are available during both these states. As a rule, you can store values using the Properties window, then start the program and expect the runtime version of the control to remember the values set during design-time.

Here are the chronological steps that must take place:

1. After setting the properties at design-time, the User Control must save these values to some location the moment the control is to revert to runtime.

2. As soon as runtime mode begins, the User Control must locate the stored property settings and restore the design-time values.

Although the idea is pretty simple, pulling it off takes a bit of work. Thankfully, VB CCE has two special events defined for the moments when the control needs to save

the design-time values and when the control needs to restore them during runtime.
You can use these two events to store and recall your private property values. The
information is saved to a special object called the Property Bag. The Property Bag can
be loaded with values and then used to recall those same values, by following these
steps:

1. Locate the UserControl Object in the User Control code window.

2. Select the WriteProperties event.

3. Now add the code shown here:

```
Private Sub UserControl_WriteProperties(PropBag As PropertyBag)
    '
    ' save design-time proportioo
    PropBag.WriteProperty "LabelBorder", intBorder, 0
    '
End Sub
```

This code uses the WriteProperty method of the PropertyBag object to save the value
of the private intBorder variable. If this variable has not been set, the default value of
"0" is stored as the LabelBorder property.

You must also add the following code to the ReadProperties event of the User Control
object. Doing so recalls the data saved using WriteProperies.

```
Private Sub UserControl_ReadProperties(PropBag As PropertyBag)
    '
    ' get design-time properties
    Label1.BorderStyle = PropBag.ReadProperty("LabelBorder", 0)
    '
End Sub
```

This code simply opens the PropertyBag object and loads the value associated with
the LabelBorder property. If no value was set, the default value of "0" will be used.

This is the end of the code section. You have just built your first custom control. Next,
you'll add a quick form to test out your new control.

Compiling and Testing the BooleanToggle Control

After you build the control, you can use VB CCE to compile it and then use it in a
standard Visual Basic project form.

1. With the control code still loaded, select File, Make ActiveXTest.ocx menu
   option. This will bring up the compile dialog box (see fig. 14.5).

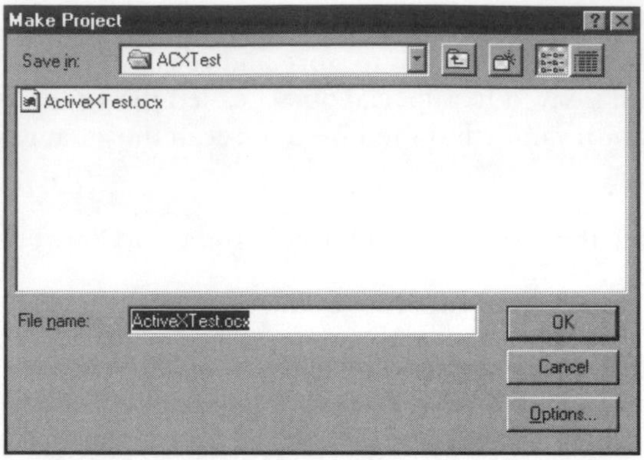

Figure 14.5

Compiling the new ActiveX control.

2. When you compile the ActiveX control, VB CCE automatically registers the control in the Windows registry. This registration enables Visual Basic 5.0 and any other ActiveX control-compliant applications to use the new control. You will know your compilation was successful when you see a new control appear in your Visual Basic toolbox.

3. After you have successfully compiled the ActiveXTest.ocx, you should close the control project. This will enable you to actually load and use the control in Visual Basic projects.

> **Warning** If you cannot see the control, you may need to use the Project, Components menu selection to load the new control. If you see the control in your toolbox, but it is disabled (grayed out), you need to close the source code for your control by selecting the User Control project in the Project window and then pressing the X in the code windows until the project is closed.

Now that you have built, compiled, and closed your BooleanToggle control project, you can create a quick project to test the new control. To create a quick test project, all you need to do is follow these steps:

1. Add a project to this project group by selecting File, Add Project, and then selecting Standard EXE and pressing OK (see fig. 14.6).

2. When the default form appears, add a command button and one of the new BooleanToggle buttons to the project.

3. Set the Caption of the Command button to Show Status. Set the Form Name to frmToggle and the Project Name to prjDemo.

Your form show look like the one in figure 14.7.

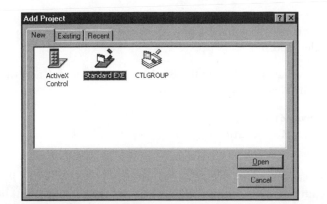

Figure 14.6

*Adding a
Standard EXE
project to the
Project Group.*

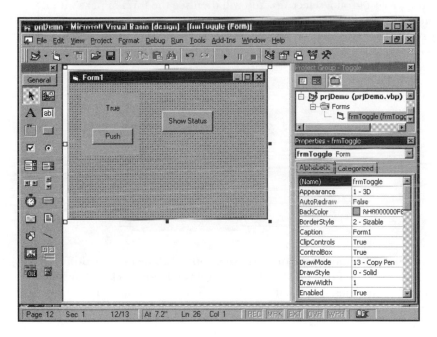

Figure 14.7

*Laying out the
BooleanToggle test
form.*

4. Now open the code window of the frmToggle form and add the following code:

```
Private Sub BooleanToggle1_Toggle()
    '
    ' respond to toggle!
    If BooleanToggle1.LabelBorder = 0 Then
        BooleanToggle1.LabelBorder = 1
    Else
        BooleanToggle1.LabelBorder = 0
    End If
    '
End Sub
```

The preceding code executes each time the user presses the Push button on the BooleanToggle control. The actual code modifies the LabelBorder property of the BooleanToggle control.

5. To execute the ShowStatus method of the BooleanToggle control, add the following code to the Command1_Click event.

```
Private Sub Command1_Click()
    BooleanToggle1.ShowStatus
End Sub
```

6. After you add this last bit of code, you can test your project by selecting Run, Start from the main menu. If you see a dialog box asking you if you want to update the project group, select Yes. You will then see the form appear with the two controls. When you press the Push button, you will see the caption and border switch back and forth. When you press the Show Status button, you will see a dialog box that shows the toggle status (see fig. 14.8).

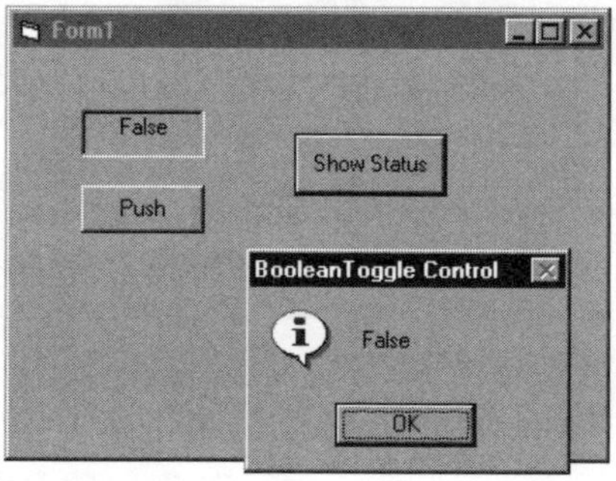

Figure 14.8

*Testing the
BooleanToggle
ActiveX control.*

This completes your quick tour of creating ActiveX controls. The next section shows you how to build a more useful control and create an installation package for both Windows and for the Internet. After that this chapter shows you how you can use these new controls in Visual Basic and in Microsoft Internet Explorer.

Building the TextEdit ActiveX Control

This section teaches you how to design and build an ActiveX control that adds new properties and functions to an existing Visual Basic control. This is sometimes called *super-scripting* controls because you are adding additional functionality. This project provides new properties to the Visual Basic text box control. These new properties add real-time input editing options to Visual Basic and Visual Basic Script projects.

The new control, called the EditText control, enables you to do the following:

◆ Automatically convert all character input to uppercase

◆ Limit input to digits or numeric data only (including ".+–")

Also, you will add properties and methods that will enable you to check numeric
input for range errors. For example, by adding Min and Max properties, you can
check that the input is within the Min and Max range.

Besides properties and methods, you will add events that fire off when input is
incorrect and when the results of the range are checking in out of bounds. After you
build this control, this chapter shows you how to create distribution packages—
including a standard Windows distribution set—and how to create a distribution set
that can be used to deliver the control over the Internet.

Laying Out the ProjEdit ActiveX Control Project

To start building the new control, follow these steps:

1. Open a new ActiveX control project in VB CCE and place a single textbox
   control on the User Control form space. Refer to figure 14.9 for the size and
   position of the control.

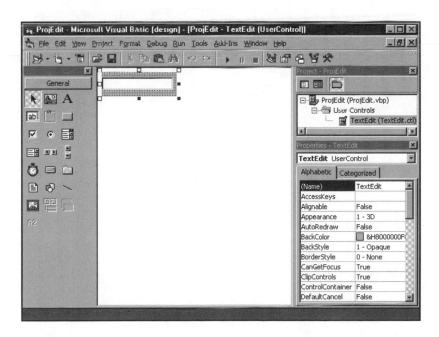

Figure 14.9

*Laying out the
EditText control.*

2. Set the User Control Name property to EditText and the Project Name Property to ProjEdit.

3. Save the control file as EditText.ctl and the Project as ProjEdit.vbp.

4. Next, open the general declarations section of the User Control and add the following code:

```
Option Explicit
'

' local storage for properties
Private intKeyFilter As Integer
Private varText As Variant
Private varMin As Variant
Private varMax As Variant

' declare an event
Public Event BadKey(KeyAscii As Integer, ValidKeys As String)
Public Event RangeError(varValue As Variant)
```

The local storage variables will map to public properties for the new control. The two event definitions will give you the ability to send messages to the host application if an invalid value is entered.

5. The next step is to add the primary code routines for the new control. In this example, you'll want to trap each keystroke and check it against the properties that define the input rules. The following code should be placed in the Text1_KeyPress event.

```
Private Sub Text1_KeyPress(KeyAscii As Integer)
    '
    ' check keypress
    '
    Dim strDigits As String
    Dim strNumeric As String
    '
    strDigits = "0123456789"
    strNumeric = strDigits & ".+-"
    '
    Select Case intKeyFilter
        Case 0 ' no filter
            ' na
        Case 1 ' uppercase
                KeyAscii = Asc(UCase(Chr(KeyAscii)))
```

```
        Case 2 ' numeric data
            If KeyAscii > 32 Then
                If InStr(strNumeric, Chr(KeyAscii)) = 0 Then
                    RaiseEvent BadKey(KeyAscii, strNumeric)
                    KeyAscii = 0
                End If
            End If
        Case 3 ' digits only
            If KeyAscii > 32 Then
                If InStr(strDigits, Chr(KeyAscii)) = 0 Then
                    RaiseEvent BadKey(KeyAscii, strDigits)
                    KeyAscii = 0
                End If
            End If
    End Select
    '

End Sub
```

The code checks each key press. The KeyFilter property is then checked to see if
any editing should be done. If one of the edit rules has been set, the code scans
the key press and reacts accordingly.

Note If the edit rule is set to Uppercase, the value is simply converted to uppercase
without any error report. However, if the numeric or digit rule is turned on, an
invalid key causes the BadKey event message to be sent out. This gives the
programmer the option of ignoring the event, adding a message, or even fixing the
keypress automatically.

Next, you need to add code to perform the range-checking of a numeric value. This is
done in two steps.

1. First, add the following code to the Text1_LostFocus event. Doing so calls the
   range-checking code when the control loses focus.

```
Private Sub Text1_LostFocus()
    '
    If intKeyFilter = 4 Then
        CheckRange
    End If
    '
End Sub
```

2. Now add the CheckRange method to the project. Note that this is defined as a Public method. This means that programmers will be able to invoke the method from within the hosting application (for instance, EditText1.CheckRange). Create the Public Sub CheckRange and enter the following code:

```
Public Sub CheckRange()
    '
    ' check the range input
    If IsNull(varMin) = False And IsNull(varMax) = False Then
        If Text1.Text < varMin Or Text1.Text > varMax Then
            RaiseEvent RangeError(Text1.Text)
        End If
    End If
    '
End Sub
```

One last routine must be added to this section of the project. The following code forces the TextBox control to resize to fit the entire User Control space. This makes the TextBox behave appropriately whenever the programmer resizes the control in design mode.

```
Private Sub UserControl_Resize()
    '
    ' make textbox fill control space
    '
    Text1.Left = 1
    Text1.Top = 1
    Text1.Width = UserControl.Width
    Text1.Height = UserControl.Height
    '
End Sub
```

1. Enter the preceding routine.

2. Save the User Control (TextEdit.ctl) and the project (ProjEdit.vbp) before you go on to the next section.

Adding Properties, Methods, and Events to the TextEdit Control

The next step is to add the property routines to the project. The following code shows the property routines for the KeyFilter property.

1. Add this code using the Tools, Add Procedure menu option. Be sure to enter
KeyFilter as the name, and select the Property option button and the Public
option button before you press "OK."

The code moves the local storage value into the property and moves the new
property value into local storage.

```
Public Property Get KeyFilter() As Integer
    '
    ' send local storage back to caller
    '
    KeyFilter = intKeyFilter
    '
End Property

Public Property Let KeyFilter(ByVal intNewValue As Integer)
    '
    ' put incoming data into local storage
    '
    If intNewValue < 0 Or intNewValue > 4 Then
        Error 380 ' invalid property value
    Else
        intKeyFilter = intNewValue
    End If
    '
End Property
```

Note   Note the use of Integer type on the property definition and the range checking. If
the value is not correct, Visual Basic raises an error. This error—Error 380—causes
the Invalid Property Value error to occur.

This procedure is the best way to report errors within ActiveX control controls. It
enables programmers to trap for errors and prevent unwanted message boxes or
other program interruptions.

2. Now add the Property routines for the Min property by entering the following
code:

```
Public Property Get Min() As Variant
    '
    Min = varMin
    '
End Property
```

```
Public Property Let Min(ByVal vNewValue As Variant)
    '
    If IsNumeric(varMin) = False Then
        Error 380 ' invalid property value
    Else
        varMin = vNewValue
    End If
End Property
```

Because you cannot be sure of the exact numeric data type passed into the Min and Max properties, it is best to use the Variant data type for these properties. You can then use the IsNumeric() function to validate the parameter and raise the Invalid Property Value error if needed.

3. After you define the Min property, use the following code to define the Max property:

```
Public Property Get Max() As Variant
    '
    Max = varMax
    '
End Property


Public Property Let Max(ByVal vNewValue As Variant)
    '
    If IsNumeric(vNewValue) = False Then
        Error 380 ' invalid property value
    Else
        varMax = vNewValue
    End If
    '
End Property
```

4. The only other property left to define is the Text property. You need to define this property to pass it from the embedded TextBox control. Enter the following code to your project:

```
Public Property Get Text() As Variant
    '
    Text = varText
    '
End Property

Public Property Let Text(ByVal vNewValue As Variant)
```

```
'
        varText = vNewValue
        Text1.Text = varText
        '

    End Property
```

Note that when the property is set, it is forced into the embedded TextBox.

5. Finally, you need to add code to the UserControl_ReadProperties and
   UserControl_WriteProperties events to keep track of property values between
   design-time and run-time modes. The code for both these events follows:

```
    Private Sub UserControl_ReadProperties(PropBag As PropertyBag)
        '
        ' load design-time info
        '
        intKeyFilter = PropBag.ReadProperty("KeyFilter", 0)
        varMin - PropBag.ReadProperty("Min", Null)
        varMax = PropBag.ReadProperty("Max", Null)
        varText = PropBag.ReadProperty("Text", UserControl.Name)
        Text1.Text = varText
        '

    End Sub

    Private Sub UserControl_WriteProperties(PropBag As PropertyBag)
        '
        ' save design-time data
        '
        PropBag.WriteProperty "KeyFilter", intKeyFilter, 0
        PropBag.WriteProperty "Text", varText, UserControl.Name
        PropBag.WriteProperty "Max", varMax, Null
        PropBag.WriteProperty "Min", varMin, Null
        '

    End Sub
```

6. After adding this last bit of code, save the control and project.

7. Now you can compile the control (select File, Make TextEdit.ocx). Remember
   that this compile step will also register the control for use on your machine. You
   should see the new control icon appear in your Visual Basic toolbox.

Finally, you are ready to create distribution sets so you can install the new control for
use in other programs.

Distributing ActiveX Controls

VB CCE ships with an Installation Wizard, a stand-alone program, that enables you to build install sets for both local install and installation over the Internet. The Internet installation option enables you to build new controls and then distribute them from a web page instead of shipping them to users or traveling to each machine in your organization with diskettes. This section shows you how to use the Wizard to build both types of install packages.

Creating a Standard Install Package

The first type of installation package you can build is the standard install. This package uses a Windows Setup program to install your ActiveX control. It is best to exit Visual Basic before you run the Installation Wizard. Follow these steps:

1. When you first start the Wizard, you are asked to select the VBP (Visual Basic Project file) that you want to use as the base of the install set. You also need to select the installation type.

   For this example, select Create a Setup Program. Also, turn on the "Generate Dependency File." Doing so creates a separate file that is used to confirm various other component modules needed for your project. Using dependency files enables the install routine to check to see what files already exist on the user's machine, thus reducing the installation time.

   After you fill out the first screen, it should look like the one in figure 14.10.

Figure 14.10

Starting the Installation Wizard.

2. The next screen enables you to select the type of setup install you want to build. You can build one for diskette install, for single-directory install, or for a multidirectory install.

The diskette version works if you need to make a physical set of disks that will be shipped to the user location. If you plan to install the project on a network, you can select the single-directory approach. This will enable you to place all the files in a single location and link to this location from the target workstation.

You can use the multidirectory approach to create an install kit that divides the package into a set of floppy disk-sized directories. This is handy for creating an install kit on a drive that is downloaded by users to diskettes or copied to diskettes for later distribution.

For this example, select the single directory option (see fig. 14.11).

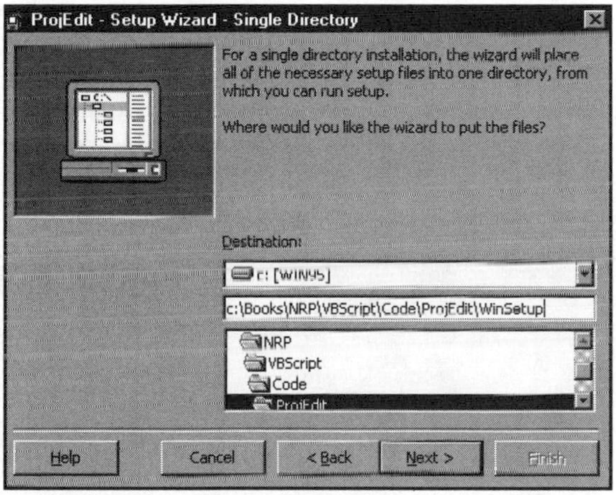

Figure 14.11

Selecting the install distribution method.

3. The next step is to select the directory to use for the installation files. It is a good idea to place the install files directly underneath the directory that contains the source code of the project (see fig. 14.12).

Warning Be sure not to select the source code directory as the target for installation files. One of the first steps in creating the install files is to remove all the existing files from the target directory. If you select your source code directory, you could lose your code files!

Figure 14.12

Selecting the target directory.

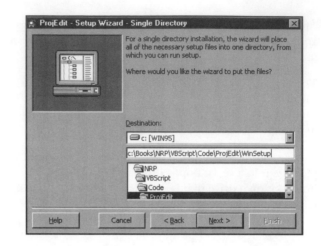

4. The next step asks you if you want to include any local ActiveX control files. You can skip this screen for this example.

5. You will be asked several other questions about the installation. For example, if you want to use this control in non-Visual Basic tools, you can include a property page DLL to gain access to your defined properties. Finally, you will see the screen that shows all the files to include in the setup (see fig. 14.13).

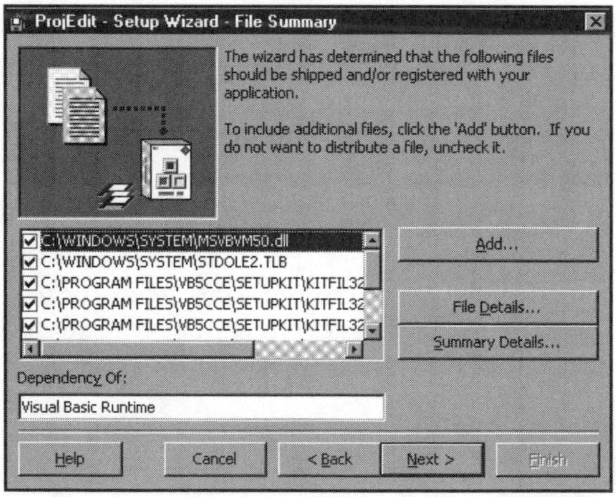

Figure 14.13

Viewing all the files in the install package.

6. When you press the Finish button, the Wizard builds the final setup kit and stores it in your selected directory. You can now run the install routine to add the new control to your system directory (see fig. 14.14).

Figure 14.14

*Starting the
Standard Setup.*

Creating an Internet Install Package

You can also use the Installation Wizard to build an Internet-based install package, by
following these instructions:

1. Start the application and select the Generate Internet option.

2. You will see a few different screens in the list of options. You are asked for a
    target directory and then asked to supply some information about supporting
    Microsoft .cab files (see fig. 14.15).

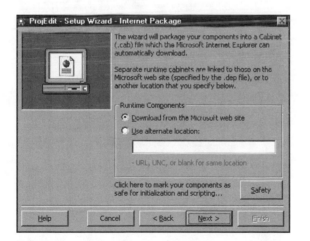

Figure 14.15

*Selecting a .cab
file location.*

.cab files are used to distribute programs and components. Users may need some
additional .cab files to install your control. If so, you can enable users to link to
the Microsoft web site to get these files, or you can indicate another site (possibly
your own).

3. For this example, select the Microsoft option.

The Wizard then collects all needed files and prepares an install directory for you. You will notice that along with the selected target directory, an additional folder, called SUPPORT is created. This folder contains the actual OCX and other files. You will also see that the install directory contains an HTML file that uses the control. By loading this file in a browser, users automatically download the control. After the control is downloaded, it can be used in any Visual Basic Script program.

The PE_Test Visual Basic Project

On the CD

You can use this new control as a part of any Visual Basic 5.0 standard EXE project. The CD that ships with this book has a short VB CCE project that uses the new control. It enables users to test each of the edit features (UpperCase, Numeric, Digits, and InRange). Figure 14.16 shows the PE_Test program in action.

Figure 14.16

Running the PE_Test program.

Because most of the processing is done in the new ActiveX control, there is very little code required to build this form. Table 14.2 shows the Form controls needed to build the PE_Test form. Refer to figure 14.17 when laying out the form.

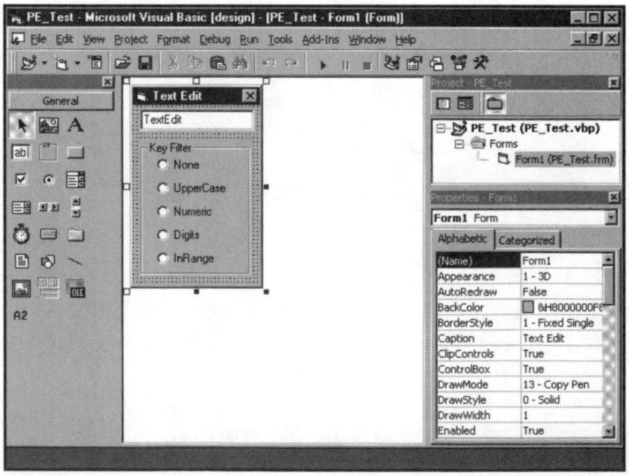

Figure 14.17

Laying out the PE_Test.FRM Form.

Table 14.2
The PE_TEST.FRM Form Controls

Control	Property	Setting
VB.Form	Name	Form1
	BorderStyle	1 'Fixed Single
	Caption	"Text Edit"
	ClientHeight	2760
	ClientLeft	45
	ClientTop	330
	ClientWidth	1965
	LinkTopic	"Form1"
	MaxButton	0 'False
	MinButton	0 'False
VB.Frame	Name	Frame1
	Caption	"Key Filter"
	Height	2055
	Left	120
	TabIndex	0
	Top	540
	Width	1695
VB.OptionButton	Name	optInRange
	Caption	"InRange"
	Height	255
	Left	240
	TabIndex	5
	Top	1680
	Width	1215

continues

Table 14.2, Continued
The PE_TEST.FRM Form Controls

Control	Property	Setting
VB.OptionButton	Name	optNone
	Caption	"None"
	Height	255
	Left	240
	TabIndex	4
	Top	240
	Width	1215
VB.OptionButton	Name	optDigits
	Caption	"Digits"
	Height	255
	Left	240
	TabIndex	3
	Top	1320
	Width	1215
VB.OptionButton	Name	optNumeric
	Caption	"Numeric"
	Height	255
	Left	240
	TabIndex	2
	Top	960
	Width	1215
VB.OptionButton	Name	optUpperCase
	Caption	"UpperCase"
	Height	255
	Left	240
	TabIndex	1

Control	Property	Setting
	Top	600
	Width	1215
ProjEdit.TextEdit	Name	TextEdit1
	Height	315
	Left	120
	TabIndex	6
	Top	60
	Width	1755

The following code for this form involves setting properties when the user presses the radio buttons and trapping for the new error events associated with the TextEdit control.

This is all the code you need for this project.

```
Private Sub Form_Load()
    '
    TextEdit1.Text = ""
    '
End Sub


Private Sub optDigits_Click()
    '
    If optDigits = True Then
        TextEdit1.KeyFilter = 3
    End If
    '
End Sub


Private Sub optInRange_Click()
    '
    If optInRange = True Then
        TextEdit1.KeyFilter = 4
        TextEdit1.Min = 5
        TextEdit1.Max = 10
        MsgBox "Enter a Number between 5 and 10"
    End If
    '
End Sub
```

```vbscript
Private Sub optNone_Click()
    '
    If optNone = True Then
        TextEdit1.KeyFilter = 0
    End If
    '
End Sub

Private Sub optNumeric_Click()
    '
    If optNumeric = True Then
        TextEdit1.KeyFilter = 2
    End If
    '
End Sub
Private Sub optUpperCase_Click()
    '
    If optUpperCase = True Then
        TextEdit1.KeyFilter = 1
    End If
    '
End Sub


Private Sub TextEdit1_BadKey(KeyAscii As Integer, ValidKeys As String)
    '
    ' report error key
    '
    Dim strMsg As String
    '
    strMsg = "Select one of the following keys:" & vbCrLf
    strMsg = strMsg & "[" & ValidKeys & "]"
    '
    MsgBox strMsg, vbCritical, "Invalid KeyPress"
    '
End Sub

Private Sub TextEdit1_RangeError(varValue As Variant)
    '
    MsgBox "Value is out of Range [ " & CStr(varValue), vbCritical,
➥"TextEdit1_InRange"
    '
End Sub
```

After you lay out the form and enter the code, save the form as PE_TEST.FRM and
the project as PE_TEST.VBP. You can then run the program to see how the TextEdit
control works within Visual Basic.

The TextEdit HTML Document

You use the ActiveX Control Pad, Microsoft Front Page, Microsoft Word HTML
Assistant, or any other text editor to create an HTML page that uses the TextEdit
Control. The following code shows a short HTML page that does just this.

Note This HTML document can be found on the CD that ships with this book. The page
was written using the CLSID code generated when the TextEdit Control was first
generated. If you rebuilt the TextEdit Control project, you may need to build this
HTML document from scratch to include the class ID that was registered on your
machine when you built the TextEdit control.

On the
CD

```
<HTML>
<!-- If any of the controls on this page require licensing, you must create a
➥license package file.
     Run LPK_TOOL.EXE in the tools directory to create the required LPK file.

<OBJECT CLASSID="clsid:5220cb21-c88d-11cf-b347-00aa00a28331">
     <PARAM NAME="LPKPath" VALUE="LPKfilename.LPK">
</OBJECT>
-->


<H1><CENTER>
HTML Example Using the PROJEDIT.OCX ActiveX Control
</CENTER></H1>
<P>
<HR>
This HTML page contains three instances of a Microsoft ActiveX Control
built using the Beta Version of Visual Basic Custom Controls Edition.
This version of VB enables users to create ActiveX controls that can be
used in VB, Access, and Internet Explorer HTML documents.<P>

You can use VBScript to control ActiveX Properties, call ActiveX Methods,
and respond to ActiveX events.<P>
<HR>
<OBJECT
     classid="clsid:4920084E-43FC-11D0-BC7F-444553540000"
     id=TextEdit1
```

```
          codebase="ProjEdit.CAB#version=1,0,0,0">
</OBJECT>
...Set to convert all alpha characters to upper case.<P>


<OBJECT
     classid="clsid:4920084E-43FC-11D0-BC7F-444553540000"
     id=TextEdit2
     codebase="ProjEdit.CAB#version=1,0,0,0">
</OBJECT>
...Set to accept only numeric data (0123456789.-+)<P>


<OBJECT
     classid="clsid:4920084E-43FC-11D0-BC7F-444553540000"
     id=TextEdit3
     codebase="ProjEdit.CAB#version=1,0,0,0">
</OBJECT>
...Set to accept only digits (0123456789)<P>


<HR>

<address>Michael C. Amundsen</address>
<address><a href= "mailto:mamund@iac.net">mamund@iac.net</a></address>
<a href = "http://www.iac.net/~mamund/">Mike Amundsen's Web Site</a>

<SCRIPT LANGUAGE="VBScript">
'
' set up controls
'
TextEdit1.KeyFilter=1
TextEdit1.Text=""
TextEdit2.KeyFilter=2
TextEdit2.Text=""
TextEdit3.KeyFilter=3
TextEdit3.Text=""
'
' global error report
'
Sub BadKeyMsg(ByVal intKey, ByVal strKeys)
    '
    strMsg="Use one of the following keys:" & chr(13)
    strMsg=strMsg & "[" & strKeys & "]"
    '
    MsgBox strMsg,16,"BadKey: " & chr(intKey)
    '
```

```
End Sub
'
' event handlers
'
Sub TextEdit1_BadKey(ByVal KeyAscii, ByVal ValidKeys)
     BadKeyMsg KeyAscii,ValidKeys
End Sub
'
Sub TextEdit2_BadKey(byVal KeyAscii, ByVal ValidKeys)
     BadKeyMsg KeyAscii,ValidKeys
End Sub
'
Sub TextEdit3_BadKey(ByVal KeyAscii, ByVal ValidKeys)
     BadKeyMsg KeyAscii,ValidKeys
End Sub
'
</SCRIPT>
</HTML>
```

You can load this completed HTML document into your Microsoft Internet Explorer
and test the new TextEdit box. Each box edits the input based on the rules set up in
the document using VBScript. If the user presses an invalid key, an error message will
appear (see fig. 14.18).

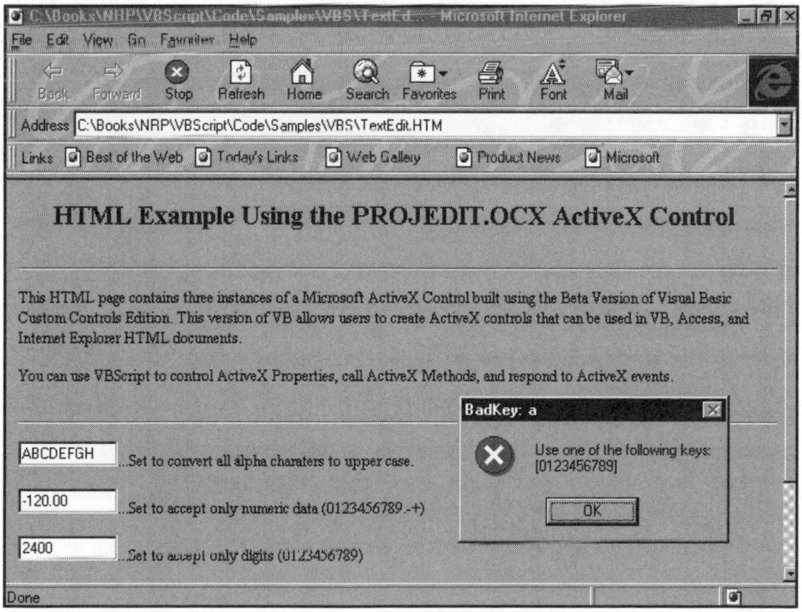

Figure 14.18

*Testing the
TEXTEDIT.HTM
document.*

You can use this control in any HTML project that requires additional data editing for the input forms.

 Note The Visual Basic 5.0 Control Creation Edition is a limited version of Visual Basic 5.0. It is limited in that it can only be used to create ActiveX controls.

Summary

This chapter presented you with information on how to use the new Visual Basic 5.0 Custom Control Edition (VB CCE). Unlike previous versions of Visual Basic, VB CCE gives you the power to create your own ActiveX controls. You can even define properties and events for these controls. With what you learned in this chapter, combined with your knowledge of VB from the VBScript you learned in previous chapters, you should be ready to create your own ActiveX controls to use with your web pages.

PART IV

Advanced Internet Programming

CHAPTER 15

Enhancing HTML Forms with VBScript

By Eric Smith

N ow that you have a good understanding of the VBScript language, it is time to put your knowledge to use. If you have ever built or visited a web site, you are certainly familiar with input forms. Forms are used for a variety of purposes. On "Ask the VB Pro," web site forms were created and used for a variety of purposes. Users, for example, can send in feedback about the site on one form and subscribe to a mailing list with another. The user enters his information into these forms and presses a button to send the data to the server. The server then processes the information and displays a response to the user.

Note You can visit the author's web sites at the following URLs:

Ask the VB Pro—http://www.inquiry.com/techtips/thevbpro

Ask the ActiveX Pro—http://www.inquiry.com/techtips/activex_pro

Although HTML forms are useful, there are a number of data fields that always need to be validated. For instance, what if the user enters a bad e-mail address? The server has to validate the form of the e-mail address before any mail is sent. If the e-mail address is bad, the user has to re-enter the information on the form. Each time the user sends the data to the server, the data has to travel over the Internet to the server and the response has to be sent back to the user. This takes time, and on a busy day the delay can be significant.

What if some of this validation could be done on the client's machine within the browser? Much of the validation could be done immediately instead of having to do it on the server. When the data is finally sent, the server "knows" that portions of the data have been validated and can be used immediately. By making an assertion that a piece of data will be validated by your web page, you can skip the validation of the data when it gets to the server. For any data that your web page does not validate, the server will need to validate it before completing the transaction.

This chapter is designed to give you some tips and techniques for enhancing your forms with VBScript, to make them quicker and more efficient to use. By adding validation and other types of code to your forms, you can make the user's experience at your site better, and because happy users make repeat visits to your site, you ensure the success of your site.

In this chapter, you learn about basic HTML forms and how and where to add VBScript code to them to make them more functional. You are also shown how to use a server program to process data from your web page. Finally, this chapter provides some tips and techniques for validating complex data, including e-mail addresses.

Examining the Basic HTML Form

Before you learn about enhancing HTML forms with VBScript, you must understand how HTML forms are created and used. If you are familiar with forms and how they work, skip to the next section, which provides a short summary of each of the tags used for building HTML forms. For more detailed information, refer to Chapter 2, "HTML Fundamentals for VBScripting."

On the CD **Note** The example used in this section is located in the \Examples\Chapter 17 folder on your hard drive and is named BasicForm.html.

This example consists of the basic form used at the "Ask the VB Pro" site for users to send in questions. The basic form illustrates all the controls that you can use on an HTML form: text boxes (single-line and multiline), check boxes, drop-down list boxes, radio buttons, and push buttons. The code for the form follows:

```
<HTML>
<HEAD>
<TITLE>Inside VBScript with ActiveX - Basic Form</title>
</HEAD>
<BODY>


<BLOCKQUOTE>
Enter the information below to submit your question.
</BLOCKQUOTE>


<HR>
<FORM ACTION=http://www.inquiry.com/pro-bin/echo.pl METHOD=POST>
<INPUT NAME="parm_proname" VALUE="VB Pro" TYPE=hidden>
<TABLE>
<TR><TD>Full Name:</TD>
<TD><INPUT TYPE=text NAME="parm_sender_name" SIZE=40
MAXLENGTH=40></TD></TR>
<TR><TD>E-Mail Address:</TD>
<TD><INPUT TYPE=text NAME="parm_sender_email" SIZE=40
MAXLENGTH=40></TD></TR>
<TR><TD>Question Topic:</TD>
<TD><INPUT TYPE=text NAME="parm_topic" SIZE=50
MAXLENGTH=50></TD></TR>
<TR><TD>VB Version:</TD>
<TD><SELECT NAME=data_Version>
      <OPTION>Select Your Version</OPTION>
      <OPTION>-----------------------------</OPTION>
      <OPTION>VBScript</OPTION>
      <OPTION>Version 3.0 Standard</OPTION>
      <OPTION>Version 3.0 Professional</OPTION>
      <OPTION>Version 4.0 Standard</OPTION>
      <OPTION>Version 4.0 Professional</OPTION>
      <OPTION>Version 4.0 Enterprise</OPTION>
</SELECT></TR>

<TR><TD>Difficulty:</TD>
<TD><INPUT TYPE=radio NAME="difficulty" VALUE="Low">Low
<INPUT TYPE=radio NAME="difficulty" VALUE="Medium" CHECKED>Medium
```

```
<INPUT TYPE=radio NAME="difficulty" VALUE="High">High
</TR>

<TR><TD>Question:</TD>
<TD><TEXTAREA NAME="data_Question" COLS=50
ROWS=3></TEXTAREA></TD></TR>
</TABLE>
<INPUT TYPE="CHECKBOX" NAME="SubscriberMailList"
VALUE="SubscriberMailList" CHECKED>
I would like to be on the Ask the VB Pro mailing list.
<CENTER>
<FONT SIZE=+1>
<INPUT TYPE=submit VALUE="Submit"> <INPUT TYPE=reset VALUE="Clear Form">
</FONT>
</CENTER>
</FORM>
</BODY></HTML>
```

Dissecting the "Ask the Pro" HTML Form

Reading through this HTML code, you can see all the basic elements of the form. Let's start with the following statement:

```
<FORM ACTION=http://www.inquiry.com/pro-bin/echo.pl METHOD=POST>
```

The <FORM> tag marks the beginning of the form. In this case, the form is tied to a real, working program that echos back your input so that you can see that the form is working.

The echo.pl program is a simple program running on a server that accepts input from HTML forms and prints it to the screen. This program is an excellent tool for testing HTML forms in this chapter. Feel free to use it for testing your own forms as you learn VBScript and HTML.

Next, let's examine the following statement:

```
<INPUT NAME="parm_proname" VALUE="VB Pro" TYPE=hidden>
```

This tag, which uses the TYPE=hidden parameter, creates a hidden field. *Hidden fields* are used to send data to the server. This field, for instance, sends the name VB Pro so that the server can provide some piece of information to the user.

 Note   Hidden fields are not required; however, using hidden fields enables you to pass data directly to the server that is not provided by the user.

Now, let's look at parts of the following statement:

```
<INPUT TYPE=text NAME="parm_sender_name" SIZE=40 MAXLENGTH=40>
```

Several tags in the form resemble this one, which creates a single-line text box. Following is a list of the parameters used in this tag and their meanings:

◆ **TYPE=text.** Indicates that the input field with this parameter should be a text box.

◆ **NAME.** Gives the text box a name that can be referenced in VBScript or server-side code.

◆ **SIZE.** Indicates how long the box should be on the screen. This value is in characters, using the font that is in effect for the input tag. If, for instance, you had an <H1> tag around the input tag, the box would be long enough and tall enough for 40 characters of size H1.

◆ **MAXLENGTH.** Indicates how many characters can be entered into the box.

The following series of tags creates a drop-down list box:

```
<SELECT NAME=data_Version>
        <OPTION>Select Your Version</OPTION>
        <OPTION>---------------------------------</OPTION>
        <OPTION>VBScript</OPTION>
        <OPTION>Version 3.0 Standard</OPTION>
        <OPTION>Version 3.0 Professional</OPTION>
        <OPTION>Version 4.0 Standard</OPTION>
        <OPTION>Version 4.0 Professional</OPTION>
        <OPTION>Version 4.0 Enterprise</OPTION>
</SELECT>
```

In the initial <SELECT> tag, the NAME parameter provides a name that can be used in code. In this case, the <SELECT> tag creates a drop-down list box.

If you want a list box that does not drop down, add the SIZE parameter, as in this example:

```
<SELECT SIZE=4 NAME=data_Version>
        <OPTION>Select Your Version</OPTION>
        <OPTION>---------------------------------</OPTION>
        <OPTION>VBScript</OPTION>
        <OPTION>Version 3.0 Standard</OPTION>
        <OPTION>Version 3.0 Professional</OPTION>
```

```
        <OPTION>Version 4.0 Standard</OPTION>
        <OPTION>Version 4.0 Professional</OPTION>
        <OPTION>Version 4.0 Enterprise</OPTION>
</SELECT>
```

By adding the SIZE=4 tag, you are creating a four-line-high text box instead of a drop-down list box. Because more than four entries exist in the box, a vertical scroll bar is automatically added by the browser.

The following three tags create a series of three radio buttons:

```
<INPUT TYPE=radio NAME="difficulty" VALUE="Low">Low
<INPUT TYPE=radio NAME="difficulty" VALUE="Medium" CHECKED>Medium
<INPUT TYPE=radio NAME="difficulty" VALUE="High">High
```

Radio buttons force the user to choose only one of a set of choices. In this case, the user chooses the difficulty of his question, which can be Low, Medium, or High difficulty. In these tags, the VALUE parameter's value is stored in the "difficulty" variable when the form is submitted.

Finally, radio buttons should never be shown without one of the choices selected. The CHECKED parameter at the end of the second <INPUT> tag forces the Medium difficulty setting to be selected when the form is displayed to the user. Other than showing the controls correctly, adding the CHECKED parameter guarantees that a value will always be selected in the "difficulty" variable. This may, in some cases, make processing this variable easier because you do not have to validate the difficulty variable.

The following tag adds a check box to your form:

```
<INPUT TYPE="CHECKBOX" NAME="SubscriberMailList"
VALUE="SubscriberMailList" CHECKED>
```

Check boxes are used for making true or false choices that are not dependent on other values. Check boxes, for instance, would be used for selecting pizza toppings. You can have pepperoni, sausage, or both. The fact that you have sausage on your pizza does not affect whether or not you can have pepperoni on the same pizza.

The parameters used in this control are similar to those used in the radio button. The NAME parameter provides a way to access the data through code. The VALUE parameter provides the value that will be placed in the variable if this check box is selected. The CHECKED parameter at the end of the tag causes this check box to be selected when it is first displayed.

The <TEXTAREA> tag, shown in the following tag, is used to create a multiline text box.

```
<TEXTAREA NAME="data_Question" COLS=50 ROWS=3></TEXTAREA>
```

In this form, the user can type his question into this large text box, created by the <TEXTAREA> tag. The user can enter an unlimited amount of text in this box. The two parameters, COLS and ROWS, determine only how large the control is on the screen, not the amount of data that the text box can hold. As with the single-line text box, the COLS and ROWS properties are expressed in character lengths, so the <TEXTAREA> tag shown before will create a box tall enough and wide enough to accommodate three rows of 50 characters.

The last controls on the form are the "Submit" and "Clear Form" buttons, shown in the following statement:

```
<INPUT TYPE=submit VALUE="Submit"> <INPUT TYPE=reset VALUE="Clear Form">
```

The Submit button, by default, sends the data in the form to the program specified in the initial <FORM> tag. The TYPE=submit parameter causes this behavior to occur.

The Clear Form button erases all the fields on the form and sets any controls back to their default values. Using the TYPE=reset parameter causes this behavior.

Now that you remember how HTML forms work, it is time to soup up the forms with VBScript.

Submitting Form Data Manually

If you tried using the form in the previous section, you probably noticed that the data was sent immediately when you pressed the Submit button. Although this is useful for non-VBScript enhanced forms, this default behavior causes problems when you want to validate the data before you send it to the server.

When you need to validate data before sending it, you need to submit the data manually. By making some changes to your form, you can use VBScript to send your data to the server. Following is a list of changes that you will need to make to your form so that you may use VBScript instead of the default Submit button:

◆ Name your form so you can access it through VBScript.

◆ Change the button's type from SUBMIT to BUTTON.

◆ Add VBScript code to submit your data to the server.

On the CD

Note The example used in this section is located in the `\Examples\Chapter 17` folder on your hard drive and is named `BasicVBScriptForm.html`.

Naming Your Form

Every element in an HTML document, including form tags, links, and graphics, can have additional parameters added to its tags. If a browser does not understand what to do with the additional parameters, the browser ignores the parameters. One of the tags is the NAME parameter. If you are creating a simple form without VBScript, you do not need to name the form. If, however, you want to add code to your form, you must add the NAME parameter to the initial <FORM> tag. Change the following line:

```
<FORM ACTION=http://www.inquiry.com/pro-bin/echo.pl METHOD=POST>
```

to:

```
<FORM NAME=frmDataEntry ACTION=http://www.inquiry.com/pro-bin/echo.pl
METHOD=POST>
```

When you add the VBScript code to your form, the name of the form is used to access the data that is within it.

Changing the Submit Button's Type

The button labeled Submit on your form is a special button because of the TYPE parameter within the <INPUT> tag. By adding TYPE=submit to this button's tag, the browser automatically calls the program in the <FORM> tag. To use VBScript code to validate the data, you have to perform the submission manually. For this reason, you need to change the Submit button to a simple button instead of a submission button. To do this, change this <INPUT> tag:

```
<INPUT TYPE=submit VALUE="Submit">
```

to the following:

```
<INPUT TYPE=BUTTON VALUE="Submit" NAME=cmdSubmit>
```

If you were to click on the Submit button now, nothing would happen. You have yet to define what this button should do, so your browser simply does nothing.

The last part of the conversion is to add a few lines of VBScript code that actually submit the data to the server when the user presses the Submit button. Add the following code to your form, just before the <BODY> tag of the HTML document:

```
<SCRIPT LANGUAGE=VBScript>
Sub cmdSubmit_onClick()
    frmDataEntry.Submit
End Sub
</SCRIPT>
```

By default, the onClick event of the cmdSubmit button is called when the user presses the Submit button. For this reason, the subroutine is named cmdSubmit_onClick. Because you are not using the ActiveX Control Pad to create this code, you must write this procedure's name manually. It is important to see how the name was derived. The ActiveX Control Pad will automatically create a template for each subroutine you add, including the line with the name of the subroutine. If you are not using the ActiveX Control Pad, you still have to use the same names in order for them to respond to events correctly.

The second line actually submits the form data to the server that was previously specified in the <FORM> tag. Because the form is named frmDataEntry, you use the Submit method of this form to send the data to the server.

At this point, you can save your HTML document and load it into Internet Explorer. If you want to submit the data and see the results, be sure your Internet connection is active. When you press the Submit button, the result is identical to having a form without any VBScript in it. Any data you entered in the form is sent to the server and is printed out. This example was designed to show you the code for validating data in HTML forms using VBScript.

Field Validation Techniques

Now that you see how to send your data to the server with VBScript, it is time to add validation code. Before you can add code, you must decide where to put it. Two common validation options are as follows:

◆ Validation as the user types

◆ Validation when the user submits the data

Both approaches have pros and cons.

Validation as the User Types

This method provides instant feedback to the user regarding what he typed into a control. If, however, the user moves around on the form as he types, he receives warning messages after each mouse click, because the data the user is entering is not complete and is thus illegal. In most cases, this method of validation is not recommended.

Validation When the User Submits the Data

This method eliminates the constant warning messages after the user leaves a field on the form. The use of this method enables the user to make all his changes at the same time.

The examples that follow use a combination of both methods in different circumstances. The first piece of validation you will write verifies that data is in each of the text fields. All fields are required on this form, so each field should be checked before the data goes to the server. All the code that is used to validate the text fields goes into the cmdSubmit_onClick subroutine that you created in the previous section.

On the CD

> **Note** The example used in this section is located in the \Examples\Chapter 15 folder on your CD and is named TextValidation.html.

The first box that needs to be validated is the name box, which here has the name parm_sender_name, which can be used in the code to retrieve the values in the box. Add the following lines of code to the cmdSubmit_onClick event subroutine. Make sure you put them before the frmDataEntry.Submit line. The subroutine should appear as follows when you are done.

```
Sub cmdSubmit_onClick()
   If Len(frmDataEntry.parm_sender_name.Value) = 0 Then
      Alert "Please enter your name."
      frmDataEntry.parm_sender_name.focus
      Exit Sub
   End If
 frmDataEntry.Submit
End Sub
```

When the user clicks the Submit button, the name box is checked before the data is submitted. Each line of code has a particular function, which is explained here:

```
If Len(frmDataEntry.parm_sender_name.Value) = 0 Then
```

The validation code first checks the length of the parm_sender_name box. If no text has been entered by the user, the length is equal to 0. If the length is 0, the lines within the If/Then statement are executed.

```
Alert "Please enter your name."
```

The Alert function automatically displays a message box with the warning icon. This is essentially a shortened version of the MsgBox function that is available in VBScript. The title of the message box is "Microsoft Internet Explorer." If this title is not appropriate, you need to use the MsgBox function instead.

```
frmDataEntry.parm_sender_name.focus
```

After the error message has been displayed, this line of code forces the cursor to jump back to the parm_sender_name box. This makes it easier for the user to make the changes because the cursor is already in the correct position on the form.

```
Exit Sub
```

Finally, because the invalid data should not be submitted, the Exit Sub statement causes the cmdSubmit_onClick subroutine to end. The use of this statement prevents you from having to worry about the frmDataEntry.Submit line, which immediately follows the If/Then block. Alternatively, you could write an Else condition for the If/Then block that would submit the data if the parm_sender_name box was not empty. The alternative coding is as follows:

```
Sub cmdSubmit_onClick()
    If Len(frmDataEntry.parm_sender_name.Value) = 0 Then
        Alert "Please enter your name."
        frmDataEntry.parm_sender_name.focus
    Else
        frmDataEntry.Submit
    End If
End Sub
```

If, however, you have a large number of conditions, as this example does, Exit Sub provides a simple way to quickly stop the subroutine before more errors are encountered.

If you understand how to do one text box's validation, you can do the rest the same way. The code to validate all the text boxes is shown here.

The example used in this section, which includes all the validation code for all the text boxes, is located in the \Examples\Chapter 17 folder on your hard drive and is named TextBoxesValidation.html.

On the CD

```
Sub cmdSubmit_onClick()
    If Len(frmDataEntry.parm_sender_name.Value) = 0 Then
        Alert "Please enter your name."
        frmDataEntry.parm_sender_name.focus
        Exit Sub
    End If
```

```
    If Len(frmDataEntry.parm_sender_email.Value) = 0 Then
        Alert "Please enter your e-mail address."
        frmDataEntry.parm_sender_email.focus
        Exit Sub
    End If
    If Len(frmDataEntry.parm_topic.Value) = 0 Then
        Alert "Please enter the question topic."
        frmDataEntry.parm_topic.focus
        Exit Sub
    End If
    If Len(frmDataEntry.data_Question.Value) = 0 Then
        Alert "Please enter your question."
        frmDataEntry.data_Question.focus
        Exit Sub
    End If
    frmDataEntry.Submit
End Sub
```

To test this form, load it in Internet Explorer and press the Submit button. You get a warning telling you that the name box is empty. Enter your name in the name box and press Submit again. You get an error saying that the e-mail address is blank. Add your e-mail address and press Submit again. You get an error saying that the topic is blank. Finally, enter a value in the topic box and press Submit again. You would expect to get an error because the question box is empty, but the data is sent to the server anyway! Why is this? Because an invisible character was placed in the multiline text box when the form first loaded. In this case, checking the text box's length against zero does not work. You will learn, however, about some alternate validation techniques later in this section.

As far as validating the other fields on the form, take a look at what you actually have to validate:

- VB Version—Need to verify that a choice other than "Select a Version" or the underline entry was selected.

- Difficulty—Already selected when the form is loaded.

- Mailing List Check Box—Selected or unselected are both valid, so no validation is necessary.

As was mentioned previously, the use of default values, such as those used in the radio buttons, saves you from validating the data later.

To validate the drop list choice, use the following code. It should be added just before the frmDataEntry.Submit line in the cmdSubmit_onClick event.

On the
CD

```
Dim sTemp
   sTemp =
frmDataEntry.data_Version.options(frmDataEntry.data_Version.selectedIndex).Text
   If sTemp = "Select Your Version" Or Left(sTemp , 1) = "-" Then
      Alert "Please select the product version."
      frmDataEntry.data_Version.focus
      Exit Sub
   End If
```

This code may look more complicated, but it is still as simple as the rest of the code. First of all, you create a temporary variable (sTemp) that holds the text currently in the drop-down list box. This variable is used later so that the code is more concise. Getting the text from the drop-down list box, however, is somewhat complicated.

```
sTemp =
frmDataEntry.data_Version.options(frmDataEntry.data_Version.selectedIndex).Text
```

This line takes care of getting the text from the drop-down list. Look at this statement, piece by piece:

- ◆ **frmDataEntry.** The form that contains all the controls, including the drop-down list.

- ◆ **data_Version.** The name of the drop-down list box.

- ◆ **options.** This is an array that contains all the entries in the drop-down box. As with all arrays in VBScript, the first entry has an index of zero. The last entry has an index that is one less than the number of entries in the box.

- ◆ **selectedIndex.** This property of the drop-down list holds the index of the currently selected item. By using this value, you can access the appropriate entry of the options array.

- ◆ **Text.** This property of each entry in the options array contains the text that is displayed in the drop-down list box. Check that property to make sure that the user selected a choice other than the first two choices.

```
If sTemp = "Select Your Version" Or Left(sTemp , 1) = "-" Then
```

This line compares the text of the drop-down list's selected item against the known contents of the first two entries of the list. Because you know that the second choice contains a series of dashes, you can just check the first character, as this code illustrates by using the Left function. If one of these two choices was selected by the user, a warning is displayed and the drop-down list is selected.

Alternatively, you could check the selectedIndex property to verify that the user selected a choice other than the first (index 0) or the second (index 1) choices. Here is the code for that method:

```
If frmDataEntry.data_Version.selectedIndex < 2 Then
   Alert "Please select the product version."
   frmDataEntry.data_Version.focus
   Exit Sub
End If
```

This example is somewhat simpler to understand because it does not use the complex object structure used by the drop-down list box. The previous example, however, checks the actual contents of the list and does not rely on the position of the item in the list. In other cases, you may not have a choice but to use the previous method.

At this point, try the form and make sure that it does not let you select "Select Your Version" or the series of dashes. You now have basic validation for your data entry form. The next section deals with specialized validation for e-mail addresses.

Validating E-Mail Addresses

One of the most common fields on Internet data entry forms is a field for a user's e-mail address. Many users, however, do not know how to format their e-mail address correctly, and you end up getting bad, unusable e-mail addresses. This section shows you some ways to validate e-mail address formats so that the user can learn how his e-mail address should be written on the Internet.

No matter what your e-mail address is, it follows the following format:

```
user@host.domain
```

◆ **user.** This is your user ID. It may be a simple word, such as easmith. CompuServe addresses use two numbers separated by a period, and many systems use first and last name, such as Eric.Smith, as the user ID.

◆ **host.** This is typically the name of your Internet domain, such as inquiry or northcomp. The host parameter must be at least one word; however, it can have multiple words separated by spaces, as in mailhost.inquiry.com or www.mcp.com.

◆ **domain.** This final portion of your e-mail address indicates the type of system you are on. Typical domains include .edu (educational institution), .com (commercial sites), .gov (government sites), and .org (non-profit organizations). If you have an e-mail address outside the United States, the last part of your e-mail address will be a two-letter abbreviation that indicates the country in which your domain is located. Following is a list of all the current country codes and domains used on the Internet:

AD	Andorra	BM	Bermuda
AE	United Arab Emirates	BN	Brunei Darussalam
AF	Afghanistan	BO	Bolivia
AG	Antigua and Barbuda	BR	Brazil
AI	Anguilla	BS	Bahamas
AL	Albania	BT	Bhutan
AM	Armenia	BV	Bouvet Island
AN	Netherlands Antilles	BW	Botswana
AO	Angola	BY	Belarus
AQ	Antarctica	BZ	Belize
AR	Argentina	CA	Canada
AS	American Samoa	CC	Cocos (Keeling) Islands
AT	Austria	CF	Central African Republic
AU	Australia	CG	Congo
AW	Aruba	CH	Switzerland
AZ	Azerbaijan	CI	Cote D'Ivoire (Ivory Coast)
BA	Bosnia and Herzegovina	CK	Cook Islands
BB	Barbados	CL	Chile
BD	Bangladesh	CM	Cameroon
BE	Belgium	CN	China
BF	Burkina Faso	CO	Colombia
BG	Bulgaria	CR	Costa Rica
BH	Bahrain	CS	Czechoslovakia (former)
BI	Burundi	CU	Cuba
BJ	Benin	CV	Cape Verde

CX	Christmas Island	GL	Greenland
CY	Cyprus	GM	Gambia
CZ	Czech Republic	GN	Guinea
DE	Germany	GP	Guadeloupe
DJ	Djibouti	GQ	Equatorial Guinea
DK	Denmark	GR	Greece
DM	Dominica	GS	S. Georgia and S. Sandwich Isls.
DO	Dominican Republic		
DZ	Algeria	GT	Guatemala
EC	Ecuador	GU	Guam
EE	Estonia	GW	Guinea-Bissau
EG	Egypt	GY	Guyana
EH	Western Sahara	HK	Hong Kong
ER	Eritrea	HM	Heard and McDonald Islands
ES	Spain	HN	Honduras
ET	Ethiopia	HR	Croatia (Hrvatska)
FI	Finland	HT	Haiti
FJ	Fiji	HU	Hungary
FK	Falkland Islands (Malvinas)	ID	Indonesia
FM	Micronesia	IE	Ireland
FO	Faroe Islands	IL	Israel
FR	France	IN	India
FX	France, Metropolitan	IO	British Indian Ocean Territory
GA	Gabon		
GB	Great Britain (UK)	IQ	Iraq
GD	Grenada	IR	Iran
GE	Georgia	IS	Iceland
GF	French Guiana	IT	Italy
GH	Ghana	JM	Jamaica
GI	Gibraltar	JO	Jordan

JP	Japan	MM	Myanmar
KE	Kenya	MN	Mongolia
KG	Kyrgyzstan	MO	Macau
KH	Cambodia	MP	Northern Mariana Islands
KI	Kiribati	MQ	Martinique
KM	Comoros	MR	Mauritania
KN	Saint Kitts and Nevis	MS	Montserrat
KP	Korea (North)	MT	Malta
KR	Korea (South)	MU	Mauritius
KW	Kuwait	MV	Maldives
KY	Cayman Islands	MW	Malawi
KZ	Kazakhstan	MX	Mexico
LA	Laos	MY	Malaysia
LB	Lebanon	MZ	Mozambique
LC	Saint Lucia	NA	Namibia
LI	Liechtenstein	NC	New Caledonia
LK	Sri Lanka	NE	Niger
LR	Liberia	NF	Norfolk Island
LS	Lesotho	NG	Nigeria
LT	Lithuania	NI	Nicaragua
LU	Luxembourg	NL	Netherlands
LV	Latvia	NO	Norway
LY	Libya	NP	Nepal
MA	Morocco	NR	Nauru
MC	Monaco	NT	Neutral Zone
MD	Moldova	NU	Niue
MG	Madagascar	NZ	New Zealand (Aotearoa)
MH	Marshall Islands	OM	Oman
MK	Macedonia	PA	Panama
ML	Mali	PE	Peru

PF	French Polynesia	SO	Somalia
PG	Papua New Guinea	SR	Suriname
PH	Philippines	ST	Sao Tome and Principe
PK	Pakistan	SU	U.S.S.R (former)
PL	Poland	SV	El Salvador
PM	St. Pierre and Miquelon	SY	Syria
PN	Pitcairn	SZ	Swaziland
PR	Puerto Rico	TC	Turks and Caicos Islands
PT	Portugal	TD	Chad
PW	Palau	TF	French Southern Territories
PY	Paraguay	TG	Togo
QA	Qatar	TH	Thailand
RE	Reunion	TJ	Tajikistan
RO	Romania	TK	Tokelau
RU	Russian Federation	TM	Turkmenistan
RW	Rwanda	TN	Tunisia
SA	Saudi Arabia	TO	Tonga
SB	Solomon Islands	TP	East Timor
SC	Seychelles	TR	Turkey
SD	Sudan	TT	Trinidad and Tobago
SE	Sweden	TV	Tuvalu
SG	Singapore	TW	Taiwan
SH	St. Helena	TZ	Tanzania
SI	Slovenia	UA	Ukraine
SJ	Svalbard and Jan Mayen Islands	UG	Uganda
SK	Slovak Republic	UK	United Kingdom
SL	Sierra Leone	UM	U.S. Minor Outlying Islands
SM	San Marino	US	United States
SN	Senegal	UY	Uruguay
		UZ	Uzbekistan

VA	Vatican City State (Holy See)	ZA	South Africa
VC	Saint Vincent and the Grenadines	ZM	Zambia
		ZR	Zaire
VE	Venezuela	ZW	Zimbabwe
VG	Virgin Islands (British)	COM	U.S. Commercial
VI	Virgin Islands (U.S.)	EDU	U.S. Educational
VN	Vietnam	GOV	U.S. Government
VU	Vanuatu	INT	International
WF	Wallis and Futuna Islands	MIL	U.S. Military
WS	Samoa	NET	Network
YE	Yemen	ORG	Non-Profit Organization
YT	Mayotte	ARPA	Old-Style Arpanet
YU	Yugoslavia	NATO	Nato Field

This list helps you to determine where your visitors are from. Now that you understand how e-mail addresses should be formatted, you can write code to validate these formats and to catch common mistakes.

Based on the standard format for e-mail addresses, a few assumptions can be made about any e-mail address that is entered in your form:

◆ Must be non-zero length

◆ Must have one and only one @ character

◆ Must contain at least one period character

◆ May not contain any spaces

The first part of the validation code checks the last three conditions by using common string manipulation functions. You have already checked the length of the e-mail address, so you do not need to repeat that task.

Checking for a Single @ Character

The quickest way to verify that only one @ character was used in an e-mail address is to write a loop that reads the entire string and looks for the @ character. The code that performs this task follows:

```
Dim i
Dim iAtCount
iAtCount = 0
sTemp = frmDataEntry.parm_sender_email.Value
For i = 1 To Len(sTemp)
   If Mid(sTemp, i, 1) = "@" Then
     iAtCount = iAtCount + 1
     If iAtCount > 1 Then
         Alert "Your e-mail address can only contain one @ character."
         frmDataEntry.parm_sender_email.focus
         Exit Sub
       End If
   End If
Next ' Next i
if iAtCount <> 1 Then
   Alert "Your e-mail address must contain an @ character."
   frmDataEntry.parm_sender_email.focus
   Exit Sub
End If
```

The For loop starts at the beginning of the e-mail address and watches for @ characters. If it gets more than one, it stops immediately and generates an error message. If the loop gets to the end of the e-mail address and no @ character was found, a different error message is shown to the user.

Checking for a Period Character

This task is essentially the same as checking for the @ character, except for the fact that finding more than one period is not necessarily an error. To add the code for this validation, change the loop that you created to check for @ characters. The code from the previous validation with a few minor changes is as follows:

```
Dim i
Dim iAtCount
Dim iPeriods
iAtCount = 0
iPeriods = 0
sTemp = frmDataEntry.parm_sender_email.Value
For i = 1 To Len(sTemp)
  If Mid(sTemp, i, 1) = "@" Then
      iAtCount = iAtCount + 1
      If iAtCount > 1 Then
         Alert "Your e-mail address can only contain one @ character."
          frmDataEntry.parm_sender_email.focus
         Exit Sub
```

```
      End If
   ElseIf Mid(sTemp, i, 1) = "." Then
      iPeriods = iPeriods + 1
   End If
Next ' Next i
if iAtCount <> 1 Then
   Alert "Your e-mail address must contain an @ character."
   frmDataEntry.parm_sender_email.focus
   Exit Sub
End If
If iPeriods < 1 Then
   Alert "Your e-mail address must contain at least one period."
   FrmDataEntry.parm_sender_email.focus
   Exit Sub
End If
```

Adding the two lines of code within the For loop that was already there saves time by checking for both error conditions in the same loop. The code to check for periods is nearly identical to the code that checks for the @ character. If the character is a period, the iPeriods counter increases by one. If, when the loop is done, the iPeriods counter is less than one, an error message is shown to the user.

Checking for Spaces

This final basic check of a user's e-mail address ensures that no spaces are embedded within the address. Because this code is even simpler than the previous two validations, there is no need for a lengthy explanation. Using the previous block of code, make the following changes:

```
Dim i
Dim iAtCount
Dim iPeriods
iAtCount = 0
iPeriods = 0
sTemp = frmDataEntry.parm_sender_email.Value
For i = 1 To Len(sTemp)
   If Mid(sTemp, i, 1) = "@" Then
      iAtCount = iAtCount + 1
      If iAtCount > 1 Then
         Alert "Your e-mail address can only contain one @ character."
         frmDataEntry.parm_sender_email.focus
         Exit Sub
      End If
```

```
    ElseIf Mid(sTemp, i, 1) = "." Then
        iPeriods = iPeriods + 1
    ElseIf Mid(sTemp, I, 1) = " " Then
        Alert "Your e-mail address may not contain any spaces."
        frmDataEntry.parm_sender_email.focus
        Exit Sub
    End If
Next ' Next i
if iAtCount <> 1 Then
    Alert "Your e-mail address must contain an @ character."
    frmDataEntry.parm_sender_email.focus
    Exit Sub
End If
If iPeriods < 1 Then
    Alert "Your e-mail address must contain at least one period."
    FrmDataEntry.parm_sender_email.focus
    Exit Sub
End If
```

After you add the three previous code blocks to your script, you are protected against the most common errors encountered in entering e-mail addresses: spaces, extra @s, and zero period characters.

On the CD

Note The example used in this section, which includes all the validation code for all the e-mail errors, is located in the \Examples\Chapter 17 folder on your hard drive and is named EMailValidation.html.

Validating Phone Numbers

Besides e-mail addresses, you can validate other fields that have a known format. Phone numbers, for instance, all share a common characteristic in that they do not contain alphabetic characters. All phone numbers, however, do not share the North American format of a three-digit area code followed by a seven-digit phone number. For this reason, only validate phone numbers for the three-seven-digit format if you know your form will only be used by users from North America. You can, however, validate phone numbers to be sure they do not contain alphabetic characters.

In the following example, the user's phone number is validated before the data is submitted to the server.

On the CD

> **Note** The example used in this section, which includes all the validation code for all the telephone number errors, is located in the \Examples\Chapter 17 folder on your hard drive and is named PhoneValidation.html.

```
Dim i
Dim sTemp
sTemp = frmDataEntry.txtPhone.Value
For i = 1 to Len(sTemp)
    If UCase(Mid(sTemp, i, 1)) >= "A" And UCase(Mid(sTemp, i, 1)) <= "Z" Then
        Alert "You cannot use alphabetic characters in your phone number."
        frmDataEntry.txtPhone.focus
        Exit Sub
    End If
Next
```

This code checks each character of the phone number to ensure that none of it is alphabetic. By uppercasing each character as you check it, you save yourself from having to check lowercase letters. Like the rest of the validation code, the user receives a warning message and the cursor is placed in the phone number box.

Reformatting Typed Text

For certain pieces of data, such as United States state abbreviations, the data should be stored in a particular format; in this case, the standard is that the two letters be uppercase. The user, however, may or may not be aware of the standard, so you need to help get the data into the right format. This example shows you how to use the onBlur event to perform these changes. The onBlur event is identical to the Exit event used when you are using ActiveX controls.

On the CD

> **Note** The example used in this section is located in the \Examples\Chapter 15 folder on your CD and is named StateUppercaser.html.

```
Sub txtState_onBlur()
    frmDataEntry.txtState.Value = UCase(frmDataEntry.txtState.Value)
End Sub
```

This piece of code is automatically called when the user moves the cursor out of the txtState text box. The Value of the text box is set equal to the uppercased version of itself. This change is immediate when the user moves out of that text box to another control on the form.

Because there could also be validation done at this point within the onBlur event, why should you wait until the user clicks the Submit button to do the validation? Here is an example to illustrate the problem that occurs with this method:

```
Sub txtCity_onBlur()
   If Len(frmDataEntry.txtCity.Value) = 0 Then
      Alert "You must enter a city name."
      frmDataEntry.txtCity.focus
   End If
End Sub
```

On the CD

Note The example used in this section is located in the \Examples\Chapter 17 folder on your hard drive and is named ValidationProblem.html.

If you load this file into your browser, you can easily see the problem that occurs if you click in the City box and then attempt to leave. VBScript keeps warning you that there is no text in the box. The subroutine, however, then puts your cursor back into the text box. The only way to stop this endless cycle is to switch pages or to exit your browser. This is another reason why it is often better to wait until the user has said he is done editing and is ready to send the data to the server.

Summary

This chapter was designed to show you how to enhance your basic HTML forms with VBScript. You learned many validation techniques, as well as why it is important to understand when events are triggered and how to use each one correctly.

One of the benefits of adding VBScript code to your forms for validation is the fact that very little needs to be downloaded besides the page. With this method, you do not have to download the ActiveX layout file or any controls. The code works fine with simple HTML forms and saves download time.

For Visual Basic Programmers:
Many of these tips and techniques are similar to those used in Visual Basic data entry forms. In addition, the idea of using the correct event is also important. Some of the main differences here are the differently named events, such as onBlur rather than LostFocus or Exit. The events, however, still work the same way. The code supplied in the previous examples also is useful for your Visual Basic programs for doing the same types of validation.

CHAPTER 16

Web Database Access

By Jeffrey P. McManus

T his chapter introduces an application that enables users to view and update information in a database through a web browser. You can create this application by using the following combination of tools:

◆ Microsoft Internet Information Server (IIS). IIS comes with Windows NT Server 4. If you have Windows NT 3.51, you can download IIS from `http://www.microsoft.com/infoserv/ iisdlfinal.htm`.

◆ Open Database Connectivity (ODBC)

◆ An ODBC-compliant database system

◆ Internet Database Connector (IDC)

◆ Any web browser

The database application enables users to enter and query records, and then adds a refinement—client-side validation by using a simple VBScript subroutine. Because it utilizes VBScript, this refinement requires that users access your application with Microsoft Internet Explorer 3.0.

Background: Client/Server Computing on the Web

Soon after the World Wide Web became popular, users running web browsers needed a way to exchange data with servers. The servers, in addition to serving HTML web pages, were increasingly called upon to perform new tasks, including database queries and updates.

CGI Scripting

Before the Microsoft Internet Information Server was available, data transfers were generally performed with a standard known as *Common Gateway Interface* (CGI). With CGI, web developers could create programs to exchange data across the web in any one of a number of different languages (including C, Perl, and Visual Basic). Such programs, although not always scripted, are usually referred to as CGI scripts.

CGI scripts are problematic mainly because of efficiency concerns. Consider a CGI script that performs an update to a database. When a web client runs a CGI script on a web server, the web server typically initiates a new process, initializes the database, makes the actual database call, and then retires until another user makes a request. This can be fine for low-volume intranet web servers where a single user's request may monopolize the computing power of the entire server. But for high-volume Internet sites, thousands of users may access the server each minute. CGI scripts can become bogged down under this great demand.

How IIS Works with ISAPI

IIS's approach to client-server transactions takes advantage of Windows NT's multithreaded architecture. Although IIS still supports traditional CGI, it also supports an application programming interface (API) known as *Internet Server Application Programming Interface,* or ISAPI. ISAPI is designed to replace CGI; an ISAPI "script" is actually a *dynamic-link library* (DLL) written in C or C++ that acts as an intermediary between IIS and the other services (such as a database) available on the server side. By writing an ISAPI extension, you can enable web browsers to perform virtually any imaginable task on the server, including database access. ISAPI is more efficient because ISAPI DLLs are loaded into memory by the server at boot time, and because an ISAPI request is handled by the operating system as a thread, instead of a full-fledged process. Threads are processed more efficiently by Windows NT; it is also easier for the operating system to handle multitasking with threads.

ISAPI DLLs cannot be developed in languages such as Visual Basic 4.0. You can, however, use VB to develop applications around an existing ISAPI DLL provided by Microsoft. This DLL, called the Internet Database Connector (HTTPODBC.DLL), serves as the core of the web database application described in this chapter. The Internet Database Connector DLL is installed with Internet Information Server in the \inetsrv\server directory. Be aware that in order for the DLL to be functional, you must move or copy it to the \inetsrv\scripts directory.

> **Note** Although you *can* develop an OLE server DLL that has the capability to interface with another existing ISAPI DLL provided by Microsoft (OLEISAPI.DLL), such an application would have more overhead than the simple query/update application described in this chapter, but could bring the full functionality of Visual Basic to your application.

Creating Your Database Access Application, Homework Helper

In this section, you'll create an example application that will make use of ISAPI technology. This application will enable students to submit questions through a web interface; the questions are then stored in the database until the teacher can answer them. To create this application, you'll go through the following steps:

◆ Configuring the ODBC data source

◆ Developing the Homework Helper Application Interface

◆ Discovering how Homework Helper Works

Configuring Your ODBC Data Source

This application requires you to set up an ODBC data source on your server. You can create an ODBC data source based on almost any database that runs on Windows. The example in this chapter uses Microsoft Access. If you don't have Access on your computer, you need to use another available ODBC-compliant database. Because part of ODBC's function is to make data sources generic to applications, the following procedure is essentially the same.

> **Note** If you want to use Microsoft Access as your database back-end, and you use Microsoft Internet Explorer Version 2.0 (the version that comes with Windows NT 4), you need to obtain an updated version of the Jet database engine. You can download the necessary files via the Internet from `ftp://ftp.microsoft.com/Softlib/MSLFILES/MSJTWNG.EXE`.

To configure an ODBC data source based on a Microsoft Access database, follow these steps:

1. Copy the Microsoft Access database `homework.mdb` to the `\wwwroot\homework` directory on your server. You don't necessarily need to place the database file in the directory structure under the server, but for this example application, it helps to keep everything in one place.

> **Note** The database `homework.mdb` has just one table, tblHelpRequest. This table has five fields: FName, LName, Email, Question, and DateTime. The DateTime field is not visible to the user; it is filled in automatically by the database engine whenever the user creates a record. (In Access, this means that the field's Default Value is set to Now.)

2. Launch the Windows Control Panel.

3. Choose the ODBC icon.

4. Click on System DSN when the Data Sources dialog box appears (see fig. 16.1).

> **Note** It's important to configure the ODBC data source for your web application as a System DSN. This is because normal ODBC data sources are visible only to the individual user who creates the data source, although System DSNs are visible to all users. This includes users who access your database through the web. System DSNs became available in ODBC 2.5. ODBC 2.5 comes with SQL Server 6.0 and with Microsoft Office 95. It also can be downloaded from `http://ftp.microsoft.com/SOFTLIB/MSLFILES/ODBC25.EXE`.

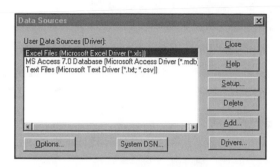

Figure 16.1

The ODBC Data Sources dialog box.

5. Click on Add. The Add Data Source dialog box will appear (see fig. 16.2).

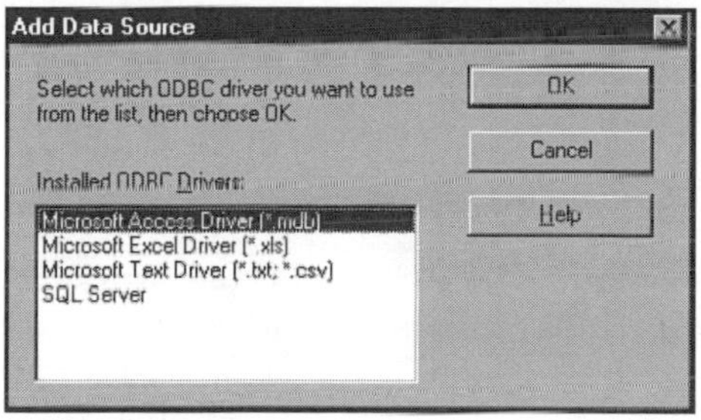

Figure 16.2

The ODBC Add Data Source dialog box.

6. Choose the Microsoft Access Driver (*.mdb) from the list, and then click OK.

7. The ODBC Microsoft Access 7.0 Setup dialog box will appear (see fig. 16.3).

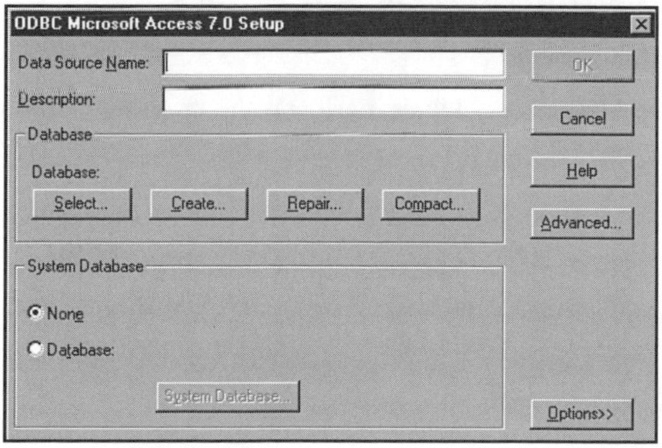

Figure 16.3

The ODBC Microsoft Access 7.0 Setup dialog box.

8. In the Data Source Name text box, type **homework**.

9. In the Description text box, type **Homework Helper**.

10. In the Database panel, click the Select button. Browse until you find the `homework.mdb` file that you previously copied to `\inetsrv\wwwroot\homework`. Click OK.

11. You're back at the ODBC Microsoft Access 7.0 Setup dialog box. In the System Database panel, click the Database radio button, then click the System Database button.

12. Browse until you find the file `system.mdw`. This file comes with Microsoft Access 7; it should exist in your Access directory. (In previous versions of Access, it is called `system.mda`.)

13. Click OK in the Browse dialog box, and then click OK in the ODBC Microsoft Access 7.0 Setup dialog box. Click in the System Data Sources dialog box. Finally, click Close in the Data Sources dialog box.

Your ODBC data source should now be configured. If you want to make sure it connects to the database properly, use another ODBC-compliant client application. Microsoft Excel works well for this purpose. The command to connect to an ODBC data source in Excel 95 is Data, Get External Data. This will provide a dialog box of ODBC data sources. If yours appears in the list, you've done it properly and you're ready to proceed.

Dissecting the Homework Helper Application

The sample application, Homework Helper, performs the most basic operations of a database application—querying and inserting records. This section describes the various files that comprise this application. The files that comprise the application are:

◆ The data-entry interface, `homework.htm`. For this example, this file resides in the directory `\wwwroot\homework`, but you can install it to any directory you want. To view this file through a web browser, use the following URL:

```
http://yourserver.com/homework/homework.htm
```

> **Note** It's important to use the http:// prefix when viewing files in this example; using the File, Open command in your browser won't work. This is because running server-side scripts requires the intervention of the web server. If you open the file in your web browser, the server doesn't get involved, and it consequently can't run your script.

◆ The IDC script file that maintains the ODBC connection and SQL data, question.idc. This file should reside in the \scripts directory under your IIS directory (typically \inetsrv\scripts).

> **Note** It's important to install scripts into a directory that has Execute access; by default, the \scripts directory has such access (the \wwwroot directory does not). You can give a directory Execute access in Internet Service Manager; choose the WWW service, click the Directories tab, and then click the Add button.

◆ The HTML template file that returns results to the user is called question.htx, and is found on the CD that comes with this book. This file should also be installed in the \scripts directory.

On the CD

◆ The IDC DLL, httpodbc.dll. This file should be installed into the \scripts directory.

◆ The Microsoft Access database file homework.mdb. This file can exist in any directory, as long as you've configured the ODBC data source correctly (as outlined in the preceding instructions).

How Homework Helper Works

This section describes the user-interface of the homework application. To submit a request, the student starts her web browser and loads the web page homework.htm. This page contains a form with a number of text boxes and a textarea control (see fig. 16.4).

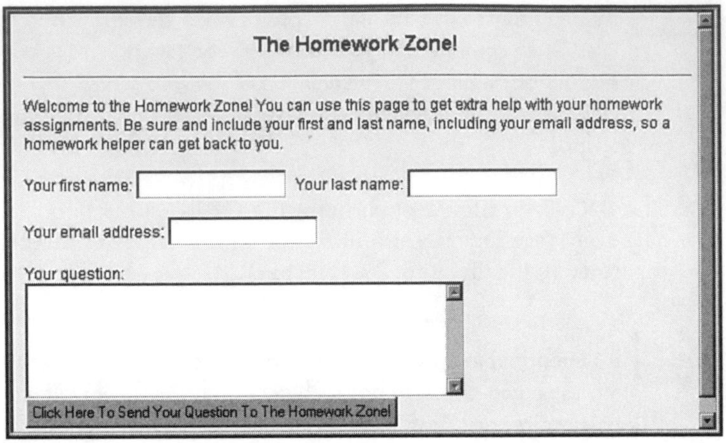

Figure 16.4

Data-entry interface in homework.htm.

The HTML for homework.htm looks like this:

```
<html>
<head>
<title>The Homework Zone</title>
</head>

<body TEXT="#000000" LINK="#FF0000" BGCOLOR="#FFF4C8">
<font face="Arial,Helvetica">
<center><font size=5><b>The Homework Zone!</b></font></center><hr>

Welcome to the Homework Zone! You can use this page to get extra help with your
homework assignments. Be sure to include your first and last name, including
your e-mail address, so a homework helper can get back to you.<p>
<form action="/scripts/question.idc" method="post" name="frmSubmit">
Your first name: <input type="text" name=txtFName> Your last name: <input
➥type="text"
name=txtLName><p>

Your email address: <input type="text" name=txtEmail><p>

Your question:<br>
<textarea cols=70 rows=5 name=txtQuestion wrap=virtual></textarea><br>.

<input type="submit" value="Click Here To Send Your Question To The Homework
➥Zone!">
</form>
```

```
</body>
</html>
```

Most of this HTML is cosmetic, except for what's in the <form> tag. You can see that when the form is submitted, it runs an IDC script, `question.idc`. The form run this script based on the contents of the <action> tag. The parameter `method="post"` means that the result generated by this form is to be sent (or "posted") back to the server.

Giving the form a name by using the parameter `name="frmSubmit"` facilitates validation using VBScript, because in order to validate the data using a VBScript procedure, your form must have a name. You'll add this procedure later in this chapter.

For now, take a look at the IDC script called by this form. The following script, `question.idc`, contains all the information required to connect to the data source and execute an SQL statement through ODBC. The file looks like this:

```
; Internet Database Connector File for Homework sample application
; October 15, 1996, Jeffrey P. McManus
; This is a comment.
;
Datasource: homework
Template: question.htx
SQLStatement:
+INSERT INTO tblHelpRequest
+(FName, LName, Email, Question)
+VALUES ('%txtFName%', '%txtLName%', '%txtEmail%', '%txtQuestion%');
```

In the preceding code, the `Datasource:` entry is the name of the ODBC data source you configured previously, and the `Template:` entry is the name of an HTML file that is displayed to the user after the database transaction takes place.

The `SQLStatement:` entry is the name of an SQL statement recognized by your database back-end. Note that this application uses a Microsoft Access database; however, you can use any ODBC-compliant database—such is the beauty of ODBC.

In this case, `SQLStatement` simply inserts values from the form and writes them to the database. You can insert the values of form fields into statements in the IDC script by using variables bounded by percentage signs (%); for example, the expression %txtFName% refers to the contents of the text control `txtFName`.

The previous code is an example of a minimal IDC file; there are other fields that can appear in a script. If, for example, you require a user to log onto a database through the web (maybe in a situation where you have an SQL Server database), you can include the Username: and Password: fields in your script, as shown in the following code.

```
; IDC file for logging on to SQL Server

; October 15, 1996, Jeffrey P. McManus
;
Datasource: homework
Username: dbuser
Password: antwerp
Template: question.htx
SQLStatement:
+INSERT INTO tblHelpRequest
+(FName, LName, Email, Question)
+VALUES ('%txtFName%', '%txtLName%', '%txtEmail%',
➥'%txtQuestion%');
```

Other optional IDC fields are documented in the IIS help file inetmgr.hlp, in \inetsrv\admin.

After the transaction takes place, another HTML page is displayed to the user. This page is based on the template question.htx:

```
<html>
<head>
<title>
Homework Zone - Question Received
</title>

<body bgcolor="#FFF4C8">
<center>
<b>Thanks for sending in your question!</b><p>

We'll reply to your question in email as soon as we can.<p>

<a href="/scripts/homework.idc">View outstanding questions</a><br>
<a href="/homework/homework.htm">Return To Homework Zone Home Page</a>
</center>
```

```
</body>
</html>
```

The output of this template isn't particularly impressive (see fig. 16.5). It just gives the user the option to return to the data entry interface (in `homework.htm`) or to run another IDC script (in `homework.idc`). But it does demonstrate how to create a multipage interface.

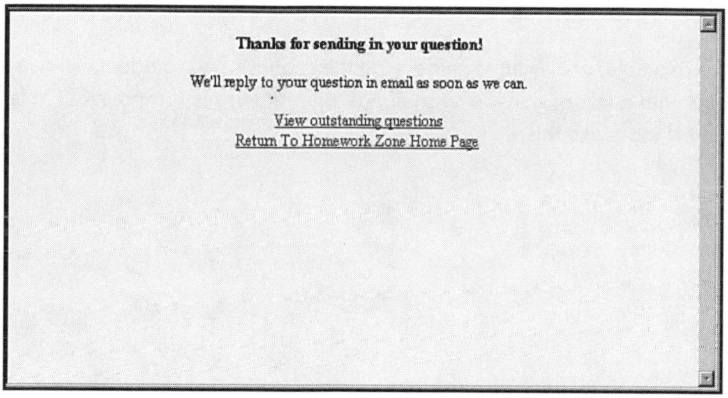

Figure 16.5

The result of script `question.idc` *and the result of template* `question.htx`.

The user can go on to view the questions that have been submitted so far by clicking on the link to the script `homework.idc`. This generates a formatted table (based on the template in `homework.htx`) containing all the records in the database. Because it's just a SQL SELECT statement, `homework.idc` is a little simpler than `question.idc`:

```
Datasource: homework
Template: homework.htx
SQLStatement:
+SELECT *
+FROM "tblHelpRequest"
+ORDER BY DateTime DESC;
```

The IDC script retrieves all the records from tblHelpRequest, ordering them in descending order by the DateTime field. Remember, the DateTime field is hidden from the user; it is filled in by the database engine each time the user creates a record.

In database queries, a wildcard character is used in place or in addition to a search parameter; such characters indicate that you want to retrieve data similar to a criteria you specify. For example, to retrieve records containing the text "hot foot," "hot dog," and "hothead," you'd use the wildcard criteria "hot%" or "hot*" depending on how your database system implements wildcard characters.

To use a wildcard character in an IDC script, you must delimit the variable name with three percent signs. This is because the percent sign is the wildcard character in ODBC.

Assume, for example, you want to retrieve all the requests from students whose first name begins with a letter you type. A minimal query interface (on your CD, it is `wildcard.htm`) looks like this:

```
<html>
<title>
Wildcard Query Example
</title>

<body>

<FORM METHOD="POST" ACTION="/scripts/wildcard.idc">
    <P>Enter the first few letters of the student's first name:
    ➡<INPUT NAME="txtFName">
    <P><INPUT TYPE="SUBMIT" VALUE="Submit">
</FORM>

</body>
</html>
```

The corresponding IDC file (`wildcard.idc`) follows. (Note that this IDC uses the same output template, `homework.htx`, as the previous example.)

```
Datasource: homework
Template: homework.htx
SQLStatement:
+SELECT *
+FROM "tblHelpRequest"
+WHERE FName Like '%txtFName%%'
+ORDER BY DateTime DESC;    + SELECT * from tblHelpRequest
```

After it queries the database, `question.idc` sends its output to the template `homework.htx`. This template formats the data into a tidy HTML table (see fig. 16.6):

```html
<html>
<head>
<title>
Homework Zone - Pending Help Requests
</title>

<body bgcolor="#FFF4C8">
<font face="Arial,Helvetica">

<table border>
<tr>
<td bgcolor="#fedea0">
Student's Name
</td>
<td bgcolor="#fedea0">
Email
</td>
<td bgcolor="#fedea0">
Question
</td>
<%begindetail%>
<tr>

<td bgcolor="#ffffff">
<%FName%> <%LName%>
</td>

<td bgcolor="#ffffff">
<a href="mailto:<%Email%>"><%EMail%></a>
</td>

<td bgcolor="#ffffff">
<%Question%>
</td>
</tr>
<%enddetail%>
</table>
<p>
Back to <a href="/homework/homework.htm">Homework Zone Home Page</a>

</body>
</html>
```

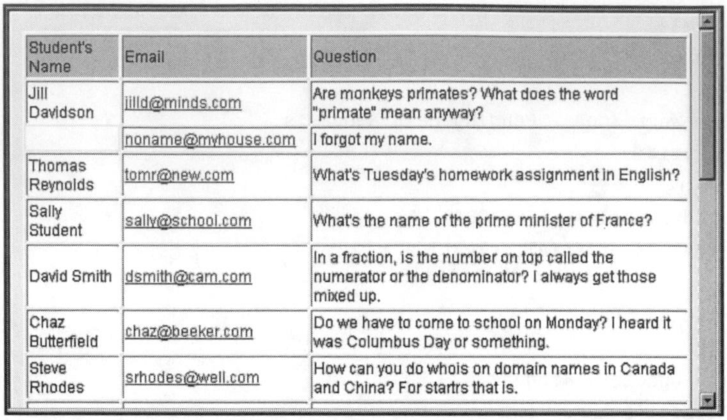

Figure 16.6

The result of script homework.idc *and the result of template* homework.htx*.*

Student's Name	Email	Question
Jill Davidson	jilld@minds.com	Are monkeys primates? What does the word "primate" mean anyway?
	noname@myhouse.com	I forgot my name.
Thomas Reynolds	tomr@new.com	What's Tuesday's homework assignment in English?
Sally Student	sally@school.com	What's the name of the prime minister of France?
David Smith	dsmith@cam.com	In a fraction, is the number on top called the numerator or the denominator? I always get those mixed up.
Chaz Butterfield	chaz@beeker.com	Do we have to come to school on Monday? I heard it was Columbus Day or something.
Steve Rhodes	srhodes@well.com	How can you do whois on domain names in Canada and China? For startrs that is.

Using Conditional Logic in the HTX File

The HTX file has the capability to perform rudimentary logic based on the output from the database. You can use this feature to perform a number of functions; in the example, conditional logic is used to display different output values if a value is missing in a particular database field.

If...Then, equality, and inequality comparisons are supported. In the template homework.htx, for example, it's possible that one or more of the fields can be null. To include a conditional statement that provides output indicating whether or not a field contains data, change the code from the following:

```
<%begindetail%>
<tr>

<td bgcolor="#ffffff">
<%FName%> <%LName%>
</td>
```

to this:

```
<%begindetail%>
<tr>

<td bgcolor="#ffffff">
<%If FName EQ ""%>
   
<%Else%>
```

```
  <%FName%>
<%Endif%>

<%If LName EQ "">
   
<%Else%>
  <%LName%>
<%Endif%>
</td>
```

This code enhancement is on your CD and is called `hwk2.htx`; it works with the files `wc2.idc` and `wc2.htm`.

Using Operators in an HTX File

HTX files don't support as many expressions as a full programming language such as Visual Basic, but there are enough basic operators to enable the incorporation of primitive logic. The available operators are:

if/else/endif	conditional logic
EQ	equivalent to
LT	less than
GT	greater than
CONTAINS	any part of the string contains another string

Using HTTP_USER_AGENT to Determine Browser Type

You can use variables generated by the interaction between the client and the server in the HTX file. Such variables are called HTTP variables. One useful HTTP variable is HTTP_USER_AGENT. This variable contains the name of the browser that is used to access your web site.

You can incorporate variables in conditional statements in your HTX file. To determine, for example, if the user is browsing with Microsoft Internet Explorer, use the following conditional statement in your HTX code:

```
<%if HTTP_USER_AGENT contains "MSIE"%>
 Continue on to the next page.
<%else%>
 Warning! This site doesn't work properly with web browsers other than
Microsoft Internet Explorer 3.0.
<%endif%>
```

The HTTP_USER_AGENT string returned by Microsoft Internet Explorer is "Mozilla 2.0 (compatible; MSIE 3.0; Windows 95)." Be careful, though, not to hard-wire your script to look for "MSIE 3.0." Newer versions may be introduced at any time and break your script.

To test if the user is browsing with a Netscape-compatible browser, your script should check to see if HTTP_USER_AGENT contains "Mozilla."

Adding VBScript Validation to the Client Web Page

Now that you have a functional web database application that accepts query and update requests from users, you can enhance it by adding a VBScript validation routine. Because the VBScript code resides in the HTML file and is executed entirely by the client, the server should never receive invalid data (as long as your validation procedure is written correctly). Catching data-entry goofs on the client side can significantly reduce the load on the server, particularly in situations where users are frequently prone to committing data-entry errors.

This enhancement involves making changes to *only* the data-entry interface homework.htm; the IDC and HTX files remain unchanged.

Note If a user's browser does not support VBScript (this includes any browser other than Microsoft Internet Explorer 3.0), then any validation routines inserted in your web page will be ignored by the browser. This is an important consideration when deploying your application. If you know that all your users only use MSIE 3.0, then there is no problem (for example, your application runs on an intranet in an organization whose standard is MSIE 3.0). Otherwise, be sure to consider that users might not be looking at your interface through a browser that understands VBScript.

The validation example shown in this section performs the most basic kind of validation—ensuring that the user does not enter a blank field. In addition to client-side validation, you may want to consider adding validation at the database engine level. In Microsoft Access, this entails setting the "Allow Zero Length" property of the E-mail and Question fields to No.

The first modification to homework.htm is to convert the input control at the bottom of the form to a conventional button control. This is necessary because the form submission will be intercepted by a VBScript validation procedure, instead of enabling the form submission control to send the form directly to the server. To do this, change the button from a SUBMIT to a plain old button. Therefore, change the code:

```
<input type="SUBMIT" value="Click Here To Send Your Question To
➥The Homework Zone!">
```

to this:

```
<input type="BUTTON" name="cmdSubmit" value="Click Here To Send
➥Your Question To The Homework Zone!">
```

Note that in addition to changing the control type from SUBMIT to BUTTON, we also give the button a name, cmdSubmit. This is so you can attach a VBScript event procedure to the button.

The VBScript validation is inserted into homework.htm just after the </form> tag (see fig. 16.7). Its code looks like this:

```
<SCRIPT LANGUAGE="VBScript">
<!--
Sub cmdSubmit_OnClick()
 Dim MyForm, ErrorFlag, ErrorMsg, vbExclamation

 vbExclamation = 48
 ErrorMsg = "Whoops! Try again!"

 Set MyForm = Document.frmSubmit
 ErrorFlag = False

 If MyForm.txtEmail.Value = "" Then
  x = MsgBox ("Please type in your email address.", vbExclamation, ErrorMsg)
  ErrorFlag = True
 End If

 If MyForm.txtQuestion.Value = "" Then
  x = MsgBox ("Don't forget to type in a question!", vbExclamation, ErrorMsg)
  ErrorFlag = True
 End If

 If ErrorFlag = True Then
  ' do nothing
 Else
```

```
  ' submit the form
  MyForm.Submit
End If


End Sub
-->
</SCRIPT>
```

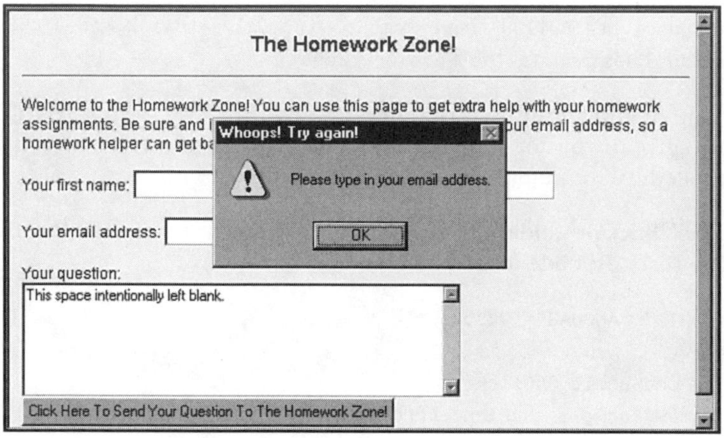

Figure 16.7

*User triggering
VBScript
validation in
modified version
of homework.htm.*

How cmdSubmit_OnClick() Works

The validation procedure examines the contents of the text boxes txtEmail and
txtQuestion. If either (or both) of the text boxes are empty, the procedure displays a
message box informing the user that input is required. The user must submit at least
an e-mail address and a homework question; if the requester fails to type in his first or
last name, it's no big deal.

The procedure revolves around the fact that VBScript can treat an HTML form as an
object variable. Most CGI applications blindly submit a form to the server. VBScript
instead programmatically evaluates the contents of the controls on the form before
sending it to the server. It then submits the form to the server using the Submit
method of the Form object.

Create a variable that refers to the form using this code:

```
Dim MyForm
Set MyForm = Document.frmSubmit
```

The Dim statement declares, or dimensions, a variable. This is the statement you use in all dialects of Visual Basic to declare a variable. Although you're not required to declare variables in Visual Basic, it can help make your code clearer.

After this Set statement has been executed, you can refer to MyForm rather than Document.frmSubmit. It's not necessary to Dim the variable, but it's good programming practice, and it saves you typing later.

After your validation procedure has run, the form must be submitted. To send the form to the server, you use the Submit method of the form object:

```
MyForm.Submit
```

The complete, revised, VBScript version of homework.htm looks like this:

```
<html>
<head>
<title>The Homework Zone</title>
</head>

<body TEXT="#000000" LINK="#FF0000" BGCOLOR="#FFF4C8">
<font face="Arial,Helvetica">

<center>
<font size=5><b>The Homework Zone!</b></font>
</center>

<hr>

Welcome to the Homework Zone! You can use this page to get extra help with your
homework assignments. Be sure to include your first and last name, including
your e-mail address, so a homework helper can get back to you.<p>

<form name="frmSubmit" action="/scripts/question.idc" method="post">

Your first name: <input type="text" name=txtFName> Your last name: <input
➥type="text" name=txtLName><p>

Your email address: <input type="text" name=txtEmail><p>

Your question:<br>
<textarea cols=70 rows=5 name=txtQuestion wrap=virtual></textarea><br>
```

```
<input type="BUTTON" name="cmdSubmit" value="Click Here To Send Your Question
➥To The Homework Zone!">

</form>

<SCRIPT LANGUAGE="VBScript">
<!--
Sub cmdSubmit_OnClick()
 Dim MyForm, ErrorFlag, ErrorMsg, vbExclamation

 vbExclamation = 48
 ErrorMsg = "Whoops! Try again!"

 Set MyForm = Document.frmSubmit
 ErrorFlag = False

 If MyForm.txtEmail.Value = "" Then
  x = MsgBox ("Please type in your email address.", vbExclamation, ErrorMsg)
  ErrorFlag = True
 End If

 If MyForm.txtQuestion.Value = "" Then
  x = MsgBox ("Don't forget to type in a question!", vbExclamation, ErrorMsg)
  ErrorFlag = True
 End If

 If ErrorFlag = True Then
  ' do nothing
 Else
  ' submit the form
  MyForm.Submit
 End If

End Sub
-->
</SCRIPT>

</body>
</html>
```

This procedure can be easily modified to accommodate more complicated validation. If, for example, you want to ensure that only users from a particular domain are allowed to submit questions, add another If...Then statement that analyzes the e-mail address:

```
If Right(MyForm.txtEmail.Value, 10) <> "wilson.edu" Then
 x = MsgBox ("Sorry, we can only accept questions from Wilson Middle School
 ➥students.",
 vbExclamation, ErrorMsg)
 ErrorFlag = True
End If
```

Although the logic provided by IDC isn't nearly as robust as one provided by a full-featured programming language, it is adequate for many basic applications requiring database access. (In fact, if you browse the Microsoft web site at www.microsoft.com, you'll find quite a few interfaces based on IDC.) Be aware that there is another ISAPI DLL available from Microsoft called OLEISAPI.DLL that acts as an interface between IIS and an OLE server DLL. Because you can write OLE server DLLs in Visual Basic 4.0, opportunities beyond IDC await you.

Note

For more information on VBScript and IDC, check out the Microsoft web site at http://www.microsoft.com/vbscript/. This site has a large amount of information on how to use VBScript in web pages, as well as links to related sites. It also contains information on how VBScript relates to other existing and emerging technologies, such as IDC. Because this stuff changes so fast, you have to keep your ear to the ground, and the web is the best way to do it.

CHAPTER 17

Server-Side Scripting

Most of this book has been dedicated to teaching you how to write scripts with HTML. In this chapter, you learn how to use the same scripting language—VBScript—to create web applications that run on the server side. This opens up a whole new world of possibilities, and provides more options for you as a developer who puts your web applications together.

This chapter begins by describing what server-side scripting is and how it differs from client-side scripting. You are introduced to .ASP files, how they work, and what sort of HTML they produce. You'll also learn how .ASP files make it possible to write code that accepts information from HTML forms.

Next you will see how to make use of each of the intrinsic objects built into Microsoft Internet Information Server 3.0. These, combined with ActiveX Server Components, make it possible to create .ASP files that offer truly dynamic pages for your users.

Finally, this chapter tells you about the GLOBAL.ASA file and offers some suggestions on debugging and error handling.

Initial Setup Requirements

Before you do anything in this chapter, you should know that server-side scripting technologies are only available to you if you are writing pages that will be executed on a Windows NT web server, and running Internet Information Server version 3.0.

If your pages are being hosted on another site that is not running the preceding configuration, you have to stick to client-side scripting and do your server-side work with CGI applications, or another technology offered by your provider.

In addition, when you are creating and testing .ASP files, you must create access to them in your browser *through the server*. In other words, you must either type the address of the page into the line at the top of the browser *or* click on a link that pulls up the page. You cannot do a File, Open or drag-and-drop the page to your browser, as you may have done when testing client-side scripts. This is because both File, Open and drag-and-drop bypasses the server altogether and the server-side parts of the .ASP file do not get processed.

> **Note**   This chapter was created with a pre-beta version of Microsoft Internet Information Server 3.0. At the time of this writing, many features were not yet implemented and some of the interfaces were not yet defined. Many of the interfaces that are defined do not work yet. This chapter is simply intended to give you a first look and an overview of this exciting new technology. Remember that some things will have changed by the time you read this and other things will certainly have been added to the ActiveX Server capabilities.

Defining a Server-Side Script

A little bit of time is spent at beginning of this chapter describing what a server-side script is, what it does, and how you can put it to use. It is easy to get confused about what happens in server-side scripting if you are used to client-side scripting, so pay careful attention to the following section. Here are the topics that will be covered:

- How ASP files differ from web pages

- What ASP files consist of

- How variables can be used

ASP Files versus Web Pages

The first thing you should know is that server-side scripting is not done in HTML pages. It is done in the .ASP page. ASP stands for **Active Server Page**. The .ASP is not a web page itself; it is a *meta-page*—meaning that the .ASP contains code that describes how to create the HTML page that will be sent to the browser. When the person browsing your site chooses View Source from the browser's menu, they do not see the .ASP. They see the HTML page it produced. That is true, even though the URL address listed at the top of the browser window will look like this:

```
www.microsoft.com/news/tech.asp
```

So the .ASP file is listed as the page you are accessing, even though the .ASP file is not what you see when you view the source. Again, what you are seeing when you View Source is the page that the .ASP *produced*.

Inside an .ASP

So what does an .ASP file look like? Take a look at the following example of a simple .ASP file.

```
<HTML>

<HEAD>
<TITLE>Unpredictable Greeting</TITLE>
</HEAD>
<%
randomize

dim greet

greet = int(rnd * 3)+1
%>
<BODY BGCOLOR=#ffffff TEXT=#0 >

<% select case greet %>
<% case 1 %>
   <h1>Hello Everybody!</h1>
<% case 2 %>
   <h1>Hey You! How ya doin'?</h1>
<% case 3 %>
```

```
    <h1>Whasssup?</h1>
<% end select %>

</BODY>

</HTML>
```

The first thing you should notice about the listing is all the <% and %> symbols. These symbols are used to enclose any server-side VBScript code that appears in the .ASP file. Anything outside the symbols is considered HTML output that may become a part of the final page.

In this page, a random number between 1 and 3 is generated and then a greeting is chosen by using a Select…Case statement. That greeting, because it is outside the <% and %> symbols is printed as if it were normal HTML header. When you bring up this page in your browser, notice that only one greeting is displayed. And if you hit refresh several times, it appears differently each time you display it. The conditional VBScript code is determining which HTML header gets displayed each time.

Now, after you bring it up in your browser, choose View Source from the Browser menu to see the source code of the page. You should see something that looks like the following example, which illustrates the HTML produced by the .ASP file in the preceding example.

```
<HTML>

<HEAD>
<TITLE>Unpredictable Greeting</TITLE>
</HEAD>

<BODY BGCOLOR=#ffffff TEXT=#0 >


    Whassup?


</BODY>

</HTML>
```

The only HTML in the final page is that which was generated from the .ASP file. The VBScript inside the <% and %> symbols, which was in the .ASP, is not visible in the final HTML page when you view the source. That's because it was executed on the server for the purpose of creating the *new* HTML file, which you see in the preceding listing.

This technique of using .ASP files to produce HTML provides several advantages. First, all that work is done on the server and only the final results are sent back to the browser. That means less information is sent over the network, enabling your page to come up faster. In addition, if there is complex or proprietary code that you don't want those who browse your pages to have access to, they won't. They only see the results, not the code that you executed to come up with the results.

> **Tip** Although the <% and %> delimiters are the preferred way of setting your server-side VBScript code apart from the rest of the page, the following is another, more familiar syntax that you can use:
>
> ```
> <SCRIPT LANGUAGE=VBScript RUNAT=Server>
>
> ...
>
> </SCRIPT>
> ```
>
> This tag is exactly the same one that you use in client-side scripting, but it has the additional RUNAT property, which specifies that the script is to be run on the server. If you don't include the RUNAT property, the script executes on the client-side.
>
> Although this syntax is probably more familiar to you, you will probably find it more cumbersome to use than the <% and %> delimiters, especially if you are beginning and ending scripts in the middle of your HTML so often.

Using Variables

Variables may be declared by using the Dim statement or implicitly by referring to a variable by name. It is usually considered better programming practice to declare your variables before you use them. Server-side scripting, however, does *not* support Option Explicit, which is used to force you to declare a variable before you use it. You must remember to declare the variable on your own.

Variables can be useful for holding information and making decisions. You may need to use variables with your HTML. How do you do that?

Actually it is easy. Whenever a block of VBScript code inside the <% and %> symbols begins with an equals sign, that tells the interpreter that the code should be replaced in the final page with the result of the calculations. So if you want to print the value of a variable called *FinalTotal*, you can do it like this:

```
<h3>FinalTotal is equal to <% = FinalTotal %> </h3>
```

If *FinalTotal* has the value 3742, the final HTML produced looks like this:

```
<h3>FinalTotal is equal to 3742 </h3>
```

You can do the same thing with a function that returns a value. If, for instance, you want to provide the current time on your page, you can use the VBScript Now function.

```
The time is now <% = Now %>
```

And you can use an entire expression inside the <% = and %> signs.

```
The result is <% = 5 + Temp * Sqr(Mass) %>
```

Suppose you wanted to extend the preceding program so that it would choose a random background, text color, and font size for the page and a random greeting? Take a look at the following example:.

```
<HTML>

<HEAD>
<TITLE>Unpredictable Greeting</TITLE>
</HEAD>
<%
Dim greet, bclr, fclr, fsz

randomize

greet = int(rnd * 3)+1
bclr = int(rnd * 2000000)+1
fclr = int(rnd * 2000000)+1
fsz = int(rnd*7) + 1
%>
<BODY BGCOLOR=#<% = hex(bclr) %> TEXT=#<% = hex(fclr) %> >
<FONT SIZE= <% = fsz %> >

<% select case greet %>
<% case 1 %>
   Hello Everybody!
<% case 2 %>
   Hey You! How ya doin'?
<% case 3 %>
   Whasssup?
<% end select %>

</BODY>

</HTML>
```

After getting a random number for the greeting, two random colors are generated. Because a long integer is the type of variable that is used to hold a color and it can have a value up to about 2 million, I generate a number between 1 and 2 million for the background and foreground text. I also generate a number between 1 and 7 to indicate the size of the font.

I then close off the VBScript code and write the BODY HTML tag, which will use all the colors that have been generated. I take the value in `bclr` and `fclr` and convert them to hexadecimal using the VBScript function `Hex`. I do this because that is what the HTML is expecting—a hexadecimal value, not a decimal value. The values are placed after `BGCOLOR=#` and `TEXT=#` properties of the BODY tag.

Finally, the font size is set and the greeting is displayed.

When you try this page out, again, keep clicking Refresh. Now not only will the greeting change, but also its size, color, and background.

ActiveX Server Scripts and Forms

Forms are an important part of any web page that wants communication to be more than a one-way street. Forms enable you to easily accept information from a user.

The problem is, after you accept information from users, what do you do with the form? Client-side scripting can't help you here. It can help you to validate and format the data before it is shipped off to the server, but it can't process the information once it is submitted.

Server-side scripting can help you put the information that you have gathered to use. Although you could use a CGI application or an ISAPI DLL to handle your user's input, an ActiveX server script is much simpler, more straightforward, and much easier for non-programmers to maintain.

The question is, how do you access information that is provided by a form? Suppose, for instance, that a page like the one in the following example is used to get information from a browsing user.

```
<HTML>
<HEAD><TITLE>Guest Book</TITLE></HEAD>

<BODY>
<H2>Sign My Guest Book</H2>
<P>
Please enter your name and e-mail address, then hit Submit.
```

```
<FORM METHOD="POST" ACTION="answer.asp">
<P>
Name: <INPUT NAME="name" SIZE="60">
<P>
E-mail: <INPUT NAME="email" SIZE="60">
<P>
<INPUT TYPE=SUBMIT><INPUT TYPE=RESET>
</FORM>

</BODY>

</HTML>
```

Nothing unusual here. Just a normal form with two fields on it to accept the user's name and e-mail address. The only thing you may notice is that instead of a CGI application or ISAPI application in the ACTION attribute, there is an .ASP. So what does the .ASP look like? See the following example, which illustrates an .ASP that responds to a form.

```
<HTML>
<HEAD><TITLE>Response To Guestbook Submit</TITLE></HEAD>
<BODY>
<H2><CENTER>Guestbook Entry Received</CENTER></H2>
<P>
Information Received:<p>
<%
Dim first, email
first = request.form("name")
email = request.form("email")
%>

Name: <% = first %><br>
E-mail: <% = email %>
</BODY>
</HTML>
```

A Request object is available to you when you create .ASP files. This object enables you to retrieve the values that the client browser passes to the server during an HTTP request. In this case, that means the values entered in the form. Other kinds of data that may be passed back to the server from the client include the information in a client certificate, cookies, a query string for database access, or environment variables.

Form is the name of the collection inside the Request object that holds the fields on the form. You must specify the name of the field you want as a string. In response, you get the value entered for that field. In this page, it is used to provide a confirmation page that reads back what the user entered.

If this were a real guest book, you could have used the TextStream or FileSystem components to save the information to the hard disk, or you could have used some other server-side ActiveX control to e-mail the information to the system administrator.

> **Tip** Make sure the METHOD property of your FORM tag is set to POST. If it is set to GET, the form's values will be returned in the Request object's QueryString collection, rather than in the Forms collection.

Intrinsic Server Objects

In the last section, you were introduced to one of the ActiveX server objects available to you while doing your server-side scripting. You used the Request object to access the information on a form.

Five intrinsic objects are built into the server itself and are always available to you when you are server-side scripting:

- ◆ Application
- ◆ Request
- ◆ Response
- ◆ Server
- ◆ Session

You should think of these objects in the same way that you think of the built-in browser objects available to you when you are client-side scripting. The following sections provide an overview of each object.

Application Object

What is an application? Microsoft IIS defines an application as any .ASP files in a folder and its sub-folders.

It is important to define an application this way because it enables you to create variables on a more global scale, that can be shared among multiple pages and that live longer than the time a page is loaded in the browser.

To create an Application object variable, all you have to do is refer to it and assign it a value. It looks like this.

```
<%
   Application("prompt") = "Please enter this information"
   Application("answer") = 42
   Application("count") = Application("count") + 1
%>
```

But when you create and access global variables, it is important to remember that your process is not necessarily the only one running on the web server. Several people could access the server at once and cause several processes to run at the same time. This gridlock can cause a problem when accessing global data. If two processes try to change the data at once, one of the changes could get lost. That's why the Application object provides two essential methods:

◆ Lock

◆ Unlock

Lock locks the global variables so that you and you alone can modify them. Unlock frees them so that others can have access. You should never keep an application locked for a long period of time or other processes that need access to the application will fail.

So what can you do with the Application object? Well, here's a really common problem. How do you tell how many people have accessed this particular page? Just add the following code to get rid of any doubt.

```
<%
Application.Lock
Application("PageHits") = Application("PageHits") + 1
Application.Unlock
%>
```

```
This page has had <%= Application("PageHits") %> hits.
```

Session Object

The Session object is similar to the Application object. It enables you to create global variables that you can access across multiple pages.

The difference is that although the Application object stores variables for the application as a whole and all users accessing it, the Session object holds information for only this user's session. Due to the nature of the Session object, no lock or unlock method is needed because the variables are specific to this user. One common use of session variables is to track all the purchases the user has indicated that they want to make. Often this is represented by a shopping cart metaphor. To create and use a variable, refer to the variable in the same way you referred to the variables with the Application object.

```
Session("NumPurchases") = Session("NumPurchases") + 1
```

The Session object has two properties: SessionID and Timeout. SessionID holds the unique ID, which the system uses to identify the session. It is a long integer. Timeout holds the number of minutes the system should wait while the user does nothing before it ends the session. Any new page request or even a refresh will reset this counter. The default is 20 minutes.

Abandon is the only Session object method. It ends the current session, destroys the current session object, and frees resources.

Request Object

The Request object is the object that you learned about in the last section. As previously mentioned, the Request object is used to get values that are passed back to the server from the client.

The Request object is usually used by accessing one of its five collections:

◆ **ClientCertificate**—The values stored in the client certificate. Enables authentication and verification of the identity of the person accessing the page.

◆ **Cookies**—Cookies saved on the client machine. Enables you to determine if a cookie exists for this site and directory and if so, to access its values.

◆ **Form**—Enables you to access the data entered by the user on a form.

◆ **QueryString**—Value of variables used for a database query. This is the information that comes after the ? on the URL indicating for what the user wants to search.

◆ **ServerVariables**—Value of a predefined list of environment variables.

Normally accessing a variable from one of these collections looks like one of these examples:

```
<%
Request.ClientCertificate("Issuer")
Request.Cookies("WestSiteCook")
Request.QueryString("Name")
%>
```

You can, however, use a shortcut and access the field. The preceding examples would look like this:

```
<%
Request("Issuer")
Request("WestSiteCook")
Request("Name")
%>
```

The danger you run into when doing it the short way, though, is that there will be two fields with the same name in two different collections. If that is the case, VBScript returns the first one to which it comes. It searches the collections in this order: QueryString, Form, Cookies, ServerVariables, and ClientCertificate. Use your best judgment.

Response Object

The Response object does just the opposite of the Request object. It provides you with information sent from the server to the client.

The Response object has one collection: cookies. Cookies enable you to modify the values in the cookie that is saved on the client machine. This enables you to update the cookies configuration information, preferences, or whatever else you decide to store in the cookie.

The Response object has four properties:

◆ **Buffer**—When set to true (usually done at the top of an .ASP file), the entire page is processed before the result is sent back to the client. That is, all scripts on the page are executed. When set to false, the page is sent back as it is created.

◆ **ContentType**—Specifies the kind of information being sent back to the client. The default is "text/HTML." If it is set to "text/plain," for instance, the file will be displayed as is without interpreting any of the tags for formatting.

◆ **Expires**—Determines how long the cached page will be used on the client before it goes back to the server and checks to see if it has been updated. Number assigned is in seconds. Zero indicates that the page should not be cached.

Alternately, you can specify an exact date and time when this page should expire, by using the **ExpiresAbsolute** property.

◆ **Status**—Consists of a three-digit code indicating the status, followed by a brief explanation. These status codes are defined by the HTTP specification.

The Response object has eight methods. These give you tight control over how the page is created.

◆ **AddHeader**—For advanced developers only. Adds a header and a value to the page. Must be used before any web page text is sent.

◆ **AppendToLog**—Appends an up to 80-character string to the log entry for this request. String cannot contain commas.

◆ **BinaryWrite**—Writes a block of binary information to the HTTP output without any ANSI or Unicode conversion. Useful if you have a custom application running on the client that uses the HTTP channel to communicate with the server.

◆ **Clear**—Removes any response body information currently in the HTML buffer. Doesn't remove response headers. Usually used in error conditions.

◆ **End**—Immediately stops processing the .ASP file and returns what is currently in the buffer. If you don't want to return anything, do a Clear first.

◆ **Flush**—Sends all the information currently in the buffer to the client immediately.

◆ **Redirect**—Causes the client browser to immediately connect to the URL you send.

◆ **Write**—Writes the string passed as HTML to the current page. You can usually write your HTML outside of the <% and %> symbols or use the <% = operator to do the same thing. But Write is especially handy inside of subroutines or functions.

Server Object

The Server object is intended to represent the server itself. It ends up housing mostly utility functions that you need as you are creating server scripts.

ScriptTimeout is the only one property of the Server object. Assign it the number of seconds that you want the server to give to the script before it decides to cancel it. The default is 90.

There are four methods:

◆ **CreateObject**—Instantiates an OLE object (or server-side ActiveX control) and returns a reference to the object so that you can make use of its properties and methods in your script.

♦ **HTMLEncode**—After sending it a string, this function produces a string that will cause the exact string sent to be displayed in the browser. So if you send it "Second Head: <h2>," HTMLEncode will return "Second Head: <h2>" that will be displayed through the browser as "Second Head: <h2>."

♦ **MapPath**—Returns the complete path of the relative or virtual path specified, relative to the current location of this web page.

♦ **URLEncode**—Encodes a string as it would look after a question mark on the URL when specifying a query string.

Using ActiveX Server Components

ActiveX Server Components, also referred to as design-time controls or OLE Automation servers, are designed to help your .ASP files as they create the web pages that your users will see.

Although ActiveX Server Components use the same COM/OLE/ActiveX technology as the ActiveX controls that you have embedded in your pages in the past, they exist only on the server and are never downloaded to the client. They also have no visible, user-interface portion. Their only purpose is to help you by providing additional functionality when creating server-side scripts.

> **Note** The ActiveX Server Components discussed in this chapter are included with Microsoft Internet Information Server 3.0 when you buy it. There will certainly be others available from both Microsoft and third-party companies soon after IIS 3.0's release. This promises to be a very exciting industry in the near future.

The Browser Capabilities Component

An example may help you to see how the ActiveX Server Components are useful.

A common problem web developers face when creating content is deciding which cool HTML features to use and which to pass on, because their users aren't likely to be using a browser that supports these features.

One solution is to create a text-only or basic-HTML-only version of your site and a separate multimedia version—enable your users to choose on the opening page which version that would like to use.

Server-side scripting offers a better solution—the Browser Capabilities Component.

Take a look at the following code example, which shows you how to create and use the Browser Capabilities Component.

```
<%
Set browser = Server.CreateObject("MSWC.BrowserType")
If browser.Tables = True Then
%>
   <TABLE>
   Table Text
   </TABLE>
<% Else %>
   <PRE>
   Pre Text
   </PRE>
<% End If %>
<% If browser.BackgroundSounds = True Then %>
   Send Sounds
<% End If %>
```

First, a new object is created with the Server object's CreateObject method. The name of the object is MSWC.BrowserType.

ActiveX Server Components offer functionality in the form of objects that contain properties and methods—just like the Intrinsic Server Object from the last section. The difference is that they must be created (sometimes called *instantiated*) before they are used. Server Components are not always available to you.

After the object is created, a pointer to it is passed back and stored in the variable browser. Notice the use of Set here. You cannot simply do an assignment because this is an object, not just a value being assigned to a variable. Whenever you are working with objects, you must use Set.

But after this line is executed, the object is available and can be used throughout the rest of the page by referring to browser.

The properties available to you in this object enable you to find out what the user's browser can do. In this case, the page checks to see if the browser supports tables. If so, the page creates a table. Normally you would put all the table information where the Table Text is in the preceding listing.

If the user's browser doesn't support tables, then you can use the next best thing— the preformatted text tag. The rest of the information inside the preformatted text flag would replace the Pre Text in the preceding listing.

The listing checks to see if background sounds are supported. If they are, the code to send the sounds would replace Send Sounds. If the browser didn't support it, it would do nothing.

So now you no longer have to have two different pages to create and maintain—you only need one. The user doesn't have to choose which type of page they want to see. You already have all the information using this object that you need to make all the decisions for them. That way you can provide all your users with the highest fidelity experience their browser will support.

What other properties are available from the Browser Capabilities Component? Here's a list of the common ones:

◆ Version—The version of the browser.

◆ Frames—Does it support frames?

◆ Tables—Does it support tables?

◆ Background Sounds—Can it play background sounds?

◆ VBScript—Does it support client-side VBScript?

◆ JavaScript—Does it support client-side JavaScript?

◆ Cookies—Does it support cookies?

How the Browser Capabilities Component Works

How does this component work its magic? Well, like most magic tricks, after you see how it's done, it won't seem very magical anymore. This component keeps track of all the browsers it knows about through the use of an INI file that is stored in your `WinNT\System32\InetSrv\Asp\Cmpnts` folder, along with the Browscap.DLL file. The INI file (see the following code example) has a list of all the browsers available and what their capabilities are. Then, when a browser connects to your site, it sends, behind the scenes, something called an HTTP User Agent Header. The HTTP User Agent Header is a string that contains the browser name and version. Here is a portion of a typical Browscap.INI file:

```
;;;last edited t-vanvan 8/19/96;;;
;;;;;;;;;;;;;;;;;;;;;;;;;;;;
;;; Microsoft Browsers ;;;
;;;;;;;;;;;;;;;;;;;;;;;;;;;;
```

```
[Microsoft Internet Explorer/4.40.308 (Windows 95) ]
browser=IE
version=1.0
majorver=#1
minorver=#0
frames=FALSE
tables=FALSE
cookies=FALSE
backgroundsounds=FALSE
vbscript=FALSE
javascript=FALSE
platform=Windows95

[Mozilla/1.22 (compatible; MSIE 2.0; Windows 95)]
browser=IE
version=2.0
majorver=#2
minorver=#0
frames=FALSE
tables=TRUE
cookies=TRUE
backgroundsounds-TRUE
vbscript=FALSE
javascript=FALSE
platform=Windows95

...

;;;;;;;;;;;;;;;;;;;;;;;;;
;;; Netscape Browsers ;;;
;;;;;;;;;;;;;;;;;;;;;;;;;

[Netscape 3.0]
browser=Netscape
version=3.0
majorver=#3
minorver=#0
frames=TRUE
tables=TRUE
cookies=TRUE
backgroundsounds=FALSE
vbscript=FALSE
```

```
javascript=TRUE
ActiveXControls=FALSE

[Mozilla/3.0b5 (Win95; I)]
parent=Netscape 3.0
platform=Win95

[Mozilla/3.0b5 (WinNT; I)]
parent=Netscape 3.0
platform=WinNT

...


;;;;;;;;;;;;;;;;;;;;;;;
;;; Oracle Browser ;;;
;;;;;;;;;;;;;;;;;;;;;;;

[Oracle 1.5]
browser=Power Browser
version=1.5
majorver=#1.5
minover=#0
frames=TRUE
tables=TRUE
cookies=TRUE
backroundsounds=FALSE
vbscript=TRUE
javascript=TRUE

[Mozilla/2.01 (Compatible) Oracle(tm) PowerBrowser(tm)/1.0a]
parent=Oracle 1.5

...
```

The Browser Capabilities Component then looks up the HTTP User Agent Header string it received from the browser in this INI file, finds the appropriate entry, and identifies the browser's capabilities.

Although this is a pretty simple way of solving the problem, it is also a pretty flexible one. When Microsoft comes out with an upgrade of Internet Explorer or Netscape comes out with an upgrade for Navigator, all you have to do is make a new entry into your INI file, copy all the information from the latest version's entry to the new version's entry, and update any information that has changed.

In addition, you can add new properties to the Browser Capabilities Component by adding new entries into the INI file. So if a new capability becomes available, add the entry and then check for it.

The Advertisement Rotator

The Advertisement Rotator is completely different from the Browser Capabilities component. It is very useful if you are lucky enough to have paying advertisers supporting your site.

The problem is this that you may want to include an advertisement on a commonly accessed page, but you don't want to sell the advertising for the page just once. You want to sell the spot several times and rotate the ad that is displayed so that each time a new user pulls up a page, the ad is different. But how do you implement that?

Well, you could create or use an existing ActiveX control and embed the control in the web page instead of the graphic. Then the control could go out and get a different image each time the page is refreshed. That works, but what if their browser doesn't support ActiveX controls?

The answer, of course, is the Advertisement Rotator server-side control. One of the nice things about a server-side control is that it works no matter what browser the user has.

The Ad Rotator Schedule File

To use the Ad Rotator component, you need to set up a support file to give it all the information it needs. The support file is called the Rotator Schedule File, and it is a text file that can have any name you like. The following example shows a typical rotator file:

```
REDIRECT/adscript/redir.asp
WIDTH 500
HEIGHT 50
BORDER 0
*
http://ads/astrox.gif
http://www.astrox.com/
Astrox Has Your Needs Covered
10
http://tiltobix/finwk1.gif
-
TiltoBix Is Your News Source
30
```

```
http://ads/candor.gif
http://www.candorPC.com/
Candor PC is the place for systems
40
http://ads/flowrme.gif
http://www.flowerMe.com/
Flower me with your love — FlowerMe, Inc.
20
```

The first line identifies a file that is executed when the user clicks on the ad box to go to the ad's home page. This redirection file will ultimately send them to the home page, but it enables you to do other things first—such as count the number of times users have clicked on ads for each company. This will be very useful information for you and the advertiser. If you leave this blank, no redirection file is used and the user is automatically taken to the ad's home page.

The next three lines are pretty self-explanatory. They determine, in pixels, the width, height, and border size of the graphic. The default values are 440, 60, and 1, respectively.

Note   There must always be one line with a star in it between the global parameters (the first four lines) and the rest of the file.

You can choose not to specify any of these global parameters, and to go with the default values instead. If you do, however, you must leave the line blank with only an asterisk in the first position. If you went with the defaults for all the global parameters, the first part of your file would look like this:

```
*
*
*
*
*
http://ads/astrox.gif
http://www.astrox.com/
Astrox Has Your Needs Covered
...
```

Now look at the rest of the file in the typical rotator code example (shown previous to the preceding code). Each entry has four lines. The first line tells the server where the graphic to be displayed can be found. This is usually on your server, but it doesn't have to be.

The second line identifies the ad's home page. This is where the user will be taken if they click on the ad. If no home page is associated with the ad, a dash can be placed on a line by itself to indicate that no home page is associated.

The third line provides a text alternative for those who don't have graphical browsers or who have graphics turned off.

Finally, the fourth line specifies a relative number that determines how often the ad comes up. In the example (the listing before last), the numbers ad up to 100, so the individual numbers can be seen as the percentage of time the ad will appear. The numbers do not have to add up to 100, though. The server simply adds the numbers together and allots the correct portion of time to each ad.

Using the Ad Rotator Component

After the schedule file is created, using the component is easy.

```
...
And now a word from our sponsor:
<% Set advert = Server.CreateObject("MSWC.AdRotator") %>
<% = advert.GetAdvertisement("/adscript/rotsched.txt") %>

Now back to our regularly scheduled program...
...
```

The first line creates the object and stores it in the variable advert. Again, notice the required use of Set here.

The second line calls the GetAdvertisement method of advert and passes the file name of the Rotator Schedule file. On this line, be sure to notice that it begins with an equal sign. That means that whatever this function returns will be placed into the final HTML file. What will that be?

```
...
And now a word from our sponsor:
<A HREF="/adscript/redir.asp?http://www.astrox.com/">
<IMG
SRC="http://ads/astrox.gif"
ALT="Astrox Has Your Needs Covered"
WIDTH=500 HEIGHT=50 BORDER=0>
</A>

Now back to our regularly scheduled program...
...
```

The anchor and image tags are returned from the GetAdvertisement function and are placed in the code where they belong. Notice that the HREF on the anchor does not go directly to www.astrox.com. It calls the redirection .ASP page with the www.astrox.com address as a query argument. This enables redir.asp to log the access before sending the user on to the home page.

Other ActiveX Server Objects

Your Microsoft Internet Information Server 3.0 comes with the two ActiveX Server Objects previously mentioned, plus a number of others. The following are some of the Server Objects:

◆ **Database Access Objects**—Active Data Objects can be used to access the database in a reliable, easy-to-use way. They can both retrieve and update data.

◆ **Content Linking**—Provides an easy way to tie pages together so that they can be viewed sequentially. Automatically generates appropriate links and tables of content for newsletters and other publications.

◆ **TextStream**—Enables you to easily access files on the server, open them, and access their contents.

The Global File

For every application on your server, you can create a GLOBAL.ASA file for that application. ASA stands for Active Server Application. The GLOBAL.ASA file provides a place where you can do two things:

◆ Declare objects that will be used throughout the application.

◆ Write scripts that will execute when the application and sessions begin and end.

The global file is optional, but it provides a handy place to do some things you couldn't do easily otherwise. If you decide to use one, it must be in the root directory of your web application, and it must be named GLOBAL.ASA.

Global Objects

An object can be created in the global file so that it is available to all objects throughout the application. The syntax used here, however, is a little different.

```
<OBJECT RUNAT=Server SCOPE=Session ID=Broser
PROGID="MSWC.BrowserType">
```

This is equivalent to this line, used earlier:

```
Set browser = Server.CreateObject("MSWC.BrowserType")
```

The RUNAT clause is required and must always be set to Server. The SCOPE clause determines whether this is being created for this session and user only or whether it should be created and the same object used for everyone who logs in. Because this is the browser object, it only makes sense to use it at the Session level. If you want an object to be available globally to all sessions, replace Session with Application.

ID is the name you want to give this object. It is the name used in future scripts that refer to it. PROGID is the name by which the system knows the object. Instead of PROGID, you can use CLASSID and refer to the object by its long serial number.

After this object is created in the global file, any script in your application can use the object as if it had already been defined in that script.

```
If browser.Tables = True Then
%>
    <TABLE>
    Table Text
    </TABLE>
<% Else %>
    <PRE>
    Pre Text
    </PRE>
<% End If %>
```

Application and Session Events

As mentioned previously when discussing objects, the global file can work at two different levels of scope. The first is session. A *session* is associated with one user accessing the site. *Application* scope applies to the application for all users accessing the application.

Application Start and End Events

If you want to write code that happens when the application first starts up or when the application ends, you can write that code here in GLOBAL.ASP.

```
<SCRIPT LANGUAGE=VBScript RUNAT=Server>
```

```
Sub Application_OnStart

...

End Sub

Sub Application_OnEnd

...

End Sub
</SCRIPT>
```

The Application_OnStart happens when the first user opens one of the application's web pages. It happens before the Session_OnStart event (see the following section).

Application_OnEnd happens just before the server is shut down and just after the Session_OnEnd event.

The only intrinsic objects available in these two events are the Application and Session objects.

Session Start and End Events

If you want to write code that happens when a session begins or ends, use the Session_OnStart and Session_OnEnd events.

```
<SCRIPT LANGUAGE=VBScript RUNAT=Server>
Sub Session_OnStart

...

End Sub

Sub Session_OnEnd

...

End Sub
</SCRIPT>
```

Session_OnStart happens when a user first opens one of the application's web pages. Session_OnEnd occurs when the user clicks on a link that takes them to a page outside the site.

The only intrinsic objects available in these two events are the Application and Session objects.

Debugging and Error Handling

Unfortunately debugging and error handling are still very tedious processes. Just like client-side scripting tracing, debugging tools just aren't the best quality yet. With the introduction and evolution of Microsoft's Internet Studio and other tools, the quality of these products is sure to improve.

In the meantime, you have to put up with error messages and line numbers appearing in your HTML page instead of the output for which you were looking. To effectively use the error message and line number information, you have to abandon Notepad and find an editor that at least provides you with the line number you are editing.

Instead of using MsgBoxes, as you would in client-side script to trace execution and variable values, you want to use the Response.Write method. This has the advantage of being interspersed with the text on your page and providing a way to trace back through the execution and the output together. You also avoid having to click the message box OK button dozens of times.

By the way, On Error Resume Next does work in client-side scripting. Just be careful with it. After you turn it on, you don't get any more error messages. Add it in only after you have your code thoroughly debugged.

CHAPTER 18

Integrating Java Applet Objects

By Art Scott and Cameron Laird

Previous chapters presented ActiveX technologies for constructing animated, programmatically powerful Internet applications and displays. Java is a complement to VBScript, a language that most readers will want to learn at least at a summary level. This chapter demonstrates the value of Java and its JavaScript relative to VBScript developers.

The Java Alternative to ActiveX

Java is an object-oriented programming language in the style of C++. Under development at Sun Microsystems through the 1990s, attention and publicity given it exploded in 1995 when it was released together with HotJava, a demonstration application for downloading and running Java applets across standard Internet networks.

Note You can visit the Sun Microsystems site at `http://java.sun.com`. Sun actively maintains this showcase of the technologies and potentials of Java. Although the site processes enormous traffic—hundreds of thousands of hits daily—from developers downloading freely distributable programming objects, it also serves as a demonstration of the commercial vision Sun has for Java.

The technical benefits Java provides that excite information technologists have to do with its portability, its network- and security-awareness, and its object-oriented purity. *Applets* are applications stored on one computer that can journey across a network and execute on another; although applets have been written for years "from scratch," it's only with the ascendance of Java that they become easy and popular enough to win their own neologism. Java's portability and network-savvy security model make it easy to write applets. The security designed into Java, in particular, promises a leap forward in development and administration of applications for desktops: Java guarantees that its applets can do no damage, in a specific but useful sense. That means not just the management, but the elimination of energy spent catching viruses, adjusting access privileges, monitoring certain kinds of intrusions, and creating novel security abstractions for each application.

Note Security in Java and ActiveX: Java and ActiveX share many characteristics, and Microsoft and others are devoting enormous resources to make them "interoperable." One of the biggest contrasts between them, though, is in their security models. When an ActiveX or Java application needs a resource outside itself, it requests the resource through network calls, validates the resource as the network returns it, and then executes it.

If, for example, you were looking at your bank account, and you wanted a detailed amortization of a prospective loan, you might click on a button that loads a loan applet. The loan applet would then operate locally on your computer, painting data-entry forms on the screen, calculating payments based on your submission, and reporting the results. How do you know, though, that the loan applet isn't infected with a virus, or is reporting your credit-card number back without your permission, or filling your hard-disk with garbage data? ActiveX resources can be *authenticated* with a *digital signature*, which assures you that the applet you receive truly is the one constructed and registered by the bank.

Java's guarantee, in contrast, is that a Java applet can only perform safe operations and positively will not write to your local disk, will not open an unauthorized network connection, will not infect other parts of your system, and so on. Java is more constricting than ActiveX; ActiveX encourages rather promiscuous use of application components, with relatively little regard to network security. Java makes ActiveX developers feel a bit claustrophobic. On the other hand, ActiveX's digital signature is a weak guarantee of safety. Even if you have complete confidence in the intentions of your bank, or other signatory, nothing in ActiveX prevents an *inadvertent* error in the loan applet's coding from damaging your local system.

What's the consequence for the individual developer? For now, it is most important to understand the two models. Sun, Microsoft, and others are actively researching and marketing variations and innovations on these schemes, and they are sure to evolve through the months and years ahead.

These benefits extend Java's use beyond that typical for ActiveX. ActiveX unites Microsoft-oriented work done with a wide variety of approaches; Java's superior portability, though, makes a far wider variety of operating systems, including Windows 95, MacOS, Windows NT, AS/400, and any Unix, all appropriate for Java development and deployment. Another strength of Java in comparison to Visual Basic and VBScript is its object-oriented purity, which permits powerful re-use of Java-coded projects. Object-orientation is orthogonal to security, but, by correctly implementing both in a single development environment, Java gives development managers hope for an order-of-magnitude improvement in maintainability over Visual Basic. Visual Basic's support of object-orientation, for example, is only partial; it does not directly support developer construction of re-usable class hierarchies.

Java, JavaScript, ActiveX, and VBScript all address opportunities to distribute applications across networks of desktops. In summary, though, Java differs from ActiveX and VBScript in subtle but crucial dimensions:

◆ Its model for applet security is much different and, most industry observers agree, far more useful. The previous note compares Java and ActiveX security. For a different perspective, see the December 1996 *SunWorld* feature article, `http://www.sun.com/sunworldonline/swol-12-1996/swol-12-javasec.html`.

◆ Its emphasis on portability and published standards offers a refreshing contrast in leadership to Microsoft's proprietary control and targeting of VBScript. Many authors have written on this subject. Briefly, the point of the whole debate is that many information technologists feel more comfortable relying on Java because it has multiple vendors rather than, for example, VBScript, which is expected always to be uniquely Microsoft's.

◆ Its engineering promises to support long-term, multiperson, and large-scale applications more easily than VBScript, which is generally better suited to unsophisticated "programming in the small." The design goals for VBScript tilt toward ease-of-first-use, accessibility to non-programmers, and similarity to Visual Basic. With modules, packages, interfaces, and pure object-orientation built into its core, Jave inherently provides more of the facilities that determine success for large-scale projects.

Sun has intended that these be advantages for Java; most important, though, is for readers to understand that these differences exist and what their domains are. Each of these have both positive and negative aspects. While the security model, for example, has generally been applauded as grounded in a stronger theory than ActiveX's commercial registry, any advantage might be lost if ActiveX proves sufficiently successful in the marketplace. With widespread adoption, ActiveX will enjoy the benefits of user familiarity and cycles of enhancement and refinement.

Note There is an enormous amount of ever-growing literature on Java versus ActiveX issues and comparisons, much of it online. We strongly urge readers curious to know more to explore `http://starbase.neosoft.com/~claird/comp.lang.java/java.html` and the documents to which it points.

The consequence for the individual practitioner is this: to partake of the constellation of advantages and disadvantages that Java represents, he or she learns the object-oriented language of *class, interface, package,* and *inheritance* that frame Java programs. VBScripting typically defines sequences of actions that respond to user events; Java authorship is definition and elaboration of classes that implement an object model of a particular domain. That is, a Java programmer describes the properties and behaviors of the objects whose interactions constitute a Java application.

A *class* is one bundle of properties and behaviors; for example, the `HelloJavaApplet.java` example manages its use of a font through the `font` class which is standard with the Java AWT (Abstract Windowing Toolkit). The public appearance of a class is its *interface.* Classes are cohesive and coherent unitary concepts; a collection of classes which co-operate to achieve a purpose, and which are bundled to that end, constitutes a *package.* In `HelloJavaApplet.java`, the package `java.awt.Font` supplies the implementation of the `font` class.

Inheritance is object-orientation's principal category for defining refinement and re-use of existing work. Thus, a particular application might particularize a supplied `transaction` class to define `customer_purchase` or `ATM_session` *sub-classes.* `HelloJavaApplet.java` refines the `java.applet.Applet` class to the `HelloJavaApplet` sub-class; in doing so, it overrides, or replaces, the `init` and `paint` definitions, which are part of the standard interface of `java.applet.Applet`.

Here is the introductory Java applet, `HelloJavaApplet.java`, which was described in the previous text. The applet's purpose is described in the code.

```
// This is the source of a complete small applet which greets the viewer
//     with a message in a particular font, and correctly handles screen
//     initialization and clean-up.
import java.awt.Graphics;        // graphics package
import java.awt.Font;            // font package
import java.awt.Color;           // color package

// create an object (rather a class) called HelloJavaApplet
public class HelloJavaApplet extends java.applet.Applet
{
        // override the initialization method to setup our font
        public void init()
        {
                // "f" inherits font types from the font class
                Font f = new Font("TimesRoman", Font.BOLD, 36);
        }

        // create a public method which takes an instance of the graphic
        ➡class
        public void paint(Graphics g)
        {
                // here we have told the graphics object to use font,
                ➡color and text
                // by location of x,y or 5,50
                g.setFont(f);
                g.setColor(Color.red);
                g.drawString("Good morning, I need some coffee.", 5, 50);
        }
}
```

Java Applet and Application Features

Java work appears in two categories: stand-alone applications, which are comparable to those coded in older languages in performance, scalability, and allied engineering factors; and applets, previously defined. Applets, like ActiveX Controls, can only be included in an HTML web page to create the following:

◆ Animation

◆ Graphical objects (bar charts, graphs, diagrams, and others)

◆ Applications made up of collections of such controls as buttons

◆ New controls

Java Applications

Java applications are stand-alone Java programs that do not require a browser. They can read and write to the reader's file system and can communicate with a server. A simple Java application might appear as follows:

```
// the complete program is enclosed within a class definition
// and the class is called "HelloJavaWorld"
class HelloJavaWorld
{
    // the program body is contained within the main() routine
    public static void main (String args[])
    {
        System.out.println("Good morning, I need some coffee.");
    }
}
```

With the Java application, your class must have one method, main(). When your application starts, main is executed. From your main method, all other program behavior is accomplished as your application requires.

How to Start with Java

It is traditional for newcomers to Java to download the standard Developers Kit distribution from Sun. The Kit can be obtained at:

```
<URL:http://java.sun.com/nav/download/index.html>
```

Other possibilities include purchase of software on CD-ROM. Applet work, as opposed to stand-alone Java applications, involves even less preparation. For most, the standard approach is to use such Java-enabled browsers as Netscape's Internet Navigator 3.0 or later, or Microsoft's Internet, to view the action of an applet. In this minimal model, a developer uses a text editor to author Java source, compiles it into byte code with javac from the SDK, and renders the resulting applet with a browser.

Activating HTML Pages with Java

It's easy to activate—that is, to animate its display, to customize it for particular characteristics of the reader, or to make it the dynamic result of a real-time calculation—an otherwise traditional HTML page by writing such code clauses as this:

```
<APPLET CODE        = HelloJavaApplet.class
                CODEBASE = "http://www.MySite.com/"
                WIDTH        = 300
                HEIGHT       = 120>
```

Your browser does not support Java Applets <!-- apology message -->
    `</APPLET>`

These clauses illustrate several items important to a Java programmer:

◆ The `CODE` attribute indicates the name of the class file, including the `*.class` extension.

◆ The `CODEBASE` attribute re-directs accesses if the file is not located within the same file directory or same web site.

◆ `WIDTH` and `HEIGHT` are required and are used to indicate the bounding box of the applet, that is, how big the applet box is within the web page. It is important to remember that the box might be smaller than the area needed by the applet, so text, graphics, and so on, might appear to be cut off.

◆ Some browsers do not support Java applets; it's an important courtesy to your prospective readers to handle such exceptions gracefully.

When Internet Component Download is called to download code through the use of `CODEBASE=`, it traverses the Internet Search Path to look for the desired component. This Path is a list of Object Store servers that the <OBJECT> and <APPLET> tags use each time they search for a component due to be downloaded. This way, even if an <OBJECT> tag in an HTML document does not specify a `CODEBASE` location to download code for an embedded OLE control, the Internet Component Download still uses the Internet Search Path to find the necessary code.

The search path is specified in a string in the registry, under the key HKEY_ LOCAL_MACHINE\Software\Microsoft\Windows\CurrentVersion\Internet Settings\CodeBaseSearchPath. The value for this key is a string in the following format:

`CODEBASE`= http://host1/path1/"; URL1; ... URL(n); ... URL(n+1); ... URL(n++)

Using Objects to Invoke Java Components

Objects can be used to invoke Java components, as in the following code example.

```
<HTML>
<HEAD>
```

```
<TITLE>My Java Applet Object Tag Page</TITLE>
</HEAD>
<BODY>

<OBJECT        ID          = jvaMyJava
               CLASSID     = "java:app.class"
               CODETYPE    = "applet/java"
               CODEBASE    = "http://www.MyWebSite.com/"
               WIDTH=350
               HEIGHT=85
               ALIGN=center
               HSPACE=20
               VSPACE=0>

    <PARAM NAME="FontName" value="Arial">
    <PARAM NAME="FontSize" value="16">
    <PARAM NAME="FontBold" value="1">
    <PARAM NAME="FontItalic" value="0">
    <PARAM NAME="FontUnderline" value="0">
    <PARAM NAME="FontStrikeout" value="0">

    Your browser does not support Java Applets <!-- apology message -->
</OBJECT>

</BODY>
</HTML>
```

Objects contribute functionality to a web page document by allowing insertion of images, video, and programs, such as Java applets and ActiveX controls. To insert an object, you use the OBJECT element, supplying attribute values that specify the object type, location, initial data, and so on. If the object has configurable properties, you can set these using the PARAM element.

Reading User Data into Your Applet

The next example uses the capabilities of the browser to read user data into your applet.

```
/////////////////////////////////////////////////
// MyCoffeeApplet.java
//
import java.awt.Graphics;
import java.awt.Font;
import.java.awt.Color;
```

```
public class MyCoffeeApplet extends java.applet.Applet
{
    Font f = new Font("TimesRoman", Fond.BOLD,36);
    String strName;

    public void init()
    {
        this.strName = getParameter("strName");
        if(this.strName == NULL)
            this.strName = "No coffee this morning ?";
        else
            this.strName = "How do you like your coffee  " + this.strName +
            ➥"?";
    }

    public void paint(Graphics g)
    {
        g.setFont(f);
        g.setColor(Color.red);
        g.drawString(this.strName, 5, 50);
    }
}
```

This applet illustrates the Java idiom of overriding the fundamental init() and paint() methods to compose an initial screen that is specific to the purpose of the applet. In this case, init() and paint(), instead of being the default no-actions, write the question, "How do you like your coffee, <NAME>?", in red TimesRoman, on the screen.

Inserting Java Applets in HTML Pages

The following listing show how to insert a Java applet into an HTML page.

```
<HTML>
<HEAD>
<TITLE> Running a simple MyCoffee Applet</TITLE>
</HEAD>

<BODY>
<P>
    <APPLET CODE     = MyCoffeeApplet.class
                 WIDTH     =300
                 HEIGHT=120>
```

```
    <PARAM NAME=strName VALUE = "Hal9000"
    </APPLET>

</BODY>
</HTML>
```

All the flush-left markup in the previous listing is conventional HTML, recognizable even to the oldest browsers. The indented tags, in contrast, are meaningful only to a Java-equipped browser (in general, it's possible to define other interpretations of <APPLET>, but they are not of interest in this book). <APPLET>...</APPLET> is a container for an applet specification. It instructs the browser to search for a class definition "MyCoffeeApplet.class," presumably byte-compiled from "MyCoffeeApplet.java"; to draw the applet in a 300 by 120 canvas; and to communicate the name "Hal9000" to the applet, bound to the variable name "strName."

This last action hints at the deeper cooperation possible between the browser and Java. The browser not only provides a blank canvas in which Java or another applet language builds its graphical output; it also can communicate an arbitrary collection of labeled PARAM values. Notice the syntax for these: HTML makes them available as <PARAM NAME=name VALUE=value> elements within the <APPLET> container. They then are available within a Java applet through use of the getParameter() method. Notice that the previous inlined code deserves to be styled appropriately for source fragments.

Java Programming Concepts

Object-orientation dominates the methodologies of software development in the 1990s. Introductions to object-orientation abound. Without duplicating their instruction here, note that the fundamental concept in object-orientation is that of *class*, an abstraction that defines a single coherent collection of characteristics and behaviors. "Automobile," "network connection," "bank transaction," and "shipping department employee" are examples of classes. Class behaviors appear as "methods"; "automobile.stop," "network connection.retrieveStatus," "bank transaction.begin," and "shipping department employee.updateBenefitSelection" are possible methods.

Understanding Classes

Java usage is purely object-oriented. A Java applet is created by subclasses of the Applet class, in the java.applet package. This Applet Package provides behavior to enable your applet to work with the browser while taking advantage of the Abstract Windowing Toolkit (AWT). The AWT is a collection of screen objects (buttons, lists, menus, graphics types, and so on) that contain methods that enable a programmer to tell how the user is interacting with the screen elements. The AWT also provides objects that handle all the normally tedious screen layout procedures. Your applet can also have other classes for its use, but it is the main applet class that executes the applet. Your Java applet will always have the following signature:

```
public class MyAppletClass extends java.applet.Applet
{
    ...
}
```

The main applet class requires the above **public** keyword for your main class. Any other classes which you define as part of your applet may be either **public** (available to the outside world) or **private** (available within the Applet class only) as you need. When Java encounters your applet within the web page, not only is your class loaded over the network, but Java creates an instance of that class and all system-based methods are sent to that instance. Different applets can use the same class, but will use different instances. This is just like creating multiple instances of a VBX or an OCX with Visual Basic where each has its own instance but uses the same code segment.

Overriding Methods

If you have downloaded the JDK from Sun, you will find many important methods that your applet can override. Overriding these methods provide added functionality to an existing method; it refines it or specializes it as needed. For instance, whenever your applet is initialized, you will want to initialize your class variables. The Java definition assures that init(), for example, will be invoked when an applet is first launched; by overriding init() with your code, you have confidence that the actions you define will occur in the proper sequence. This echoes a C developer's starting point of writing a main() routine, but the structure of class-method-overriding enforces disciplines that enhance the reliability of application development. Again, we refer the interested reader to the literature on object-orientation; in this chapter, we subordinate explanation of why Java is as it to description of how to use it.

There are at least five important methods that you might want to override. These applet methods are:

◆ initialization

◆ starting

◆ stopping

◆ destroying

◆ painting

The next few sections discuss how to implement these overrides.

> **Note**
>
> In reading the following sections, remember that "override" doesn't involve a normative judgment that a standard method is deficient; rather, it's the label for the standard object-oriented process of constructing complex applications. "Overriding" is akin to editing in a standard create-critique cycle of authorship.
>
> A different metaphor for overriding is the architectural one. It's conventional to think about stacking "building blocks" together. In an object-oriented world, it's also possible to work from the other direction and put ("override") special-purpose building blocks within an existing construction plan. The default methods are placeholders, keeping the architecture together until our overridings can be fit into their positions.

Overriding the Initialization Method

Initialization occurs when the applet is either first loaded or is reloaded. Here you will want to override this method to create needed objects, images, fonts, parameters, and so on.

```
// override the initialization method to setup our font
public void init()
{
    // "f" inherits font types from the font class
    Font f = new Font("TimesRoman", Font.BOLD, 36);
}
```

Overriding the Starting Method

Starting occurs after an applet has been initialized. Starting also covers restarting of the applet. An applet is stopped if the client follows a link to another web page—and by the same token, is re-started when the client returns to this page. This may occur many different times.

```
// override the starting method to setup our font
public void start()
{
    ...
}
```

Overriding the Stopping Method

Stopping occurs when the client leaves the current web page where your applet resides. By default, when the client leaves the current web page, the applet continues running and using up system resources. By overriding stop, you can suspend execution of the applet and then restart the applet when the client is again viewing the current web page.

```
// override the stopping method to setup our font
public void stop()
{
    ...
}
```

Overriding the Destroying Method

Destroying enables the applet to clean up after itself just before the browser exits. You might want to kill any running objects. This method is generally used to release any resources. Destroy() is reminiscent of finalize(). Browsers apply destroy() only to applets, though, whereas the garbage collector guarantees that it applies finalize() to each object it collects. We tabulate the contrast, then, between them as follows:

◆ destroy()

    A. Applied by browser

    B. To applet

    C. On applet exit

◆ finalize()

    A. Applied by garbage collector

    B. To every object

    C. At time of collection

```
// override the destroy method to setup our font
public void destroy()
{
    ...
}
```

Overriding the Painting Method

Painting is how the client draws something on the monitor. That something may be text, a line, background, or an image. "Paint" also is a keyword for the default method the browser defines for achieving that action, a method designed to be overriden by developer definitions. Painting may happen many times while the applet is displayed. If the browser is moved or re-sized or if another application is moved in front of the

browser and then the browser is again moved to the front of the monitor, paint()
is called. That's part of the contract the browser offers the developer; it's the
developer's responsibility, then, to override the default paint() with the actions
specific to a particular application:

```
// create a public method which takes an instance of the graphic class
public void paint(Graphics g)
{
    // here we have told the graphics object to use font, color, and text
    // by location of x,y or 5,50
    g.setFont(f);
    g.setColor(Color.red);
    g.drawString("Good morning, I need some coffee.", 5, 50);
}
```

Combining Java and VBScript

There are constraints on use of both Java and VBScript. The security model of the
former limits the knowledge available to a particular applet, and limits what it can do
with that knowledge. The security model for VBScript is quite different, and poten-
tially advantageous to developers. On the other hand, Internet Explorer is the only
prominent browser which supports VBScript. There are a variety of other advantages
and disadvantages to each. What is sometimes wise is to use them co-operatively. You
can, for example, have VBScript refer to the Java applets previously described:

```
<HTML>
<HEAD>
<TITLE>A ActiveX Control Pad New Page</TITLE>
</HEAD>
<BODY>

<OBJECT ID="MyTextBox" WIDTH=120 HEIGHT=30
   CLASSID="CLSID:8BD21D10-EC42-11CE-9E0D-00AA006002F3">
    <PARAM NAME="VariousPropertyBits" VALUE="746604571">
    <PARAM NAME="Size" VALUE="2540;635">
    <PARAM NAME="Value" VALUE="Your Name">
    <PARAM NAME="FontCharSet" VALUE="0">
    <PARAM NAME="FontPitchAndFamily" VALUE="2">
    <PARAM NAME="FontWeight" VALUE="0">
</OBJECT>
```

```
<OBJECT ID="MyCommandButton" WIDTH=135 HEIGHT=32
CLASSID="CLSID:D7053240-CE69-11CD-A777-00DD01143C57">
    <PARAM NAME="Caption" VALUE="Enter your Name">
    <PARAM NAME="Size" VALUE="2858;662">
    <PARAM NAME="FontCharSet" VALUE="0">
    <PARAM NAME="FontPitchAndFamily" VALUE="2">
    <PARAM NAME="ParagraphAlign" VALUE="3">
    <PARAM NAME

<SCRIPT LANGUAGE="VBScript">
<!--
Dim strName

Sub MyCommandButton_Click()
    strName = MyTextBox.Text

    if strName = "" then
        MsgBox "You should enter a name."
    else
        MyJavaApplet.strName = strName
end sub
-->
    </SCRIPT>

</BODY>
</HTML>
```

The **ID** attribute is declared as part of the object declaration. And the Java Object's properties and methods can be called directly from the code. With this example, VBScript filters transactions by the name a user enters.

Notice how simple is VBScript's invocation of the Java applet. All that VBScript knows about it is the method from the applet's interface:

MyJavaApplet.strName = strName.

JavaScript—A Different Alternative to VBScript

JavaScript is another complement to VBScript, a tool that largely overlaps VBScript in its applicability, but sometimes is useful in combination with VBScript. VBScript is generally easier to use and understand, and we don't recommend JavaScript at its current level of maturity. However, we do offer a sample of its operation.

```
<HTML>
<HEAD>
<TITLE> A JavaScript Page</TITLE>

<SCRIPT LANGUAGE="JavaScript">
    parent.vrmlFrame.document.open("X-WORLD/X-VRML");
    parent.vrmlFrame.document.writeln("#VRML V1.0 ASCII");
    parent.vrmlFrame.document.writeln("Separator {");
    parent.vrmlFrame.document.writeln("Material { diffuseColor 0 .7 0}");
    parent.vrmlFrame.document.writeln("Sphere { radius 5 }");
    parent.vrmlFrame.document.writeln("Translation { translation 0 10 0 }");
    parent.vrmlFrame.document.writeln("AsciiText { string \ "Hello World\"}");
    parent.vrmlFrame.document.writeln("}");
    parent.vrmlFrame.document.close();
</SCRIPT>
</HEAD>

<BODY>
<FORM>
<INPUT TYPE="submit" VALUE="Create VRML" ONCLICK="do_it()">
</FORM>

</BODY>
</HTML>
```

Java Visions: What Java Means for Internet Development

From the perspective of this book, Java is important because it permits construction of applets—modular, re-usable objects that VBScript readily accesses. Beyond this, though, Java promises several other exciting prospects.

Java could well enable a software industry different from our current shrink-wrapped one. Its platform-independence holds out the hope that applications will work not just on conventional desktops, but on Unix engineering workstations, processors embeddable in household appliances, AS/400 business computers, and everywhere else, streamlining use and distribution of all applications. Microsoft already is including the Java Virtual Machine in its contemporary operating systems, so that not only will disparate computers speak a common language, but Java applets will be immediately available to Microsoft Office parts, VB, VC++, and so on.

The incrementalism and transportability of Java are already being exploited to shorten the cycles of product delivery and customer response. These encourage use of the Internet as a distribution channel, which should lower the barriers to entry into the retail software market. The strong object-orientation of Java might do the same, as it permits specialization and refinement. The vision is of a world different from ours, where a single word processing application, for example, holds a dominating share of the market; in the future, it's possible that the word processing function will be achieved as the co-operative result of combining separate commercially available and extremely competitive objects which individually specialize in text-editing, painting, spell-checking, and so on. Finally, Java holds out the hope of such new models of commerce as pay-per-use.

These are speculations. What's certain for now, though, is that Java is part of a number of successful projects at a variety of scales of operation; that its ubiquity can simplify many web developments; and that it integrates increasingly well with VBScript programming.

PART V

Appendices

Installing Microsoft Internet Explorer 3.0

By Eric Smith

This appendix will help you install the necessary tools to view and edit the examples used throughout this book.

After you install the necessary tools, go back to Chapter 2, " HTML Fundamentals for VBScripting," to learn how to view HTML documents on your hard drive and over a remote Internet connection.

Installing Microsoft Internet Explorer

On the CD

For your convenience, the accompanying CD-ROM contains the complete version of Microsoft's Internet Explorer. If you don't already have this browser installed on your computer, follow these steps:

> **Note** Microsoft Internet Explorer 3.0 is the browser that is used throughout this book to demonstrate aspects of VBScript and ActiveX. The browser runs on both Windows 95 and Windows NT, version 4.0

1. Insert the *Inside VBScript with ActiveX* CD-ROM .

2. Choose Start, Run.

3. Type *drive***:\TOOLS\MSIE**, where *drive* is the letter of your CD-ROM drive.

   Before you can install Internet Explorer 3.0, you must agree to Microsoft's Internet Explorer License Agreement, which is shown in figure A.1.

Figure A.1

Microsoft Internet Explorer's license agreement. You must click Yes to continue the installation process.

```
Internet Explorer License Agreement

 END-USER LICENSE AGREEMENT FOR
 MICROSOFT INTERNET EXPLORER

 IMPORTANT READ CAREFULLY: This Microsoft
 End-User License Agreement (EULA) is a
 legal agreement between you (either an
 individual or a single entity) and Microsoft
 Corporation for the Microsoft software
 product identified above, which includes
 computer software and associated media and
 printed materials (if any), and may include
 online or electronic documentation (SOFTWARE
 PRODUCT or SOFTWARE). By installing, copying,
 or otherwise using the SOFTWARE PRODUCT,
 you agree to be bound by the terms of this
 EULA. If you do not agree to the terms of
 this Agreement, you are not authorized to
 use the SOFTWARE PRODUCT.

 The SOFTWARE PRODUCT is protected by
 copyright laws and international copyright
 treaties, as well as other intellectual

        [ I Agree ]      [ I Disagree ]
```

> **Warning** Although this license agreement is straightforward, you should read software license agreements completely. Typically, license agreements tell you if you can make backup copies of the software, technical support availability for the software, and other important information. In some cases, software manufacturers have hidden important clauses in license agreements that might cause problems. For instance, a major development tools vendor had a clause in its license agreement that prohibited users from developing competing tools with their software. Although the clause was thrown out in court, only the careful readers caught the clause and protected themselves from legal action.

4. To continue the installation process, click I Agree. If you agree to the license agreement, click the I Agree button to continue. If you do not agree to the license agreement, click I Disagree and the installation program terminates immediately. You can also click I Disagree to terminate the installation program, if you accidentally started the installation program. Figure A.2 shows the window that displays as the installation program extracts the files required in the setup process.

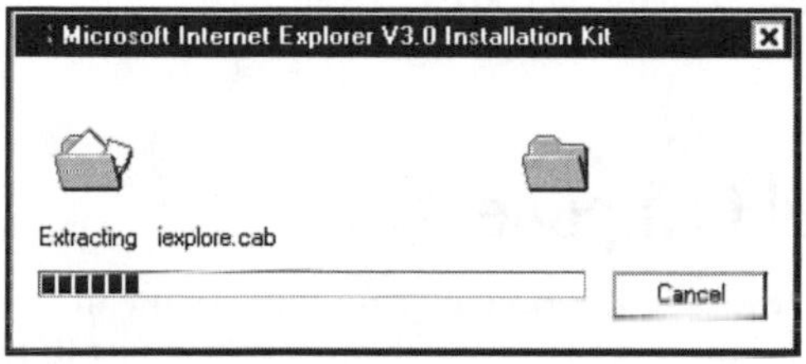

Figure A.2

This window appears briefly while the installation program extracts files required in the setup process.

5. After Internet Explorer copies some temporary files used during installation, the installation program prompts you for the directory where you want to store Internet Explorer. This window is displayed in figure A.3. From this window, you can specify a folder in which to create the folder called "Microsoft Internet."

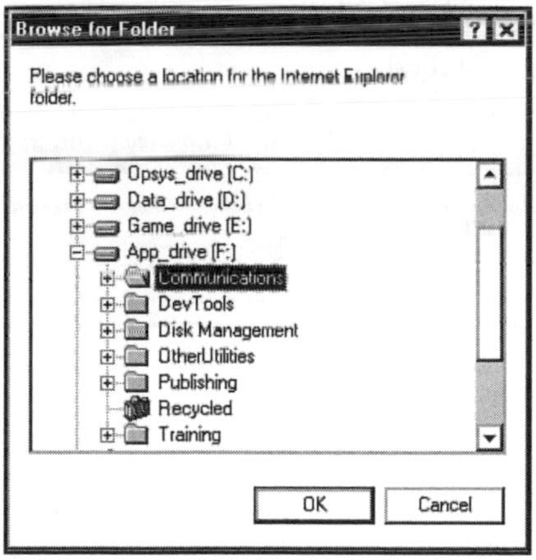

Figure A.3

This window prompts you for a folder in which the Microsoft Internet folder should be created.

Note The directory name for Internet Explorer, by default, is Microsoft Internet. This name cannot be changed during the installation process.

If you have already installed Internet Explorer on your computer, you will not be shown the window in figure A.3, which enables you to choose a directory in which the Internet Explorer folder will be created.

However, if you are installing Internet Explorer for the first time, the window shown in figure A.3 displays to enable you to choose the directory for the browser software's directory.

Installing Optional Components

On the CD

Internet Explorer now has several additional components that can be installed at the same time that you install the Internet Explorer browser. The CD-ROM included with this book contains the complete package of Internet Explorer and its add-on products, which include Internet Mail and News, ActiveMovie, and the HTML Layout Control. Whether or not to install optional components is part of the Internet Explorer installation process; therefore, the numbering of the following list picks up where the list in the previous section left off.

6. The window shown in figure A.4 enables you to choose whether or not you want to install these additional components. To install any of the components just mentioned, press the Yes button. If you click the No button, none of the additional components will be installed.

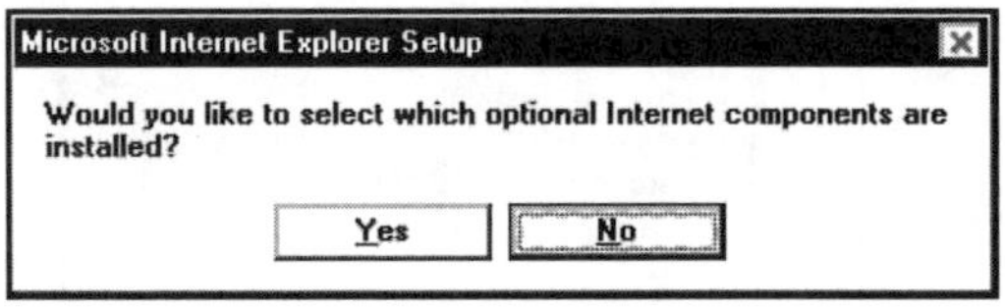

Figure A.4

You can choose to install optional components for Internet Explorer by clicking the Yes button in this window.

> Microsoft Internet Explorer Setup   [X]
>
> Would you like to select which optional Internet components are installed?
>
> [Yes]   [No]

7. If you choose to install Internet Explorer's optional components, the window shown in figure A.5 displays. You have a choice of installing four optional components. Descriptions of each of these components are included here to help you choose the components that you want on your computer.

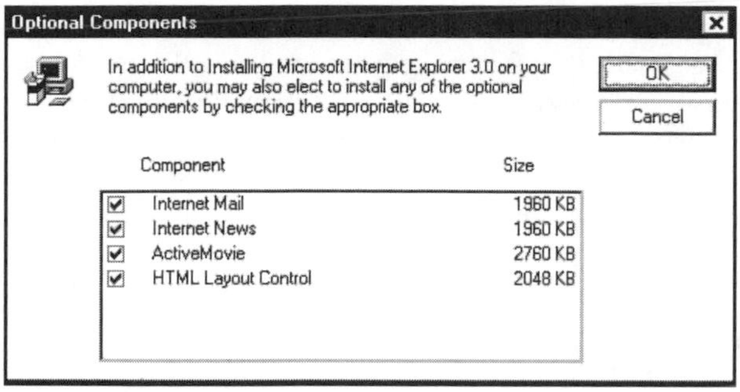

Figure A.5

These Optional Components can be installed when Internet Explorer is installed.

◆ **ActiveMovie.** This component is a relatively new technology introduced by Microsoft. With the large number of video standards that are emerging on the Internet, ActiveMovie seeks to combine them together with a common programming interface. Not only does ActiveMovie support all the major video formats, such as MPEG, Video for Windows, and Apple's QuickTime movie format, but it also supports *streaming video*, which enables video to be played over the Internet on demand without having to wait for the entire file to download. This technology simplifies retrieving content from the Internet because you do not have to get separate applications to view each of the types of video that ActiveMovie supports. For more information on ActiveMovie and related media technologies, visit the Microsoft Interactive Media page at http://www.microsoft.com/imedia.

◆ **HTML Layout Control.** This is a revolutionary method for creating web pages. Instead of the relatively simple formatting provided by standard HTML codes, the HTML Layout Control enables you to view pages that are displayed exactly as the designer wanted. You can learn more about how to create these pages by using the ActiveX Control Pad, which is described in Chapter 3, "The ActiveX Control Pad." However, to view pages created with the ActiveX Control Pad, you must have the HTML Layout Control installed. For more information on this control, visit its home page at http://www.microsoft.com/ie/ie3/layout.htm.

◆ **Internet Mail.** This program enables you to send and retrieve mail by using an Internet mail server, which is made available by your Internet service provider. With the Internet Mail program, which integrates into Internet Explorer, you can work online or offline with your mail. If you do not already have a mail program on your system, try this one. For more information on the Internet Mail program's features, visit its home page at http://www.microsoft.com/ie/ie3/imn.htm.

◆ **Internet News.** A large percentage of the traffic on the Internet is due to the large amount of content generated every day in newsgroups. Each newsgroup is devoted to a particular subject. Because literally thousands of newsgroups exist, whatever interests you is probably covered by at least one group. To read news, your Internet service provider must be set up to receive the newsgroups you want to read. After you know that your Internet provider supports newsgroups, the Internet News program from Microsoft enables you to easily view the groups and articles, as well as keep track of previously read articles. For more information on the Internet News program's features, visit its home page at `http://www.microsoft.com/ie/ie3/imn.htm`.

8. Check the boxes next to the components you want to install, and then press the OK button to continue. If you press the Cancel button now, the installation program stops and no new software is installed on your computer.

9. At this point, the installation program will begin installing software on your computer. The window shown in figure A.6 will list the components you chose to install. As the installation program proceeds, the component being installed will be highlighted in this window.

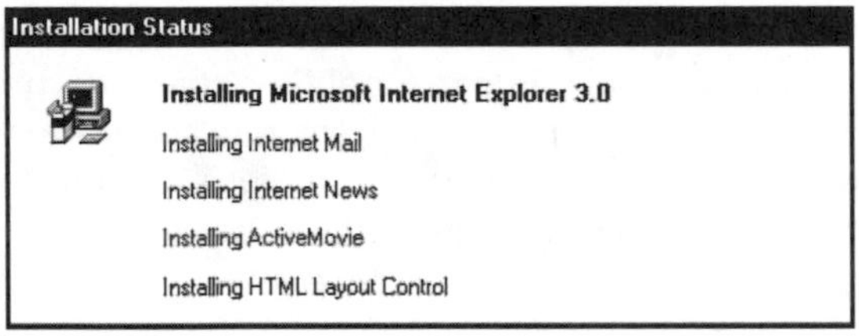

Figure A.6

Internet Explorer's Installation Status screen, with the component currently being installed shown in boldface.

```
Installation Status

   Installing Microsoft Internet Explorer 3.0
   Installing Internet Mail
   Installing Internet News
   Installing ActiveMovie
   Installing HTML Layout Control
```

10. The next window in the installation displays as the installation program copies the necessary files to your hard drive (see figure A.7). The Cancel button on this window enables you to abort the installation if necessary.

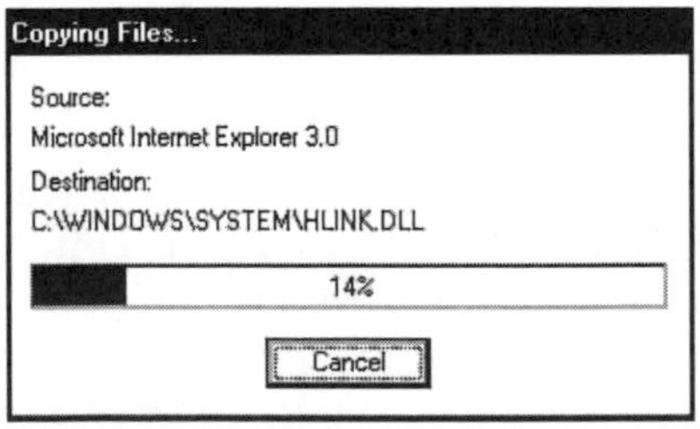

Figure A.7

This window displays the files required by a component as they are copied to your hard drive.

```
Copying Files...

Source:
Microsoft Internet Explorer 3.0
Destination:
C:\WINDOWS\SYSTEM\HLINK.DLL

                  14%

              [ Cancel ]
```

11. As with most newer Windows software, installing Internet Explorer requires changes to the Registry and other system files. The final window, shown in figure A.8, prompts you to reboot your computer. Click Yes to reboot and finish the installation.

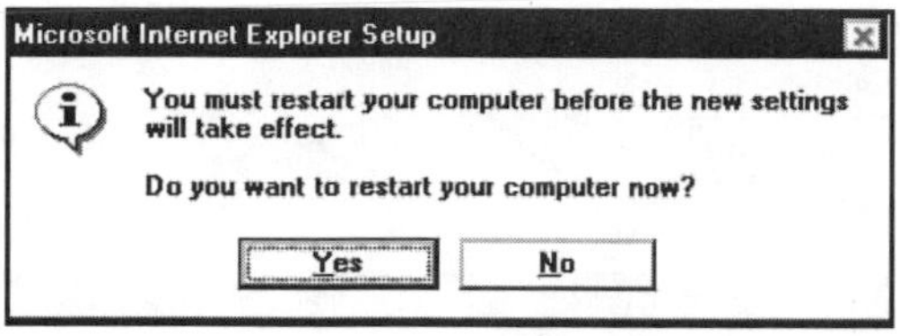

Figure A.8

This window prompts you to reboot your computer.

After your system reboots, you will see that Internet Explorer's installation program has created shortcuts to the following programs:

◆ Internet Explorer—located in the Programs menu within the Start menu

◆ Internet Explorer—located in the Internet Tools folder within the Accessories folder

◆ Internet Setup Wizard—located in the Internet Tools folder within the Accessories folder

◆ Internet Setup Wizard—labeled **The Internet** on the desktop

Note The Internet Setup Wizard is not the same program as the Internet Explorer. The Internet Setup Wizard enables you to easily create a connection to your Internet provider or to the Microsoft Network. If you have already done this and have connections available in Dial-Up Networking, you do not need to run the Internet Setup Wizard. For more information about the Internet Setup Wizard, you can start the program by pressing the Help button.

Running Internet Explorer

At this point, Internet Explorer is ready to run. To verify that the installation was successful, do the following:

1. Connect to your Internet provider by using Dial-Up Networking. If you have not set up Dial-Up Networking yet, contact your Internet service provider for specific instructions on how to configure your system.

2. When you have done so, start Internet Explorer by choosing it from your Start menu.

After Internet Explorer has started, it connects to the Microsoft Internet Explorer Welcome page, shown in figure A.9.

Figure A.9

Microsoft's Internet Explorer Welcome page.

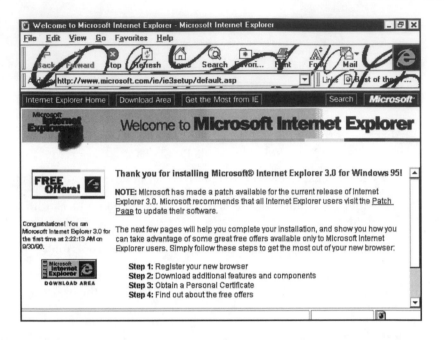

If you can see the Internet Explorer Welcome page, congratulations! Internet Explorer is installed correctly. If your computer has a sound card, you will hear background music when the Welcome page loads. Use the buttons shown on the Welcome page to proceed through the final steps in the installation of Internet Explorer. All these steps are optional. You will be able to register your browser, download additional software for use with Internet Explorer, receive a free personal security certificate, and find out about free offers from Microsoft for Internet Explorer users.

Note The first time Internet Explorer is loaded, it will load the Internet Explorer's Welcome page shown in figure A.9. However, the next time you use Internet Explorer, you will be taken to the Microsoft home page. If you want to return to the Welcome page at a later time, load the following page:

```
http://www.microsoft.com/ie/ie3setup/default.asp
```

If you do not see the Internet Explorer Welcome page, check the following things to determine the problem:

1. Did you restart your computer after Internet Explorer finished the installation process? You must do this before attempting to use Internet Explorer to view pages on the Internet.

2. Are you connected to your Internet service provider? When a Dial-Up Networking connection has been made successfully, the small pop-up window will say **Connected to <connection name>** and the timer will be running. If the connection is not active, restart the connection by using the steps mentioned previously.

3. Is your Dial-Up Networking configured correctly? If you do not know, contact your Internet service provider to verify that your network settings are correct.

After you have completed the tour, press the Home button on the Internet Explorer toolbar. The Home button immediately takes you to your specified home page. Because the Internet is so large, and because it can be easy to get lost, the Home button transports you to a convenient and familiar starting point.

Internet Explorer's home page is set to Microsoft's home page, which is located at `http://home.microsoft.com`. When you start Internet Explorer, it attempts to connect to this page. In the next section, you learn more about the options available in Internet Explorer, including an option that enables you to change your home page. You also learn about the other buttons on the Internet Explorer toolbar.

Exploring Internet Explorer

In this section, you learn more about the options and functions of Internet Explorer 3.0. Because this book uses Microsoft's browser exclusively, you must be familiar with the following features of Internet Explorer:

◆ The toolbar

◆ Internet Explorer's menus

◆ Address and Quick Links toolbar

The Toolbar

As with most Windows applications, Internet Explorer contains a toolbar that lists its commonly used functions. This toolbar's graphic design is quite different from other familiar Microsoft Office 95 applications. Instead of a three-dimensional look, its buttons are black-and-white pictures. As you move your mouse over each button, the picture changes from black-and-white to color. When the picture changes to color, you can click it to execute your action. This toolbar design is known as the Office 97 toolbar and is appearing in new versions of Microsoft's software. Figure A.10 shows the Internet Explorer toolbar.

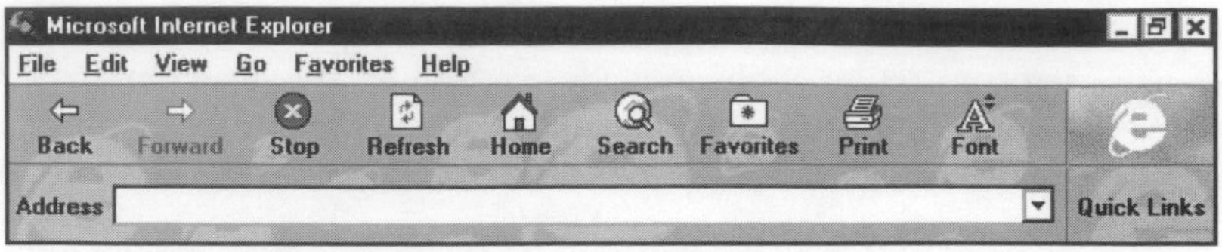

Figure A.10

Internet Explorer toolbar.

Back and Forward Buttons

As you traverse various pages on the Internet, you quickly find that good navigation tools are important. When viewing various pages, you may need to move to a previous page before either returning to the current page or following another path. Because Internet Explorer keeps a history of the pages you load each time you use it, the Back and Forward buttons enable you to move to a previous page and then forward to the page currently loaded.

Stop Button

If you are using a dial-up connection to access the Internet, you may notice that some pages require more time to load. This is because graphics and other elements on the page such as multimedia are large in size and take a long time to download from the Internet. An entire page need not be loaded to use the page. If you want to stop loading the current page, just press the Stop button.

Refresh Button

The Refresh button is very useful in programming web pages. The button instructs the browser to erase the current page and reload it completely from its original source, whether that is your hard drive or the Internet. This button is important when you test a page, make a change to the HTML source code, and want to see what you have just done. Press the Refresh button to try the page again. You can also use the Refresh button to reload a page from the Internet. This is useful if you need to stop the page from previously loading.

Home Button

The Home button returns you to a predefined starting page. Internet Explorer's default home page is `http://home.microsoft.com`, Microsoft's home page. As you soon learn, the default home page is one of many options you can change through Internet Explorer's Options window.

Search Button

As with the Home Button, the Search button can be used in the Options window to access your favorite search or super search engine. Although the Internet has experienced explosive growth in the past few years, the advent of the search engine has made it easy to find documents almost anywhere on the Internet. Yahoo (http://www.yahoo.com), Lycos (http://www.lycos.com), and AltaVista (http://www.altavista.digital.com) are three of the most popular search engines. Most of these engines work by accessing site addresses that webmasters have submitted. Webmasters will typically submit their site's address to many search engines so that more people can find and utilize their sites. After a site has been submitted to a search engine, the software indexes each page of a site. By following the links on a page, the search engine can find additional pages to index. The results of this process are then made available for keyword searches by users of the search engine. For instance, you may be looking for information about used car prices. By using a search engine, you could simply enter in the words "used car prices" and the search engine would return you a list of pages that had those keywords. More often than not, the first few links will give you the results you wanted.

> **Tip**
> Literally hundreds of search engines exist on the Internet and enable you to search for anything from a bed and breakfast in Connecticut to a long-lost roommate in Colorado. To help manage the proliferation of search engines, several sites have been created that serve as super search engines. These sites contain a well-organized format that enables you to access all search engines from a single site. You can use clnet's super search engine at http://www.search.com, and Microsoft's super search engine at http://www.msn.com/access/allinone.asp.

Favorites Button

More commonly known as *bookmarks*, the Favorites button opens a window to the site addresses that you have saved during your browsing sessions. From the Favorites window, you can double-click any of the items to go to that particular site.

Many Windows 95 Explorer-like features appear when you click the alternate mouse button (the right mouse button for right-handed users, and the left mouse button for left-handed users) in the window. For instance, you can create folders to store your bookmarks or move bookmarks between folders.

To add an entry to your Favorites folder, perform the following steps:

1. Go to your favorite web page. For instance, you could go to http://www.inquiry.com/thevbpro, which is Ask the VB Pro, or you could go to http://www.mcp.com, which is Macmillan Computer Publishing. (Of course, you may have other favorite pages you like to visit.)

2. Press the Favorites button and choose Add To Favorites from the menu shown in figure A.11.

3. In the window that is displayed (shown in figure A.12), you can change the name for this Favorite. In many cases, the name that is displayed will not be an accurate name for the link you are saving. Feel free to change the text shown in the box to better describe the site you are saving. When you are done changing the text, press the OK button.

4. You can now see the new Favorite by pressing the Favorites button again. The link you just saved will be alphabetized within the menu that appears after you press the button, as shown in figure A.13.

Print Button

The Print button prints the current page to your printer. As with most Windows applications, the Print button prints to the default printer without asking for additional options. To specify a different printer or a larger number of copies, choose Print from the File menu.

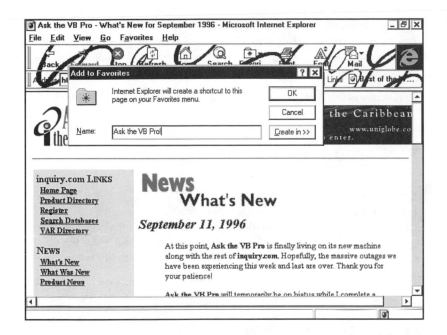

Figure A.12

Before the Favorite is added, you can change its name.

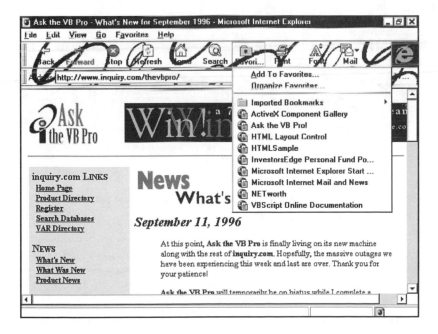

Figure A.13

The new Favorite has been added and is instantly shown in the Favorites menu.

Although you can usually print entire pages, some elements on web pages will not print. Typically, you should only count on being able to print the text and simple graphics on a page. Animated graphics only print one frame of the animation, for instance. Applets written in Java or Shockwave will not print, nor will video clips.

Also, if you are viewing a page that uses frames, choosing Print will only print the active frame. You can choose a frame by clicking in it with the left button and then pressing the Print button. Clicking a frame will cause it to become active and enable it to be printed.

Font Button

Most web page fonts are scaled in relation to each other. Newer browsers also contain specific fonts and font sizes that can be specified within the page. Depending on the layout of the page you are viewing, you might want to enlarge or reduce the font size. The Font button cycles through the available font sizes without requiring you to change the value in a separate window.

To help illustrate this feature, figure A.14 is shown with the smallest scaled font size, and figure A.15 shows the same content with the largest font size. As you can see, the proportions are maintained between the different fonts on the page. The large text on the page is always larger than the small text.

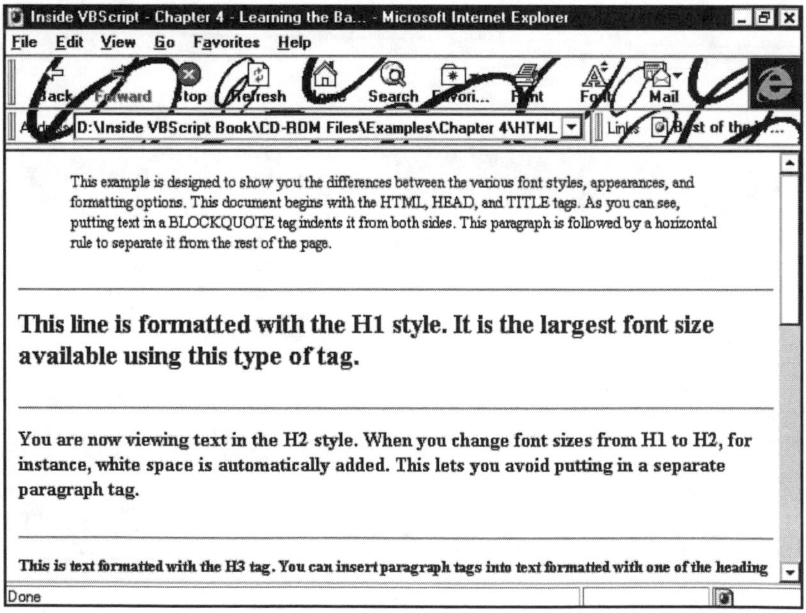

Figure A.14

Document shown using the smallest font size.

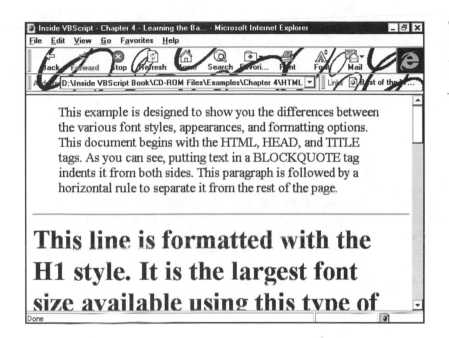

Figure A.15

Document shown using the largest font size.

Internet Explorer's Menus

Although the Internet Explorer toolbar provides quick access to the most commonly used functions, the power of Internet Explorer is located in the menus. You learn about each of the menu choices in this section and how to use these menus to customize your browser.

File Menu

As with most Windows software programs, Internet Explorer's first menu is the File menu. In general, the menu choices under the File menu are used to manipulate the currently loaded file or web page. The choices under Explorer's File Menu consist of the following items:

- ◆ New Window
- ◆ Open
- ◆ Save As File
- ◆ Send To
- ◆ Page Setup

◆ Print

◆ Create Shortcut

◆ Properties

◆ Close

New Window

It is convenient to be able to have multiple pages loaded at the same time, especially as you are browsing the web. For instance, you may be comparing products and want to view the product descriptions side by side. For this reason, the New Window menu choice will create another Internet Explorer browser that can be pointed to another web page. This browser is independent of the first; that is, if you change pages in the first browser, the second will not change. However, any Favorites you create in either browser will be available to any browser window. This is because the Favorites are stored in a common location on your computer.

 To switch between Internet Explorer windows, you can use the Windows 95 Taskbar at the bottom of the desktop. You can also use Alt+Tab to quickly toggle between windows.

Open

This menu item brings up a dialog box that enables you to type in or choose a document to view (see fig. A.16). You can enter either a URL or a file name. When you press OK or the Enter key, the document loads in the current Internet Explorer window.

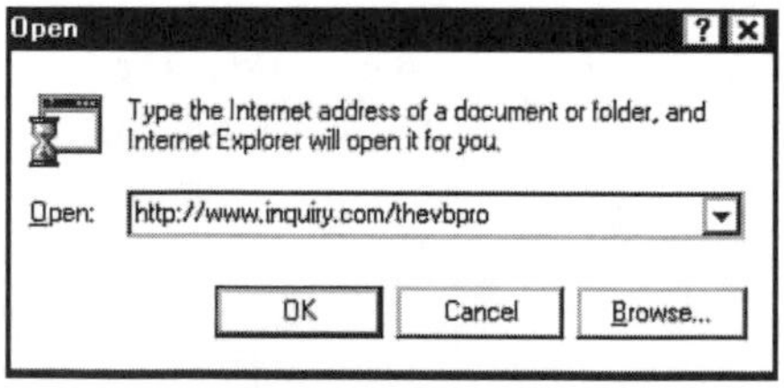

Figure A.16

Internet Explorer's Open dialog box.

Save As File

This menu item enables you to save the text portion of the current document. The standard Windows 95 Save dialog box prompts you for a location in which to save the current document.

By saving a document, you only save the text portion. Any graphics, sounds, or other elements on the page must be saved separately.

Send To

As with most newer Windows 95 applications, Internet Explorer supports the Send To function that is also found in the Explorer desktop. By adding shortcuts to the Send To folder under the Windows 95 directory, you can direct an HTML document to Word, Notepad, Exchange, or any other application.

Page Setup and Print

These two menu options work together to determine how your document prints. From the Page Setup window, you can set margins, create headers and footers, and choose a printer. In addition to these options, Internet Explorer can create a table of page links at the end of the document. When you print a page from Yahoo's directory, for instance, the final page of the document lists the full URLs for each link on the page. This creates a handy reference guide for surfing the Internet.

Create Shortcut

In some cases, you may want to have a quick way to access a web page immediately without having to start Internet Explorer manually. By using the Create Shortcut menu choice, Internet Explorer will create a link to the current page and place this link on your desktop. This enables you to start Internet Explorer by using the shortcut and proceeding immediately to that page.

To create a shortcut to a favorite page, follow these steps:

1. Load your favorite page in your browser window. Figure A.17 shows Internet Explorer loaded with Macmillan Computer Publishing's home page.

2. Choose Create Shortcut from the File menu, and the message shown in figure A.18 will be displayed.

3. If you look at your Windows desktop, you will see a shortcut to Macmillan's site on your desktop. If you exit Internet Explorer and double-click this shortcut, Internet Explorer will load that page immediately.

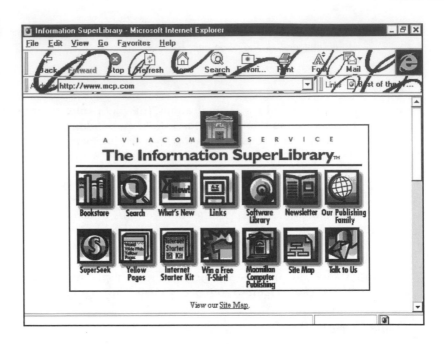

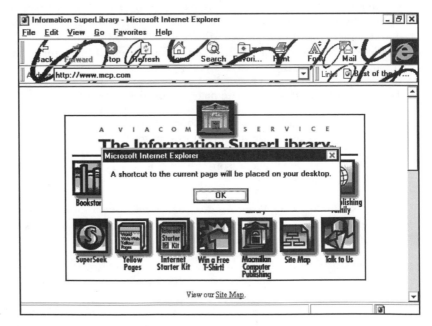

Properties

From this menu item, you can view statistics and security information about the current document. Figure A.19 shows the General tab of the Page properties window. Figure A.20 shows the information available when you visit a secure site, such as `https://www.microsoft.com`. A secure site is one whose web server uses encryption to protect the data that is going back and forth from your browser. Encryption uses secret, virtually unbreakable codes to protect your information as it travels over the Internet. Typically, secure web sites' URLs are prefixed with `https` instead of just `http`. The *s* on the end indicates a secured server.

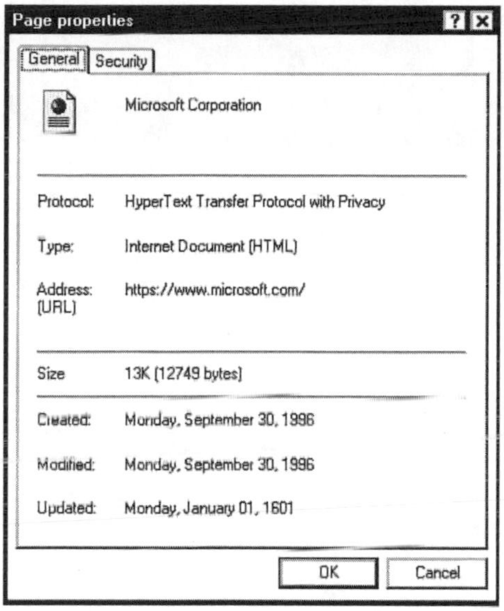

Figure A.19

The General tab shown in the Page properties window.

Close

This menu choice causes the current Internet Explorer window to close. If you have multiple windows open, this choice only causes the current window to close.

Edit Menu

Although the File menu choices operate on the document as a whole, the Edit menu deals specifically with the content of the document. Many of these menu choices will be familiar to users of other Windows software, as the initial menu choices are common to many applications. The shortcut keys, such as Ctrl+C and Ctrl+V, are identical to the rest of Microsoft's Office 95 suite and Windows 95. This similarity makes it easy to begin using these menu choices immediately.

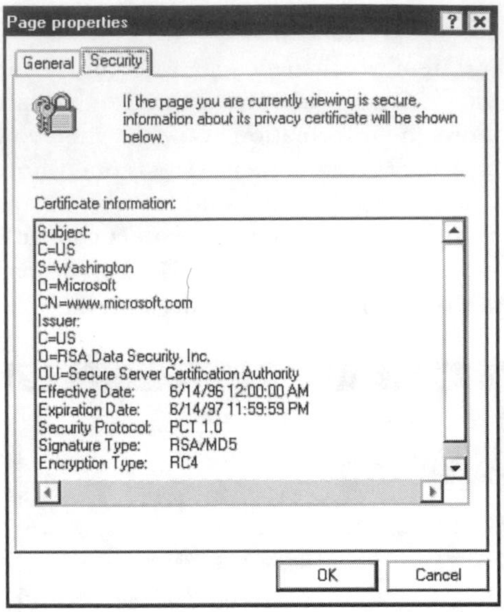

Figure A.20

The Security tab shown in the Page properties window.

The following menu choices are on the Edit menu:

♦ Cut

♦ Copy

♦ Paste

♦ Select All

♦ Find (on this page)

Cut, Copy, Paste, and Select All

As with almost all Windows applications, you have the ability to cut, copy, and paste to and from Internet Explorer. These functions work normally in the Address box (discussed later), but only Select All and Copy can be used when editing content in the main document window.

To cut content from a document, highlight it and choose Cut from the Edit menu. However, the content you selected will simply be copied. Documents you view with Internet Explorer, whether they are on your local hard drive or on the Internet, cannot be edited directly with Internet Explorer. The Cut menu option was included in Internet Explorer primarily to be consistent with other Windows applications.

To copy content from a document, highlight it and choose Copy from the Edit menu. When you choose Paste in another application, the content is pasted as plain text without any formatting.

Finally, if you want to select all the text content on a page, you can choose Select All. For a large page, this is an easier way to select all the text without having to scroll down the page.

Find (on this page)

Internet Explorer provides a simple text-search capability to find keywords in the current document shown in Internet Explorer. This differs from the Search toolbar button and menu choice, which actually redirects the browser to search engines on the Internet.

View Menu

The View menu contains the menu choices that modify the appearance of the page within Internet Explorer. Although these options and choices do not actually change the document, they can be used to change the appearance within your browser window.

The following menu choices are on the View menu:

◆ Toolbar

◆ Status Bar

◆ Fonts

◆ Stop

◆ Refresh

◆ Source

◆ Options

Toolbar and Status Bar Options

By toggling each of these menu items, you can display or hide the toolbar and the status bar. The toolbar is the line of buttons at the top of the Internet Explorer window. The status bar is the bar at the bottom of the window.

Fonts

This submenu offers the same functions as the Fonts toolbar button. You can choose one of five different font groups for the documents in Internet Explorer. Because fonts are displayed in proportion to each other, all the fonts on a document will shrink when you choose the Small group. For more information on how fonts can be sized in Internet Explorer, refer to the previous section that dealt with the Fonts toolbar button.

Stop and Refresh

These two menu items are identical to the toolbar buttons of the same names, which are explained in the previous section of this appendix that dealt with the Internet Explorer toolbar.

Source

This menu item opens Notepad with the current document and enables you to view the source HTML behind the page. This is an extremely useful tool for debugging page layouts.

Options

This dialog box enables you to set all the options in Internet Explorer. The following list details the tabs and the options that can be set:

◆ **General.** Here, you can control various viewing options and specify content that should not be downloaded, such as graphics or sound.

◆ **Connection.** You can specify that a dial-up networking connection should be created when Internet Explorer places a request for a page on the Internet. You can also specify proxy server information from this dialog box.

◆ **Navigation.** This tab enables you to change not only your home page, but also the page to which the Search button goes. You can also change the Quick Links, which are located beneath the Internet Explorer toolbar. This feature enables you to put your five favorite pages within easy reach. You can also control how many days worth of history Internet Explorer saves between browsing sessions. Internet Explorer stores links for a certain number of days before it removes them from the History folder, located in your Windows directory.

◆ **Programs.** This tab's options control your Internet mail and news program choices. You can also choose the browser you want to use for downloading files. Finally, you can force Internet Explorer to make itself the default web browser each time it loads. This option is a result of the ongoing browser wars between

Netscape and Microsoft. Each company's browser automatically makes itself the default web browser when it is installed. This option essentially notifies you that another browser has made itself the default browser.

◆ **Security.** Internet Explorer contains the Content Advisor, which can control what web pages can be loaded. After a supervisor password is set, you can control how much sex, nudity, violence, and offensive language to allow on a page before Internet Explorer objects. These ratings are based on the RSAC (Recreational Software Advisory Council) system, but other rating systems can be loaded for use. The RSAC system is an extension of a system developed to rate video games. Each category (sex, nudity, violence, and language) is given a rating from zero to four, with four being the most objectionable. However, because ratings are a new extension of HTML, this method might not always prevent a child's access to a site with objectionable content. For the rating system to work correctly, each page on a web site has to have a special tag added to it. Because this is time-consuming, very few sites have yet to implement ratings throughout their sites. Until more sites have implemented the ratings system, direct parental supervision is still the only sure way to prevent access to offensive sites.

Tip   For more information on the RSAC system, visit their home page at http://www.rsac.org.

Besides the actual content of the page, you can also restrict content based on the type of content, whether it be Java applets, ActiveX controls, or ActiveX scripts. Finally, Internet Explorer supports a security system that enables controls and pages to be given security certificates, which identify the creator of the page. Although a certificate does not ensure that the page will work correctly, it does assure you of the actual creator of the page.

◆ **Advanced.** Internet Explorer maintains local copies of pages for quicker access. The options on this tab specify how much disk space this cache should take, as well as how often to reload the pages from their original sources. If a page that is stored locally has expired, Internet Explorer will automatically load it from the original source the next time you request that page.

Internet Explorer also warns you of various events that happen as you are browsing. Most of these events are normal, but you may want to leave these warnings enabled while you are learning how to use the browser. Finally, this tab contains some other options that deal with how pages are displayed.

For more information on any option in this or any other Options tab, click the question mark icon in the title bar and then click the option you want to learn about.

Tip All options on the tabs can be set from the Control Panel Internet applet.

Go Menu

Besides duplicating the functions of the Back, Forward, Home, and Search toolbar buttons, the Go menu enables you to quickly access Microsoft's Internet Explorer home page for product updates. The Go menu maintains a record of the most recent pages you have visited. To view all the pages you have visited, choose the Open History folder at the bottom of the menu. The display is similar to the Favorites view and enables you to reload a previously loaded page.

Favorites Menu

The Favorites menu lists the favorite sites you have saved while navigating the Internet. You can access the entire Favorites folder by choosing the Open Favorites Folder. This is the same function provided by the Favorites toolbar button. You can also add a new favorite site from the Favorites menu.

Help Menu

Microsoft has included an extensive Help file with Internet Explorer. As with other Windows 95 Help files, you can either use the Index tab or use the Find function to locate specific keywords.

Other Window Features

The last two elements in Internet Explorer are the Address and Quick Links toolbars. These toolbars can be arranged by dragging them into the position that you desire. By default, the toolbars will be stacked on top of each other. If your window is wide enough, you can arrange the toolbars next to each other to save vertical space for more content. To drag the toolbar into a different position, click the toolbar name and move it into its new position. The cursor changes to a four-way arrow to signal when you can begin dragging. The toolbars can be stacked on top of each other, or if your window is wide enough, placed next to each other.

The Quick Links toolbar contains five icons:

♦ **Best of the Web.** This link displays a page on the Microsoft Network web site with links to some of the best sites on the Internet, as selected by the staff of the Microsoft Network. The links shown on this page are ones that were previously featured on the Today's Links pages.

♦ **Today's Links.** This page, which is updated daily, contains links to other great web sites. Sites shown on this page may eventually be added to the Best of the Web pages.

◆ **Web Gallery.** This link brings you to a part of Microsoft's site devoted to all the technologies related to the Internet and the World Wide Web. This is a good page to keep because you can access everything from ActiveX control directories to browser Plug-Ins.

◆ **Product News.** This link calls up the Internet Explorer home page. You can retrieve the latest version of all the Internet Explorer files and add-ins from this page.

◆ **Microsoft.** This link transports you to the Microsoft home page.

Note	The Quick Links icons can be changed from their default definitions within the Options dialog box, located under the View menu.

Summary

This chapter has attempted to give you an overview of the features of Internet Explorer 3.0. As with all software packages, the best way to learn how to use the tool is to use the software. You can only learn so much from looking at pictures in a book. Now that you have your browser installed, get out there and surf the web!

GLOSSARY G

32-bit structure   A program or computer that processes 32 bits (or 4 bytes) of information at a time. By extension, a 32-bit operating system is an operating system that is capable of processing 32 bits at a time. Windows 95 and Windows NT are 32-bit operating systems; Windows 3.1 is a 16-bit operating system.

8.3 rule   In DOS and Windows 3.1, file names can't have more than eight characters; file-name extensions can't have more than three characters. This rule doesn't apply to files in newer, 32-bit versions of Windows such as Windows 95 and Windows NT, and in other operating systems like the Macintosh OS and Unix.

A

absolute link (URL)   An HTML hyperlink containing the complete URL, including the directory path. Example: `<A HREF="http://www.domain_name.com/name.html>`. This is as opposed to a link (such as `<A HREF="name.html">`) that does not contain a fully-qualified path. See also *relative link*.

Acrobat   Adobe Systems' software suite for creating and publishing portable electronic documents that will look the same on any computer. Acrobat is a stand-alone application; there is also an ActiveX version downloadable from the ActiveX gallery.

active content   Web content that has the ability to change dynamically or interact with users, based on scripts or objects embedded in the web page.

ActiveX   A set of component technologies that enables software components to interact with one another in a networked environment, regardless of the language in which they were created.

ActiveX controls are 32-bit, which means that they only function under Windows 95 and Windows NT.

ActiveX Control Pad   An application to assist VBScript developers in inserting ActiveX controls into web pages.

ActiveX gallery   A location on the Microsoft web site where you can preview and download ActiveX controls from Microsoft and a number of other developers.

ActiveX scripting   Synonymous with VBScript.

add-on   (Also called *add-in*, *plug-in*, or *helper application*.) An accessory or utility program that extends the capabilities of an application program.

algorithm   A specific set of procedures for solving a problem in a finite number of steps. Computer programs are based on algorithms.

alignment   The horizontal arrangement of lines of text, graphics, or other elements on a page with respect to the left and right margins.

Alta Vista   Digital Equipment's search engine and site. http://www.altavista.com

analog format   A form of representation in which the indicator is varied continuously (for example, analog sound files on a computer). Contrast with *digital format*. Colloquial definition: the real-life version of something that is often represented digitally.

anchor   The start or destination of a hyperlink.

animated GIFs   A GIF graphic file comprised of multiple images. The images, when presented sequentially, can appear to be in motion. You can construct your own animated GIFs using software such as GIF Construction Set.

animation   A series of images created in successive positions to create the effect of movement by the characters or other elements.

ANSI   Acronym for American National Standards Institute, which defines the standards for (among other things) the character set used by Microsoft Windows. (Compare with *ASCII*, an earlier standard character set used by MS-DOS.)

antialiasing   The smoothing of pixelated (jagged) edges in a graphic image. Many graphics applications include an option to antialias images.

API   Application Programming Interface, a method by which a programmer can write function calls to perform predefined tasks. Windows programs generally perform data processing through calls to the Windows API; many other APIs exist.

application programs   Programs that perform functions directly for a user. Includes word processors, spreadsheets, databases, presentation programs, and desktop publishing programs. Often referred to as simply *applications* or *programs*.

argument   A value passed to a procedure. For example, in the statement

```
Print "cheese"
```

the text value "cheese" is an argument to the Print method.

array   A set of sequentially indexed elements having the same type of data. Each element of an array has a unique identifying number, called an index.

ASCII (American Standard Code for Information Exchange)   Pronounced *ask-ee*. The original 128-character set, or a file containing only those characters and no special formatting. Compare with *ANSI*.

asynchronous   An operation that can proceed without waiting for another related process to complete. A factory production line is synchronous; cars navigating a freeway interchange are (ideally) asynchronous.

attribute   HTML code included in an opening tag to provide extra information about the behavior of the tag and the text, graphic, or other element it describes. For example, in the HTML tag `<BODY BGCOLOR="#FFFFFF">`, the `BGCOLOR` code is an attribute tag.

audio   Audible sound. See also *sound, video*.

Authenticode   A technology used by Microsoft Internet Explorer to verify that downloaded software (such as ActiveX controls) came from a reputable source.

AVI (Audio/Video/Interactive)   The Microsoft file format for Video for Windows movies.

B

background   The solid color, image, or textured pattern behind the text and graphics on a web page.

bandwidth   A measure of the carrying capacity of a network, including the Internet. Some kinds of information, such as graphics, take up much more bandwidth; other kinds, such as text, take up much less. Larger bandwidth means that data moves through the data to your computer faster. For most individual users who dial in to access the Internet, one way to increase bandwidth is to upgrade to a faster modem.

banner   An advertisement on a web page; usually a commercial advertisement that links to the advertiser's site or to another page dedicated to the product being advertised. Banners are almost always composed of bitmapped GIF graphics, sometimes with animated GIFs.

batch processing   Performing the same function on many files or documents at the same time.

baud   A measure of the speed at which data is transmitted. *Baud rate* indicates the number of bits of data transmitted in one second. One baud is one bit per second. Common modems today have baud rates of 14,400 or 28,800. See also *bandwidth.*

beta testing   The last stage of development for a computer program before it is released. During beta testing, the program is released to a select group of users for testing.

binary numbers   The number system having a base of 2. Preferred for computers for precision and economy. See also *bit.*

bit   A binary digit, the smallest piece of information used by a computer. Bits can be turned on or off and used in various combinations to represent different kinds of information. Eight bits form a byte.

bit-wise comparison   A bit-by-bit comparison of identically positioned bits in two numeric expressions.

bitmap   A "paint" or "photo" file. Graphic image formed by an array of screen dots (pixels). Also known as a *raster image.*

blocking   Occurs when you initiate an operation and an individual process waits until the operation has finished.

bookmark   An URL that has been saved using a command in a web browser program for easy access later. Bookmarking URLs prevents the user from having to type in long web page addresses over and over again.

Boolean expression   An expression that evaluates to either True or False.

bridge   A piece of networking hardware that joins two disparate networks using a common protocol.

broadcast   Sending information that can be received by all nodes on a network such as the Internet. See also *multicast, narrowcast.*

browse   To look over a collection of information casually, especially in an effort to find something of interest, as in browsing through directories (folders) to find a specific file. See also *browser*.

browser   A program, such as Netscape Navigator or Microsoft Internet Explorer, used to view information on the World Wide Web.

bullets   Simple graphics that call attention to something. Usually, they look like tiny buttons without words and are used to set apart items in an unnumbered list.

by reference   A way of passing the address, rather than the value, of an argument to a procedure. This enables the procedure to access the actual variable. As a result, the variable's actual value can be changed by the procedure to which it is passed.

by value   A way of passing the value, rather than the address, of an argument to a procedure. This enables the procedure to access a copy of the variable. As a result, the variable's actual value can't be changed by the procedure to which it is passed.

byte   A measurement of computer storage. Usually 8 bits.

C

C, C++   Programming languages preferred by many professional programmers. C is characterized by a syntax that is harder to learn than BASIC, while enabling the programmer greater control over the computer's functions than BASIC. C++ is a superset of C, adding object-oriented language features.

cache   Pronounced "cash." Special section of RAM or disk memory set aside to store frequently accessed information.

Café   Symantec's Java development environment. It is available at `http://www.symantec.com/product/index_devtools.html`.

Catapult   The code name for the Microsoft Proxy Server. See also *Microsoft Proxy Server*.

CDK   Control Development Kit, the software development kit used by C++ programmers to create OCX controls. Superseded by the ActiveX Development Kit.

CGI (Common Gateway Interface)   A format and syntax for passing information from browsers to servers via forms or queries in HTML. It can be written in nearly any programming language, but is generally written in Perl, C, or C++. Programs written in this syntax are sometimes known as CGI scripts. See also *ISAPI*.

character code   A number that represents a particular character in a set, such as the ASCII character set. For example, the ASCII code for the lowercase letter "e" is 101.

class   The formal definition of an object. The class acts as the template from which an instance of an object is created at runtime. The class defines the properties of the object and the methods used to control the object's behavior.

class module   A module containing the definition of a class (its property and method definitions).

clear GIF   A completely invisible GIF. It can be any size, but is usually only a single pixel. Used to create white space on a web page for better placement of text by changing the Height and Width attributes of the image tag.

client   A computer that primarily receives information destined for use by an end user. Compare to *server*, a machine that is configured to distribute information to a number of client computers.

client-side image map   An image map that is interpreted by the browser, rather than the server. See also *server-side image map*.

collection   An object that contains a set of related objects. Think of a collection as an array of objects.

COM (Component Object Model)   A specification for reusable software components. ActiveX controls fall under the DCOM, or Distributed Component Object Model specification, which in turn falls under the COM specification.

comment   Text within a piece of code that is not interpreted or executed. In BASIC, comments are set off with a single apostrophe (') or the Rem statement. In HTML, comments are enclosed in comment tags "<!--" and "-->".

comparison operator   An operator that tests a quantitative relationship between two or more values or expressions.

compressed file   A data file that has been modified to consume less space than it did before modification. Prior to use, it must be decompressed. On Windows computers, the most common general compression format is the ZIP format, although many compressed files are saved in an executable (EXE) format.

constant   A variable that does not change in the course of a procedure or a program. Visual Basic supports the use of constants, but VBScript does not. However, you can "fake" constants in VBScript by using a naming convention—for example, many programmers type constants in all-capital letters to indicate that their values do not change.

contact link   Also known as a *mail link*. A hypertext link that makes it easy for visitors to a web site to contact people "behind" the web site. It could link to the site developer's e-mail address, to a mail form, or to a page with a directory of e-mail addresses for key company contacts.

control   A programmable element of the user interface. Examples of controls are the text box, the combo box, and the command button. In Visual Basic, "control" also can refer to certain programmable objects that are not part of the visible user interface, such as the timer control or the ActiveX preload control.

cookies   A technique for storing persistent information on a web browser. When a process running on a web server needs to temporarily store information on a user's computer, it passes a cookie to the browser, which then stores it for the duration of the session with that server.

cross-platform   A computer program with versions for more than one operating system, such as Unix, Macintosh, and Windows. Can also mean applications, such as those created in Java, that run on different operating systems with little or no modification.

custom control   A generic term referring to ActiveX, OCX, or VBX controls.

cyberspace   Refers to the entire world of online information and services, but specifically to the Internet. Coined by William Gibson in his novel *Neuromancer*.

D

data ranges   Each Variant subtype has a specific range of allowed values:

◆ Byte: 0 to 255.

◆ Boolean: True or False.

◆ Integer: -32,768 to 32,767.

◆ Long: -2,147,483,648 to 2,147,483,647.

◆ Single: -3.402823E38 to -1.401298E-45 for negative values; 1.401298E-45 to 3.402823E38 for positive values.

◆ Double: -1.79769313486232E308 to -4.94065645841247E-324 for negative values; 4.94065645841247E-324 to 1.79769313486232E308 for positive values.

◆ Currency: -922,337,203,685,477.5808 to 922,337,203,685,477.5807.

◆ Date: January 1, 100 to December 31, 9999, inclusive.

◆ Object: Any Object reference.

◆ String: Variable-length strings may range in length from 0 to approximately 2 billion characters (approximately 65,535 for Microsoft Windows version 3.1 and earlier).

◆ Error: Contains an error number (see also *error*).

data types   The different types of variables that can be processed by a programming language. VBScript has only one data type, the Variant, which has many subtypes; variants can contain textual, numeric, or other information.

database administrator   The person responsible for maintaining a database system—usually a client-server system.

database program   Enables collection of data in an organized format, permitting manipulation of the data in a variety of ways (examples: Sybase, Oracle, Microsoft Access). Sometimes abbreviated RDBMS (for Relational Database Management System).

date expression   Any expression that can be interpreted as a date. This includes any combination of date literals, numbers that look like dates, strings that look like dates, and dates returned from functions. A date expression is limited to numbers or strings, in any combination, that can represent a date from January 1, 100 through December 31, 9999.

Dates are stored as part of a real number. Values to the left of the decimal represent the date; values to the right of the decimal represent the time. Negative numbers represent dates prior to December 30, 1899.

date literal   A value that can be interpreted by Visual Basic as a date. In Visual Basic and VBScript expressions, dates are delimited by number signs (#).

Valid formats include the date format specified by the locale settings for your code or the universal date format. For example, #12/31/1992# is the date literal that represents December 31, 1992. Other valid date formats are dependent on your computer's international language settings.

In VBScript, the only recognized format is that of U.S. English, regardless of the actual locale of the user; that is, the interpreted format is mm/dd/yyyy.

date separators   Characters used to separate the day, month, and year when date values are formatted. In U.S. English, the date separator is a forward slash (/).

dates and times   In Visual Basic and VBScript, dates and times are stored internally as different parts of a real number.

The value to the left of the decimal represents a date between January 1, 100 and December 31, 9999, inclusive. Negative values represent dates prior to December 30, 1899.

The value to the right of the decimal represents a time between 0:00:00 and 23:59:59, inclusive. In expressions involving date arithmetic, a single day is equal to 1.

DBMS   Database Management System, an application that enables a programmer to store and access data in tables.

DCOM   Distributed Component Object Model, a protocol that permits software objects to interact over networks (including the Internet). Previously called "Network OLE."

DDE   Dynamic Data Exchange. An older Microsoft protocol for interprocess communications in Windows; made obsolete by OLE Automation. You cannot access DDE from VBScript code.

default   The condition set automatically in a program when no selection has been made explicitly.

DES   Data Encryption Standard, a cryptographic standard. This technology is used by software developers in the encryption features of their software products.

desktop   In a graphical environment, a representation of your day-to-day work as though you are looking at an actual desk littered with folders full of work to do.

desktop publishing program   Application programs, such as PageMaker and QuarkXPress, used for typeset publications, such as newsletters and magazines.

dialog box   An on-screen message box that conveys or requests information.

digital format   The form of something, such as an image or sound, when stored as computer data.

dingbats   Ornamental characters, such as bullets, stars, and flowers, used to decorate a page.

Director movie   An animation, presentation, or interactive title created in Macromedia Director.

directory (subdirectory)   A list of computer files contained on a disk or drive. May be nested to facilitate organization of data on the disk or drive. On Macintosh, Windows 95, and Windows NT 4.0 systems, directories and subdirectories are called *folders*.

dithering   A method employed to simulate natural shading in images with a limited color range. Shades are represented with combinations of different colored dots (pixels) on-screen in various patterns. Often used to give the appearance of smoother transitions between shades of color.

DLL   Dynamic Link Library. This is a type of Windows file that can be called from an application. DLLs can hypothetically be shared between applications.

DNS   Domain Name Service, a piece of software that converts Internet IP network addresses to textual names.

document source   The HTML code behind a page displayed on the web. This information can usually be viewed through a web browser.

domain   The name of a computer that acts as a server.

domain name   A unique identifier that assigns a name to a specific Internet address. Domain names are a way of translating numeric computer names, known as IP addresses, into easily-remembered textual addresses. For example, the IP address of your computer might be 128.47.84.12, but you can refer to it as myserver.com if the computer has been mapped to that domain name. The right-most part of a domain name is known as the *zone*; it tells what type of institution the name is related to: .org (organization), .com (commercial), .edu (educational), .net (network operations), .gov (U.S. government), or .mil (U.S. military). Most countries also have a domain; for example, .us (United States), .uk (United Kingdom), and .au (Australia). See *DNS*.

DOS (Disk Operating System)   The underlying control system for many personal computers. Usually refers to MS-DOS, the operating system for IBM-compatible computers.

download   The process of transferring information from a remote computer to your computer. On the Internet, you can use a file transfer utility (such as FTP) to download or upload files. You also download files using a web browser.

dpi (dots per inch)   A measure of image resolution that measures the number of addressable dots in an inch. Most laser printers, for example, can print at a resolution of 300 to 600 dpi.

drag and drop   A method for moving text or graphics to other locations. Point to the item with the cursor, hold down the mouse button, and then drag the item to its new location. Release the mouse button, and the item has now moved. This process can also be used to launch applications. Many HTML editors also set links to images and graphics using drag and drop.

dynamic (adj.)   Marked by continuous activity or change.

E

e-mail address   A domain-based address used for sending electronic mail (e-mail) to a specified destination. Must include an @ sign and extension, such as `.com` or `.org`; for example, `president@whitehouse.gov`.

element   A component of a hierarchical structure (for example, in a web site). Also used to mean any individually manipulatable shape in a graphic. In this usage, the term *element* is synonymous with the term *object*.

embedded   An object that resides in another object. ActiveX controls and Java applets, for example, are said to be embedded in HTML pages through the use of the <OBJECT> tag.

Empty   A special value that indicates that a variable has never been initialized. In Visual Basic expressions, Empty can be the equivalent of either zero or a zero-length string ("").

end tag   In HTML programming, this identifies the end of an element. It is also called the *close tag*.

end user   A person who uses a computer program or device to perform a function such as word processing.

Enum   Shorthand for enumeration.

environment   An operating system. Windows 95, OS/2, and Macintosh OS are examples of environments.

error number   A whole number in the range 0 to 65,535, inclusive, that corresponds to the Number property of the Err object. When combined with the Name property of the Err object, this number represents a particular error message.

event   An occurrence that takes place while an application runs. Events are usually user-initiated; button clicks, windows opening, and menu commands are examples of events. Visual Basic programs are often designed to respond to events. Procedures triggered to run when events take place are called *event procedures*.

event procedure   Code that is run as the result of an event, such as a click on a command button. See also *event*.

expression   A combination of keywords, operators, variables, and constants that yield a string, number, or object. An expression can perform a calculation, manipulate characters, or test data.

extension, file name extension   (1) Tags or attributes introduced by a browser company, such as Netscape or Microsoft, which are not part of the current HTML specification and are usually only supported by that browser. (2) The latter portion of a filename on a DOS or Unix machine, such as .doc for document or .gif for Graphic File Format. Macintosh file names don't require extensions; however, all files that are to be displayed by a browser must include an extension.

F

FAQs (Frequently Asked Questions)   A list of questions and answers with basic information about a web site or other Internet resource.

Fetch   The most popular Macintosh program for file transfer between client and server.

firewall   A piece of software that runs alongside an Internet server in order to improve security. See also *proxy server*.

first-generation browsers   Early versions of browsers that pre-date the capability to recognize plug-ins, tables, animated GIFs, background colors, or background images. The original Mosaic is an example of such a browser.

folder   A list of computer files contained on a disk or drive. May be nested to facilitate organization of data on the disk or drive. Called directories or subdirectories on DOS and Unix systems.

font   One complete collection of letters, punctuation marks, numbers, and special characters with a consistent and identifiable typeface, weight, posture, and font size. Sometimes used to refer to typefaces or font families. In Windows, the native font format is called TrueType.

font family   A set of fonts in several sizes and weights that share the same typeface.

form   A user interface, usually comprised of input controls such as text boxes and buttons. In HTML, *form* refers to a page that takes information inputted into a web browser and submits it to a web server. In Visual Basic, a form is the basis of the user interface.

frames   An HTML extension that enables more than one HTML document to be displayed on a web page by splitting the web browser's window into distinct sections.

FTP (File Transfer Protocol)   A method for transferring files from one machine to another on the Internet.

FUD   Fear, Uncertainty, and Doubt, an industry term applied to the marketing practice of marketing by systematically obsfucating the future of technology.

G

gamma curve controls   A dialog box that permits the user to control smooth transitions in contrast over limited areas of tonal range in an image. For example, you may want to lower the contrast in the image's brightest highlights.

Gibraltar   The code name for Microsoft's Internet Information Server.

GIF (Graphics Interchange Format)   A bitmapped, compressed graphics format popularized by the online service CompuServe.

GIF87a and GIF89a   Versions of the GIF (Graphical Interchange Format) graphics format. GIF87a is the original specification of the standard; GIF89a is an enhanced specification that adds support for transparency and animation. Microsoft Internet Explorer and Netscape Navigator support inline display of GIF89a images.

global   Of, relating to, or applying to a whole (as a computer program or web site).

Gopher   A technology similar to the World Wide Web that enables you to find information across the Internet by using a series of nested menus.

graphic   A representation of an object on a two-dimensional surface.

graphical environment   An environment that includes the use of graphics rather than only text.

GUI   Graphical User Interface, a method of displaying a computer interface with pictures instead of only text.

H

halo   A word usually used to describe the off-color ring surrounding a transparent GIF image resulting from stray-edge pixels that don't quite match the color specified as transparent. Also known as *UHS* (Ugly Halo Syndrome).

hits   Visits to a web site. The most traditional systems for counting hits on a web page count all the graphics and external links as hits when one user views a page. For example, a page with three graphics and two external links would count as five hits when one user viewed the page.

home page   The first page seen when someone accesses a web site—the "title page." On a small site (for example, a personal site), this may be the only page. On a larger site (business or organization, for example), it is the central page and includes links to other pages within the site.

host   A computer capable of connecting to others on the Internet. Generally refers to servers, particularly web servers.

Host Address   The address of a computer on the Internet, usually expressed as four byte values; for example, 204.70.203.106.

Host Name   The textual name of a computer on the Internet, such as `microsoft.com` or `eff.org`.

HTML (HyperText Markup Language)   A language used to create hypertext documents on the World Wide Web. HTML is a subset of the SGML standard.

HTML converters   Programs that convert documents from various formats into HTML documents. The Microsoft Word Internet Assistant is a type of HTML converter.

HTML editors   Programs that can be used to alter or create HTML pages. HTML editors can be text or WYSIWYG editors. (See *WYSIWYG*.)

HTML Layout Control   A Microsoft ActiveX control designed to extend the functionality of style sheets within Microsoft Internet Explorer.

HTTP (HyperText Transfer Protocol)   The protocol that governs how a web server and a web browser communicate and Exchange data.

hyperlinks (links)   A highlighted piece of text that moves a user from one hypertext document to another (or from one anchor to another).

hypermedia   Links between pictures, sounds, and text in the same or related files or web sites.

hypertext   A word or series of words with related HTML programming linking the words to other locations. Users who click these words can skip from one document to the next, or from one area of a document to another area in the same document.

I

icon   Small, "high-concept" images meant to give the reader a message that takes less time to read and is more universally understood than if the same message were spelled out in words.

IETF   Internet Engineering Task Force. An international group of engineers who assist in the process of developing new Internet standards.

IIS   Internet Information Server, Microsoft's web server. Provided as a component of Windows NT Server, this web server is programmable through ISAPI.

image maps   Images that are divided into different regions linked to different URLs. Each area of the image can be linked to any URL; the user can jump to different destinations by clicking different parts of the image. See also *client-side image map, server-side image map*.

in-process server   OLE Automation Server that runs in the same process as the application calling it.

inline images   Images that can be viewed directly by the browser and don't require a plug-in or separate window for viewing. Most browsers can view JPEG and GIF images inline.

interaction   Mutual or reciprocal action or influence.

interface   In programming, the set of functions and data exposed by an object. For example, the interface of an ActiveX object is comprised of the object's properties, methods, and events.

interlacing   Enables an image to load in several stages of resolution. Creates the illusion that graphics (and, therefore, whole pages) load more quickly and gives the reader a chance to see a "fuzzy" recognizable image quickly enough to know whether to wait or move on.

Internet   An international collection of interconnected computer networks. The Internet implies a collected set of standards for interoperability between disparate types of computers and networking systems, including, for example, protocols for network connectivity (TCP/IP), file transfer (FTP), and electronic mail (SMTP/POP).

Internet Assistants   Microsoft Office add-ons that convert Microsoft Office documents into HTML. There are Internet Assistants for Access, Word, Excel, PowerPoint, and Schedule+ documents.

Internet Explorer   Microsoft's web browser. Supports Java and ActiveX, and runs on Windows 3.1, Windows 95, Windows NT, and Macintosh. http://www.microsoft.com/ie/default.asp

InterNIC Information Services   A nonprofit organization that registers domain names and addresses so no two sites use the same name or number. Registered domain names are used by domain name services running on the Internet (see also *DNS*).

intranet   A "private internet"—a local or wide-area network using TCP/IP protocol and making use of Internet services such as FTP and the World Wide Web, but closed to the Internet at large.

IP (Internet Protocol)   Allows information to be passed from one network (set of computers) to another by using a unique string of numbers (address) for each network.

IRC   Internet Relay Chat, an Internet protocol for real-time, multi-user online chat.

ISAPI (Internet Services API)   The Microsoft API for communicating with Microsoft Internet Information Server. Communicating with MSIIS through ISAPI involves writing a DLL that communicates to the server; the API governs how the function calls are made. Internet Database Connector (IDC) is an example of an ISAPI extension.

ISDN (Integrated Services Digital Network) connections, ISDN lines   Digital technology for Internet connections and other telecommunications that offers higher bandwidth and better signal quality than telephone lines.

ISP (Internet Service Provider)   An organization or company that provides Internet access to individuals or companies.

ISPx   A national or local company that sells access to the Internet. Well-known examples include Netcom and AT&T, although many smaller regional service providers also exist.

ISV   Independent Solution Provider, a company or individual that builds custom software.

J

Java   A programming language developed by Sun Microsystems that executes on any computer platform. This makes it possible to place applications on remote computers that will run on any computer connected to that remote computer. Small Java applications, called *applets*, are used on many web pages to perform operations that can't normally be accomplished in HTML code. Not every web browser is capable of handling Java applets, but the current versions of Netscape and Microsoft Internet Explorer can.

Java applet   A small application created with the Java programming language that can be embedded in an HTML page to execute animations or interactive applications.

JDK   Java Development Kit, Sun Microsystem's Java development kit. http://www.javasoft.com/nav/developer/index.html

JPEG   A compressed file format in which to save graphics for use on the web if they are full-color, continuous-tone images (such as photographs) larger than approximately 150 pixels square. Gets its name from the committee that originated it, the Joint Photographic Experts Group.

K

Kbps (Kilobits per second)   A measurement of communication speed (of modems, for example).

kilobyte (KB)   1,024 bytes of data.

L

LAN   Local area network, a series of computers connected together to enable them to share resources.

landscape view   A page of text or graphics that is wider than it is tall.

LED (Light Emitting Diode)   A small electronic device made from semiconductor materials; emits light when current flows through it. Sometimes used for computer displays.

lifetime   The period of time a variable exists, depending on the level at which it was declared. Global and static variables persist until the application is done running, while variables declared at the procedural level are only valid while the procedure they were declared in is still running. See also *procedure level, scope.*

ligature   In typography, two or more characters designed and cast as a distinct unit for aesthetic reasons (commonly fi, ff, fl, ffi, ffl, ae, and oe).

link (hyperlink)   A connection between locations in the same file (web site) or between different files created by the HTML Anchor or link tag. See also *hypertext, hyperlink.*

load, loading   To transfer program instructions or data from a disk or drive into the computer's random access memory (RAM).

load-time dynamic linking   Functions used in a dynamic link library through the use of an import library.

local links   Links that go to HTML documents or other files within your web site (as opposed to external links, which take browsers to pages outside your site).

locale   The set of information that corresponds to a given language and country. A locale affects the language of predefined programming terms and locale-specific settings. There are two contexts where locale information is important: the code locale affects the language of terms such as keywords and defines locale-specific settings such as the decimal and list separators, date formats, and character sorting order. The system locale affects the way locale-aware functionality behaves; for example, when you display numbers or convert strings to dates. You set the system locale using the Control Panel utilities provided by the operating system.

localization   The process of translating software for international use. This entails, among other things, translating the textual elements of the user interface into the local language. In Windows, the operating system is responsible for some elements of localization, such as the format of date and time values.

logical styles   HTML markup tags that provide emphasis or indicate a particular kind of device or action. See also *physical styles.*

loop, looping   A set of program instructions that execute repeatedly until a condition is satisfied. In Visual Basic, the Do...While and For...Next statements are looping structures.

lossy compression   So called because not all original image detail is preserved when the file is compressed (there is some "loss" of data, but the image looks acceptable to the human eye). JPEG is an example of a lossy format.

Lycos   A broad and comprehensive World Wide Web search engine.

Lynx   A character-mode World Wide Web browser that displays only text.

M

macro   A stored list of commands to perform tedious and often-repeated tasks.

markup language   Special characters embedded within a text file to instruct a computer program how to handle or display the contents of the file itself. HTML is a markup language.

megabyte (MB)   1,024 kilobytes, or 1,048,576 bytes.

menu, menu bar   A list of options presented to a user by a program or web site. In graphical programs, the menu may appear as a bar that is actually an image map of the site, enabling the user to click on a menu item and jump to the linked page automatically.

metacharacter   A specific character within a text file that signals the need for special handling. In HTML, angle brackets (< >), ampersand (&), pound sign (#), and semicolon (;).

method   A public, exposed function in an ActiveX control.

MFC   Microsoft Foundation Classes, a software library that enables C++ programmers to write applications. Included with the Visual C++ development environment.

Microsoft Internet Explorer   See *Internet Explorer*.

Microsoft Office Viewers   Enable users to view Word, Excel, and PowerPoint documents over the Internet in their native form without converting them to HTML. Can be used in conjunction with a browser. Especially useful on intranets.

Microsoft Proxy Server   A piece of server-side software that works with Microsoft Internet Information Server. The purpose of a proxy server is to enhance the security of an Internet server, permitting the server to selectively deny access to certain types of users and control the data that flows in from the Net. Formerly code-named "Catapult."

MIDI (Musical Instrument Device Interface)   Pronounced *middy*. Protocol for the exchange of information between computers and musical synthesizers. After being placed into computer-represented form, all the aspects of the digitized sound can be edited and altered.

MIME (Multipurpose Internet Mail Extensions)   An extension to Internet e-mail that enables the transfer of nontextual data, such as graphics, audio, and video.

modem   A device that converts (modulates) electrical pulses from a computer to signals suitable for transmission over a telephone line. Acronym for MODulator-DEModulator.

Moiré   Pronounced *mwah-ray*. Optical illusion perceived as flickering that some-times occurs when high-contrast line patterns are placed too close together.

Mosaic   The first graphical World Wide Web browser. Currently manufactured by Spyglass (`http://www.spyglass.com/products/smosaic/`).

Mozilla   An early name coined for Netscape products that derives from "Mosaic meets Godzilla." The word and associated image often appear in Netscape products or in references to them.

MSDN   Microsoft Developer Network, a subscription service provided by Microsoft for developers who use Microsoft tools.

multicast   Sending information that can be received by multiple nodes on a network such as the Internet. See also *broadcast, narrowcast*.

multimedia   The presentation of information on a computer by using video, sound, graphics, and other media.

N

nanosecond   One-billionth of a second.

narrowcast   Information aimed at specific viewers who can be assumed to have identical browser and hardware configurations and high-speed connections. See also *broadcast, multicast*.

navigational icons   In this case, navigation refers to the use of hyperlinks to move through a web site. Navigational icons show the user where to find information. These icons often move viewers through sequential pages and back again.

Navigator   Netscape's web browser. `http://home.netscape.com`

NCSA (National Center for Supercomputing Applications)   Department at the University of Illinois where Mosaic, the first web browser, was developed.

nested, nesting   When one code structure occurs within another, it is said to be nested. HTML tags and Visual Basic looping and decision structures are often nested.

netiquette   "Internet etiquette." Written and unwritten rules for behavior on the Internet.

Netscape Navigator   See *Navigator*.

NNTP   Network News Transfer Protocol, an Internet standard for non-real-time conferencing.

node An individual connection point in a network, usually an individual computer or terminal.

Normandy A Microsoft server product that permits multi-user conferencing over intranets or the Internet.

Nothing In Visual Basic, a special value that indicates that an object variable is not associated with an object. Evaluates to zero or an empty string ("") in an expression.

NSAPI Netscape Server Application Programming Interface, an API for extending the Netscape web server.

Null A value indicating that a variable contains no valid data. Null is the result of an explicit assignment of Null to a variable or an operation between expressions that contain Null. A variable will typically be set to Null in a database context, in situations where a field contains no data or a recordset contains no records.

numeric expression Any expression that can be evaluated as a number. Elements of the expression can include any combination of keywords, variables, constants, and operators that result in a number.

O

object Generally, a self-contained piece of code embedded in another application. Objects provide various interfaces (such as properties, methods, and collections) to permit programmers to access them.

VBScript objects are either ActiveX controls or Java applets. Objects are inserted into an HTML page through the use of the <OBJECT> tag.

object model A blueprint documenting the interfaces made available by an object. The Microsoft Internet Explorer Scripting Object Model lists the properties and methods of the web browser accessible from VBScript.

object type A type of object exposed by an application through OLE Automation, for example, Application, File, Range, and Sheet. Refer to the application's documentation (Microsoft Excel, Microsoft Project, Microsoft Word, and so on) for a complete listing of available objects.

OCX OLE Custom Control, a type of software object designed to be embedded in applications. This term has been supplanted by the term "ActiveX," but the underlying technology is similar.

OEM Original Equipment Manufacturer, a term used to identify the original manufacturer of a piece of hardware when that hardware is sold by another company.

OLE   Originally an acronym for Object Linking and Embedding, now refers to a broad range of interoperability protocols and standards.

OLE Automation object   An object that is exposed to other applications or programming tools through OLE automation interfaces. Applications that expose an OLE automation interface can be programmed just like other types of software objects (see also *object*).

operator   A logical or mathematical symbol that serves as part of an expression in code. Plus and minus signs are examples of math operators; the greater-than symbol (>) is an example of a logical operator.

out-of-process server   OLE Automation Server that runs in a different process than the application calling it. See also *in-process server*.

P

Packet   A transmitted block of data. Meaningful in low-level network programming; individual packets are handled by the network protocol, not by the application (or the programming language).

On the CD

palette   An array of colors that exist in a particular indexed image. Netscape and Microsoft have created palettes that best utilize colors for cross-platform display. Copies of both palettes can be found on the CD-ROM included with this book.

pan, panning   Rotating a camera to keep an object in view or to give a wider view of the object. Computer programs simulate panning for the same purpose.

PDF (Portable Document File)   A file that carries all font and layout specifications with it, regardless of the platform on which it is viewed. The best solution for putting print documents on the web when those print documents must be as close as possible to their paper counterparts. Generally requires a viewer such as Adobe Acrobat.

Perl (Practical Extraction and Reporting Language)   First developed by Larry Wall for Unix systems, this language is frequently used for writing CGI scripts.

persistence   The ability to store and recall the state of an application.

PGP   Pretty Good Privacy, an encryption technology that can be included in Internet applications.

phosphor   Electrofluorescent material used to coat the inside face of a cathode ray tube. This determines the color temperature of an image displayed on a monitor.

physical styles   HTML markup tags that specifically control character styles, such as Bold <B> or Italic <I>. Contrast with *logical styles*.

pi   Pi is a mathematical constant equal to approximately 3.1415926535897932.

PICT   A metafile that can contain both raster and vector images. Probably the most common Macintosh graphics format. Enables use of JPEG compression when saving a file on a Macintosh. However, neither a web browser nor any other program will recognize a PICT file as a JPEG file.

pixel   Pronounced *picks-L* (short for picture element). Smallest element (dot) a computer can display on-screen. Images created for the web are most commonly measured in pixels. Spacing attributes in HTML tags are also commonly measured in pixels. A pixel measured on a screen is the equivalent of a dot (as in dots per inch) on a printed page.

plain text   A text format that does not include formatting codes that maintain layout and appearance of text.

platform   Computer hardware or operating system standard, such as IBM PC-compatible or Macintosh personal computers.

plug-in   An accessory or utility program that extends the capabilities of an application program, such as the RealAudio player. See also *add-on*.

PNG   Pronounced *ping*. Bitmapped file format, designed especially for network graphics. PNG is a new format meant to be a patent-free replacement for GIF, but it is not yet widely readable by browsers.

POP   Post Office Protocol, the Internet protocol that governs a client application downloading mail from a mail server.

Port   A channel over which an Internet application communicates. Internet servers conventionally devote a port to a particular application; for example, web servers usually send and receive data on port 80.

portrait view   A page of text or graphics that is taller than it is wide.

PPP   Point-to-Point Protocol, a dial-up protocol for accessing the Internet using a modem.

PPTP   Point-to-Point Tunneling Protocol, a Microsoft standard that permits the use of the Internet as a virtual private network (VPN). This allows users to access files on a private network by dialing into the public Internet. Windows NT 4.0 currently supports PPTP.

procedure   A collection of statements in a programming language. VBScript contains two types of procedures: Function procedures, which can return a value, and

Sub procedures, which do not. Procedures in VBScript can be intrinsic to the language (such as the MsgBox function) or defined by the programmer.

procedure level   Describes the scope of code within a Function or Sub procedure. Variables declared at the procedure level can only be accessed by the procedure (that is, they are said to have procedural scope) and they disappear when the procedure is done executing (that is, they are said to have procedural lifetime). See also *lifetime, scope.*

program flow   Elements of a program that determine whether a piece of code is executed and, if it is executed, how many times it is executed. The If...Then...Else statement is an example of conditional program flow. The Do While...Loop statement is an example of a loop.

progressive JPEG   Like interlaced GIF, progressive JPEG enables an image to load in stages of increasingly higher resolution.

properties   The characteristics of an object defining its state, appearance, or value.

properties page   A dialog box that displays an ActiveX control's properties. Also called *property sheet.*

property   An exposed, public attribute in an ActiveX control. A named attribute of an object. Properties define object characteristics such as size, color, and screen location, or the state of an object, such as enabled or disabled.

protocol   A set of rules for how programs work. These rules generally include requirements for formatting data and error checking.

proxy server   A piece of server-side software that enhances the security of an Internet server, permitting the server to selectively deny access to certain types of users and control the data that flows in from the Net. Also known as a *firewall.* See *Microsoft Proxy Server.*

Q

QuickTime   A multimedia format used by software tool vendors and content creators to store, edit, and play synchronized graphics, sound, video, text, and music. Developed by Apple Computer, QuickTime technologies include QuickTime Movies, an audio-video format, and QuickTime VR, a format for displaying three-dimensional virtual reality.

In Netscape 3.0, QuickTime operates as a plug-in application.

R

RAM (Random Access Memory)   Computer memory that stores ongoing work or any operating systems and applications actually running at the moment.

RAS   Remote Access Service, the Windows technology that enables a computer to (among other things) connect to the Internet through a telephone dial-up connection. A RAS connection is integrated into the computer's networking protocol.

raster image   See *bitmap*.

raw code   Refers to the HTML code behind a web page.

RealAudio   A compressed sound technology that enables streaming sound play on web pages.

Registry   Windows system database containing software and hardware information. The Windows 95 and Windows NT registries are actually quite different.

relative link   Link set using the path within a Web site directory structure, omitting the domain name. For example: `<a HREF=file_name.html>` or `<a HREF=/resources/file_name.html>`. Contrast with *absolute link*.

resolution   The number of picture elements per unit in an image. For example, the resolution of a full-screen image on a 15-inch, 640 by 480 monitor is 72 dpi. See also *dpi*.

RFC   Request for Comment, a method for hashing out Internet technology standards. Generally, every major Internet technology will have its own RFC.

ROM (Read-Only Memory)   Non-volatile computer memory, programmed a specific set of system instructions.

router   A device that reads the destination address on information sent over a network and sends the information to the next step in its route.

RTF (Rich Text Format)   A text format used by a variety of word processors (such as Microsoft Word and Windows 95 WordPad) that permits font and paragraph formatting.

runtime   The time when code is running—as opposed to design-time, when you are writing the code. Some object properties can be changed only at runtime, while some can be changed either at design-time or runtime.

runtime dynamic linking   Functions used in a dynamic link library through the process of loading a DLL and calling a function through its procedure address.

runtime error   An error that occurs when code is running. A runtime error results when a statement attempts an invalid operation.

S

SCODE   A long integer value that is used to pass detailed information to the caller of an interface member or API function. The status codes for OLE interfaces and APIs are defined in FACILITY_ITF.

scope   Defines the visibility of a variable, procedure, or object. For example, a variable declared as Public is visible to all procedures in all modules in a project. Variables declared in procedures are visible only within the procedure and lose their value between calls.

scrolling   Moving the window horizontally or vertically to make information that extends beyond the viewing area visible.

SDK   Software Development Kit. Often, software companies (most notably Microsoft) distribute SDKs that permit developers to write to APIs (see *API*). The ActiveX SDK permits Visual C++ developers to create ActiveX controls.

search engine   (1) A web site that contains search programs capable of retrieving other web pages based on user queries. (2) A program created to search the contents of a particular web site for information related to a specific topic or keyword supplied by a user. Prominent search engines include Lycos, Yahoo!, and Excite.

seed   An initial value used to generate pseudorandom numbers. For example, the Randomize statement creates a seed number used by the Rnd function to create unique pseudorandom number sequences.

serif, sans serif   Serif fonts have cross-strokes across the ends of the main strokes of characters. Sans serif fonts have no cross-strokes.

server (web server)   A computer connected to the Internet that "serves" files. The server is generally located on a remote computer and responds to requests from client computers.

server-side image map   An image map that requires a corresponding CGI script on the server. See *image map*.

SGML (Standard Generalized Markup Language) A sequence of characters organized physically as a set of entities and logically into a hierarchy of elements. A document definition, specification, and creation mechanism that makes platform and display differences across multiple computers irrelevant to the delivery and rendering of documents. HTML is a subset of SGML.

shareware Software that can be freely shared with others, provided certain restrictions regarding distribution are followed, as specified by the author. Often involves payment of a fee to the author for continued use.

Shockwave A plug-in technology that enables web browsers to display animated Macromedia Director files. Such files are compressed with a program called Afterburner. Shockwave plug-ins are available for both Mac and PC.

SLIP Serial Line Interface Protocol, a dial-up protocol for accessing the Internet using a modem.

SMTP Simple Mail Transfer Protocol, the Internet technology for sending electronic mail through a mail server.

sockets A set of subroutines that gives software applications access to the TCP/IP network protocol. The Windows implementation of sockets is a standard known as *winsock.*

spawn Initiate a new process.

special characters (1) Typed characters such as ~ or &. On web pages, these characters must be created as HTML entities, or by using special character tags. (2) With the exception of the underline (or underscore) character, these characters should not be used in filenames.

spell checker A program that checks text against a file of correctly spelled words and indicates when words don't match (that is, when they are presumably misspelled).

splash screen The opening screen that appears when you start a program. Usually includes information about the manufacturer.

spreadsheet A program that simulates an accountant's worksheet on-screen and enables the embedding of hidden formulas to perform calculations on data (examples: dBase, Excel, and Paradox).

SQL Structured Query Language. A language for issuing requests to database servers.

SSL Secure Sockets Layer. A Windows technology for using a computer securely over the Internet.

start tag   In HTML programming, a start tag identifies the start of an HTML element; it can include attributes. Start tags usually must be followed by an end tag. The HTML tag <BODY> and <B> are start tags.

static   Characterized by lack of movement, animation, or progression. Opposite of *dynamic.*

stdin   Standard input stream, commonly used by CGI to receive incoming data.

stdout   Standard output stream, commonly used by CGI to send data out to a client application.

still graphics   Representations of objects without animation.

streaming   "Streaming" technology starts to play sound, video, or other data as soon as enough material has downloaded so that the rest will download before the movie or sound file finishes playing. An example of a streaming audio application is RealAudio.

string   A series of text characters.

string comparison   A comparison of two sequences of characters. Unless specified in the function making the comparison, all string comparisons are binary. In English, binary comparisons are case-sensitive; text comparisons are not.

structural element   An element that determines how your document looks; for example, a heading is a structural element, but paragraph text is not.

style sheet   A collection of formatting descriptions designed to give web pages a consistent style.

surf, surfing   Used to describe the action of moving from one place to another on the Web with no apparent plan or pattern.

Sweeper   A code name for a collection of standards designed to unify Internet and Windows technology standards. Now referred to as Active Internet Platform (AIP).

synchronize   To arrange events so that they happen at the same time.

synchronous   See *blocking.*

syntax   The grammar of a language.

system administrator   Also known as a sysadmin or network administrator. The person or group responsible for configuring and maintaining a network or web server.

T

T1 line   A high-speed, dedicated connection to the Internet. Transmits a digital signal at 1.544 megabits per second.

T3 line   A high-speed, dedicated connection to the Internet. Transmits a digital signal at 44.746 megabits per second.

tables   HTML table tags organize text or graphics in relation to one another on a web page.

tags   An element of HTML markup, usually enclosed in angle brackets (< >).

TCP/IP (Transmission Control Protocol/Internet Protocol)   A network protocol designed to permit many different types of networks to work together. TCP/IP is the network protocol used by all computers on the Internet.

third-party (programs, plug-ins)   Developed by a company other than the company who developed the program with which they function.

thread   Support for multithreading depends on the operating system; Windows NT and Unix are both systems that support multithreading.

title bar   An area at the top of a window that displays the window's caption or name.

Tivoli   Code name for Microsoft Index Server, a piece of software that enables a web server to provide searching capabilities to users.

tools   (1) Icons or palette items in a graphical program that perform specific functions when selected. (2) Useful software programs.

transparent GIF (tGIF)   Generally means a GIF that appears as a graphic that "floats" over the background because the image's background is transparent. Transparency can be set to any single color section.

typeface   The distinctive design of a set of type. See also *font.*

U

Unicode   16-bit fixed-width character encoding that covers all characters in use on a computer system today.

Unix   Pronounced *U-nicks.* A popular networked operating system. Many web servers and other Internet-related computers run on Unix.

upload   The process of moving information from your computer to a remote computer, as in uploading web site files to a server.

URL (Uniform Resource Locator)   Pronounced as either *earl* or *U-R-L*. Server and path information that locates a document on the Internet; for example, `http://www.domain_name.com`.

user   A person who visits a web site.

utility software   Software used in maintaining and improving the efficiency of a computer system.

V

validation   The process of ensuring that a user's input is valid before processing that input.

variable   A named storage location that can contain data that can be modified during program execution. Each variable has a name that uniquely identifies it within its level of scope. Variables also have a specific lifetime depending on where and how they were declared (see also *lifetime, scope*).

Variable names must begin with an alphabetic character, can't contain an embedded period or type-declaration character, must be unique within the same scope, and must be no longer than 255 characters.

VBScript   Visual Basic Script, one of the web programming languages understood and interpreted by Microsoft Internet Explorer.

VBX   Visual Basic Extension. VBXes are 16-bit component software objects, sometimes referred to by the general term "custom controls." VBX technology has been made largely obsolete by 32-bit OCX and ActiveX controls.

vector graphics   Images whose shapes are described by geometric formulae. Vector files are resolution-independent, meaning that they are always drawn at the best possible resolution of the device generating them. Because even a fairly complex geometric shape can be described in a few lines of text as a formula, vector images tend to be much smaller than a typical equivalent bitmap image, which has to be described using several bits of data for each pixel in the image.

video   Information displayed on a TV screen or computer terminal. See also *audio*.

viewer   An application launched by a browser to display elements such as sound files or video that cannot be displayed by the browser. One such viewer is the Microsoft Word Viewer, which lets you view Word documents, even if you don't have Word installed on your computer.

viewing window   A defined area of the screen through which portions of text or other information can be seen.

virtual memory   A method of extending the apparent size of a computer's random access memory (RAM) by using part of the hard disk as an extension of RAM.

virtual reality   An artificial environment experienced through sensory stimuli (sights and sounds) provided by a computer, and in which one's actions partially determine what happens in the environment.

Visual J++   Microsoft's Java Applet/Application development environment.

VRML (Virtual Reality Modeling Language)   Enables the creation of three-dimensional models and walk-through spaces within the context of a web browser or other application. Graphics can be mapped to the surfaces of 3-D models, and links can be attached to surfaces. Links can display a media type, take users to another model or another part of the current model, or perform any of the functions of any web hyperlink.

W

WAN   Wide Area Network. A network that is comprised of several computers connected together, but at remote locations (for example, at different divisions of the same company located in different cities). The Internet is an example of a Wide Area Network.

web browser   A software application that lets you view World Wide Web data. Microsoft Internet Explorer is an example of a web browser.

web designer   Anyone, professional or hobbyist, who creates web pages. Also called *web developers*.

web page   One file in a collection of files that make up a web site. Usually used to describe the first page that appears in a web site.

web server   A piece of software responsible for sending web pages and associated data to web browsers using the HTTP protocol. Major commercial web servers include Microsoft's Internet Information Server, Netscape's FastTrack and Enterprise Servers, and O'Reilly's WebSite.

web site   A specific location on the Internet, housed on a web server and accessible through an URL. Consists of one or more web pages.

webmaster   The individual responsible for administering a web site.

WININET   The DLL that exposes the Internet API, found in the Sweeper SDK.

winsock   High-level Windows interface to the TCP/IP protocol.

wizard   A program sequence within software products that leads you step-by-step through a task.

World Wide Web Consortium (W3C)   An industry consortium that seeks to promote standards for the evolution of the Web and interoperability between WWW products by producing specifications and reference software. The international group is jointly hosted by the MIT Laboratory for Computer Science in the United States and by INRIA in Europe.

WWW   World Wide Web, the collection of files in the HTML format that reside on computers connected by the Internet.

WYSIWYG   Stands for "What You See Is What You Get;" pronounced *wizzy-wig*. Describes programs that attempt to show on-screen what the final document will look like.

X, Y, Z

Yahoo!   An Internet search engine. `http://www.yahoo.com`

zip   A compression method primarily used on Windows and DOS computers. Uses the `.zip` file extension.

zipped archive   A file that consists of many compressed files.

zoom, zooming   Enlarging a document view so it fills the screen, or making it smaller so more overall detail can be seen.

INDEX I

C

G

Getting Started with the CD-ROM

This page provides instructions for installing software from the CD-ROM.

Windows 95/NT 4 Installation

Insert the disc into your CD-ROM drive. If autoplay is enabled on your machine, the CD-ROM setup program starts automatically the first time you insert the disc.

If setup does not run automatically, perform these steps:

1. From the Start menu, choose Programs, Windows Explorer.

2. Select your CD-ROM drive under My Computer.

3. Double-click SETUP.EXE in the contents list.

4. Follow the on-screen instructions that appear.

5. Setup adds an icon named CD-ROM Contents to a program group for this book. To explore the CD-ROM, double-click on the CD-ROM Contents icon.

Macintosh Installation

Insert the disc into your CD-ROM Drive. Double-click on the CD-ROM Contents icon.

How to Contact New Riders Publishing

If you have a question or comment about this product, there are several ways to contact New Riders Publishing. You can write us at the following address:

New Riders Publishing
Attn: Publishing Manager
201 W. 103rd Street
Indianapolis, IN 46290

If you prefer, you can fax New Riders Publishing at 1-317-817-7448.

To send Internet electronic mail to New Riders, address it to support@mcp.com.

You can also contact us through the Macmillan Computer Publishing CompuServe forum at GO NEWRIDERS. Our World Wide Web address is http://www.mcp.com/newriders.

MACMILLAN COMPUTER PUBLISHING USA

A VIACOM COMPANY

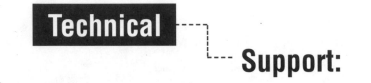

Technical

Support:

If you need assistance with the information in this book or with a CD/Disk accompanying the book, please access the Knowledge Base on our Web site at **http://www.superlibrary.com/general/support**. Our most Frequently Asked Questions are answered there. If you do not find the answer to your questions on our Web site, you may contact Macmillan Technical Support **(317) 581-3833** or e-mail us at **support@mcp.com**.